The Encyclopedia of American Law Enforcement

Facts On File, Inc.
An imprint of Infobase Publishing
132 West 31st Street
New York NY 10001

ISBN-10: 0-8160-6290-0
ISBN-13: 978-0-8160-6290-4

Library of Congress Cataloging-in-Publication Data

Newton, Michael, 1951–
The encyclopedia of American law enforcement / Michael Newton.
p. cm.
Includes bibliographical references.
ISBN 0-8160-6290-0 (hc : alk. paper)
1. Law enforcement—United States—Encyclopedias. 2. Law enforcement—United States—History—Encyclopedias. 3. Police—United States—Encyclopedias. 4. Police—United States—Biography. I. Title.
HV8133.N48 2007
363.20973′03—dc22   2005035914

Facts On File books are available at special discounts when purchased in bulk quantities for businesses, associations, institutions, or sales promotions. Please call our Special Sales Department in New York at (212) 967-8800 or (800) 322-8755.

You can find Facts On File on the World Wide Web at http://www.factsonfile.com

Text design by Joan McEvoy
Cover design by Dorothy Preston

Printed in the United States of America

VB Hermitage 10 9 8 7 6 5 4 3 2 1

This book is printed on acid-free paper.

For all officers who sacrifice their lives
in the line of duty

Every society gets the kind of criminal it deserves. What is equally true is that every community gets the kind of law enforcement it insists on.

—Robert F. Kennedy

Revolt and terror pay a price. Order and law have a cost.

—Carl Sandburg

Crime is contagious. If the Government becomes a lawbreaker, it breeds contempt for law; it invites every man to become a law unto himself; it invites anarchy. To declare that in the administration of the criminal law the end justifies the means—to declare that the Government may commit crimes in order to secure the conviction of a private criminal—would bring terrible retribution.

—Louis Brandeis

Contents

Introduction

When I began work on this book in 2004, approximately 870,000 sworn law enforcement officers were employed by various municipal, county, state, and federal agencies in the United States. They patrolled 3.8 million square miles (including Puerto Rico), inhabited by 289 million people—leaving each officer outnumbered by a factor of 332 to one.

Police work is clearly one of the world's most dangerous professions. In 2002, the latest year with statistics available at press time, 1.4 million violent crimes were reported throughout the United States, and police suffered more than their share of the mayhem. An average 58,000 officers are assaulted each year, sustaining 16,500 significant injuries. A total of 883 officers were killed on duty between January 2000 and July 2004, but broader estimates for line-of-duty deaths remain confused and contradictory. The National Law Enforcement Officers Memorial Fund lists 16,656 officers killed between 1792 and 2003, while another source, the Officer Down Memorial Page, pegs the total at 17,392 in January 2005.

In fact, while conflicting statistics abound, no definitive list of officers killed on duty presently exists. We do know that the 1970s—sometimes described as years "when nothing happened"—were America's most deadly decade for police, with 2,240 officers slain. The worst single year, with 271 police fatalities, was 1974; the worst day to date was September 11, 2001, with 72 officers killed in terrorist attacks. California remains the most dangerous state for police, with a minimum of 1,357 officers killed on duty, while Vermont is the safest (claiming only 17). New York City devours more police lives than any other American metropolis, 579 at press time. Law enforcement is a daunting, often thankless job—yet sometimes one with great emotional rewards for those who make the grade and keep the faith.

The Encyclopedia of American Law Enforcement presents the first-ever comprehensive overview of American police work. Its 654 entries include profiles of 149 law enforcement agencies, short biographies of 362 significant individuals, 20 descriptions of famous or notorious incidents, and 119 essays on general subjects ranging from agents provocateur to the FBI's Z-Coverage mail surveillance program. The text surveys all aspects of U.S. law enforcement, from investigative techniques to modern crisis points (corruption, suicides, etc.). Broad trends in crime are examined, but specific criminals are generally excluded from the text, except where their cases had a lasting impact on American police work (e.g., Ernesto Miranda). No effort has been made to sugarcoat the history of law enforcement in America, nor is the work a "hatchet job" designed to scandalize. The individuals and facts speak for themselves.

Entries in the work are arranged alphabetically. Cross-references are indicated by use of SMALL CAPITALS in the text. A selected bibliography lists major works consulted during preparation of the book, while a separate appendix lists 152 Internet Web sites for various police agencies and other relevant groups. Neither the author nor Facts On File/Checkmark Books are responsible for the content or conflicting opinions expressed on those pages. I owe special thanks to the following for their assistance with this work: the American Society for Prevention of Cruelty to Animals; David Frasier at Indiana University; Chief Penny Harrington; and Heather Newton.

Every effort has been made to ensure accuracy. Readers wishing to suggest corrections or propose material for future editions may contact the author via Facts On File or at http://www.michaelnewton.homestead.com.

Entries A–Z

Acton, Thomas C. (1823–1898)

A native of New York City, born in 1823, Thomas Acton left school as a youth to support his widowed mother and siblings, but he studied law in private and later won admission to the state bar. In lieu of private practice, he launched a career in public service, starting in the county clerk's office. In May 1860 he was appointed to serve on New York's board of police commissioners, a post Acton held until 1869. His service coincided with the deadly Draft Riots of July 1863, wherein protests against Civil War military conscription became a full-scale racist assault upon blacks by white mobs. After police superintendent John Kennedy was nearly killed by rioters, Acton assumed personal frontline command of the force, ordering patrolmen to pursue and attack rioters, rather than waiting for them to wreak havoc. (One field commander ordered his men to "kill every man [in the mob] who has a club.") While deemed brutal by some, Acton's methods quelled the outbreak after three grim days and prevented the rioters from demolishing Wall Street.

After the riots, Acton became embroiled in a bitter quarrel with the city's volunteer fire department, whose leaders resented his efforts to establish a professional (paid) team of firefighters. Acton retired from public service on May 1, 1869, and died in 1898, at age 75. A library in Saybrook, Connecticut, is named in his honor.

Adams, Francis W. H. (1904–1990)

A native of Mount Vernon, New York, Francis Adams was born on June 26, 1904. He earned a bachelor's degree from Williams College in 1925, followed by an LL.B. from New York City's Fordham Law School three years later. After six years in private practice, Adams was appointed to serve as chief assistant U.S. attorney for the Southern District of New York. The next year, 1935, saw him promoted to U.S. attorney, then once again as special assistant to the U.S. attorney general. Adams returned to private practice in 1937, then accepted a post as arbitrator for the War Labor Board during World War II.

In 1953 mayor-elect Robert Wagner asked Adams to serve as commissioner of the NEW YORK CITY POLICE DEPARTMENT. Adams accepted, based on Wagner's promise of a free hand in rooting out departmental CORRUPTION, and he took office on January 1, 1954. Over the next 18 months, Adams added 2,000 officers to the department, put more cops on the street by eliminating many desk jobs and extracurricular units (the band and glee club), and launched "Operation Efficiency" to monitor patrolmen on their beats. By the time he left office on August 1, 1955, serious crime in New York City had declined 13 percent.

Still, Adams was not done with public service. In 1963 he was chosen as assistant counsel to the blue-ribbon Warren Commission, appointed by President Lyndon Johnson to investigate the JFK assassination. For the commission's final report, Adams was assigned to join counsel Arlen Spector in writing a chapter on the number and direction of shots fired at President John Kennedy in Dallas. However, Adams disbelieved the so-called magic bullet theory that described one rifle slug apparently defying all known laws of physics, and he left Spector to write the chapter alone. Enduring controversy surrounds the Warren Report, but it left Adams unscathed. He returned to private practice in Manhattan and died in 1990, at age 86.

agents provocateurs

Agents provocateurs ("provocative agents," in French) are spies employed by unscrupulous law enforcement agencies to provoke criminal activities by suspect groups or persons, thus resulting in their prosecution. Such ENTRAPMENT is illegal, but has nonetheless been widely used by various police departments and federal agencies throughout U.S. history. Agents provocateurs are usually (but not always) civilians hired by law enforcement to infiltrate "radical" groups, where they transcend the role of common INFORMANTS by proposing crimes, supplying weapons or contraband items, and breaking the law themselves to incriminate their "comrades."

The FBI, particularly, was notorious for using agents provocateurs in its illicit COINTELPRO campaigns of 1956–71. A few examples from the period include:

Alfred Burnett: A twice-convicted felon in Seattle, Washington, Burnett was awaiting trial for robbery in January 1970, when he was suddenly released from jail over the objections of his parole officer. He subsequently pled guilty in that case but remained at large, again despite his parole officer's demand that Burnett be jailed for failure to appear for sentencing on another charge. The FBI's Seattle field office overruled the parole officer in each case, naming Burnett as an informant who supplied the Bureau with "valuable information" on ghetto violence and the Black Panther Party. More specifically, he was assigned to locate Jimmy Davis, a Panther suspected of involvement in recent BOMBINGS. Burnett never found Davis, but he paid a friend of the fugitive, 22-year-old Larry Ward, to bomb a local realtor's office on May 14, 1970. Burnett supplied the bomb, then alerted G-men and city police to the impending crime. (He later told reporters, "The police wanted a bomber and I gave them one.") Local police killed Ward at the scene, but later blamed FBI agents for his death. John Williams, chief of the SEATTLE POLICE DEPARTMENT's intelligence unit declared, "As far as I can tell, Ward was a relatively decent kid. Somebody set this whole thing up. It wasn't the police department." As Burnett went off to serve his robbery sentence, G-men had him transferred from state prison to a federal lockup for added security.

Larry Grathwohl: Once ranked among "the most militant members" of the 1960s Weather Under-

ground, Grathwohl was in fact an FBI informant whose actions, by his own admission, went far beyond simply observing and reporting crimes. Habitually armed with a pistol and straight razor, Grathwohl advertised himself to fellow Weathermen as a demolitions expert and offered bomb-making lessons to radicals of the "New Left." He went further still, and later confessed to the *New York Times* that he participated in the 1969 bombing of a Cincinnati public school. On March 6, 1970, a federal grand jury in Detroit indicted Grathwohl and 12 other Weathermen for conspiracy to bomb various military and police facilities. A subsequent indictment, issued on December 7, 1973, dismissed all charges against Grathwohl and another defendant, while adding more radicals to the list. Despite the serious charges, including the March 1970 firebombing of a Cleveland policeman's home and conspiracy to plant bombs in four states, none of the defendants were ever tried. Grathwohl, meanwhile, vanished into the federal WITNESS SECURITY PROGRAM and later published a sensational account of his exploits titled *Bringing Down America: An FBI Informer with the Weathermen* (1976).

Charles Grimm: In 1970 Grimm joined protests against the Vietnam War at the University of Alabama in Tuscaloosa. Unknown to fellow demonstrators, he received stipends from both the FBI and local police. Three days after the KENT STATE UNIVERSITY SHOOTINGS, on May 7, Grimm burned Dressler Hall on the Tuscaloosa campus. One week later, he lobbed Molotov cocktails into a city street, and on May 18 he joined in stoning police officers at the university. When questioned later about those crimes, Grimm claimed that his FBI handlers had full knowledge of his activities and that they in fact ordered him to destroy Dressler Hall. FBI spokesmen denied that charge, but no investigation of Grimm's allegations was pursued.

William Lemmer: A mentally unstable military veteran, threatened with a psychological discharge before he voluntarily left the service, Lemmer subsequently penned a letter to his estranged wife, blaming the group Vietnam Veterans Against the War (VVAW) for the breakup of their marriage. In the same letter, Lemmer threatened to silently eliminate VVAW members, using "tennis shoes" and a "length of piano wire." Police in Gainesville, Florida, caught Lemmer with two loaded pistols, and a local doctor recommended psychiatric treatment. None of that dissuaded

FBI agents from hiring Lemmer to infiltrate the VVAW, where he promoted schemes to attack the 1972 Republican National Convention in Miami with crossbows, firebombs, automatic weapons, and homemade grenades. Eight VVAW activists were indicted based on Lemmer's revelations, but their trial in 1973 only showcased the role of government provocateurs in criminal entrapment. Prosecutors produced no weapons other than slingshots purchased from a sporting goods shop, and Major Adam Klimkowsi, chief of the MIAMI POLICE DEPARTMENT's Special Investigations Unit admitted under oath that one of his agents proposed acquisition of machine guns to the defendants, who flatly rejected his offer. Lemmer's exposure as an FBI plant finally doomed the government's case, and jurors acquitted all eight defendants.

Reinhold Mohr: Two years after the Kent State shootings, in April 1972, members of the VVAW warned police in Kent, Ohio, that "there's a nut running around out there with a bunch of automatic weapons." The subject, alleged student radical Reinhold Mohr, had offered the illegal weapons to the VVAW's local chapter as a means of "furthering the armed struggle against imperialism." Caught with a machine gun and a rocket launcher in his car, Mohr identified himself as a member of the Kent State University police force. He also drew support from FBI agents who said Mohr had "only followed orders" in peddling illegal weapons. Mohr was released without charges to pursue his law enforcement career.

William O'Neal: Twice arrested during early 1968, for auto theft and impersonating an FBI agent, O'Neal escaped trial and earned substantial income by infiltrating the Black Panther Party for FBI handlers. In that role, he helped disrupt peace talks between the Panthers and Chicago's Blackstone Rangers, resulting in a string of shooting incidents that wounded several persons. Local Panther boss FRED HAMPTON rejected O'Neal's plans to bomb city hall and to construct a homemade electric chair for police informants, but O'Neal took advantage of Hampton's absence to bullwhip dissident Panthers and to lead other party members in armed robberies. In December 1969 he supplied local police with a floor plan of Hampton's apartment, prior to a raid that killed Hampton and colleague Mark Clark. Subsequent investigation proved that Hampton was asleep, probably drugged, when he was shot in bed by officers of the CHICAGO POLICE DEPARTMENT.

Horace Packer: Employed by Seattle FBI office to infiltrate the Students for a Democratic Society and its Weather Underground offshoot at the University of Washington, Packer admitted under oath that he supplied student radicals with illegal DRUGS, weapons, and components for Molotov cocktails. He also furnished (and the FBI paid for) the paint used to vandalize Seattle's federal courthouse during demonstrations staged in February 1970. That incident became a key element in conspiracy charges filed against eight defendants. At trial in Tacoma, Packer testified that his Bureau handlers told him to "do anything to protect my credibility" as an informant. Pursuant to those orders, Packer "smoked dope all the time" and used other illegal drugs, including cocaine, LSD, amphetamines, and mescaline while active on FBI business. He was arrested several times and violated terms of a suspended sentence he received for his role in an attack on campus ROTC headquarters. Packer's credibility collapsed in court when he admitted on the witness stand that he would lie to convict the defendants. Charges against the "Seattle Eight" were later dismissed.

Alton Roberts: A violent member of the Mississippi KU KLUX KLAN, Roberts murdered two civil rights workers in June 1964 and received a 10-year federal sentence for that crime in 1967. While free on bond pending appeal, he accepted some $35,000 from the FBI and Jewish businessmen to solve a series of racist bombings in the Magnolia State. To that end, Roberts arranged for Klansman Thomas Tarrants to bomb a home in Meridian, where local police lay in ambush. The resultant firefight killed Tarrants's female accomplice, while leaving Tarrants, a policeman, and a bystander gravely wounded.

Gary Rowe: Another Klansman serving on the FBI's payroll, Rowe participated in many acts of racist violence with full knowledge and approval of his FBI handlers. In May 1961 he led attacks on integrated freedom riders in Birmingham, where police commissioner Eugene "Bull" Connor granted Klansmen time to beat demonstrators without official interference. Two years later, Rowe failed a polygraph test wherein he denied responsibility for a church bombing that killed four young girls. In March 1965 he was present in the car from which two other Klansmen shot and killed civil rights worker Viola Liuzzo. Defendants in that case named Rowe as the triggerman, but murder charges filed against him in Lowndes County were later dismissed. Rowe also boasted of killing a black man in 1961, under circumstances that remain obscure.

Melvin Smith: On December 8, 1969, four days after Chicago police killed Fred Hampton and Mark Clark, officers of the LOS ANGELES POLICE DEPARTMENT staged a similar raid on the local Black Panther office. A four-hour firefight ensued, leaving six Panthers wounded and 13 in custody. Seven months later, the 13 were tried on charges of conspiracy to murder policemen and to possess illegal weapons (though none were found in the raid). The defendants were surprised when one of their comrades, Melvin "Cotton" Smith, appeared as a prosecution witness. Revelation of his role as an FBI/LAPD informant who promoted acquisition of illegal arms influenced jurors to acquit the Panthers on the most serious charges, though nine were strangely convicted of plotting to stockpile guns that police could not find.

Thomas Tongyai: Nicknamed "Tommy the Traveler" for his wide-ranging rambles around New York state, Tongyai toured various universities while drawing paychecks from the FBI and local police. In the process, he exhorted crowds to kill policemen, build bombs, and demolish campus buildings. Habitually armed with firearms and grenades, Tongyai offered training courses in marksmanship and bomb-making for radicals. His role as an agent provocateur was exposed when a group of his protégés bombed the ROTC office at Hobart College. Tongyai escaped indictment and retired from UNDERCOVER WORK to become a policeman in Pennsylvania.

See also: CONNOR, THEOPHILUS EUGENE ("BULL"); FEDERAL BUREAU OF INVESTIGATION.

Ahrens, Robin (1952–1985)

Born in St. Paul, Minnesota, on May 6, 1952, Robin Ahrens earned a B.A. in fine arts from Utah State University in 1974. She taught school in Idaho until 1980, then moved to Virginia and enrolled at James Madison University, earning a media specialist degree in 1983. She entered the FBI Academy on October 14, 1984, but her graduation was delayed until June 1985, by an injury suffered in training. On June 28, 1985, Ahrens was assigned to her first active-duty post at the Phoenix, Arizona, field office. Barely three months later, on October 4, Ahrens joined a group of agents assigned to arrest a suspected armored car bandit. The raid was tragically confused: G-men mistook Ahrens for an armed accomplice of their suspect and shot her, inflicting wounds that claimed her life on October 5. The first

female FBI agent killed on duty, Ahrens was memorialized by having the new Phoenix field office named in her honor. One agent involved in her death was fired for "faulty and atrocious judgment," while a second resigned.

See also: FEDERAL BUREAU OF INVESTIGATION.

air marshals

While Israel has long stationed plainclothes armed guards on its commercial airline flights, the United States did not follow suit until hijackings became commonplace, during the administration of President Richard Nixon (1969–74). Few details have been published concerning the Federal Air Marshal Service (FAMS), since its operations are designed to catch would-be skyjackers by surprise. We know that the FAMS was originally part of the U.S. Transportation Department's Transportation Security Administration (TSA), and its numbers were limited. According to the FAMS Web site, only 33 air marshals were employed nationwide on September 11, 2001, when terrorists hijacked four airliners and used them as crude missiles to attack the Pentagon and World Trade Center in New York.

After "9/11" President George W. Bush authorized a personnel increase of undisclosed proportions at FAMS, resulting in a deluge of some 200,000 job applications. From that mass of prospects, an unknown number of applicants (6,000 according to one report) were screened, hired, trained, and certified for deployment on domestic and international flights. On September 2, 2003, Secretary Tom Ridge announced that the FAMS would be shifted from Transportation to his own HOMELAND SECURITY DEPARTMENT, attached to the Bureau of Immigration and Customs Enforcement (ICE). Michael Garcia, acting assistant secretary of the bureau, told reporters, "ICE offers the air marshal service multiple investigative resources, such as additional access to intelligence, better coordination with other law enforcement agencies, and broader training opportunities."

It was a boost badly needed after August 2002, when *USA Today* reported a "flood" of resignations from the FAMS. The report claimed that "at least 250" marshals had resigned, while TSA spokesman James Loy pegged the actual number at "fewer than 80" defectors. Complaints from inside the service that summer included 12- to 16-hour working days, with 10-day consecutive tours of duty resulting in illness and marshals sleeping on the job. *USA Today* quoted a July 17 e-mail sent to various managers by the FAMS human resources officer, seeking appointment of an employee relations aide "given the volume of resignations we have been receiving." A second memo from the FAMS operations control center acknowledged a "long list of notifications for transfers and resignations." One current marshal told reporter Blake Morrison, "We were promised the Garden of Eden. We were given hell. If they don't make major changes fast, they're going to have no one left but the bottom of the barrel."

Ridge's September 2002 announcement included plans to hire 5,000 additional air marshals. Progress seemed sluggish, though, with the *Washington Times* reporting in 2004 that air marshals covered less than 5 percent of daily U.S. flights, with numbers still declining. While the total number of active air marshals remained top-secret, anonymous FAMS executives claimed that "fewer than 3,500" were employed to guard 35,000 daily flights. Allowing for time off and sick leave, the same sources said that only 500 to 1,000 flights were protected on any given day. David Adams, spokesman for FAMS, refused to join in any public speculation. "People could figure out the ratio of which [flights] are covered and which ones are not," he said. "That's our position. The amount of personnel is classified and we won't release it." Meanwhile, a vague briefing paper from Homeland Security, issued on the second anniversary of the 9/11 attacks, asserted that "thousands of air marshals fly on tens of thousands of flights each month on a wide variety of routes and aircraft."

Whatever their numbers, FAMS administrators note that their marshals—self-described as "the quiet professionals"—are trained at the William J. Hughes Technical Center in Atlantic City, New Jersey. The program includes courses in "behavioral observation, intimidation tactics and close quarters self-defense." And while their expertise has never been tested in combat, FAMS also reports that marshals "are held to a higher standard for handgun accuracy than officers of any other federal law enforcement agency."

See also: TERRORISM.

Alabama Bureau of Investigation

In January 1936, one month after the ALABAMA HIGHWAY PATROL was created, Chief Walter McAdory named two of his 74 patrolmen as "special investigators." No record remains today of their work, but the unit was expanded several years later to become the Highway Patrol's Investigation and Identification Division (I&I), assigned to conduct various investigations not only for the Highway Patrol, but also for the governor's office, the state attorney general, and other Alabama executive agencies. I&I agents also assisted the FBI, county sheriffs, circuit solicitors, and various municipal police departments with criminal investigations on request. Much of its work during World War II involved reports of ESPIONAGE, sabotage, and draft evasion. In 1943 I&I

became Alabama's central fingerprint repository, under an order from Governor Chauncey Sparks, requiring all county sheriff's to fingerprint all arrestees, providing copies of their prints to I&I and to the FBI in Washington.

In 1947 Governor James Folsom issued a new executive order, creating a Bureau of Investigation and Identification (BII), wholly divorced from the Highway Patrol. Folsom made the BII responsible for criminal investigation and enforcement of state liquor laws, but he dissolved the unit two years later, dispersing its agents among various Highway Patrol divisions statewide. Although that move was meant to improve coordination between investigators and uniformed patrol officers, Folsom reversed himself again in 1950, reconstituting the BII under pressure from various prosecutors, sheriff's, and other Alabama law enforcement spokesmen. Governor Gordon Persons continued the seesaw tradition in 1952, when he revoked Folsom's order, reactivating the BII.

There matters rested until 1954, when L. B. Sullivan, director of Alabama's Department of Public Safety, created a new Investigative and Identification Division, combining administrative, highway patrol, and driver's license services as the department's fifth division. In 1971 the new I&I was officially divided into three units: auto theft, narcotics and criminal investigations. Governor George Wallace replaced I&I with the present Alabama Bureau of Investigation on October 15, 1974.

See also: FINGERPRINTS.

Alabama Highway Patrol

The Alabama Highway Patrol (AHP) was created in December 1935, with 74 uniformed patrolmen under chief Walter McAdory. A month later, two of those officers were assigned to full-time (but unspecified) investigative work, while the remainder continued on routine patrol, enforcing state traffic laws and responding to accident calls. As in other states, AHP officers were also available to help county sheriffs and municipal police in situations where they found themselves shorthanded, but the force attracted little attention outside Alabama until 1963, with the inauguration of Governor George Wallace.

Elected on a promise to preserve racial segregation "forever," Wallace drew support from the KU KLUX KLAN and soon transformed the AHP into a notorious vehicle for crushing civil rights demonstrations. Under Col. ALBERT J. LINGO—a self-styled "good friend" of the Klan, known to friends as "hell on niggers"—Wallace renamed the AHP as Alabama State Troopers, ordering Confederate battle flags mounted on the front bumper of each patrol car. Lingo's troopers were notorious for

Alabama state troopers attack civil rights marchers in Selma on "Bloody Sunday," in March 1965. (Library of Congress)

use of EXCESSIVE FORCE against blacks and integrated demonstrators, frequently collaborating with hard-line racist lawmen such as Birmingham's Eugene "Bull" Connor and Sheriff JAMES G. CLARK, JR. in Selma. State attorney general Richmond Flowers and FBI files confirm that Lingo personally intervened on multiple occasions to subvert prosecution of Klan terrorists, including those responsible for a fatal church bombing in Birmingham on September 15, 1963. Information flowed freely from Lingo's "antisubversive squad" to Klan leaders throughout Alabama, and troopers figured prominently in violence against peaceful demonstrators, as in Selma's "Bloody Sunday" of March 1965. Lingo also supported Wallace by reinstating the revoked driver's licenses of potential white voters convicted of driving while intoxicated. During 1968's presidential campaign, a state trooper destroyed the film of a reporter who photographed Wallace shaking hands with Klan "wizard" Robert Shelton.

While Lingo left the AHP in 1966 to seek election as Jefferson County sheriff, defeated by black votes, the state patrol remained a political tool (or weapon) for Governor Wallace. His 1970 gubernatorial campaign included TV ads attacking incumbent Albert Brewer's integration of the AHP. One ad depicted a white woman stopped for speeding on a lonely road at night, cringing as a black state trooper peers through her window. It finally took a near-miss with death from an assassin's bullet to crack Wallace's hard-line racism and lift the burden of his foibles from the AHP.

In recent years, the AHP has suffered from the same budget cuts and personnel shortages that plague other American law enforcement agencies. By 2003, with 4.6 million registered vehicles and 4.2 million licensed drivers cruising Alabama highways, the AHP had only 320 uniformed officers—a net loss of 40 from its 369 in 1968. (The recommended minimum, meanwhile, was 574.) The loss of personnel, accompanied by a 150-mile travel limit for troopers on duty, was occasioned by a state budget shortfall of some $675 million. Additionally, moved by concerns over TERRORISM, several troopers resigned to become federal AIR MARSHALS, while 24 were serving on active U.S. military duty in December 2003.

See also: BOMBING AND BOMB SQUADS; CONNOR, THEOPHILUS EUGENE ("BULL"); FEDERAL BUREAU OF INVESTIGATION.

Alaska Bureau of Investigation

The Alaska Department of Public Safety, Division of ALASKA STATE TROOPERS, has 350 commissioned troopers statewide. A subdivision of that force, founded in 1971 to handle specific cases, is the Alaska Bureau of Investigation (ABI). ABI headquarters is located in Anchorage, hosting a Computer and Financial Crimes Unit, a Missing Persons Clearinghouse, and a four-officer Wildlife Investigation Unit. Substations are found in Fairbanks, Mat-Su, and Soldotna. In addition to the cases specified above, ABI agents also police fellow troopers themselves. In 2004, for example, ABI officers were assigned to investigate Sgt. Brian Wassman's fatal shooting of 54-year-old James Dorff at Delta Junction and a two-year rash of SEX CRIMES allegedly committed in Aniak by Trooper Daniel Scott. (Neither case had been resolved at press time for this volume.)

See also: COMPUTER CRIMES.

Alaska State Troopers

Law enforcement duties in Alaska were shared by the U.S. Army and Navy from the mid-19th century until the gold rush of 1898, when primary responsibility passed to the U.S. MARSHALS SERVICE. In 1941 the territorial legislature established the Alaska Highway Patrol to enforce traffic codes, but no police authority was granted to patrolmen. Four years later, in the face of thriving rural crime, Highway Patrol officers were deputized as "special deputy" U.S. marshals, a status they maintained until the Highway Patrol gained full police authority in 1948. Five years later, new legislation established the Alaska Territorial Police with 36 sworn officers assigned to remote outposts. Statehood, in 1959, saw the ATP renamed Alaska State Police, with 23 new officers (including 13 former U.S. marshals). The unit's name changed once again, in 1967, to Alaska State Troopers. The same year witnessed creation of Alaska's Public Safety Training Academy.

At press time for this volume, 350 commissioned state troopers were posted throughout Alaska, with headquarters detachments located in Anchorage, Fairbanks, Ketchikan, Palmer, and Soldotna. Those 350 officers patrol a region one-fifth the size of the continental United States, some 586,412 square miles of diverse terrain and climate, including rugged mountains, huge glaciers, forests, tundra, and 6,640 miles of coastline.

Within the state, more than 3 million lakes and 3,000 rivers present additional challenges for transportation and recovery of evidence. Specialized bureaus within the Alaska State Troopers include the ALASKA BUREAU OF INVESTIGATION and the 82-member Alaska Bureau of Wildlife Enforcement. Other responsibilities include administration of the Village Public Safety Officer Program and search-and-rescue missions.

Algiers Motel shootings

The Detroit ghetto riot of July 1967 left 43 persons dead and 1,189 injured. As in other riots from that "long hot summer," most of the fatalities were African Americans shot by police or members of the NATIONAL GUARD for alleged looting, sniping, or curfew violations. Many of those deaths are suspect, but none more so than the triple killing that occurred at the Algiers Motel on the night of July 25–26.

Unverified reports of sniping were rife throughout the Detroit riots, peaking after nightfall on July 25. Around midnight, authorities responded to reports of shots fired from the Algiers Motel, a Woodward Avenue establishment known for its transient "pleasure loving" clientele. In short order, the motel was surrounded by a strike force including officers of the DETROIT POLICE DEPARTMENT, the MICHIGAN STATE POLICE, National Guardsmen, and five private security guards. Sweeping from room to room, the raiders corralled 15 patrons, including three black youths—17-year-old Carl Cooper, 19-year-old Aubrey Pollard, Jr., and 18-year-old Fred Temple—found in a room with two scantily clad white females.

Witnesses disagree over what happened next. Civilian survivors and some of the officers present agreed that the motel was ransacked in a fruitless search for guns, and that most of its patrons were beaten during interrogations laced with racial epithets and sexual insults. (One officer broke the stock of his shotgun over a helpless victim's head.) Other officers and Guardsmen denied any use of EXCESSIVE FORCE during the raid. By the time most of the patrons were released at 2:00 A.M., Cooper, Pollard, and Temple were dead, killed by close-range gunshots in two separate rooms. Detroit newspapers initially described the three dead teenagers as "snipers" killed in a battle with police, but that story changed as proof emerged that none of them were armed.

On July 31, 1967, Detroit Patrolman Robert Paille admitted shooting Fred Temple and testified that Patrolman David Senak "shot almost simultaneously at the same man." (Senak denied it, but acknowledged killing another black man in the riots, on July 24.) Patrolman Ronald August admitted shooting Aubrey

Pollard, while the shooter(s) in Carl Cooper's death remain unknown today. Aside from those confessions, one National Guardsman identified August as Pollard's killer, while three guardsmen fingered Senak for beating various victims, and two motel tenants named Paille as the officer who beat them. Murder warrants were issued for August and Paille on August 2, 1967, while one of the private security guards (Melvin Dismukes) was charged with felonious assault. Patrolman Senak, though not charged with any crime as yet, was still suspended and eventually left the force.

The Algiers Motel cases proceeded by fits and starts. On August 15, during a preliminary hearing on the murder charges, Judge Robert DeMascio ruled Paille's confession inadmissible on constitutional grounds. Two days later, DeMascio dismissed the charge against Paille but allowed August's case to proceed. On August 23 Paille, Senak, and Dismukes were arrested on new charges of "conspiracy to commit a legal act in an illegal manner." Judge Frank Schemanske dismissed those charges after another hearing, on December 1, 1967. Meanwhile, David Senak was jailed for felonious assault on two prostitutes in October 1967, but that case was also dismissed. On May 3, 1968, federal prosecutors indicted August, Dismukes, Paille, and Senak for conspiracy to violate the civil rights of Pollard, Temple, and eight surviving Algiers Motel victims, but that case likewise came to nothing. Dismukes was acquitted of assault in May 1968, and Ronald August was later acquitted of killing Aubrey Pollard. A civil lawsuit filed by Temple's mother in January 1968, naming 10 defendants, was later dismissed.

No one was ever punished for the Algiers Motel killings, except for the motel's proprietors. On October 3, 1967, Detroit authorities filed litigation to padlock the place as a public nuisance. The courts agreed, and the Algiers Motel was subsequently bulldozed out of existence.

Alvord, Burt (1866–1910)

The son of a traveling judge, born in 1866, Burt Alvord was 15 years old and living in Tombstone, Arizona, during the famous O.K. CORRAL GUNFIGHT. Though still a child, he recognized the underlying motive for that battle and the string of homicides that followed—namely, control of the county sheriff's office, which in turn meant control of local vice and the collateral duty of collecting taxes, which might wind up in the sheriff's pocket rather than in the local treasury. Five years later, in 1886, Alvord took his first step toward that coveted post, becoming chief deputy to newly elected Sheriff JOHN HORTON SLAUGHTER in Cochise County.

At first Alvord seemed intent on building up a reputation as a dedicated lawman, running down rustlers and thieves, but he soon turned to crime on the side. Sheriff Slaughter grew suspicious, but he had no evidence that would support indictments, and Alvord took over the sheriff's office when Slaughter retired in 1890. A few years later, Alvord switched to full-time rustling, operating from Mexico, but he returned to law enforcement of a sort in 1899, serving as a constable in Wilcox, Arizona. Local residents raised no objection to his reputation as a gunman, including several known murders, and they were presumably unaware of Constable Alvord's latest sideline—at least, for a while.

Alvord was barely settled in Wilcox when he joined another corrupt lawman, Deputy Billie Stiles, in a series of train robberies. (Stiles claimed to have murdered his own father when he was but 12 years old.) Their gang was captured in September 1900, following a holdup near Cochise, but Stiles orchestrated a jailbreak and they were soon back in business. Alvord and Stiles were jailed again in 1903, but once again they managed to escape. Tiring of life on the run, Alvord contrived to fake their deaths, sending caskets filled with their alleged remains back to Tombstone, but authorities there saw through the ruse and continued their manhunt.

In 1904 a squad of ARIZONA RANGERS followed Alvord into Mexico and cornered him at a site known as Nigger Head Gap. A brief shootout left Alvord wounded, and he was returned to Arizona for trial, serving two years in prison on various charges. Nothing certain is known of his life following parole: Alvord was reportedly seen in Jamaica and sundry towns in Latin America before 1910, when allegedly he died as a laborer on the Panama Canal.

As for Billie Stiles, he seemed to have made a clean getaway. In January 1908 a Nevada deputy sheriff named William Larkin shot and killed a wanted fugitive from justice. As Larkin rode back to the dead man's house, his victim's 12-year-old son drew a shotgun and blasted Larkin dead from his saddle. Subsequent investigation proved that "Larkin" was in fact the elusive Billie Stiles, gunned down by a boy the same age as he was when he shot his own father.

See also: TRAIN ROBBERY.

Amber Alerts

Nine-year-old Amber Rene Hagerman was kidnapped from her Arlington, Texas, neighborhood while riding her bicycle on January 17, 1996. A neighbor witnessed the abduction and described the vehicle to police, but no system existed to broadcast that description through the city or beyond. Amber's corpse was found on January 21, her death propelling efforts to establish the emergency alert system that today bears her name—also recognized as an acronym for *America's Missing Broadcast Emergency Response.*

Amber Alerts are used to notify civilians that a child has been abducted and is deemed to be in danger. The present system includes bulletins broadcast over radio and television, on the Internet, and via lighted highway billboards that include such information as the child's description, a description of the kidnapper, his vehicle, and license number (where that information is available). Authorities in various states credit Amber Alerts with the recovery of children and teenagers snatched by sex offenders and/or would-be murderers.

A National Amber Alert Plan was written into federal law by Congress in 2003, and by April 2004 every U.S. state except Hawaii had an Amber Alert system in place.

A similar system, albeit operating on a smaller scale, is the "Code Adam" alert (named for six-year-old Adam Walsh, kidnapped from a Florida shopping mall and murdered in July 1981). Code Adam alerts are distributed within buildings (such as malls or apartment houses) where a child is reported missing, thereby triggering heightened security precautions on the premises. By that means, authorities hope to prevent kidnappers and their victims from escaping, but no practical results have thus far been reported by the media.

An electronic sign shows an Amber Alert over Interstate 80 in Omaha, Nebraska, Wednesday, December 11, 2002. A search for a nine-month-old girl triggered Nebraska's first Amber Alert warning after a white 1995 Jeep Grand Cherokee with the girl in the backseat was taken from a Texaco station while the girl's grandmother was paying for gas. (AP Photo/ Nati Harnik)

Police and child-protection activists warn that it is possible to overuse Amber Alerts, thereby generating an atmosphere wherein such alerts are ignored. Critics acknowledge that some 800,000 children are reported missing in the United States every year, but note that a majority of those are either runaways who soon return or children "kidnapped" by their parents during bitter custody disputes. To avoid "crying wolf," the National Center for Missing and Exploited Children suggests the following criteria for broadcast of Amber Alerts:

1. A recognized law enforcement agency must determine that a child has been abducted.

2. That agency should also have reason to believe the missing child faces a risk of death or serious bodily harm.

3. Sufficient descriptive information on the child, the suspected abductor or his/her vehicle must be available to make the public alert worthwhile.

At press time for this volume, the driving force behind nationwide Amber Alerts was the Polly Klaas Foundation (PKF), acting through a subsidiary called AmberAlertNow.org. The PKF is named for 12-year-old Polly Klaas, abducted from her California home and murdered by a paroled sex offender on October 1, 1993.

American Civil Liberties Union (ACLU)

Founded in 1920, the ACLU was created by New Yorker Roger Baldwin to replace his wartime National Civil Liberties Bureau. For the better part of a century it has provided free legal defense to clients of various races, religions, and political persuasions in cases where their constitutional rights are infringed by some official action. With clients ranging from the far left to the neo-Nazi right, the ACLU is ever controversial and has endured harassment from various U.S. law enforcement agencies.

FBI files released under the Freedom of Information Act reveal that the ACLU was under constant federal surveillance for nearly half a century, from Baldwin's initial 1924 meeting with J. EDGAR HOOVER to the date of Hoover's death in 1972 (and perhaps beyond). While Hoover feigned sympathy in his first conversation with Baldwin, he hated the "liberal" ACLU and all it stood for, particularly when its spokesmen criticized the FBI. Ever resourceful, though, Hoover found ways to block that criticism at the source, corrupting the ACLU's leadership even as he kept the group under surveillance, indexing names of its members for wartime custodial detention. FBI records disclose that Morris Ernst, general council of the ACLU, exchanged more

than 300 personal letters with Hoover between 1939 and 1964, keeping Hoover informed of every move the group made. Obsessed with purging Communists from the ACLU, Ernst passed along everything from membership lists to office gossip. An internal ACLU report cleared Ernst of any "overt improprieties" in 1977, but executive director Aryeh Neier called Ernst's dealings with the FBI "inexcusable and destructive of civil liberties."

Even so, Ernst was not the worst INFORMANT. Irving Ferman, director of the ACLU's Washington, D.C., chapter, was described in the same 1977 report as having maintained "the most intensive and extensive and secretive" FBI relationship of any ACLU leader—a relationship described as "friendly and somewhat clubby." Between 1952 and 1959 Ferman delivered reams of documents and correspondence to the Bureau, later conceding from retirement that "perhaps he was violating his trust with the organization." Assistant FBI Director Louis Nichols was sufficiently impressed to praise Ferman for being "as much a soldier as those of us serving the Bureau."

The ACLU's federal lawsuit, filed in 1977, unearthed 41,728 pages of FBI reports dating back to 1917, when Roger Baldwin led the American Union Against Militarism. Spying had intensified in 1940, after ACLU spokesmen opposed a $100,000 congressional appropriation for the FBI. Reports filed in the wake of that faux pas noted that Ernest Besig, ACLU director for northern California, was "not a Communist [but] enough of a troublemaker not to be left alone." In Southern California, meanwhile, G-men deemed that "every person" in the ACLU's office "is a Communist." Exposure of illegal FBI wiretaps in a 1949 ESPIONAGE case prompted criticism from ACLU board member James Fry, but other leaders of the group dissented, praising the Bureau's efforts to purge America of Reds. The ACLU's annual report for 1953 found "a heartening expression of principle" in one of Hoover's ghost-written magazine articles, concluding erroneously that FBI civil rights violations "seem to be happily infrequent." Lou Nichols lied outright to ACLU staff counsel Herbert Levy, telling him that Hoover considered the ACLU a "very worthwhile organization," and ACLU director Louis Joughin suppressed a pamphlet published by the Philadelphia chapter, advising citizens of their rights during an FBI interrogation. Joughin, in his wisdom, deemed the warning "unjustified" and "unwise."

The ACLU's one-sided love affair with Hoover's FBI ended in March 1971, after antiwar protesters stole and published thousands of COINTELPRO documents outlining the Bureau's illegal harassment of various political groups. On October 29–30, 1971, the ACLU hosted a sharply critical conference on FBI activities, convened at Princeton University. FBI surveillance and infiltration of the ACLU allegedly ended with Hoover's death in May 1972, but in light of past history some ACLU members remain unconvinced.

The union's collaboration with FBI agents was not replicated in dealings with state and local law enforcement agencies. Nationwide, ACLU lawyers have consistently led the offensive against EXCESSIVE FORCE, POLICE RIOTS, racial PROFILING, and "THIRD-DEGREE" TACTICS. Union spokesmen also played a leading role in the campaign for establishment of CIVILIAN REVIEW BOARDS to investigate claims of police misconduct. In July 2002 the ACLU opposed new bids by Attorney General JOHN ASHCROFT to expand DOMESTIC SURVEILLANCE under terms of the USA PATRIOT ACT. Interviewed by the *San Francisco Chronicle,* ACLU spokespersons declared that they had "drawn a line with respect to privacy, political and associational rights that government must not cross even with the best of intentions. President George W. Bush responded from Washington that limits on domestic spying would cripple his administration's "war on terrorism." The debate continues.

See also: CUSTODIAL DETENTION INDEX; FEDERAL BUREAU OF INVESTIGATION.

American Protective League

Spawned by xenophobic hysteria during World War I, the American Protective League (APL) was organized by Chicago advertising executive Albert Briggs in 1916. Conceived as a private intelligence corps to police aliens and "radicals," the APL attracted 100,000 members in its first three months, topping 250,000 by the end of 1917. Its first step toward legitimacy, in February 1917, was an offer posed to Hinton Claybaugh, agent-in-charge of the FBI's Chicago field office. Claybaugh accepted the APL's plan to spy on wealthy Germans by putting its members to work as chauffeurs and the like. When Briggs returned a month later, offering the Bureau a fleet of 75 cars, Claybaugh passed the proposal upstairs. FBI chief A. BRUCE BIELASKI discussed the prospect with Attorney General THOMAS GREGORY, and both welcomed the APL as a quasi-official JUSTICE DEPARTMENT auxiliary force.

The bargain made sense at first glance, since the FBI had only 265 agents to cover the entire United States. More eyes and hands were needed, but the deal caused trouble from day one. First, the TREASURY DEPARTMENT complained that APL detectives carried badges identifying them as "SECRET SERVICE" agents. Bielaski and Briggs changed the badges in time for their first joint action in Chicago, raiding offices of the Industrial Workers of

the World in September 1917. By early 1918 reports surfaced of APL members burglarizing homes and offices, but Bielaski ignored it, since his G-men sometimes did the same. The next public FBI-APL collaboration occurred in March 1918, with a city-wide sweep for Chicago draft dodgers. The "slacker" roundup was deemed successful enough to warrant further raids in Birmingham (assisted by the KU KLUX KLAN), Cleveland, Dayton, Detroit, Philadelphia, St. Louis, and San Francisco. Beginning on September 3, 1918, 35 FBI agents, 2,000 APL vigilantes and scores of local police spent three days sweeping the streets of Manhattan, Brooklyn, Newark, and Jersey City, jailing an estimated 75,000 suspects. When the dust settled, only one in 200 of those detained proved to be "slackers."

Denunciation from the press and U.S. Senate scuttled any plans for further raids and stripped the APL of its quasi-official status. Two months later, on November 11, 1918, the armistice canceled any need to hunt draft dodgers in America. The APL formally disbanded on February 1, 1919.

anarchism

In its purest form, anarchism is the belief that all forms of government should be abolished. Historically, some anarchists have gone beyond mere advocacy and attempted to secure that goal by physical attacks on government officials and institutions in Europe and the United States. Before the advent of Bolshevism, with the Russian revolution of 1917, "radicals" and "enemy aliens" in the United States were often branded anarchists regardless of their actual philosophy. The label was also broadly applied to social reformers and labor organizers, as a later generation of activists would be falsely branded "communists."

America's anarchist panic dated from 1880, with the onset of a major immigration wave from Italy. New arrivals included several prominent anarchist spokesmen, such as Luigi Galleani, Enrico Malatesta, and Carlo Tresca. On May 4, 1886, the Chicago HAYMARKET BOMBING killed eight policemen and an uncertain number of civilians, while wounding more than 260 others at a rally for striking workers. Eight alleged anarchists (none of them Italian) were convicted of conspiracy, though evidence produced at trial proved none of them had thrown the bomb. By 1890 a new nativist, antiradical movement arose in America, expanding nationwide from its East Coast epicenter.

Fear of anarchism increased with each reported act of violence. In 1900 Italian anarchist Gaetano Bresci left his adopted home in New Jersey to assassinate King Umberto I of Italy. The following year, anarchist Leon Czolgosz shot and killed President William McKinley

Anarchist Leon Czolgosz assassinated President William McKinley in 1901. (Author's collection)

ings rocked America in 1919. Attorney General A. MITCHELL PALMER retaliated with sweeping raids from coast to coast, counting famed anarchists Emma Goldman and Alexander Berkman among those deported to Russia. Still the bombings remained unsolved, despite unsubstantiated claims of a confession from New York anarchist Andrea Salsedo (killed in FBI custody on May 3, 1920). Two activist friends of Salsedo, Nicola Sacco and Bartolomeo Vanzetti, were framed for murder by Massachusetts authorities, convicted on perjured testimony and executed despite international protests in 1927.

America's last significant act of anarchist violence was the Wall Street bombing of September 16, 1920. In that case, a horse-drawn wagon filled with dynamite and iron sash weights exploded at the intersection of Wall and Broad Streets, in downtown Manhattan, killing 30 victims outright and wounding at least 300 (10 of whom later died). Pamphlets found a block from the bomb site, signed by the "American Anarchist Fighters," demanded that U.S. authorities "Free the political

in Buffalo, New York. McKinley's successor in office, THEODORE ROOSEVELT, signed legislation to stifle the anarchist press in 1908. Four years later, two immigrant labor organizers were framed on murder charges (but finally acquitted) during a textile strike at Lawrence, Massachusetts. Colorado's LUDLOW MASSACRE of 1914 prompted three anarchists to plot the murder of industrialist John D. Rockefeller (and thus sparked creation of the New York City bomb squad). Two more anarchists were arrested (some say framed) in New York the following year, for plotting to blow up St. Patrick's Cathedral.

"Progressive" president Woodrow Wilson reserved some of his harshest words and legislation for "enemy aliens" on the eve of America's entry into World War I. The Bolshevik revolution of 1917 gave nativists a new reason to tremble, but communism and anarchism (or "syndicalism") were confused in many minds, including that of a fledgling clerk at the JUSTICE DEPARTMENT named J. EDGAR HOOVER. War's end brought no cessation of violence, as a wave of strikes, riots and bomb-

Anarchist leader Alexander Berkman was deported to Russia in 1919. (Author's collection)

he was responsible for the publicity campaign that outlawed marijuana.

Anslinger's career at the FBN was marked by a long-running feud with FBI director J. EDGAR HOOVER. Both men courted publicity, and Hoover blamed Anslinger for using copycat initials to promote his agency—though, in fact, the "FBI" name was not adopted until 1935, five years after the FBN's creation. The greatest bone of contention was Anslinger's public warnings of an international drug-dealing syndicate. Strong evidence supported those claims, including WIRETAP transcripts linking exiled New York mobster "Lucky" Luciano to the transatlantic heroin trade, but Hoover was incapable of any compromise with enemies, a stance that led him to dismiss all reports of ORGANIZED CRIME in the States as "baloney." Deputy attorney general William Hundly recalled, years later, that Hoover "got in a big pissing match with Harry Anslinger over at Narcotics, who he didn't like, and Anslinger had the Mafia coming up out of the sewers the same way Hoover had the Communists coming out of the sewers. So Hoover got himself locked into saying there was no Mafia."

That stance proved embarrassing in 1950–51, when Anslinger assisted Senator ESTES KEFAUVER's investigation of organized crime; again in 1957, when Mafia leaders from across the United States were arrested in conference at Apalachin, New York; and finally when mob defector Joe Valachi testified before the U.S. Senate in the early 1960s. Anslinger retired from the FBN in 1962 and published a book, *The Murderers,* which detailed the growth of international drug cartels since the 1920s. He remained outspoken on the subject until his death in 1975.

See also: FEDERAL BUREAU OF INVESTIGATION.

U.S. authorities deported anarchist Emma Goldman to Russia in 1919. (Author's collection)

prisoners or it will be sure death for all of you." J. Edgar Hoover took personal charge of the case, declaring that he would not rest until the bombers were identified, but the crime remains officially unsolved today.

See also: BOMBING AND BOMB SQUADS; FEDERAL BUREAU OF INVESTIGATION.

Anslinger, Harry J. (1892–1975)

A Pennsylvania native, born in 1892, Harry Anslinger attended Pennsylvania State University before joining the U.S. War Department in 1917. He earned a law degree from Washington College prior to transferring, in 1926, to a post at the TREASURY DEPARTMENT. Three years later, he was named Commissioner of PROHIBITION, but Anslinger held that post for barely a year, then found himself named commissioner of the FEDERAL BUREAU OF NARCOTICS (FBN). Anslinger retained that post until his retirement in 1962, crusading tirelessly for stiffer penalties against all manner of DRUG and narcotic offenses. More than anyone else in government,

Appel, Charles A. (1895–?)

A native of Washington, D.C., born in 1895, Charles Appel trained as a combat aviator in World War I and later attended George Washington Law School, graduating in 1924. He joined the FBI in October 1924, specializing in document examination. Appel recommended establishment of an FBI laboratory years before Director J. EDGAR HOOVER finally approved the concept in 1932, with Appel placed in charge. For several months Appel was the lab's only full-time employee. His testimony in the Lindbergh KIDNAPPING helped persuade jurors that suspect Bruno Hauptmann penned various ransom notes. On the side, Appel also served as the FBI's unofficial historian, writing laudatory accounts of the Bureau's exploits for both public and in-house consumption. He retired from the FBI on December 3, 1948.

See also: FEDERAL BUREAU OF INVESTIGATION.

Arizona Department of Public Safety

Pursuant to legislation passed in 1968, Governor Jack Williams created the Arizona Department of Public Safety (ADPS) by executive order on July 1, 1969. The ADPS combines functions of the former Arizona Highway Patrol, the Law Enforcement Division of the state's Department of Liquor Licenses and Control, and the state Department of Law's Narcotics Division. Its mission statement is: "To protect human life and property by enforcing state laws, deterring criminal activity, assuring highway and public safety, and providing vital scientific, technical, and operational support to other criminal justice agencies."

With headquarters in Phoenix and offices located in more than 30 communities spanning Arizona's 15 counties, the modern ADPS consists of four divisions—Agency Support, Criminal Investigations, Criminal Justice Support, and Highway Patrol. In addition to normal enforcement of traffic safety laws, the Highway Patrol administers safety programs for commercial vehicles, school buses, and tow trucks; provides specialized training in handling and disposal of hazardous materials; and oversees state aviation programs for law enforcement, emergency medical evacuation, and search-and-rescue operations. The Criminal Investigations Division handles cases of auto theft, narcotics trafficking, ORGANIZED CRIME, gang activity, intelligence, financial and COMPUTER CRIMES. It also guards Arizona's governor and provides specialized high-risk response (see SWAT TEAMS) to "acts of extraordinary violence and domestic preparedness incidents." Four bureaus within the Criminal Investigations Division include Intelligence, Narcotics Investigation, Special Enforcement, and the Rocky Mountain Information Network.

Arizona Rangers

Three law enforcement agencies have operated under variations of this name between the mid-19th and early 20th centuries. Provisional Governor Lewis Owings created the Arizona Territorial Rangers in April 1860, commanded by Captain James Henry Travis with headquarters at Piqos Altos. After Confederate supporters announced Arizona's secession from the Union (on March 16, 1861) the Rangers disbanded and joined the Confederate army en masse. During the postwar decades, Arizona suffered Indian wars, cross-border raids from Mexico, and enough domestic crime to rank some portions of the territory as unfit for full-time human settlement.

Arizona's sixth territorial governor, Frederick Tritle, was in office barely two months before he penned

a letter to Captain John Jackson on April 24, 1882, authorizing formation of the 1st Company of Arizona Rangers. The unit's first assignment was to scout the border for Indian warriors and the slayers of a recently murdered teamster, using "your own discretion as to movements until further orders." Funding was nonexistent, and Congress rebuffed Tritle's bid for federal appropriations in May 1882. Private subscriptions from Tombstone and elsewhere kept the unit going until late 1882 or early 1883, when it passed from existence with little to show for its efforts.

The third and final incarnation of the Arizona Rangers dates from March 21, 1901, when state legislators authorized creation of a company including one captain, one sergeant, and twelve privates. Burton Mossman was commissioned captain of the Rangers on August 30, 1901, with headquarters at Bisbee. New legislation in March 1903 increased the Ranger staff to 26 men, including one lieutenant, and increased pay across the board. In addition to pursuing livestock rustlers and other outlaws, the Arizona Rangers also intervened when Mexican miners struck for higher wages and improved working conditions. Resistance to the statewide force from county sheriffs gained momentum over several years, with two abolition movements defeated in 1907. Finally, state legislators passed a bill to abolish the Rangers on February 15, 1909, and while Governor Joseph Kibbey vetoed the law, anti-Ranger forces had sufficient strength to enact it without his approval. The last Arizona Ranger, Captain Harry Wheeler, was officially discharged on March 25, 1909. No other statewide law enforcement agency existed in the Grand Canyon State until 1931, with creation of the 15-member Arizona Highway Patrol.

Army Criminal Investigation Command

Discipline is a paramount concern in any military organization, and the U.S. Army is no exception. Field commanders were generally responsible for discipline between 1775 (with creation of the Continental Army) and March 1863, when a new Provost Marshal General's Bureau (PMGB) was established to enforce military conscription and arrest deserters in the Civil War. Wartime investigation of crimes committed by Union soldiers fell to private organizations, until General George McClellan commissioned Major ALAN PINKERTON to lead the army's first Criminal Investigation Division (CID).

The first CID dissolved at war's end, while the PMGB remained essentially unchanged until World War I. New demands then prompted creation of the Military Police Corps (MPC) in October 1917. That unit survives today as the Army's uniformed police force, but General John Pershing, commanding the American Expeditionary Force in France, also created a new CID within the Military Police Corps, in October 1918. Specifically designed to solve and prevent crimes within U.S.-occupied territory, the CID shrank with the rest of America's army between World War I and World War II. As the Army expanded once more, during 1942–43, so did the rate of crimes committed or suffered by U.S. military personnel. Yet another Criminal Investigation Division was established within the Provost Marshal General's Office in January 1944, coordinating various investigations between individual commands.

Over the next two decades, CID operations were decentralized until 1964, when a Defense Department study titled *Project Security Shield* called for renewed centralization on the World War II pattern, to increase coordination and efficiency. Full-scale reorganization began in 1965 and culminated in September 1969, with creation of the U.S. Army Criminal Investigative Agency, again directed by the Provost Marshal General. In September 1971, pursuant to orders from Defense Secretary Melvin Laird, the Criminal Investigation Command was created as a major command, vested with control of all Army criminal investigations and investigative resources worldwide. The modern CID (still known in Army circles by its obsolete initials despite the name change) has authority to investigate any crime affecting the U.S. Army anytime, anywhere in the world. Its commander answers directly to the Army's Chief of Staff and to the Secretary of the Army.

Headquartered at Fort Belvoir, Virginia—which also houses the U.S. Army Crime Records Center—the CID also has operational bases at various Army facilities. Its crime lab is located at Fort Gillem, Georgia, while other units are based at Fort Benning, Georgia; at Fort Lewis, Washington; and in Seckenheim, Germany. Primary mission requirements for the CID include investigating serious crimes; conducting "sensitive" investigations; collecting, analyzing and disseminating criminal intelligence; providing forensic laboratory support; protecting key Army personnel on and off the battlefield; and providing logistical security for army materials from the manufacturer to their final use in peacetime or in combat.

See also: FORENSIC SCIENCE.

arson

Arson is the deliberate setting of fires with criminal intent. According to a 1998 report from the Federal Emergency Management Administration, arson is the leading cause of fire-related property damage in the United States, also resulting in an average 500 deaths per year nationwide. The National Fire Protection Agency claims that arson accounted for 8.6 percent of all structure fires and 12.4 percent of all vehicle fires reported in 2002. The FBI's *Crime Classification Manual* lists seven motives for deliberate fire-setting. They include:

Vandalism: Subcategories of this motive include willful and malicious mischief (wherein motive may be determined by choice of targets) and peer-group pressure (most commonly seen in juvenile [see JUVENILE CRIME] offenders).

Excitement: Variants of this motive include fire-setting by thrill-seekers, by arsonists craving attention, by those seeking recognition as "heroes" (including some firefighters), or sexual deviants who achieve satisfaction from the act of setting fires.

Revenge: A more "rational" form of fire-setting, this type may target individuals, specific groups or institutions, or society in general. It may also include acts of intimidation, as in the case of fires set to discourage particular activities (e.g., the testimony of a witness, purchase of specific property, etc.).

Crime concealment: Fire destroys evidence, and various arsonists have used it to conceal acts of murder, suicide, burglary, theft or embezzlement, and to destroy crucial records pertaining to disputed property or activities.

Profit: These fires are normally set to obtain an insurance payoff, to liquidate property, to dissolve a failing business, to eliminate unwanted inventory, or to eradicate competition.

Extremism: Fires in this category include acts of TERRORISM and discrimination (if indeed there is any discernible difference between the two acts), and arson incidents committed during riots. Religious fanaticism may be a factor, in addition to political or racial concerns. (In 1999 a self-styled Satanist confessed to burning more than 30 Christian churches across the Midwest.)

Serial arson: Only compulsive repetition seems to distinguish this category from the "excitement" motive already discussed. FBI taxonomists confuse the issue by creating a subcategory for spree arsonists (who set multiple fires without an emotional "cooling off" period between incidents), and by adding a *mass* arson category for offenders who set multiple simultaneous fires at one location. The latter clearly has nothing to do with "serial" arson, which by definition involves successive and separate incidents.

Arson investigators—commonly involving both police and fire department personnel—start their task by studying the complex chemical process that is fire. Each fire consists of three basic elements: fuel, oxygen and heat. The physical state and shape of the fuel, available oxygen, and the transmission of heat all play critical roles in development of a specific fire. Investigators must also understand the basics of building and/or vehicle construction, including materials used and the nature of any fire-protection systems in place, which determine the course of a fire's development and progress.

The first step in any fire investigation is determining a blaze's point of origin. Only when that point has been determined may authorities discover how and why a fire began. This "backwards" investigation must be fully documented via field notes, diagrams and sketches, photographs, and collection of fire scene evidence. If investigators can eliminate accidental causes—faulty equipment, careless smoking or storage of flammable liquids, electrical failures, and spontaneous combustion—they are ready to proceed in search of a deliberate incendiary cause for the fire. That evidence may include traces of accelerants (gasoline, kerosene, etc.) or the remnants of an incendiary/explosive device recovered from the fire scene. Various mechanical sensors and specially trained dogs assist investigators in the discovery of accelerants and other clues at a fire scene. That evidence, in turn, may prove vital in tracing the arsonist (or, in the alternative, for use in attempts at psychological PROFILING of an unknown fire-setter).

Collection of evidence at any crime scene must conform to rigorous FORENSIC SCIENCE standards if that evidence is to withstand legal challenges in court. Photographs and fire-scene sketches document the points where evidentiary items were discovered, and each fire department or law enforcement agency follows established procedures to preserve the chain of custody between discovery and trial. Modern computer software, such as the FireFiles system, provides arson investigators with case-management tools to organize various details of each case, track evidence from collection through analysis, and to help in preparation of technical reports.

See also: FEDERAL BUREAU OF INVESTIGATION.

Ashcroft, John David (b. 1942)

A Chicago native, born on May 9, 1942, and raised in Missouri, John Ashcroft was the son and grandson of fundamentalist Pentecostal ministers. He carried that conservative upbringing with him through college and law school, then into the political arena, first as a failed congressional candidate in 1972, then as Missouri's state auditor (1973–75). While serving as the state's attorney general (1976–85), Ashcroft fought court-ordered school integration (1977) and also opposed a voluntary busing program for racial parity in St. Louis (1983). He served two terms as Missouri's governor (1985–93), and was elected to the U.S. Senate in 1994. During his single Senate term, Ashcroft sponsored the unsuccessful "Human Life Amendment" (banning abortion even in cases of incest and rape), opposed appointment of black federal judges, and voted consistently against federal GUN CONTROL and firearms safety legislation. His popularity in Missouri is suggested by the fact that Ashcroft lost his 2000 reelection bid to an opponent who died before election day.

Ashcroft was spared from political obscurity by his friendship with the Bush family. President George H. W. Bush had considered Ashcroft for the post of U.S. attorney general in 1991, but his nomination was ultimately deemed too controversial. President George W. Bush had no such qualms in 2001, though Ashcroft was admittedly his second choice (after Montana governor Mark Racicot declined the position). Ashcroft's critics challenged his confirmation on grounds that included his civil rights record, his opposition to abortion and gun control, and his acceptance of an honorary degree from far-right Bob Jones University (where interracial dating was banned until the 1990s and students are taught that the pope is the Antichrist of Revelation). Confirmed despite that opposition, Ashcroft vowed that his religious views would have no impact on his official performance—and then spent $8,000 for drapes to hide a bare-breasted statue of Justice at his headquarters in Washington. (Ashcroft later told reporters he "knew nothing" of the decision.)

Ashcroft avoided any major controversy until the terrorist attacks of September 11, 2001, whereupon he unleashed a national campaign of arrests targeting Muslims as alleged "material witnesses" to the attacks. He also campaigned for new powers of DOMESTIC SURVEILLANCE, complaining that current legislation unduly limited federal WIRETAPS. Many of Ashcroft's goals were accomplished with passage of the USA PATRIOT ACT, but Congress stopped short of granting his ultimate wishes: power to detain and deport on suspicion alone any aliens branded "suspected terrorists" or "who may pose a risk to the national security"; elimination of deportation hearings; and waiver of appeals from deportation orders. Addressing an assembly of American mayors on October 25, 2001, Ashcroft issued a warning to "enemy" aliens: "If you overstay your visa even by one day, we will arrest you. If you violate a local law, and we hope that you will, and work to make sure that you are put in jail and be kept [*sic*] in custody as long as possible."

Despite his commitment to pursuing terrorists, Ashcroft also found time for collateral campaigns. One pitted him against the state of Oregon, where Ashcroft sought federal injunctions in November 2001 to invalidate a state law approving physician-assisted SUICIDE. Governor John Kitzhaber and state attorney general Hardy Myers struck back with litigation of their own; they were victorious in April 2002, when a federal court denied Ashcroft's authority to nullify state laws. Back in Washington, meanwhile, Ashcroft issued a curious order on December 7, 2001, forbidding FBI agents from checking the names of suspected terrorists against federal firearms purchase records. Bewildered FBI spokesmen told the media, "This is a sticky one for us. The JUSTICE DEPARTMENT sees things differently than we do." Matthew Nosanchuk, a Justice lawyer under ex–Attorney General JANET RENO, spoke more bluntly, accusing Ashcroft and company of "rejecting their own authority and acting as lawyers for the gun lobby."

Ashcroft's concern for the privacy of gun owners did not extend to the Muslim community. Appearing on ABC's *This Week* in December 2002, he warned that "[p]eople who hijack a religion and make out of it an implement of war will not be free from our interest." At the same time, however, Ashcroft sought to work behind an airtight screen of secrecy. While in the Senate, during 1998, Ashcroft had accused Janet Reno of "stonewalling" when she withheld federal prosecutors' memos from Congress; in April 2002 Ashcroft claimed the same privilege for himself, prompting Rep. Dan Burton, chairman of the House Judiciary Committee, to express "concern that you have one standard for a Democrat attorney general and another standard for yourself." Ashcroft, unfazed by the criticism, responded in terms reminiscent of J. EDGAR HOOVER: "To those who scare peace-loving people with phantoms of lost liberty, my message is, your tactics only aid terrorists, for they erode our national unity and diminish our resolve."

Critics disagreed, including spokesmen for the AMERICAN CIVIL LIBERTIES UNION and 17 other civil rights organizations who joined forces in a lawsuit filed against Justice on December 4, 2001. That action challenged Ashcroft's arrest and detention without criminal charges of an estimated 1,000 unnamed "suspects" and "material witnesses" in the wake of the Septem-

ber 11 attacks. As if determined to further alienate his opponents, Ashcroft chose Christmas Day 2001 for his announcement that Justice would withdraw $500,000 in federal grants earmarked for nationwide DNA testing to determine whether or not inmates in controversial cases had been wrongfully convicted. The money would be better used for other things, Ashcroft decided—including a new plan to fingerprint, photograph, and register Middle Eastern visitors to the United States.

Ashcroft submitted his resignation on November 10, 2004, one week after President Bush was reelected for a second term. His five-page letter to the White House claimed that "the objective of securing the safety of Americans from crime and terror has been achieved," but media reports cited failing health as Ashcroft's reason for resigning. He remains controversial in retirement. Prof. Viet Dinh, a former Ashcroft aide who helped draft the PATRIOT Act, called his ex-boss "one of the most powerful, if not the most powerful and effective, attorneys general in the history of this nation," while the ACLU panned Ashcroft as "one of the most divisive forces in the entire Bush administration."

See also: FEDERAL BUREAU OF INVESTIGATION; TERRORISM.

ASPCA Humane Law Enforcement Department

The American Society for the Prevention of Cruelty to Animals (ASPCA) was founded by wealthy New Yorker Henry Bergh on April 10, 1866. Ten days later, the state legislature passed America's first animal protection statute, which permits the ASPCA to investigate complaints of animal cruelty and to arrest offenders. Thus was born the ASPCA's Humane Law Enforcement (HLE) Department, with jurisdiction limited to New York state.

HLE agents are duly sworn New York State peace officers, operating from ASPCA headquarters in New York City. At last count, the department employed 14 uniformed and plainclothes officers with full powers of arrest. They work closely with the NEW YORK CITY POLICE DEPARTMENT and other agencies to apprehend suspected animal abusers, including the operators of illegal cockfights and dogfights. In the last year with full statistics presently available (2003), HLE agents investigated 3,509 cruelty complaints, arrested 277 suspects, issued 335 summonses, and seized 407 abused animals. In each adjudicated case, the courts barred convicted defendants from owning or having any future contact with animals. Convicted abusers were also sentenced to forfeit any animals owned, perform community service, pay monetary fines, and/or pay restitution to the ASPCA.

The ASPCA's creation spawned many imitators, including 25 more humane organizations across the United States and Canada. Several other states and cities now have humane society investigators on staff, though none are formally associated with New York's ASPCA. For several years, the exploits of humane enforcement officers in Florida, Michigan, New York, and Texas have been featured on the Animal Planet television network, in such reality series as *Animal Cops* and *Animal Precinct.*

assassination

Assassination is defined as the murder of a prominent person. Some purists insist that the term is properly applied only to heads of state and other public office holders, but modern usage generally includes slayings of celebrities, social activists, and recognized leaders of ORGANIZED CRIME. Four U.S. presidents have thus far

Assassin John Wilkes Booth led the conspirators who plotted Lincoln's murder. (Author's collection)

been assassinated, including Abraham Lincoln (1865), James Garfield (1881), William McKinley (1901), and John Kennedy (1963). Failed murder attempts were also made against Presidents Andrew Jackson (1835), THEODORE ROOSEVELT (1912), Franklin Roosevelt (1933), Harry Truman (1950), Gerald Ford (twice in September 1975), and Ronald Reagan (1981). Murder of a U.S. chief executive was not a federal crime until August 28, 1965, when Congress enacted a statute penalizing assassination of the president, vice president or president-elect. (It is also a crime to threaten those officials with bodily harm.) Protection of the president, vice president, and major presidential candidates during election years is handled by the U.S. SECRET SERVICE.

Other significant assassinations or attempted assassinations throughout U.S. history include:

William Seward: Secretary of state, wounded by accomplices of President Lincoln's assassin in Washington, D.C., on April 14, 1865.

President Abraham Lincoln was assassinated in April 1865. (Author's collection)

Henry Frick: Prominent industrialist, shot and stabbed in his New York City office by a Russian-born anarchist on July 23, 1892. (Frick survived his wounds.)

Frank Steunenberg: Ex-governor of Idaho, killed by a bomb at his home on December 30, 1905, allegedly for his prior involvement in brutal STRIKE-BREAKING in 1899.

Anton Cermak: Mayor of Chicago, fatally wounded in the February 1933 attempt on Franklin Roosevelt's life, in Miami, Florida. Some researchers now believe Cermak was the primary target, marked for death by Chicago mobsters.

Huey Long: U.S. senator from Louisiana, fatally wounded by a gunman in Baton Rouge on September 8, 1935. The shooter's motive—and, indeed, his guilt—remains controversial.

Harry Moore: Black civil rights leader in Florida, killed by a KU KLUX KLAN bomb at his home in Mims, on Christmas Day 1951.

Assassin Charles Guiteau shot Garfield to settle a personal grudge. (Author's collection)

James Garfield was America's second murdered president, in September 1881. (Author's collection)

Medgar Evers: Black civil rights leader in Mississippi, killed by a KKK sniper at his home in Jackson, on June 12, 1963.

John Connally: Governor of Texas, wounded by the same fusillade of rifle fire that killed President Kennedy in Dallas, on November 22, 1963.

Malcolm X: Black nationalist leader shot and killed in New York City, allegedly by rival Black Muslims, on February 21, 1965.

Martin Luther King, Jr.: Black civil rights leader, killed by a sniper's bullet in Memphis, Tennessee, on April 4, 1968.

Robert Francis Kennedy: U.S. senator and brother of President John Kennedy, fatally shot in Los Angeles moments after winning the California presidential primary election, on June 5, 1968.

George Wallace: Governor of Alabama and a presidential candidate, critically wounded by gunfire

President William McKinley fell victim to an anarchist's bullet in September 1901. (Author's collection)

John F. Kennedy was the most recent victim of a U.S. presidential assassination, in November 1963. (Library of Congress)

at a campaign rally in Laurel, Maryland, on May 15, 1972.

Vernon Jordan: Black civil rights leader, shot and critically wounded in Fort Wayne, Indiana, on May 29, 1980.

Most U.S. assassinations are officially described as the work of lone individuals driven by personal grudges, mental illness, or adherence to some extreme belief system. Nonetheless, suspicion of conspiracy lingers in various cases, especially the 1960s murders of John and Robert Kennedy, Malcolm X, and Martin Luther King. In 1979 the House Select Committee on Assassinations reported that both John Kennedy and Dr. King were "probably" killed as the result of organized conspiracies, but that finding resulted in no further criminal charges.

See also: ANARCHISM.

Aten, Ira (1863–1953)

An Illinois native, born at Cairo on September 3, 1863, Ira Aten was transplanted with his family to Round Rock, Texas, following the Civil War. There, in July 1878, he glimpsed outlaw Sam Bass, while Aten's father—a Methodist preacher—ministered to the mortally wounded outlaw. Ira joined the TEXAS RANGERS five years later, and engaged in his first shootout with rustlers near Laredo in May 1884. That battle landed him in jail, detained for 27 days on false charges by a corrupt local sheriff, but upon his release Aten received a promotion to corporal. The subsequent capture of outlaws Rube Boyce and Jim Epps won Aten another promotion, to sergeant.

Aten's best-known case, the three-month pursuit of escaped convict Judd Roberts in 1887, produced multiple gunfights. Aten twice wounded Roberts in separate engagements, before finally killing the fugitive in July. That exploit won Aten promotion to major, but higher rank did not remove him from the line of fire. With three other lawmen, he killed rustlers Alvin and Will Odle near Vance, on Christmas Day 1889. Even retirement, in the closing days of 1889, did not bring peace to Aten's life. Appointed to serve as sheriff of Fort Bend

County, Aten found himself embroiled in a hotly contested election in November 1891. Following a series of public insults and challenges, he wounded two land-grabbing brothers from Tennessee, Andrew and Hugh McClelland, and once again was briefly jailed while his opponents fled the state.

Finally retired from law enforcement, Aten served as superintendent of the 600,000-acre XIT Ranch from 1895 to 1904, then moved to California with his wife. He died there, at Burlingame, on August 5, 1953.

Atlanta Police Department

Georgia's premier city (then named Marthesville) hired its first town marshal—now remembered only as "Antonio"—in 1844. The city was renamed Atlanta two years later and employed its first team of nocturnal patrolmen in January 1853, increased to 20 officers over the next five years. The first board of police commissioners was organized in 1873, naming Thomas Jones as Atlanta's first chief of police. The force acquired its first motor vehicles in 1911, and established its first organized training course four years later.

Race has always been a law enforcement issue in Atlanta, which served as national headquarters of the KU KLUX KLAN from 1915 to 1961. Many Klansmen joined the all-white force, some rising to command positions, and Atlanta's police union was essentially a KKK recruitment vehicle until its abolition in 1947. As late as 1949, detectives and patrolmen openly attended Klan meetings in Atlanta, often unmasked, and were sometimes featured as guest speakers. At one such gathering, in 1948, Patrolman "Trigger" Nash was honored for killing his 13th black victim "in self-defense." Nash told his brother Klansmen that "he hoped he wouldn't have all the honor of killing the niggers in the South, and he hoped the people would do something about it themselves." Atlanta detective Sam Roper, formerly chief of the GEORGIA BUREAU OF INVESTIGATION (GBI) under Governor Eugene Talmadge, served from 1949 to 1952 as national leader of America's largest Klan faction, and reports persist that many Ku Klux crimes went unsolved through collaboration with racist police.

Atlanta hired its first black patrolmen in 1948, but restricted their assignment to the all-black neighborhood of Auburn Avenue. The city boasted 15 black officers by 1955, and Howard Baugh became Atlanta's first black superior officer in 1961, but another year passed before black officers were authorized to arrest white suspects. Still, they were not assigned to regular patrols until 1966, and two-man patrol teams were not integrated until 1969. The first black female officer, Linnie Hollowman, was hired two years later.

Integration of the force and election of a black mayor did not spare Atlanta from ongoing racial controversy in the 1970s and 1980s. A series of brutal murders terrorized Atlanta's black community from 1979 to 1982, prompting criticism of police who included adult ex-convicts on a published list of Atlanta's "missing and murdered children," while arbitrarily excluding 30-odd minors who fit the established victim profile. Black suspect Wayne Williams was finally convicted of killing two adult males from the list, then named without charges or trial as the slayer of 20 black children, but evidence in that case remains ephemeral, and many black Atlantans regarded Williams as a scapegoat, charging that white racists committed the murders. That viewpoint was strengthened in 1985, with revelation that Klansmen had confessed at least to one of the slayings on tape, in conversations recorded (and later withheld from the Williams defense team) by agents of the GBI. Despite that evidence and other revelations suggesting that Williams may be innocent, his appeals and public pleas for a renewed investigation have been uniformly rejected over the past two decades.

A different kind of scandal hit the Atlanta P.D. in early 1993, when seven policemen and two civilians were charged with a series of burglaries targeting local nightclubs. The crew stole an estimated $300,000 in 1992–93 and murdered one club owner at his home. Five officers were subsequently convicted on various felony charges, drawing prison terms ranging from five years to life. Other scandals from the 1990s include more traditional incidents of CORRUPTION, domestic violence and EXCESSIVE FORCE during arrests. In one case, investigators from the department's INTERNAL AFFAIRS division (locally known as the Office of Professional Standards) ignored criminal allegations against six officers until federal charges were filed. As reported in the *Atlanta Journal Constitution*, those officers "had good reason to believe OPS would ignore or tolerate their criminal behavior. . . . Despite many allegations of brutal treatment or violent behavior, these officers remained on the force until they faced federal corruption charges."

By the dawn of the new millennium, Atlanta's police administrators faced budgetary problems common to many departments across the country. Recruitment was down, with 340 vacancies (18.9 percent of available positions) in 2000. While the department was authorized to fill 1,802 jobs, its personnel declined from 1,615 in 1992 to 1,462 in 1999. Low salaries were blamed for the decline, ranging from a rookie's pay of $30,783 to a 10-year maximum of $42,262 (slightly higher in each case for college graduates). By contrast, wages for the SEATTLE POLICE DEPARTMENT started at $38,500 and reached $49,000 after six years; the SAN DIEGO POLICE DEPARTMENT paid rookies $36,525, increasing to $56,305 after four years. Retirement benefits for Atlanta officers likewise lagged behind the national average, while three administrators of the Atlanta Police Pension Fund were indicted for fraud in 1999, charged with collecting some $15 million in illegal commissions.

Attica Prison riot

On September 9, 1971, inmates at New York's maximum-security Attica Correctional Facility rioted in protest against "unmitigated oppression wrought by the racist administrative network of this prison throughout the years" and the "ruthless brutalization and disregard for the lives of the prisoners here and throughout the United States." Twelve injured prison employees escaped during the early hours of the riot, including one guard (William Quinn) who later died from his wounds. Inside the prison, another 38 hostages were confined by their inmate captors in D Yard, abused by some convicts while others sought to protect them as bargaining chips. A four-day siege ensued, broken on September 13, when Governor Nelson Rockefeller, citing "a matter of principle," dispatched 1,000 members of the NATIONAL GUARD and NEW YORK STATE POLICE to reclaim the prison by force. When the gunsmoke cleared, 10 more hostages and 29 inmates were dead, with dozens more wounded.

Reporters initially blamed the deaths on inmate rioters, proclaiming that hostages were found with their throats slashed, some of them castrated and otherwise mutilated. Those reports were later disproved, leaving William Quinn as the only prison employee killed by inmates. All other fatalities were inflicted by police and National Guardsmen firing shotguns and high-powered rifles during a six-minute barrage that filled D Yard with some 2,200 lethal projectiles. Billed in some contemporary reports as America's worst single incident of violence since the Civil War, the Attica assault was certainly a case of DEADLY FORCE employed without discrimination or proper safeguards.

Nearly as bad were the incidents of post-riot retaliation, painfully detailed in official reports of the incident. Hundreds of inmates were stripped and beaten while crawling nude on the ground, and leaders of the riot were singled out for special punishment. One inmate leader, Frank Smith, was forced to lie nude on a table for hours, a football wedged under his chin, warned by state police that if the ball fell from its place he would be shot. Despite official recognition of widespread abuse, no officers were ever disciplined for using EXCESSIVE FORCE at Attica.

The riot's aftermath was painful for all sides. Eleven widows of hostages killed in the riot were pressured to accept paltry death benefits, all but one accepting after a covert meeting with Corrections Commissioner Russell Oswald, who promised to "take care of them." Surviving hostages were granted six months off with pay to recuperate from the trauma, but acceptance of the deal meant they—and the 10 hostage widows—were legally barred from seeking further damages in court. The lone holdout, Lynda Jones, filed suit against the state and in May 1985 won $1,060,000 after a court determined that police gunfire on September 13, 1971, "was haphazard and directed indiscriminately at the group of prisoners and hostages." Governor Hugh Carey officially closed the book on Attica in 1976, when he commuted the life prison term of inmate John Hill (convicted of killing William Quinn). At the same time, Carey ignored a state prosecutor's recommendation that certain officers be disciplined for their behavior in the riot, and he sealed the state's records concerning the Attica riot until 2026.

In January 2000, state officials and attorneys representing several D Yard inmates announced a $12 million settlement for violence inflicted on the convicts by police (although the state still denied any fault). A federal judge approved the deal on February 14, prompting hostage survivors to meet five days later, organizing a protest group called Forgotten Victims of Attica (FVA). In March 2000 state legislator Daniel Burling proposed paying each Attica widow and hostage survivor $90,000, a sum reduced in budget negotiations to $50,000 or a total outlay of $550,000. FVA spokesmen rejected the offer, while pressing five demands. They include:

1. An official apology for wrongful death of hostages shot by police, for physical injury to others and emotional trauma to all FVA members, as well as state "duplicity" in negotiating compensation.

2. Release of all state records on the riot from their 50-year seal to answer unresolved questions, dispel public misinformation, expose an alleged cover-up and correct any denials of due process.

3. Long-term state-funded counseling for all employees affected by the riot.

4. A private memorial service conducted on prison property each September 13 by FVA members.

5. Financial compensation in an unspecified amount "deemed fair by the victims."

B

Baca, Elfego (1865–1945)

Hispanic folk hero Elfego Baca was born in New Mexico (1865) and raised in Kansas, where his father was imprisoned for killing two cowboys in a gunfight. At age 19 Baca returned to New Mexico's Socorro County, where his brother-in-law was employed as a deputy sheriff. Seeking to follow the same path, Baca purchased a mail-order badge and a pair of six-guns, waiting impatiently for a chance to challenge the local racists who routinely harassed and murdered Mexican Americans.

He got his chance on November 30, 1884, when a drunken cowboy in Frisco (now Reserve) forced several Hispanics to dance by shooting at their feet. Baca arrested the bully, but quickly found himself besieged in Frisco's jailhouse by friends of the cowboy. A flurry of gunfire left one cowboy dead and another wounded, while Baca holed up overnight in the jail with his prisoner. Next morning he surrendered the cowboy to Frisco's justice of the peace, who fined the man five dollars and released him. Meanwhile, 80 armed cowboys led by ranch boss Tom Slaughter cornered Baca in a small shack, riddling it with bullets and lobbing sticks of dynamite in a futile bid to flush him from cover. Baca fought back for some 36 hours, dodging 4,000 bullets, killing at least four assailants and wounding several others before certified lawmen arrived to lift the siege.

Twice tried for murder in Socorro, Baca was acquitted on all counts and emerged from the courtroom a hero to Mexican Americans. He subsequently studied law and won admittance to the state bar in 1894. His career as an attorney and politician included terms as mayor of Frisco, county clerk, district attorney, and deputy sheriff of Socorro County. In 1915 a personal enemy, Celestine Otero, tried to murder Baca in El Paso, Texas, but his aim proved faulty, and Baca killed him with two shots to the chest.

Four years later, Socorro County voters chose Baca as their sheriff. His reputation preceded him, and several notorious fugitives voluntarily surrendered after Baca sent letters to their families, demanding that they submit to arrest. Baca died with his boots off in Albuquerque in 1945, but his legend lived on, memorialized by Walt Disney productions in a television series starring Robert Loggia.

Baird, Carl (c. 1953–1994)

Carl Baird had been chief of police in tiny Walpole, New Hampshire, for less than two years when he left his post on February 10, 1994. The move was sudden, and local wags could not agree on whether Baird had resigned or been fired by the town's board of selectmen. The debate was still raging on February 12, when the 41-year-old ex-chief entered Walpole's town hall for the last time. Confronting one of the selectmen, 51-year-old Roger Santaw, Baird drew a pistol and fired several shots into Santaw's chest, killing him where he stood.

Baird fled immediately, racing to his car and leaving Walpole, driving west across the state line to Vermont, stopping only when he reached Danby, some 35 miles away. Vermont authorities found him there, slumped at the wheel of his car, dead from a single self-inflicted gunshot to the head. In the aftermath of tragedy, locals acknowledged that Baird and Santaw were longtime adversaries, their conflict resulting in Baird's ouster from office, but the cause of their feud remained obscure. In retrospect, Baird was described by those who knew him as "a quiet person who never showed much emotion."

Baltimore Police Department

Baltimore Towne was created by Maryland's colonial legislature in August 1729, but another half century passed before the city hired its first constables in 1784. State legislators authorized recruitment of armed police officers on March 16, 1853. Union military forces assumed control of Maryland in June 1861, since Maryland remained a slave state throughout the Civil War, but law enforcement tasks in Baltimore returned to state control in March 1862. The city's first police call boxes were installed in 1885, and the department acquired its first patrol wagon in October of that year. A Harbor Patrol division was also created in 1885, followed by a Traffic Division in 1908 and the city's first police academy in 1913. Seven years later, Charles Gaither won appointment as Baltimore's first police commissioner. The department created an Accident Investigation Unit in February 1930, opened its Laboratory Division in June 1950, and deployed its first K-9 UNIT on March 1956. A separate Park Police unit merged with the main force in January 1961.

The undisputed "Big Man" of Baltimore law enforcement was Donald Pomerleau, who ruled the department from 1966 to 1982. On the day of his appointment as police commissioner, Pomerleau created a covert Red squad, officially known as the intelligence section of BPD's Inspectional Services Division (ISD). ISD's charter proclaimed its "primary mission" the "active surveillance of individuals or groups outside the normal criminal behavior," conducted as an "attempt to spot potential areas of violence." In fact, a 1968 report from Pomerleau himself declared: "The primary purpose of the Intelligence Section is to serve as the eyes and ears of the Police Commissioner." To that end, over the next decade, ISD conducted DOMESTIC SURVEILLANCE on at least 125 organizations, ranging from the AMERICAN CIVIL LIBERTIES UNION and the American Friends Service Committee to the militant Black Panther Party. Tactics included WIRETAPS, "BLACK BAG JOBS" and use of paid INFORMANTS, tactics borrowed from collaborating agents of the FBI. Beyond the often-illegal surveillance, ISD targets complained of physical intimidation, false arrests, ENTRAPMENT, and threats to their employment.

In April 1970 Baltimore police charged lawyer Arthur Turco and 17 of his Black Panther clients with murdering police informant Eugene Anderson.

Anderson's alleged executioners, identified as Mahoney Kebe, Arnold Loney, and Donald Vaughn, all turned state's evidence against their former comrades, describing Turco as the plot's mastermind. At trial, the three were exposed as FBI informants favored with grants of immunity, government paychecks, plus free room and board. Star witness Kebe's testimony proved so contradictory and laced with lies that the presiding judge declared a mistrial, after striking Kebe's comments from the record. A new prosecutor drastically reduced all charges, confessing in court that the state's case lacked substantive evidence of murder or conspiracy, blaming his predecessor for "improper prosecution practices." Offered dismissal of his murder charge in return for a guilty plea to simple assault, Turco reluctantly agreed, thus ending his 10-month ordeal in Baltimore's city jail (subsequently condemned as unfit for human occupancy).

Spurred by that case and others, Maryland's Senate Committee on Constitutional and Public Law opened preliminary hearings on Baltimore police practices in January 1975. Commissioner Pomerleau initially refused to testify, penning a letter that claimed that "the Senate is being used as an instrument to disrupt the last bastion of order in Baltimore." He further called the probe illegal and "immoral," presenting "a daily rehashing of past activity solely based on the statements of those who would like to change our system of government other than by the lawful process of the law." When Pomerleau at last consented to appear, in October 1975, he treated the committee to a sample of his actions in a case involving misconduct by the son of a community leader:

> I called that individual's mother and said, "You know, I think it would be wise if you came into the office and bring your son with you." And we had a discussion and that individual, when I read to him what I had in two different source statements, got on his knees and said, "Please don't do that to me," and the mother assured me that she would make some proper input.

While the senate committee's report of January 1976 substantially verified most complaints from ISD victims, Mayor William Schaefer and Governor Martin Mandel publicly praised Pomerleau, seconded by local businessmen who voted him Baltimore's "Man of the Year." It required state legislation, passed in 1978, to shut down ISD's illegal activities, but Pomerleau remained for another four years, retiring in 1982.

Problems persist in Baltimore, despite Pomerleau's passing. Racial tension continues between police and minorities, surfacing in several courtroom cases of "jury nullification" in the early 21st century. Officer Brian

Sewell was indicted in October 2000 for his attempted FRAME-UP of a robbery suspect, including perjured testimony and crack cocaine planted on the suspect to support drug charges, but that indictment was dropped after crucial evidence vanished from BPD headquarters. In June 2004 ex-police commissioner Edward Norris and his former chief of staff at BPD headquarters, John Stendrini, were sentenced to six months in prison and fined $10,000 each for using $30,000 in departmental funds to pay for lavish dinners, posh hotel rooms, and sexual encounters with various women. Supporters of the two defendants expressed disappointment at their "severe" punishment, but welcomed news that Norris and Stendrini would serve their time at a federal "country club" prison in Florida, commonly known as "Club Fed."

See also: FEDERAL BUREAU OF INVESTIGATION; RED SQUADS.

bank robbery

Famed stickup artist Willie Sutton was once quoted as saying he robbed banks because "that's where the money was." Sutton denied that comment to his dying day, but its author—whoever he was—captured the essence of bank robbery and the greed that inspires its practitioners.

America's first bank robber, Englishman Edward Smith, was actually a burglar who invaded New York's City Bank of Wall Street on the night of March 19, 1831, stealing $245,000. He managed to spend $60,000 before his arrest, drawing a five-year prison term from a judge who found his crime unique. America's first homicide during a bank heist occurred in 1855, when teller George Gordon was beaten to death by a nocturnal thief who stole $130,000. PINKERTON detectives secured a confession from suspect Alexander Drysdale by convincing him that Gordon's ghost had returned to haunt him.

Nocturnal burglary remained the norm for East Coast bandits in the 19th century, their operations peaking with the Bliss Bank Ring in New York City. That three-man gang laid out extensive bribes to keep police from interfering with their raids. A total of $132,000 was paid to myopic lawmen for a single job in 1869, permitting the gang to steal $1.75 million from the Ocean Bank. Out west, meanwhile, a more direct and dangerous method of looting banks was pioneered by the James-Younger gang, graduates of William Quantrill's Civil War guerrilla band. The gang "invented" daylight bank robbery at Liberty, Missouri, stealing $15,000 in gold coins and $45,000 in bonds on February 14, 1866. Copycats were soon active from California to the Midwest, risking their lives in pursuit of easy money. The James-Younger gang met its Waterloo in 1876, at Northfield, Minnesota, but that bloody fiasco and others like it failed to discourage a new generation of bandits. The Dalton brothers, cousins of the Youngers, enjoyed a brief run before they overstepped themselves in 1892 and were slaughtered while trying to rob two banks simultaneously at Coffeyville, Kansas.

Every year since 1866 had witnessed multiple bank holdups in the United States, their frequency mounting over time, but the last great era of headline-grabbing "social bandits" passed with the Great Depression of the 1930s. Between 1930 and 1936 Americans were captivated by the exploits of such "PUBLIC ENEMIES" as John Dillinger, "Baby Face" Nelson, "Pretty Boy" Floyd, and "Machine Gun" Kelly. Few Americans sympathized with bankers in those days of foreclosures and lost savings, but the mounting death toll of police and civilian bystanders finally provoked congressional action. Robbery of federally insured banks became a federal crime in May 1934, with FBI agents empowered to hunt down those responsible.

The demise of Dillinger and company demoted American bank robbers from their status as off-color folk heroes, but bandits continued to perfect their trade during and after World War II. "Phantom burglars" Stanley Patrek and Joseph Stepka looted banks in New York and New Jersey between October 1944 and May 1945, using oxyacetylene torches to crack vaults and safes. The January 1950 robbery of a Brinks vault in Boston set a new record for U.S. bank heists, with the theft of $1,218,211 in cash plus $1,557,184 in checks and money orders. Perpetrators of that crime were added to the FBI's "Ten Most Wanted" list, the same vehicle that took Willie Sutton off the street in 1951.

The early 1970s witnessed a rash of incidents wherein bankers and their families were held hostage, compelled under threat of death to serve as proxies for their captors. Bank president Robert Kitterman, his wife and daughter were murdered at Gallatin, Missouri, in January 1973, after Kitterman removed $10,000 from his bank. In the wake of that crime, *Newsweek* magazine revealed 77 similar cases during 1972, with an average ransom of $77,000. Few of the holdups resulted in murder, however, and the fad soon passed in the wake of the Kitterman slaughter, while security specialists debated the hopeless task of guarding every banker's home in the United States around the clock.

Bank robberies are routine in modern America, with 7,546 reported in 2000 (including 23 murders) and 8,565 in 2001 (with eight persons killed). By 2002 FBI agents logged bank heists at a rate of one every 52 minutes. Offenders were jailed at a much higher rate than "normal" thieves—58 percent in 2001, versus 25 percent for robbers overall—but most of their loot goes unrecovered. (Between 1996 and 2000 authorities regained only $94.4 million of some $470 million stolen from U.S. banks, about 20 percent.) In this age of COMPUTER CRIME, some of the largest bank thefts are accomplished without guns or personal risk, sometimes by high-tech holdup men in distant foreign lands.

See also: FEDERAL BUREAU OF INVESTIGATION; "TEN MOST WANTED" FUGITIVES.

Barr, William Pelham (b. 1950)

New York native William Barr was born on May 23, 1950. He received his B.A. and M.A. degrees from Columbia University in 1971 and 1973, respectively, then earned his doctorate in jurisprudence from George Washington University in 1977. During his period of study for that doctorate, Barr was employed by the Central Intelligence Agency (1973–77), then served as a legal clerk for the U.S. Court of Appeals in Washington, D.C. (1977–78). Nine years of private legal practice were interrupted by a brief term on President Ronald Reagan's domestic policy staff (1982–83), ending when he joined the JUSTICE DEPARTMENT under President George H. W. Bush. At Justice Barr served variously as assistant attorney general for the Office of Legal Counsel (1989–90), deputy attorney general (1990–91) and acting attorney general (August to November 1991). He assumed office as attorney general on November 20, 1991.

In that post Barr soon developed a disdain for FBI Director WILLIAM STEELE SESSIONS that rivaled the hostile attitude of predecessor RICHARD LEWIS THORNBURGH. Communications from retired agents confirmed Barr's opinion that Sessions was abusing his office, whereupon an investigation was launched by the Justice Department's self-policing Office of Professional Responsibility (OPR). The OPR's report deemed Sessions's misconduct serious enough that the president should consider removing him from office, but Bush ignored that recommendation, leaving the problem for President Bill Clinton and Attorney General JANET RENO. Meanwhile, Barr actively opposed investigation of the Iran-contra scandal and in December 1992 he rejected congressional demands for an independent prosecutor to investigate possible criminal involvement by government officials in loans to Iraq. Two weeks later, President Bush pardoned six former aides convicted of perjury during investigations of the conspiracy. Barr left office on January 15, 1993, and returned to private practice.

Bartels, John R., Jr. (b. 1937)

Brooklyn native John Bartels, Jr. was born on September 12, 1937. He graduated from Harvard Law School in 1960, and four years later joined the U.S. JUSTICE DEPARTMENT as a federal prosecutor in the Southern District of New York (1964–68). He subsequently served as an adjunct professor at Rutgers University School of Law (1969–71), then returned to law enforcement as chief of the Justice Department's ORGANIZED CRIME Strike Force in Newark, New Jersey. In 1973 he was appointed deputy director of President Richard Nixon's new Office of Drug Abuse Law Enforcement. On September 12 of that year, Nixon named Bartels the first director of the DRUG ENFORCEMENT ADMINISTRATION (DEA).

Interdicting the flow of illegal DRUGS is never easy, and it was doubly difficult in an administration closely tied to organized crime, while Nixon and his aides fought to contain the mushrooming Watergate scandal. Bartels and the DEA soon became lightning rods for controversy, involving both the agency's aggressive (some said illegal) methods and Bartels's personal brand of administration. Nixon's successor, President Gerald Ford, forced Bartels out of office in May 1975, whereupon it was revealed that Bartels had stonewalled federal inquiries into DEA operations. That embarrassment did not prevent his selection as New York's state Republican chairman, nor his selection in March 2002 to serve on the directorial board of Star Scientific Inc.—a company engaged in manufacture of tobacco products.

Bates, Edward (1793–1869)

Born at Belmont, Virginia, on September 4, 1793, Edward Bates attended Charlotte Hall Academy in Maryland. Despite his pacifist Quaker religion, he served as a sergeant in a volunteer brigade during the War of 1812. At war's end, in 1814, he moved to St. Louis, Missouri, and studied law, winning admittance to the state bar in 1817. He was elected circuit prosecuting attorney in 1818, and two years later served as a delegate to Missouri's constitutional convention. Subsequent political offices included Missouri state attorney general (1820–21), U.S. district attorney (1821–26), Missouri state representative (1822, 1834), U.S. representative from Missouri (1827–29), Missouri state senator (1830), and judge of the St. Louis land court (1853–56). In 1850 Bates declined appointment as President Millard Fillmore's secretary of war, and ten years later waged an unsuccessful fight to wrest the Republican presidential nomination away from Abraham Lincoln. Despite that conflict, Lincoln appointed Bates to serve as U.S. attorney general, assuming office

Attorney General Edward Bates (Author's collection)

1926, when he finally became the NYPD's first black sergeant. Nine years later, he became the department's first black lieutenant, then won promotion as parole commissioner in 1941. Another riot sparked by misuse of DEADLY FORCE, in 1943, brought Battle back to Harlem's streets as peacemaker, drawn from his office by the personal request of Mayor Fiorello La Guardia. Battle retired from public service in 1951, and 12 years later was honored as "the father of all Negroes in the Police Department." He died on August 7, 1966, at age 83.

Bean, Roy (1825–1902)

Kentucky native Roy Bean was born in 1825. After a brief teenage sojourn in New Orleans, he struck off for Mexico at age 22, where he tried his hand as an outlaw. Murder charges drove him back across the border, settling in Southern California with his brother Joshua. Trouble persisted for the Beans, as Joshua was murdered in Los Angeles and Roy was sentenced to hang for some now-forgotten offense. His life was spared when the rope snapped, leaving him with a lifelong stiff neck and a strong incentive to flee California.

Bean drifted back to Mexico, where his transgressions were forgotten in the tumult surrounding America's Civil War. He joined a Confederate guerrilla band, stealing as much for personal profit as for the lost cause of slavery. After Appomattox he settled in Texas, opened a saloon in the small town of Vinegaroon, and wangled an appointment as a justice of the peace. The title and a dog-eared law book later followed Bean to Langtry, Texas, where he held court at the bar of the Jersey Lily Saloon (named for actress Lillie Langtry).

With a placard billing himself as "Law West of the Pecos," Bean dispensed liquor and "justice" by turns. Both proved unpalatable on occasion, as when Bean released the slayer of a Chinese laborer with the remark: "Gentlemen, I find the law very explicit on murdering your fellow man, but there's nothing here about killing a Chinaman. Case dismissed." Other defendants had less luck in the barroom court, with an uncertain number hanged on Bean's order for various offenses. While Bean was totally devoid of legal education, he served Langtry as a draw for tourists and maintained at least a semblance of order. So it was that local voters kept him in office from 1884 to 1896, when a clearly fraudulent landslide for Bean tipped the election to his opponent.

Bean, unimpressed, continued to hold court in the Jersey Lily until his death in 1902. The minor scandal faded over time, and Hollywood lit a candle to Bean's memory in 1956, with the television series *Judge Roy Bean* (starring Edgar Buchanan). Sixteen years later,

on March 5, 1861. He resigned in September 1864, in the midst of the Civil War, and returned to private practice in Missouri. Bates died at St. Louis on March 25, 1869.

Battle, Samuel J. (1883–1966)

A native of North Carolina, born to former slaves in 1883, Samuel Battle left Dixie to attend a Connecticut trade school, then found work as a porter in New York City's Grand Central Station. He passed the NEW YORK CITY POLICE DEPARTMENT's qualifying test in 1910, but administrators of the all-white force stalled for nearly a year—citing a nonexistent "heart condition"—before they finally accepted Battle as the NYPD's first black officer. Assigned to the Harlem ghetto in 1913, Battle performed so well that his superiors encouraged him to study for the sergeant's exam, then backpedaled with phony claims that promotion depended on approval of his white classmates. Battle tipped the scales in 1919, when he rescued a white patrolman from blacks enraged by the police shooting of an unarmed ghetto youth.

Despite Battle's completion of the training course with top grades, superiors delayed his promotion until actor Paul Newman came closer to capturing Bean's eccentric nature in a feature film, *The Life and Times of Judge Roy Bean.*

Becker, Charles (c. 1870–1915)

Charles Becker was once described as "the crookedest cop who ever stood behind a shield"—no small achievement in New York City, during the reign of TAMMANY HALL. So infamous was Becker, in fact, that he was featured in a novel and later inspired the first American gangster movie, but his reputation did not save him in the end.

A son of German immigrants, Becker worked as a saloon bouncer before he joined the NEW YORK CITY POLICE DEPARTMENT in 1893. He was still a uniformed patrolman in the 1890s, when novelist Stephen Crane saw him beating a young prostitute, furious at the girl for withholding Becker's standard bribe. That scene was immortalized in Crane's novel *Maggie: A Girl of the Streets,* but Becker had moved on by then to other breaches of decorum. When a New Jersey matron asked him for directions on the street and could not understand his mumbled response, Becker arrested her for drunkenness. He and a partner later killed a bystander while firing at a burglar, then tried to cast their victim as the fugitive. Some critics even charged that Becker drowned his first wife in the bathtub, though her death was formally blamed on pneumonia.

A protégé of Tammany leader Tim Sullivan, Becker was promoted to lieutenant in 1911, assigned as an aide to Commissioner RHINELANDER WALDO. Becker also ran NYPD's Special Squad Number 1, supervising the smooth flow of graft from criminal activities along Broadway, in the Tenderloin, and Hell's Kitchen districts. Although assigned by Waldo to suppress gambling, Becker collected some $640,000 in bribes (about $10 million today). He enjoyed a lavish lifestyle in New York and paid cash for a $9,000 Tudor home in the Bronx.

One gambler who forked over half of his profits to Becker was Herman Rosenthal, proprietor of a club on West 54th Street. He balked at paying more, though, when Becker raised his rates in 1912, prompting a raid that demolished his casino. Rosenthal retaliated by exposing Becker, first to a reporter from the *New York World,* then to Manhattan district attorney Charles Whitman. Mob gunmen ambushed Rosenthal on July 16, outside the Hotel Metropole, and left him dying from four gunshot wounds. Becker, ironically, was chosen to investigate the case.

Witnesses had seen four gunmen flee the murder scene—and better yet, had memorized the license number of their car. Its owner was identified and named the shooters as Frank Cirofici, Harry Horowitz, Louis Rosenberg, and Jacob Siedenschner—all known enforcers for mob boss "Big Jack" Zelig. Zelig himself was killed by gangland rivals in October 1912, but the incarcerated hitmen named Lieutenant Becker as the brains behind the murder. Convicted at his first trial, Becker saw the verdict overturned on appeal, but a second jury also found him guilty. Any hope of executive clemency vanished with prosecutor Charles Whitman's election as governor, and Becker kept his date with the electric chair on July 7, 1915. Afterward, his loyal third wife commissioned a silver plaque for the lid of Becker's casket, reading:

> CHARLES BECKER
> MURDERED JULY 7, 1915
> BY GOVERNOR WHITMAN

The plaque was removed under threat of prosecution for criminal libel, but some defenders still champion Becker's cause to this day, proclaiming him the victim of a FRAME-UP spawned by his "vigorous work" in suppressing ORGANIZED CRIME. In 1912 director D. W. Griffith used the Rosenthal case as inspiration for his pioneering gangster film, *The Musketeers of Pig Alley.* As recently as 1992 authors Michael Radelet, Hugo Bedau, and Constance Putnam listed Becker among 400-plus Americans wrongly convicted of capital crimes.

Behan, John H. (1846–1912)

Missouri native John Behan was born in 1846. He saw Arizona for the first time as a Union soldier in the Civil War and liked it well enough to stay after his discharge from the army. From 1867 onward he worked as a deputy sheriff in Yavapai County, served two terms in the Arizona legislature and one term as a territorial representative to Congress from Mohave County. With the rapid growth of Tombstone, Behan put down roots there, opening a livery stable with partner John Dunbar.

In Tombstone Behan divided his time between business, gambling, romance, and law enforcement. His wife left him in 1875, but he subsequently shared quarters with actress Josephine Marcus. He served once again as a deputy sheriff, but allied himself with the Clanton-McLaury gang of rustlers and stage robbers. From 1880 onward Behan was a dedicated enemy of the EARP BROTHERS and their comrade, gambler-gunman John "Doc" Holliday. The conflict was both personal and political, sparked by rivalry between Behan and City Marshal Virgil Earp, exacerbated when Josie Marcus left Behan to become Wyatt Earp's lover. Holliday, meanwhile, described Behan as "a deadly enemy of mine, who would give any money to have me killed."

Matters worsened with the creation of Cochise County in January 1881. Both Behan and Wyatt coveted the lucrative sheriff's position, and Earp had the early edge with support from Governor John Fremont. Behan persuaded Earp to quit the race, with a promise that he (Behan) would name Wyatt undersheriff after the election, whereupon they would split the various fees and fines collected countywide. Earp agreed, but Sheriff Behan reneged on his promise, throwing his weight behind Earp's rivals at every opportunity. Wyatt Earp countered by wangling an appointment as deputy U.S. marshal, though he seldom seemed concerned with law enforcement. Following a spate of gold mine robberies, Behan complained to Governor John Gosper that the Earps "seemed unwilling to heartily cooperate with him in capturing and bringing to justice these outlaws." Today some historians suggest that the Earps and Holliday were those outlaws—or, at least, their protectors.

The Tombstone conflict culminated in the bloody O.K. CORRAL GUNFIGHT of October 1881, and while Behan missed the shootout, he charged the Earps and Holliday with murder afterward. They were acquitted, but the matter did not rest there. Morgan Earp was subsequently shot and killed from ambush, and while Holliday was "almost certain" of Behan's guilt in that crime, the Earps retaliated by killing suspected triggerman Frank Stillwell. Behan filed murder charges once again, pursuing the Earps in vain for several months, while they picked off various enemies throughout the district. No one was ever punished for the rash of killings, though Behan later told federal investigators that "he himself had done more to quell the disturbance than anyone else."

Despite persistent rumors of CORRUPTION, Behan pursued a life of public service beyond Tombstone and the O.K. Corral. He ran Arizona's state prison for a time, then served as a Customs inspector, fought in the Spanish-American War, joined the U.S. military brigade sent to China during the Boxer Rebellion, and finally worked as a code clerk for the Arizona legislature. He died in Tucson, from Bright's disease, on June 7, 1912. His funeral featured an honor guard from the Arizona Pioneer Society.

See also: CUSTOMS SERVICE.

Bell, Griffin Boyette (b. 1918)

Georgia attorney Griffin Bell was born at Americus on October 31, 1918. He served 14 years as a federal judge (1962–76) before taking office as U.S. attorney general under President Jimmy Carter on January 26, 1977. His administration was the first to actively pursue UNDERCOVER campaigns against ORGANIZED CRIME and in cases of official CORRUPTION, including the ABSCAM and UNIRAC ("union racketeering") investigations. Bell also secured the first-ever indictments of high-ranking FBI officials, including former director L. Patrick Gray and acting associate director W. MARK FELT, for authorizing illegal break-ins and other outlawed techniques of DOMESTIC SURVEILLANCE. Bell resigned on April 16, 1979, before the defendants in that case were convicted, and returned to private practice in Atlanta. In 1980 he led America's delegation to the Madrid Conference on Security and Cooperation in Europe, and two years later Bell served as a cochair of the Attorney General's National Task Force on Violent Crime. He also headed investigations into E. F. Hutton's financial management in 1985 and the Exxon Valdez oil spill of 1989. Bipartisan respect for Bell was demonstrated when President George H. W. Bush appointed him to a senior position on the Commission on Federal Ethics Law Reform in the late 1980s. In December 2003 Defense Secretary Donald Rumsfeld named Bell as one of four civilians designated to review legal proceedings against suspected terrorists confined at Guantánamo Bay, Cuba.

See also: FEDERAL BUREAU OF INVESTIGATION; GRAY, LOUIS PATRICK, III.

Bennett, William John (b. 1943)

Born in Brooklyn, New York, on July 31, 1943, William Bennett grew up in a strict Catholic home. He graduated from Williams College (Massachusetts) in 1965, completed his Ph.D. studies at the University of Texas, Austin, in 1970, and earned his J.D. from Harvard University Law School a year later. Bennett occupied various teaching and school administrative positions over the next decade, before President Ronald Reagan appointed him to head the National Endowment for the Arts (1981–83). Reagan next appointed Bennett as secretary of education (1985–88), where his views proved controversial.

When President George H. W. Bush created the Office of National Drug Control Policy in 1989, Bennett sought and secured directorship of the new agency. Bush dubbed Bennett America's "Drug Czar"—a title that many criticized as violating the U.S. Constitution's ban on royal titles (Article I, Section 9)—and while some federal agents termed the underfunded War on Drugs an "intellectual fraud," Bennett talked tough to reporters. An example from 1990 delivers his prescription for casual users:

> *Non-addicted users still comprise the vast bulk of our drug-involved population. There are many millions of them. . . . Users who maintain a job and a steady income should face stiff fines. . . . These are the users who should have their names published in local papers. They should be subject to driver's license suspension, employer notification, overnight or weekend detention, eviction from public housing, or forfeiture of the cars they drive while purchasing drugs.*

Chief among Bennett's goals was a clean-up of Washington, D.C., but the cocaine arrest of Mayor Marion Barry proved so embarrassing that Bennett resigned after 18 months in office.

From drug enforcement, Bennett moved on to head the Republican Party (November 1990) and become a leading spokesman for America's "New Right," publishing ultraconservative books such as *The Book of Virtues* (1996) and *The Death of Outrage* (1998). His posture as a moral icon suffered major damage in 2003, with media revelations that Bennett had lost $8 million gambling over the past decade, $1.4 million of that in two months (and $500,000 during a two-day spree in Las Vegas, during April 2003). In retrospect, his most telling observation on ethics may have been delivered on July 10, 2003, when Bennett told CNN News: "Hypocrisy is better than no standards at all."

Berkeley Police Department

The city of Berkeley, California, was incorporated in 1878, policed by a town marshal and supporting constables. Legendary lawman AUGUST VOLLMER was elected marshal in 1905, elevated to serve as Berkeley's first chief of police four years later. A true visionary, Vollmer instituted a strict code of ethics which banned "THIRD-DEGREE" TACTICS along with acceptance of "gratuities, rewards or favors." While other departments relied on EXCESSIVE FORCE to obtain confessions from suspects, Vollmer demanded strict professionalism and relied on cutting-edge scientific advances to win convictions in court. During his 25-year tenure as chief, Vollmer established BPD's basic records system and first Modus Operandi (MO) system (1906), pioneered FORENSIC SCIENCE techniques (1907), established the world's first police academy (1907), organized the first motorcycle patrol (1911), introduced patrol cars (1913), established the first School of Criminology at the University of California (1916), required intelli-

gence tests to screen police recruits (1918), introduced "LIE DETECTORS" (1920), added psychiatric screening for recruits (1921), created the first Junior Traffic Police program (1923), established one of the first single-fingerprint files (1924), and hired Berkeley's first female officer (1925).

The image of Berkeley's "college cops" persisted for decades after Vollmer's departure. In the 1960s Berkeley P.D. required two years of college education for recruits, and rookies completed an average 260 hours of classwork in their first year on the job. Department alumni include Earl Warren (later California's attorney general, then governor, finally Chief Justice of the U.S. SUPREME COURT) and Chicago police superintendent ORLANDO WILSON. In the turbulent Sixties, BPD officers were known for their skillful handling of mass demonstrations without resorting to violence, while similar situations in other cities led to riots. When violence *did* occur, as during the Sproul Hall arrests of 1964 and at the "People's Park" in 1969, accusations of excessive force were generally leveled at officers from other agencies. Local NAACP leader Frankie Jones told *Time* magazine (February 18, 1966), "I have seen police at work all over, and there's not a police department in the United States that excels this one." Author and ex-FBI agent William Turner agreed two years later that "physical brutality is not an issue in Berkeley."

That is not to say that Berkeley had no problems in the 1960s, or that some do not persist today. In 1965 Chief Addison Fording awarded college credit, with corresponding promotions and pay hikes, to officers who attended far-right activist Fred Schwarz's Christian Anti-Communism Crusade training school. Successor William Beall, Jr. stressed arrests for jaywalking and CONSENSUAL CRIMES in an apparent effort to boost departmental statistics, but the effort backfired. In 1967 Berkeley police jailed 474 persons for DRUG offenses, an increase of 220 percent over 1966, but most of the cases collapsed in court, where all but 74 defendants were released and 57 of those convicted escaped with probation. More recently, in July 1999, spokesmen for Pacifica radio station KPFA charged that staff members were beaten by Berkeley police during a labor dispute with company management. On balance, however, such complaints are rare in Berkeley, and are even more rarely sustained.

See also: FEDERAL BUREAU OF INVESTIGATION; FINGERPRINTS.

Berrien, John Macpherson (1781–1856)

A native of Rocky Hill, New Jersey, born August 23, 1781, John Berrien moved with his family to

Savannah, Georgia, as an infant. He graduated from Princeton University in 1796, but by then his roots were firmly planted in Georgia soil. Bates studied law in Savannah and was soon admitted to the Georgia bar, establishing a practice in Atlanta during 1799. In 1809 he was elected solicitor for Georgia's eastern judicial circuit, then served as a judge in the same circuit (1810–21), interrupted by volunteer service in the War of 1812. Bates subsequently served in the Georgia state senate (1822–23) and in the U.S. Senate (1825–29), resigning the latter post to become President Andrew Jackson's attorney general on March 9, 1829. He resigned that post in turn on June 22, 1831, and returned to private practice for the next decade. More service in the U.S. Senate followed (1841–52), broken by a brief term as a justice of Georgia's state supreme court in 1845. Bates served as chairman of the dissident American Party convention at Milledgeville, Georgia, in 1855 and died soon after, at Savannah, on January 1, 1856. Modern counties bear his name in Georgia and Michigan.

Attorney General John Berrien (Author's collection)

Bertillon System

Named for French ethnologist Alphonse Bertillon (1853–1914), the first system of classifying criminals was based on a series of body measurements (skull, foot, torso, and left middle finger) and other characteristics. Bertillon then divided the measurements into small, medium, and large groupings, from which he placed any given individual into one of 243 categories. Further classification by eye and hair color expanded the categories to 1,701. After initially dismissing Bertillon's system as a joke, Parisian police formally adopted it in 1881, followed by French authorities at large.

Under Bertillon's method, each prisoner was measured, photographed, and physically described in writing on cards six feet six inches tall by five and one-half inches wide. The completed card was indexed and placed in a specific category. A file of 10,000 records might hold only 40 individuals in a particular class, thus making comparison simpler than it sounds. Each new offense was added to the felon's card, thereby creating a permanent record.

From France the system spread rapidly to other countries and debuted in the United States via the Illinois state prison system in 1887. New York's state prisons followed six years later, and the system was eventually used in 19 states and Canada by police and penologists alike. For the first time in recorded history, authorities could positively identify individuals upon successive encounters. New York established America's first Bureau of Identification on May 9, 1896, operating from the State Capitol building. Two months later, the first training class in Bertillon measurements and criminal photography convened at Sing Sing prison, where classification of 8,000 inmates began in September 1896.

The system's impact on police work was impressive, though advance claims that it would eliminate career criminals as a class proved unduly optimistic. Spokesmen for the National Chiefs of Police Union tried to establish the first National Bureau of Investigation in Chicago, during 1897, but their effort went unrealized until creation of the FBI. Bertillon's system remained the standard method of criminal identification until finally replaced by FINGERPRINTS.

See also: FEDERAL BUREAU OF INVESTIGATION.

Biaggi, Mario (b. 1917)

A son of Italian immigrants, born in New York City on October 26, 1917, Mario Biaggi spent six years as a mail carrier (1936–42) before he joined the NEW YORK CITY POLICE DEPARTMENT. He earned the first of 27 citations for bravery in 1943, when he shot and killed a prisoner who tried to stab him with an ice pick.

Successive awards fueled his rise through the NYPD ranks, but mounting rumors surrounded his acts of alleged heroism. In 1959, while off duty, Biaggi shot and killed a man whom he claimed had kidnapped him with murder in mind. Some superiors doubted Biaggi's version of the incident, but his story prevailed and won him NYPD's highest award—the Police Medal of Honor for Valor—in 1960. Later that year, Biaggi won a scholarship to New York Law School. He took a leave of absence from the force to study law, graduating in 1963, then retired from NYPD in 1965, allegedly disabled by a leg wound he suffered in 1946.

Biaggi passed the New York bar exam in 1966, on his third attempt, and soon established a successful practice. In 1967 he served as president of the National Police Officers Association of America and was elected to the association's Hall of Fame. In 1968 he won a seat in Congress, where he served nine terms. Still, scandal pursued him, beginning when Biaggi pled the Fifth Amendment under questioning about the immigration bills he sponsored for selected individuals. That gaffe came back to haunt him in an unsuccessful campaign to become New York's mayor, in 1973, but worse trouble lay in store for Biaggi. Federal prosecutors indicted him in 1987 on charges that Biaggi took bribes to arrange government contracts for a Brooklyn ship-repair company. Jurors convicted him of bribery and obstructing justice on September 22, 1987, whereupon he was fined and sentenced to prison.

That case was still on appeal in 1988, when Biaggi faced a second trial on federal racketeering charges. Jurors convicted him on 15 counts on August 4, 1988, and Biaggi ultimately served two years in prison. He resigned from Congress on his way to jail, but demonstrated his audacity with another (unsuccessful) campaign in 1992.

Biddle, Francis Beverley (1886–1968)

Born in Paris to American parents on May 9, 1886, Francis Biddle was the fourth and last attorney general to serve President Franklin Roosevelt. He assumed office on September 5, 1941, two months before U.S. entry into World War II. That event provided the first real test of Biddle's authority over FBI Director J. EDGAR HOOVER. Biddle approved detention of "dangerous" German and Italian immigrants, but refused Hoover's request for mass arrests of Communists since the Soviet Union was a U.S. ally. Biddle also ordered the abolition of Hoover's CUSTODIAL DETENTION INDEX in July 1943, on grounds that the "classification system is inherently unreliable." He added that the FBI's "proper function" was to investigate those "who may have broken the law," with that purpose "not aided by classifying per-

sons as to dangerousness." Biddle ordered that all Custodial Detention dossiers should be clearly stamped as canceled and unreliable, with a warning that "[t]here is no statutory authorization or other present justification" for maintaining such files.

Hoover generally defied Biddle, preserving the banned files as a renamed "Security Index" in August 1943, instructing all FBI field offices that in future all such dossiers must be "strictly confidential and should at no time be mentioned or alluded to in investigative reports or discussed with agencies or individuals outside the Bureau." Biddle likewise disapproved of Hoover's wide-ranging investigations into legitimate political dissent, but he rarely took steps to curtail DOMESTIC SURVEILLANCE and was overruled on those occasions by FDR (who condoned or secretly ordered various illicit FBI activities). In 1941, when Biddle ordered an end to surveillance of labor unions and liberal groups, Hoover complained to Roosevelt that Biddle's restrictions would hamper "investigations into situations involving potential danger to the Government of the United States" and "will make utterly impotent the work of the FBI in subversive fields." (FDR sided with Hoover.) Later, when Biddle declined to prosecute certain right-wing critics of the New Deal whom Hoover branded subversive, Hoover told Roosevelt that FBI investigations had been "blocked by the Attorney General again and again." Furthermore, he said, "until some of the Attorney General's instructions have been changed . . . agents could not operate." (Again, Biddle was overruled.)

Six weeks after FDR's death, on June 30, 1945, President Harry Truman demanded and received Biddle's resignation. Successor THOMAS CAMPBELL CLARK would prove to be more pliable, ranked by Hoover as one of his favorite attorneys general. Biddle, meanwhile, was appointed by Truman to serve as a judge on the International Military Tribunal at Nuremberg, Germany, presiding over the trial of Nazi war criminals. Biddle subsequently returned to private practice in Massachusetts, and died of a heart attack at Hyannis on October 4, 1968.

See also: FEDERAL BUREAU OF INVESTIGATION.

Bielaski, A. Bruce (1884–1964)

A Maryland native, born in 1884, Alexander Bruce Bielaski got his start in law enforcement (with brother Frank) as a member of the PINKERTON Detective Agency. He received a law degree from George Washington University in 1904 and joined the U.S. JUSTICE DEPARTMENT that same year, rising through the ranks to serve as second in command to FBI chief STANLEY FINCH. Attorney General GEORGE WOODWARD WICKERSHAM named Bielaski to replace Finch on April 12, 1912, and the new chief enjoyed five relatively uneventful years, until America entered World War I in 1917.

Pursuit of draft dodgers thereafter consumed Bielaski's attention, while a manpower shortage prompted his unwise approval for collaboration with the vigilante AMERICAN PROTECTIVE LEAGUE (APL). Controversy surrounding the FBI-APL "slacker" raids of 1918 drove Bielaski to resign on February 10, 1919, and return to private legal practice. He was kidnapped by bandits while touring Mexico in 1921, but escaped in time to spare his family from paying a $10,000 ransom. Bielaski subsequently worked as covert PROHIBITION agent in New York City and led ARSON investigations for the National Board of Fire Underwriters (1929–59). He died in February 1964.

See also: FEDERAL BUREAU OF INVESTIGATION.

Birmingham Police Department

Birmingham has long been Alabama's largest city and manufacturing center, ruled by "Big Mules" of the steel industry and politicians who served them. Police knew their place in that hierarchy, devoted in equal measure to suppressing organized labor and maintaining the hallowed southern tradition of white supremacy.

Both goals were served, from 1915 through the 1960s, by collaboration with the violent KU KLUX KLAN. The 1920s KKK boasted 14,000 members in Birmingham, including Police Chief Thomas Shirley. Shirley was such an enthusiastic Klansman, in fact, that he served on the Klan's Imperial Kloncilium (national executive council) and urged leaders of the NASHVILLE POLICE DEPARTMENT to form their own Klan, as an adjunct to local law enforcement. (When finally dismissed in 1926, Shirley campaigned and won election as Jefferson County's sheriff.) Historian William Snell asserts that under Shirley and his successors, most "if not all" Birmingham policemen were also members of the Klan.

That symbiosis, masking Klan TERRORISM with virtual immunity, continued into the Great Depression and beyond World War II. In 1930 Alabama Klan leader John Murphy told Congress that his knights collaborated with Birmingham police and FBI agents to mount surveillance on suspected communists. Real or imagined Communist Party members were often arrested in Birmingham, then beaten by police or delivered to Klan whipping squads. On May Day 1933 police, Klansmen, and White Legionnaires fought a pitched street battle with 3,000 hunger marchers. Future arrests were facilitated by the Downs Ordinance—named for police commissioner William Downs, an ex-sheriff and prominent Klansman—which prescribed fines and jail time for any person possessing more than one copy of any "radical literature."

As bad as things already were in Birmingham, they worsened under public safety commissioner Eugene "Bull" Connor (1937–53, 1957–63). A bitter racist who once jailed a U.S. senator for walking through the "colored" entrance of a public edifice, Connor was so in synch with local vigilantes that he managed to predict the bombings (see BOMBING AND BOMB SQUADS) of black homes and churches in advance. Unfortunately, his omniscience did not extend to catching the terrorists; in fact, his willful negligence earned Birmingham the nickname "Bombingham," while its central black district was dubbed "Dynamite Hill." (In one case, where a black witness identified the city's latest bomber as a uniformed policeman, furnishing the number of his patrol car, FBI agents stepped in to jail the witness on a federal perjury charge.) In May 1961 Connor authorized Klan riots against integrated "freedom riders," promising the racists 15 minutes access to their victims without police interference. Two years later, he unleashed attack dogs and high-pressure hoses on demonstrators led by Dr. Martin Luther King, and thus helped ensure passage of 1964's Civil Rights Act.

Harassment of civil rights workers and "liberals" did not end with Connor's removal from office in 1963. Four years later, Birmingham police mounted surveillance on Vice President Hubert Humphrey, tracking his movements and eavesdropping on his telephone calls. Birmingham's primary civil rights organization, the Alabama Christian Movement for Human Rights, was still under full-time surveillance in 1969, police employing WIRETAPS and INFORMANTS to chart the progress of nonwhite "subversives."

Birmingham's police force has long since been racially integrated, with a mission statement pledging an effort "to exceed the citizen's expectations in all matters." Some residents, however, still wonder *which* citizens are favored by authorities. Criticism was fierce in August 2004, when police armed with automatic WEAPONS ended an armed stand-off by pumping at least 24 bullets into Benjamin Griggs, a mentally ill Vietnam War veteran. Coroner Jay Glass found himself unable to accurately count the intersecting wounds in Griggs's corpse, but Rev. Abraham Woods Jr. termed the shooting "complete overkill. They just blasted him away. One or two well-placed shots would have immobilized him or killed him, and they know that."

While it is often difficult to second-guess police responses in such cases, any perceived transgression in Birmingham, given its history, is viewed in some quarters as cause for alarm. Two years before the Griggs incident, in December 2001, Carlos Williams missed his court date on a charge of breaking into a parked car. Declared a fugitive, Williams was later shot and killed before his assembled family by Officer Lorenzo Hughes, who encountered Williams in the course of an unrelated investigation. Hughes claimed that Williams argued with him, then "reached for a gun," forcing Hughes to shoot him seven times in the head and four times in the torso. In fact, Williams was found to be unarmed.

See also: CONNOR, THEOPHILUS EUGENE ("BULL"); FEDERAL BUREAU OF INVESTIGATION.

Bismarck Police Department

Bismarck is the capital of North Dakota and the state's second-largest city (after Fargo), with some 55,000 inhabitants. Its total police force comprises 85 sworn officers (including three command positions) and 30 civilian personnel, divided into Field Services (72 officers and six civilians) and Support Services (10 officers and 23 civilians). Field Services is further divided into Patrol, Traffic (including Animal Control), and Investigations. Support Services includes the following sections: Training, Crime Prevention/Community Services, Records and Identification, Reception, Facility Maintenance, the Police Youth Bureau, and Office Assistance. The department states its mission as follows:

The men and women of the Bismarck Police Department are dedicated to provide our citizens and visitors with a safe environment to live, work and play. We take pride in being a very responsive law enforcement agency when addressing community needs. We will continue to preserve Bismarck's excellent quality of life by building partnerships with our citizens in resolving community problems. We strive for excellence by providing our employees with a positive, supportive and professional environment, which promotes innovative and creative thinking.

Black, Jeremiah Sullivan (1810–1883)

Jeremiah Sullivan was born at The Glades, in Pennsylvania's Somerset County, on January 10, 1810. He completed a common school education, then read law privately and won admission to the Pennsylvania bar in December 1830. Twelve years later, Sullivan was named president judge for the court of common pleas in his district, a post he held until winning election as chief justice of Pennsylvania's state supreme court (1851–57). President James Buchanan appointed Black as U.S. attorney general on March 6, 1857, then later as secretary of state (1860–61). President Andrew Johnson named Black to the U.S. SUPREME COURT in 1861, but the Senate denied confirmation. Almost as a consolation prize, Black was appointed as Supreme Court reporter in December 1861, from which position he published *Black's Reports*, Volumes 1 and 2. In 1867 Black joined

Attorney General Jeremiah Black (Author's collection)

Attorney General HENRY STANBERY in drafting Johnson's veto message for the first Military Reconstruction Act, which both men deemed unconstitutional. (Congress passed the bill over Johnson's veto.) Black died at York, Pennsylvania, on August 19, 1883.

"black bag jobs"

In FBI parlance, "black bag jobs" are illegal break-ins conducted for purposes of planting microphones, installing WIRETAPS, or obtaining information by some other means (including theft or photocopying of documents and mail). The term was coined because agents engaged in such activity were said to operate inside "black bags," without the knowledge or approval of superiors. In fact, most such illegal entries were performed pursuant to official orders, but the fiction preserved "plausible deniability" in case G-men were caught committing crimes.

It is unknown precisely when Bureau agents began to indulge in burglary, since records of criminal activity are often missing or deliberately misleading. In the 1970s FBI spokesmen called to account for the agency's crimes admitted a total of 239 illegal break-ins between 1942 and 1966, but that record was clearly incomplete. During investigations of the Teapot Dome scandal (1923–24) G-men burglarized the offices of Montana senators Thomas Walsh and Burton Wheeler, to subvert prosecution of corrupt government officials, and there is no reason to suppose those break-ins were the Bureau's first.

Burglary was a regular feature of FBI investigations under Director J. EDGAR HOOVER, whose only concern for violations of law was that the Bureau should avoid exposure and embarrassment. In 1942 G-men invaded offices of the American Youth Congress and photographed correspondence from First Lady Eleanor Roosevelt. Three years later, the *Amerasia* ESPIONAGE case collapsed in court upon revelation of illegal entries by the FBI and Office of Strategic Services. Attorney General HERBERT BROWNELL formally approved warrantless break-ins and bugging in "national security" cases on May 20, 1954; one day later, Hoover privately extended the authorization to any "important" criminal case. By 1957 leaders of ORGANIZED CRIME were targeted for burglary under the FBI's Top Hoodlum Program. Assistant Director WILLIAM SULLIVAN described the ethos of illegal break-ins in a memo to colleague CARTHA DELOACH, dated July 19, 1966. That memo read:

> The following is set forth in regard to your request concerning what authority we have for "black bag" jobs and for the background of our policy and procedures in such matters.
>
> We do not obtain authorization for "black bag" jobs from outside the Bureau. Such a technique involves trespass and is clearly illegal; therefore it would be impossible to obtain any legal sanction for it. Despite this, "black bag" jobs have been used because they represent an invaluable technique in combating subversive activities of a clandestine nature aimed directly at undermining and destroying our nation.
>
> The present procedure in the use of this technique calls for the Special Agent in Charge of a field office to make his request for the use of the technique to the appropriate Assistant Director. The Special Agent in Charge must completely justify the need for the use of the technique and at the same time assure that it can be safely used without any danger of embarrassment to the Bureau. The facts are incorporated in a memorandum which, in accordance with the Director's instructions, is sent to Mr. [Clyde] Tolson or to the Director for approval. Subsequently this memorandum is filed in the Assistant Director's office under a "Do Not File" procedure.
>
> In the field the Special Agent in Charge prepares an informal memorandum showing that he obtained Bureau authority and this memorandum is filed in his safe until the next inspection by Bureau Inspectors, at which time it is destroyed. . . .
>
> We have used this technique on a highly selective basis, but with wide-ranging effectiveness, in our operations. We have several cases in the espionage field, for example, where through "black bag" jobs we determined that suspected illegal agents actually had concealed on their premises the equipment through which they carried out their clandestine operations.
>
> Also through the use of this technique we have on numerous occasions been able to obtain material held highly secret and closely guarded by subversive groups and organizations which consisted of membership lists and mailing lists of these organizations. . . .
>
> Through the same technique we have recently been receiving extremely valuable information concerning political developments in the Latin American field, and we also have been able to use it most effectively in a number of instances recently, through which we have obtained information concerning growing [deleted] intelligence activities directed at this country.
>
> In short, it is a very valuable weapon which we have used to combat the highly clandestine efforts of subversive elements seeking to undermine our Nation.

Hoover penned an order across the bottom of Sullivan's memo, declaring "No more such techniques must be used"—but they continued nonetheless. In July 1970 the White House–approved Houston Plan echoed Sullivan's memo, outlining a series of "clearly illegal" techniques to be used against political "enemies" of President Richard Nixon. Hoover initially balked at participating in the program, then agreed with the proviso that Attorney General JOHN NEWTON MITCHELL should personally approve each instance of G-men breaking the law. Eight months later, the tables were turned, when burglars invaded the FBI office at Media, Pennsylvania, and escaped with thousands of classified documents detailing the Bureau's illicit COINTELPRO operations. Hoover canceled those programs a month later, while publication of the stolen documents sparked a flurry of lawsuits, including a $27 million action filed by leaders of the Socialist Workers Party (targets of 92 documented break-ins between 1960 and 1966).

It was finally another break-in, planned in part by ex-FBI agent G. GORDON LIDDY, which doomed the Nixon administration. In August 1973, as the Watergate scandal unfolded, Nixon told reporters that similar burglaries had been carried out "on a very large scale" under predecessors John Kennedy and Lyndon Johnson. The next day, FBI spokesmen acknowledged using the same "old, established investigative technique" for 30-odd years in "national security" cases, but they clung to the fiction that illegal break-ins had ceased in July 1966. The U.S. Senate's CHURCH COMMITTEE report on FBI abuses (1976) tabulated 697 bugging incidents and 26,287 illegal mail-openings between 1958 and 1974, but the senators strangely accepted Director CLARENCE MARION KELLEY's assertion that G-men committed only 239 burglaries between 1942 and 1966. Retired agent M. Wesley Swearingen challenged Kelley's statement, claiming personal knowledge of more than 500 break-ins committed in Chicago alone, during 1952–57.

Critics found a certain irony in Kelley's May 1976 statement that the FBI should never again occupy the "unique position that permitted improper activity without accountability," when his own agents were accused of using COINTELPRO-style techniques against the American Indian Movement and Puerto Rican nationalists. In November 1980 former acting associate director MARK FELT and former assistant director Edward Miller were convicted of authorizing illegal break-ins around New York City in the 1970s, but President Ronald Reagan pardoned both defendants four months later. Soon, Reagan's own administration was using identical techniques against political dissenters, notably the Committee in Solidarity with the People of El Salvador.

It would be comforting to think that FBI leaders have finally abandoned use of illegal techniques, after skirting or breaking the law for almost a century, but recent events provide no such assurance. After the events of September 11, 2001, in the fervor of a global "war on terrorism" that includes sweeping new surveillance powers under the USA PATRIOT ACT, civil libertarians suggest that illicit activities by federal, state and local agencies may be more common than ever before.

See also: FEDERAL BUREAU OF INVESTIGATION.

"Bloody Christmas"

In December 1951 officers of the LOS ANGELES POLICE DEPARTMENT arrested seven young Mexican-Americans who were subsequently beaten in their cells for allegedly assaulting or insulting policemen (reports of the incident vary). Visiting reporters captured the events on film, and the resultant "Bloody Christmas" scandal forced prosecutors to indict eight officers, while 36 more were subjected to interdepartmental discipline. Author James Ellroy later dramatized the incident as a centerpiece of his novel and film, *L.A. Confidential.*

"blue flu"

Coined in 1970, the term *blue flu* refers to orchestrated absenteeism by police officers or firefighters who claim illness while in fact supporting union contract demands or similar labor actions. (The *blue* refers to typical U.S. police uniforms.) Such "sick-outs" have occurred throughout the country over the past four decades, but none to date have rivaled the chaos resulting from Boston's police strike of September 1919, when 80 percent of the BOSTON POLICE DEPARTMENT's officers left work to demand affiliation with the American Federation of Labor. Federal intervention crushed that strike, but modern outbreaks of "blue flu" have avoided such drastic remedies. Some recent examples include:

Yale University: Twenty campus police officers—95 percent of those scheduled for duty—called in sick on February 14, 1998, supporting contract demands by the Yale Police Benevolent Association. University administrators responded by withholding pay from officers who could not document illness and warned that "any future participation in similar activity may subject them to disciplinary action, which could include termination." The sick-out climaxed two years of police contract disputes at Yale.

Los Angeles: "Blue flu" struck the LOS ANGELES COUNTY SHERIFF'S DEPARTMENT as 249 officers ignored court injunctions and called in sick on October 7, 2003 (election day). Their action temporarily closed four county courthouses in El Monte, Pomona, and West Covina, while substations in Compton, East Los Angeles, and City of Industry were left with critical personnel shortages.

East Orange, New Jersey: After working for five years without a pay raise, 50 officers of the 284-member East Orange Police Department (including all 20 members of the department's school unit) staged a sick-out protest on October 22, 2003. The one-day strike came after city officials appealed an arbitrator's decision granting pay raises of 12.5 percent over seven years, retroactive to expiration of the last contract on January 1, 1999. Officers were also angered by the language of a recent report from New Jersey's Public Employment Relations Commission, which compared police work to coal mining and employment at convenience stores. Sgt. Bilal Hall, speaking for the FRATERNAL ORDER OF POLICE, called that comparison "an insult to officers and to family members of officers who have been slain in the line of duty."

Wilmington, Delaware: Officers of the WILMINGTON POLICE DEPARTMENT, affiliated with the Fraternal Order of Police, staged a sick-out in July 2004, resulting in double shifts for non-striking officers. DELAWARE STATE POLICE and New Castle County officers filled positions vacated by "blue flu" victims, while city leaders maintained that "public safety has not been compromised."

New York City: Labor unrest within the NEW YORK POLICE DEPARTMENT climaxed in August 2004 with threats of a sick-out on August 30, the first day of the Republican National Convention in Manhattan. Police Commissioner Raymond Kelly blamed reports of the job action on an anonymous letter, and spokesmen for the Patrolmen's Benevolent Association denied any involvement with the threat, which failed to materialize on cue.

body armor

History does not record the first use of protective body armor in battle, but shields, helmets, and injury-resistant clothing certainly date from the earliest days of armed human conflict. Leather and wood were used extensively before technology allowed the manipulation of various metals, and steel remained the epitome of armor for generations thereafter. Bandits and police fought their epic battles of the 1930s wearing crude steel plates in fabric vests that slipped over their heads like sandwich signs, and such cumbersome gear remained the norm until bullet-resistant fabrics like DuPont's Kevlar, Honeywell's GoldFlex and Zylon, or the European firm Akzo's Twaron were developed in the 1960s and 1970s.

The National Institute of Justice (NIJ) rates body armor on a scale of ballistic protection levels. Armor is tested not only for resistance to penetration, but also for minimization of blunt force trauma (either from projectile impact or direct blows in hand-to-hand fighting). Blunt trauma is measured by the dent inflicted on a soft clay pad behind the armor being tested, with a maximum depth of 1.7 inches permitted for physical safety. The NIJ's armor rankings are:

I—Blocks .38 Special round-nose lead bullets traveling at 850 feet per second (fps), .22-caliber Long Rifle ammunition at 1,050 fps. This armor also protects the wearer against birdshot charges from a shotgun but is not recommended for use against any higher-velocity ammunition.

IIA—Consisting of 16 to 18 layers of Kevlar, this armor is designed to cope with most threats encountered in urban shooting situations. It will stop various rounds including 9-mm full metal jacket (FMJ) bullets traveling at 1,090 fps and .357 Magnum jacketed hollow-point (JHP) projectiles traveling at 1,250 fps.

II—With 22 to 24 layers of Kevlar, this armor should stop bullets including 9-mm FMJ rounds traveling at 1,175 fps and .357 Magnum jacketed soft-point (JSP) rounds traveling at 1,395 fps. It also deflects most shotgun pellets.

IIIA—Offering 30–32 layers of Kevlar, this armor stops projectiles including 9-mm FMJ rounds traveling at 1,400 fps (the usual muzzle velocity for most 9-mm submachine guns) and .44 Magnum rounds at the same velocity. Its blunt-trauma protection rating is the highest offered by soft armor, thus allowing for more effective return fire in a shootout.

III—To repel most rifle bullets, this armor abandons soft fabrics and employs 1/4-inch specially treated steel, 1/2-inch ceramic plates, or one-inch polyethylene plates. Blunt trauma should be minimized, but the armor is heavier and not concealable.

IV—Finally, to protect against armor-piercing rifle bullets, this armor is crafted from 3/4-inch ceramic plates.

Special circumstances require special armor, beyond those listed above. Bomb-disposal personnel require full-body coverage in the event of an explosion, typically combining both ballistic-resistant and fire-retardant fabrics (some of which protect the wearer from projectiles traveling up to 2,250 fps). A typical bomb-disposal suit includes a fully armored coat (including sleeves), removable collar and groin protector, armored trousers (often open at the rear for comfort, providing front coverage only), a helmet with fragment-resistant face shield, an armored chest plate, with special boots and gloves (available for cases where an explosive device must be disarmed, rather than simply transported). "Bomb blankets" are also available to screen personnel or to shroud small devices and contain shrapnel in the event of a blast.

Manufacturers are quick to stress that no body armor is ever 100 percent bulletproof. Likewise, special stab-resistant fabrics or fabric combinations may be needed to deflect blades, in the event of an assault with knives or other edged weapons. Armor-piercing ammunition has been banned from civilian sale in the United States for many years, but sufficient quantities of "cop-killer" bullets are still available to render many forms of concealable armor superfluous. Factors to consider in selecting body armor include:

Threat assessment: The type of protection required obviously varies from person to person. A motorcyle patrol officer needs less (or different) protective clothing than a bomb-disposal technician. If an assailant's weapons are known, armor may be adjusted accordingly.

Comfort: Uncomfortable armor is more likely to be removed and abandoned, thus making it useless when a crisis finally arrives. A compromise between comfort and coverage must be attained in order for the gear to be effective.

Concealability: If an assailant knows his target is wearing a protective vest, he may fire at the head or lower body and inflict fatal wounds without regard to the armor. Various situations such as diplomatic functions or corporate gatherings may also require discretion on the part of those wearing protective gear.

Cost: The better the armor, the higher its price. Urban officers forced to purchase their own Kevlar vests have more limited options (and consequent greater exposure than wealthy corporate CEOs or military personnel whose equipment is funded by taxpayers.

Coverage: Some vests offer only front-and-back protection, while others wrap around the wearer's torso to include side coverage. Various other garments, including whole business suits, may be crafted from thin layers of bullet-resistant fabric (albeit with some sacrifice of fashion points). Tactical vests, worn outside the clothing by officers on SWAT TEAMS and other assault units, offer 50 percent more protection on average than vests designed to be worn under shirts or jackets.

Mobility: Armor becomes a handicap if it retards the wearer's movements, making him or her a proverbial "sitting duck." Whether fleeing an attack or fighting back, a certain amount of mobility is required for survival.

Temperature: A primary concern for wearers of protective clothing, heat buildup may prove uncomfortable in some situations or debilitating in others (such as desert combat). Whenever possible, armor intended for long-term use should be tailored to the environment where it will be worn. Some modern (more expensive) vests include built-in cooling systems for extra comfort.

Weight: Heavy armor induces fatigue with prolonged wear, and it also reduces mobility. In most cases this issue arises with Class III or IV armor and in bomb-disposal suits. Ceramic and polyethylene plates weigh less than steel, and may be prepared if they provide equivalent protection from incoming projectiles.

In addition to "bulletproof" clothing, various tactical shields are also available. Special canine "vests" are sold for police dogs in firefight situations, and projectile-resistant fabric may be crafted into a variety of other shapes. Some of the more common forms include use as upholstery (for office furniture or car seats) and in backpacks or briefcases (which may be used to shield an otherwise uprotected target).

Boggs, John C. (1825–1909)

A native of Greencastle, Pennsylvania, born October 18, 1825, John Boggs worked in an iron foundry before the siren song of gold lured him across the continent to California in 1849. He failed at mining, then turned to guarding gold procured by others, serving as a watchman in the mining town of Auburn during 1853. His promotion to constable coincided with a crime wave in Auburn and Placer County, as roving bands of outlaws terrorized miners and the teamsters who transported their gold.

Never one to worry much about the niceties of legal jurisdiction, Boggs ranged far afield from Auburn in 1856, to pursue bandit Tom Bell (né Hodges). Boggs led the posse that captured Bell on October 4, 1856, and raised no objection to the summary hanging that smacked of LYNCHING. Two years later, Boggs pursued another badman, Richard "Rattlesnake Dick" Barter, with such zeal that he (Boggs) was nicknamed "the Nemesis of Rattlesnake Dick." Personal hatred fueled the manhunt, since Barter several times escaped from Boggs's jail and once eluded his pursuer following a standup fight in April 1858. Their final clash, on July 11, 1859, left one deputy dead and another crippled for life, but Barter was mortally wounded. Searchers found him the next morning, clutching a note that read: "If J. Boggs is dead, I am satisfied."

Despite his reputation as a crime fighter, Placer County voters rejected Boggs when he ran for sheriff in 1860, 1862, and 1873. Sheriff C. C. Crosby appointed Boggs to serve as undersheriff in 1877, and Boggs finally won election to the coveted top office two years later. His tenure was a brief one, though. He resigned in March 1880, after jurors acquitted two recently captured train robbers and a third suspect escaped from jail. Boggs died in 1909, at age 84.

bombing and bomb squads

While no reliable statistics presently exist, most official sources concur that hundreds or thousands of bombings and bomb scares occur throughout the United States every year. Motives range from personal to sociopolitical, while the explosive devices employed run the gamut from crude homemade incendiaries to sophisticated bombs with complex timers and multiple detonators. Bombs are favored by terrorists of every political and/or religious persuasion, as well as some members of ORGANIZED CRIME. Aside from their destructive force, successful bombs also permit their builders to be absent from the crime scene when detonation occurs, and their explosions eradicate much incriminating evidence (FINGERPRINTS, tool marks, serial numbers, etc.). Bombing targets in recent American history include abortion clinics, financial institutions, schools, government buildings, commercial enterprises large and small, private homes and vehicles, churches, and synagogues.

Police respond to bombings and bomb scares in various ways. Most large departments have bomb squads with officers specially trained and equipped to deactivate or safely detonate explosive devices. The federal response to bombing was erratic prior to 1972, when a new Federal Bombing Statute defined responsibility for such cases. Under that law, U.S. postal inspectors investigate mail-bombings and bombing attacks on post offices; the FBI handles bombings of federal property (excluding postal and TREASURY DEPARTMENT facilities); and the BUREAU OF ALCOHOL, TOBACCO, FIREARMS AND EXPLOSIVES (ATF) investigates all other domestic bombings unless the crimes are designated acts of TERRORISM—in which case they revert to FBI jurisdiction. Bomb threats involving alleged nuclear devices have been handled since 1974 by a special Nuclear Emergency Search Team (NEST), comprising more than 1,000 volunteer scientists, engineers, and technicians employed at various nuclear labs and regulatory agencies, collaborating with the U.S. Army's 52nd Ordnance Group (specially trained to deactivate nuclear weapons).

While the system outlined under law looks efficient on paper, it sometimes breaks down in reality. One problem is the FBI's highly selective definition of which bombings count as "terrorist" acts, permitting the Bureau to sidestep cases it wants to avoid. A prime example lies in the realm of antiabortion violence, which during 1977–2000 included 40 bombings, 163 arson attacks, 80 attempted bombings or arsons, and 526 bomb threats against women's clinics nationwide. While most observers regarded those attacks as terrorist in nature, often carried out by organized group's like the "pro-life" Army of God, FBI Director WILLIAM WEBSTER announced in December 1984 that clinic bombings did not fit the Bureau's definition of domestic terrorism. (G-men were forced to investigate clinic bombings in 1995, with passage of the federal Free Access to Clinic Entrances Act, but their conviction rate remains at zero.) Various bombings perpetrated by the KU KLUX KLAN and neo-Nazi groups were likewise ignored by FBI headquarters until FBI agents completed their investigation and suspects were indicted. According to ATF historian James Moore, the FBI "liked those cases . . . so much that, notwithstanding their minor assistance in no more than three [of 10] investigations, they issued an official report taking full and exclusive credit for almost all of them."

While most American bombings are fairly inept exercises, some prove deadly and vastly destructive. Amid thousands of blasts detonated by nativists, racists, racketeers, revolutionaries, foreign agents and self-styled patriots, the following cases stand out.

July 1854—Nativist bombers destroyed Catholic churches in Dorchester, Massachusetts, and Sidney, Ohio. No suspects were apprehended.

May 3, 1886—The HAYMARKET BOMBING climaxed a violent strike at Chicago's McCormick Reaper factory, killing seven policemen and wounding 68 more. While the bomber was never identified, eight supposed anarchists were convicted of murder, with seven condemned and four ultimately executed. Few modern observers believe the defendants were guilty, and the last three surviving in prison were pardoned in 1893.

Spring 1919—Suspected anarchists mailed parcel bombs to prominent persons across the U.S. Most were intercepted by postal inspectors, but one injured a servant employed by a former senator in Georgia. On June 3 bombs exploded at homes in eight cities, but the only casualties were two apparent bombers who died at the home of Attorney General A. MITCHELL PALMER. That explosion spurred Palmer's "Red raids" of 1919–20, but the bombings remain unsolved.

September 16, 1920—A wagon filled with dynamite and iron sash weights exploded on Wall Street, in downtown Manhattan, killing 40 persons and wounding nearly 300 more. Once again anarchists were blamed, but no suspects were ever identified.

May 18, 1927—Tax protester Andrew Kehoe bombed an elementary school in Bath, Michigan, killing himself, a teacher, and 37 children. Another 43 students were injured in the blast.

April 1928—Rival gangsters lobbed so many bombs and hand grenades at one another in the days preceding Chicago's primary election that reporters dubbed it the "pineapple primary."

December 25, 1951—Civil rights leader Harry Moore and his wife died in the bombing of their home at Mims, Florida. While several deceased Klansmen are suspected, the crime remains officially unsolved.

November 1, 1955—A bomb exploded on board United Airlines Flight 629, en route from Denver to Portland, Oregon, killing all 44 persons aboard. FBI agents arrested John Gilbert Graham, who confessed planting the bomb to kill his mother for her life insurance.

September 16, 1963—Ku Klux Klansmen bombed the all-black Sixteenth Street Baptist Church, a focal point of recent civil rights demonstrations in Birmingham, Alabama. Four adolescent girls died in the blast. Although state police and FBI agents concealed vital evidence, one bomber was

An anarchist bombing devastated New York's Wall Street financial district in September 1920. (Author's collection)

Bombings like this one, at a black housing project in Miami, occurred throughout the South during the civil rights era.
(Florida State Archives)

convicted in 1977. Two others were imprisoned in 2001–02.

February 26, 1993—Muslim extremists detonated a car bomb in the underground garage of New York's World Trade Center, killing six persons and injuring more than 1,000. A global search for suspects ultimately sent 16 defendants to prison with terms ranging from 25 to 240 years.

April 19, 1995—A massive truck bomb demolished the Alfred P. Murrah Federal Building in Oklahoma City, killing eight federal agents and 160 other victims. Prosecutors convicted two self-styled "patriots," Timothy McVeigh (executed June 11, 2001) and Terry Nichols (sentenced to life imprisonment). A third suspect, known only as "John Doe No. 2," remains at large today, while critics speculate on a broader conspiracy involving various private "militias."

See also: ANARCHISM; FEDERAL BUREAU OF INVESTIGATION.

Bonaparte, Charles Joseph (1851–1921)

A grandnephew of French emperor Napoleon Bonaparte I, born in 1851, Charles Bonaparte was appointed by President THEODORE ROOSEVELT to serve on the Board of Indian Commissioners in 1902. He later served as Secretary of the Navy (1905) and as assistant to Attorney General PHILANDER KNOX, dedicated to pursuing "bad men in public office." Bonaparte succeeded Knox as attorney general on December 17, 1906 and continued the JUSTICE DEPARTMENT's policy of prosecuting corrupt officials, a campaign that won him few friends in Congress. Finally, denied the use of SECRET SERVICE agents and legally barred from recruiting his own detectives, Bonaparte defied Congress by creating a team of "special agents" on June 30, 1908. Congressional critics were outraged, but there was little they could do to block the move after Roosevelt issued a presidential order supporting Bonaparte on July 26, 1908.

The original detective force had no formal name or function, described by historian Francis Russell as "an odd-job detective agency with fuzzy lines of authority and responsibility." Bonaparte vowed that his men would abstain from an investigation of private morality, confining their attention to antitrust cases and similar federal crimes. That promise was forgotten with passage of the MANN ACT in 1910, but Bonaparte was already gone, leaving office on March 4, 1909. He returned to private legal practice in his native Baltimore, working there until his death in 1921. The "special" force that he created was the embryonic FBI.

Bonfield, John (c. 1836–1898)

John Bonfield joined the CHICAGO POLICE DEPARTMENT late in life, at age 41, but within a year of his enlistment he was elevated from patrolman to lieutenant, with a corresponding post in the Detective Force. Some said his meteoric rise was due less to Bonfield's ability than his familial connections, including one brother who served as the mayor's corporate counsel and another employed as bailiff for Chicago's criminal court.

Under police chiefs Austin Doyle (1882–85) and FREDERICK EBERSOLD (1885–88) Bonfield became a renowned STRIKEBREAKER and hunter of supposed anarchists, notorious for unleashing his troops to club and arrest striking workers. When bystanders caught in the melee filed lawsuits for damages, Bonfield explained to Mayor Carter Harrison, "I am doing it in mercy of the people. A club today to make them scatter may save use of the pistol tomorrow. The wholesale arrests we have made have dampened the enthusiasm of the strikers and their friends." His tactic backfired in 1886, with the deadly HAYMARKET BOMBING, and most historians today consider Bonfield's solution to that case a clumsy political FRAME-UP.

In January 1889 a series of exposés in the *Chicago Times* accused Bonfield of protecting gamblers. One of his former UNDERCOVER officers, Patrick Tyrell, described his own demotion to a beat in the 12th Precinct's "Terror District" after he embarrassed Bonfield on a burglary case. According to Tyrell, quoted on January 8, "Bonfield has no claims of ability fitting him for the place, only that he is a malicious bigot. There is no record of any important case that he has ever worked up except to hunt ignorant anarchists and create a scare about them." Stung by the charges, Bonfield arrested the newspaper's editor and principal owner, held them briefly without bail, then resigned under fire. The department called him back in 1893, to help maintain order around the World's Fair, but it was a temporary assignment. Bonfield subsequently opened a private detective agency, but mismanagement drove him into bankruptcy. He died in 1898.

See also: ANARCHISM.

Border Patrol

Established by an act of Congress on May 28, 1924, the U.S. Border Patrol was initially attached to the Bureau of Immigration, its 450 original officers assigned to catch illegal aliens and those who smuggle them into the country. Over time the patrol expanded to include more than 9,500 persons, but its primary mission remains unchanged. After the terrorist attacks of September 11, 2001, the Border Patrol was transferred to a newly created Department of Homeland Security, as part of

U.S. Customs and Border Protection. Between 1994 and 2004 Border Patrol agents arrested 11.3 million persons, exceeding the current combined populations of Iowa, Kansas, and Missouri.

Officers of the Border Patrol are currently assigned to 6,000 miles of U.S. territory adjoining Canada and Mexico, plus 2,000 miles of coastal water around Florida and Puerto Rico. Agents spend 19 weeks in training at the Border Patrol Academy in Glynco, Georgia, or at the Federal Law Enforcement Training Center in Charleston, South Carolina. Their training includes courses on immigration law, statutory authority, police techniques and Spanish, followed by 24 weeks of on-the-job training (including further instruction in immigration law and Spanish) before they "solo." The modern Border Patrol's jurisdiction is divided into 20 sectors, listed alphabetically below:

Blaine Sector (Washington), covering Alaska, Oregon, and the western half of Washington state.

Buffalo Sector (New York), spanning 450 miles of Canadian border from the Ohio/Pennsylvania state line to Jefferson County, New York. Buffalo also covers most of New York State, plus all of Maryland, Pennsylvania, Virginia, and West Virginia.

Del Rio Sector (Texas), spanning 59,541 square miles of Texas, along a 300-mile-wide strip of the U.S.-Mexican border.

Detroit Sector (Michigan), including the states of Illinois, Indiana, Michigan, and Ohio.

El Centro Sector (California), covering Imperial and Riverside Counties in Southern California.

El Paso Sector (Texas), covering 125,500 square miles that includes the whole state of New Mexico and two west-Texas counties, El Paso and Hudspeth.

Grand Forks Sector (North Dakota), covering Iowa, Kansas, Minnesota, Missouri, Nebraska, and North and South Dakota.

Havre Sector (Montana), patrolling 452 miles of Canadian border with Montana, plus the full states of Colorado, Utah, Wyoming, and part of Idaho.

Houlton Sector (Maine), covering the entire state.

Laredo Sector (Texas), encompassing 116 counties (101,439 square miles) in northeastern and southwestern Texas, with its northern boundary extending to the Oklahoma state line.

Marfa Sector (Texas), the Southwest's largest, covering 118 counties (more than 135,000 square miles) in Texas and Oklahoma, with 420 miles of river border on the Rio Grande.

McAllen Sector (Texas), spanning 18 counties (17,000 square miles) in southeastern Texas.

Miami Sector (Florida), including the states of Florida, Georgia, North and South Carolina.

New Orleans Sector (Louisiana), spanning 362,310 square miles and a seven-state area, including Alabama, Arkansas, Kentucky, Louisiana, Mississippi, Tennessee, and part of the Florida panhandle.

Ramey Sector (Puerto Rico), covering Puerto Rico and the U.S. Virgin Islands.

San Diego Sector (California), restricted to San Diego County on the Mexican border.

Spokane Sector (Washington), covering eastern Washington and Idaho, plus western Montana to the Continental Divide.

Swanton Sector (Vermont), including the state of Vermont with three New Hampshire counties and five counties in New York (24,000 square miles), plus 261 miles of land and water boundaries.

Tucson Sector (Arizona), patrolling the state of Arizona outside La Paz, Mojave, and Yuma Counties.

Yuma Sector (Arizona), covering three Arizona counties excluded from the Tucson Sector, plus four counties in southern Nevada and the eastern part of three California counties (Imperial, Los Angeles, and Riverside).

See also: CUSTOMS SERVICE; HOMELAND SECURITY DEPARTMENT; CITIZENSHIP AND IMMIGRATION SERVICE; TERRORISM.

Boston Police Department

Boston, Massachusetts, established its first night watch unit in 1631, consisting of one officer and six patrolmen. Seventy years later, in 1701, a town meeting ordered night watchmen to remain on duty from 10:00 P.M. until daybreak, forgoing use of tobacco during their tours of duty. The Boston Police Department was formally established in 1854, but its greatest fame (or notoriety) came in 1919, when a strike in favor of unionization prompted Governor Calvin Coolidge to mobilize the state militia, publicly declaring that "[t]here is no right to strike against the public safety by anybody, anywhere, anytime." Coolidge's equation of Boston policemen with anarchists and "radicals" was ironic, since the department had recently formed its first RED SQUAD to harass suspected Bolsheviks.

In September 2004 Boston PD was rocked by exposure of a "double-dipping" scandal, wherein 396 of the city's 2,035 officers had illegally collected double pay for overlapping shifts on 724 occasions during

2002–04. The unearned pay spanned ranks ranging from patrolmen to captains, including a commander of BPD's Paid Detail Assignment Unit. According to reports published in the *Boston Globe,* at least 150 officers collected double pay on multiple occasions, with one cheating the city on 23 separate occasions. The incidents occurred while officers were "moonlighting," working private security details under contract with various business establishments, including supermarkets, shopping malls, department stores, and so forth. Big Dig (construction of Boston's massive traffic tunnel) was the hardest hit, billed for 121 shifts in which officers were also paid for working somewhere else. While some department spokesmen dismissed the problem as faulty bookkeeping, Police Commissioner Kathleen O'Toole told reporters that deliberate cheaters might be prosecuted for theft. "We will aggressively discipline anybody who is found to have violated the laws and regulations of this department," she declared. "There's nothing more important than integrity." (No charges had been filed at press time for this volume.)

More traditional—and more disturbing—cases of police malpractice also surface in Boston from time to time. On December 3, 2003, BPD Sergeant Harry Byrne received a 70-month sentence in federal prison, convicted of beating a college student and soliciting false testimony from four other officers to conceal his use of EXCESSIVE FORCE. (Byrne's sentence also included two years of supervised parole upon release and $7,700 restitution to his victim.) Ten months later, in October 2004, another federal jury convicted Sergeant Joseph Lemoure and Officer Joseph Polito on charges including obstruction of justice, conspiracy to obstruct justice, perjury, subornation of perjury, and witness tampering. Their case involved the June 2000 beating of victim Peter Fratus, after which the two defendants lied to INTERNAL AFFAIRS investigators and fabricated testimony from three nonexistent witnesses to excuse the assault. Upon conviction, Lemoure faced a maximum sentence of 40 years, while Polito faced up to 30 years in prison.

See also: ANARCHISM.

bounty hunters

Bounty hunters are civilians who track and apprehend fugitives from justice in expectation of monetary rewards offered by local, state, or federal authorities. Most such offers specify payment for information leading to arrest and conviction of the individuals in question, while urging civilians to avoid direct contact and report any suspects to regular law enforcement agencies. For some profit-seekers, however, a phone call is never enough.

Bounty hunters were more common in the Old West, where jurisdictional limitations prevented sworn peace officers from pursuing fugitives across county or state boundaries, and frequent notice that suspects were wanted "Dead or Alive" cast some civilian operators as little more than contract killers. (The last such reward offer, branding certain 1930s bank robbers as "Wanted Dead," was quickly withdrawn by embarrassed Texas legislators.) Modern bounty hunters are primarily "skip tracers," bail-bondsmen or their "recovery agents" who pursue bail-jumping fugitives. They draw authority from the U.S. SUPREME COURT's ruling in *Taylor v. Taintor* (1872), which declared that defendants free on bail have voluntarily surrendered custody of themselves (and by extension, waived most of their constitutional rights) to the individuals posting bond. Thus, since bounty hunters employed by bondsmen are not government agents, *Taylor v. Taintor* specifically exempts them from most statutes concerning trespass and KIDNAPPING (as long as they seize the right target). They may invade hotels or private homes without a warrant and without announcing themselves, need not inform a suspect of his/her legal rights, may seize evidence under circumstances barred to sworn peace officers, and may use "reasonable force" (including DEADLY FORCE, if fired upon) to effect an arrest. Deaths are rare in such cases, though two persons were killed in August 1997, when five bounty hunters raided a home in Phoenix, Arizona.

Spokesmen for the National Association of Bail Enforcement Agents claim that civilian bounty hunters are more efficient than sworn officers at retrieving bail-jumpers. According to the NABEA, civilian agents capture 88 percent of known U.S. "skips," while police retrieve 10 percent (typically by accident, in traffic stops or by arrests for some new offense), and 2 percent are never caught. An estimated 200 to 300 full-time bounty hunters operate across America, earning an average $36,000 per year (10 percent of the posted bond for each fugitive captured), while another 1,700 track fugitives part-time. Few training courses are offered for recovery agents, and those that exist stress legal constraints over tactics. Despite legal protections under *Taylor v. Taintor,* bounty hunters must still exercise caution. In 1996 a New York woman mistakenly seized and transported to Alabama by skip tracers won a civil judgment for $1.2 million against her careless kidnappers.

Bradford, William (1755–1795)

Philadelphia native William Bradford was born on September 14, 1755. He earned his bachelor's and master's degrees from Princeton University, then studied law privately before the outbreak of the American Revolution in 1776. Volunteering as a private in the Continental Army, he rose through the ranks to serve as a lieutenant colonel, deputy quartermaster general, deputy muster-master general, and finally as a colonel. Admitted to the bar in September 1779, Bradford subsequently served as Pennsylvania's state attorney general (1780–91) and as a justice of the state's supreme court (1791–94). President George Washington appointed Bradford as the nation's second U.S. attorney general in January 1794, and he died in office on August 23, 1795. Pennsylvania's Bradford County is named in his honor.

Bradley, Cyrus Parker (1819–1865)

A product of New England Puritan stock, born at Concord, New Hampshire, on November 14, 1819, Cyrus Bradley ran Chicago's largest warehousing company before he entered public service. Appointed as the city's fire marshal in 1850, he put the fire department on a solid professional footing and organized its first Benevolent Association. Bradley later won election as city collector, with a parallel appointment to serve as a Cook County deputy sheriff. Mayor Levi Boone selected him as Chicago's first police chief in 1855, swayed chiefly by Bradley's promise to enforce the Sunday-closing laws, which Marshal James Donnelly ignored.

Historian Bonnie Forkosh calls Bradley "one of the most energetic and able men ever connected with the fire and police service in Chicago," but his tenure was a brief one. Politics ruled the Windy City, then as now, and new mayor Thomas Dyer replaced Bradley in 1856. Undaunted, Bradley created his own private force, the Chicago Detecting and Collecting Police Agency, which proved more efficient than the city force at recovering stolen property.

Bradley emerged from retirement in April 1861 to serve as the first superintendent of Chicago's new police commission, recruiting 33 new officers, establishing standard height and weight requirements, and supplying patrolmen with their first uniforms. Still, politics ensnared him, driving Bradley from office on July 23, 1864. He died the following year.

Bradley, Tom (1917–1998)

Born at Calvert, Texas, on December 29, 1917, African-American Tom Bradley moved to Los Angeles with his family at age six. An excellent student and star athlete in high school, he won an athletic scholarship to the University of California, Los Angeles, but left school in his junior year (1941) to join the LOS ANGELES POLICE DEPARTMENT. Bradley rose through the ranks to become a lieutenant, but entrenched RACISM inside LAPD convinced him he would never gain a higher rank. He earned a law degree from Southwest College in 1956 and quit the police force in 1961 to enter private practice.

Leaders of L.A.'s black community marked Bradley as an ideal political candidate, backing his successful race for a city council seat in 1963. Bradley lost his first campaign for mayor in 1969, but came back strong to win in 1973, thus becoming the first black mayor of a major American city. Voters reelected him four times, presenting Bradley with a solid vote of confidence. (His two attempts to occupy the governor's mansion, in 1982 and 1986, were unsuccessful.) While in office, Bradley clashed repeatedly with old-line white leaders of LAPD, including controversial chief DARYL FRANCIS GATES. Mayor Bradley retired from politics in 1992, a year after the RODNEY KING case and resultant ghetto riots highlighted the tense nature of Los Angeles race relations. Bradley died on September 29, 1998.

Branch Davidian siege

The Branch Davidian sect is a fundamentalist Christian denomination organized in the 1930s, after Bulgarian immigrant Victor Houteff led a small group of defectors from the parent Seventh-Day Adventist (SDA) Church. Houteff established his own Davidian SDA Church outside Waco, Texas, and leadership passed to his widow with Houteff's death in 1955. Mrs. Houteff predicted the return of Christ at Easter 1959, and the failure of that prophecy produced another rift, various members departing while a hard core of 50 believers—renamed Branch Davidians—remained at the Waco compound ("Mount Carmel") under "prophet" Ben Roden. Roden died in 1978, ceding leadership to his widow, Lois, but her subsequent death left son George Roden vying for control of the sect with 25-year-old Vernon Howell, alias "David Koresh." A period of bitter conflict, including a nocturnal shootout at Mount Carmel in November 1987, left Koresh in charge of the sect. His behavior grew increasingly bizarre, including collection of high-powered weapons, recruitment of a private security team (the "Mighty Men"), and a 1989 decree that only he (Koresh) was entitled to marry or have sex.

By November 1992 agents from the BUREAU OF ALCOHOL, TOBACCO AND FIREARMS (ATF) had multiple reports on file that Koresh was stockpiling illegal weapons and explosives. For three months they planned a "surprise" raid on the Mount Carmel compound, but Koresh was apparently forewarned. When ATF agents stormed the sect's camp on February 28, 1993, a deadly firefight erupted, killing four agents and six Branch Davidians, leaving another 26 persons wounded (including Koresh). ATF leaders then requested FBI assistance, and the Bureau's SWAT TEAM was dispatched to Waco. Deeming a fresh attack potentially disastrous, the two agencies laid siege to Mount Carmel with 700 agents and a fleet of armored vehicles. By early April 1993 FBI leaders feared that the standoff, complete with sensory assaults from floodlights and loudspeakers blaring at night, might drag on forever, their embarrassment compounded day by day. The Branch Davidians, meanwhile, apparently viewed the siege as fulfillment of Koresh's prediction that an "apocalyptic" showdown with the U.S. government would presage Christ's return.

FBI strategists approached Attorney General JANET RENO on April 16, 1993, with a plan to break the siege by unleashing tear gas within the Davidian complex. Reno first rejected the plan, then changed her mind on April 17, after G-men promised that no potentially inflammatory gas canisters would be used. The tanks moved in at 6:02 A.M. on April 19, receiving gunfire as they sprayed gas into the cluster of occupied buildings. Gassing proceeded for six hours, until flames were sighted at 12:07 P.M. Gunfire echoed from within the compound at 12:25, and fire soon devoured the rambling structure. Nine Davidians escaped the blaze; Koresh and 75 others lay dead in the rubble, including at least 17 children (some accounts say 25) below the age of 15 years.

Investigators claimed that the fire was set deliberately by cult members, presumably to initiate mass SUICIDE. Autopsy results showed that Koresh died from a gunshot to the forehead, while second in command Steve Schneider was shot in the mouth. Seventeen others, including five children, were also shot before the flames reached them, and a two-year-old boy was apparently stabbed to death. Eleven surviving Davidians were charged with murder and conspiracy to murder federal agents. All were acquitted of those counts at trial, but five were convicted of manslaughter and received 40-year prison terms. Four others were sentenced to terms between three and 20 years for lesser crimes.

A series of investigations followed the Waco disaster. At the first hearing, before the House Judiciary Committee on April 28, 1993, Reno and other key officials defended their assault as the only means of protecting Davidian children from physical and sexual abuse inside the compound. A separate report, issued by former assistant attorney general Edward Dennis, Jr. on October 8, 1993, acknowledged various FBI tactical errors but concluded that "[u]nder the circumstance, the FBI exhibited extraordinary restraint and handles the crisis with great professionalism." Four days later, a *New York Times* editorial dismissed the Dennis report as a "whitewash." Outside Washington, members of the rapidly growing militia movement armed and trained in anticipation of similar showdowns, and terrorist Timothy McVeigh chose the second anniversary of the Mount Carmel blaze as his target date for bombing Oklahoma City's Alfred P. Murrah Federal Building, with a loss of 168 lives.

A new Congress, dominated by Republicans, reviewed the Waco incident in July 1995, and its report, issued 12 months later, was predictably more critical of Janet Reno's choices, calling her acceptance of the tear-gas plan "premature, wrong, and highly irresponsible." Criticism aside, there were no consequences for agents involved in the Branch Davidian siege. Two ATF agents in charge of the initial raid were fired, then reinstated on appeal. No FBI agents were disciplined, and Attorney General Reno defended their conduct of the final assault until August 1999, when Bureau spokesmen finally admitted lying for the past six years about their use of military-style inflammatory tear gas canisters. Despite their promises to Reno beforehand, volatile grenades had been used at Mount Carmel, but agents now insisted they had "bounced off" the buildings without setting fire to the compound. Reno declared herself "very, very upset" by the admission of deceit, but the renewed debate produced no disciplinary action, either for the Waco siege or for misleading the attorney general. A lawsuit filed by Davidian survivors, seeking $675 million in damages for the wrongful death of those killed at Waco, was dismissed by a federal judge in September 2000, with a ruling that ATF and FBI agents were not responsible for the fire or loss of life.

See also: BOMBING AND BOMB SQUADS; FEDERAL BUREAU OF INVESTIGATION; TERRORISM.

Breckenridge, John (1760–1806)

America's fifth attorney general was born near Staunton, Virginia, on December 2, 1760. Breckenridge served in the Continental Army during the American Revolution, and was elected to the Virginia House of Delegates before war's end (though he was denied a seat because of his youth). After cessation of hostilities, he studied law and was admitted to the Virginia bar in 1785. Seven years later, Breckenridge won election to Congress, but he resigned before commencement of his term and moved to Kentucky, there serving as a state legislator (1788–90), U.S. district attorney (1793–94), state attorney general (1793–97), speaker of the Kentucky State House of Representatives (1799–1801), and in the U.S. Senate (1801–05). He resigned from the Senate to serve as attorney general under President Thomas Jefferson, assuming office on August 7, 1805. Breckenridge died in office on December 14, 1806. Kentucky's Breckenridge County bears his name.

Brewer, Jesse (b. 1921)

Alabama native Jesse Brewer attended his home state's all-black Tuskegee Institute before joining the U.S. Army to fight as an infantry captain in Italy during World War II. After his discharge from the service, he joined the CHICAGO POLICE DEPARTMENT but soon grew disillusioned with that agency's CORRUPTION and resigned. Moving westward, Brewer settled in Los Angeles and applied for a job with the LOS ANGELES POLICE DEPARTMENT. There, while passing all of his preliminary tests, he was rejected by an LAPD physician on grounds of "inadequate muscular development." TOM BRADLEY, a black L.A. cop who was initially rejected for a nonexistent heart murmur, counseled Brewer to appeal the decision and seek an independent medical exam. When that proved him fit, he was admitted to the police academy, where fellow cadets chose him as president of their class.

By 1955 Brewer was LAPD's first black motorcycle officer, considered an elite assignment, but he still faced roadblocks from departmental RACISM. Three oral review boards under Chief WILLIAM PARKER rejected his bid to become a lieutenant, but Brewer prevailed on his fourth attempt in 1967 (the year after Parker's death). In 1973 he served as chief of security for Tom Bradley's mayoral campaign, leading a team of 20 black LAPD officers. Brewer subsequently rose to the rank of assistant chief under DARYL GATES, working tirelessly to counter the aggressive police tactics, which Brewer privately dubbed "appalling."

Brewster, Benjamin Harris (1816–1888)

New Jersey native Benjamin Brewster was born in Salem County on October 13, 1816. He graduated from Princeton College at age 18 and commenced private study of law the same year, winning admittance to the bar in 1838. In 1846 President James Polk appointed Brewster to adjudicate Cherokee Indian claims against the U.S. government. Brewster subsequently served as Pennsylvania's state attorney general (1867–68) and as a state presidential elector (in 1876). On January 3, 1882, he took office as U.S. attorney general under President Chester Arthur, serving in that post until Grover Cleveland's inauguration on March 4, 1885. Brewster died in Philadelphia on April 4, 1888.

Broderick, John (1894–1956)

A native of New York City's crime-ridden Gashouse District, born in 1894, John Broderick was a veteran brawler, nicknamed "The Boff" for his crushing left hook. Before joining the NEW YORK CITY POLICE DEPARTMENT in 1923, he worked first as a strong-arm STRIKEBREAKER, then as a firefighter. His well-known "fistic ability" won Broderick a swift promotion to the NYPD's Gangster Squad during PROHIBITION, where his commander called for hoodlums to be beaten, rather than arrested. "When we get through with them," Broderick was told, "they're either going to be too scared to shake down the storekeepers, or they're gonna be in the hospital."

With those orders in mind, Broderick and partner Johnny "Dutchman" Cordes compiled a fearsome reputation on the streets, and in the gossip columns. Broderick was fond of stuffing gangsters into trash cans, bestowing bruises and humiliation equally on small-time thugs and mob bosses like Jack "Legs" Diamond. He invaded one mob funeral to spit in the corpse's eye, and in 1931 captured two crazed killers—"Two-Gun" Crowley and "Fats" Duringer—without firing a shot. Three years later, Broderick and Cordes duked it out with a crew of "sluggers" (the "mugger" label had yet to be coined) who pistol-whipped subway passengers.

Broderick's style of police work naturally took its toll. Civil libertarians complained incessantly, but Broderick was shielded by Mayor Fiorello La Guardia, who shared his hatred of mobsters. On a personal note, Broderick broke his right hand so often that his X-rays became training tools for interns at Bellevue Hospital. Edward G. Robinson portrayed a thinly veiled version of Broderick in *Bullets or Ballots* (1936), but age and modern standards finally caught up with The Boff and forced his retirement in 1947. He died nine years later, at age 72.

See also: CORDES, JOHN H. F.

Brown, Lee Patrick (b. 1937)

An African-American native of Oklahoma, born October 4, 1937, Lee Brown moved with his family to California at age five. His hardworking parents instilled Brown with strict Christian values, prompting him in later life to name his personal heroes as Jesus, Gandhi, and Martin Luther King, Jr.

Brown earned his B.A. in criminology from California State University, Fresno, in 1960 and joined the San Jose Police Department, where he rose from a patrolman's rank to perform UNDERCOVER WORK on vice and narcotics cases. He subsequently earned a master's degree in sociology from San Jose State College and a Ph.D. in criminology from UC Berkeley. Hired to teach at Oregon's Portland State University, Brown established that institution's Department of Criminal Justice. In 1972 he was named director of the criminal justice department at Howard University, in the nation's capital.

Brown returned to hands-on law enforcement work in 1975, serving as sheriff of Multnomah County, Oregon. In 1978 he became Atlanta's first black public safety commissioner, fated to serve during a brutal rash of SERIAL MURDERS. (The solution of that case, in 1981, left many locals convinced of a police whitewash or frame-up.) Brown moved to Texas in 1982, serving as chief of the troubled HOUSTON POLICE DEPARTMENT, where he spent the next nine years attempting to reverse a legacy of RACISM and EXCESSIVE FORCE with new techniques of community policing. At the same time, Brown worked closely with the University of Texas Health Sciences Center to create a Center for the Study of Interpersonal Violence, examining acts of violence as a community health issue.

Brown's success in Houston won him appointment as police commissioner of New York City in 1989. Mayor David Dinkins sought to reform the NEW YORK CITY POLICE DEPARTMENT, with strong emphasis on community policing, and Brown did his best to oblige, despite opposition from the ranks. As New York's first outside police commissioner since 1966, when controversial Howard Leary was imported to implement a CIVILIAN REVIEW BOARD, Brown suffered thinly veiled mistrust from officers who dubbed him "Out-of-Town Brown." Still, he overcame budget constraints to expand NYPD's personnel roster, including more aggressive recruitment of women and Hispanics, while veteran officers were retrained in innovative community policing techniques. Within a year of his arrival, New York's crime statistics declined for the first time in nearly four decades.

Brown retired as police commissioner on August 3, 1992, and returned to Houston, as a criminal justice professor at Texas Southern University. In 1993 President Bill Clinton named Brown director of the Office of National Drug Control Policy. He left that post in 1996 to teach at Houston's Rice University, subsequently transferring to serve as the Radoslav A. Tsanoff Professor of Public Affairs in the department of sociology at the James A. Baker, III Institute of Public Policy. In 1998 he was elected the first African-American mayor of Houston.

See also: FRAME-UPS.

Brownell, Herbert, Jr. (1904–1996)

A native of Peru, Nebraska, born on February 20, 1904, Herbert Brownell, Jr. graduated from the University of Nebraska in 1924 and spent most of his remaining life in New York. He was admitted to the bar in 1927, soon after graduating from Yale University's law school, and entered private practice with a prestigious Manhattan firm. Brownell served in New York's state assembly (1933–37) and as chairman of the Republican National Committee (1944–46). In 1948 he managed the unsuccessful presidential campaign of THOMAS DEWEY. Brownell's longtime service to the party was rewarded five years later, when President Dwight Eisenhower named Brownell to lead the JUSTICE DEPARTMENT. Brownell took office as attorney general on January 21, 1953.

His term spanned the worst of the Red Scare generated by Senator Joseph McCarthy, and Brownell had no qualms about fanning the flames of hysteria. On November 6, 1953, before an audience of Chicago businessmen, he accused ex-President Harry Truman of coddling traitors in government and cited FBI reports on the "spying activities" of economist Harry Dexter White as proof of those claims. (In fact, Bureau files contained no evidence against White, merely unsupported accusations.) On November 17 Brownell expanded his charges before the Senate Internal Security Subcommittee, accompanied by FBI Director J. EDGAR HOOVER. Once again, the witnesses declined to support their sweeping accusations with anything resembling proof.

On May 20, 1954, in response to urgings from Hoover, Brownell issued a secret memo that approved illegal break-ins and bugging in cases of "national security." According to Brownell, "For the FBI to fulfill its important intelligence function, consideration of internal security and the national safety are paramount and, therefore, may compel the unrestricted use of this technique in the national interest." Recognizing that his order violated many state and federal laws, Brownell warned Hoover that he "would be in a much better position to defend the Bureau in the event there should be a technical trespass if he had not heretofore approved it." One day later, Hoover unilaterally expanded Brownell's order to include "important" criminal cases, thus granting his agents authority to burglarize any targets he selected.

Two years later, in March 1956, Brownell invited Hoover to address Eisenhower's cabinet on the subject of racial turmoil in the South. Hoover used the occasion to praise the segregationist Citizens' Councils and to dismiss the growing, increasingly violent KU KLUX KLAN as "pretty much defunct." He blamed recent unrest on the U.S. SUPREME COURT's school desegregation rulings of 1954–55, noting that behind fears of "mixed education . . . stalks the specter of racial intermarriage." Hoover denounced the NAACP and other civil rights groups for preaching "racial hatred," then produced a chart on the decline of LYNCHING to support his claim that FBI intervention in Dixie was pointless.

Brownell left office on November 8, 1957, subsequently serving as the U.S. member of the Permanent Court of Arbitration at The Hague. From that post he returned to private practice in New York. Cancer claimed his life in New York City, on May 1, 1996.

See also: FEDERAL BUREAU OF INVESTIGATION.

"Buddy Boys" scandal

In 1986 the NEW YORK CITY POLICE DEPARTMENT suffered one of its cyclical CORRUPTION scandals, this one involving officers of Brooklyn's 77th Precinct. Known to department insiders as "The Alamo," for its hopeless siege mentality, the 77th Precinct was tacitly recognized as a dumping ground for trouble-prone officers, transferred in lieu of embarrassing dismissal. By the 1980s the 77th was riddled with graft, staffed by officers (and a few supervisors) who actively robbed drug dealers and users, relieving them of cash and narcotics (which were then resold). The scandal earned its nickname jointly from collaboration among corrupt police in the 77th Precinct, and for the outside warnings they received of ongoing investigations by NYPD's INTERNAL AFFAIRS Division—"buddy boys" united to preserve a blue wall of silence.

Thirteen officers were ultimately indicted and convicted on charges of stealing and dealing drugs. (Many, apparently, were also users, on and off the job.) An after-the-fact mayoral report suggested sweeping changes in NYPD's selection and promotion procedures to ward off future trouble. Police Commissioner BENJAMIN WARD proposed a job-rotation plan, whereby one-fifth of the officers in each precinct would be transferred annually, but a work slowdown ("BLUE FLU") quickly scuttled that effort. A salutary side effect of the "Buddy Boys" scandal emerged from the neighboring 75th Precinct, where a group of honest officers went public with charges against their corrupt colleagues. Chief among those fingered was Officer Michael Dowd, whose city salary somehow supported a $35,000 sports car and four suburban homes, one valued at $300,000.

Budzyn, Walter, and Larry Nevers

Thirty-five-year-old Malice Wayne Green was clearly in no shape to drive on the night of November 5, 1992. Later blood tests would prove that he was high on both alcohol and cocaine when he got behind the wheel, but he might still have made it home alive, with any luck. In the final analysis, it was geography that got him killed.

Detectives Walter Budzyn and Larry Nevers, employed by the DETROIT POLICE DEPARTMENT, were staking out a West Side crack house, seeking an armed robbery suspect, when Green pulled up to the curb in front. The officers approached him and identified themselves, requesting Green's driver's license. According to Budzyn and Nevers, Green reached for his glove compartment, apparently with something clenched in his fist. The officers assumed that "something" was DRUGS, and they ordered Green to open his hand. He allegedly refused and a struggle ensued. Five more policemen rolled up while the fight was in progress. Neighbor-hood witnesses—many of them crack addicts with no love for police—later described Green being pummeled by multiple officers, kicked in the head at least once, and slammed repeatedly across the head with heavy metal flashlights. His autopsy report disclosed at least four distinct and separate blows to the skull.

An outcry swept Detroit, claiming that racist cops had murdered Green for no good reason other than the color of his skin. Such accusations are routine in ghetto racial confrontations, but in Green's case there appeared to be substantial evidence supporting the claim. On November 16 four officers present at the scene of Green's death were indicted on various criminal charges: Budzyn and Nevers were charged with second-degree murder; Robert Lessnau faced charges of assault with intent to do great bodily harm; and Sgt. Freddie Douglas (the only black officer present) was slapped with dual charges of voluntary manslaughter and willful neglect of duty (for failure to stop the assault). Exactly one month later, the four defendants were fired in a move which Dewey Stokes, national president of the FRATERNAL ORDER OF POLICE, described to the press as "a little harsh." Mayor Coleman Young, meanwhile, told reporters that Green was "literally murdered by police."

Three of the four indicted officers went to trial before Judge George Crockett in Detroit, on June 18, 1993. The arrangements were unusual, to say the least: two separate juries, one each for Budzyn and Nevers, while Lessnau waived his right to jury trial and left Judge Crockett to decide his fate. (Sgt. Douglas won separation of his case from the others, and his manslaughter charge was dismissed on December 23, 1992.) Defense attorneys advanced the theory that Green had not been fatally beaten, but rather died from the combined effects of liquor and cocaine. Assistant prosecutor Doug Baker called the death a clear-cut case of homicide, telling jurors, "It was simply the exercise of raw power over one human being by others." The trial spanned 13 weeks, including more than 200 exhibits and testimony from 50 witnesses. At one point, in July, Oakland County medical examiner Ljubisa Dragovic seemed to support the defense, submitting that blows to the head alone had not killed Malice Green; instead, Dr. Dragovic said, a combination of the beating plus cocaine and alcohol produced a fatal seizure.

If defense attorneys were cheered by that testimony, there was little else about their case to inspire confidence. Larry Nevers admitted striking Green "four or five times" with his flashlight, but insisted that Green was trying to grab Nevers's pistol. County paramedics, meanwhile, confirmed the beating but had seen no move by Green in the direction of any officer's gun. Walter Budzyn denied striking Green with his flashlight, but several civilian witnesses contradicted that testimony.

Judge Crockett acquitted Lessnau, but the twin juries convicted Budzyn and Nevers of second-degree murder on August 23, 1993. At their sentencing, on October 12, Budzyn received a prison term of eight to 18 years, while Nevers drew a term of 12 to 25 years.

Mindful of death threats from black prison gangs, Budzyn and Nevers were sent to serve their time at a federal minimum-security prison in Texas. Even there, however, while sharing a cell, the disgraced officers remained fearful. A January 1993 newsletter, prepared by Nevers for his supporters at large, claimed that he and Budzyn had befriended two other inmates who would henceforth serve as bodyguards. Michigan's appellate court denied requests for a new trial in 1995, and the state supreme court followed suit a year later.

Ex-Sergeant Douglas, meanwhile, faced trial on misdemeanor negligence charges in June 1994. Jurors convicted him on July 1, and Douglas was freed on bond pending an appeal which upheld the conviction. Nonetheless, in March 1995 Douglas was reinstated to his former rank with back pay, after a police trial board effectively overruled the jury's verdict, finding no evidence that Douglas witnessed Green's beating by Budzyn and Nevers.

On July 31, 1997, the Michigan supreme court overturned Budzyn's conviction and ordered a new trial, on grounds that his mostly black jury may have been inflamed by a group viewing of the film *Malcolm X* while the trial was in progress. That film included newsreel footage of Los Angeles policemen beating RODNEY KING, while a voice-over from Malcolm X described the white race as "the greatest murderer on Earth." The state's high court allowed Larry Nevers's conviction to stand however, on grounds that overwhelming evidence of guilt outweighed whatever influence a movie may have had on his jury, but federal judge Lawrence Zatkoff reversed Nevers's conviction five months later, on December 30.

Walter Budzyn was convicted of involuntary manslaughter at his second trial, on March 19, 1998. One month later, he received a prison term of four to 15 years with credit for time already served. Judge Thomas Jackson then vacated Budzyn's sentence on May 20, 1998, releasing him on the basis of time spent in prison before his retrial. The seesaw battle continued on January 11, 1999, when Michigan's court of appeals reinstated Budzyn's latest sentence and shipped him back to prison. Larry Nevers was convicted of involuntary manslaughter on April 18, 2000. On May 17 he received a prison term of seven to 15 years, with credit for time served.

bugging

"Bugging"—the covert installation of electronic listening devices—is a form of surveillance employed by law enforcement agencies for decades to collect information on criminal suspects and spies, as well as countless individuals with no involvement in any illegal activity. In conjunction with WIRETAPS, bugs supply much of the material credited to unnamed "confidential sources" or "reliable sources" in FBI files, and the same techniques have been widely employed by municipal and state police. Because installation of eavesdropping equipment frequently involves break-ins on private property, bugging operations conducted without warrants clearly violate the U.S. Constitution's Fourth Amendment.

FBI Director J. EDGAR HOOVER recognized the illegality of most bugging raids—dubbed "BLACK BAG JOBS"—and while he rarely shied away from breaking state or federal laws, he required that each illegal operation be cleared in advance by headquarters. Whether agents in the field obeyed that dictum is impossible to say, since Hoover also created elaborate procedures for hiding illicit orders and contraband intelligence in the Bureau's vast files. Exposure of a bug could jeopardize prosecution in some cases, but Attorney General ROBERT HOUGHWOUT JACKSON promised Hoover in June 1940 that "confidential sources" would not be compromised "without the prior approval of the Bureau." Another 11 years passed before Hoover sought guidance on bugging procedures from Attorney General J. HOWARD MCGRATH, in October 1951. McGrath replied on February 26, 1952, that "I cannot authorize installation of a microphone involving a trespass under existing law," but FBI bugging continued. On May 20, 1954, Attorney General HERBERT BROWNELL, JR. authorized break-ins and bugging in "national security" cases, a grant of power which Hoover unilaterally extended to "important" criminal cases. By late 1957 the FBI's Top Hoodlum Program had extended illegal bugging to leaders of ORGANIZED CRIME.

Various presidents from Franklin Roosevelt to Richard Nixon authorized illegal surveillance of political adversaries, allies, journalists, public figures, and others who had committed no crimes and were suspected of none. Bugging of Dr. Martin Luther King, Jr. was authorized by Attorney General ROBERT FRANCIS KENNEDY, and President Lyndon Johnson enjoyed listening to FBI tapes of King's sexual encounters with various women. In 1964 Johnson also ordered bugging of various hostile delegates to the Democratic National Convention. A July 1970 memo from Nixon aide Charles Huston outlined a series of "clearly illegal" DOMESTIC SURVEILLANCE campaigns, and while Hoover voiced doubts about the plan, he told Attorney General JOHN NEWTON MITCHELL that the FBI would "implement the instructions of the White House at your discretion." To protect himself from criticism, Hoover added that he would "continue to seek your specific authorization" each time G-men were asked to break the law.

New federal legislation, meanwhile, had expanded FBI authority to use bugs and wiretaps. The Omnibus Crime Control and Safe Streets Act of June 1968 approved bugs and taps under court order, while preserving the president's power to order surveillance in cases of "national security." Two years later, in October 1970, the Racketeer Influence and Corrupt Organization (RICO) Act broadened the scope of eavesdropping against organized crime. Legal requirements notwithstanding, the FBI continued illicit bugging on a daily basis. Subsequent disclosures by the U.S. Senate's CHURCH COMMITTEE revealed 697 incidents of bugging during the Bureau's COINTELPRO campaigns, between 1960 and 1974. (FBI claims that statistics on COINTELPRO bugging between 1956 and 1959 were "not available" are scarcely credible, but the figures remain undisclosed.)

Today, most FBI bugging is carried out by units variously known as Technical Support Squads (TSS) or Special Operations Groups (SOG). The New York City field office maintained 15 such teams in the 1980s, and their schedule was so crowded that some G-men claimed the initials TSS stood for "Tough Shit Squads," after the number of requests for bugs and wiretaps commonly delayed by heavy workloads. A decade later, new technology had projected bugging into cyberspace and sparked new controversy, after FBI agents used surveillance software to monitor keystrokes on a New Jersey mobster's personal computer. Prosecutors used the evidence thus collected to charge Nicodemo Scarfo, Jr. with running a $5 million bookmaking and loansharking operation in the Garden State.

No reliable statistics are presently available for bugging operations carried out by state, county, or city police departments across the U.S. Based on FBI admissions of activities within a single agency, it seems certain that thousands of bugs have been planted around the country over the past century, in pursuance of criminal investigations and domestic surveillance conducted by various RED SQUADS. Lawsuits have resulted in some cases, as detailed elsewhere in this volume, but the AMERICAN CIVIL LIBERTIES UNION and other watchdog groups remain concerned that the activities may be ongoing.

See also: FEDERAL BUREAU OF INVESTIGATION.

Bureau of Alcohol, Tobacco, Firearms and Explosives

Congress imposed its first tax on imported liquor in 1789, leaving enforcement to the TREASURY DEPARTMENT under Secretary Alexander Hamilton (who pro-

posed the tax to cover debts from the Revolutionary War). Two years later, a federal tax was also imposed on liquor produced in the United States. That action sparked the short-lived Whiskey Rebellion of 1794, and launched some opponents into lifelong careers as bootleggers. In July 1862 Congress created an Office of INTERNAL REVENUE to collect federal taxes, waiting another year before it authorized employment of "three detectives to aid in the prevention, detection and punishment of tax evaders." The unit's first great triumph was the breakup in 1875 of a "Whiskey Ring," including grain dealers, corrupt politicians, and revenue agents who had defrauded the U.S. government of several million dollars in liquor taxes.

While bootlegging continued through the years—and goes on to the present day—the next great challenge came with ratification of the Eighteenth Amendment to the U.S. Constitution in 1919. That amendment, enforced by the Volstead Act (1919), ushered in the "noble experiment" of PROHIBITION on January 17, 1920. Ironically, before it was repealed in 1933, the federal ban on alcoholic beverages vastly increased the number of active saloons nationwide, while encouraging pervasive police CORRUPTION and plaguing America with a national network of ORGANIZED CRIME. If local police and politicians were easily bribed by bootleggers, so too were members of Treasury's Prohibition Bureau. Few federal "revenuers" met the standard of Chicago's ELIOT NESS and his "Untouchables," and indictments were frequent. In Cincinnati alone, 71 law enforcement officers and politicians were indicted for Prohibition violations during March 1925, with 58 pleading guilty as charged a month later. Nationwide, between January 1920 and June 1930, 1,587 federal Prohibition agents (nearly 10 percent of the force) were "dismissed for cause."

When Prohibition agents *did* enforce the law, their performance was erratic at best. Agent Clarence Pickering, stationed along the Canadian border, later admitted personally killing 42 suspected smugglers while on duty. Most agents were less violent, and few were truly qualified to serve. When Congress placed the Prohibition Bureau under Civil Service in April 1927, three-fourths of all applicants failed the qualifying test. By November 1928 two-thirds of the bureau's positions were empty. Only 1,282 agents, inspectors and chemists were fully qualified by May 1929, while nearly half as many more (604) were temporary appointments, including political hacks and some hangers-on with criminal records.

Large-scale illicit distilling survived Prohibition's repeal in December 1933, interdicted briefly by a new Federal Alcohol Control Administration (1933–35), then by Treasury's Federal Alcohol Administration and the JUSTICE DEPARTMENT's competing Alcohol Tax

Unit (ATU). Those redundant agencies merged in 1940, keeping the ATU label at Treasury, while collection of tobacco taxes and enforcement of the 1934 National Firearms Act (mandating federal registration and taxation of such "gangster" WEAPONS as machine guns, sawed-off shotguns, and silencers) fell to Treasury's Miscellaneous Tax Unit. The MTU was disbanded in 1952, its responsibilities shifted to ATU, renamed the Alcohol and Tobacco Tax Division. That incarnation survived until 1968, with passage of a new federal GUN CONTROL act (banning mail-order sales and "destructive devices"), whereupon the Bureau of Alcohol, Tobacco and Firearms (ATF) was born.

ATF responsibilities grew from there, with passage of the Federal Bombing Statute (1972) and Anti-ARSON Act (1982). Responsibility for bombing cases was formally split between ATF, the FBI and U.S. postal inspectors, depending on the bomber's target and official designation of the crimes as acts of TERRORISM. In pursuance of its duties, ATF created a state-of-the-art Integrated Ballistic Identification System, pioneered detection of explosives and accelerants with specially trained K-9 UNITS, and instituted a Gang Resistance Education and Training (GREAT) program which teaches children to resist recruitment by street gangs.

Such wide-ranging responsibilities, particularly in a nation seemingly obsessed with firearms, has often placed ATF in the spotlight of controversy. Its agents frequently have been accused of ENTRAPMENT and of using EXCESSIVE FORCE during arrests, including several headline cases wherein ATF officers raided the wrong premises or shot suspects "armed" with inoperable antique weapons. The most sensational case occurred in February 1993, when ATF agents raided the Branch Davidian religious compound at Waco, Texas, sparking a shootout that claimed 10 lives and left 26 persons wounded. The fiery climax of that siege, involving armored vehicles and FBI agents, left 76 cult members dead on April 19, 1993. No illegal weapons were found in the ruins, leaving ATF leaders to claim they were equally concerned with alleged SEX CRIMES inside the sect's compound. That argument, while emotionally persuasive, ignored the fact that ATF has no jurisdiction in such cases.

A new age of terrorism in the 21st century changed ATF's complexion once again. Following the catastrophic attacks of September 11, 2001, a wholesale reorganization of federal law enforcement agencies was launched by President George W. Bush and Attorney General JOHN ASHCROFT. Despite a long-standing, often bitter rivalry between ATF and the FBI, ATF was transferred to Justice on January 24, 2003, renamed the Bureau of Alcohol, Tobacco, Firearms and Explosives. Under provisions of the Homeland Security Act, ATF's tax and trade functions remained with Treasury, administered by a new Alcohol and Tobacco Tax and Trade Bureau.

See also: BOMBING AND BOMB SQUADS; BRANCH DAVIDIAN SIEGE; FEDERAL BUREAU OF INVESTIGATION; POSTAL INSPECTION SERVICE.

Bureau of Indian Affairs Police

The Bureau of Indian Affairs (BIA) has primary responsibility for administration and management of various Indian reservations—some 55.7 million acres overall—held "in trust" by the federal government for Native Americans. Washington and the BIA recognize 562 tribal governments throughout the United States, and while FBI agents are sometimes called to investigate crimes committed on reservation land, the BIA also maintains at least 33 tribal police departments on various reservations around the country. Working in conjunction with the JUSTICE DEPARTMENT, BIA leaders have determined that jurisdiction over crimes committed in "Indian country" involves three criteria: (1) the perpetrator's status (Indian or non-Indian); (2) the victim's status (ditto); and (3) the type of crime involved. In general, the cases break down as follows:

Tribal courts hear most misdemeanor cases, including crimes committed by Indians against Indian or non-Indian victims and cases of Indians involved in CONSENSUAL CRIMES.

State courts try cases wherein neither party is an Indian, or when non-Indian offenders are involved in consensual crimes on a reservation.

Federal courts hear all felony cases, regardless of the victim's or offender's race (including felony consensual crimes committed by Indian offenders), and most cases involving non-Indian offenders with Indian victims.

Burlington Police Department

Burlington, located on the eastern shore of Lake Champlain, is Vermont's largest city, with a population of 38,000 and a greater metropolitan area of some 150,000 residents. Various civic organizations rank it among the most "livable" U.S. cities, and a fair amount of credit for that fact belongs to Burlington's police department.

Organized in 1865, Burlington P.D. is the state's largest municipal law enforcement agency, with 130-plus employees, pledged to "policing with the citizens of Burlington to achieve a safe, healthy and self-reliant community." Toward that end, department spokesmen report that they "problem-solve with citizens, businesses, our institutions of higher learning, students, and other partners to reduce crime and disorder." Still, problems persist in some areas, including police interaction with disaffected "street kids," producing occasional complaints of false arrest and EXCESSIVE FORCE. Thus far, no disciplinary action has resulted from such incidents.

Burns, William J. (c. 1860–1932)

A Baltimore native, born "around 1860" and raised in Columbus, Ohio, where his father served as police commissioner, William Burns enjoyed a checkered law enforcement career. He started young, solving cases that his father's men could not crack, and in 1885 identified the culprits who had rigged Ohio's state election. Four years later Burns joined the U.S. SECRET SERVICE, pursuing counterfeiters until he transferred in 1903, to the Department of the Interior. There, over the next three years, he investigated land fraud and secured indictments against several prominent persons, including Oregon Senator John Mitchell. (Critics say Burns stacked the Mitchell jury with political enemies, thus securing a false conviction.)

William Burns led the FBI during a period of notorious corruption. (Author's collection)

With those victories behind him, Burns retired to form the William J. Burns Detective Agency, second in size only to ALLAN J. PINKERTON's rival firm. Both agencies were known primarily as private police forces (or goon squads) employed by wealthy industrialists at various STRIKE-BREAKING chores nationwide. A classic case from that era involved a bombing (see BOMBING AND BOMB SQUADS) of the *Los Angeles Times,* wherein Burns implicated members of the Iron and Bridge Workers Union. (Some critics now regard that prosecution as a frame-up.)

Burns returned to Washington, D.C., in 1922 as part of President Warren Harding's venal "Ohio Gang," serving under Attorney General HARRY MICAJAH DAUGHERTY as chief of the FBI. Burns took office on August 22 and named young J. EDGAR HOOVER his chief assistant. Together, they pursued a course of stalking "radicals" and "Reds" that had begun under Attorney General A. MITCHELL PALMER. As to the definition of a Bolshevik, Burns told Congress that Red strategy in America "principally consists of urging the workingman to strike, with the ultimate purpose of bringing about a revolution in this country."

While the Harding regime settled into a morass of CORRUPTION, climaxed by revelation of the Teapot Dome scandal, Burns and his G-men harassed labor unions and personal critics, investigated Harding's Democratic opponents, and generally took advantage of an atmosphere wherein the JUSTICE DEPARTMENT was nicknamed the "Department of Easy Virtue." After Daugherty left office in disgrace, Attorney General HARLAN STONE demanded Burns's resignation on May 9, 1924. He left the next day, and Hoover filled his post, but resignation did not end Burns's involvement with Teapot Dome. Back at the helm of his old detective agency, Burns harassed and shadowed jurors in the trial of Bernard Fall, ex-secretary of the interior, to the point that a mistrial was declared and Burns narrowly escaped conviction on a charge of criminal contempt.

That near-miss drove Burns into retirement at Sarasota, Florida, where he spent his last years penning "true" accounts of his more famous cases. At his death, on April 14, 1932, the *Washington Post* hailed Burns as "probably the most famous individual in the detective business during his active years."

See also: FEDERAL BUREAU OF INVESTIGATION; FRAME-UPS.

Butler, Benjamin Franklin (1795–1858)

New York native Benjamin Butler was born at Kinderhook Landing on December 17, 1795. He read law with future president Martin Van Buren and became Van Buren's partner upon admission to the bar in 1817. Butler subsequently served as district attorney for Albany

Attorney General Benjamin Butler (Author's collection)

County (1921–24) and in 1825 was one of three commissioners appointed to revise New York's state statutes. Thereafter, he served as a state legislator (1827–33) and as a commissioner employed to adjust New York's border with New Jersey. President Andrew Jackson named Butler as the nation's 12th attorney general, assuming office on November 18, 1833. He resigned that post in 1838, then served two terms as U.S. attorney for the Southern District of New York (1838–41 and 1845–48). During his second term, in 1837, Butler was named principal professor at the University of New York. He died in Paris, France, on November 8, 1858.

Butler, Smedley Darlington (1881–1940)

Born July 30, 1881, Smedley Butler fled his Pennsylvania Quaker home at age 16 to join the U.S. Marine Corps and fight in the Spanish-American War. He subsequently served in Nicaragua and earned his first Congressional Medal of Honor in 1914, for action at Vera Cruz, Mexico. In 1915 Butler earned a second Medal of Honor in Haiti, becoming one of only 19 U.S. servicemen twice honored with the nation's highest military award. Military colleagues dubbed him "Old Gimlet Eye" and "The Fighting Quaker" for his ruthless courage in battle.

In January 1924 the Corps loaned Butler to Philadelphia Mayor W. Freeland Kendrick, as the city's new police commissioner. PROHIBITION had infested the City of Brotherly Love with CORRUPTION and ORGANIZED CRIME, a problem Butler attacked in his usual style. Two days after his appointment, Butler's raiders had closed three-fourths of Philadelphia's 1,300 speakeasies. He also organized a "bandit squad" to pursue racketeers, instructing his officers to "shoot a few of them, and make arrests afterward." Inside the PHILADELPHIA POLICE DEPARTMENT, Butler abolished formal training and decreed that every officer would henceforth "learn his job right on the beat." He also upset established promotion techniques, hand-picking selected patrolmen for promotion over those who failed to satisfy.

Butler's insistence on equal treatment for all citizens, rich or poor, won him no friends among the Philadelphia elite. Mayor Kendrick sent him back to the Marine Corps in 1925, where he remained a lightning rod for controversy. Butler served a tour of duty in China during 1927 and returned to the United States a major general. In January 1931 he accused Italian dictator Benito Mussolini of running down a child with his limousine, an accusation that prompted formal U.S. apologies and nearly earned Butler a court-martial. He retired from the Marine Corps nine months later and pursued an unsuccessful campaign for a U.S. Senate seat in 1932. The same year saw him lead the Bonus March on Washington, D.C., where veterans of World War I were teargassed and beaten by troops under General Douglas MacArthur.

A year later, Butler was approached by right-wing industrialists and officers of the America Legion who proposed that he lead a coup to overthrow President Franklin Roosevelt's New Deal administration. Butler reported the plot to Congress instead, and moved on to serve as spokesman for the left-wing League Against War and Fascism. His book *War Is a Racket* (1935) sounded an early warning against the insidious growth of America's military-industrial complex. Butler died on June 21, 1940, still the most decorated Marine in U.S. history. Camp Smedley Butler, on Okinawa, is named in his honor.

Byrd Committee

In 1937 Virginia senator Harry Byrd chaired a committee appointed to investigate the relative efficiency of various federal executive agencies. Included in its survey were the FBI, U.S. Postal Inspectors, the SECRET SERVICE, the INTERNAL REVENUE SERVICE, and Customs. Scholars from the Brookings Institution reviewed statistics submitted by the several agencies (convictions, cash recoveries, etc.), reporting that both the Secret Service and postal inspectors produced conviction rates outstripping the FBI's by a factor of five or six to one. FBI statistics initially looked better on paper, but the Brookings scholars found them falsely inflated by an average of 33 percent. The committee's final report had more to say about J. EDGAR HOOVER's abuse of statistics.

The Director of the Federal Bureau of Investigation referred in March 1936 to the "armed forces of crime which number more than 3 million active participants." Three months later he stated that "the criminal standing army of America" numbered 500,000, "a whole half-million of armed thugs, murderers, thieves, firebugs, assassins, robbers, and hold-up men." About six months afterward he gave the total criminal population of 3,500,000 and the number of crimes as 1,500,000. Five months later he stated that 4,300,000 persons were engaged by day and night in the commission of felonies and estimated that 1,333,526 major felonies were committed in the United States during the year 1936. . . .

In an address about a year ago [April 23, 1936], he stated that "the files of the Bureau of Investigation show that there are actually 3 million convicted criminals. Beyond this there are enough more with police records to demonstrate that an average of one out of every twenty-five persons in the United States of America has at least had his brush with law-enforcement agencies and is inclined toward criminality."

In the same address he declared that "there are today in America 150,000 murderers roaming at large"; but it appears from [the FBI's] Uniform Crime Reports that in 987 cities with a population of 35,450,666 the police were cognizant of only 3,582 cases of criminal homicide, and of these, 2,936 or 81.9 per cent had according to the police, been cleared by arrest.

The committee attributed Hoover's vacillating statistics to "guesswork," although their frequent spurious precision suggested deliberate fabrication. The Byrd Committee concluded its review by noting a persistent American "fear that a strong Federal police force might be used as an instrument of oppression," further warning that concentration of police power in federal hands "may weaken the incentives for better State and local enforcement."

See also: CUSTOMS SERVICE; FEDERAL BUREAU OF INVESTIGATION; POSTAL INSPECTION SERVICE.

Byrnes, Thomas F. (1842–1910)

Born in Ireland during 1842, Thomas Byrnes immigrated to the United States with his parents as a child. The family settled in New York City, where Byrnes later worked for a gas company and joined the Union Army in the early days of the Civil War. Discharged in 1863, he joined the NEW YORK CITY POLICE DEPARTMENT as a patrolman, rising to the rank of captain by 1870. Eight years later, he tracked and captured the burglars who stole $3 million from the Manhattan Bank, recovering most of their loot in the process. That coup set Byrnes on the path to fame and fortune, with his promotion to chief of detectives.

On the day of his appointment, Byrnes opened an office on Wall Street, cultivating friendships with the city's wealthy elite that endured for the remainder of his NYPD career. He specialized in doing favors for the rich and powerful, recovering personal items stolen by pickpockets and foiling a KIDNAPPING plot against robber baron Jay Gould. Byrnes established a "deadline" for hoodlums along Fulton Street, north of Manhattan's financial district, and forbade known criminals to cross it on pain of arrest or worse. His attention to the wealthy, and the profits that accrued from it, soon earned Byrnes the nickname "Wall Street Johnny." Newspaper columnists also dubbed him "the Great Detective," while calling his plainclothes officers "Immortals."

As chief of detectives, Byrnes pioneered the fine art of manipulating statistics, later used by J. EDGAR HOOVER to guarantee ever-increasing FBI appropriations. Byrnes broadcast the fact that during four years prior to his appointment, his predecessors had arrested 1,943 criminals and sent them away for a total of 505 years in prison. Byrnes's detectives, in his first four years as chief, jailed 3,324 felons for 2,488 years—an increase worthy of pay raises, even if it failed to cut the city's crime rate. Byrnes also expanded the NYPD's "Rogue's Gallery," collecting 7,000 mug shots, which he later published in a groundbreaking volume, *Professional Criminals of America* (1886).

In 1888 Byrnes was promoted again, to fill the new post of chief inspector that made him the number-two man in the NYPD. That autumn he dared British serial killer "Jack the Ripper" to visit New York, but the still-unknown slayer refused to oblige. Four years later, another appointment elevated Byrnes to serve as superintendent of police. He instantly ordered a series of show raids on vice dens, closing a reported 444 brothels in seven months, and transferred half of NYPD's captains and inspectors to new commands, while organizing a privately funded "vigilance league" to investigate civic CORRUPTION. Still, there was more flash than substance to Byrnes on the job, and he somehow compiled a personal fortune of $350,000 (equivalent to $8 million in 2005) on a yearly salary of $5,000. Graft was rampant under Byrnes, and he suspended officers who testified frankly before the LEXOW COMMITTEE in 1894. His own testimony before that panel proved evasive, referring vaguely to investment tips from Jay Gould and others which had fattened his own bank account.

That performance made Byrnes a target for police commissioner THEODORE ROOSEVELT, who told his friend Henry Cabot Lodge, "I think I shall move against Byrnes at once. I thoroughly distrust him and cannot do any thorough work while he remains." Under pressure from Roosevelt, Byrnes resigned on May 27, 1895, leaving his friends on Wall Street to plaintively ask, "Who will protect us now?"

C

Cahill, Thomas J. (1910–2002)

Chicago native Thomas Cahill was born in 1910. Two years later, his immigrant parents returned to their native Ireland, but Cahill made it back to the United States in 1930. He worked as an iceman, then joined the SAN FRANCISCO POLICE DEPARTMENT in 1942 and teamed with partner Frank Ahern, earning a reputation as an expert on ORGANIZED CRIME. During 1950–52 Cahill and Ahern worked part time for Senator CAREY ESTES KEFAUVER in his probe of interstate gambling, prompting Kefauver's remark that "[t]hese two men have more information on the Mafia than any police department in the nation."

Reform mayor George Christopher tapped Ahern as chief of police in 1956, succeeded by Cahill at his unexpected death in 1958. Over the next 12 years—still a record tenure for San Francisco police chiefs—Cahill rebuilt the force in his image and established a national reputation in police work. In 1965 he was the only police executive named to President Lyndon Johnson's Commission on Law Enforcement. Three years later, J. EDGAR HOOVER introduced Cahill to graduates of the FBI Academy as "the greatest police administrator in America." In 1969 Cahill was elected president of the INTERNATIONAL ASSOCIATION OF CHIEFS OF POLICE.

For all the praise and commendations, there was another side to Chief Cahill, as well. He opposed creation of a police Community Relations Unit for years (finally relenting under NAACP pressure, in March 1962) and threatened to resign if a CIVILIAN REVIEW BOARD was created in San Francisco. He never criticized participants in POLICE RIOTS on May 13, 1960 (during protests against the House Committee on Un-American Activities) or January 10, 1968 (an antiwar protest against President Johnson), but in 1966 he tried to fire black officer Lindsay Crenshaw, wrongfully arrested by Oakland police after gunmen shot up Crenshaw's car. (Cahill charged Crenshaw with "conduct unbecoming an officer.") Cahill also scorned hippies ("no asset to the community") and established a two-man Special Obscenity Squad to raid Bay Area bookstores and theaters.

Cahill retired from the force in 1970, but he kept collecting honors. San Francisco's Hall of Justice is named in his honor, and the IACP gave Cahill its Professional Achievement Award in 1997. He died in San Francisco on October 12, 2002.

California Highway Patrol

The California Highway Patrol (CHP) was created by state legislative action on August 14, 1929. That statute granted statewide authority to enforce traffic laws on state and county highways. During its first decade the CHP expanded to include 730 uniformed officers. A "new" Department of the California Highway Patrol was established in October 1947, and CHP responsibilities have expanded since then to include bus and truck inspections, airborne operations, plus investigation and prevention of vehicle theft. In 1995 the CHP absorbed the California State Police (a small force analogous to the U.S. CAPITOL POLICE, assigned to protect the governor and state capitol building in Sacramento). Under terms of that merger, the CHP assumed responsibility for guarding the governor, secretary of state, state treasurer's office, state controller's office, and the state superintendent of schools.

The CHP's most dramatic and tragic incident to date occurred at Newhall, California, on April 6, 1970. That night, officers answered a report of a man waving a gun outside a local restaurant. On arrival, they met felons Bobby Davis and Jack Twinning, who engaged in a five-minute shootout with CHP officers, killing Patrolmen George Alleyn, Walt Frago, Roger Gore, and James Pence. A nine-hour manhunt ensued, during which Twinning broke into a private home, then killed himself when cornered. Davis was captured, convicted of murder, and sentenced to die, but a 1972 U.S. SUPREME COURT ruling against the death penalty commuted his sentence to life imprisonment. The Newhall incident prompted drastic changes in CHP training and selection of defensive WEAPONS for its officers.

Callahan, John T. (1895–1976)

Born in 1895, John Callahan graduated from Yale University in 1920, then attended Fordham Law School. After a period of private practice and employment with the Federal Trade Commission, he joined President Franklin Roosevelt's new SECURITIES AND EXCHANGE COMMISSION during the Great Depression. Callahan was assigned to the SEC's Division of Trading and Exchanges, where he pursued stock swindlers and manipulators with partner Edward Jaegerman. Together, the so-called Rover Boys investigated more than 500 federal cases. Callahan was eventually promoted to serve as the SEC's general counsel. He retired in 1968 and died eight years later, at age 81.

Camarena, Enrique "Kiki" (1948–1985)

A Mexican native, born at Mexicali in 1948, Enrique Camarena immigrated as a youth and joined the U.S. Marine Corps in 1972. Discharged two years later, he worked as a firefighter and police officer before joining the DRUG ENFORCEMENT ADMINISTRATION (DEA) in 1976, serving first at Calexico, California (across the border from his hometown), then in Fresno (1977–80) and Guadalajara (1980–85). In Guadalajara he organized "Operation Miracle," merging DEA and Mexican efforts to corral drug smugglers. The program captured 20 tons of marijuana in one raid (May 1984), but failed to crack the billion-dollar cocaine empire ruled by Rafael Caro Quintero.

In an effort to do more, Camarena expanded his UNDERCOVER WORK, soon discovering that Commandante Miguel Aldana Ibarra of the Mexican Judicial Police protected the Caro cocaine ring. Camarena's revelations sparked congressional hearings in Washington, probing the full extent of Mexico's official CORRUPTION, but Camarena did not live to see the findings published.

Identified as a DEA agent, Camarena was kidnapped with *federale* Captain Alfredo Zavala Avelar, outside a bar in Guadalajara. Their mutilated corpses were found on March 5, 1985, near the Villahermosa estate of former Mexican legislator Manuel Bravo Cervantes. (Pathologists determined that Camarena died on or about February 9.) When police tried to question Cervantes, a gunfight ensued, claiming the lives of Cervantes, his wife, and two children.

Investigation revealed that Camarena and Zavala were kidnapped on orders from Rafael Caro Quintero and tortured to death at his home. Three participants in the murders, including former policeman Raúl López Álvarez, were extradited to Los Angeles. Upon conviction of murder and racketeering, the three received sentences exceeding 200 years in prison. Another suspect, Humberto Álvarez-Machaín, was snatched from Mexico by civilian BOUNTY HUNTERS but freed following acquittal at trial in L.A. Mexican authorities later convicted two dozen defendants of various crimes related to Camarena's slaying, but Caro Quintero escaped punishment for the murder itself, instead receiving a 34-year sentence for smuggling weapons and holding workers in peonage on his marijuana farms.

Camarena left a wife, two sons, and various awards for service, including the DEA's highest award, a posthumous Administrator's Award of Honor. In 1990 actor Benecio del Toro portrayed Camarena in a television miniseries, *Drug Wars: The Camarena Story*. The DEA's annual golf tournament in Miami is named in Camarena's honor.

See also: DRUGS.

Canton, Frank A. (1849–1927)

Frank Canton's career as a frontier lawman had rocky beginnings. A Virginia native, born Joe Horner in 1849, he moved to Texas with his family in childhood and became a cowboy after the Civil War, driving herds from northern Texas to the Kansas railheads. Rustling and BANK ROBBERY seemed more appealing than hard labor in the early 1870s, but Horner soon ran into trouble. In October 1874 he killed one U.S. soldier and wounded another at Jacksboro, Texas. Six years later, Horner was jailed for robbing a bank at Comanche, Texas, but he escaped in 1880 and fled to Nebraska, where he changed his name and resolved to go straight.

Phase one of Canton's new life was a job as RANGE DETECTIVE (hired gun) for the Wyoming Stock Grower's Association. Johnson married in 1885 and tried his hand at farming, then won election as Johnson County's sheriff, but fickle voters turned him out after his second term. Canton rejoined the stock association in time for the Johnson County War of 1892, but a near-miss murder trial persuaded him that it was time to leave Wyoming. He surfaced next in Oklahoma, serving as a deputy U.S. marshal in Oklahoma under Judge ISAAC CHARLES PARKER in 1895–97. Canton subsequently left his family to serve the U.S. MARSHALS SERVICE in Alaska, where he maintained his reputation as a fearless town-tamer. There, he befriended author Rex Beach and served as the prototype for Beach's two-fisted heroes in such novels as *The Spoilers* (1906), which was filmed six times, most notably with John Wayne in 1942.

After narrowly surviving the Alaskan winter of 1898, Canton returned to Oklahoma and resumed his lawman's duties. He was appointed to serve as adjutant general of Oklahoma's NATIONAL GUARD in 1907 and held that post until his death in 1927, his outlaw days long since forgotten.

capital punishment

Capital punishment—death inflicted by duly authorized authorities, as opposed to simple murder or LYNCH-ING—ranks among the oldest punishments imposed for criminal behavior. It also ranks, with GUN CONTROL and abortion, among the most controversial issues in modern America.

Execution was ordered for a wide variety of offenses in colonial America. The earliest legal executions were recorded from Virginia, where authorities hanged George Kendall for ESPIONAGE (1608) and Daniel Frank for theft (1622). By 1636 the Massachusetts Bay Colony had 13 capital crimes on its statute books, including such antiquated offenses as witchcraft. The U.S. Constitution's Eighth Amendment (1791) banned imposition of "cruel and unusual" punishment, but that failed to spare African slaves, who were sometimes burned alive for rebelling against their masters. Pennsylvania capped the 18th century by legislating various degrees of murder, some of which did not invoke the death penalty.

Rhode Island was the first state to ban rowdy public executions, in 1833, followed by New York two years later. Michigan was the first state to abolish capital punishment (except for treason), in 1846. Rhode Island and Wisconsin followed suit in 1852–53. Vermont began a slow trend toward state (versus local) imposition of death penalties, in 1864, but 90 years later, four states—Delaware, Louisiana, Mississippi, and Montana—still left a defendant's fate in the hands of local judges. New York was the first state to replace hanging with electrocution, in 1888, but two years passed before the electric chair claimed its first U.S. victim. While "the chair" gained popularity, Nevada bucked the trend in 1924, taking a lesson from World War I to execute condemned inmates with lethal gas.

A wave of abolitionist sentiment swept the United States during 1907–17, wherein eight states (Arizona, Kansas, Minnesota, Missouri, North Dakota, Oregon, South Dakota, and Tennessee) repealed their capital punishment statutes. All but two later restored the death penalty, however, as a means of countering popular vigilantism. American executions peaked in 1935, with 199 inmates put to death nationwide, and declined thereafter through the early 1960s. Victor Feguer, hanged for kidnapping and murder in 1963, was the last federal prisoner executed in the 20th century. A 1966 Gallup poll revealed that 58 percent of all Americans opposed capital punishment, and an unofficial moratorium began after Colorado executed Luis Monge in 1967. Five years later, the U.S. SUPREME COURT issued its landmark ruling in *Furman v. Georgia,* deeming current death penalty statutes unconstitutional (and thereby commuting the sentences of 629 condemned inmates nationwide). Henceforth, the court decreed, death could not be imposed for crimes where no victim was slain, and "special circumstances" (torture, contract killing, murder of a peace officer, etc.) were required to execute a defendant for murder.

Thirty-five states responded to *Furman* by immediately passing new, more specific death penalty statutes. Some of those were likewise found defective in the high court's eyes, and the law surrounding capital punishment continues to evolve. Arguments surrounding the relative cruelty of execution prompted many states, beginning with Oklahoma in 1977, to replace gas chambers and electric chairs with lethal injections. Nonetheless, Utah defendant Gary Gilmore chose a firing squad in 1977, when he broke the 10-year moratorium on U.S. executions. Between Gilmore's execution and January 4, 2005, another 943 inmates were executed (10 of them women). Modern executions peaked in 1999, with 98 inmates killed. The federal government resumed executions in June 2001 with terrorist Timothy McVeigh. A Gallup poll from May 2003 showed 74 percent of Americans supporting capital punishment, a figure that declined slightly to 71 percent in May 2004. Law enforcement officers traditionally support capital punishment by even larger margins.

Arguments for and against capital punishment are familiar to most Americans. Apologists often base their support on Old Testament religious grounds of "an eye for an eye," while maintaining that executions deter violent crime, that death is more humane than life imprisonment, that jailing prisoners for life costs more than killing them, and that prisoners awaiting death have an added incentive to "make peace with God." Opponents deem capital punishment a human rights violation with no proven deterrent value, imposed by a legal system whose foibles include RACISM, occasional

FRAME-UPS, and simple errors that may send innocent persons to death row. Critics also contend that execution—now preceded in all states by a system of mandatory appeals—may actually prove more expensive than housing an inmate for life.

Modern breakthroughs in FORENSIC SCIENCE highlight one glaring weakness of capital punishment—specifically, mistaken verdicts cannot be remedied once a defendant has been executed. Since 1990 more than 100 U.S. prison inmates have been exonerated by DNA evidence, proved innocent of crimes for which they were convicted and in some cases condemned. In Illinois alone, where 13 death row inmates were released, exposure of pervasive official misconduct in capital cases prompted Governor George Ryan to commute the death sentences of 167 inmates in January 2003. While police and the National District Attorney's Association denounced Ryan's "liberal" gesture, DNA exonerations continued nationwide, and a study conducted by the University of Maryland (2003) revealed that defendants accused of killing white victims since 1977 were condemned more frequently than slayers of nonwhite victims. Until such issues are resolved, critics insist, the moral doubts surrounding capital punishment outweigh its supposed benefits.

See also: TERRORISM.

Capitol Police

The U.S. Capitol Police force dates its existence from 1801, when John Golding was hired as the first watchman for Congress in Washington, D.C. Golding and his immediate successors had no police powers, instead relying on U.S. Marines for help when confronting intruders. President John Quincy Adams established a four-man Capitol watch force in 1827, then expanded its authority and renamed it the U.S. Capitol Police a year later, after his own son was attacked and beaten in the Capitol Rotunda. The new officers wore no uniforms, received little training, and often doubled as tour guides, relying on the District of Columbia's Auxiliary Guard to cope with emergencies.

New construction on Capitol Hill in 1851 brought a corresponding expansion of the Capitol Police, while a fire at the Library of Congress that same year prompted authorization of further personnel. By 1854 the force was uniformed and armed with hickory canes, though badges were withheld until the Civil War. In 1867 the House and Senate sergeants at arms took control of the force, expanding its roster, raising salaries, and designing new uniforms. A new Capitol Police Board headquarters was built in 1873, at which time the force included one captain, three lieutenants, 27 privates, and eight watchmen. Threats of

TERRORISM and ASSASSINATION in the 20th century have prompted the Capitol Police to become increasingly vigilant and professional.

One exception to that rule was Officer James Pickett, relieved of duty in 2001 for an ill-conceived "joke" that risked panic in Washington. Following the terrorist attacks of September 11, deadly anthrax had been mailed to various members of Congress and other targets along the Eastern Seaboard in a rash of crimes that claimed six lives (and which remains unsolved today). During that scare, Pickett left a quantity of white powder at his duty post, with a note inviting passersby to "Please Inhale." First suspended, then fired, Pickett faced a maximum prison sentence when he was convicted in November 2002, but the court was lenient. On February 11, 2003, he received a sentence of two years probation and 200 hours of community service.

The role of the Capitol Police received national attention in 2006 following an incident involving Congresswoman Cynthia McKinney, a Democrat from Georgia. On March 9 McKinney entered the Capitol and bypassed a security checkpoint without wearing her identifying lapel pin. An officer of the Capitol Police, who did not recognize McKinney, detained her, and McKinney struck the officer with her fist in response. Public outcries supporting and criticizing McKinney followed, and Capitol Police officials discussed legal action, though none had been taken as of this writing.

carjacking

The theft of automobiles from their owners by force is not a new phenomenon, but it appeared to reach near-epidemic proportions in the last decade of the 20th century. On September 15, 1992, FBI headquarters announced creation of a special unit to suppress "carjacking" in the nation's capital and environs. Washington, D.C., and Maryland had logged more than 300 such incidents since January 1992, with thousands more reported nationwide. Federal legislation was enacted that November, imposing a life prison term for any carjacking resulting in death, but it seemed to have no impact on the new crime wave. An FBI report published on March 6, 1999, declared that 49,000 carjackings had occurred each year from 1992 through 1996, with an average of 27 victims killed each year. Despite federal action, local and state police investigate the vast majority of U.S. carjackings and any murders that result. In 1997 Louisiana state legislators passed a new law exempting from punishment any citizen who shoots or otherwise kills a would-be carjacker.

See also: FEDERAL BUREAU OF INVESTIGATION.

Carroll, Joseph F. (1910–1991)

Born in 1910, Joseph Carroll joined the FBI at age 30 and served as an agent for seven years, thereafter resigning to lead the newly created U.S. Air Force Office of Special Investigations. That pose made Carroll responsible for ESPIONAGE and counterintelligence activities, as well as internal reviews of the Air Force itself. In 1959 he was appointed to serve as Air Force chief of staff in Europe. Two years later, following the Cuban Bay of Pigs fiasco, President John Kennedy chose Carroll to head a new Defense Intelligence Agency, coordinating activities of the U.S. intelligence community to avoid redundancy and avoid future embarrassment. Carroll retired in 1969 and died in 1991.

Chamberlain, Paul (b. 1941)

The son of a career soldier, born in 1941, Paul Chamberlain initially planned to become a physician, but his goals changed in 1962, when he found part-time work as a clerk in the FBI's Los Angeles field office. He soon abandoned premed studies and graduated from the FBI Academy in 1965, serving variously in the Tulsa, San Antonio, and Los Angeles field offices. In 1980 he solved the KIDNAPPING of a wealthy California banker's son, prompting a $500,000 expression of gratitude that enabled Chamberlain to quit the FBI and found his own private investigative agency, Paul Chamberlain International. Specializing in executive kidnapping and extortion, Chamberlain built his company over the next decade from a one-man operation to a $10 million firm with 50-plus field consultants. Chamberlain and his company remained active at press time for this volume, taking full advantage of various FBI and commercial contacts to turn a profit in the modern age of TERRORISM.

See also: FEDERAL BUREAU OF INVESTIGATION.

Chandler, George Fletcher (1872–1964)

A native New Yorker, born in 1872, George Chandler quit Syracuse University after two years to study at Columbia University's College of Physicians and Surgeons. He graduated in 1895 and spent 11 years in private practice before joining the New York NATIONAL GUARD as a lieutenant and assistant surgeon. Once infected with the military bug there was no turning back. Chandler won promotion to captain in 1910, then joined the regular U.S. Army and graduated from officer candidate school in 1915. During 1916–17 he joined General John Pershing's pursuit of bandits along the Tex-Mex border, followed by service as a stateside surgery instructor during World War I.

That conflict was still in progress when Governor Charles Whitman tapped Chandler to serve as superintendent of the newly created NEW YORK STATE POLICE. Despite a total lack of law enforcement training, Chandler used his military background to design uniforms, write training manuals, and map out patrol districts. By the time he resigned and returned to private medical practice in 1923, Chandler had established the NYSP as a respected professional agency with a competent command staff to carry on his traditions.

Chattanooga Police Department

Tennessee's legislature established the town of Chattanooga in December 1839, and its first constable was appointed soon afterward. Incorporated as a city with a new form of government in 1851, Chattanooga relied on a marshal and his assistants, dubbed "policemen," to keep order and maintain a city jail constructed on a $200 budget. City marshals were appointed until 1863, when Union troops occupied Chattanooga and the city lapsed into a crime wave resembling the atmosphere of a western frontier settlement. The federal provost marshal restored municipal government in October 1865, followed by creation of a volunteer police force one month later. In 1866 state legislators created a local police district, authorizing employment of one commissioner, two sergeants, and 24 officers. The city marshal's office was restored in 1869 and maintained control of the Chattanooga police force until a new charter was passed in 1883.

The new charter actually *decreased* police protection in Chattanooga, creating a force with one chief (James Allen), one assistant chief, and 10 patrolmen (split into two squads of five working 12-hour shifts). Political infighting and the bizarre death of one chief struck by lightning (Dock Mitchell, July 1893) produced frequent changes of command during the 1890s, but the department grew with Chattanooga, gaining a chief of detectives in 1895 and a new headquarters three years later. Chief John Mosely resisted political pressure on his department during the early 1900s, but the effort cost him, as enemies in power blocked his recommendations for higher police education and physical fitness standards. Chief William Hackett announced a general "housecleaning" in 1915, weeding out some corrupt and inept officers, but department leaders faced new CORRUPTION challenges with the advent of PROHIBITION five years later.

Chattanooga was a center of racist TERRORISM against blacks in 1949–60, rocked by a series of still-unsolved bombings, floggings and other crimes that sparked rumors of police collusion with the KU KLUX KLAN. In February 1960 black officers were assigned for the first time to patrol cars in two districts, but that progress was offset in the eyes of some critics by establishment of a K-9 UNIT in 1961, initially (and perhaps mistakenly) viewed as a weapon for use against civil rights protesters. Chattanooga's first police academy was not established until December 1962.

In 1967 the Chattanooga P.D. entered a four-year period of labor disputes and scandals, marked by periodic outbreaks of "BLUE FLU" and charges of corruption leveled at high-ranking officers. The department's image suffered, although none of the criminal charges were substantiated in court. Police commissioner Gene Roberts brought a "new broom" to the job in 1971, appointing a new chief (Jerry Pitts), designing new uniforms, hiring the department's first female patrol officers, and creating an ARSON investigation unit.

Challenges continued in the 1980s, a decade marked by more Klan violence, black rioting, and mandatory drug testing for all department employees (staunchly opposed by police union spokesmen in 1985, and canceled when a federal court found it to violate the Constitution's Fourth Amendment). The death of Chief Ralph Cothran in November 1995 left the department without a chief until 1997, when J. L. Dotson replaced him. Vigorous reform efforts ensued, climaxed in March 2001, when the Chattanooga P.D. was officially accredited by the Commission on Accreditation for Law Enforcement Agencies, placing it in the top 3 percent of U.S. departments. Those standards are reviewed at three-year intervals, and accreditation was affirmed in 2004.

Cheyenne Police Department

As Wyoming's capital and largest city, home to the world's largest rodeo, Cheyenne presents an unusual mixture of Old West atmosphere and 21st-century civilization. The Cheyenne Police Department is a self-described "progressive" agency with 94 sworn officers and 31 civilian personnel. It offers a full range of services, including mounted patrols (both horse and mountain bike), a SWAT TEAM and hostage negotiation unit, a K-9 UNIT, a Special Enforcement Unit focused on drug-related crimes, an Arson and Explosives Investigative Unit, a crime lab and a Victims Assistance Program. An unusual feature is Cheyenne's Citizens' Police Academy, offering a 13-week course (one night class per week) to provide civilians with an overview of the police department's methods. Cheyenne P.D.'s mission statement includes a pledge to "provide the highest level of protection and service to the community of Cheyenne, through partnership with its citizens, and to provide that protection and service in a professional, ethical, honest and timely manner."

See also: DRUGS.

Chicago Police Department

Residents of Chicago, Illinois, built their first jail in 1833, but no police force was created to arrest offenders. That move came four years later, with election of a High Constable and appointment of one subordinate constable for each of the city's six wards. Mayor Levi Boone authorized creation of a police force with 80 to 90 officers in 1855, dictating that all recruits must be native-born citizens. State legislators established a municipal police board in 1861, placing control of the department in the hands of three commissioners (and thus ensuring its subservience to political interests). In 1875 a new statute replaced the board with a single commissioner, appointed by Chicago's mayor.

Chicago patrolmen walked their beats until 1880, when horse-drawn patrol wagons entered service. A special mounted patrol of 40 men and horses was created for the crowded Loop in 1906, while limited auto patrols were launched in March of that year. Chicago PD established its Identification Bureau in 1884, soon boasting an unparalleled "Rogue's Gallery" of criminal mug shots. A year later, concern for the safety of female prisoners prompted employment of two matrons for each police precinct in April 1885. A special Murder Bureau was established in 1905, followed by appointment of the force's first JUVENILE CRIME specialists in 1917.

Such progress paled, however, in the face of Chicago PD's obsession with anarchists and "radicals." Police STRIKEBREAKING was routine throughout the latter 19th century, culminating in the deadly HAYMARKET BOMBING of 1886. In the wake of that incident, Captain Michael Schaak organized the department's first RED SQUAD, employing civilian INFORMANTS dubbed "specials," fabricating claims that Chicago was infested by an army of 83,000. World War I and its subsequent Red Scare increased Chicago PD's penchant for DOMESTIC SURVEILLANCE, expanding over the next half century to the point where journalist Frank Donner dubbed Chicago "the national capital of police repression." Assaults on public meetings were routine, logging 313 arrests in the first six months of 1930 alone. The same year saw Lt. Make Mills boast that his intelligence files contained information on 5,000 local "communists" and "75,000 names all over the United States." By 1960 the Red squad admitted keeping 17,000 files on local individuals, 141,000 out-of-towners, and some 14,000 organizations.

While part of the force dedicated itself to ESPIONAGE, the rest seemed intent on setting new records for CORRUPTION. PROHIBITION's advent set Chicago PD adrift in a sea of bootleg money, provoking a national scandal as officers protected mobster Al Capone and various rivals. Some local crime historians still claim police were active participants in 1929's St. Valentine's Day massacre, and other officers were exposed as hit men for ORGANIZED CRIME in the 1960s. In fairness to Chicago, though, it may be said that Capone's flamboyant reputation during 1925–33 highlighted local graft, while equally corrupt police departments in Cleveland, Detroit, New York City, and elsewhere avoided the spotlight by virtue of dealing with more circumspect racketeers. (New York racketeer "Lucky" Luciano once described Capone's Chicago as a "goddamn crazy place. Nobody's safe on the streets.") Renewed corruption scandals in 1960 prompted the hiring of ORLANDO WILSON to reorganize the Chicago PD, but it left political harassment and oppression unimpeded.

Chicago's problem was highlighted by a series of events in the latter 1960s. First, in 1966, three officers belonging to the KU KLUX KLAN were jailed for planning the ASSASSINATION-by-bazooka of Mayor Richard Daley. Two years later, the Democratic National Convention was disrupted by antiwar demonstrations and televised examples of EXCESSIVE FORCE that prompted federal investigators to coin the term *POLICE RIOT*. Behind the scenes, Chicago PD officers became embroiled in the FBI's illicit COINTELPRO operations, mounting violent attacks on the Black Panther Party which culminated with FRED HAMPTON's murder in December 1969. Frank Donner describes Chicago PD's guerrilla war against dissent as "flamboyantly illegal and in many instances criminal." Routine activities included "BLACK BAG JOBS," warrantless BUGGING and WIRETAPS, blackmail, plus thefts of property and cash. Sworn testimony indicates that a police unit led by Sgt. Joseph Grubisic also repeatedly urged physical attacks on leftists by a right-wing vigilante group, the Legion of Justice.

Litigation exposed Chicago PD's spy network in the early 1970s, around the same time FBI headquarters allegedly dismantled its COINTELPRO apparatus. In autumn 1974, spurred by formation of a local Alliance to End Repression, CPD's Intelligence Division admitted destroying secret files on 105,000 individuals, 1,300 organizations, and 200 informants. At least 500 files on individuals survived the purge, containing an estimated 400,000 pages of derogatory information. A local grand jury condemned police spying in September 1975, but Mayor Jane Byrne still defended the practice through early 1981. A settlement that March barred police from gathering political intelligence "in the absence of prior evidence of criminal intent," but officers violated the agreement by filming a protest against nuclear weapons in April 1982. Six months later, auditors enumerated 92 transgressions of the 1981 agreement. Ongoing violations through November 1985 resulted in cash damage awards totaling $701,500 to various surveillance targets.

Civil libertarians question the supposed cessation of political spying in Chicago after 1985, but they also found other causes for concern. The 1990s brought a series of dismissals targeting officers involved with street gangs, while 15 others were convicted and imprisoned in drug-related bribery cases. Repeated FRAME-UPS in Cook County and environs prompted Governor George Ryan to commute the sentences of 167 death row inmates in January 2003. Six months later, former inmate Aaron Patterson filed a $20 million federal lawsuit claiming that Chicago police tortured him to extract a murder confession, and that State's Attorney Richard Devine concealed evidence of brutal police malpractice. His case remained pending at press time for this work.

See also: ANARCHISM; FEDERAL BUREAU OF INVESTIGATION.

choke holds

"Choke holds"—also known as "carotid takedowns" or "bar arm holds"—include various grips applied to the neck of a subject, designed to subdue physical resistance. Their popular name notwithstanding, choke holds properly applied do not prevent the subject from breathing. Rather, they pinch the carotid arteries and thus induce unconsciousness by starving the brain of oxygenated blood. Danger arises if the grip is (a) improperly applied, thereby strangling the subject; or (b) held too long, resulting in brain damage or death.

Choke holds were popular with the LOS ANGELES POLICE DEPARTMENT until 1981, when a class action lawsuit was filed over 10 deaths recorded between August 1975 and March 1980. All 10 victims were male, eight of them African American. Dr. E. Karl Koiwai reviewed those cases on behalf of the International Judo Federation, which found no corresponding deaths in judo competitions worldwide. Koiwai concluded that the holds were improperly applied in most cases, sometimes using batons or flashlights as "choke sticks" with resultant lethal damage. Drug intoxication also played a role in four cases, by increasing the subjects' strength or tolerance for pain. Most big-city police departments now discourage officers from using choke holds, but reports of their application continue, including several fatalities reported from U.S. correctional facilities.

Christopher Commission

The Independent Commission on the LOS ANGELES POLICE DEPARTMENT—better known by the name of its chairman, attorney-diplomat Warren Christopher—was created to investigate the 1991 RODNEY KING beating incident and to generally conduct "a full and fair examination of the structure and operation of the LAPD."

The commission's report, published in July 1991, found that:

- "There is a significant number of officers in the LAPD who repetitively use excessive force against the public and persistently ignore the written guidelines of the department regarding force."

- "The failure to control these officers is a management issue that is at the heart of the problem. The documents and data that we have analyzed have all been available to the department; indeed, most of this information came from that source. The LAPD's failure to analyze and act upon these revealing data evidences a significant breakdown in the management and leadership of the Department. The Police Commission, lacking investigators or other resources, failed in its duty to monitor the Department in this sensitive use of force area. The Department not only failed to deal with the problem group of officers but it often rewarded them with positive evaluations and promotions."

The commission found a particular problem with repeat offenders at LAPD. Of 1,800 officers slapped with accusations of EXCESSIVE FORCE between 1986 and 1990, more than 1,400 had only one or two complaints, while 183 officers had four or more charges against them, 44 had six or more, 16 had eight or more, and one had 16 allegations. Incredibly, the 44 officers with six or more complaints consistently received positive performance evaluations, and their personnel files contained no information as to whether the brutality complaints had been "sustained" by LAPD's INTERNAL AFFAIRS Division. During the same five-year period, however, L.A.'s city attorney had settled 83 police brutality complaints with payments of $15,000 or more.

The Christopher Commission closed its report by recommending "a new standard of accountability. . . . Ugly incidents will not diminish until ranking officers know they will be held responsible for what happens in their sector, whether or not they personally participate." Warren Christopher subsequently served President Bill Clinton as secretary of state (1993–97).

Church Committee

Idaho senator Frank Church served as chairman of the U.S. Senate's Select Committee on Government Intelligence Agencies, better known as the Church Committee, active during the term of the 94th Congress (1975–77). The committee took public and private testimony from hundreds of witnesses and collected thousands of classified files from the FBI, the CIA, the INTERNAL REVENUE SERVICE, the National Security Agency, and other federal investigative bodies. The panel issued 14 reports before

it dissolved, but much of the original reference material remained secret until 1992, when passage of the JFK Assassination Records Collection Act declassified more than 50,000 documents.

After interrogating FBI officials, INFORMANTS, and harassment victims, the Church Committee had this to say about J. EDGAR HOOVER's motives for conducting illegal COINTELPRO campaigns:

Protecting national security and preventing violence are the purposes advanced by the Bureau for COINTELPRO. There is another purpose for COINTELPRO which is not explicit but which offers the only explanation for those actions which had no conceivable rational relationship to either national security or violent activity. The unexpressed major premise of much of COINTELPRO is that The Bureau has a role in maintaining the existing social order, and that its efforts should be aimed toward combating those who threaten that order.

With respect to FBI claims that COINTELPRO activities ended in May 1971, Senator Church and his colleagues reported:

The Committee has not been able to determine with any greater precision the extent to which COINTELPRO may be continuing. Any proposals to initiate COINTELPRO-type action would be filed under the individual case caption. The Bureau has over 500,000 case files, and each one would have to be searched. In this context, it should be noted that a Bureau search of all field office COINTELPRO files revealed the existence of five operations [conducted after May 1971]. A search of all investigative files might be similarly productive.

More disturbing than concealment of records, however, was the committee's discovery that "[a]ttitudes within and without the Bureau demonstrate a continued belief that covert action against Americans is permissible if the need for it is strong enough." Based on that conclusion, the committee declared in its final report that:

The American people need to be assured that never again will an agency of the government be permitted to conduct a secret war against those citizens it considers threats to the established order. Only a combination of legislative prohibition and Departmental control can guarantee that COINTELPRO will not happen again.

Closing on a pessimistic note, the Church Committee noted that "[w]ether the Attorney General can control the [FBI] is still an open question."

63

With respect to the IRS, Church and company found that most abuses involved illicit collaboration with the FBI in COINTELPRO-type campaigns. However, the IRS also maintained its own Special Services Staff (SSS) assigned to target various groups and individuals for "special" tax investigations. A list of 8,000 individuals and 3,000 groups, compiled between 1969 and 1973, included such targets as the AMERICAN CIVIL LIBERTIES UNION, the National Association for the Advancement of Colored People, the National Urban League, the American Library Association, the Ford Foundation, and the federal government's own Head Start program.

See also: FEDERAL BUREAU OF INVESTIGATION.

Cincinnati Police Department

Civic leaders of Cincinnati, Ohio, established a "night watch" to guard against fire and burglars soon after the village was incorporated, in 1802. Establishment of a bona fide police force came in 1859, with appointment of the city's first police commissioner. The 1920s brought startling new challenges as PROHIBITION spawned unprecedented CORRUPTION and a resurgent KU KLUX KLAN recruited 19,000 members in the Cincinnati metropolitan area. As elsewhere nationwide, those recruits included numerous policemen (plus Lieutenant Colonel Dan Caldwell of the Ohio NATIONAL GUARD).

Complaints of police RACISM persist to the present day in Cincinnati, where ghetto rioting erupted in April 2001, sparked by Officer Stephen Roach's fatal shooting of a black youth named Timothy Thomas. That outbreak—and another following Roach's acquittal in September 2001—came in the midst of a federal lawsuit filed by the AMERICAN CIVIL LIBERTIES UNION and other groups, complaining of police malpractice in the deaths of 15 blacks below the age of 40 during 1995–2001. A policy review by the U.S. JUSTICE DEPARTMENT produced a report in August 2002, suggesting various means of improvement in police procedures. With that report and the lawsuit in mind, Cincinnati politicians and police administrators signed a collaborative agreement with Washington, in which Cincinnati PD agreed to formation of a community focus group on "community-police oriented policing"; revision of department policies on use of force; creation of an independent CIVILIAN REVIEW BOARD to investigate complaints. Under the new policy guidelines, reports must be filed every time an officer draws a sidearm from its holster, nonlethal WEAPONS must be substituted for DEADLY FORCE whenever feasible, and a federal judge must monitor compliance with the agreement.

Citizenship and Immigration Service

Despite the welcoming message engraved on the Statue of Liberty, federal authorities have long harbored ambiguous feelings toward immigrants arriving in America. The U.S. SUPREME COURT established immigration control as a federal prerogative in 1875, overturning various state laws enacted since the Civil War. RACISM inspired the Chinese Exclusion Act of 1882 and played a significant role in the Alien Contract Labor Laws of 1885 and 1887, barring certain immigrants from the United States. A "Gentleman's Agreement" capped Japanese immigration in 1902, while the more general Immigration Act of 1882 excluded convicts, mental defectives, and persons likely to require public assistance.

Those statutes required enforcement, initially directed by the TREASURY DEPARTMENT, whose Customs inspectors collected the 50-cent head tax imposed on new arrivals in 1882. Special "Chinese inspectors" held the color line, while the Immigration Act of 1891 barred polygamists and persons suffering from "loathsome" or contagious diseases. That statute also created the Office of the Superintendent of Immigration at Treasury, supervising a new team of U.S. Immigrant Inspectors stationed at principal ports of entry. Since most immigration laws were theoretically designed to safeguard American jobs, the Bureau of Immigration was transferred from Treasury in February 1903 to a newly created Department of Commerce and Labor. Rules for naturalization—assigned by Congress since 1802 to "any court of record"—were standardized by law in 1906, whereupon the Bureau of Immigration became the Bureau of Immigration and Naturalization. Immigration and Naturalization split in 1913, when Commerce and Labor were divided into separate cabinet posts, then merged again in June 1933, as the Labor Department's Immigration and Naturalization Service (INS).

World War I brought new duties, including pursuit of "enemy aliens," while the Immigration Acts of 1921 and 1924 imposed ever stricter quotas on new arrivals. Denials of entry became so common that an Immigration Board of Review was created in the mid-1920s, transferred to the U.S. JUSTICE DEPARTMENT during World War II. Statutes from the 1920s kept immigration rates low until 1952, with passage of a new Immigration and Nationality Act. Anti-communist immigrants also found their passage eased by the Displaced Persons Act (1948), the Refugee Relief Act (1953), the Hungarian Refugee Act (1956), the Refugee-Escapee Act (1957), and the 1960s Cuban Adjustment Program. At the same time, INS launched various deportation programs (notably "Operation Wetback") designed to curb illegal immigration, but the nation's insatiable appetite for cheap labor frustrated most such efforts.

INS responsibilities expanded with passage of the Immigration Reform and Control Act in 1986, which included procedures for legitimizing illegal aliens in the U.S. Since the terrorist attacks of September 11, 2001, the INS has worked closely with the BORDER PATROL and other federal agencies of the HOMELAND SECURITY DEPARTMENT to monitor immigrants and resident aliens from Muslim nations. The agency is currently named the Citizenship and Immigration Service and exists as part of the Department of Homeland Security.

See also: CUSTOMS SERVICE; TERRORISM.

Civiletti, Benjamin Richard (b. 1935)

Born at Peekskill, New York, on July 17, 1935, Benjamin Civiletti earned his bachelor's degree from Johns Hopkins University in 1957 and received his LL.B. in 1961 from the University of Maryland's law school. Admitted to the Maryland bar that same year, he served as clerk for federal judge W. Calvin Chesnut in Maryland (1961–62) and as assistant U.S. attorney for Maryland (1962–64). After 13 years of private practice in Baltimore, Civiletti joined President Jimmy Carter's JUSTICE DEPARTMENT as assistant attorney general in charge of the criminal division (1977–78) and deputy attorney general (1978–79). On August 16, 1979, Civiletti took office as the 73rd U.S. attorney general, remaining in that post until President Ronald Reagan's inauguration on January 19, 1981.

Civiletti made his primary contribution to Justice two weeks before he left office, on January 5, with the issuance of new guidelines governing FBI UNDERCOVER operations. Those rules, created in the wake of controversy surrounding the Bureau's BRILAB and CORKSCREW campaigns in 1980, remain in force today with only minor alterations. Henceforth, direct approval from the FBI's director and its Undercover Operations Review Committee was required for any investigation lasting longer than six months and/or involving any of various "sensitive" areas—i.e., foreign governments; religious or political organizations; public officials; the news media; domestic security; any case where an agent might break the law (except for buying or selling stolen property and/or concealing his/her identity); any case where an agent will pose as a lawyer, doctor, journalist, or member of the clergy; any case where an agent may attend meetings between the target and his/her attorney; or any case involving significant risk of physical injury or financial loss.

See also: FEDERAL BUREAU OF INVESTIGATION.

civilian review boards

Prior to the troubled 1960s, most U.S. law enforcement agencies were responsible for policing themselves. Complaints of EXCESSIVE FORCE or other malpractice were (at least theoretically) investigated by departmental leaders or an INTERNAL AFFAIRS unit specially tasked to deal with disciplinary problems. The complaints and outcome of internal inquiries were commonly kept secret from the public. Local prosecutors or FBI agents might investigate notorious cases, but indictments were rare, convictions rarer still.

The 1960s brought social protest to the streets and into conflict with police, where the official response was frequently violent. At the same time, U.S. SUPREME COURT rulings amplified the basic rights of criminal suspects, while the AMERICAN CIVIL LIBERTIES UNION and other groups turned a spotlight on incidents of police malfeasance. Increasingly, from coast to coast, demands arose for civilian panels to investigate complaints of abusive policing—in short, to crack the "blue wall of silence" that enveloped too many distressing cases.

Opposition to the plan from law enforcement leaders was immediate, outspoken, and continues in some quarters to this day. (The mayor of Louisville, Kentucky, vetoed a civilian-review ordinance passed by his board of aldermen in May 2000.) Public opponents of civilian review included FBI director J. EDGAR HOOVER, most big-city police chiefs, plus such organized lobbies as the POLICE BENEVOLENT ASSOCIATION and the INTERNATIONAL ASSOCIATION OF CHIEFS OF POLICE. Contrary arguments varied, but the general thrust was a two-pronged attack, denigrating proponents of civilian review (as "Reds," "cop-haters," "bleeding hearts," etc.) while challenging their insight into law enforcement. The first complaint was not entirely without substance, since advocates of civilian review were predominantly "liberal," including victims of police abuse and their attorneys, but the second argument—that "only cops can understand why these things happen"—seemed to claim a special privilege, even immunity, for law enforcement officers which critics felt was undeserved and dangerous to free society at large.

After years of protests, litigation, and negotiations, many large U.S. police departments today accommodate some form of "civilian advisory process." Review boards do not necessarily possess authority to discipline abusive officers, but most have some process for making their findings public. Some police spokesmen argue that cities with civilian review boards pay out more in settlement of litigation claims than towns that have none. Supporters of the system, meanwhile, view that fact as validation of their efforts to reveal and remedy abuse.

Jurisdictions with civilian review boards in place at press time for this work included: Albany, New York; Albuquerque, New Mexico; Austin, Texas; Baltimore,

Maryland; Berkeley, California; Boise, Idaho; Cambridge, Massachusetts; Cincinnati, Ohio; Cleveland, Ohio; Dade County, Florida; Dallas, Texas; Dayton, Ohio; Evergreen University, in Washington; Flint, Michigan; Indianapolis, Indiana; Iowa City, Iowa; Kansas City, Missouri; Key West, Florida; King County, Washington; Knoxville, Tennessee; Las Vegas, Nevada; Long Beach, California; Los Angeles and Los Angeles County, California; Miami, Florida; Minneapolis, Minnesota; New Haven, Connecticut; New York City; Novato, California; Oakland, California; Omaha, Nebraska; Orange County, Florida; Philadelphia, Pennsylvania; Pittsburgh, Pennsylvania; Portland, Oregon; Riverside, California; Rochester, New York; Sacramento, California; St. Louis, Missouri; St. Petersburg, Florida; Salt Lake City, Utah; San Diego and San Diego County, California; San Francisco, California; San Jose, California; Santa Cruz, California; Sausalito, California; Seattle, Washington; Seminole County, Florida; Syracuse, New York; Tucson, Arizona; University of California, Berkeley; and Washington, D.C.

Cizanckas, Victor I. (1937–1980)

Founded in 1830, the police department of Stamford, Connecticut, was approaching its sesquicentennial when a festering CORRUPTION scandal erupted in the 1970s. City leaders sought a new chief to reform and revitalize the department, finally settling on Chief Victor Cizanckas of the Menlo Park (California) Police Department. Fearing charges of a whitewash or political maneuvering behind the scenes, Stamford's city council named Cizanckas chief for life in 1977, with a mandate to root out malfeasance at any cost.

Cizanckas arrived none too soon in a city where illegal gambling netted $35 million per year for ORGANIZED CRIME, while police extorted payoffs from racketeers by means which Cizanckas admitted were "not very subtle." Working in collaboration with federal prosecutors, Cizanckas fired many officers tainted by graft, while restructuring the department for greater efficiency. He hired civilian employees to handle various office jobs formerly done by sworn officers, and disbanded the Traffic Division entirely, proclaiming that "traffic was not a police function." Spokesmen for a patrolmen's union dropped their opposition to Cizanckas's reforms upon realizing that obstruction was widely viewed as support for corruption.

Cizanckas sadly would not live to see his goals achieved in Stamford. Three years after tackling the job, he died in his sleep at age 43, leaving others to carry on the work he had begun. Today, nearly two decades after that beginning, Stamford PD has managed to maintain its newfound reputation for integrity.

Clark, James G., Jr. (b. 1924)

Born in 1924, Sheriff Jim Clark of Dallas County, Alabama (Selma), emerged in the mid-1960s as a symbol of racist defiance against black civil rights, on a par with ALBERT LINGO of the Alabama State Troopers and Birmingham's EUGENE "BULL" CONNOR. Together, those men personified a brutal era of southern law enforcement—and, ironically, ensured the passage of those very civil rights laws they opposed.

Clark's law enforcement career was uneventful until early 1957, when Dr. Martin Luther King and other activists accused him of whitewashing an elderly black man's death outside Selma. Six years later, members of the Student Nonviolent Coordinating Committee launched a black voter-registration drive in Selma, prompting Clark to recruit a civilian "posse" composed of KU KLUX KLAN members and sympathizers. Armed with clubs, bullwhips, and cattle prods, Clark's posse joined Al Lingo's troopers to "operate in tandem as a mobile anti-civil rights force," ranging far beyond their legal jurisdiction. During 1964–65 Clark and his men surfaced on the racial battlefields of Gadsden, Hayneville, Marion, Notasulga, and Tuscaloosa, assaulting and threatening civil rights workers. In February 1965, when he appeared with Lingo in Marion and watched police kill one unarmed demonstrator, Clark told reporters, "Things got a little too quiet for me over at Selma tonight, and it made me nervous."

On March 7, 1965—memorialized as "Bloody Sunday"—Clark's posse and Lingo's troopers attacked a group of peaceful marchers in Selma, sending more than 60 to the hospital with wounds from clubs and bullwhips. That fiasco earned him a personal reprimand from Governor George Wallace, along with a federal court order to cease "any further use whatsoever of the Dallas County posse." Still, he found time to fraternize with the Klan, sharing derogatory information he received on murder victim Viola Liuzzo in April 1965, from the DETROIT POLICE DEPARTMENT, and visiting the jury room during deliberations on three Klansmen who fatally beat a white minister, Rev. James Reeb. Clark's comments to the jury were not recorded, but the panel voted to acquit all three in record time.

Clark's intransigent RACISM doomed his reelection bid in 1966, as newly enfranchised black voters turned out to defeat him. He fought to the bitter end, suppressing some 1,600 "irregular" ballots cast for his opponent, but court orders placed those votes on record and retired Clark from his job. Ex-sheriff Clark then joined the John Birch Society as a traveling speaker who condemned civil rights as a "communist" plot, but his appeal faded with time and the society's dwindling membership. In 1978 Clark was indicted for smuggling three tons of marijuana into Alabama, valued at $4.3

million. He pled guilty and received a two-year federal prison sentence in December 1978. At the time of his plea, Clark also faced unrelated charges from New York, including three counts of fraud and one count of racketeering.

Clark, Thomas Campbell (1899–1977)

A native Texan, born in Dallas on September 23, 1899, Tom Clark earned his bachelor's degree from the University of Texas, then served in the U.S. Army during World War I. Clark received his LL.B. from the University of Texas in 1922, then spent five years with his father's law firm before winning election as district attorney of Dallas County in 1927. Ten years later, he served as an attorney for the Bureau of War Risk Litigation, followed by a term as special assistant in the JUSTICE DEPARTMENT's Antitrust Division (1938). During World War II Clark served as West Coast chief of the Antitrust Division (1940–42), coordinator of alien enemy control for Japanese relocation in the Western Defense Command (1942), chief of the War Frauds Unit (1943), first assistant to the Antitrust Division (1943), and assistant attorney general of the Criminal Division (1943–45).

President Harry Truman named Clark U.S. attorney general at war's end, assuming office on July 1, 1945. A staunch anticommunist in the postwar era, Clark initiated the SMITH ACT prosecution of Communist Party leaders in 1948 and gave FBI Director J. EDGAR HOOVER a virtual free hand in illegal DOMESTIC SURVEILLANCE techniques. (An aide explained that Clark "didn't want to know who was tapped and who wasn't tapped" by Hoover's G-men.) Unfortunately, Clark was not so zealous when it came to prosecuting leaders of ORGANIZED CRIME. In May 1947 he personally dismissed fraud charges filed against leaders of the Chicago syndicate, and three months later arranged early parole for the same gangsters, already serving time in federal prison for extortion. When Congress sought to investigate the latter case, Clark withheld parole records. Nearly two decades later, an FBI bug in Chicago caught one of those paroled, notorious mobster Murray "The Camel" Humphreys, explaining how the early parole was arranged. "The trick was to get to Tom Clark," Humphreys said. "Finally, a deal was made: If he had the thick skin to do it, he'd get the next appointment to the Supreme Court." (FBI leaders suppressed the tape, which surfaced after Hoover's death.)

That promise was kept in October 1949, when President Truman appointed Clark to the nation's highest court. The *Chicago Tribune* greeted the announcement with a call for Clark's impeachment, noting the ex-attorney general's "utter unfitness for any position of public responsibility, and especially for a position on the Supreme Court." Clark displayed his "thick skin" by remaining on the court until 1967, resigning then to avoid potential conflicts of interest when his son became attorney general under President Lyndon Johnson. Clark died in New York City on June 13, 1977.

Clark, William Ramsey (b. 1927)

Ramsey Clark, son of Attorney General and SUPREME COURT justice THOMAS CAMPBELL CLARK, was born in Dallas, Texas, on December 18, 1927. He served in the U.S. Marine Corps during 1945–46, then earned his B.A. from the University of Texas in 1949, followed by an M.A. and J.D. from the University of Chicago in 1950. Clark was admitted to the Texas bar in 1951 and to practice before the U.S. Supreme Court five years later. After a decade in private practice (1951–61), he joined the JUSTICE DEPARTMENT as assistant attorney general for the Lands Division (1961–65) and deputy attorney general (1965–66). Under President John Kennedy, Clark played a key role in the civil rights field. He led members of the U.S. MARSHALS SERVICE who defended James Meredith during the OLE MISS RIOT of 1962, coordinated federal efforts in Birmingham the following year, and played a key role in drafting the Civil Rights Act of 1964.

President Lyndon Johnson appointed Clark to serve as acting attorney general on October 3, 1966, and Clark assumed the office full-time on March 2, 1967. He clashed instantly with FBI Director J. EDGAR HOOVER, whom Clark dismissively labeled "the old man down the hall." Staunchly opposed to illegal DOMESTIC SURVEILLANCE techniques, Clark issued sweeping directives against such behavior, except in special cases dealing with national security. (In that vein, Clark rejected Hoover's plea to bug the hotel rooms of presidential candidates at the 1968 Democratic National Convention.) Hoover retaliated with a torrent of memoranda, prompting Clark to observe that "Hoover would memo you to death. An attorney general could have spent literally all his time preparing memos back to the director."

The feud between Clark and Hoover soon transcended procedural details, plumbing the depths of bitter enmity. Clark denounced Hoover's pursuit of the Communist Party as a "terribly wasteful use of very valuable resources," while lampooning the director's "self-centered concern for his own reputation." Hoover fired back in kind, branding Clark "a jellyfish" and the worst attorney general of the century, confiding to journalists that Clark was "nothing but a hippie. I went over there once and his wife was barefoot. What kind of person is that?"

Despite their quarrels, Clark stopped short of reforming the FBI. He once declared prosecution of renegade G-men his "highest priority," but none were indicted while Clark held office. He likewise failed to investigate complaints from within the FBI itself of Hoover's profiteering and autocratic rule. Clark *did* propose appointment of a "single oversight officer" to supervise all federal investigative agencies, noting that "from many standpoints it was desirable for Mr. Hoover to be removed from running the FBI," but President Johnson dismissed the plan as "too ambitious and too heavy to take on." In the end, Johnson regretted his choice of Clark, telling friends, "I thought I had appointed Tom Clark's son. I was wrong."

Notwithstanding that lack of support, Clark remained through the end of Johnson's administration, stepping down with the rest of LBJ's team on January 20, 1969. A controversial visit to North Vietnam in 1972 failed to help Clark with abortive U.S. Senate campaigns in New York, in 1974 and 1976. He remains an outspoken critic of U.S. foreign policy and has published a book analyzing alleged U.S. war crimes in the 1991 Gulf War. Clark provided legal advice and counsel to former Iraqi president Saddam Hussein during his trial. In the past he represented others accused of war crimes and genocide such as Slobodan Milosevic, Radovan Kavadzic (in Yugoslavia), and Elizaphan Ntakirutimana (in Rwanda), as well as Karl Linnas, a Nazi concentration camp commander.

See also: FEDERAL BUREAU OF INVESTIGATION.

Clegg, Hugh H. (1898–1979)

Born on July 17, 1898, in Mathiston, Mississippi, Hugh Clegg joined the FBI on August 12, 1926. He rose rapidly through the ranks, serving as special agent in charge of the Atlanta, Chicago, and Washington, D.C., field offices. In 1932 he was appointed to serve as assistant director under J. EDGAR HOOVER. Three years later, Clegg became the first head of the FBI Academy, serving simultaneously as assistant director of the Bureau's Training and Inspection Divisions. In 1940–41 he studied wartime intelligence and security techniques in England, with the British intelligence service. Following retirement from the FBI in 1954, Clegg served as an assistant to the University of Mississippi's president from 1956 to 1971 (a tenure that included the OLE MISS RIOT of September 1962). He died at Anguilla, Mississippi, on December 12, 1979.

Cleveland Police Department

Founded in 1866, the police department of Cleveland, Ohio, was born in a place and era beset by politi-
cal CORRUPTION. Boss Mark Hannah's "Ohio Gang" ruled the state—and for a time, the nation, under hand-picked presidents William McKinley (1897–1901) and Warren Harding (1921–23). At home in the Buckeye State, crime flourished with official blessings, as long as bribes were paid, and police ignored ORGANIZED CRIME, preserving their energy for harassment of blacks, labor unions, and "Reds."

A seeming deviation from that norm occurred in 1921, with Mayor Fitzgerald's order for Cleveland police to suppress the KU KLUX KLAN. Although some officers unquestionably ranked among the Klan's 2,500 members in Cleveland, police pressure kept the order from flourishing there, despite a statewide membership approaching 200,000. Perhaps, in retrospect, it was decided that Cleveland's men in blue needed no white-robed vigilantes to keep residents of the squalid Hough ghetto "in their place."

And Cleveland police had other concerns during PROHIBITION, when their city was a major hub of mid-western bootlegging, run by a sophisticated crime syndicate that bribed everyone from City Hall to rookies on the beat. Cleveland was wide open for liquor, gambling, and vice throughout the "dry" era and into the 1930s, acquiring such a sordid reputation that its voters rebelled in 1935, electing reform mayor Harold Burton to clean up the town. His new broom was ELIOT NESS, of Chicago "Untouchable" fame, a straight-arrow lawman who found himself confronted with a Herculean task.

Police reform was job one for Ness, and he started in December by personally firing two veteran patrolmen caught drinking on duty. Their dismissal without pensions, close to Christmas, caused a furor on the force, but Ness was adamant. "Either we have a decent, law-abiding community, or we don't," he told reporters. "Either we have decent, law-abiding policemen to show us the way, or we don't." A few days later, Ness attacked departmental corruption by demoting several officers and transferring 122 away from their longtime cronies. He reorganized the Detective Bureau, where promotion had long depended on political contacts, and fired the bureau's chief outright. On December 30 Ness hired John Flynn, a lawyer with military experience, to root out graft in the department, effectively creating Cleveland PD's first INTERNAL AFFAIRS division.

Ness ultimately failed to wipe out Cleveland's mob, thanks in equal part to corrupt officers like Captain Louis Cedek (who warned casinos in advance of pending raids) and to the foresight of mob boss Moe Dalitz, who anticipated Ness's actions and moved most of the action outside city jurisdiction. Still, he rooted out much of the police department's ingrained corruption—

Captain Cedek was convicted and imprisoned on four counts of bribery—and revolutionized traffic patrols to the point where Cleveland was (briefly) regarded as "America's safest city." Ness did not curtail the city's active RED SQUAD, which continued operation through the troubles 1960s. Author Hank Messick, researching local mobsters for a book in 1964, was bluntly told that he would get cooperation from police only if he revised his focus to report on "communists and niggers taking over Cleveland."

Four years later, on July 23, 1968, a deadly shootout between police and black militants left seven dead and 15 wounded, sending activist Fred "Ahmed" Evans to death row on murder charges. Local newspapers headlined the "Massacre of Police," but evidence collected in that case left disturbing questions unanswered. Blood tests on two slain officers proved both were legally drunk when they died. A third dead officer was riddled with shotgun pellets, but since Evans and his cohorts had no shotguns, some unknown person crudely changed the cause of death on Patrolman Louis Golonka's autopsy report from "shotgun" to "gunshot" wounds. Finally, black civilian James Chapman was hailed in the press as a hero, gunned down by Evans et al. while trying to rescue wounded policemen—but a week after the shootout, famed medical examiner Cyril Wecht disputed that story. Wecht found that Chapman was killed by a point-blank shot to the head, informing defense attorneys, "The police officers are lying. This young man was killed execution-style from very close range." In short, by some unknown policeman at the scene.

Cleveland PD today is organized in three divisions, including Administrative Operations, Field Operations (uniformed patrol, traffic, etc.), and Special Operations—subdivided into Technical Support and various Detective Bureaus (ARSON, auto theft, fraud, homicide, SEX CRIMES, etc.). Despite its troubled history and ongoing tension in minority areas, the department pledges "to protect the life and property of all citizens against criminal activity and to create an environment of stability and security within the community."

Clifford, Nathan (1803–1881)

New Hampshire native Nathan Clifford was born at Rumney on August 18, 1803. After graduating from the Hampton Literary Institution, he studied law privately and won admittance to the New Hampshire bar in 1827. He thereafter settled in Maine, where he served as a state legislator (1830–34), state attorney general (1834–38), and as a U.S. representative (1839–43). President James Polk named Clifford his attorney general on October 17, 1846, a post he held

Attorney General Nathan Clifford (Author's collection)

until March 17, 1848. Clifford subsequently served as U.S. envoy extraordinary and minister plenipotentiary to Mexico (1848–49), where he negotiated treaty terms annexing California as a U.S. territory. Clifford then returned to private legal practice in Maine for nine years, interrupted when President James Buchanan appointed him to the U.S. SUPREME COURT in 1858. Justice Clifford died in office, while at home in Maine, on July 25, 1881.

Clum, John P. (1851–1932)

A native New Yorker, born in 1851, John Clum left Rutgers College after one year to join the U.S. Army at age 20. Posted to the Signal Corps in New Mexico, he left military service in 1874 to become the government's Indian agent at the San Carlos Reservation. His arrival coincided with raiding by Apache renegades that prompted General George Crook to display the heads of seven offenders on the reservation's parade ground. Clum sympathized with the Apaches and moved to reduce the aggravating military presence by creation of a reservation police force, led by the warriors Eskinospas, Goodah-Goodah, "Sneezer," and Talkalai.

Unfortunately, Clum's plan proved so successful that "white fathers" in Washington, D.C., decided to consolidate all reservation-bound Apaches at San Carlos. In February 1875 the Fort Verde Reservation was closed, its 1,500 residents forced to march overland to San Carlos through the worst of winter. Five months later, another 800 Apaches were uprooted from Fort Apache and transferred to San Carlos. In May 1876 Clum received orders to corral all "wild" Chiricahuas in New Mexico, but he captured only 325, while an estimated 940 escaped. Federal planners closed the Warm Springs Reservation and moved its inhabitants to San Calos in spring 1877, prompting a violent insurrection by Mimbreño war chief Victorio.

Clum resigned his position in July 1877 and moved to Tombstone, Arizona, where he edited the *Tombstone Epitaph*. In that position he reported on conflicts between Sheriff JOHN H. BEHAN and the EARP BROTHERS, culminating in Tombstone's notorious gunfight at the O.K. CORRAL. Unlike many others, Clum survived the local feud and later moved to California. He died in Los Angeles in 1932.

Coast Guard

Created in August 1790 with 10 small ships, the U.S. Coast Guard is unique among America's armed forces as the only branch organized to enforce federal laws. Initially known as the Revenue Marine and the Revenue Cutter Service, the unit was assigned to enforce tariff and trade statutes, prevent smuggling, and to protect the collection of federal revenue. It also served as the nation's only armed service afloat for four years, until the U.S. Navy was created in 1794.

Over the next century, Congress expanded the agency's duties to include suppression of piracy and slavery, charting the U.S. coastline, exploring and policing Alaska, and protecting the marine environment. The Coast Guard gained its current name in 1915, when new legislation merged the Revenue Cutter Service and the Life-Saving Service into a single unit. Further responsibility was added with absorption of the Lighthouse Service in 1939. Seven years later, Congress transferred the Bureau of Marine Inspection and Navigation to the Coast Guard, thereby placing merchant marine safety and licensing under the unit's purview. Today its broad charter requires the Coast Guard to "enforce or assist in the enforcement of all applicable laws on, under and over the high seas and waters subject to the jurisdiction of the United States." Drug enforcement remains a major aspect of that duty, coupled with suppression of TERRORISM since September 2001.

COINTELPRO

The FBI's official history, reported on the Bureau's Internet Web site, provides the following information on so-called COINTELPRO (*counterintelligence program*) operations in the midst of a section devoted to "The Vietnam War Era":

No specific guidelines for FBI Agents covering national security investigations had been developed by the [Richard Nixon] Administration or Congress; these, in fact, were not issued until 1976. Therefore, the FBI addressed the threats from the militant "New Left" as it had those from Communists in the 1950s and the KKK in the 1960s. It used both traditional investigative techniques and counterintelligence programs ("Cointelpro") to counteract domestic terrorism and conduct investigations of individuals and organizations who threatened terroristic violence. Wiretapping and other intrusive techniques were discouraged by Hoover in the mid-1960s and eventually were forbidden completely unless they conformed to the Omnibus Crime Control Act. Hoover formally terminated all "Cointelpro" operations on April 28, 1971.

That passage, pretending to describe a campaign of criminal activity perpetrated under the COINTELPRO label, is in fact a classic piece of FBI disinformation. Within a span of 113 words it rewrites history concerning illegal WIRETAPS (banned by Congress in 1934 and by U.S. SUPREME COURT rulings in 1937 and 1939); falsely identifies the targets of COINTELPRO harassment as terrorists; implies that COINTELPRO campaigns occurred only during the first 28 months of the Nixon administration (January 1969 to April 1971); falsely claims that J. EDGAR HOOVER "discouraged" illegal surveillance techniques; and claims (again, falsely) that such techniques have not been used by G-men since 1971.

The first official COINTELPRO campaign was launched by FBI headquarters on August 28, 1956, targeting the Communist Party, with its goals described in a memo from Alan Belmont, head of the Bureau's Internal Security Section.

During its investigation of the Communist Party, USA, the Bureau has sought to capitalize on incidents involving the Party and its leaders in order to foster factionalism, bring the Communist Party (CP) and its leaders into disrepute before the American public and cause confusion and dissatisfaction among rank-and-file members of the CP.

Generally, the above action has constituted harassment rather than disruption, since, for the most part, the Bureau has set up particular incidents, and the attack has been from the outside. At the present time, however, there is existing within the CP a situation resulting from the developments at the 20th Congress of the CP of the Soviet Union and the Government's attack on the Party principally through prosecutions under the Smith Act of 1940 and the Internal Security Act of 1950 which is made to order for an all-out disruptive attack against the CP from within. In other words, the Bureau is in a position to initiate, on a broader scale than heretofore attempted, a counterintelligence program against the CP, not by harassment from the outside, which might serve to bring the various factions together, but by feeding and fostering from within the fight currently raging.

On May 8, 1958, Hoover sent Attorney General WILLIAM ROGERS a progress report on the FBI's effort to "promote disruption within the ranks of the Communist Party," including use of paid infiltrators to spark "acrimonious debates" and "increase factionalism." A flurry of anonymous letters also sought to generate "disillusionment [with] and defection" from the party. Six months later, on November 8, 1958, Hoover briefed President Dwight Eisenhower's cabinet on the continuing effort, distributing a 36-page "Top Secret" summary. That booklet read, in part:

To counteract a resurgence of Communist Party influence in the United States, we have a . . . program designed to intensify confusion and dissatisfaction among its members. During the past few years, the program has been most effective. Selective informants were briefed and trained to raise controversial issues within the Party. In the process, they may be able to advance themselves to high positions. The Internal Revenue Service was furnished the names and addresses of Party functionaries. . . . Based on this information, investigations have resulted in 262 possible income tax evasion cases. Anticommunist literature and simulated Party documents were mailed anonymously to carefully chosen members.

FBI files later revealed that during the years 1957–60, 266 individual COINTELPRO campaigns were mounted against the Communist Party in America. In 1960 alone those campaigns involved 114 illegal wiretaps, 74 warrantless bugs, and 2,342 pieces of private mail read by G-men in violation of federal law. Hoover "discouraged" none of it; in fact, he required that headquarters approve each specific criminal act in advance.

On January 10, 1961, Hoover briefed President John Kennedy and Attorney General ROBERT FRANCIS KENNEDY on the campaign's progress, including

penetration of the Party at all levels with security informants; use of various techniques to keep the Party off-balance and disillusion individual communists concerning communist ideology; investigation of every known member of the CPUSA in order to determine whether he should be detained in the event of a national emergency. . . . As an adjunct to our regular investigative operations, we carry on a carefully planned program of counterattack against the CPUSA. . . .

One of those "carefully planned programs," launched on October 4, 1966, was dubbed Operation Hoodwink. As described in the kick-off memo, Hoodwink was "designed to provoke a dispute between the Communist Party, USA, and La Cosa Nostra" (otherwise known as the Mafia). Ideally, G-men hoped that American communists and members of ORGANIZED CRIME would "expend their energies, time, and money attacking each other. This would help neutralize the activities of both groups which are detrimental to this country." The FBI's New York City field office recommended a method of sparking the feud.

This technique consists of anonymously forwarding one leaflet to a local La Cosa Nostra leader attacking the labor practices of one of his enterprises. The leaflet would ostensibly be published by a local Party unit. A note with the leaflet would give the impression that it has received wide circulation.

Instead of vetoing the suggestion, with its clear potential for provoking lethal violence, Hoover suggested an even more aggressive campaign in a memo dated October 5, 1966. It read:

New York is authorized to mail the anonymous letters and leaflet set out . . . as the beginning of a long-range program to cause a dispute between La Cosa Nostra (LCN) and the Communist Party, USA. . . . To strengthen this alleged attack, add a last sentence to the leaflet: "Let's show the hoodlums and the bosses that the workers are united against sweatshops."

Take the usual precautions to insure this mailing cannot be associated with the Bureau and advise of tangible results. New York should also submit follow-up recommendations to continue this program.

The Party has been the subject of recent bombings, a typical hoodlum technique. Consider a spurious Party statement blaming the LCN for the bombings because of "Party efforts on behalf of the workers." This statement could be aimed at specific LCN members if appropriate.

In developing this program, thought should also be given to initiating spurious LCN attacks on the

CPUSA, so that each group would think that the other was mounting a campaign against it. The Bureau very much appreciates New York's careful analysis of this program and the initial "low-key" method suggested.

It is difficult to guess what actions Hoover may have deemed excessive, when bombing (see BOMBING AND BOMB SQUADS) and other acts of deadly violence were considered "low-key." The campaign failed to produce a gang war as desired, but the FBI was still trying in 1968, when similar spurious letters were sent from alleged CP members to the mob-affiliated Teamsters' Union in Philadelphia.

Hoover's campaign to disrupt the Communist Party proved so successful that a second COINTELPRO operation was launched in 1960, this one targeting a wide spectrum of Puerto Rican nationalists. Hoover's initial memo on the subject, dated August 4, 1960, advised his subordinates that:

The Bureau is considering the feasibility of instituting a program of disruption against organizations which seek independence for Puerto Rico through other than lawful, peaceful means.

Because of the increasing boldness apparent in the activities of such organizations, their utter disregard for the will of the majority, the inevitable communist and/ or Soviet effort to embarrass the United States, and the courage given to their cause by Castro's Cuba, we must make a more positive effort, not only to curtail, but to disrupt their activities.

San Juan and New York should give this matter studied consideration and thereafter furnish the Bureau observations, suggestions and recommendations relative to the institution of a program to reach the Bureau no later than 3-25-60 [sic]/

In considering this matter, you should bear in mind the Bureau desires to disrupt the activities of these organizations and is not interested in mere harassment. No action should be taken in this program without Bureau authority at any time.

There followed a familiar war of nerves, including use of infiltrators to "raise controversial issues at meetings, raise justifiable criticisms against leaders and take other steps which would weaken" various nationalist groups; circulation of anonymous letters and planted news stories to sow dissent among *independistas;* and pursuit of other means by which "the nationalist elements could be pitted against the communist elements to effectively disrupt some of the organizations." When nationalist leader Juan Mari Bras suffered a near-fatal heart attack on April 21, 1964, FBI memos gloated that one of the Bureau's anonymous letters "certainly did nothing to ease his tensions for he felt the effects of

the letter deeply. . . . This particular technique has been outstandingly successful and we shall be on the lookout to further exploit our achievements in this field." Another memo, dated December 15, 1967, boasted that COINTELPRO operations in Puerto Rico had served to "confuse the independentist leaders, exploit group rivalries and jealousies, inflame personality conflicts, emasculate the . . . strength of these organizations and thwart any possibility of pro independence unity."

Far from ending in April 1971, illegal disruption campaigns against Puerto Rican nationalists groups and leaders escalated over the next two decades, becoming markedly more violent after COINTELPRO veteran RICHARD W. HELD took charge of the San Juan field office in 1978. The new phase of psychological warfare included vigilante bombings, beatings and murders of nationalist leaders, investigated but never solved by the FBI. Sworn affidavits taken from G-men in 1985 acknowledged use of illegal bugs and wiretaps, while a former secretary with the San Juan field office blamed agents for a 1978 firebombing at the home of Juan Mari Bras. Agent Held was rewarded for the campaign in 1988, with promotion to serve as agent-in-charge of the San Francisco field office.

The Bureau's third formal COINTELPRO target, beginning in October 1961, was the Socialist Workers' Party (SWP). Any claim that COINTELPRO actions were reserved for "terrorists" is laid to rest by Hoover's memo of October 12, 1961, inaugurating his new campaign with a complaint that the SWP

has, over the past several years, been openly espousing its line on a local and national basis through the running of candidates for public office and strongly directing and/or supporting such causes as Castro's Cuba and integration problems in the South. The SWP has been in frequent contact with international Trotskyite groups stopping short of open and direct contact with these groups. . . . It is felt that a disruption program along similar lines [to COINTELPRO-CPUSA] could be initiated against the SWP on a very selective basis. One of the purposes of this program would be to alert the public to the fact that the SWP is not just another socialist group but follows the revolutionary principles of Marx, Lenin and Engels as interpreted by Leon Trotsky. . . . It may be desirable to expand the program after the effects have been evaluated.

In fact, the "new" COINTELPRO-SWP was not new at all. FBI records, later released under the Freedom of Information Act, reveal that between 1943 and 1963 G-men logged 20,000 days of monitoring wiretaps on SWP telephones and 12,000 days monitoring bugs illegally planted in SWP homes and offices. The same

20-year period witnessed 208 FBI break-ins against the SWP, with 9,864 party documents stolen or photographed during burglaries. Separate COINTELPRO records, perhaps including some overlap with the previous statistics, confirm 46 disruptive campaigns against the SWP through 1971, with 80-plus break-ins staged to photograph more than 8,000 documents during the same period.

Some of the Bureau's specific anti-SWP campaigns included disruption of the party's support for FRAME-UP victim Robert F. Williams, a black civil rights leader falsely charged with KIDNAPPING in North Carolina, and a successful effort to drive SWP member Morris Starsky from his teaching post at Arizona State University. According to a memo from the Phoenix field office, dated October 1, 1968, Professor Starsky

> by his actions, has continued to spotlight himself as a target for counterintelligence action. He and his wife were both named as presidential electors by and for the Socialist Workers Party when the SWP in August, 1968, gained a place on the ballot in Arizona. In addition they have signed themselves as treasurer and secretary, respectively of the Arizona SWP. Professor STARSKY's status at Arizona State University may be affected by the outcome of his pending trial on charges of disturbing the peace. He is alleged to have used violent, abusive and obscene language against the Assistant Managing Director of Gammage Auditorium at ASU during the memorial service for Martin Luther King last April. Trial is now scheduled for 10/8/68 in Justice Court, Tempe, Arizona.

Rather than await the outcome of that trial, G-men mailed a series of scurrilous letters to the university's faculty committee, signed by "concerned ASU alumni" and accusing Starsky of various unethical or criminal activities. Starsky's dismissal from the faculty was rated a success for the Bureau's COINTELPRO-SWP. Parallel COINTELPRO operations were also undertaken against an SWP affiliate, the Young Socialist Alliance (YSA), and records from those campaigns prove that the operation did not end in April 1971 as the FBI claims. In fact, a memo sent to headquarters on June 20, 1973, referred to the Bureau's recent receipt of "items stolen from the YSA office" in New York City.

Next on tap for the COINTELPRO treatment were various factions of the KU KLUX KLAN. Spurred by President Lyndon Johnson, the FBI inaugurated its COINTELPRO—white hate groups on September 2, 1964. By the time action was suspended in April 1971, G-men had undertaken 287 separate operations against Klansmen in various states. "Snitch-jacketing" (the false portrayal of loyal Klansmen as FBI informants) was a favorite technique, apparently prompting Mississippi racists to murder one of their colleagues in August 1965, but the KKK was spared the more aggressive techniques employed against racial minorities and targets on the political left. INFORMANTS such as Gary Rowe were encouraged to spread dissension in Klan ranks by any means possible, including serial adultery with the wives of brother Klansmen, but G-men often sheltered Klan spies who committed acts of violence against southern blacks or civil rights workers.

Aside from a 1968 incident wherein an AGENT PROVOCATEUR was paid to arrange the police ambush of two Mississippi bombers, leaving one dead and the other gravely wounded, FBI anti-Klan operations consisted largely of petty harassment. Familiar anonymous letters accused Klan leaders of financial and/or sexual impropriety. The FBI prepared a joke book titled *United Klowns of America*, described in headquarters memos as "light in presentation" but still "a serious effort at counterintelligence." G-men also created a front group, the National Committee for Domestic Tranquility, that was described in FBI reports as "a Bureau-approved vehicle for attacking Klan policies and disputes from a low-key, common sense, and patriotic perspective." Claiming active chapters in 11 states, the paper group published a regular newsletter urging Klansmen to quit the KKK and support "our boys" fighting in Vietnam. The FBI had 2,000 Klan informants on its payroll by September 1965, when G-men assisted the House Committee on Un-American Activities with a public investigation of the KKK. Friendly authors such as Don Whitehead described a series of physical confrontations between FBI agents and Klansmen, prompting Hoover to boast that Klan members were "afraid to 'mix' with our Agents," but the only such incident reliably documented involved G-men firing random shots into a saloon patronized by Mississippi Klansmen.

The Bureau's last official COINTELPRO operation, targeting "Black Nationalist-Hate Groups," was launched on August 25, 1967, with a memo from Hoover that read:

> The purpose of this new counterintelligence endeavor is to expose, disrupt, misdirect, discredit, or otherwise neutralize the activities of black nationalist, hate-type organizations and groupings, their leadership, spokesmen, membership, and supporters, and to counter their propensity for violence and civil disorder. The activities of all such groups of intelligence interest to this Bureau must be followed on a continuous basis so we will be in a position to promptly take advantage of all opportunities for counterintelligence and to inspire action in instances where circumstances warrant. The pernicious background of such groups, their duplicity, and devious

maneuvers must be exposed to public scrutiny where such publicity will have a neutralizing effect. Efforts of the various groups to consolidate their forces or to recruit new or youthful adherents must be frustrated. No opportunity should be missed to exploit through counterintelligence techniques the organizational and personal conflicts of the leadership of the groups and where possible an effort should be made to capitalize upon existing conflicts between competing black nationalist organizations.

The scope of Hoover's plan was demonstrated by a list of target organizations ranging from the wholly nonviolent Congress of Racial Equality and Southern Christian Leadership Conference (SCLC) to the more militant Student Nonviolent Coordinating Committee (SNCC) and the separatist Nation of Islam. Of the lot, only the latter group truly qualified as a "black nationalist" group, and none of the others came close to preaching "race hatred," except in Hoover's private definition of the term (generally encompassing any black critics of racial segregation).

The campaign undertaken in 1967 was merely an extension of the FBI's harassment directed at sundry black activists since 1919. Marcus Garvey was an early victim of such methods, imprisoned in 1925, and his case was far from unique. As in previous COINTELPRO campaigns, G-men concocted anonymous letters and leaflets, cartoons and press leaks to embarrass black leaders. Adultery was a favorite charge, highlighting the white racist's preoccupation with black sexuality. False arrests and frame-ups were common, as the Bureau coordinated its efforts with local police departments across the U.S. Agents provocateurs encouraged various targets to break the law, often supplying guns or other contraband at FBI expense in order to facilitate arrests.

On February 29, 1968, a new memo warned Bureau field offices of a "tremendous increase in black nationalist activity," demanding that the COINTELPRO campaign launched six months earlier "should be expanded and [its] goals should be reiterated in the field." Four days later, another headquarters memo reminded all G-men of their duty to "prevent the coalition of militant black nationalist groups"; "prevent the rise of a 'messiah' who could unify, and electrify, the militant black nationalist movement"; "prevent violence on the part of black nationalist groups"; "prevent militant black nationalist groups and leaders from gaining respectability"; and "prevent the long-range growth of militant black nationalist organizations, especially among youth."

The four groups named specifically as "primary targets" in Hoover's memo of March 4, 1968, were the SCLC, SNCC, the Nation of Islam, and the Revolutionary Action Movement (RAM), but the director's focus was already shifting toward the California-based Black Panther Party, soon named by Hoover as "the greatest threat to the internal security of the country." FBI files from the late 1960s reveal that Hoover's commitment to "prevent violence" by black militants was a cynical sham. In fact, from Southern California to Chicago and New York, G-men did everything within their power to *cause* violence between rival groups—pitting Black Panthers against one another, promoting street warfare between Black Panthers and Ron Karenga's US (United Slaves) and the Blackstone Rangers, encouraging members of the militant Jewish Defense League to attack black spokesmen whom the FBI accused of anti-Semitism. Multiple deaths in several states resulted directly from the Bureau's effort to "exploit conflicts" between militant groups.

When not promoting murder, FBI agents indulged in more conventional forms of harassment, including collaboration with local police in a systematic campaign of raids and false arrests. FBI memos from 1967 boast that RAM members were "arrested on every possible charge until they could no longer make bail" and thus "spent most of the summer in jail." The following year, police cooperating with an FBI agent provocateurs invaded the Chicago Black Panther office and killed chairman FRED HAMPTON while he slept. In California, Panther member Elmer Pratt was framed for murder and spent most of three decades in prison.

The FBI's last official COINTELPRO campaign began with a memo dated May 9, 1968, which read in part:

Our Nation is undergoing an era of disruption and violence caused to a large extent by various individuals generally connected with the New Left. Some of these activists urge revolution in America and call for the defeat of the United States in Vietnam. They continually and falsely allege police brutality and do not hesitate to use unlawful acts to further their so-called causes. The New Left has on many occasions viciously and scurrilously attacked the Director and the Bureau in an attempt to hamper our investigation of it and to drive us off the college campuses. With this in mind, it is our recommendation that a new Counterintelligence Program be designed to neutralize the New Left and the Key Activists. The Key Activists are those individuals who are the moving forces behind the New Left and on whom we have intensified our investigations.

The purpose of this program is to expose, disrupt and otherwise neutralize the activities of this group and persons connected with it. It is hoped that with this new program their violent and illegal activities may be reduced if not curtailed.

Contrary to the Bureau's stated goals, FBI informants and agents provocateurs significantly increased violence on the part of various New Left organizations. A partial list of those felons who received their salaries and orders from the FBI includes: *Horace Packer,* who admitted supplying student radicals in Seattle with drugs, weapons and components for Molotov cocktails; *Alfred Burnett,* who built and supplied the bomb carried by Vietnam veteran Larry Ward on the day he was ambushed and killed by Seattle police, in May 1970; *Robert Hardy,* who supplied "90 percent" of the burglary tools used by radicals to invade a New Jersey draft board; *Charles Grimm,* a participant in ARSON and student riots at the University of Alabama; *Larry Grathwohl,* who bombed a Cincinnati school in 1969; *William Lemmer,* arrested with illegal weapons and held for psychiatric evaluation after infiltrating an antiwar group; *Reinhold Mohr,* jailed while trying to sell Ohio activists a rocket launcher and machine gun; and *Howard Godfrey,* employed by G-men to lead California's Secret Army Organization, whose violent acts included bombings and the attempted murder of a university professor. With such individuals on the payroll, it is perhaps no surprise that former New Left radicals blame the FBI for a majority of bombings and similar acts attributed to the movement.

The Nixon administration assisted FBI efforts against the New Left with multiple conspiracy charges against movement leaders, resulting in trials described by historian William Manchester as "an unparalleled series of judicial disasters for the government." In terms of curbing leftist influence, the Bureau's campaign was a resounding failure. Most of the 862 alleged bombings or bombing attempts investigated by G-men between January 1969 and April 1970 remain unsolved today, perhaps because investigation would expose the crimes committed by agents provocateurs. Of 13,400 persons arrested in New Left demonstrations during May 1971, 12,653 were discharged without trial; 122 were convicted, while another 625 pled guilty or no contest—but all such pleas were voided and expunged by a federal court in 1974, on grounds of police coercion. In January 1975 the victims of those mass arrests were awarded $12 million in punitive damages. The New Left, meanwhile, collapsed in 1972 after its raison d'être was removed by American withdrawal from Vietnam.

The FBI's harassment network suffered terminal embarrassment in March 1971, after burglars invaded the Bureau's office in Media, Pennsylvania, and stole several thousand COINTELPRO documents, which soon found their way to the press. Hoover formally canceled all COINTELPRO activities a month later, although their full scope would not be revealed until several years after his death. According to records exposed by the CHURCH COMMITTEE in 1975, the FBI mounted at least 2,218 separate COINTELPRO actions against various groups and individuals between 1957 and 1971; those campaigns included at least 1,884 illegal wiretaps and 583 warrantless bugs, plus 55,804 pieces of mail illegally opened and read by G-men.

It would be comforting to accept the FBI's claim that such methods have not been used since April 1971, but evidence to the contrary is plentiful. The Church Committee found that during 1972-74, despite the alleged ban on all COINTELPRO techniques, FBI agents installed another 421 illegal wiretaps and 114 warrantless bugs, while stealing another 2,042 pieces of personal mail. As embarrassing as those disclosures were, they still had no apparent effect on covert Bureau policy. Organizations such as the American Indian Movement (AIM), Earth First!, the Committee in Solidarity with the People of El Salvador, and various Puerto Rican nationalist groups suffered attacks indistinguishable from COINTELPRO techniques throughout the 1970s, 1980s, and early 1990s. On November 26, 1973, some 31 months after all such programs supposedly ended, Agent Richard W. Held penned a memo to headquarters, suggesting that "Los Angeles and Minneapolis consider possible COINTELPRO measured to further disrupt AIM leadership." Terrorism remains a frequent excuse for extralegal measures on the part of federal agents, and sweeping provisions of the USA PATRIOT ACT suggest that the use of such methods may be increasing.

See also: FEDERAL BUREAU OF INVESTIGATION.

Colburn, Wayne B. (1919–1983)

Born in 1919, Wayne Colburn served in the U.S. Marine Corps after high school, then joined the SAN DIEGO POLICE DEPARTMENT in March 1943. He was soon recalled to Marine service in World War II, but returned to police work in San Diego during 1951. Over the next 11 years he rose through the SDPD ranks, from sergeant to lieutenant, then captain, and finally inspector supervising the entire Patrol Division. That same year, 1962, witnessed a change as Colburn left his San Diego post to join the U.S. MARSHALS SERVICE, commanding the newly formed Southern District of California. CORRUPTION charges snared service director Carl Turner in 1969, and Attorney General JOHN NEWTON MITCHELL named Colburn to replace him in January 1970.

Colburn's tenure would not be an easy one. By 1972 the Watergate scandal had enveloped President Richard Nixon's administration, and ex–Attorney General Mitchell would soon be on his way to prison, while Nixon was forced to resign in disgrace. Before that climax, though, the Marshals Service—and its new Special Operations Group (SOG), created by Colburn—ran into conflict with the American Indian Movement (AIM). After initial skirmishes at Alcatraz Island and the Twin Cities Naval Air Station in 1971, Colburn's marshals joined the FBI to confront a major AIM siege at Wounded Knee, South Dakota in 1973. Gun battles there left two AIM members dead and one marshal paralyzed for life, while FBI charges against various AIM leaders were thrown out of federal court on grounds of official misconduct.

The Wounded Knee fiasco cast a pall over Colburn's tenure with the Marshals Service. Attorney General RICHARD KLEINDIENST granted the service full bureau status on May 10, 1973, but successor ELLIOT LEE RICHARDSON revoked that order on October 17, 1974. Through all the waffling, appointment of marshals remained a political function, with candidates nominated by members of the U.S. Senate. Colburn retired in May 1976 and died at his California home on June 21, 1983.

See also: FEDERAL BUREAU OF INVESTIGATION.

Collins, Ben (d. 1906)

Nothing is known of this Native American lawman's early years. He was presumably born in the Oklahoma Indian Territory, where he served first as an Indian policeman, then won appointment as a deputy U.S. marshal in 1898. His refusal to compromise with wealthy white miscreants produced complaints, which Collins balanced with a series of sensational arrests. In 1905 Collins tried to arrest Port Pruitt, a prominent resident of Emet, but Pruitt refused to submit and drew a pistol. Collins was faster, firing a shot that left Pruitt partially paralyzed. Pruitt's charges of attempted murder were later dismissed, but he harbored a deadly grudge, offering $500 to any gunman who would eliminate Collins.

The first candidate, a friend of Collins, took a $200 down payment from Pruitt, then reported the plot to Collins and left Oklahoma with Pruitt's money. A few months later, on August 1, 1906, Collins was shot and killed from ambush by ex-lawman and contract assassin James "Killin' Jim" Miller (a principal in the FRAZER-MILLER FEUD). Miller was indicted for murder, but the charge was later dropped. A lynch mob hanged him at Ada, in February 1908, following another murder-for-hire.

Collins, Morgan (1865–?)

Born in 1865, Morgan Collins initially hoped to become a physician. He studied at Bennett Medical College but failed to graduate, although his knowledge of forensic medicine would serve him well in his second-choice career. Collins joined the CHICAGO POLICE DEPARTMENT in 1888, under Republican mayor John Roche, in an age when new recruits were chosen mainly on the basis of political affiliation. His career was interrupted briefly in 1897, when Chief Joseph Kipley fired all the city's Republican cops, but Collins soon returned to duty and rose to a captain's rank at the GOP-dominated East Chicago Avenue Station. Reform mayor William Dever, though a Democrat, chose Collins to replace Chief CHARLES C. FITZMORRIS in April 1923.

By that time, Chicago was overrun by bootleggers and racketeers who fattened on the black-market profits spawned by PROHIBITION. Public murders in broad daylight were routine, and the deposed regime of Mayor William "Big Bill" Thompson had set new standards for civic CORRUPTION. Dever cast himself as a reformer, and Collins was the broom he selected to sweep Chicago clean. Collins promised the city "full jails and a populous morgue," but his first challenge was internal. Soon after his appointment, Collins fired five captains, threatened others with dismissal if they could not curb the city's rising crime rate, and returned 200 sergeants from desk jobs to street patrol. "The people of Chicago," he declared, "are entitled to a dollar's worth of protection for each dollar of the $11 million they pay annually for the support of the police."

When mobster Johnny Torrio offered Collins $1,000 per day to ignore bootleg traffic, Collins responded with a press conference condemning graft and sweeping raids that closed 4,600 of the city's 6,565 illegal saloons by early 1924. As violence escalated, he issued a "shoot-to-kill" order on mobsters, equipping his men with open-topped cars to facilitate running gun battles. Still, it was politics as usual in Chicago, Democrats lobbying Mayor Dever for a chief of their own, complaining that "[n]ever in its history was the Police Department so closely hooked up with the underworld as it is today."

Dever supported Collins and ordered more speakeasy raids, but neither man could buck the Windy City tide indefinitely. Voters returned Big Bill Thompson to office in 1927, and Collins was soon replaced by Chief MICHAEL HUGHES. Leaving the police department after 39 years, Collins told reporters, "I have faced the hardest job of any police chief in Chicago. The Prohibition law and the racketeers that exist in its violation presented a problem that no other police chief in the history of the world had to face."

Colorado Bureau of Investigation

In 1951 Colorado legislators began a long-running debate over creation of a central crime bureau and laboratory for the Rocky Mountain State. Five separate bills were introduced that year, to launch the project, but all met defeat in the General Assembly. Over the next 16 years, the DENVER POLICE DEPARTMENT provided lab and identification services for smaller departments on a limited basis, but that service proved inadequate to cope with rising crime rates. Finally, in 1967, the Colorado Bureau of Investigation (CBI) was created as an adjunct to the state attorney general's office. Later legislation transferred the CBI to Colorado's Department of Local Affairs, then (in July 1984) to the Department of Public Safety.

While the CBI's headquarters remain in Denver, branch offices subsequently opened in Montrose (1973), in Pueblo (1981), and in Durango (1999). Functions of the CBI include: criminal investigations and fugitive apprehension; forensic crime scene investigations; gaming investigations; investigation of ORGANIZED CRIME; providing scientific laboratory services; maintaining sex offender registrations; compiling and distributing a list of missing children; establishing and maintaining a statewide law enforcement telecommunications system; processing criminal and civil identification files and records; supporting a computerized data base for law enforcement information sharing; conducting instant background checks on the transfer of firearms; operating the statewide uniform crime reporting system.

Colorado State Patrol

Colorado boasted only three law enforcement agencies in April 1935, when state legislators created a new Colorado State Highway Courtesy Patrol within the Department of Highways. Five months later, 44 men were chosen from a pool of 7,500 applicants for training at Camp George West, then scattered statewide upon graduation. Over the next decade, manpower increased to 118, including a chief, assistant chief, six captains, 10 sergeants and 100 patrolmen. In 1947 the unit was renamed the Colorado State Patrol.

Creation of the CSP produced a groundswell of public opposition, especially from civil libertarians and organized labor unions who recalled the LUDLOW MASSACRE of April 1914. Various state officials also feared that the new unit would undermine their authority, prompting legislators to clearly define the CSP's responsibilities. As detailed in the 1935 Patrol Act, "it shall be their duty to promote safety, protect human life and preserve the highways of Colorado by the intelligent, courteous, and strict enforcement of the laws and regulation of this state relating to highways." Courtesy

remains a watchword with the CSP, at least in theory, while criminal investigations are carried out by local agencies or the COLORADO BUREAU OF INVESTIGATION.

computer crimes

Computer crime is not a new phenomenon. The first record of computer-related crimes dates from 1958, and 374 cases of "computer abuse" were logged by 1976 (including four cases of frustrated owners shooting their own computers). The first federal prosecution of computer crime occurred in 1966. Today, with new advances in technology and the advent of the Internet, U.S. law enforcement agencies and civilian watchdog groups receive complaints numbering in the tens of thousands each year. A representative sampling of "cybercrimes" includes:

Hacking: Whether performed by bored, precocious "nerds" or sophisticated gangs linked to ORGANIZED CRIME, illicit penetration of corporate and government computers by unauthorized insiders is today viewed as a significant threat to national security and global communications infrastructures, "Idealistic" hackers deny any interest in monetary gain and insist their penetrations are designed to preserve "freedom of information," but purely mercenary hackers (sometimes dubbed *crackers* to emphasize their criminal motives) dedicate themselves to large-scale theft of cash, confidential information and the like. Another problem area, dubbed "darkside hacking" by computer aficionados, involves deliberate cybervandalism of systems and Web sites. By their own estimate, federal investigators detect barely 10 percent of all attempted intrusions each year.

Theft of cash: In 1994 Russian hacker Vladimir Levin stole more than $10 million from Citibank Corporation without ever setting foot in the U.S. Internet transfers of cash and securities between banks and other financial institutions are routine today, subject to interference and diversion by cyberbandits who invade corporate systems, steal passwords and bank account numbers, and divert huge sums to accounts under their own control. Techniques such as "lapping" (employee diversion of incoming cash to a bogus account) and "kiting" (use of normal processing delays to create the appearance of assets where none exist) victimize financial institutions from within. Another form of internal theft, "salami slicing," occurs when employees shave small sums from numerous sources over time. Automatic teller machines, meanwhile, lose an estimated $200 million per year to various frauds. At the same time, Internet credit card fraud, involving theft or counterfeiting of credit and debit card numbers by the hundreds of thousands, levies a staggering toll against various targets. The problem's gravity may be judged by Visa Corporation's report for 1997, listing losses of $490 million as an improvement over previous years.

"Phreaking": Akin to hackers, both in spirit and technique, "phreakers" are those who employ various devices to cheat telephone companies on long-distance calls. Once again, some "purists" profess to regard their actions as a blow for freedom of communication, while others cheerfully turn a profit on sale of charge-evasion devices and stolen calling card numbers. No precise figures for telephone fraud are available, but industry spokespersons suggest that long-distance fraud costs the industry $4 billion to $8 billion yearly. All forms of telecommunications fraud combined may top $15 billion per year, with wireless fraud alone exceeding $1 billion.

"Data diddling": Employed in a variety of settings, this technique involves manipulation or falsification of computer data for personal profit or other illegal ends. One case, reported in 1997, involved crackers who penetrated the computers of maritime insurance companies, inserting registration data for nonexistent ships and buying large insurance policies on the mythical vessels, then "sinking" them to collect the payoffs.

Extortion and/or blackmail: As before the computer's invention, these crimes involve coercion of tribute payments to prevent some threatened action by the extortionist or blackmailer. On June 12, 1996, the *Times* of London reported that various banks and investment firms in the U.S. and Britain had "secretly paid ransom to prevent costly computer meltdown and a collapse in confidence among the customers." None of the threats or the payoffs (up to £13 million per incident) had been reported to police. Florida resident Michael Pitelis was jailed in August 2000 for attempting to extort $1 million from a Massachusetts corporation, threatening to expose software secrets. That same month, Kazakhstan native Oleg Zezov was charged with blackmailing the Bloomberg financial news company for $200,000. In May 2001 Russian operator Alexei Ivanov faced charges of victimizing firms across the U.S. with similar threats.

Bootlegging and piracy: Lumped together by prosecutors as "INTELLECTUAL PROPERTY THEFT," these offenses include any unauthorized duplication and/or distribution of copyrighted material. The items most often bootlegged include computer software, motion pictures and music, but any material covered by U.S. or international copyrights is likewise subject to misappropriation. Profit motives were once deemed essential for prosecution in such cases, but enactment of the No Electronic Theft (NET) Act on December 16, 1997, criminalized software piracy and other forms of bootlegging whether the items were sold or given away as a "public service."

Malicious programming: Since the 1980s thousands of computer viruses and worms have been unleashed upon the Internet by programmers around the world. Some are benign, with no more impact on their host computers than a brief, amusing video display, while others cause global damage to corporate and personal computers estimated in billions of dollars. Certain nations spawn a disproportionate number of virus writers—160 separate viruses were traced to Bulgaria alone during 1989–93—but no part of the world is presently immune. While most malicious programs are broadcast at random, often in the form of infected e-mail attachments, some are written with specific targets in mind. Corporate victims fall prey most often to disgruntled employees, while government computer systems may be targeted by foreign agents or domestic activists. "Logic bombs"—destructive codes that lie dormant within a computer until triggered by a specific signal—have been found in the systems of several U.S. agencies.

Espionage: Whether corporate or political, spying thrives on the Internet. In 1986 a systems administrator at the Lawrence Berkeley Laboratory in California found that crackers from "Chaos," a West German group, had hijacked the computer account of a former employee and used it to steal U.S. military data for sale to Russia's KGB. Three Chaos members were indicted for espionage, while a fourth died mysteriously. The survivors were convicted in 1990, drawing prison terms of 20 months to five years. Eight months later, a group calling itself "Masters of Downloading" claimed to have cracked the Pentagon's communications network, stealing software for a military satellite system and threatening its sale to terrorists, but the threat was never carried out.

Cyberstalking: While most of the crimes discussed so far are financially or politically motivated, cyberstalking is distinctly personal. As malicious individuals in daily life stalk celebrities, relatives, ex-lovers, and friends, so their counterparts in cyberspace spew venom online. E-mail "bombing" is one common harassment technique, swamping the target with unwanted "spam." Other forms of cyberstalking include posting personal data or photos online or hacking of personal computers. Cyberangels, a civilian volunteer group pledged to opposing online stalkers, reports an average of 650 complaints each day to the group's website.

Child pornography and solicitation: Production and sale of child pornography was banned by federal law in 1977, with "children" legally defined in 1984 as any person under 18 years of age. Further U.S. legislation has since been enacted to ban advertisement of child pornography (1986); use of computers to transmit, sell or receive child porn (1988); possession of three or more images depicting sex with children (1990); inducement of minors to participate in pornography (1996); and possession of any image that *appears* to depict sex with children, even when the models are adults or where "virtual" children are used in place of live models (1996). To date, despite prosecution of defendants including teachers, priests, judges and other public officials, legislation seems largely ineffective in curbing child pornography, particularly that which is produced outside the U.S.

"Mousetrapping": Designed to create a captive audience for otherwise unwelcome advertising, "mousetrapping" involves the creation of alluring Web sites with built-in snares that prevent online viewers from escaping once they log onto the site. The undisputed king of American mousetrapping, Pennsylvania operator John Zuccarini, has reportedly earned millions from his many Web sites, while logging more than 60 lawsuits from the Federal Trade Commission.

Identity theft: This offense differs from credit card fraud in both its scope and potential damage to victims. Felons who obtain sufficient personal data about an intended target, whether from online sources or primitive "dumpster diving," are often able to create their own persona with someone else's name, Social Security number, and other vital information. While certain bizarre cases of celebrity impersonators rank among the most notorious incidents—a West Indian immigrant spent years posing as the son of comedian Bill Cosby—middle-class victims suffer the greatest damage. In one egregious case the ex-convict impostor ran up more than $100,000 in credit card debts, obtained a federal home loan, and purchased various high-ticket items before filing bankruptcy, all in his victim's name. The victim and his wife spent more than $15,000 to restore their credit and reputations, while the thief escaped with a brief jail term (for using a false name to purchase a gun) and paid no restitution. That case and others like it prompted Congress to pass legislation on identity theft in 1998.

Internet fraud: These crimes occur so often and evolve so rapidly that no detailed accounting is possible, but certain broad categories are noteworthy. Online *auctions* generate more fraud complaints than any other Internet activity, most commonly when buyers bid on some valuable piece of merchandise and receive counterfeits or nothing at all. Retail fraud involves the same basic scams, including nondelivery or bait-and-switch techniques. Business opportunity fraud advertises spurious "work at home" schemes, generating millions of "spam" e-mail messages daily, bilking thousands of gullible victims for wasted "processing fees." Money laundering, while not a fraud upon the average consumer, uses financial institutions and charities to "wash" vast sums including profits from organized crime and forbidden political contributions. Investment fraud includes manipulation of securities via the "pump-and-dump" technique (inflating prices of worthless stocks before they are sold) and "cybersmear" campaigns that deflate stock prices by attacking a firm's reputation. In extreme cases such activities not only defraud traders and damage individual companies, but may also affect the stock market as a whole. Cyberfraud allegations are investigated by the Internet Fraud Complaint Center, a joint operation of the FBI and the JUSTICE DEPARTMENT's National White Collar Crime Center.

computer databases

Gone are the days when police departments were isolated by geography and forced to toil without assistance on baffling crimes. Today, any forces with a computer and a telephone line can tap vast databases of information to assist in linking unsolved cases, retrieving criminal records, or identifying corpses and missing persons. Some agencies still refuse to participate, for personal or political reasons, but most have greeted the 21st-century cyber age with open arms. The major databases presently available to police nationwide include (alphabetically):

AFIS (Automated Fingerprint Identification System): Administered by the FBI Laboratory in Washington, D.C., AFIS maintains computerized fingerprint records of more than 35 million individuals. Subjects include convicted felons and persons booked on criminal charges, together with U.S. military personnel and employees in various jobs that require fingerprinting (various government posts, public education, etc.). The various uses of AFIS include swift identification of suspects in custody (who may give false names) and unidentified corpses, as well as screening of job applicants and participants in various public benefits programs (Aid to Families with Dependent Children, etc.).

CODIS (*Combined DNA Index System*): Another program administered by the FBI Laboratory, CODIS began in 1990 and today maintains thousands of DNA profiles available at need for comparison with genetic evidence collected by local law enforcement agencies. CODIS is presently divided into two sub-indexes: the Forensic Index contains DNA profiles from evidence found at crime scenes, while the Offender Index contains profiles for individuals convicted of sex crimes and other violent offenses. Matches from the Forensic Index are used to link (or exclude) suspected serial crimes, while "hits" from the Offender Index often link known felons to crimes as yet unsolved.

DRUGFIRE: This FBI program mirrors the ATF Bulletproof and IBIS databases, preserving computerized images of bullets recovered in various criminal cases. As indicated by its title, the early program dealt primarily with drug-related murders and nonfatal shootings, but evidence from other cases (sniping, gang-related crimes, etc.) is now also included for comparison.

FISH (*Forensic Information System for Handwriting*): Used in the examination of questioned documents, various FISH software programs convert handwriting features into mathematical algorithms, storing exemplars from known subjects for comparison against future samples of unknown origin. The U.S. SECRET SERVICE pioneered this program, which is also used today by the German law enforcement agency Bundeskriminalamt (BKA). BKA spokesmen claim that of 90,000 subjects whose handwriting is stored in their database, "the system has determined that no two writers write alike, nor do they share the same combination of handwriting characteristics." Other students of handwriting—particularly those employed by defense attorneys—strongly dispute the reliability of handwriting evidence, whether the "matches" are made by computers or human examiners.

IBIS (*Integrated Ballistics Identification System*): Administered by the BUREAU OF ALCOHOL, TOBACCO, FIREARMS AND EXPLOSIVES (ATF), IBIS parallels the FBI's DRUGFIRE database without that program's relatively narrow focus on drug-related shootings. Subdivisions of the database include *Bulletproof* (with digital images of bullets recovered from victims or crimes scenes) and *Brasscatcher* (with images of cartridge cases). In either case, impressions left by a gun's barrel, firing pin, or extractor permit examiners to confirm or refute links between newly discovered ballistics evidence and previous shootings. While incapable of indentifying triggermen (or women), IBIS can made a positive match between bullets from multiple crime scenes and a particular weapon in custody.

NCIC (*National Crime Information Center*): Launched by the U.S. JUSTICE DEPARTMENT in the early 1980s and presently headquartered in Clarksburg, West Virginia, NCIC is the mother of all law enforcement computer databases. Its archived information (submitted by various federal, state, local, and foreign agencies) includes detailed criminal records, information on fugitives from justice, details of stolen property (descriptions, serial numbers, etc.), and missing persons. Information stored by the NCIC is catalogued as follows:

- *Wanted persons* include those with outstanding federal warrants; persons who have committed or been linked to felonies or serious misdemeanors in various jurisdictions (including probation and parole violators); subjects of "temporary felony wants"; juveniles who have been adjudicated delinquent and who have escaped from custody (even though no arrest warrants were issued); and individuals charged with offenses committed in foreign countries, which would be felonies if committed in the United States.

- *Individuals charged with serious or significant offenses* include violent felons with three or more convictions and any other convicted criminals whose records and fingerprints are submitted to NCIC.

- *Missing persons* include subjects of any age who are reported missing and whose physical or mental disability places them in danger; persons missing under circumstances indicating a risk to personal safety (i.e., abduction); persons missing after a catastrophe; and any missing minors (as defined in the jurisdiction of their residency).

- *Potential assassins* identified by the U.S. Secret Service as posing potential danger to the president of the United States or any other authorized protectee.

- *Members of violent criminal gangs,* including those identified as gang members by self-admission or testimony of reliable informants; persons who frequent gang areas, associate with known gang members and display gang symbols or tattoos; and persons arrested multiple times with known gang members for offenses consistent with gang activity.

- *Members of terrorist organizations,* identified by the same criteria applied to violent gang members above, or via information gathered by various intelligence agencies worldwide. "Terrorist" groups are broadly defined as any that attempt to intimidate or coerce a civilian population, influence government policies through violence or coercion, or to affect the conduct of governments by criminal action (including kidnapping).

- *Unidentified persons* on file include any unidentified deceased person; any person living or dead whose identity cannot be ascertained (e.g., amnesiacs, infants, etc.); unidentified catastrophe victims; and unidentified body parts recovered under various circumstances.

- *Stolen vehicles,* vehicle parts, and/or vehicles sought by police in connection with felonies or serious misdemeanors.

- *Stolen license plates.*

- *Stolen boats.*

- *Firearms* reported stolen and those whose ownership has not been established.

- *Stolen articles,* including any item readily identified by serial numbers or other distinctive features.

- *Securities*—including stock certificates, bonds, bills, debentures and bank notes—which have been stolen, embezzled or counterfeited, identified by serial numbers.

Comstock, Anthony (1844–1915)

A reputed descendant of Christopher Columbus, born at New Canaan, Connecticut, on March 7, 1844, Anthony Comstock served with the Union Army in the Civil War. That experience apparently heightened his fundamentalist religious fervor and prompted a postwar move to New York City, where he joined the YMCA as a crusader against "obscenity." By 1872 he led the Society for Suppression of Vice, dedicated to supervising public morality. Pressure from Comstock and his followers secured passage in March 1873 of a federal statute banning transportation of any "obscene, lewd, or lascivious" material through the U.S. mail. The Comstock Law further provided:

That whoever, within the District of Columbia or any of the Territories of the United States, shall sell, or shall offer to sell, or to lend, or to give away, or in any manner to exhibit, or shall otherwise publish or offer to publish in any manner, or shall have in his possession, for any such purpose or purposes, an obscene book, pamphlet, paper, writing, advertisement, circular, print, picture, drawing or other representation, figure, or image on or of paper of other material, or any cast instrument, or other article of an immoral nature, or any drug or medicine, or any article whatever, for the prevention of conception, or for causing unlawful abortion, or shall advertise the same for sale, or shall write or print, or cause to be written or printed, any card, circular, book, pamphlet, advertisement, or notice of any kind, stating when, where, how, or of whom, or by what means, any of the articles in this section, can be purchased or obtained, or shall manufacture, draw, or print, or in any wise make any of such articles, shall be deemed guilty of a misdemeanor, and on conviction thereof in any court of the United States, he shall be imprisoned at hard labor in the penitentiary for not less than six months nor more than five years for each offense, or fined not less than one hundred dollars nor more than two thousand dollars, with costs of court.

To guarantee enforcement of his law, Comstock took an unpaid position as a postal inspector in New York, personally arresting abortionists, pornographers, birth-control advocates and anyone else he deemed "immoral." Although he had no legal jurisdiction outside the Post Office, Comstock's raids were virtually unchallenged until 1913, when he launched a campaign to ban the nude portrait *September Morn,* by Paul Chabas. The debate surrounding that censorship drive occupied Comstock until his death, on September 21, 1915.

See also: POSTAL INSPECTION SERVICE.

Conlisk, John B., Sr.

Richard Lindberg, unofficial historian of the CHICAGO POLICE DEPARTMENT, describes John Conlisk, Sr. as "arguably the most powerful man" on the force, despite the fact that "few outside City Hall knew who he was." Conlisk served as top administrative aide to five police chiefs between 1931 and 1960—John Alcock, James Allman, John Prendergast, Timothy O'Connor, and Kyran Phelan—during which time he processed every transfer and promotion order, authorized all budgets, requisitions and payment vouchers. In 1955 Conlisk rejected Mayor Richard Daley's offer to become chief of police, preferring to retain his post behind the scenes. Chief ORLAND WILSON fired Conlisk in 1960, then surprised observers by promoting Conlisk's son (John, Jr.) to serve as deputy chief. Conlisk, Jr. had risen to the department's top spot by 1968, when televised POLICE RIOTS marred the Democratic National Convention. Five years later, he resigned in the midst of a CORRUPTION scandal that saw 37 officers indicted for bribery and conspiracy.

Connecticut State Police

Created in 1903, the Connecticut State Police began life as a five-man squad created to combat illicit liquor manufacturing and sale. Those early officers traveled by rail and kept in touch haphazardly, by telegraph or private telephone. When motorcycles were provided during World War I, they ran in all weather, patrolmen stuffing their uniforms with newspaper to ward off winter chills. Radio communication lagged behind the advent of patrol cars, requiring a central dispatcher to telephone various rural gas stations, which hoisted small flags to attract patrolmen on their rounds. Twelve-hour shifts remained routine into the 1960s, but the CSP was modernized in other ways, leading the state with its adoption of new law enforcement technology.

During its century of service to Connecticut, the CSP established one of the country's first K-9 UNITS, organized a team of scuba divers trained by the U.S. Navy, and established divisions including Major Crimes, Casino and Gambling, ORGANIZED CRIME, Emergency Services, Extradition, Intelligence, and a FORENSIC SCIENCE laboratory run by Dr. Henry Lee (known for his controversial testimony in the O.J. Simpson case). Since Connecticut sheriffs have no authority outside of courthouse security and prisoner transport, CSP officers combine highway patrols with rural law enforcement duties delegated in other states to county officers. Their duties thus include wide-ranging cases such as ARSON investigations, homicides, robberies, SEX CRIMES, street gangs, drug-related offenses and welfare fraud. In most cases, troopers are expected to carry out full-scale investigations on their own, without delegating the work to specialized units, and responding officers remain involved from start to finish even in complex cases such as SERIAL MURDER.

See also: DRUGS.

Connolly, John J., Jr. (b. 1940)

Boston native John Connolly, Jr., born in 1940, was a childhood neighbor and admirer of future mob boss James "Whitey" Bulger. By 1975, as an agent of the FBI's Boston field office, Connolly was assigned to recruit "Top Echelon INFORMANTS" in the Bureau's campaign against ORGANIZED CRIME. In the process, he forged an alliance with Bulger's ruthless Winter Hill Gang against the New England Mafia, forging an illicit combination that had tragic consequences for all concerned.

Recruitment of Bulger as an informant made Connolly a "star" within the FBI, a status he enjoyed until his retirement in 1990. Bulger's tips helped G-men score impressive victories against the Irish gang's Italian rivals, but those triumphs had a price. Presumably unknown to their superiors, Connolly and several other Boston agents were corrupted in the process. On an FBI salary of $60,000 per year, Connolly bought a $400,000 home in Boston and a $300,000 summer retreat on Cape Cod. The cash came from Bulger, and Connolly (with other G-men) repaid that largess by warning Bulger of impending sting operations and shielding him from prosecution on various charges, including multiple murder. At least four innocent defendants suffered FRAME-UPS and were jailed for life on false murder charges during 1965, while Bulger and his triggermen went free. (Two of the scapegoats died in prison, while two others—Peter Limone and John Salvati—survived to win exoneration after 30 years in custody.)

Bulger's free ride ended after Connolly retired to accept a lucrative post with Boston Edison. A new task force, including agents from the DRUG ENFORCEMENT ADMINISTRATION, built a narcotics case against Bulger in 1995, but friendly G-men tipped him once again and he escaped. (At this writing, in November 2004, Bulger remains a fugitive on the FBI's "TEN MOST WANTED FUGITIVES" list, with a $1 million price on his head.) Details of the FBI's protection racket were exposed in 1998, during pretrial hearings for Bulger associate Stephen Flemmi. Connolly was indicted a year later for accepting bribes and sharing the money with his former superior, Agent John Morris. A second indictment, filed in 2002, charged Connolly with leaking information to Bulger and Flemmi that led to three murders.

Connolly faced trial in Boston on May 6, 2002, charged with eight counts of racketeering, conspiracy, obstructing justice and making false statements. Codefendant Stephen Flemmi was charged with two counts of conspiracy. Prosecution witnesses included John Morris, various convicted mobsters and confessed murderers. Morris, testifying under a grant of immunity, wept on the stand as he admitted taking $7,000 from Bulger and soliciting $5,000 more from a Mafia bookie who doubled as an FBI informant. Connolly's lawyer denounced every witness, telling jurors, "You've never seen a bigger group of thieves and liars in your life," while prosecutor Michael Sullivan called Connolly "a Winter Hill gang operative masquerading as an FBI agent." The panel convicted Connolly on May 28, 2002. Judge John Tauro handed Connolly a 10-year prison term on September 16 and denied pleas for time to settle his affairs. At last report, Connolly still faced wrongful-death litigation from relatives of three Boston murder victims, who seek $35 million in damages from Connolly and the FBI.

See also: FEDERAL BUREAU OF INVESTIGATION.

Connor, Theophilus Eugene ("Bull") (1897–1973)

Born at Selma, Alabama, on July 11, 1897, Eugene Connor dropped out of high school to work as a railroad telegrapher and radio sportscaster (where he earned his famous nickname for fabricating plays—i.e., "shooting the bull"—during broadcasts). Elected to the state legislature in 1934, three years later he became Birmingham's commissioner of public safety, commanding the city's police and fire departments. Connor held that post until 1953, declining to seek reelection following a 1951 sex scandal. Voters returned him to office in 1957, on a pledge to maintain strict racial segregation in the face of mounting civil rights protests, and he held the job until Birmingham changed its form of municipal government in 1963.

Connor's die-hard RACISM quickly placed him in collaboration with the violent KU KLUX KLAN, protecting nightriders responsible for 40-plus bombings (see BOMBING AND BOMB SQUADS) between 1948 and 1963. Under Connor, the city was dubbed "Bombingham," while its largest black neighborhood earned the nickname "Dynamite Hill." On the rare occasions when he addressed the problem, Connor invariably blamed blacks for bombing their own homes and churches. An FBI memo filed on December 7, 1957, following the demolition of a black-owned house, reported that "Connor did not intend to solve this bombing." Seven months later, FBI headquarters ordered the Birmingham field office to "hold contacts with Connor to a minimum in view of his unsavory background." Connor reciprocated in October 1958, instructing his police to share no information with G-men on civil rights cases. (During the last decade of Connor's reign, Birmingham police were unofficially barred from attending the FBI National Academy.)

That breakdown in communication hardly mattered at the time, since FBI INFORMANTS in the Klan kept agents fully advised on Connor's negligence where TERRORISM was concerned. One such spy alerted Washington to Connor's May 1961 agreement to let Klansmen assault integrated freedom riders without police interference. Rather than warn the demonstrators, though, FBI agents provided Birmingham police (including officers with known Klan ties) with an itinerary of the buses, thus facilitating brutal attacks in Birmingham and Anniston. After the May 14 riot in his city, Connor explained the absence of police by claiming that most of his had stayed home for Mother's Day. Two years later, when a black witness identified one of Birmingham's

phantom bombers as an on-duty patrolman, FBI agents charged the witness with perjury and JUSTICE DEPARTMENT prosecutors sent him to prison for a year.

Stripped of his office by popular vote and court orders in summer 1963, Connor won election a year later to serve as president of Alabama's Public Service Commission. He held that post until 1972, when a series of strokes left him disabled and forced his retirement. A final stroke claimed his life on February 26, 1973.

See also: FEDERAL BUREAU OF INVESTIGATION.

consensual crimes

Consensual crimes—sometimes called "victimless" crimes—are statutory offenses in which all participants consent, generally without infringing on the rights or privacy of nonparticipants. The label covers a broad range of activity, including illegal gambling, prostitution, homosexual activity, DRUG offenses, traffic in "obscene" materials, and so forth.

Those who support prosecution of consensual crimes typically argue their case from a viewpoint of fundamental morality. Indeed, relegation of most such cases to police "vice" squads reveals the moralistic tenor of the statutes. Apologists maintain that consensual crimes are immoral (from a religious perspective), that they somehow undermine society or "the family," and that they fatten the coffers of ORGANIZED CRIME. Critics answer that religious fundamentalism has no place in American law, and that government regulation of various proscribed activities would drive gangsters out of the business. (The latter claim is undercut by recurring evidence of mob involvement in legal gambling across the United States.)

No recent figures are available for the public cost of prosecuting consensual crimes, but author Peter McWilliams provides a somewhat dated tabulation in his entertaining volume *Ain't Nobody's Business If You Do*. Writing in 1996, McWilliams noted that some 750,000 Americans were then incarcerated for consensual crimes, another 2 million were on parole for such offenses, an average of 4 million were arrested each year "for doing something that hurts no one but, potentially, themselves." In 1994 alone, "discretionary" arrests jailed 25,300 persons for vagrancy, 128,000 for "loitering," 713,200 for public drunkenness where no vehicles were involved, and 1.35 million for various drug offenses. An estimated $29 billion per year was spent in the 1990s to capture drug offenders, while enforcement of various other "vice" statutes pushed the public cost above $50 billion.

Proponents of legalization say most of that money and effort is wasted. In fact, they say, it does more harm than good by creating a vast untaxed black-market economy, identical to that which blossomed during PROHIBITION. Supporters of the status quo, meanwhile, sometimes become enmeshed in contradictions—demanding lower taxes and increased spending for law enforcement, or in extreme cases hailing rampant immorality as a cherished omen of the biblical last days yet urging police to suppress it. Based on history, there seems to be no prospect for a resolution of that conflict.

Cook, David J. (1840–1907)

Indiana native David Cook was born on August 12, 1840. He journeyed westward at age 17, winding up in Colorado, where he joined a cavalry regiment and found himself assigned as a detective, tracking Civil War deserters, spies, and smugglers. Fresh out of uniform in 1866, he was appointed to serve as Denver's city marshal, then won election as Arapaho County sheriff in 1869. His sterling record in that post won Cook appointment as a deputy U.S. marshal, followed by service as a major general of the Colorado state militia (1873–82). His achievements in the latter post included suppression of anti-Chinese rioting in 1880. His memoir, *Hands Up! or Twenty Years of Detective Work in the Mountains and on the Plains* (1897), remains a classic of frontier literature, detailing Cook's arrest of some 3,000 fugitives, including 50 murderers. Cook died in Denver on April 29, 1907.

Corbitt, Michael J. (b. 1944), and
James Dennis Keating (b. 1937)

Born on March 17, 1944, in Oak Park, Illinois, Michael Corbitt was raised in the Chicago suburbs of Willow Springs and Summit. A high school dropout who left home at 17, he found his first employment with a vending machine company, installing gambling paraphernalia in Cook County dives owned by members of ORGANIZED CRIME. From there, he moved on to run a gas station, and at age 21 joined the Willow Springs Police Department, an agency whose reputation for CORRUPTION belied its small size. In Willow Springs, patrolmen could be fired for failing to warn illegal gambling houses and brothels of impending raids by county sheriff's deputies. During his first year on the job, Corbitt was one of three Willow Springs officers briefly detained by county deputies to prevent them from alerting vice operators to raids in progress. No charges were filed, and he returned to duty the next day, but the incident provided Corbitt's introduction to James Keating, a sheriff's deputy who shared Corbitt's taste for easy money.

Keating, born on March 10, 1937, was the son of a Chicago cop who followed in his father's footsteps, join-

ing the CHICAGO POLICE DEPARTMENT in 1962. He was fired a month later, allegedly for beating a prisoner, and went to work as a detective for the Santa Fe Railroad. In 1964, with help from a political "rabbi," Keating found a job with the Cook County Sheriff's Police and soon gravitated to the vice and gambling unit, where graft proliferated. Known among his fellow officers as "the most personable guy you could meet," Keating always had his hand out and his eyes open for another scam, another opportunity to pad his bank account. By 1984 he was earning $34,000 per year on the job, supplementing that income with an estimated $2,000 to $8,000 each month on the side. His specialty was selling protection to bookies, gamblers, pimps—anyone, in short, who had reason to fear the police.

While Keating was learning the ropes on vice, Mike Corbitt was well on his way to becoming a local hero. In April 1967 he shot it out with three burglars in a Willow Springs cabinet shop, wounding one and forcing him to drop a bag containing some $2,000 in loot. Eighteen months later Corbitt shot and killed an alleged voyeur who resisted arrest and grabbed Corbitt's gun. A few months later, Corbitt transferred to the Summit Police Department, but returned to Willow Springs when Mayor John Rust offered him the chief's job. Sadly for Corbitt, Rust died before the April 1969 election, and his successor named Corbitt a lowly sergeant instead. In September 1971 Corbitt killed a drunken trucker who was shooting up a Willow Springs saloon. The death was ruled justifiable, and in 1973, with the election of Mayor William Bucki, Corbitt finally attained the chief's position he craved.

Already working countless crooked deals with Keating—himself lately promoted to lieutenant in the sheriff's office—Corbitt broadened his horizons as chief by openly consorting with known mobsters, collecting a fleet of fast cars, and enjoying an open credit line at Las Vegas casinos. A striking figure at 6 feet 2 inches and some 240 pounds, Corbitt preferred cowboy garb or an open shirt and gold chains to the traditional police uniform, and his lifestyle was equally unorthodox. When Chicago gangster Joe Tesca lost his legs in a Florida car bombing, Corbitt flew south to say good-bye in person, remaining at Tesca's bedside until the mobster died. It was clearly no joke, then, when Corbitt told a reporter that "Willow Springs is unique."

One of the men who made it all happen for Corbitt and Keating was Alan Masters, a local attorney and "fixer" in the grand Chicago tradition. Some Willow Springs police illegally referred drunk drivers to his office and got kickbacks in return, while others knew Masters as a contact in the murky realm of vice and gambling. In the mid-1970s Masters sold his own $45,000 home to Keating at a substantial discount;

when Keating turned around and sold it for $88,000 in 1981, Masters handled the closing. Before year's end, Masters handled divorce proceedings for Jim Keating and one of his subordinates, Lt. Howard Vanicki (the latter free of charge). In 1982, when Keating was promoted to serve on the sheriff's intelligence unit, a local mobster remarked, "Everyone was pleased, because he wasn't greedy and he would do almost anything."

And *almost anything,* as it turned out, included planning murders for his friends.

Mike Corbitt's lucrative career hit a snag in April 1981, when Mayor Frank Militello was elected on a promise to clean up Willow Springs, beginning with the graft-ridden police force. His first move, in May, was to fire Corbitt and 15 other officers, but Corbitt fought the dismissal in court, defiantly hanging onto his job for another 13 months. In June 1981 a grand jury subpoenaed Corbitt's financial records, going back six years, but he had covered his tracks well enough to avoid indictment. While the court battle dragged on, Corbitt told his underworld friends not to worry: If worse came to worst, he expected to be appointed as chief of police in Summit, where he would soon resume business as usual.

Alan Masters, meanwhile, faced divorce proceedings from his second wife, Dianne, in early 1982. On March 19 he filed a missing-person report with the Cook County sheriff's office, claiming that Dianne had vanished after a late dinner with fellow trustees of Moraine Valley Community College. Masters offered a $10,000 reward to the public, while Lt. Vanicki was assigned to investigate the case, supervised by Jim Keating. When Vanicki told reporters that Dianne "did not voluntarily disappear," hinting that Masters himself was involved, Keating reprimanded his subordinate for "not being objective" and threatened to remove him from the case.

Detectives caught a break on December 11, 1982, when a scuba diver hired to find cars found Dianne's car in a Willow Springs canal. Her corpse was in the trunk, partially nude, but with expensive jewelry intact. Autopsy results showed blunt-force trauma to the skull, followed by two close-range shots from a .22-caliber pistol. Prosecutors blocked attempts by Alan Masters to cremate his wife's remains, but he collected $100,000 life insurance, together with another $6,500 on her car.

In Willow Springs, new chief of police James Ross collaborated with FBI agents engaged in "Operation Safebet," a sting operation targeting corrupt police. One who accepted Bureau bribes was James Keating, who described Alan Masters as "the man who runs things" in Willow Springs. Keating noted that Dianne's disappearance had canceled a scheduled divorce hearing. At that, G-men noted, Keating "chuckled and thought it was kind of humorous, because it was so convenient." Operation Safebet included investigation

of a car-insurance scam, wherein some 70 vehicles were "stolen" and ditched in the same canal where divers found Dianne Masters in her Cadillac. One of the other cars belonged to Mike Corbitt's brother-in-law, Chicago policeman Anthony Barone. Barone cracked under interrogation and described the fraud as Corbitt's brainchild.

On August 29, 1985, James Keating was jailed on federal charges of bribery and racketeering. Alan Masters paid for Keating's defense, but jurors convicted him in May 1986, and he received a 15-year prison term. One year later, on May 20, 1987, Michael Corbitt was indicted on federal charges of bribery and extortion related to the Safebet sting. Convicted on all counts, Corbitt produced 40 letters from local politicians, priests, and teachers begging the court for leniency. He received a four-year sentence, then surprised prosecutors three months later by admitting that he had dumped Dianne Masters's car in the canal where it was found. He further admitted to plotting her murder with husband, Alan, but claimed he backed out of the scheme and didn't know her corpse was in the trunk when he sank her Cadillac.

On June 13, 1988, federal prosecutors indicted Corbitt, Keating, and Masters for plotting Dianne's murder, soliciting hired killers and concealing the crime. Keating was specifically accused of offering $25,000 to one potential shooter (who declined the job), while Corbitt was charged with dumping Dianne's corpse and car. The three defendants were also charged with bribery in their referral-kickback scheme, while Keating stood accused of splitting various gambling protection bribes with Masters. Masters also faced a charge of mail fraud for collecting Dianne's life insurance.

Trial convened on May 18, 1989, and jurors rendered their verdicts on June 13. They acquitted Masters of mail fraud but convicted him on two racketeering counts, including bribery of police and conspiring to murder his wife. Keating was likewise convicted on two counts, for accepting bribes and soliciting the hitman who refused to kill Dianne. Corbitt was convicted of bribery and dumping Dianne's vehicle. At sentencing on August 24, Masters drew a 40-year prison term and a $250,000 fine; Corbitt and Keating got 20 years each, those sentences running concurrently with their previous jail terms.

Cordes, John H. F. (1890–1966)

A child of immigrant parents, born in 1890 and raised in New York City's Greenwich Village, John "Dutchman" Cordes quit school at age 13 to become a runner on Wall Street. Later, he earned money as a professional bicycle racer and a police recruiter for the O'Brien Civil Service Institute. He tried out for the NEW YORK CITY

POLICE DEPARTMENT in April 1915, on a bet from one of his prospective clients, and was accepted for training as a patrolman. (The slaughterhouse laborer who challenged him was rejected.) During his tenure with NYPD, Cordes twice won the department's coveted Medal of Valor.

The first award derived from an incident in March 1923, when Cordes entered a Lexington Avenue cigar store with a robbery in progress. Unarmed, he suffered two gunshot wounds before disarming one of the bandits, killing the man with his own pistol. Cordes pursued and captured the second felon, then nearly died when he was shot again, this time by a drunken off-duty policeman who mistook him for a robber. Four years later, again unarmed, Cordes earned his second medal by capturing two hoodlums who kidnapped a wealthy bootlegger.

Shootouts aside, Cordes was best known to New Yorkers via gossip column articles describing his exploits with partner JOHN BRODERICK. Together, the detectives earned a reputation for manhandling notorious racketeers and brawling bare-knuckled with subway muggers, always emerging from their latest fracas with some earthy comment for the press. On the softer side, Cordes personally vowed to find straight jobs for every felon he arrested, when they were paroled from prison. He retired in 1949 as a detective lieutenant and died in 1966.

corruption

While no concise definition of police corruption presently exists, and public discussions of the problem range from penny-ante bribes to unjustified use of DEADLY FORCE, we shall here define *corruption* as encompassing illegal acts committed by law enforcement officers for personal profit. Such crimes may include acts of violence, ranging from armed robbery and strongarm extortion of criminal suspects to contract murder for hire, but the more common forms involve bribery ("graft") and theft of contraband for private sale.

In general terms, police corruption may be either *external,* wherein outside elements pay officers to ignore or perform illegal acts, or *internal,* wherein officers initiate crimes on their own behalf. Classic graft involves bribery of officers to secure immunity from punishment. At one end of the scale it includes petty bribes to forestall traffic tickets or misdemeanor arrests; at the other, members of ORGANIZED CRIME pay out millions to protect illegal gambling, prostitution, and DRUG networks. CONSENSUAL CRIMES generate vast amounts of graft, as during PROHIBITION, where purveyors of popular contraband treat bribes as standard costs of doing business.

Internal corruption goes beyond passively waiting for the offer of a bribe. Officers involved in such activities may rob or burglarize business establishments (like Antoinette Frank in New Orleans or MARK DOUGLAS

MCKENNA's team in Atlanta, Georgia), pilfer confiscated items from police evidence rooms for resale on the street (like Rafael Perez in Los Angeles), rob smugglers to sell their illicit merchandise (like the Miami "RIVER COPS"), or even serve as hired assassins (like WILLIAM ERNEST LEASURE and RICHARD FORD in Los Angeles). A brief and incomplete survey of recent corruption scandals nationwide includes the following:

1990—Seven members of the LOS ANGELES COUNTY SHERIFF'S DEPARTMENT's elite narcotics squad were convicted of stealing $1.4 million in confiscated drug money.

1991—Forty-seven residents of Cleveland, Ohio—including 30 police officers—were indicted for extortion, gambling, dealing narcotics and obstructing justice.

1991—Gary, Indiana's entire vice squad was indicted on charges of extortion, drug-dealing, robbing drug pushers during phony raids, and one count of murder.

1991—William Hart, former chief of the DETROIT POLICE DEPARTMENT, was convicted with deputy chief Kenneth Weiner for embezzling $2.6 million from a special fund earmarked for UNDERCOVER WORK.

1991—Detective Allen Schott was arrested and charged with robbing two banks in Camden, New Jersey.

1994—Ten members of the NEW ORLEANS POLICE DEPARTMENT were indicted for selling drugs and confiscated weapons. One member of the team received a death sentence for ordering the contract murder of a female witness.

1994—The nine-member Greenpoint (New York) Police Department was disbanded over allegations of pervasive corruption, drunkenness, and drug abuse.

1995—New Orleans officer Antoinette Frank was convicted of robbing a local restaurant and murdering three victims in the process, one of them her own off-duty partner.

1995—Officers in Jersey City, New Jersey, were charged with selling themselves 113 impounded cars at discount prices.

1995—An officer of the SAN DIEGO POLICE DEPARTMENT was convicted of burglarizing a software company.

1999—Scandal rocked the LOS ANGELES POLICE DEPARTMENT's gang-ridden Rampart Division, where members of the elite CRASH unit (Community Resources Against Street Hoodlums) stole confiscated cocaine, planted guns on unarmed shooting victims, and concocted FRAME-UPS of innocent persons.

2003—FBI agents launched a full-scale investigation of the Tacoma (Washington) Police Department, after Chief David Brame killed his estranged wife and himself. Multiple allegations of bribery surround that case.

Courtright, Timothy Isaiah (1845–1887)

Born in 1845, in either Illinois or Iowa, Timothy Courtright was one of the Old West's more colorful figures, best known for his handsome face, twin pistols and the blond hair that caused acquaintances to call him "Longhair Jim." During the Civil War, Courtright served as a Union scout under General Logan, then drifted into Texas and became marshal of Fort Worth in the early 1870s. Little is known of his early law enforcement career, but rumors persist that Courtright supplemented his income by shaking down gamblers and saloonkeepers. Fired for drunkenness in 1878, he moved on to serve briefly as marshal in Mesilla, New Mexico, before signing on as a guard for the American Mining Company. In 1883 he killed two would-be robbers, the shootout bringing him to the attention of his old wartime commander, now a prosperous New Mexico rancher.

Although employed as a "foreman" on Logan's ranch, Courtright's real job was eliminating squatters. Raiding a camp at American Valley in 1883, Longhair Jim and another gunman killed two unarmed settlers, but this time there were witnesses and Courtright fled the state. Manhunters tracked him to Fort Worth and jailed him pending extradition, but his knowledge of the local lockup served him well. Courtright escaped with the aid of two smuggled six-guns, absconding to South America. He remained outside the United States until 1886, when word reached him that the prosecution's witnesses had scattered. He then returned for trial in Socorro, where charges were dropped, and Courtright returned to Fort Worth, where he founded the T.I.C. Commercial Detective Agency. A shortage of work left him bankrupt, while brief employment as a strikebreaker failed to cover his debts. Desperate for money and increasingly ill-tempered, his natural mean streak aggravated by liquor, Courtright returned to his old trade of extorting "protection" money from Fort Worth's saloons.

That racket was effective only if everyone paid, however, and Courtright met stiff resistance from Luke Short, another notorious gunman and owner of the White Elephant Saloon. Short refused to pay Courtright's "insurance," leaving Longhair Jim to brood over the insult in his cups. On February 8, 1887, Courtright called Short out of the White Elephant, and they fought in the street, Short's first bullet detaching the thumb of Courtright's gun hand. Three more shots drilled Courtright's chest and forehead, killing him instantly. No charges were filed against Short, leaving him free to resume business as usual.

See also: STRIKEBREAKING.

Cowley, Samuel P. (1899–1934)

A native of Franklin, Idaho, born July 23, 1899, Sam Cowley was a devout Mormon who conducted missionary work in Hawaii during 1916–20. He graduated from George Washington University's law school in 1928, licensed to practice law in Utah and the District of Columbia. Cowley joined the FBI in March 1929 and was assigned to headquarters in October 1932. He was promoted to inspector on July 1, 1934, placed in charge of the Midwest "flying squad" that pursued bandit John Dillinger and suspects deemed responsible for the KANSAS CITY MASSACRE.

Cowley's role in the Dillinger manhunt assumed greater importance as a personal rift developed between FBI Director J. EDGAR HOOVER and Chicago G-man MELVIN HORACE PURVIS, JR. On November 27, 1934, Cowley and Agent Herman Hollis killed Dillinger cohort George "Baby Face" Nelson in a shootout near Barrington, Illinois. Hollis was killed outright in the battle, while Cowley suffered mortal wounds and died the following day. After Purvis resigned from the Bureau in April 1935, Hoover launched a campaign to erase his name from FBI history, publicly crediting Cowley with the apprehension of Dillinger and Charles "Pretty Boy" Floyd. Briefly (and falsely) credited with killing Dillinger himself, Cowley was posthumously enshrined as the mastermind behind the FBI's pursuit. After Cowley's murder, his widow served for 12 years as an FBI clerk.

See also: FEDERAL BUREAU OF INVESTIGATION.

Crime Stoppers

Albuquerque, New Mexico, launched the first Crime Stoppers program in September 1976 as a crime-fighting partnership of law enforcement, the media, and the civilian community. At press time for this book, some 1,200 local Crime Stoppers programs were active in 20 nations worldwide, including the United States, Canada, Great Britain, Australia, South Africa, Central America, and the Caribbean. Local chapters operate as nonprofit charities managed by volunteer directors, accepting information to assist police in solving or preventing various crimes. Thus far, Crime Stoppers tips have reportedly produced 600,000 arrests, plus seizures of DRUGS and stolen property valued in excess of $7 billion.

Crime Stoppers list apathy, fear of reprisals, and reluctance to get involved as the primary reasons for civilian noninvolvement in crime fighting. The program overcomes those obstacles by relieving informants of the responsibility to speak with police or testify in court directly, while offering cash rewards for information leading to arrest and indictment of felony offenders. Tips to Crime Stoppers are not themselves sufficient evidence to warrant an arrest, but they often provide detectives with the leads required to launch and pursue a successful investigation. Subsequent surveillance by police confirms or refutes the allegations of criminal activity, and search or arrest warrants are issued on the basis of direct police observations. Media outlets collaborates with Crime Stoppers by publicizing descriptions of unknown offenders, staging reenactments of crimes to jog the memory of witnesses, and to generally keep unsolved crimes in the public eye.

Crittenden, John Jordan (1787–1863)

John Crittenden was born near Versailles, in Kentucky's Woodford County, on September 10, 1787. He graduated from Virginia's William and Mary College in 1806,

Attorney General John Crittenden (Author's collection)

then studied law and won admission to the bar in 1807. From private practice in Kentucky he advanced to the post of attorney general for Illinois Territory (1809–10) and was elected to the Kentucky state legislature (1811–17), with service interrupted by service in the War of 1812 as an aide to Kentucky's governor (1812–13). Crittenden's postwar public service included terms as a Kentucky legislator (1813–17, 1825–29), U.S. district attorney for Kentucky (1827–29), U.S. senator from Kentucky (1817–19, 1835–41), and Kentucky secretary of state (1834–35). President William Harrison named Crittenden attorney general on March 5, 1841, but his tenure expired prematurely with Harrison's death one month later.

Crittenden thereafter returned to the U.S. Senate (1842–48), then resigned to serve as governor of Kentucky (1848–50). On July 22, 1850, President Millard Fillmore appointed Crittenden to his second term as U.S. attorney general, assuming office on August 14 and remaining until March 7, 1853. Two years later, Crittenden won election to the U.S. Senate for the third time (1855–61) and spent the early Civil War years in the U.S. House of Representatives (1861–63). Crittenden was running for reelection to the House when he died at Frankfort, Kentucky, on July 26, 1863.

Cummings, Homer Stillé (1870–1956)

Born in Chicago on April 30, 1870, Homer Cummings earned his bachelor's degree in 1891 and his LL.B. in 1893, both from Yale University. He was admitted to the Connecticut bar in 1893 and soon immersed himself in Democratic Party politics. Cummings twice won election as mayor of Stamford (1900–02, 1904–06), but otherwise he failed in races for the U.S. House of Representatives (1902), the U.S. Senate (1916), and the White House (1920). Still, he was selected as a delegate to every Democratic National Convention between 1900 and 1948. President Franklin Roosevelt chose Cummings as his first attorney general, installed on March 4, 1933. He served until January 1939, his term coinciding with the FBI's expansion into headline "gangbusting" and covert DOMESTIC SURVEILLANCE of alleged "subversive" activities.

Driven by such incidents as the Lindbergh kidnapping and the KANSAS CITY MASSACRE, Cummings declared a federal war on crime that perfectly suited FBI Director J. EDGAR HOOVER's desire to broaden Bureau authority. On April 19, 1934, Cummings announced a 12-point crime program complete with legislation to expand FBI powers and transform various local offenses into federal crimes. Congress rejected some of the Cummings-FDR proposals, but FBI agents were finally granted authority to carry firearms and make arrests (activities some G-men had pursued illegally since 1908). The 73rd Congress also added more laws to the U.S. criminal code than all previous Congresses combined. Among the new federal offenses were BANK ROBBERY; murder of a federal agent or employee of a federally insured bank; possession of unregistered "gangster" weapons (including machine guns, sawed-off shotguns, and silencers); and a mixed bag of interstate crimes including KIDNAPPING, extortion, racketeering, and transportation of stolen property.

As the "crime war" wound down and a new war loomed in Europe, President Roosevelt ordered sweeping FBI investigation of "subversive" behavior including "general activities—Communist and Affiliated Organizations, Fascist, Anti-Fascist movements, and activities in Organized Labor organizations." Hoover received his orders from FDR on September 1, 1936, and launched his campaign four days later, belatedly informing Cummings on September 10. Cummings endorsed the plan and broadened its scope, instructing Hoover to collaborate with the State Department and military and naval intelligence.

Finally broken by his failure to help Roosevelt "pack" the SUPREME COURT with liberal justices, Cummings resigned on January 2, 1939. He returned to private practice in Washington, D.C., and remained active in Democratic politics, serving as a presidential elector from Connecticut in 1940 and 1944. He died in Washington on September 10, 1956.

See also: FEDERAL BUREAU OF INVESTIGATION.

Cunningham, Thomas (1838–1900)

Legendary California lawman Tom Cunningham began his journey to the wild frontier from Ireland, where he was born on August 17, 1838. His parents immigrated to New York City 10 years later, hiring Tom out to his brother-in-law as an apprentice harness maker. At age 16 he fled Brooklyn and made his way to Northern California, settling in Stockton to ply the only trade he knew. Cunningham joined Stockton's volunteer fire department in 1857, rising to serve as chief in 1865 and winning election to Stockton's city council the same year.

He shifted careers to law enforcement six years later, with a successful campaign to become sheriff of San Joaquin County. Over the next 27 years he pursued and captured a series of notorious bandits, including outlaw-poet Charles Boles (alias "Black Bart"). Dubbed the "Thief Taker of San Joaquin," Cunningham was also an early pioneer of systematic criminology, spending some $20,000 to compile 42,000 mug shots and PROFILING habits of various fugitives to aid in their capture. He also personally designed a new jail for San Joaquin County, nicknamed "Cunningham's Castle" for its twin watchtowers, and he constructed an extensive criminal museum in the old county courthouse. Cunningham retired as sheriff in January 1899 and died a year later, at age 62.

Curtis, Edwin Upton (1861–1922)

The son of a Massachusetts businessman, born in Roxbury on May 26, 1861, Edwin Curtis graduated from Maine's Bowdoin College in 1882, followed by study at Boston University Law School. Immersed in Republican politics while he practiced law, Curtis first won election as Boston's city clerk, then served as mayor (1895–99). Although he retired after one term in office, Curtis remained active in government as a member of the Metropolitan Park Commission, as assistant U.S. treasurer for Boston, and as collector of the Port of Boston. In 1918 lame-duck governor Samuel McCall appointed Curtis to serve as Boston's police commissioner.

The appointment came at an inauspicious time. As strikes, Red scares, and panic over ANARCHISM wracked America in the wake of World War I, Boston police complained about their salaries (frozen at roughly half the yearly income of a common laborer). Curtis wangled a $200 raise from Boston's city council in May 1919, but the small boost failed to keep up with postwar inflation. Two months later, police spokesmen announced their affiliation with the American Federation of Labor. No current statute forbade police unions, but Curtis was adamant in opposition, threatening to fire any officer who joined the AFL. While Mayor Andrew Peters sought an amicable compromise, Curtis fulfilled his threat, dismissing 19 union members from the force. On September 9, 1919, by an overwhelming vote of 1,134 to 2, Boston police walked out on strike.

Curtis had organized a small volunteer patrol force before the strike started, but he unaccountably instructed them to start duty on September 10, more than 12 hours after the regular force went home. Chaos resulted, with sporadic vandalism escalating into full-scale rioting and looting overnight. At midday on September 10 Mayor Peters bypassed Curtis and his volunteers, mobilizing the NATIONAL GUARD to restore order in Boston. One patrolman and several civilians died in skirmishes that day, but order was restored. Governor Calvin Coolidge dispatched more Guardsmen on September 11, and curiously emerged as the "hero" of the strike, using his belated action as a springboard to the vice presidency in 1920.

Despite intervention by AFL leaders, Curtis refused to reinstate the 19 officers he had dismissed. Coolidge supported Curtis, proclaiming: "There is no right to strike against the public safety by anybody, anywhere, anytime." Despite calls for his resignation, Curtis hung on to rebuild the BOSTON POLICE DEPARTMENT with non-union officers. He died in office on March 28, 1922.

Attorney General Caleb Cushing (Author's collection)

Cushing, Caleb (1800–1879)

Child prodigy Caleb Cushing was born at Salisbury, Massachusetts, on January 17, 1800. He entered Harvard University at age 13 and graduated in 1817, then studied law and was admitted to the Massachusetts bar in 1821. His public service included multiple terms in the Bay State's house of representatives (1825, 1833–34, 1845–46, 1850), the state senate (1827), and as a U.S. representative (1835–43). In 1843–44, as America's commissioner to China, he secured the first treaty between that country and the United States. Four years later, at his own expense, Cushing raised a regiment to fight in the Mexican War and led it with the rank of colonel. At war's end, he was appointed associate justice of the Massachusetts supreme court, a post he held until March 7, 1853, when President Franklin Pierce named him U.S. attorney general. Cushing left that office, with the rest of Pierce's cabinet, on March 6, 1857, and returned to the Massachusetts state legislature (1857–59). In 1860 President James Buchanan dispatched him as a confidential intermediary to South Carolina's secessionists. Six years later, Cushing served as one of three commissioners employed to revise and codify federal statutes. In 1868 he negotiated the right-of-way for U.S. ships crossing the Isthmus of Panama, and four years later served as U.S. counsel at the Geneva Convention. President Ulysses Grant named Cushing as his minister to Spain in January 1874, a post Cushing held until April 1877. He died at Newburysport, Massachusetts, on January 2, 1879.

Custodial Detention Index

Following the outbreak of World War II in September 1939, FBI Director J. EDGAR HOOVER devised a new program targeting "individuals, groups and organizations engaged in . . . subversive activities, or espionage activities, or any activity that was possibly detrimental to the internal security of the United States." Immediate subjects of interest were all "persons of German, Italian, and Communist sympathies," together with others whose "interest may be directed primarily to the interest of some other nation than the United States." Those "whose presence at liberty" was deemed "dangerous to the public peace and safety of the United States Government" were to be "discreetly" listed in a new Custodial Detention Index, slated for mass arrest if America entered the war.

Lacking any legal authority for his new program, Hoover sought and received secret approval from Attorney General ROBERT JACKSON in June 1940. Jackson's successor, FRANCIS BIDDLE, authorized arrest of German and Italian enemy aliens in 1942, but U.S. citizens were not affected and Communists were likewise omitted since the Soviet Union was an American ally. In July 1943 Biddle ordered Hoover to discontinue the program, noting that the Bureau's "classification system is inherently unreliable" and that the FBI's proper law enforcement function "is not aided by classifying persons as to dangerousness." Hoover avoided Biddle's order with an August 1943 memorandum informing subordinates that "[h]enceforth the cards known as Custodial Detention cards will be known as [the] Security Index." Fearing discipline for insubordination, Hoover warned that the new list must be "strictly confidential and should at no time be mentioned or alluded to in investigative reports or discussed with agencies or individuals outside the Bureau." Under its new name the index endured for another 28 years, finally abolished in autumn 1971.

See also: FEDERAL BUREAU OF INVESTIGATION.

Customs Service

The U.S. Customs Service was established by Congress in July 1789, to enforce the new nation's first tariff regulations. Over the next 125 years its collections funded most of the federal government's operations, including purchase of vast new territories in the West and creation of various national roads. Revenue from the Customs Service also built Washington, D.C., along with the country's military and naval academies, various lighthouses, and the Transcontinental Railroad. Although the fledgling United States once faced impending bankruptcy, Customs revenues alone reduced the national debt to zero by 1835.

Today the Customs Service ensures that all imports and exports conform to U.S. laws and regulations. Aside from its primary task of collecting revenue, Customs also guards against smuggling, and interdicts contraband shipments. Customs plays a key role in the federal "War on Drugs," as evidenced by statistics from 2000, when Customs agents seized 90 percent of all heroin captured in the United States, 85 percent of all cocaine intercepted, and 51 percent of all marijuana confiscated on arrival. In addition to its own statutory duties, Customs presently enforces more than 400 other federal laws on behalf of 40 collaborating agencies (motor vehicle safety and emission standards, protection of endangered species, consumer safety, pesticide controls, etc.). According to statistics issued from headquarters, Customs returned $16 to the U.S. TREASURY DEPARTMENT for every dollar spent on its operations. Under the HOMELAND SECURITY DEPARTMENT regulations established in 2001, Customs also cooperated extensively with the U.S. BORDER PATROL to apprehend illegal aliens in the United States.

See also: DRUGS.

D

Dallas Police Department

Created in the early 1880s, the spokesmen for the Dallas (Texas) Police Department describe their force as an agency which "has created an atmosphere of ethical, caring behavior." Critics take issue with that claim, however, and point to the department's long, troubled record of CORRUPTION, RACISM, and alleged brutality as a legacy to be lived down, rather than heralded with praise.

In the 1920s Dallas was state headquarters for the powerful Texas KU KLUX KLAN, and the hometown of "Imperial Wizard" Hiram Evans. The Dallas PD was as heavily infiltrated by Klansmen as any police department of the Deep South, resulting in a near-zero conviction rate for the masked perpetrators of countless Klan floggings, castrations, abductions, and murders. Forty years later, while inviting Texas journalist Penn Jones to print a regional KKK newspaper in 1961, Dallas police lieutenant George Butler confided to Jones that "half the force" still consisted of Klansmen. While that claim may have been exaggerated, Dallas PD remained lily-white until the 1950s, and its first black civilian personnel were hired in December 1963. Meanwhile, Dallas pioneered in the use of "JACK-IN-THE BOX" TEAMS, fatally ambushing suspected burglars who were nearly always black or Hispanic.

Dallas was wide open for illegal gambling in the 1920s and 1930s, with local kingpins Herbert Noble and Benny Binion (later a Las Vegas icon) protected from arrest by the generosity of their payoffs to local police. Even murder could be whitewashed for a price in Dallas, creating an atmosphere that lured Chicago mobsters after World War II. The aforementioned Lt.

Butler became a hero of sorts in the late 1940s, secretly recording mob overtures to Dallas County's sheriff and securing indictments against Chicago's Paul Jones, but while Butler emerged as a star witness before the federal Kefauver Commission (1950–51), Jones explained the charges as resulting from Butler's own excessive demands for graft. In any cast, Chicago transplant Jack Ruby enjoyed warm relations with Dallas PD, operating without interference from his notorious Carousel Club until 1963.

Few Americans noticed in 1962, when a report from Michigan University's Police-Community Relations Institute declared that "the Dallas department has enjoyed for many years a nationwide reputation for outstanding efficiency." If that reputation existed, in fact, it took a fatal hit in November 1963, with the ASSASSINATION of President John Kennedy and subsequent events. Dallas police mishandled the case from its outset, misidentifying the alleged murder weapon and apparently beating suspect Lee Harvey Oswald in custody. Two days after the assassination, on November 24, Oswald was scheduled for transfer from police headquarters to the county jail (under personal supervision of George Butler), but Jack Ruby intervened to murder Oswald in the department's own basement, in full view of television cameras. Investigation of Ruby's multiple connections to Dallas PD left some observers speculating that Officer J. D. Tippit—allegedly gunned down by Oswald within an hour of Kennedy's murder—may have been an active participant in the president's assassination.

Scandal, low pay, and a paucity of qualified applicants combined to create a severe manpower shortage for Dallas PD by 1966. Of 1,033 applicants that year, only 375 passed the department's written test; 248 of those failed the physical exam; and only 29 survived a background check for prior arrests and other problems such as drug or alcohol abuse. That shortage has been overcome today, with 2,977 sworn officers and 556 civilian personnel on active duty with Dallas PD, but numerous problems remain. An investigation by the *Dallas Morning News* in 2004 found that the department "has hired a number of officers with questionable backgrounds, including some with legal troubles or repeated difficulties in completing training."

Administrative problems were the key for Gary Sykes, director of Plano's Institute for Law Enforcement Administration, who described Dallas PD to the *Morning News* as a "department in trouble. In that kind of atmosphere, things just don't get done very well and morale suffers. If you see that kind of ongoing chaos at the top of the organization, that's a de-motivator. If they don't care, why should we care? That's the attitude that gets established." And that chaos had filtered down through the ranks, according to retired Sgt. Sam Johnson, formerly in charge of the department's management research unit. According to Johnson, "You've got guys on phantom special assignments everywhere. They're not answering calls."

Still, elusive officers were the least of Dallas PD's problems in the 1990s and early 21st century. Officers Swany Davenport and Randy Harris were convicted in December 1992 of shaking down local crack cocaine dealers, extorting some $50,000 in payoffs during 1990–91. A decade later, in 2001, the department was rocked by an even more sinister scandal. That investigation revealed that 20-plus defendants had been victimized by FRAME-UPS involving Hispanic suspects arrested and deported for possessing DRUGS. The cocaine in question proved to be fake, prompting the indictment of four officers who fabricated and planted the "evidence." Assistant police chief Dora Saucedo-Falls, in charge of narcotics investigations at the time, escaped criminal charges but was demoted and transferred to the department's communications division in December 2004. Her chief assistant, Deputy Chief John Martinez, resigned after refusing to accept a similar demotion.

D.A.R.E

Drug Abuse Resistance Education—D.A.R.E.—is a highly acclaimed program designed to help children avoid involvement with DRUGS, gangs, and violence. Launched in Los Angeles during 1983, the program has proved so successful that it now operates in some 80 percent of American school districts and at least 54 foreign countries, reaching an estimated 36 million children in any given year. Led by local police offi-

cers, D.A.R.E. features classroom lessons and discussions that teach children from kindergarten through 12th grade to resist negative peer pressure and avoid involvement in criminal activity. The nonprofit parent program, D.A.R.E. America, presently operates from headquarters in the Los Angeles suburb of Inglewood, California. Since 1988 members and participants have celebrated a National D.A.R.E. Day by presidential proclamation. D.A.R.E. America's Web site describes the virtues of the program thusly:

> D.A.R.E. "humanizes" the police: that is, young people can begin to relate to officers as people.
>
> D.A.R.E. permits students to see officers in a helping role, not just an enforcement role.
>
> D.A.R.E. opens lines of communication between law enforcement and youth.
>
> D.A.R.E. Officers can serve as conduits to provide information beyond drug-related topics.
>
> D.A.R.E. opens dialogue between the school, police, and parents to deal with other issues.

D.A.R.E. classroom instructors are officers uniquely experienced in working with juveniles, gangs, and drug cases. Each received 40 hours of additional instruction on teaching methods before class assignments are issued.

Daugherty, Harry Micajah (1860–1941)

Ohio native Harry Daugherty was born in Fayette County, at Washington Court House, on January 16, 1860. He attended local public schools, then studied at the University of Michigan and graduated from that institution's law school in 1881. After nine years of private practice in his hometown, Daugherty won election to the state assembly (1890–94) and thus became affiliated with the corrupt political machine dubbed the "Ohio Gang." He was a close friend of Warren Harding and managed Harding's successful campaign for the White House in 1920. As a reward for that service, Harding named Daugherty attorney general on March 4, 1921.

Harding's regime is remembered today as one of the most corrupt in U.S. history, and Daugherty's performance was no exception. He quickly transformed the JUSTICE DEPARTMENT into a "Department of Easy Virtue" that became a national laughingstock. Daugherty's top priority appeared to be concealing crimes committed by other members of the Harding administration, including the notorious Teapot Dome Scandal. To that end, acting in concert with FBI chief WILLIAM I. BURNS and assistant chief J. EDGAR HOOVER, he launched a campaign of surveillance and character assassination against various congressional critics, including Senators Thomas Walsh and Burton Wheeler.

Harding's death in August 1923 brought Calvin Coolidge to the White House, while increasing heat from Congress and the courts placed Daugherty in an untenable position. Coolidge demanded his resignation on March 28, 1924, and Daugherty was subsequently indicted on charges of conspiracy to defraud the U.S. government, but two hung juries spared him from prison and the charges were dismissed in 1927. (He was not acquitted, as some accounts maintain.) Daugherty died at Columbus, Ohio, on October 12, 1941.

See also: FEDERAL BUREAU OF INVESTIGATION.

Daughtry, Sylvester, Jr. (b. 1945)

An African-American native of North Carolina, born in 1945, Sylvester Daughtry, Jr. joined the GREENSBORO POLICE DEPARTMENT in 1968, when integration of southern police departments was still a relatively new idea. Despite complaints of RACISM within the department, highlighted by lax handling of violent KU KLUX KLAN members in 1979, Daughtry advanced through the ranks on pure merit, winning promotion to sergeant in 1973, lieutenant in 1977, captain in 1980, and assistant chief in 1983. Before his final appointment as Greensboro's first black police chief, in 1987, Daughtry earned a bachelor of science degree from North Carolina Agricultural and Technical State University in Greensboro. He also graduated from the FBI National Academy and the FBI National Executive Institute.

Chief Daughtry worked tirelessly for 12 years to reform and modernize the Greensboro PD, elevating its professional standards to the point where his department was the first southern police force to receive accreditation from the Commission of Accreditation for Law Enforcement Agencies (CALEA). In 1993–94 he served as the second black president of the INTERNATIONAL ASSOCIATION OF CHIEFS OF POLICE. (Atlanta's LEE PATRICK BROWN was the first, in 1990–91.) Daughtry retired from the Greensboro force in January 1998 and was elected one year later to serve as executive director of the CALEA. His many honors and awards include the North Carolina A&T State University Alumni Association's award for achievement and excellence in law enforcement, plus the U.S. attorney general's William French Smith Award for outstanding contribution to cooperative law enforcement. Daughtry's professional associations include the life membership in the IACP, plus the National Organization of Black Law Enforcement Executives and the Police Executive Research Forum.

Davidson, Alaska P. (1868–)

Born in 1868, Alaska Davidson completed only three years of public school education but was still described by her friends as "very refined." On October 11, 1922, Chief WILLIAM J. BURNS appointed her to serve as the FBI's first female "special investigator." Davidson trained in New York before her transfer to the Washington, D.C., field office, but no record of her work survives today. J. EDGAR HOOVER assumed control of the Bureau in May 1924 and ordered each field office to evaluate its personnel, with an eye toward dismissing unqualified agents. Washington's agent-in-charge reported that his office had "no particular work for a woman agent," whereupon Hoover demanded and received Davidson's resignation on June 10, 1924.

See also: FEDERAL BUREAU OF INVESTIGATION.

Davis, Edward Michael (1916–2006)

The LOS ANGELES POLICE DEPARTMENT's Web site claims that Chief Edward Davis (1969–78) "is recognized as the foremost police innovator of our generation." While the source of that recognition goes unnamed, his innovations are beyond dispute. During his tenure Davis launched LAPD's Neighborhood Watch program, created the department's first K-9 UNIT, inaugurated an Asian Task Force to cope with gangs in Chinatown, used undercover officers to purchase DRUGS on high school campuses under the School Buy Program, and introduced high-tech equipment with the force's Multimedia Instruction for Law Enforcement (MILE) and Development and Evaluation of Firearms Training (DEFT) programs.

There was, of course, also another side to Davis.

A Southern California native (born in 1916) who described himself as "just a country boy doing my best to protect the city," Davis was in fact an ultrarightist who, under Chief WILLIAM HENRY PARKER (1950–66) ran the John Birch Society's FIRE AND POLICE RESEARCH ORGANIZATION. While LAPD historians call him "shrewd" and "outspoken," his public pronouncements as chief were often outrageous. A staunch opponent of GUN CONTROL, he warned a 1975 National Rifle Association gathering that L.A. was "a cesspool of pornography, fruit bars, and bottomless bars, thanks to the United States and California Supreme Courts." Unhappy farm workers, he quipped, should join the gay rights movement to create a "United Fruit Party." If LAPD hiring standards were adjusted for women, minorities, and gays, Davis fumed, "I could envision myself on the [police academy] stage at graduation day giving a diploma to a 4'1" transvestite moron who would kiss me instead of saluting."

In 1971, after the AMERICAN CIVIL LIBERTIES UNION obtained an injunction barring Davis from public comment on an impending police lawsuit, the chief called a press conference where he appeared with a bandanna wrapped around his face. "Bar your doors," he muttered, "buy a police dog, call us when we're available and pray. I am under a gag rule imposed by the American Civil Liberties Union. I'm one of the few men in the country without freedom of speech. I'm not saying they're Communists, but I've noticed that when the Communist Party takes a deep breath, the ACLU's chest goes out."

Civil libertarians were more concerned with Davis's methods than his mouth, however. Soon after taking office, he revived LAPD's Red squad, renamed it the Public Disorder Intelligence Division (PDID), and unleashed its members on a freewheeling campaign of illegal DOMESTIC SURVEILLANCE, including widespread use of INFORMANTS and criminal AGENTS PROVOCATEURS. On Davis's watch, the PDID collaborated with members of the FBI's secret COINTELPRO team, harassing leftists of all kinds and black militants in particular. A favorite target was the Black Panther Party, whose members suffered FRAME-UPS and worse under Davis. The campaign reached its nadir when G-men and LAPD officers recruited members of the United Slaves—a supposed black nationalist group led by a police informer—to ambush and murder Black Panthers. LAPD's raid on a 1975 rock concert, resulting in 511 marijuana arrests, was small-time by comparison, though Mayor TOM BRADLEY cited "a serious question about the priorities in assignment of personnel."

Davis retired from LAPD on January 1, 1978, to pursue a career in the state senate. His reputation paved the way to Sacramento, where he subsequently underwent a startling change of heart. In 1984 Davis not only admitted that PDID "probably" committed criminal acts under his leadership, but he also joined in sponsoring a landmark gay rights initiative.

See also: FEDERAL BUREAU OF INVESTIGATION; RED SQUADS.

Davis, James Edgar (1889–1949)

A Texas native, born in 1889, James Davis arrived in Los Angeles at age 22, shortly after his discharge from the U.S. Army. Within a month, he joined the LOS ANGELES POLICE DEPARTMENT as a patrolman. It took him 10 years to make sergeant, in 1921, but after that his rise was meteoric, including stints as a detective lieutenant (1922–24), and captain of the graft-ridden vice squad (1924–26). In his first term as chief (1926–29), Davis fired 240 officers for "bad conduct," but PROHIBITION-era CORRUPTION still flourished without significant interference from LAPD, despite tough talk from Davis and vows to nab rumrunners "dead, not alive."

A model for successor WILLIAM HENRY PARKER, who served as his personal aide, Chief Davis was described by the then-conservative *Los Angeles Times* as "a burly, dictatorial, somewhat sadistic, bitterly antilabor man who saw communist influence behind every telephone pole." In pursuit of those alleged subversives, Davis expanded the department's RED SQUAD under Capt. William Hynes, who worked as a professional strikebreaker and AGENT PROVOCATEUR before joining the force in 1922. Soon, the AMERICAN CIVIL LIBERTIES UNION filed multiple lawsuits against LAPD, calling its Red squad "the most lawless and brutal" in America.

It was the Vice squad, though, that cost Davis his job the first time. Bribery scandals and the election of reform mayor John Porter brought a demotion for Davis in 1929. He rode out the storm, biding his time until Frank Shaw's election in 1932 assured a return to wholesale graft throughout L.A. Reinstalled as chief by Shaw, Davis revived the Red squad once again, erected LAPD's first police academy with convict labor, and announced a "bum blockade" to rid Los Angeles of persons with "no definite purpose in coming into the state." Meanwhile, ORGANIZED CRIME flourished citywide, under the stewardship of Benjamin "Bugsy" Siegel, Mickey Cohen, Jack Dragna, and others who paid well for immunity.

In 1938 it was the overzealous Red squad that finished Davis's career. Angered by a new police watchdog group, the Citizens' Independent Vice Investigating Committee, LAPD captain EARL KYNETTE bombed one of the group's spokesmen, nearly killing him. Revelation of the attempted murder sent Kynette to prison and put reformer Fletcher Bowron in the mayor's office. Bowron disbanded the Red squad (briefly) and forced Davis—along with 45 other high-ranking officers—into retirement. Davis rebounded as chief of security for Douglas Aircraft, holding that post until a heart attack sidelined him during World War II. He died from a stroke while visiting Montana, on June 29, 1949.

Davis, Lawrence O.

In the troubled 1960s, Sheriff L. O. Davis of St. Johns County, Florida, (St. Augustine) epitomized the hardline RACISM of such contemporaries as Birmingham's EUGENE "BULL" CONNOR. Committed to resisting change at any cost, Davis publicly allied himself with white terrorists and seldom missed an opportunity to harass or demean the black community.

Although he was elected sheriff in 1949, most Americans heard of Davis for the first time in 1963, when four black members of the NAACP were severely beaten at a local KU KLUX KLAN rally. Davis arrived in time to save their lives, then arrested the four unconscious victims for assault. Four Klansmen were also jailed, but their charges were soon dismissed, while the battered blacks were tried and convicted of assaulting their would-be murderers. In early 1964, with an election pending, Davis visited St. Augustine's Lincolnville ghetto to announce his disdain for black votes. "I used the word 'nigger,'" he told reporters, "so they'd know I meant it."

If there was any doubt concerning Davis's bigotry, he proved it by fraternizing with the KKK at every opportunity. Davis appeared at Klan rallies, allowed Klan meetings in his jail, and loaned patrol cars to visiting out-of-town Klansmen. As demonstrations heated up in St. Augustine, he also deputized 169 members of the city's Ancient City Hunting Club, led by convicted bootlegger Holsted Manucy, to assist sheriff's officers and the ST. AUGUSTINE POLICE DEPARTMENT. FBI reports and congressional investigators named the club as a front for the KKK, while Manucy was identified as the Klan's local "exalted cyclops." In February 1964, a Klansman sought on bombing charges in Jacksonville fled to St. Augustine, where FBI agents reported that Davis "was . . . instrumental in helping the Klan hide" him.

After numerous riots, shootings, and incidents of police brutality, civil rights workers filed a complaint against Sheriff Davis, before federal judge Bryan Simpson. Davis committed perjury in Simpson's court, initially denying that he deputized any Klansmen, then admitting that he had at least four KKK members on staff as full-time deputies. He also lied concerning weapons seized from civil rights protesters. After showing photographs of clubs and guns, claiming they had belonged to rowdy blacks, Davis confessed that they were seized from "anti-demonstrators"—and that all had been returned by him to their owners. Judge Simpson was outraged to find Manucy's name on Davis's roster of "special" deputies, flaring, "That man is a convicted felon in this court!" Davis finally confessed that he had passed out badges to any white man who requested one.

Still, it was Davis's treatment of prisoners that angered Simpson most. The sheriff's use of clubs and cattle prods was bad enough, but conditions in his jailhouse were medieval—50-plus prisoners crammed into cells built for four, men and women packed together in outdoor, unshaded corrals, where shallow pits in the earth served as communal toilets. Judge Simpson ordered the abusive conduct discontinued, declaring: "More than cruel and unusual punishment is shown. Here is exposed, in its raw ugliness, studied and cynical brutality, deliberately contrived to break men physically and mentally."

For all his glaring faults, Davis was still beloved by most white voters in St. Johns County. The local sheriff's Web site still declares him "kindly," claiming that "with Sheriff Davis' leadership the community held together" under stress from outside agitators in the 1960s. Davis easily won reelection in 1964 and 1968, but he was removed from office by Governor Claude Kirk in 1970, citing allegations of CORRUPTION. Local jurors acquitted Davis of those charges, but his time was past. In 1972 he failed to recapture his office from Kirk's appointee, Dudley Garrett.

See also: BOMBING AND BOMB SQUADS; FEDERAL BUREAU OF INVESTIGATION.

deadly force

According to the Officer Down memorial page at http://www.odmp.com, 17,392 American peace officers have died on duty since 1792. That tabulation includes deaths resulting from accidents and illness (such as strokes or heart attacks) with lives lost to adversarial action. Limited statistics exist for civilians killed due to deadly force by police.

According to the U.S. Bureau of Vital Statistics, American police killed 2,806 persons in the line of duty between 1952 and 1963. Police deaths from all causes during the same 12-year period totaled 1,406. Officers of the DETROIT POLICE DEPARTMENT shot and killed 16 persons during 1958–61, while losing five of their own. Members of the NEW YORK CITY POLICE DEPARTMENT killed 30 citizens (versus four officers lost) between July 1, 1964 and June 30, 1965.

How accurate are such statistics? An academic paper published in 1999 found significant discrepancies between tabulation of deadly force applications in police supplementary homicide reports (SHR) and those counted by the National Vital Statistics System (NVSS) of the National Center for Health Statistics. For the 23 years between 1976 and 1978, SHR files recorded 6,686 citizens killed by police in the line of duty, while NVSS files placed the tally at 8,658. According to the Internet's "Officer Down" Web site, 4,208 peace officers died on duty from various causes during the same period. The discrepancy—1,972 deaths, or some 23 percent of the total—is unexplained but could be the result of underreporting of police homicides nationwide.

A perennial sore point for cop-watchers is the number of nonwhite civilians killed by police in America. Of the 2,806 persons killed during 1952–63, 1,382 (49.3 percent) were identified by federal statisticians as "nonwhite"—a label that did not include Hispanics. Of the 30 killed by NYPD during 1964–65, 12 were black and five had Spanish surnames. Detroit's 16 dead for 1958–61 included 12 African Americans. That margin apparently shifted during 1976–98, if we can trust the available statistics. Police SHR files for the period list 4,832 white victims, 3,592 blacks, 173 "other," and

61 of "unknown" race. The NVSS files, meanwhile, include 4,158 whites, 2,359 blacks, and 179 "other."

Even presumably efficient federal agencies such as the FBI have trouble keeping track of their on-duty homicides and losses. G-men were not legally empowered to carry firearms until June 18, 1934, although many were armed as a matter of course from 1908 onward. In May 1936 Senator Kenneth McKellar asked Bureau director J. EDGAR HOOVER, "How many people have been killed by your department since you have been allowed to use guns?" Hoover replied, "I think there have been eight desperadoes killed by our agents and we have had four agents in our service killed by them." In fact, however, only six fugitives had been shot by FBI agents since June 1934, while three agents died on duty. The director's tabulation was accurate only if he started counting in April 1934, two months *before* his men were authorized to carry guns.

Most law enforcement agencies have rules in place dictating when and where deadly force may by employed. Some departments require written reports every time an officer draws a weapon, whether or not shots are fired. Nonetheless, cases like those of AMADOU DIALLO in New York and EULIA LOVE in Los Angeles provoke furious reactions from minority communities, while the deadly BRANCH DAVIDIAN SIEGE of 1993 directly spawned the antigovernment "militia" movement.

See also: FEDERAL BUREAU OF INVESTIGATION.

Deitsch, Philip M. (1840–1903)

German native Philip Deitsch, born in 1840, followed a wave of immigration that brought him to Ohio as a child. He joined the CINCINNATI POLICE DEPARTMENT in 1863, pulling the strings required to win promotion as a sergeant one month later, and as a lieutenant in his third month on the job. In 1873 Deitsch left the CPD to wear a federal badge, as an agent of the U.S. Revenue Service.

As political CORRUPTION ensured Deitsch's meteoric rise, so it would ultimately change his life. By 1885 Cincinnati was immersed in one of its cyclical scandals, this one involving false registration of some 1,250 fraudulent voters. A civilian Committee of One Hundred sought help from the state legislature, which enacted a bill to reorganize the graft-ridden Cincinnati force. All but 51 of the department's 289 patrolmen were fired in one swoop, while Deitsch was hired (ironically, some said) to rebuild the scandal-ridden CPD.

His style was rigid paramilitary discipline, including new uniforms and equipment, strict medical examinations, physical training in a new gymnasium, and precision drill exercises. A new system of patrols reduced an officer's workday from 12 to eight hours, while Deitsch's

new training programs set an unprecedented national standard. In his spare time, Deitsch was fond of mounting a white stallion to ride in various civic parades. He died in Cincinnati on January 23, 1903, at age 62.

Delaware State Police

Delaware state legislators debated creation of a state police force in 1906, but action was postponed until 1919, when a one-man Highway Traffic Police "force" was created to patrol the Philadelphia Pike around Wilmington. Three more officers and motorcycles joined the team in 1920, serving directly under the State Highway Commission. PROHIBITION and proliferation of motor vehicles brought a change in January 1923, when Governor William Denney recommended creation of a larger state police force. Four months later, legislation was enacted creating the State Highway Police (DSP).

From humble beginnings in an old construction shack at Bellevue, with 14 sworn officers, the force expanded to include five stations, 24-hour service, and a fledgling K-9 UNIT (for pursuit of prowlers) by 1925. Communication was facilitated by adoption of a semaphore system and collaboration from 42 service stations that possessed telephones. "Highway" was officially deleted from the force's name in 1931, and a teletype system was established in 1934, linking the DSP to agencies in eight other states. A Bureau of Identification was established in 1935, followed by radio communications in 1936. Motorcycles were replaced with cars in 1938, as 24 new recruits joined the force, and the DSP was formally divided into Traffic and Criminal sections. A manpower shortage in World War II prompted the hiring of seven female clerks in 1943 (although active recruitment of female officers did not begin until 1974).

Modern times brought more changes. In 1969 the DSP adopted the state's first self-imposed code of police ethics. A year later, it created a full-time Drug Unit. The year 1971 witnessed creation of an Aviation Unit, plus active recruitment of black and Spanish-speaking officers. The DSP's first SWAT TEAM was established in 1975, followed by acquisition of an Automated Fingerprint Identification System (AFIS) in 1987 and creation of a specialized statewide homicide unit in 1989. The same year brought heightened awareness of white-collar crime, with formation of the Financial Organized Crime Asset Seizure Team (FORCAST). At 80 years and counting, the DSP is recognized as one of the Eastern Seaboard's outstanding law enforcement agencies.

DeLoach, Cartha Dekle (b. 1920)

A Georgia native, born July 20, 1920, Cartha DeLoach graduated from Florida's Stetson University and remained there for law school, but failed to complete his graduate studies. He joined the FBI as a clerk in August 1942, elevated to the rank of special agent 11 weeks later. G-men lost their automatic draft deferment in 1944, whereupon DeLoach joined the navy and spent the last nine months of World War II in the athletic department of an Oklahoma naval air station.

Rejoining the Bureau upon his discharge, DeLoach rose through the ranks to serve as inspector for the Training and Inspection Division (1951–53), as an aide to associate director CLYDE TOLSON (1953–54), in the Crime Records Division (1954–65), and as assistant to the Director for Investigations (1965). During that tenure DeLoach also acted as FBI liaison with the Central Intelligence Agency, where (in the words of ex-agent Robert Lamphere) he "reflected [J. EDGAR HOOVER's] negative attitude toward the CIA by working to exacerbate the problems between the two agencies, rather than damp them down."

By 1964 DeLoach was also Hoover's liaison to President Lyndon Johnson, summoned to perform special favors such as the illegal BUGGING of anti-Johnson delegates at the Democratic National Convention. Around the same time, in pursuit of funds to build a new FBI headquarters, DeLoach used unseemly pressure on Senate critics of the plan. Frank Elison, an aide to Senator Carl Hayden, accused DeLoach of "attempted blackmail," informing author Robert Kessler that DeLoach threatened disclosure of "information about my sex life . . . and that the senator might be disturbed." When Elison stood firm, DeLoach "started backing off" and claimed he was "only joking."

On December 31, 1965, Hoover promoted DeLoach to serve as deputy associate director, the third-highest FBI post. Widely regarded as Hoover's heir apparent, DeLoach surprised FBI-watchers by retiring from the Bureau in July 1970 and moving to New York as Pepsico's vice president for corporate affairs. In 1985 he "retired" again, moving to South Carolina as chairman of the board for Lighthouse Mortgage Corporation. Ten years later, he published *Hoover's FBI,* a memoir hailing his late boss as "a rare individual" possessed by "a nobility of purpose" that outshone his minor faults.

See also: FEDERAL BUREAU OF INVESTIGATION.

Denver Police Department

Colorado state legislators issued a city charter for Denver in November 1859, followed by election of William Sisty as the first city marshal. Over the next 15 years, eight men served as city marshal or chief of police, positions that sometimes merged, while at other times competing for authority. No uniforms existed, but badges were provided in 1864, followed by clubs in 1870 and official caps in 1871. Heavy-handed political influence produced a high turnover in personnel until 1873, when salaries and uniforms were standardized. Mug shots of "noted" criminals were authorized two years later, followed by institution of mounted patrols in December 1875.

Denver PD had no chief in November 1880, when anti-Chinese riots rocked the city, but Officer Dave Cook won the post after leading a 15-man team to break a mob of 2,000 rioting miners. He immediately issued 13 rules of behavior to reform the department, including two regulations for sleeping on duty and three against on-duty drinking. Denver acquired its first patrol wagon in 1886, and two years later hired a matron (Sadie Likens) to supervise female prisoners.

The 20th century brought new challenges, including pervasive CORRUPTION during PROHIBITION and the rise of a powerful KU KLUX KLAN that boasted 45,000 Colorado members, with 23,000 in Denver alone. Known Klansmen in Denver included the mayor, police chief William Candlish (appointed on orders from "Grand Dragon" J. G. Locke), a police inspector, scores of officers, and at least four local judges. The right-wing attitudes spawned by that infestation lingered for decades afterward, manifested in a widespread system of illegal DOMESTIC SURVEILLANCE during in the 1950s and beyond.

Denver PD created its RED SQUAD to spy on local "subversives" in 1954. In the late 1960s the unit collaborated with FBI agents to arrest and harass black militants and antiwar protesters. Unlike the FBI's COINTELPRO campaigns, however, Denver's spy unit was not exposed until March 2002, when its cover was blown by the AMERICAN CIVIL LIBERTIES UNION. Mayor Wellington Webb admitted that local police had adopted an "overbroad interpretation" of their intelligence duties, resulting in "cases where it may not have been justifiable to include certain individuals or organizations in our intelligence gathering activities." In fact, city spokesmen grudgingly confessed, the DPD had amassed dossiers on 208 different organizations and at least 3,200 individuals. Denver officials, slapped with multiple lawsuits for civil rights violations spanning a half century, offered the public their promise that all illegal surveillance has been terminated. Skeptics remain unconvinced, and the ACLU filed a new lawsuit for full disclosure of police surveillance files in January 2004.

Battered but unbowed, Denver PD leaders maintain that their department is committed to honesty and integrity, and dedicated to enforcing the law and maintaining peace, in partnership with the community." Their vision includes "consistent and equitable enforcement of the law"; "maintaining the highest standards of professional ethics, leadership, and integrity at all levels of the department"; "openness and accessibility within our community"; and ultimately the creation of "a community with a collective intolerance for crime, violence, neighborhood decay and disorder."

See also: FEDERAL BUREAU OF INVESTIGATION.

Detroit Police Department

Michigan state legislators established the Detroit Police Department in 1865, run by a four-man commission whose members were appointed by the governor for eight-year terms. That system continued until May 1901, when John Gillespie was named as the city's first solo police commissioner. Gillespie's force consisted largely of slow-witted political hacks, with an average IQ of 57 for patrolmen and 55 for sergeants. With salaries of $2.50 per 12-hour shift, many officers also welcomed bribes from racketeers and gamblers. Their "investigative" skills were limited to crude "THIRD-DEGREE" TACTICS, and many complaints were resolved with a baton during brutal "curbstone courts."

In early 1916 Mayor Oscar Marx replaced Gillespie with James Couzens, a former director of Ford Motor Company, whose police experience consisted of hiring private detectives to spy on Ford workers and harass union organizers. Despite that suspect background, Couzens called for a "disciplined city," demanding that his men enforce all statutes without fear or favor. He seemed to mean it, and that posed a problem for civic leaders, who sought a hands-off policy for Detroit's red-light district in the name of "public welfare." Couzens later complained, "When they asked me to clean up Detroit they didn't mean it. They wanted me to clean it up and not clean it up. They wanted me to make it nice enough for the reformers and let it stay rotten enough to appease the bums."

In October 1917, when Couzens called Detroit "the best policed city in the United States," a local tabloid countered with reports that murders had increased by 53 percent under his regime (from 59 to 89), while robberies nearly tripled (from 308 to 843) and auto thefts quadrupled (from 1,097 to 4,405). Nearly 300 policemen were hauled before Couzens on various charges in the last six months of 1917, 89 of them for drinking on duty, but he fired only 29. Fifty-four holdups were recorded in the first six weeks of 1918, and Couzens virtually conceded defeat in mid-February, enlisting state troopers to patrol the streets at night. Statewide PROHIBITION, beginning in May 1918, inaugurated a 15-year reign of CORRUPTION surpassing anything Detroit had seen before. Police turned a blind eye while the number of saloons increased tenfold, one observer christening Detroit "a city on a still."

Detroit P.D. created its first RED SQUAD—the Special Investigation Bureau (SIB)—in 1930, primarily to help Henry Ford and other Motown industrialists combat the United Auto Workers union. Common tactics included mass arrests, raids on political meetings, random beatings and mounted charges into union picket lines. SIB officers also worked closely with members of the Black Legion, a spin-off faction of the KU KLUX KLAN that practiced TERRORISM in the form of bombings (see BOMBING AND BOMB SQUADS), floggings, and murder. After the Legion was exposed, with 50-odd members shipped off to prison, Police Commissioner Heinrich Pickert was revealed as a secret member. He dodged that bullet by "frantically promot[ing] all those police officers who could compromise him," but Pickert was finally driven from office in 1939, after a local grand jury investigation disclosed widespread graft in the department. Indictments were filed against the mayor, Wayne County's prosecutor, Detroit's police superintendent and eight uniformed officers.

RACISM was another problem for Detroit P.D., showcased during a deadly race riot in June 1943. The outbreak left 34 persons dead, 25 of them black, and police so obviously sided with white rioters that future SUPREME COURT justice Thurgood Marshall issued a report comparing Detroit police to Hitler's Gestapo. A typical passage from Marshall's report described police handling of "looters":

> Throughout Monday the police, instead of placing men in front of stores to protect them from looting, contented themselves with driving up and down Hastings Street from time to time, stopping in front of the stores. The usual procedure was to jump out of the squad car with drawn revolvers and riot guns to shoot whoever might be in the store. The policemen would then tell the Negro bystanders to "run and not look back . . ." On several occasions, persons running were shot in the back. In other instances, bystanders were clubbed by police. To the police, all Negroes on Hastings Street were "looters."

Little had changed in Detroit by July 1967, when another riot rocked the city's ghetto. Of 43 persons killed in that riot, 34 were killed by police or by members of the NATIONAL GUARD. One Detroit policeman faced murder charges for his role in the execution-style slaying of three unarmed blacks at the Algiers Motel, but an all-white jury later acquitted him. The late 1960s also witnessed a revival of Detroit PD's Special Investigation Bureau, assigned to conduct surveillance on black militants and antiwar protesters of the "New Left." The SIB's political bias was revealed in 1965, when its leaders released derogatory material on murdered civil rights worker Viola Liuzzo to Alabama sheriff JAMES G. CLARK, JR. and leaders of the KKK.

Detroit voters adopted a new city charter in 1974, creating a five-member Board of Police Commissioners with broad supervisory powers, but the move failed to cure the department's problems. In June 2003 federal investigators probing police misconduct told Police Chief Jerry Oliver that they "have never seen problems as embedded and entrenched as in the DPD." Oliver, appointed in 2001, agreed that "the last couple of months here have been a real eye-opener." Among the problems cited were excessive use of DEADLY FORCE, illegal detention of witnesses, and other instances of misconduct that had cost the city $130 million in police-related lawsuits between 1987 and 2000. Fourteen persons died needlessly in police custody during 1998–2001, prompting the federal civil rights investigation and imposition of a consent decree mandating strict judicial oversight of all police activities.

See also: ALGIERS MOTEL SHOOTINGS.

Devens, Charles (1820–1891)

Boston native Charles Devens was born on April 4, 1820. He graduated from Harvard University in 1838, then studied law at Cambridge and engaged in private

Attorney General Charles Devens (Author's collection)

practice during 1841–49. He also served in the Massachusetts state senate (1848–49) and as a U.S. Marshal (1849–53) (see U.S. MARSHALS SERVICE), before returning to private practice in Worcester (1854–61). During the Civil War he served first as the major of an independent rifle battalion, later as colonel of the 15th Massachusetts Volunteers, brigadier general, and brevet major general. Devens was wounded twice in combat, at Fair Oaks and Chancellorsville. He left military service in 1866 and briefly resumed legal practice, before he was appointed justice of the Massachusetts superior court (1867–73) and then to the state supreme court (1873–77). President Rutherford Hayes named Devens attorney general, assuming office, holding that post from March 12, 1877, to March 7, 1881. Upon leaving Washington, Devens returned to his seat on the Massachusetts supreme court (1881–91). He died in office, at Boston, on January 7, 1891.

Devery, William (1855–1919)

The son of a New York City bricklayer, born in 1855, William Devery was nicknamed "Big Bill" for his girth and brutal exploits as a Bowery bartender. At age 23 he paid the standard bribe required by TAMMANY HALL for a patrolman's job with the NEW YORK CITY POLICE DEPARTMENT. The same graft-riddled system promoted him to sergeant in 1884, and in 1891 to captain of the Eldridge Street Station, in the midst of the Lower East Side's red-light district.

In that post, Devery distinguished himself as one of the NYPD's most corrupt field commanders, granting a virtual license to illegal brothels and gambling clubs. He was a bitter adversary of Rev. CHARLES H. PARKHURST and other reformers. Devery once threw a complaining minister out of his office, and told local dive owners: "There is a lot of silk-stocking people coming from uptown to bulldoze you people, and if they open their mouths you stand them on their heads." On one occasion, when a local ward heeler gathered 500 thugs to chase a team of Parkhurst's investigators from the precinct, Devery's detectives stood by laughing on the sidelines. In 1894 Devery was an unrepentant witness before the Lexow Committee, emerging unscathed from that inquiry into official CORRUPTION.

Four years later, Tammany leaders tapped Devery to serve as chief of NYPD, replacing John McCullagh (who refused to fire a patrolman who raided a protected casino). Parkhurst was outraged, telling journalists, "I know him as a man knows a serpent, by studying the trail where a serpent has crawled past. Devery's precinct is a moral cesspool. . . . The Lexow investigation had its direct origin in the damnably vicious condition of the precinct that was captained by a man who has just been made the responsible head of the biggest police force in America." NYPD historians James Lardner and Thomas Reppetto describe the new chief's style:

Devery was an informal administrator. He ran the force mostly from in front of a saloon on Ninth Avenue, where he would hold court until two or three in the morning. Sometimes he would go on a prolonged drunk, riding around town in a hack throwing handfuls of silver at sidewalk crowds.

The year 1900 was a watershed for Devery. August brought racial disturbances in the Tenderloin district, where Devery cleared the streets with club-swinging charges and prompted the *New York Herald* to coin the term *police riot*. Governor THEODORE ROOSEVELT sponsored legislation to create a single police commissioner for New York City, thus hoping to unseat Devery, but the chief had other plans. First, he ran for district attorney of Manhattan, then resigned when voters spurned him. Next he sought election as Tammany district leader in Chelsea, supported by bands of armed thugs and flagrant bribery, including free river cruises and picnics for some 18,000 constituents. Devery won that contest easily, but Tammany's leaders had second thoughts in the face of his mass popularity, refusing to certify the election results.

Ironically, the snub turned Devery into a reformer of sorts, angrily denouncing the political machine he had served throughout his police career. Former critics backed his mayoral campaign in 1903, against Tammany's man, but Devery lost by a landslide. Thereafter, he slipped into obscurity and died in 1919, on the eve of PROHIBITION.

Dewey, Thomas Edmund (1902–1971)

Born at Owosso, Michigan, on March 24, 1902, Thomas Dewey graduated from the University of Michigan in 1923 and received his law degree two years later from New York's Columbia Law School. As New York City's chief prosecutor in the 1930s, Dewey earned a "gangbuster" reputation for pursuing leaders of ORGANIZED CRIME. He convicted Mafia boss Charles "Lucky" Luciano on prostitution charges in 1936, convicted Nazi leader Fritz Kuhn of embezzlement in 1939, and sent labor racketeer Louis "Lepke" Buchalter to death row for murder in 1941. However, some observers of the Luciano trial deemed it a FRAME-UP, and Luciano himself claimed that his 1946 parole was secured through a $75,000 donation to Dewey's political war chest.

By that time, Dewey was serving his first term as New York's governor (1943–47) and had his eyes fixed firmly on the White House. His first bid for the Republican nomination failed in 1940, but the GOP selected him in 1944 and again in 1948. President Franklin Roosevelt smothered Dewey in the first contest, but his prospects seemed better in 1948—so much so, in fact, that the *Chicago Daily Tribune* printed advance headlines trumpeting Dewey's defeat of incumbent Harry Truman. Truman's upset victory stunned Dewey and FBI director J. EDGAR HOOVER, who had thrown the Bureau's covert weight behind Dewey in return for a promise of appointment to the U.S. SUPREME COURT. (Chagrined by the electoral upset, Hoover feigned a bout of pneumonia to avoid Truman's inauguration ceremony.)

Dewey abandoned his presidential aspirations after 1948, but served as a consultant to GOP candidate Dwight Eisenhower in 1952. Completing his third term as governor in early 1955, Dewey retired to private law practice, employed through the latter 1950s and early 1960s as general counsel for Schenley Industries, a whiskey-making firm run by PROHIBITION-era bootlegger Lewis Rosenstiel. Dewey died in New York, from a heart attack, on March 16, 1971.

See also: FEDERAL BUREAU OF INVESTIGATION.

Diallo, Amadou (1975–1999)

Guinean native Amadou Bailo Diallo, born in September 1975, settled in the United States to train as a computer technician. Prior to enrollment in college, he supported himself by selling videotapes and clothing on the streets of New York City. Early on the morning of February 4, 1999, Diallo was approached near his apartment building by four white officers of the NEW YORK CITY POLICE DEPARTMENT's Street Crime Unit. The plainclothes officers later claimed that Diallo matched the description of a rapist at large, further asserting that they "loudly" identified themselves as police. Diallo pulled a wallet from his coat pocket, at which point Officer Sean Carroll shouted, "Gun!" and all four officers opened fire with pistols, striking Diallo 19 times out of 41 shots fired. Examination of his corpse proved that Diallo was unarmed.

The extreme application of DEADLY FORCE prompted a Bronx grand jury to indict all four policemen on charges of second-degree murder and reckless endangerment. In an echo of the RODNEY KING case from Los Angeles, defense attorneys sought and won a change of venue to Albany, claiming that a fair trial was impossible in New York City. All four defendants were acquitted on February 25, 2000, sparking massive protest demonstrations against racial PROFILING and use of EXCESSIVE FORCE. Federal prosecutors from the U.S. JUSTICE DEPARTMENT declined to file civil rights charges against the four officers, whereupon Diallo's parents sued the city and

NYPD for $81 million on April 18, 2000. (City officials settled out of court for $3 million on January 6, 2004.) Singer Bruce Springsteen composed a song about Diallo's case, "American Skin/41 Shots," which prompted calls for a boycott of Springsteen concerts from spokesmen for the Patrolmen's Benevolent Association in June 2000. As a result of the Diallo killing and lawsuit, NYPD disbanded its Street Crime Unit in April 2002.

diplomatic immunity

Diplomatic immunity is a form of legal immunity recognized between governments, codified by the 1961 Vienna Convention on Diplomatic Relations, which grants diplomats safe passage without fear of arrest or lawsuits under a host country's laws. Diplomats may be expelled from host countries, and a home country may waive immunity, but that is rarely done and only then in cases of serious crime unconnected to the diplomat's mission. Legal guidelines permit a home country to try its own diplomats for crimes committed abroad, though once again, that option is rarely exercised.

Immunity is not equally applied in all cases. In general terms, a nation's diplomatic agents, members of the administrative and technical staff, together with their recognized family members, may not be arrested, subpoenaed or prosecuted for any offense, and their homes may not be searched (although they may receive traffic citations). Members of the diplomatic service staff and consular officials enjoy immunity only for actions directly related to their official duties. Diplomatic-level staff of various international organizations (the United Nations, NATO, etc.) enjoy full diplomatic immunity, while their general staff and support staff are protected only on official business.

Diplomatic immunity is sometimes abused, though major infractions are much more common in fiction than real life. New York City officials file innumerable protests with the U.S. State Department over nonpayment of parking tickets by United Nations officials, but serious crimes such as rape or murder would doom the careers of diplomats from most civilized nations, and would likely result in waiver of immunity or prosecution at home. The sole exception, in cases of ESPIONAGE, typically results in expulsion and branding of the guilty diplomat as persona non grata.

DNA

Often described as the building block of life on earth, deoxyribonucleic acid (DNA) is the substance that transmits genetic traits. Discovered in the 1960s, DNA was first used as legal evidence in 1985 and sent a criminal (British serial killer Colin Pitchfork) to prison

for the first time in January 1988. Since then, the science of DNA analysis and comparison—sometimes called "DNA fingerprinting"—has assumed strategic importance in many criminal cases where conviction or acquittal hinges on traces of blood, semen, hair, or other evidence containing genetic material.

To the best of current scientific knowledge, only identical twins display precisely the same DNA, but all human DNA has certain traits in common, and a relatively small percentage of it—some 13 percent—varies from one person to another. The key to analyzing DNA evidence lies in comparing genetic evidence found at crime scenes with a suspect's DNA in those segments that differ.

As a new form of evidence in the 1980s and early 1990s, DNA faced challenges from courts and attorneys who questioned the value of testing as positive evidence. Most jurors still have only a vague understanding of DNA analysis and require a crash course in the testing procedure at trial, before they can reach an informed verdict. Even then, attorneys for opposing sides have no recourse against jurors who misunderstand the evidence or simply refuse to consider it. A prime example was the case of O. J. Simpson, acquitted of double murder in 1995 despite damning DNA evidence collected from the crime scene and his home. In the wake of Simpson's acquittal, one juror told reporters, "I didn't understand the DNA stuff at all. To me it was just a waste of time. It was way out there and carried absolutely no weight with me."

Exoneration of those falsely accused or imprisoned is perhaps the greatest public service performed by DNA analysts, since it remedies injustice and informs authorities (if they were not already conscious of the fact) that unknown criminals remain at large. DNA cleared its first innocent suspect, a British citizen accused of two rape-murders, in 1985. Since the late 1980s more than 100 U.S. prison inmates have been liberated after DNA analysis proved they were innocent of murder, rape, and other heinous crimes. At least 10 have been freed from death row, condemned for the crimes of others, and those cases—including several deliberate FRAME-UPS by corrupt authorities—have sparked new debates over CAPITAL PUNISHMENT in America. Nationally, according to FBI analysts, DNA testing exonerates primary suspects in 30 percent of all cases examined.

Dodge, Fred J. (1854–1938)

A California native, born in 1854, Fred Dodge grew up among the Digger Indians and learned their tracking skills in childhood. Various odd jobs preceded his recruitment in 1879 as an undercover agent for the Wells Fargo express company. His first assignment was in Tombstone, Arizona, posing as a gambler, where Dodge had a ringside seat for the bloody conflict between the EARP BROTHERS and the Clanton gang.

Over the next decade, though still ostensibly a civilian, Dodge joined in most of the major manhunts for outlaws across Arizona Territory. He finally dropped his façade in 1888, joining the full-time staff of Wells Fargo's Southern Division, including Texas and the Oklahoma Indian Territory. There, after a May 1891 TRAIN ROBBERY, Dodge launched a pursuit of the Dalton gang that would consume most of his time and energy for the next 17 months. After failing to plant an informant in the gang, Dodge joined U.S. deputy marshal HENRY ANDREW THOMAS to create a "Dalton Posse," jointly funded by five railroads and three express companies. Dodge and Thomas believed they were "close," but time ran out for the Dalton's in Coffeyville, Kansas, riddled by outraged townspeople on October 5, 1892.

Eradication of the Daltons brought no rest for Dodge, however. Within a year of the Coffeyville shootout, train robberies reached epidemic proportions in Indian Territory, "coming too fast and thick for one man to work them all." Still, Dodge perse-

Bank robber Robert Dalton and his brothers eluded Fred Dodge, before meeting his fate in Coffeyville, Kansas, in 1892. (Author's collection)

vered, jailing more than his share of outlaws. He bought a Texas farm in 1896, but remained active with Wells Fargo until 1918, when he finally retired from the chase. Dodge died at home on December 16, 1938, a respected local character of whom the local paper wrote:

He had no patience with the rising tendency to glorify early day outlaws as picturesque heroes. He knew them for what they were. We cannot mourn his passing. He was very tired and had earned his rest.

See also: INFORMANTS.

Dodge City Peace Commission

In February 1883 Luke Short, an associate of the EARP BROTHERS and gambler-gunfighter Doc Holliday, purchased the Long Branch Saloon's gambling concession in Dodge City, Kansas. Gambling was banned by law in Dodge, but various casinos—including one run by Mayor

Outlaw Grattan Dalton (Author's collection)

Alonzo Webster at the Alamo Saloon—went unmolested where their owners paid regular fines as a kind of "sin tax." In April 1883 a new reform administration was elected, vowing to clean up the town with ordinances on vagrancy and prostitution. Marshal Jack Bridges and city clerk Lou Hartman invaded the Long Branch on April 28, arresting three "singers" on prostitution charges, leaving Short to fume at news that only his casino had been raided, while the Alamo remained unscathed.

Two days later, Short exchanged gunfire with Hartman on the street, but neither man was wounded. Short was jailed, then freed on bond, while raiders struck at several more saloons—still carefully avoiding the Alamo. Short briefly retreated to Kansas City, where he cabled Governor George Glick and received a promise of support. Next, Short reached out to his quick-draw friends, including Holliday, Wyatt Earp, and Bat Masterson, requesting their help in Dodge City. Holliday's tuberculosis prevented him from answering the call, but the *Kansas City Journal* of May 15 reported other gunmen flocking to a "tea party" in Dodge. Earp arrived on May 31, with comrades Johnny Green, Dan Tipton, Johnny Milsap, and "Texas Jack" Vermillion. Luke Short arrived with Bat Masterson on June 4, and the "Dodge City War" was settled five days later, with a compromise for peaceful coexistence among rival crime bosses.

Before leaving town, Wyatt Earp and his comrades posed with Short for a group photograph, published six weeks later in the *National Police Gazette* with a tagline identifying those pictured as members of the "Dodge City Peace Commission." Whether they ever used that name in fact is open to debate, but violence was avoided through the threat of overwhelming force. Short subsequently sold out his share in the Long Branch, in November 1883, and moved on to further adventures in Fort Worth, Texas.

See also: MASTERSON BROTHERS.

domestic surveillance

Most law enforcement agencies engage in some degree of domestic surveillance, defined here as investigation of citizens motivated primarily by the subjects' race, religion, political beliefs, or similar traits that violate no law. Civil libertarians note that such surveillance is commonly unwarranted, produces no criminal indictments, and historically has violated various statutes concerning "BLACK BAG JOBS," BUGGING, and WIRETAPS. Domestic surveillance sometimes crosses the line into active harassment, or even illegal ENTRAPMENT, including various cases of deliberate FRAME-UPS.

Congressmen who opposed formation of the FBI in 1908 expressed determination that "[n]o general system of spying upon and espionage of the people, such as has prevailed in Russia, in France under the Empire, and at one time in Ireland, should be allowed to grow up." Attorney General CHARLES JOSEPH BONAPARTE dismissed those fears as groundless, insisting that innocent persons should have no qualms about policemen studying their every move. And in fact, while the fledgling Bureau was theoretically restricted to investigating specific federal crimes, its first known file on private political expression dates from 1911. Sadly, it would not be an isolated case.

World War I witnessed the FBI's first authorized dabbling in "national security" cases, with a General Intelligence Division (GID) under young J. EDGAR HOOVER established in 1918 to track "enemy aliens." By 1922 Hoover had compiled 450,000 index cards on various groups and individuals, selected chiefly on the basis of their race (nonwhite) or "leftist" politics. Attorney General HARLAN FISKE STONE disbanded the GID in 1924, naming Hoover as the FBI's director on condition that he drop all political investigations, but Hoover kept his files and broke his word before the week was out. Over the next 48 years he collected dossiers on thousands of Americans, ranging from laborers and housewives to presidents and justices of the U.S. SUPREME COURT. Most had committed no crimes, but their inclusion in the Bureau's files was justified on grounds of "national security," providing G-men with limitless blackmail potential.

President Franklin Roosevelt legitimized part of that spying on August 25, 1936, when he requested an FBI report on Communist and fascist groups in the U.S. On September 5 Hoover ordered all FBI field offices to report "any information relating to subversive activities on the part of any individual or organization, regardless of the source from which this information is derived." There was no turning back for Hoover, who increased the scope of FBI domestic spying every year until his death. In 1956 he launched the first of several COINTELPRO operations explicitly designed to go beyond surveillance, actively disrupting and "neutralizing" groups of which he disapproved. And while COINTELPRO-type activities allegedly ended in 1971, later revelations demonstrate that identical tactics were still in use by FBI agents as late as 1990.

Domestic surveillance reportedly declined after 1991, with the collapse of the Soviet Union, but threats of TERRORISM soon replaced the cold war fear of "Reds." The disastrous attacks of September 11, 2001, renewed calls for sweeping surveillance to prevent future assaults. That outcry eased passage of the USA PATRIOT ACT, including broad surveillance powers for the federal government. On May 30, 2000, Attorney General JOHN DAVID ASHCROFT announced that G-men henceforth would be permitted to spy on domestic groups without producing any evidence of criminal behavior. Critic Laura Murphy, of the AMERICAN CIVIL LIBERTIES UNION, replied: "The government is rewarding failure. When the government fails, as it increasingly appears to have done before September 11, the [George W.] Bush administration's response is to give itself new powers rather than seriously investigate why the failures occurred."

While federal agencies like the FBI and Central Intelligence Agency are the best known practitioners of domestic surveillance in America, many state and local police departments have tried their hand at spying via RED SQUADS and other units established to shadow "subversives." A prime example is the DENVER POLICE DEPARTMENT, still facing litigation over surveillance campaigns that spanned a quarter century or more.

See also: FEDERAL BUREAU OF INVESTIGATION.

Dondero, John A. (1900–1957)

A New York native, born November 11, 1900, John Dondero graduated from the City College of New York in 1923, with a degree in chemical engineering. His career took a surprising turn at a Manhattan dinner party in the early 1930s, where he shared a table with pioneer fingerprint expert John Faurot. They discussed the problems caused by inks that smeared when fingerprints were taken, and Dondero—inspired by the hospital footprints of his infant daughter—soon developed a new inkless fingerprinting pad. Dondero soon quit his job and teamed with Faurot to create the Faurot Forensic Company, manufacturing crime-detection equipment with an emphasis on fingerprinting. In 1944 Dondero helped identify all but one of 168 victims killed in a tragic circus-tent fire at Hartford, Connecticut. After World War II, collaborating with the NEW YORK CITY POLICE DEPARTMENT, he founded a school to teach fingerprinting techniques.

Dondero died in August 1957, but his contributions to FORENSIC SCIENCE are posthumously honored via the International Association for Identification's John A. Dondero Memorial Award. The award, bestowed for a year's most significant contribution to identification and related sciences, has been granted to only 18 recipients since its creation in 1958. The first honoree was FBI director J. EDGAR HOOVER.

See also: FEDERAL BUREAU OF INVESTIGATION; FINGERPRINTS.

Dotson, David

Iowa native David Dotson ran away from home at age 14 and lived on his own thereafter. He served in the U.S. Air Force as an operational intelligence specialist, was discharged in 1955, and joined the LOS ANGELES POLICE

DEPARTMENT three years later. While employed as a patrolman, Dotson earned an associate's degree from College of the Canyons, using his relatively advanced education to rise steadily through the department's ranks. Dotson was assigned to the LAPD's Use of Force Review Board in 1980 and retained that post after his 1985 appointment to serve as one of three assistant chiefs under Chief DARYL FRANCIS GATES. From 1987 to 1992 Dotson also managed the department's internal disciplinary system.

His involvement with investigations of EXCESSIVE FORCE and DEADLY FORCE brought Dotson into conflict with LAPD colleagues who championed "aggressive law enforcement." In 1986, alarmed by the apparent lackadaisical investigation of police killings by Inspector Chuck Higbie's Officer Involved Shooting Team, Dotson spoke directly to Higbie's superior, James Hardin, commander of the Robbery/Homicide division. LAPD historian Joe Domanick describes what happened next:

"Look," [Dotson] told Hardin, when they met, "these investigations are terrible. I want you to tell Higbie to get with the goddamn program and start using the same investigative techniques we use in our other investigations." . . . Higbie, according to David Dotson, replied with clarity and unequivocation: "Tell him," he said to Hardin, "that we don't have time for that shit, tell'm that it's crazy, tell'm I'm doing what Gates wants me to, and tell'm to mind his own fucking business." "And by God," says David Dotson, "after that I minded my own business." David Dotson had learned that Chuck Higbie, as he himself put it, was "a creation of the chief, answerable only to the chief." That Chuck Higbie "was," in short, "above the law."

Dotson served as acting chief of the LAPD for 60 days in 1991, when Gates was suspended in the wake of the RODNEY KING beating, and while he took the civil service test to replace Gates permanently, he was not selected for the post. An extramarital affair surfaced around that time, involving a woman 28 years Dotson's junior, coupled with claims (never substantiated) that Dotson had failed to investigate misconduct charges against a deputy chief. Fearing demotion by Chief Gates, which would have cost him $1,300 in monthly pension benefits, Dotson retired before Gates returned in early 1992.

Effectively blackballed by Gates with other California law enforcement agencies, Dotson tried his hand at writing, affiliated with the Western Knight Center for Specialized Journalism. Writing for the *Los Angeles Times* in February 2000, he noted that LAPD could not be reformed while administrators blamed their problems on a few "bad apples," stressing instead that the department's internal difficulties were "cultural in nature." In interviews with *The Nation* that same year, Dotson cited LAPD's continuing resistance to reform by "outsiders." "And that's the root of this problem," he said, "this huge, inert mass that is the sealed-off, resistant internal culture of the LAPD. Until that is broken down there will be little reform."

Douglas, John Edward (b. 1945)

A Brooklyn native, born in 1945, John Douglas was rejected by Cornell University and carried a "D" average at Montana State College before he joined the U.S. Air Force in 1966 to avoid infantry service in the Vietnam War. While stationed in New Mexico, Douglas finished his bachelor's degree and became close friends with a local FBI agent. On leaving the air force in 1970, Douglas joined the Bureau, serving with the Detroit and Milwaukee field offices before he returned to the FBI Academy for training as a hostage negotiator. There he met instructor Robert Ressler, assigned to the Behavioral Science Unit devoted to psychological PROFILING of unknown offenders. Douglas transferred to the BSU in 1977 and joined Ressler in creating the Violent Criminal Apprehension Program (VICAP). Ressler retired in 1990 and Douglas replaced him as head of the unit, holding that post until his own retirement in 1995.

While involved on the periphery of many infamous SERIAL MURDER cases, often described as the real-life model for fictional G-man Jack Crawford in *The Silence of the Lambs,* Douglas never pursued or arrested a serial killer himself. Still, the job had its dangers, including a schedule so hectic and stressful that it drove Douglas to a near-fatal brain hemorrhage in December 1983. In retirement, Douglas has pursued a lucrative new career in true-crime writing, TV talk-show appearances, and private consultation on cases including the Jon-Benét Ramsey murder. His best-selling books pioneered a trend among retired FBI profilers who have followed his lead with publication of memoirs.

See also: FEDERAL BUREAU OF INVESTIGATION.

Drug Enforcement Administration

Prosecution of CONSENSUAL CRIMES is rarely effective in curbing illicit activities, as evidenced by PROHIBITION and America's haphazard "War on Drugs." The latter effort is assessed by most observers as an abject failure, undermined in equal parts by politics, CORRUPTION and wholesale public defiance. In 2004 federal sources reported that some 74 million Americans—26 percent of the total population—had used illegal drugs (up from 4 million, or 2 percent, in 1960), and that 10 per-cent or less of all drugs smuggled into the United States were captured by authorities.

While most police agencies play some role in the endless drug "war," federal efforts provide the best genealogy of U.S. drug enforcement. The Harrison Narcotics Act of 1914 taxed and regulated various drugs, leaving enforcement to the TREASURY DEPARTMENT's Bureau of Internal Revenue during 1915–27 and its Bureau of Prohibition during 1927–30. Treasury's Federal Narcotic Control Board, established in 1922, was renamed the FEDERAL BUREAU OF NARCOTICS (FBN) in 1930, with HARRY J. ANSLINGER appointed as the first commissioner of narcotics. The FBN survived until 1968, collaborating through its last two years with the Bureau of Drug Abuse Control, a subdivision of the Food and Drug Administration in the Department of Health, Education and Welfare. Those agencies merged and transferred to the JUSTICE DEPARTMENT in 1968, as the new Bureau of Narcotics and Dangerous Drugs (BNDD). In January 1972 President Richard Nixon created a new Office of Drug Abuse Law Enforcement at the Justice Department, renamed the Drug Enforcement Administration (DEA) on July 1, 1973. Three months later, a report from the Senate Committee on Government Operations listed six presumed benefits of the new agency:

1. Eliminating interagency rivalries that hampered federal drug enforcement, especially antagonism between the U.S. CUSTOMS SERVICE and the BNDD.

2. Giving the FBI its first major role in drug enforcement, by providing the DEA with "expert" information on ORGANIZED CRIME.

3. Establishing a focal point for drug enforcement efforts by federal, state, local, and foreign authorities.

4. Naming a single administrator to coordinate drug investigations and guard against corruption or abuse within the system.

5. Consolidating federal drug enforcement operations to maximize efficiency and eliminate redundancy.

6. Establishing the DEA as a "superagency" to spur greater federal efforts against drug trafficking.

President Nixon named JOHN R. BARTELS, JR. as the DEA's first administrator, confirmed by the Senate in October 1973. Bartels established the agency's first field intelligence unit that same month, including agents of the NEW YORK STATE POLICE and detectives from the NEW YORK CITY POLICE DEPARTMENT. Before year's end, the DEA established a National Narcotics Intelligence System, which contained 4.5 million records by 1998, with 5,000 items incoming per week. Drug smuggling in the Southwest prompted creation of the El Paso Intelligence Center in 1974, combining elements of the DEA, FBI, Customs, COAST GUARD, Immigration and Naturalization, the INTERNAL REVENUE SERVICE, and the Bureau of Alcohol, Tobacco and Firearms. Still, by the DEA's own admission, joint efforts with Mexican authorities "did not, in the long term, prevent the development of powerful drug trafficking organizations based in Mexico."

Soon after his January 1981 inauguration, President Ronald Reagan named Francis Mullen, a former FBI assistant director, to lead the DEA. That surprise move sparked criticism in Congress, where investigators described Mullen's appointment as a reward for his role in concealing Labor Secretary Raymond Donovan's underworld ties during Senate confirmation hearings. On January 28, 1982, Attorney General WILLIAM FRENCH SMITH announced a federal "War on Drugs," commanded by Vice President George H. W. Bush, but Reagan simultaneously cut the DEA's budget by 12 percent, requiring dismissal of 211 agents and 223 support personnel. By March 1982 the AMERICAN CIVIL LIBERTIES UNION, Coast Guard officers, and others had publicly condemned the Reagan drug war as a "fraud in terms of being serious proposals to reduce crime."

DEA-FBI collaboration in the past two decades has produced an uneven record. The jointly-sponsored Drug Demand Reduction Program, launched in June 1984, had no appreciable impact on U.S. drug consumption, but certain criminal investigations proved more successful. In 1985 G-men helped identify the killers of DEA agent ENRIQUE "KIKI" CAMARENA, producing 22 indictments in California and 24 convictions in Mexico. In November 1986 another joint effort indicted leaders of the Medellín, Colombia, cocaine syndicate; reputed leader Carlos Lehder Rivas was captured and extradited to the United States in February 1987. A year later, in February 1988, Panamanian dictator Manuel Noriega and 16 associates were indicted on drug smuggling and money laundering charges. In 1992 the DEA and FBI collaborated with ATF and the Coast Guard to create a National Drug Intelligence Center based at Johnstown, Pennsylvania.

Crime "wars" are typically judged on statistics, and the DEA's long struggle has produced some epic seizures: 75,066 pounds of hashish in San Francisco, on May 24, 1988; 389,113 pounds of marijuana in Miami, on August 8, 1988; 47,554 pounds of cocaine at Sylmar, California, on September 29, 1989; and 1,071 pounds of heroin in Oakland, California, on May 20, 1991. Still, it is a losing battle. Federal sources estimate that 12.3 tons of heroin entered the U.S. during 1995–98, while the Latin American Information Center pegged

U.S. cocaine imports (in December 2000) at 295–395 tons per year.

See also: DRUGS.

drugs

Prior to the 1870s no laws existed anywhere in the United States restricting manufacture, sale, or use of any drugs. Anti-Chinese hysteria prompted legal bans on opium in California and Nevada during 1875–76, but neither statute proved effective. Congress tried its hand in 1883, imposing a federal tax on opium and leaving the TREASURY DEPARTMENT to enforce it. On January 12, 1888, Treasury Secretary Charles Fairchild told Congress, "Although all possible efforts have been made by this Department to suppress the traffic, it has found it practically impossible to do so."

That failure should have been an object lesson, but politicians typically respond to failure with more legislation and greater expenditures of cash, and federal drug enforcement was no exception to the rule. The 1906 Pure Food and Drug Act restricted use of opiates, while the Harrison Narcotics Act of 1914 imposed higher taxes and regulated sales. Still, a Treasury study in 1922 found no decrease in drug trafficking. Four years later, a Federal Narcotics Control Board was created to oversee antidrug operations. In 1924 Congress outlawed importation or manufacture of heroin in any form, a ban that remains in effect despite studies in 1925 and 1967 that found the drug "does not differ in any significant pharmacological effect from morphine."

President Herbert Hoover created the FEDERAL BUREAU OF NARCOTICS in July 1930, naming HARRY J. ANSLINGER as its first commissioner. For reasons never clear, Anslinger launched a national campaign against marijuana, prompting 46 states and the District of Columbia to ban the drug between 1935 and 1937. Congress left federal enforcement to Treasury with the Marijuana Tax Act of 1937, while Anslinger carried his "reefer madness" campaign to the American Medical Association. Physicians initially contradicted his claims of marijuana's danger to society, but that viewpoint shifted radically after Anslinger prosecuted some 3,000 doctors for drug violations in 1937–39. By contrast, only three physicians went to trial in 1939–49, after the AMA adopted Anslinger's stance on marijuana.

Federal drug legislation continued to proliferate during and after World War II. Congress passed the Opium Poppy Control Act in 1942, followed by the 1951 Boggs Act (imposing harsher penalties for drug offenses) and the 1956 Narcotics Control Act (stiffening penalties once again, while it ensured federal primacy in suppressing illegal drug traffic). In 1968 President Nixon merged Anslinger's FBN with the Bureau of Drug Abuse

Control to create the Bureau of Narcotics and Dangerous Drugs (BNDD). The name change also brought a bureaucratic change of scene, as the BNDD was removed from Treasury and assigned to the JUSTICE DEPARTMENT. Accordingly, Congress abandoned the tax motive in 1970, basing its new Controlled Substances Act on the concept of federal dominance in interstate commerce. December 1970 saw President Richard Nixon honored by the International Narcotic Enforcement Officers' Association "in recognition of the outstanding loyalty and contribution to support narcotic law enforcement." In July 1973 Nixon created the DRUG ENFORCEMENT ADMINISTRATION (DEA), merging the BNDD with the Office of Drug Abuse Law Enforcement and the Office of National Narcotics Intelligence.

While drug seizures, arrests and prosecutions continued apace, the next major offensive was announced by Attorney General WILLIAM FRENCH SMITH in January 1982, with his public declaration of a national "War on Drugs." Vice President George H. W. Bush was named commander of the effort, but it was a curious campaign from the start. President Ronald Reagan launched the "war" with a 12 percent cut in the DEA's budget, while federal criminal prosecutions dropped 60 percent overall from levels maintained under President Jimmy Carter. Senator Joseph Biden called for a full-scale investigation by the General Accounting Office (GAO), whereupon Reagan and Attorney General Smith declined to furnish necessary documents. By March 1982 COAST GUARD spokesmen had publicly branded the new war on drugs "an intellectual fraud." Reagan countered criticism in 1988 by creating a new National Drug Enforcement Policy Board and an Office of National Drug Control Policy. The latter agency's commissioner was dubbed America's "Drug Czar," despite a constitutional ban on royal titles in the federal government.

Each year brings new reports of record drug seizures across the United States, but a February 2002 report from the GAO revealed that such statistics are deceptive. GAO investigators reviewed 26 cocaine seizures reported during 1998–2000, revealing that various seizures were counted twice to inflate the image of "success." Joint seizures carried out by the Defense Department, Coast Guard and the CUSTOMS SERVICE were commonly claimed by two or more agencies simultaneously, thus presenting a distorted image to the public. One motive for the deception was clearly economic, based on federal appropriations for anti-drug operations: in fiscal 2000 the Coast Guard received $756 million for drug interdiction, while Defense got $545 million and Customs received $436 million. Manipulation of statistics also occurred at DEA headquarters, where agency spokesmen claimed credit for 2,876 undocumented arrests. DEA accountants claimed that $30.2 million in criminal assets were seized during its high-profile *Libertador operation,* but GAO investigators found that $30 million of that total had been seized a month or more before the operation began.

Statistics on the human and financial cost of U.S. drug wars are likewise subject to debate, but they include the following: On April 25, 1993, the *Los Angeles Times* reported that almost 60 percent of all federal prison inmates were incarcerated on drug charges. The same survey found that federal drug sentences had increased in length by 22 percent since 1986, while sentences imposed on violent criminals *decreased* by 30 percent. Libertarian author Peter McWilliams reports that U.S. authorities spent $29 billion in 1991 alone to capture and prosecute drug offenders nationwide. Military agencies spent another $11 billion during the same year, to ferret out users within their own ranks. In 1994, 1,350,000 persons were arrested in America for drug offenses (among 15 million arrests overall). Critics of current government policy cite those statistics as evidence of futility in prosecuting CONSENSUAL CRIMES.

Durk, David (b. 1940)

The son of a New York eye surgeon, born in 1940, David Durk attended Amherst College and spent a year at Columbia University's law school before joining the NEW YORK CITY POLICE DEPARTMENT "on a lark," in June 1963. At the police academy Durk met and befriended another recruit, FRANK SERPICO, who shared his passion for crime-fighting and Durk's subsequent disillusionment over pervasive departmental CORRUPTION. Both were known as troublemakers early on—soon after his assignment to the 18th Precinct, Durk refused an order from his sergeant to clean the borough chief's office—but the rookies soon diverged in style. While Serpico grew long hair and affected exotic attire, Durk remained well groomed and dressed in suits, striving to retain good relations with his colleagues on the force.

It was a losing battle. Serpico soon asked Durk for advice on how to cope with daily bribe offers. Durk counseled him to report the offers, working his way up the chain of command ("people with flags in their offices") as one superior after another proved corrupt or apathetic. With Serpico, Durk persuaded Inspector Paul Delise to sit for a *New York Times* interview on police graft, but the partners diverged on tactics when the KNAPP COMMISSION was created to investigate the charges. Serpico was anxious to testify, while Durk refused. Angered by his hesitation, commission chief counsel Michael Armstrong told Durk, "You're just like everybody else. When it doesn't serve your agenda, you're not willing to testify—you're not willing to make the kind of sacrifice that you don't hesitate to ask of others. You expect guys to get out there and be heroes. You condemn everyone else because, according to you, they weren't willing to upset their good relations with the police, and here you are telling me that you won't upset your good relations with the police."

Still, Durk preferred to work behind the scenes, in an effort to save his career. With the Knapp hearings in progress, he persuaded other witnesses to testify, including Patrolman Robert Leuci, who described the links between NYPD and organized gamblers. Durk subsequently retired from the force but remained active in fighting CORRUPTION behind the scenes. Exposure of the 1986 "BUDDY BOYS" SCANDAL was due in large part to his efforts, convincing honest cops to grant newspaper interviews.

Dyer Act

The National Motor Vehicle Theft Act—more commonly known as the Dyer Act (after its primary sponsor, Missouri congressman Leonidas Dyer)—passed Congress in October 1919 in response to a new auto theft "crime wave." The law imposed harsh sentences, up to 10 years imprisonment plus fines, on anyone who drove a stolen car across state lines in the United States.

Aside from pacifying troubled motorists, the Dyer Act was also a financial godsend for the FBI, which frequently claimed credit for stolen cars recovered by local police. FBI leaders used the rigged statistics to obtain increased appropriations, Chief WILLIAM J. BURNS telling Congress in 1922 that the value of autos recovered "amounts to more than our appropriations" for the year. J. EDGAR HOOVER refined the technique during his 48 years as FBI director. In 1976, for example, Hoover supported his pleas for a budget exceeding $256 million by claiming his G-men had recovered 30,599 stolen cars and convicted 3,694 car thieves in 1969. The Dyer Act also provided an FBI "handle" on headline-grabbing cases where it had no other jurisdiction, including the 1930s pursuit of such bandits as John Dillinger and Clyde Barrow.

See also: FEDERAL BUREAU OF INVESTIGATION.

E

Earp Brothers

History and Hollywood have cast the five Earp Brothers—James, Morgan, Virgil, Warren, and Wyatt—as classic heroes of the American frontier, standing firm against ruthless outlaws to make the Wild West a more civilized place. The truth, as usual, is rather different and is glimpsed more commonly between the lines, behind the stage settings and clouds of gunsmoke that surround this famous family.

The Earps were Illinois natives, James born in 1841, Virgil in 1843, Wyatt in 1848, Morgan in 1851, and Warren in 1855. James was badly wounded as a Union soldier in 1863, and the whole family moved to California the following year. There Wyatt worked as a stagecoach guard, bartender, and gambler until 1871, when he was jailed for horse-theft. Posting $500 bail, he fled the state to hunt buffalo, then drifted to Wichita, Kansas, where James and wife, Bessie, ran a combination brothel and saloon. Bessie Earp appeared in Wichita police files as a known prostitute between May 1874 and March 1875, Earp critics noting that her disappearance from official records coincided with Wyatt's employment (in April 1875) as a Wichita policeman. Wyatt lasted 11 months on the job, fired and fined $30 in March 1876 for assaulting William Smith, a candidate for city marshal.

Moving on to Dodge City, Wyatt joined the local police force in May 1876, followed shortly by brother Morgan. James and Bessie soon arrived to resume their familiar trade in flesh and liquor, while Wyatt and colleague William "Bat" Masterson protected the action. Both were sworn policemen, but Dodge City residents knew them better as card sharks and procurers, dubbed

Morgan Earp (Author's collection)

"the Fighting Pimps." Wyatt left Dodge City in May 1879, after he and Masterson beat two drunks so badly that "their own mothers would have had a hard time

Since most of the Earps wore badges, members of the Clanton gang soon found themselves unwelcome in Tombstone, unless they were spending their money in Earp-run saloons, casinos, and brothels. Both sides were suspected in a fatal stagecoach robbery outside town, in March 1881, and violent clashes escalated until October 26, when the two factions met in the infamous O.K. CORRAL GUNFIGHT. Morgan and Virgil Earp were wounded, along with Doc Holliday, while three members of the Clanton gang were dispatched to Boot Hill. Murder charges were filed against the Earps, then thrown out by a friendly judge. Morgan was killed in a local pool hall on March 17, 1882, and the resultant "vengeance ride" by Wyatt, Warren, Doc Holliday, and others claimed an uncertain number of lives before the last Earps departed Arizona.

Wyatt and Holliday returned to Dodge City in 1883, teaming with Bat Masterson, gambler-pimp Luke Short, and others to create the DODGE CITY PEACE COMMISSION. In fact, the group was anything but peaceful, launching

Virgil Earp (Author's collection)

picking out their sons." A stop-off at Mobeetie, Texas, saw Wyatt collaborate with outlaw/lawman Dave Mather to sell phony gold bricks, before he was run out of town by the sheriff. Settled next in Tombstone, Arizona, Wyatt gathered his brothers as usual, enlisting tubercular gambler-gunman John "Doc" Holliday to help out with poker and gunplay. As historian John Faragher described the scene:

> Southeastern Arizona at the time was torn by conflict between the Republican business community and the mostly Democratic ranchers of the arid countryside. The "Cowboys," as the Republican Tombstone Epitaph labeled the ranchers, were led by Newman "Old Man" Clanton and his hot-headed sons and were backed by such violent gunmen as "Curly" Bill Brocius and Johnny Ringo. The trouble in Tombstone was just one episode in a series of local wars that pitted men of traditional rural values and Southern sympathies against mostly Yankee capitalist modernizers. As the hired guns of the businessmen in town, the Earps became the enemies of the Clantons.

Wyatt Earp (Author's collection)

a campaign of intimidation against owners of rival bordellos and gambling dens. After successfully defending their investments, Wyatt moved on to Idaho Territory, running various saloons with brother James and lending his hand to a claim-jumping gang. Tiring of those pursuits, Wyatt drifted back to California and remained there for the rest of his life, except for four years spent in Alaska (1897–1901), where he banked $80,000 as a gold-rush bartender. Warren Earp returned to Arizona as a "cattle detective" in 1900, but a gunfight in Wilcox claimed his life before year's end. Virgil died of pneumonia at Prescott, Arizona, in 1906, while James survived another 22 years in San Francisco.

By that time, Wyatt had begun work on his autobiography with author Stuart Lake. Wyatt died on January 13, 1929, and thus never saw his checkered life become the stuff of American legend, revised and inflated beyond all recognition through a long series of novels, films, and television shows. Nor was the process of mythologizing focused solely on Wyatt. Brother Morgan was credited with killing gunman William Brooks at Wichita in 1880, when in fact Brooks was lynched for rustling in July 1874. Within a quarter century of Wyatt's death, the Earp crime family had been transformed into rugged heroes, while their gang war with the Clanton crowd was enshrined as an epic triumph of good v. evil.

See also: MASTERSON BROTHERS.

Ebersold, Frederick

German immigrant Frederick Ebersold joined the Union Army at the outbreak of the Civil War and fought heroically beside General William Sherman at the battle of Shiloh. He subsequently joined the CHICAGO POLICE DEPARTMENT and rose to command the Harrison Street Precinct, which produced six chiefs between 1875 and 1907. Although Ebersold was a staunch Republican, Democratic mayor Carter Harrison chose him to replace retiring Chief Austin Doyle in October 1885.

Harrison may have supposed that Ebersold's background would please Chicago's many German voters, but it had the opposite effect on xenophobic Capt. JOHN BONFIELD. Obsessed with anarchists and "enemy aliens," Bonfield opposed Ebersold's "soft" stance on organized labor and gathered a clique of like-minded officers to undercut the new chief at every opportunity. Their feud split the department into hostile camps before tragedy struck with the HAYMARKET BOMBING of 1886. Even before that incident, a Bonfield partisan, North Side inspector Michael Schaak pronounced Ebersold's detective squad "incompetent." Neglecting his own central role in the problem, Schaak later wrote, "The department was rent and paralyzed with feuds

and jealousies between the chief and his subordinates. This too was at a time when the people of Chicago were in a condition of mind bordering on panic. [Ebersold] had neither a proper conception of his duties nor the ability to perform them."

Chicago police historian Richard Lindberg concludes that Ebersold had no significant role in the subsequent frame-up of Haymarket suspects, chiefly because Bonfield and Schaak withheld information on their frenetic search for the bombers. Still, it is difficult to understand how Ebersold could have missed entirely the citywide arrests and coercion of suspects, coupled with cash payments to 40-odd families in return for false testimony. Ebersold left office in 1888, with the advent of Mayor John Roche.

See also: ANARCHISM; FRAME-UPS.

Egan, Edward (1930–1995)

A native New Yorker, born January 3, 1930, Eddie "Popeye" Egan won international recognition as a detective of the NEW YORK CITY POLICE DEPARTMENT in 1962, when he and partner SALVADOR GROSSO cracked the infamous "French Connection" heroin ring. That episode and its resultant publicity lured both officers into show business, where they established lucrative secondary careers. Egan capitalized to good effect on his reputation as "the toughest cop in New York."

His first appearance on screen, appropriately, was a small role in *The French Connection* (1971), while his own character—renamed "Popeye" Doyle—was portrayed in Oscar-winning style by actor Gene Hackman. From there, he went on to act in films including *Prime Cut* (1972), *Badge 373* (1973), and *Cold Steel* (1987). Egan appeared even more often on the small screen, with roles in TV movies that included *Night of Terror* (1972), *Cop on the Beat* (1975), *To Kill a Cop* (1978), *Crazy Times* (1981), *Murder Me, Murder You* (1983), *Out of the Darkness* (1985), *Houston Knights* (1987), and *True Blue* (1989). Between 1975 and 1985, Egan also guest-starred or played continuing roles in the television series *Joe Forrester, Eischied, Police Story,* and *Mike Hammer.* He retired to Florida in 1984 and died of cancer in Miami on November 4, 1995.

Einstein, Isadore (1880–1938), and Moe W. Smith (?–1961)

The imposition of national PROHIBITION in 1920 brought unprecedented lawlessness to the Unites States, as rival gangs battled for bootleg territories, then joined forces to create the nation's first ORGANIZED CRIME syndicate. Thousands of gangland murders were recorded before the "Noble Experiment" ran its course in 1933—at least 696 in Chicago alone—but Prohibition also had its comic side. And many of the laughs were provided by a pair of U.S. Treasury Department agents known as Izzy and Moe.

Isadore "Izzy" Einstein, born in 1880, was a former dry-goods salesman, employed as a postal clerk when America went "dry" in January 1920. Federal administrators laughed when he asked for a badge, noting that he "didn't look like a Prohibition agent," but that fact would prove to be his greatest strength. Auditioned almost as a joke, Einstein scored big on his first day, infiltrating and closing a 52nd Street speakeasy which a dozen straitlaced agents before him had failed to crack. After a few weeks on the job, Einstein recruited a friend, cigar store employee Moe Smith, to be his partner. This time, Izzy's supervisors did not argue.

Together, Izzy and Moe raided saloons throughout New York City, slipping past security guards in the guise of two overweight working men out for a night on the town. As their fame spread in gangland, they later adopted disguises including rubber noses, black-face makeup, and false beards. They also fashioned funnels, worn beneath their vests or jackets, to collect the alcoholic evidence required for convictions in court. Over a five-year period, Izzy and Moe confiscated 5 million bottles of liquor and arrested 4,392 suspects, scoring a phenomenal conviction rate of 95 percent. Some accounts claim the pair raided 48 saloons on their busiest day, while other reports peg the total at 65.

The comic style of Izzy and Moe left some offenders laughing on their way to jail. On his first raid, Einstein reportedly flashed his badge and asked, "How about a good stiff drink for a thirsty revenue agent?" When the bartender asked where he'd purchased the badge, Izzy replied, "Give me a drink and I'll take you to the place sometime." On another occasion, invading a Coney Island saloon in the dead of winter, Einstein doused himself with cold water and stumbled in shivering, while Smith cried, "Quick! Some liquor before he freezes to death!" (The bartender complied, and went to jail.) At a bar in Van Cortlandt Park, the duo wore mud-spattered football uniforms, announcing that the season was over and they were ready to "break training." In yet another club, when two bootleggers wagered over whether Izzy's surname was Einstein or Epstein, Izzy won the bet—and bagged his men.

With notoriety came far-ranging assignments, as supervisors requested help from Izzy and Moe in other cities. Everywhere they went, the partners shamed their hosts, busting saloons in record time. On visits to Chicago and St. Louis, they cracked speakeasies within 21 minutes of their arrival in town. Atlanta was easier still (17 minutes), Pittsburgh took all of 11 minutes, and they barely had to leave the train in New Orleans, scor-ing their first drinks in 35 seconds. Back in New York, the two partners were often chastised for their lack of decorum by superiors who valued dignity over results.

Einstein and Smith left the Prohibition Bureau in November 1925, under circumstances that remain obscure today. Treasury spokesmen said they were dismissed "for the good of the service," while Einstein claimed, "I fired myself," rather than transfer to Chicago. Izzy published an autobiography, *Prohibition Agent No. 1,* in 1932 and died six years later. Moe Smith survived in obscurity until 1961. A 1985 made-for-TV movie based on their careers, *Izzie and Moe,* cast Jackie Gleason as Einstein and Art Carney as Smith.

Enright, Richard Edward (1871–1853)

Campbell, New York, native Richard Enright was born on August 30, 1871. He worked as a telegrapher prior to joining the New York City Police Department in 1896. Enright rose to the rank of lieutenant and served as president of the Police Lieutenants' Benevolent Association (forerunner of the Patrolmen's Benevolent Association), but his criticism of Commissioner Arthur Woods from that forum stymied his hopes for advancement. Woods bypassed Enright for promotion to captain on three occasions, pushing Enright to the bottom of the civil service list. He might have remained a lieutenant forever, but for the election in 1917 of Mayor John "Red Mike" Hylan.

An irascible politician who appreciated Enright's views and plain-spoken manner, Hylan broke all precedent by choosing Enright to replace Chief Frederick Bugher at the helm of the NYPD. To achieve that coup, Hylan bypassed 122 higher-ranking officers, most of whom instantly became Enright's enemies. Still, Enright was adept at departmental politics, NYPD historians James Lardner and Thomas Reppetto noting that the new chief's "vindictiveness knew no bounds." Former rivals of Enright's from the PLBA were special targets of malice, including Lt. Lewis Joseph Valentine (three times denied promotion to captain) and Lt. Floyd Horton (denied membership in the department's Honor Legion after he died in a shootout with felons).

Enright's methods as chief were unique, if not always effective. He disbanded NYPD's prototype Internal Affairs unit, preferring an "honor system" to prevent corruption, and solicited private donations to help patrolmen purchase their required equipment. While joining the FBI and the vigilante American Protective League in street sweeps for "slackers" during World War I, Enright lobbied to have his officers exempted from the military draft. He hired a handful of female officers, but generally preserved the NYPD as a bastion of white male superiority. Enright's creation of a special anti-gambling squad ultimately proved futile, and NYPD was soon awash in fresh graft from bootleggers, with the advent of PROHIBITION, forcing Enright to discipline dozens of command-grade officers who turned a blind eye to booze-runners.

Enright retired from the NYPD in December 1925, then tried his hand briefly at magazine publishing before he launched a business selling burglar alarms to New York City merchants. In 1933 he helped create a small detective force for President Franklin Roosevelt's National Recovery Administration, persevering despite jealous opposition from FBI director J. EDGAR HOOVER. Before an accidental fall claimed his life in 1953, Enright founded and directed the United Service Detective Bureau, a private investigation agency in New York City.

See also: FEDERAL BUREAU OF INVESTIGATION.

entrapment

In legal parlance, "entrapment" occurs when law enforcement officers stage some criminal activity to ensnare unidentified suspects. Unlike bona fide "sting" operations—which offer contraband or some illicit opportunity to known criminals—entrapment commonly targets subjects with no history of criminal behavior, and thus generates crimes that otherwise would not occur, for the sole purpose of logging arrests. Most U.S. jurisdictions bar entrapment as a matter of policy.

A classic case of entrapment emerged from Seattle, Washington in 1970, where FBI agents employed career felon Alfred Burnett to provide "valuable information" on ghetto violence and the Black Panther Party. After a series of local bombings (see BOMBING AND BOMB SQUADS), Burnett was ordered to identify the individuals responsible. Unable to link any Panthers with the crimes, Burnett paid Larry Ward, a 22-year-old Vietnam war veteran, $75 to bomb a Seattle realtor's office. Burnett also supplied the bomb, then alerted G-men to the impending attack. As Burnett later explained in court, "The police wanted a bomber and I gave them one."

On the night of May 14, 1970 officers of the SEATTLE POLICE DEPARTMENT ambushed Ward and killed him at the realtor's office. Ward carried no weapon other than Burnett's bomb, and Burnett later claimed that he "distinctly told" the FBI that Ward would be unarmed. Seattle's mayor had advocated killing bombers as a deterrent to future attacks, but police spokesmen professed surprise at the stakeout's result. John Williams, chief of the SPD's intelligence unit, blamed FBI agents for Larry Ward's death, saying, "As far as I can tell, Ward was a relatively decent kid. Somebody set this whole thing up. It wasn't the police department." Bur-

net later pled guilty on a bank robbery charge and was transferred to federal prison by his FBI handlers for reasons of security. The Seattle bombings remain unsolved.

See also: FEDERAL BUREAU OF INVESTIGATION.

environmental crimes

Environmental crime includes any transgression of laws enacted to protect the ecosystem from destruction or pollution. In the United States it spans a wide range of federal, state, and local statutes governing air and water pollution, dumping of waste or toxic materials, destruction of natural habitats and protection of endangered species. Federal statutes are administered by the ENVIRONMENTAL PROTECTION AGENCY, and offenders may be arrested by the FBI, prosecuted by the U.S. JUSTICE DEPARTMENT. State, county, and municipal law enforcement agencies enforce their own laws and ordinances, but local officials sometimes oppose federal guidelines and (particularly in the western states) set themselves deliberately at odds with statutes restricting construction, oil drilling, mining, logging, and other pursuits deemed critical to regional economies. The outcome of that seesaw conflict depends in large part on who controls the White House and the Congress.

See also: FEDERAL BUREAU OF INVESTIGATION.

Environmental Protection Agency

Congress established the EPA in July 1970, in response to mounting public demands for cleaner air, land, and water. Its difficult mission combines repair of damage already done to the U.S. environment with prevention of further damage. Its 18,000 employees operate from headquarters in Washington, D.C., with 10 regional offices and 17 laboratories scattered across the country. More than half the EPA's employees are highly educated engineers, scientists, and environmental protection specialists who often find themselves mired in a swamp of self-serving federal and state politics.

Statutes presently enforced by the EPA include the Water Pollution Control Act (1948); the Air Pollution Control Act (1955); the Clean Air Act (1963); the Wilderness Act (1964); the Motor Vehicle Air Pollution Control Act (1965); the Water Quality Act (1965); the Solid Waste Disposal Act (1965); various Clean Air Act Amendments (1966, 1977, 1990); the Clean Waters Restoration Act (1966); the Endangered Species Preservation (1966); the Air Quality Act (1967); the Scenic Rivers Preservation Act (1968); the National Environmental Policy Act (1969); the Endangered Species Conservation Act (1969); the Clean Air Extension Act (1970); the Water Quality Improvement Act (1970);

the Resource Recovery Act (1970); the Wilderness Acts (1970, 1978); the Water Pollution Control Act (1972); the Marine Mammal Protection (1972); the Endangered Species Act (1973); the Safe Drinking Water Act (1974); the Toxic Substances Control Act (1976); the Resource Conservation and Recovery Act (1976); the Clean Water Act (1977); the Surface Mining Control and Reclamation Act (1977); the Alaska Land Protection Act (1980); the Comprehensive Environmental Response, Compensation, and Liability Act (1980); the Nuclear Waste Repository Act (1982); the Hazardous and Solid Wastes Amendments Act (1982); the Water Quality Act (1987); and the California Desert Protection (1994).

Unfortunately, the EPA's work is often frustrated by political leaders in Washington who seek votes and financial support from special interests tied to polluting industries.

Erdmann, Ralph

In Texas, where he plied his trade as a circuit-riding medical examiner, Dr. Ralph Erdmann was nicknamed "Dr. Death." He won that sobriquet from prison inmates and defense attorneys, based on his courtroom testimony that sent dozens of accused murderers to death row. Apparently a tireless public servant, Erdmann operated in 40 of the Lone Star State's 47 counties, once charging prosecutors $171,000 for 400 autopsies in a single year. His medical verdicts invariably supported police theories in the cases he examined—so dependably, in fact, that one attorney later told reporters, "If the prosecution theory was that death was caused by a Martian death ray, then that was what Dr. Erdmann reported."

And therein lay the problem.

Erdmann's reputation began to unravel in 1992, when relatives of one deceased man obtained a copy of Erdmann's autopsy report, noting the weight of a spleen surgically removed years earlier. The corpse was exhumed, revealing that no autopsy had been performed. Lubbock attorney Tommy Turner was named as special prosecutor to review Erdmann's work, examining 100 autopsies wherein he found "good reason to believe at least 30 were false." In fact, as one judge noted, some police departments refused to use Erdmann because "he wouldn't do the work. He would ask what was the police theory and recite results to coincide with their theories"—in short, a long series of FRAME-UPS.

When Erdmann *did* operate, he made bizarre mistakes which prosecutors struggled to conceal from jurors. In one case, Odessa prosecutors had to dismiss murder charges after Erdmann lost the victim's head, bearing a fatal bullet wound. In another case, he claimed to have examined the victim's brain, but exhu-

mation revealed no cranial incisions. Yet another case found Erdmann mixing organs from two bodies in the same container and offering false testimony as to cause of death. Turner's investigation disclosed that Erdmann sometimes allowed his 13-year-old son to probe wounds during autopsies, and that on several occasions his wife sold bones removed from murder victims.

Erdmann did not always find a suspect guilty, though. If police believed a death was accidental, he would skew the evidence in that direction just as happily. One such case involved 14-month-old Anthony Culifer, smothered with a pillow by his mother's boyfriend. Erdmann blamed the death on pneumonia, his finding reversed by a second autopsy nine years later. In a similar case, Erdmann claimed that a woman strangled by her ex-boyfriend had accidentally choked to death on vomit. (The killer was eventually convicted, while a judge ordered Erdmann to pay the victim's family $250,000.) Still, it was Erdmann's testimony in capital cases that proved the most dangerous, though, with at least four defendants executed on his word alone. Statewide, 20 more condemned inmates appealed their verdicts after Erdmann's misconduct was revealed.

In 1992 Erdmann pled guilty to seven felony counts in Randall County, including perjury and falsifying autopsy results. As part of the plea bargain, Erdmann surrendered his medical license, received a sentence of 10 years' probation with 200 hours of community service, and was ordered to repay $17,000 in unearned autopsy fees. He moved to Seattle, Washington, where police caught him with a cache of weapons in June 1995, thus violating terms of his probation. Texas extradited Erdmann to serve his time, and while he was eligible for release after 30 months, public protests blocked his first parole bid in March 1997.

Erler, Robert John, Jr. (b. 1944)

At 6:18 A.M. on August 12, 1968, an anonymous caller told the sheriff's office in Fort Lauderdale, Florida, "I just killed three people! Please catch me before I kill more!" Despite pleas to "come and get me," the male caller refused to give his name or location, signing off with a warning: "I'm going to kill more tonight, too!"

A short time later, security guards at Fort Lauderdale's airport found a woman slumped in her car in a public parking lot. She had been shot five times in the head at close range, but she still clung to life. Rushed to a nearby hospital, she was identified as 42-year-old Dorothy Clark, from Clarkston, Georgia. While surgeons fought to save her, Patrolman Robert Erler, Jr. of the Hollywood Police Department found another body lying in a field near a local industrial park, allegedly directed to the scene by an excited motorist. The victim was Clark's 12-year-old daughter Merilyn, shot five times in the head and certified dead at the scene. Police felt certain they had found two of the caller's victims, but no third body was ever located to round out the score.

Patrolman Erler was a rookie, born July 1, 1944, in Adam, Arizona, whose family moved to Phoenix when he was a child. A black-belt karate expert who joined the army after high school, he enrolled in Special Forces training but received an early hardship discharge when his father fell terminally ill. Married in Phoenix, Erler soon moved to Florida and entered local law enforcement. Starting off with the tiny police force in Dania, he clashed with black officers over their off-duty flirtations with white barmaids. Erler resigned in Dania after coming home one night to find a black cop in his home, conversing with his wife. He soon transferred to Hollywood P.D. and received his first real training, from all appearances adjusting well to his new job. Now he was in the midst of a murder investigation, assigned to supervise a voice-recognition campaign reviewing tapes of the "Catch-Me Killer's" phone call.

By August 19 Dorothy Clark had recovered sufficiently to describe her attacker as a blond, crew-cut young man in a police uniform. He had approached her car while Clark and her daughter slept on Dania Beach, shining a flashlight in their eyes and demanding money. Upon receiving that description, Bob Erler—a short-haired blond—announced his resignation with the claim that his mother needed help at home in Arizona. He was gone a week before one of his coworkers identified the unknown caller's voice as Erler's. Detectives checked his patrol log for August 12 and found that Erler had no name or license number for the witness who supposedly found Merilyn Clark's corpse. They also determined that the field where she lay was too dark at night for any passing motorist to see a body lying on the ground.

The case broke when Dorothy Clark picked Erler's photo as a likeness of her attacker, and prosecutors issued a warrant for his arrest on September 13. Captured in Phoenix two days later, he was held on $85,000 bond pending extradition to Florida. Indicted for second-degree murder, Erler based his defense on sparse physical evidence and conflicting statements from Dorothy Clark. She failed to spot him in a lineup on September 24, and defense attorneys were still seeking an elusive alternate suspect when Erler's trial began on January 27, 1969.

Clark's story on the witness stand hardly resembled her first report to police. She now described Erler approaching her car on Dania Beach with a warning that laws forbade sleeping in public. Instead of forcing them to move along, however, Erler had invited the

Clarks to his mobile home, easing their qualms with the advice that he was married, with an infant son. They saw no wife or child upon arriving at the trailer, but Merilyn still went to sleep on a couch. Then, Clark testified, Erler had turned to her with a demand for sex, drawing a gun and forcing her to watch him masturbate when she refused. That done, he escorted the Clarks to their car at gunpoint, only then demanding cash. Clark had turned to her daughter, remarking, "Boy, I sure can pick them," and remembered nothing more until she woke in the hospital, more than three weeks later.

Erler testified in his own defense, denying any part in the crime, but jurors convicted him on January 31, recommending a sentence of 99 years. The judge agreed, adding another six months for good measure. Confined at Raiford prison, Erler refused protective isolation and suffered repeated attacks by inmates who despised him both as a child-killer and policeman. Finally transferred to a medium security lockup at Belle Glade, Erler escaped in August 1973 and made his way to Miami, where he organized a loose-knit criminal gang.

On March 31, 1974, authorities in Mathison, Mississippi, were called to examine a parcel at the local post office. Inside the package, addressed to "Bruce Strickland," they found marijuana and a pistol. Police were waiting when Erler arrived to collect it, sporting black-dyed hair and fake I.D. A high-speed chase ensued, ending when Erler crashed his car, and a gunshot to the buttocks prevented his escape on foot. Returned to prison under tight surveillance, Erler experienced a jailhouse religious conversion, confessing his attack on the Clarks and withdrawing his appeal of that conviction. Soon he was recognized as leader of the Christian Men's Fellowship at Florida's state prison, where he also organized an inmate Jaycee chapter. In 1977 Erler was transferred to an Arizona lockup, where he continued his ministry, baptizing more than 100 convicts in a prison irrigation ditch. A year later, Arizona's parole board recommended his release, but Florida authorities insisted that he serve a minimum of 25 years. That demand notwithstanding, Erler was freed on July 19, 1983, to resume preaching as a free man. "Religion," he told reporters, "is the best armor that a man can have, but it is the worst cloak."

espionage

Most national governments engage in some manner of espionage—spying—against other countries and on their own citizens (termed DOMESTIC SURVEILLANCE). Under U.S. law in the 20th century, "intelligence" functions were clearly divided between foreign and domestic operations. Agents of the Central Intelligence Agency operated abroad and were barred by law from spying inside the United States (a rule which they often ignored), while the FBI held sole responsibility for catching foreign spies inside the country. After the terrorist attacks of September 11, 2001, that structure changed, with passage of the USA PATRIOT ACT and creation of the HOMELAND SECURITY DEPARTMENT. CIA agents are now empowered to operate inside the United States and to share FBI files on "normal" criminal cases—a situation viewed by civil libertarians with substantial concern.

While FBI agents were assigned to enforce the Espionage Act of 1917 during World War I, their operations under that statute had less to do with bagging foreign spies than silencing critics of military conscription. Secret agents were caught on occasion, but the Bureau's first major espionage case arrived in 1935, when G-men in New York City uncovered a German spy ring run by Guenther Rumrich. The breakthrough was tempered by embarrassment, since Rumrich's network had been active since 1927, and another three years elapsed before 18 suspects were indicted on June 20, 1938. Even then 14 escaped, leaving Rumrich and three others to receive 10-year prison terms in December 1938.

In November 1938 President Franklin Roosevelt approved J. EDGAR HOOVER's bid to expand FBI espionage work in collaboration with the Army's Military Intelligence Division and the Office of Naval Intelligence. FBI statistics reveal a dramatic surge in spy cases around that time, from an average of 35 per year in 1937 to 634 in 1938 and a "projected total" of 772 in 1939. No figures are available for World War II, but statistics provided to author William Breuer for his book *Hitler's Undercover War* (1989) portray a less impressive conviction rate. According to the Bureau's own figures, it convicted only 100 spies between 1937 and 1945, including 68 U.S. citizens, 25 Germans, and one each from Austria, Canada, Colombia, Portugal, Russia, South Africa, and Spain. The war's most dramatic spy investigation, the Amerasia case of 1945, was thrown out of court because G-men and agents from the Office of Strategic Services committed illegal break-ins to obtain evidence.

Counterespionage work was no easier in the cold war. Ex-communist Elizabeth Bentley volunteered her services as an FBI informant in 1945, describing her wartime work with the Jacob Golos spy ring, but again the Bureau was embarrassed at having missed a network active in New York since 1938. Bentley's testimony failed to secure a single indictment, a problem she suffered again with charges filed against alleged spies William Remington and Harry Dexter White. G-men caught Judith Coplon red-handed in 1949, passing classified documents to a foreign agent, but she escaped punishment because of the FBI's addiction to illegal WIRETAPS. Alleged traitor Alger Hiss, likewise, could not be convicted on the ever-changing testimony of professional witness Whitaker Chambers, though he was finally imprisoned for perjury. Even the FBI's 1951 "triumph" in the case of Julius and Ethel Rosenberg stands tainted today, in light of revelations that Ethel's conviction was a frame-up conducted in a vain attempt to make Julius name accomplices.

The FBI has fared better with espionage cases since Hoover's passing. Unfortunately, some of those caught in the net were traitorous G-men themselves, including RICHARD W. MILLER (1984), Supervisor Earl Pitts (1986), and Agent ROBERT HANSSEN, who spent a quarter century spying for Russia before his arrest in 2001. A report from the General Accounting Office, published on August 15, 2001, revealed that even when spies were discovered, FBI spokesmen sometimes failed to alert the JUSTICE DEPARTMENT. In other cases, revelations were made so late they proved worthless, the suspects already beyond reach of U.S. authorities.

See also: FRAME-UPS; INFORMANTS.

Evarts, William Maxwell (1818–1901)

A native of Boston, born February 6, 1818, William Evarts graduated with honors from Yale University in 1837. He subsequently studied law at Harvard and with an attorney in New York City, where he was admitted to the bar in 1841. From 1849 to 1853 Evarts served as assistant U.S. district attorney for the Southern District of New York. An ardent Republican, Evarts was a delegate to the Republican National Convention that nominated Abraham Lincoln for president in 1860, then ran unsuccessfully for the U.S. Senate in 1861. Six years later, he served as a delegate to the New York state constitutional convention. In early 1868 Evarts was principal counsel to President Andrew Johnson in his impeachment trial before the U.S. Senate. After defeating that challenge, Johnson rewarded Evarts by naming him attorney general, a post Evarts held from July 20, 1868, to March 5, 1869. In 1872 he served as U.S. counsel before the Swiss tribunal adjudicating claims from the wartime sinking of the Confederate warship *Alabama* in European waters. Four years later, following the controversial election of 1876, Evarts represented the GOP and candidate Rutherford Hayes before the electoral commission that named Hayes the winner (even though Samuel Tilden led Hayes in both popular and electoral votes). Once again, Evarts was rewarded for his service to the White House, this time by appointment to serve as secretary of state (1877–81). Evarts subsequently served as America's delegate to the International Monetary Conference in Paris (1881) and

Attorney General William Evarts (Author's collection)

in the U.S. Senate (1885–91). Poor health thereafter prompted his retirement from public life, and he died in New York City on February 28, 1901.

excessive force

"Police brutality" is a subject guaranteed to raise the hackles of conservatives and liberals alike. Most law enforcement officers will privately admit that certain colleagues use more violence than is necessary during some arrests, but a majority insist that such abuse is "understandable" or even necessary to preserve "respect." Only in isolated cases, such as that of ABNER LOUIMA in New York City, will most cops acknowledge a need for criminal sanctions.

Police brutality is broadly divided into two categories: excessive force during or after an arrest, and "THIRD-DEGREE" TACTICS used to extract confessions in custody. Violence is a daily hazard and by-product of police work, expected in situations where officers confront resentful citizens or felons bent on remaining at large. Methods of subduing violent subjects constantly

evolve with the development of new nonlethal WEAPONS, while other techniques (like the sometimes-deadly choke hold) are abandoned. In general terms, "necessary" force is that which any reasonable person—in this case, specially trained police officers—might deem necessary to subdue a subject without inflicting gratuitous injury or summary punishment. Most observers agree that force becomes *excessive* when it continues beyond the arrest (with subjects handcuffed or otherwise physically restrained) and/or when it inflicts severe or life-threatening injury.

Different observers naturally disagree on how much force is "necessary" to subdue a prisoner or maintain "order in the streets." Most northern residents were outraged in February 1946, when black combat veteran Isaac Woodward was jailed for using a "white" restroom in South Carolina, then beaten and blinded by Batesburg police chief Linwood Shull, who gouged out Woodward's eyes with a nightstick. (Shull was acquitted at trial and retained his job.) In the early 1960s southern police drew criticism for their use of attack dogs, high-pressure hoses, and electric cattle prods against nonviolent civil rights marchers (many of them children). Later that same decade, televised POLICE RIOTS in Los Angeles, Chicago, and elsewhere made it clear that excessive force is a national problem. Thirty years later, videotapes of the RODNEY KING beating revealed that little had changed.

Complaints of excessive force are the prime motivation behind public calls for CIVILIAN REVIEW BOARDS created to investigate charges of police misconduct. Many observers feel that police INTERNAL AFFAIRS departments have failed to curb abusive practices, and may in some cases whitewash unnecessary violence. The controversy will doubtless endure as long as police officers and civilians clash on urban battlefields from coast to coast.

See also: CHOKE HOLDS.

Explorer Program

The Explorer Program is a young adult division of the Boy Scouts and Girl Scouts of America, not to be confused with the separate and distinct Explorer Scouts. As described by scouting spokesmen, the Explorer Program "is often misunderstood or mislabeled because the program focuses on service and is usually seen and not heard." Specifically, young Explorers of both sexes receive "training and leadership in businesses, industries, churches, schools, government agencies, professional societies, civic clubs, labor unions, sports clubs, and other community organizations." The program's law enforcement branch exists specifically "to educate and involve youth in police operations, to interest them in possible law enforcement careers and to build mutual understanding."

Scout troops throughout the United States maintain Explorer units ("posts"), which send teenagers on police ride-along programs and otherwise involve them in the daily work of law enforcement under predetermined guidelines. Explorers normally do not participate in arrests or other dangerous situations, and they are not authorized to collect crime scene evidence, perform interrogations, or otherwise intrude upon active police investigations. They are, in effect, apprentices without authority or WEAPONS, and must still complete standard police training courses as adults before entering service as sworn peace officers.

Despite its laudable aims, the Explorer Program came under fire in the late 1990s, following reports that various participants (mostly female) had engaged in sex with sworn officers and in some cases were sexually molested against their will. On June 25, 2003, federal investigators published results of a $1 million research project scrutinizing charges filed against police involved with the Explorer Program. Professors Samuel Walker and Dawn Irlbeck conducted the study from their base at the University of Nevada's Criminal Justice Department, declaring that 25–30 reports of Explorer sexual abuse had been filed within the past 12 months alone. The cases cited included:

East Ridge, Tennessee: Officer Keith Maynard, age 31, was suspended from duty in 2002, charged with two counts of statutory rape and two counts of aggravated child molestation, accused of having sex with a 15-year-old female Explorer. Upon conviction in November 2004, Maynard received concurrent 30- and 20-year prison terms, facing a minimum of 15 years in custody before parole.

Haltom City, Texas: A 28-year-old policeman, John Ross Ewing, was indicted in March 2003 on charges of sexually assaulting two male Explorers,

ages 15 and 16, in his apartment. Ewing was convicted on three felony counts in September 2003; he received a 20-year prison term on one count, with 10-year terms suspended on two others.

San Bernardino, California: Freddie Lee Johnson, a 34-year-old deputy, pled guilty in April 2003 on charges of having sex with a 16-year-old girl on a scout-related camping trip. The girl woke in her tent to find Johnson atop her, and she submitted from fear that "if I said anything I would get in trouble and I would have to leave the sheriff's department." Johnson was sentenced to spend 60 weekends in jail.

Anaheim, California: Officer Jason David Rosewarne, 31, was relieved of duty as Explorer Program adviser and resigned from the force in 2002, facing charges of oral copulation with a 17-year-old female. Rosewarne was indicted on that charge in October 2002, but the British native escaped trial by fleeing to London, where he claimed dual citizenship.

Several departments also acknowledged illegally using Explorers on pornography sting operations, sending them into adult bookstores to purchase items legally restricted to adults. In other areas, Explorers were allowed to drive marked patrol cars, thus placing them in potential danger situations. All such activities are specifically banned by Explorer Program guidelines.

Law enforcement leaders note that such cases are still relatively rare. In 2002 some 43,000 Explorers were assigned to police and sheriff's departments around the nation, with 30 complainants constituting only .006 percent of the total. Still, as a Boy Scouts of America national spokesman told reporters in June 2003, "One child, 12 children, it's always one too many."

Fargo Police Department

Despite its comic treatment in the Oscar-winning movie *Fargo* (1996), law enforcement is serious business in North Dakota's largest city. Predictable problems arise with some 93,000 inhabitants, policed by 124 sworn officers and 36 support personnel. In addition to a full range of programs, including bicycle patrols, a K-9 UNIT and multi-agency SWAT TEAMS, Fargo P.D. provides certain unusual services. One of those is performed by Refugee Liaison Officer Julie Hinkel, who works extensively with immigrants from such war-torn nations as Albania, Bosnia, Somalia, and Sudan, resolving issues that include housing, alcohol abuse, domestic violence, and conformity with sexual age-of-consent laws.

Another interesting feature of Fargo P.D. is its Citizens' Police Academy, providing 20-member classes with lectures and "realistic hands-on training" in such areas as domestic violence investigation, use of force during arrests, narcotics investigation, SEX CRIMES, police firearms training, crime scene processing, gang investigations, traffic stops, and Fargo's Community Watch program. In the words of departmental spokesmen, the classes "expose citizens to many of the challenges that face our officers. The goal of the class is to provide education and awareness to members of the community about what the Fargo Police Department is, what we do, and how we accomplish our mission."

Federal Bureau of Investigation (FBI)

While Congress created the U.S. JUSTICE DEPARTMENT in 1870, with responsibility for prosecuting federal crimes, no enforcement arm was provided to investigate those crimes or apprehend offenders. With passage of the Interstate Commerce Act (1887) and Sherman Antitrust Act (1890), various attorneys general filled the gap by hiring agents of the Pinkerton Detective Agency on a part-time, case-by-case basis, but that relationship was severed in 1892, when Pinkerton's brutal STRIKEBREAKING activities prompted a ban on temporary hiring of detectives already employed in the private sector. For the next 16 years, Justice borrowed SECRET SERVICE agents from the TREASURY DEPARTMENT, until further abuses led Congress to ban that practice in May 1908. One month later, on June 29, Attorney General CHARLES JOSEPH BONAPARTE defied congressional opponents to create an unnamed squad of "special agents" at Justice. President THEODORE ROOSEVELT approved that action in July, and STANLEY WELLINGTON FINCH was named first chief of the still-nameless unit on July 26, 1908. Attorney General GEORGE WOODWARD WICKERSHAM officially christened the Bureau of Investigation (BI) on March 16, 1909.

At first, the new unit had little to do beyond investigating crimes on federal property. That changed with passage of the MANN ACT in 1910, designed to curb "white slavery" (prostitution) carried out across state lines. Despite public promises that Mann Act prosecutions would target only commercial vice rings, BI agents soon digressed into selective harassment of "immoral" individuals such as black boxing champion Jack Johnson, convicted in 1913 of crossing state lines with his white fiancée. Another boost to Bureau power came in 1917, with passage of the federal Selective Service Act. Chief A. BRUCE BIELASKI augmented his small force with vigilantes from the American Protective League for a series of nationwide "slacker" raids in 1917–18, jailing thousands of suspected draft dodgers (most of whom were found upon examination to be innocent). At the same time, BI agents used the wartime Espionage Act to justify harassment of socialists, conscientious objectors, and various "radical" labor unions. Postwar hysteria involving Bolsheviks and anarchists, intensified by a series of still-unsolved bombings, spurred a series of "Red raids" and deportations during 1919–20, directed from Washington by Attorney A. MITCHELL PALMER and his young assistant, J. EDGAR HOOVER.

PROHIBITION and Warren Harding's inauguration as president confronted Bureau agents with new challenges and temptations in the 1920s. While Attorney General HARRY MICAJAH DAUGHERTY transformed Justice into a graft-ridden "Department of Easy Virtue," Director WILLIAM J. BURNS had a similar impact on the BI, filling its ranks with political hacks and "dollar-a-year" men like GASTON B. MEANS, who were often criminals themselves. J. Edgar Hoover, named assistant BI director in August 1921, avoided the worst scandals while leading his General Intelligence Division in pursuit of communists, socialists, and other vaguely defined "subversives." Hoover raised no objections in September 1922, when Daugherty and Burns devoted the Bureau to Pinkerton-style strikebreaking activities, and a year later Hoover led the BI's efforts to block investigation of the Teapot Dome scandal. Still, he somehow avoided all blame when Daugherty and Burns were fired in early 1924. On May 10, Attorney General HARLAN FISKE STONE named Hoover acting director of the Bureau, confirmed as permanent director on December 10.

Hoover reorganized the BI from top to bottom, winnowing corrupt agents (along with blacks and women) from the personnel roster, striving for a new image of competency and professional conduct. Among those steps was Hoover's institution of the first training courses for Bureau agents (January 1928) and creation of a National Division of Identification and Information to compile nationwide crime statistics (June 1930). On June 1, 1932, the BI was renamed the U.S. Bureau of Investigation, and two months later the agency published its first issue of the periodical *Fugitives Wanted by Police*. The first national radio program based on BI cases premiered in October 1932, but the Bureau still remained unknown to most Americans for another eight months.

On June 10, 1933, President Franklin Roosevelt merged the USBI with the fading Prohibition Bureau to create a new Division of Investigation at Justice. Exactly one week later, Americans were stunned by the KANSAS CITY MASSACRE, which claimed the lives of two DI agents, three local policemen, and federal fugitive Frank

"Jelly" Nash. That incident, coupled with a series of high-profile bank robberies and kidnappings, launched a federal "war on crime" with Hoover's agents at the forefront. Over the next three years, invested with new weapons and authority, the FBI (officially renamed for the last time July 1, 1935) killed or captured a roster of "PUBLIC ENEMIES" including such desperadoes as John Dillinger, "Baby Face" Nelson, and "Machine Gun" Kelly (falsely credited with giving FBI agents their "G-man" nickname). Along the way, Hoover cultivated a small army of friendly journalists who would praise every move he made for the next 35 years.

The Great Depression and World War II saw a shift in FBI emphasis from straightforward crime-fighting to the pursuit of "subversives" that was always Hoover's passion. President Roosevelt sanctioned the far-flung campaign of DOMESTIC SURVEILLANCE on August 24, 1936, with secret orders authorizing Hoover to investigate communists, fascists, and virtually anyone who criticized the Roosevelt administration. From that date until his death on May 2, 1972, Hoover enjoyed virtual carte blanche from six presidents to spy on, harass, and disrupt hundreds of organizations from coast to coast. At their worst, in the COINTELPRO campaigns of 1956–71, FBI efforts to preserve Hoover's version of "national security" included thousands of "BLACK BAG JOBS," illegal WIRETAPS and occasional FRAME-UPS of targets whose worst offenses were political dissent, support for civil rights, or criticism of the FBI.

Illegal FBI activities were publicly exposed March 1971, when members of a Citizens' Committee to Investigate the FBI burglarized the Bureau office in Media, Pennsylvania, escaping with thousands of COINTELPRO documents which later surfaced in the media and before members of Congress. Hoover's death spared him from most of the ensuing criticism, but the U.S. Senate's CHURCH COMMITTEE fully documented FBI abuses during public hearings in 1975–76. Those revelations, paired with scandals of the Watergate era (1972–74), prompted Congress to impose a 10-year term-limit on Hoover's successors as Bureau director. Attorney General EDWARD HIRSCH LEVI, in March 1976, imposed new limits on FBI political investigations, while Directors CLARENCE MARION KELLEY (1973–78) and WILLIAM H. WEBSTER (1978–87) increased Bureau efforts to curb ORGANIZED CRIME. Challenges during the last quarter of the 20th century included sting operations targeting political CORRUPTION, COMPUTER CRIME, white-collar crime, and TERRORISM. At the same time, public confidence was shaken by a series of incidents including the BRANCH DAVIDIAN SIEGE in Texas, President Bill Clinton's dismissal of Director WILLIAM STEELE SESSIONS on charges of abusing his authority, reports of unprofessional conduct at the FBI's crime lab, and the arrest of double-agent ROBERT HANSSEN for selling Bureau secrets to Russia.

The FBI's relationship with state and local police nationwide has endured many of the same highs and lows. At its best, the FBI provides invaluable support for small police departments in terms of fingerprint searches, analysis of forensic evidence, pursuit of fugitives, and PROFILING of unknown suspects at large. On the downside, local police suggest that G-men sometimes claim credit for cases solved by other agencies, thus inflating FBI statistics (and congressional appropriations). The FBI National Academy, founded in 1935, provides advanced training for some 1,200 officers per year, a total of 29,000 by 2001. That training elevates the quality of law enforcement nationwide to new levels of professionalism, but some critics charge that it also skews loyalty away from an officer's home department, toward the FBI. During J. Edgar Hoover's long feud with Los Angeles police chief WILLIAM HENRY PARKER, officers of the LOS ANGELES POLICE DEPARTMENT were barred from enrollment at the National Academy.

On balance, while FBI spokesmen strive to draw a clear dividing line between the Hoover years and FBI activities since 1972, some serious problems remain. Domestic surveillance of ethnic and political minorities under President Ronald Reagan (1981–89) was virtually indistinguishable from the same activity under Presidents Lyndon Johnson (1963–69) and Richard Nixon (1969–74). The FBI's parochial attitude, spawning petty feuds with other U.S. intelligence agencies, is cited as a major fault in antiterrorist investigations prior to September 11, 2001. Likewise, as passage of the USA PATRIOT ACT after "9/11" exalted national security over personal liberty and privacy, some observers suggest that COINTELPRO-type activities may once again be on the rise, diverting G-men from their role as crimefighters, casting them as arbiters of "loyalty" and political orthodoxy.

See also: ANARCHISM; BANK ROBBERY; BOMBING AND BOMB SQUADS; FINGERPRINTS; FORENSIC SCIENCE; KIDNAPPING; PINKERTON, ALLAN J.

Federal Bureau of Narcotics (FBN)

The FBN was organized in 1930, under HARRY J. ANSLINGER, as an agency of the U.S. TREASURY DEPARTMENT. Anslinger, unlike FBI director J. EDGAR HOOVER, recognized the threat of ORGANIZED CRIME and its ties to narcotics trafficking, but his zeal went even further, launching a crusade to ban marijuana as a national "menace" which (allegedly) turned placid smokers into wild-eyed berserkers. In pursuit of ever more restrictive legislation, the FBN lobbied successfully for passage of the 1937 Marijuana Tax Act, the 1942 Opium Poppy Control Act, the 1951 Boggs Act (imposing harsh penalties for drug offenses), and the 1956 Narcotics Control Act (stiffening penalties, while it ensured federal primacy in suppressing illegal drug traffic).

In 1962 the White House Conference on Narcotics and Drug Abuse recommended dismantling the FBN in favor of programs including drug treatment and prevention of drug diversion from legitimate channels, but the agency survived (minus Anslinger) until 1968, when President Lyndon Johnson transformed it into the Bureau of Narcotics and Dangerous Drugs. The name switch also brought a bureaucratic change of scene, as the BNDD was moved from Treasury to the JUSTICE DEPARTMENT. In July 1973 the agency was renamed once again, becoming the DRUG ENFORCEMENT ADMINISTRATION.

See also: DRUGS; FEDERAL BUREAU OF INVESTIGATION.

Felt, W. Mark (1913–)

A native of Twin Falls, Idaho, Mark Felt graduated from the University of Idaho in 1935 and moved to Washington, D.C., the following year, where he studied law at night while working in the offices of Idaho's U.S. senators. Admitted to the District of Columbia bar in 1940, Felt soon obtained a post on the Federal Trade Commission, then joined the FBI in January 1942. From the beginning of his Bureau service, Felt was fast-tracked for FBI stardom, spending barely six months in the field before his transfer to headquarters as a supervisor in the ESPIONAGE Section. In 1947 he became a firearms instructor at the FBI Academy.

In 1954, after a stint investigating employees of the Atomic Energy Commission, Felt returned to FBI headquarters as an inspector's aide, followed by tours of duty in New Orleans, Los Angeles, Salt Lake City, and Kansas City. Along the way, in 1957–58, he helped create the Bureau's "Top Hoodlum Program," marking J. EDGAR HOOVER's first grudging (and secret) acknowledgment of ORGANIZED CRIME in America. September 1962 saw Felt named deputy assistant director of the Training and Inspection Division, promoted again to chief inspector in November 1964. In 1971 Felt was promoted once again, to deputy associate director, ranking third in line of command behind Hoover and CLYDE ANDERSON TOLSON. When Hoover died in 1972 and Tolson subsequently retired, Felt became acting associate director under L. PATRICK GRAY III. Felt served briefly as acting director after Gray's resignation, in April 1973, then retired from the Bureau on June 22, 1973. (In the midst of the Watergate scandal Felt was named as a possible "Deep Throat" informer for the

Washington Post, but he denied leaking any information to the press.)

Trouble caught up with Felt five years after he retired. It began in August 1976, when JUSTICE DEPARTMENT investigators in New York found evidence of illegal "BLACK BAG JOBS" committed by G-men between 1956 and 1973. That discovery in turn led searchers to the files of Squad 47, a special FBI unit assigned to track New Left fugitives during the Nixon years. Agents of Squad 47 had routinely burglarized private homes, leaving memos indicating that their crimes were approved by Gray, by Felt, and by Assistant Director Edward Miller. A federal grand jury indicted all three on April 10, 1978.

Gray denied all knowledge of the break-ins, and his case was severed from the others (dismissed in December 1980). Felt and Smith faced trial in 1980 for conspiring to violate the civil rights of five persons whose homes were burglarized by Squad 47. Felt claimed that the FBI was entitled to make secret, warrantless searches "in cases of national security involving foreign-directed terrorism [*sic*]," and furthermore that Gray issued blanket approval for illegal break-ins. Gray predictably denied it, while ex-President Nixon and five former attorneys general likewise denied approving any criminal activity by G-men. Jurors convicted Felt and Miller on November 6, 1980; one month later, they were fined $8,500 each. President Ronald Reagan—himself a former FBI informant—pardoned both defendants on March 26, 1981, claiming that Felt and Miller had served "with great distinction" and acted "in good faith" while pursuing radical leftists. The next day, Richard Nixon sent each man a bottle of champagne.

Ironically, in 2005, Felt confessed that he was the informant who exposed the Watergate break-in to reporters at the *Washington Post.* The incident eventually led to the resignation of President Richard Nixon and sparked decades of speculation over the identity of "Deep Throat." Felt was often called out as a suspect but always denied he was the infamous informant. The *Vanity Fair* article that officially outed Felt as "Deep Throat" noted that Felt's family had persuaded him to come forward in order to take advantage of potentially profitable book and media deals that they assumed would result from the revelation.

See also: FEDERAL BUREAU OF INVESTIGATION; INFORMANTS.

Finch, Stanley Wellington (1872–1951)

A native of Monticello, New York, born July 20, 1872, attended five different colleges before joining the U.S. JUSTICE DEPARTMENT as a clerk in 1893. In short order

he was promoted to bookkeeper, examiner, special examiner, and finally chief examiner. Finch graduated from Washington's National University Law School in 1908, around the same time that Attorney General CHARLES JOSEPH BONAPARTE defied Congress to create the fledgling FBI (although the agency would not adopt that name for 27 years). Bonaparte named Finch to lead the new unit on July 26, 1908, maintaining his title as chief examiner. Finch supervised the Bureau's early expansion in pursuit of "white slavers," under the MANN ACT, and remained at his post until replaced by A. BRUCE BIELASKI in April 1912.

After leaving the Bureau, Finch continued his crusade as the Justice Department's special commissioner for suppression of prostitution, recruiting wealthy philanthropists to establish a network of halfway houses for ex-working girls. Finch resigned in 1913, then returned to Justice nine years later, as special assistant to the attorney general in the Anti-Trust Division (1922–25). Yet another retirement proved temporary, and Justice lured Finch once more, to serve as an inspector for the U.S. Bureau of Prisons (1931–34). In January 1935 Attorney General HOMER CUMMINGS reinstated Finch as an auditor, but Finch regained his old chief examiner's rank in January 1940, thus bringing his career full-circle before he finally retired, later that year. Finch died in 1951.

See also: FEDERAL BUREAU OF INVESTIGATION.

fingerprints

Fingerprints are the marks made by ridges on the pads of human fingers, impressed on solid surfaces with natural bodily oils or other media (ink, grease, blood, etc.). When found at crime scenes, fingerprints are analyzed—a process known as dactylography—in order to identify potential suspects.

"Modern" fingerprint identification dates from 1788, when German analyst J. C. A. Mayer declared for the first time that each fingerprint is unique, but practical identification awaited the near-simultaneous work of William Herschel in India, Henry Faulds in Japan, and Francis Galton in England. Official fingerprinting made its way to the United States in 1902, when Dr. Henry DeForrest introduced it to the New York Civil Service. By 1908 the U.S. armed forces had adopted fingerprinting for all personnel, and America witnessed its first criminal conviction based on fingerprints three years later.

Basic fingerprint patterns include arches (plain or tented), loops (radial or ulnar), and whorls. Despite widespread acceptance of the premise that no two fingerprints are identical, controversy endures among jurists and some alleged experts. In the January 2002

Philadelphia trial of three alleged narcotics traffickers and murderers, federal judge Louis Pollak barred testimony suggesting that crime scene fingerprints were "identical" to those of the defendants, ruling that the unique nature of individual prints had never been scientifically tested. Prosecutors appealed that decision, and Pollak later reversed himself, but a hearing held on the original decision in February 2002 produced acrimonious disagreement between FBI experts and British analyst Allan Bayle, who called the Bureau's six-week training course in dactylography "a joke." Bayle noted specifically that FBI analysts required only 10 "Galton points" of comparison for a fingerprint match, while Australian courts require 12 and British authorities demand 16 identical features.

See also: FEDERAL BUREAU OF INVESTIGATION.

Fire and Police Research Organization

This controversial group, also sometimes called the Firemen's and Policeman's Protective League in some published reports, was known to its members simply as "Fi-Po." Beginning in the 1950s, it recruited police and firefighters in Southern California, with particular focus on the LOS ANGELES POLICE DEPARTMENT. Author Robert Conot described Fi-Po as a "little John Birch Society," while Frank Donner named it as an actual branch of that right-wing extremist group, "the spearhead of the Birch operation" to infiltrate LAPD.

In any case, Fi-Po was welcomed by Chief WILLIAM HENRY PARKER, and was run throughout most of his administration by future LAPD chief EDWARD MICHAEL DAVIS. Its newsletter, the *Fi-Po News,* promoted farright rallies, lobbied for passage of new laws restricting "subversive" activities, and railed against the views expressed by moderates or liberals. Fi-Po members were constantly warned to beware of "the communist conspiracy operating within the borders of the state," epitomized by a cast of villains ranging from folk singers to presidents. On April 18, 1963, the *Fi-Po News* told readers: "We know the United States will be a socialistic nation that will eventually fall under the domination

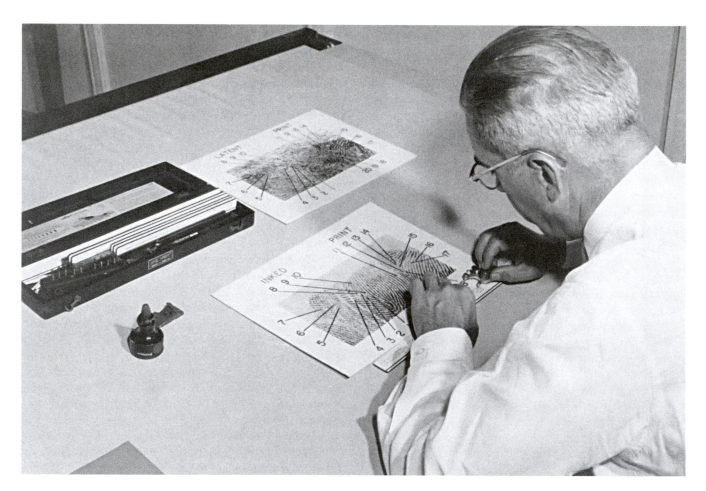

An FBI officer examines an enlargement of a fingerprint sample at the FBI Headquarters in Washington, D.C. (Bettmann/Corbis)

of Russian rule if we continue our 'New Frontier' progress. . . . According to Khrushchev's openly published schedule of conquest . . . we have at least two more years of 'freedom.'"

Fi-Po disbanded in 1975, transferring its files to another right-wing extremist group, the Community Churches of America. Run by Rev. W. S. McBirnie and operating from a Glendale post office box, the CCA and its "Voice of Americanism" offered its members "Newsclippings showing the creeping influence of homosexuality, New Age, and Communism are summaried [sic] in DOCUMENTATION!, which you will receive until Jesus comes, which may be as early as 1995."

Fisk, James

California native James Fisk graduated from the University of California, Los Angeles, in 1939 and joined the LOS ANGELES POLICE DEPARTMENT one year later, at a time when African-American recruits were frequently rejected on spurious medical grounds. He passed muster on merit, and rose through the ranks to serve as a Vice Squad lieutenant in the early 1950s. In 1965, following the Watts ghetto riot, Chief WILLIAM HENRY PARKER tapped Fisk to lead a new four-man Community Relations unit. Parker explained that Fisk was the only LAPD officer he knew who had "any interest in blacks." White colleagues responded by dubbing Fisk "the nigger inspector."

The assignment was a mixed blessing for Fisk, who later told author Joe Domanick, "At the time, having good relations with the black community was to be considered a traitor." Following Parker's death in 1966, Chief THOMAS REDDIN expanded the Community Relations unit from four to 120 officers. Fisk's innovative methods as commander of the team included obtaining a government grant to hire ex-convicts as police liaisons to the black community, and arranging race-sensitivity seminars for high-ranking LAPD officers through the University of Southern California. Chief EDWARD MICHAEL DAVIS credited Fisk's team for averting riots in Los Angeles after the April 1968 murder of Dr. Martin Luther King, Jr., but Fisk would rise no higher within the department. Although he twice surpassed all other candidates on civil service tests for chief, the job was never offered to him.

Fitzmorris, Charles C. (1884–?)

A native of Fort Wayne, Indiana, born in 1884, Charles Fitzmorris won a trip around the world at age 16, in a contest sponsored by the *Chicago American*. He returned to work for the newspaper as an office boy, then as cub reporter. While covering city hall he met Mayor Carter Harrison and wangled a job as the mayor's private secretary in 1911. During the "Red Summer" race riots of 1919 Fitzmorris toured the West Side battle zone with NATIONAL GUARD officers, reporting on the carnage to his boss. A year later, he sought and won appointment to replace JOHN GARRITY as chief of the CHICAGO POLICE DEPARTMENT.

With unanimous backing from the city council and the Chicago Crime Commission, Fitzmorris cast himself as a reformer, committed to streamlining the force and purging it of CORRUPTION. Within 72 hours of his appointment, Fitzmorris transferred hundreds of officers to new precincts, while warning CPD captains to clean up their precincts or look for new jobs. He demoted the detective bureau's chief, promoted a heroic lieutenant (twice wounded in gunfights) to replace him, and transferred 75 of the division's 100 officers to other details. A second wave of transfers in May 1921 shifted 800 cops, while Fitzmorris redrew all existing precinct boundaries.

Those moves were not entirely unopposed. Corrupt officers plotted behind the chief's back, while State's Attorney Robert Crowe obstructed Fitzmorris at every turn. Crooked judges leapt into the fight when Fitzmorris criticized their lax treatment of convicted racketeers and murderers: in September 1921, Judge John David fined the chief $100 and slapped him with a five-day sentence for contempt. Days later, Fitzmorris publicly admitted that his officers had failed to enforce state PROHIBITION statutes. He estimated that 2,500 cops were involved to some degree in the illicit liquor trade, including one lieutenant and three sergeants, whose legal defense costs in criminal cases were paid from a secret department slush fund.

Little had changed for the better in Chicago by April 1923, when Fitzmorris left the department to serve Mayor William Thompson as city comptroller. We can only speculate on his involvement in the morass of corruption that enveloped the Thompson regime and bound it to ORGANIZED CRIME, but after racketeers bombed Fitzmorris's home in January 1928, insiders hinted that the crime was prompted by disputes over division of gambling and liquor payoffs. Fitzmorris retired from his post and from public life six months after the blast wrecked his house.

Florida Highway Patrol

State law enforcement in Florida dates from November 1931, when Governor Doyle Carlton ordered the State Road Department to hire 12 weight inspectors. A state Division of Traffic Enforcement was added in January 1934, led by Inspector E. A. Sherman. The Traffic Division was abolished in 1938, to save money in the

Great Depression, but civic groups lobbied for a new highway patrol to serve the motoring public. In 1939 legislators created a Department of Public Safety with two divisions, the Florida Highway Patrol and a Division of State Motor Vehicle Licenses. Sixty officers were authorized to patrol the Sunshine State at salaries ranging from $1,500 to $2,000 per year.

As the number of Florida automobiles increased, so the Highway Patrol grew larger, with 171 officers employed by 1950. Three hundred were authorized for 1951, but budget shortages left 45 positions unfilled at year's end. Money was so tight, in fact, that the FHP could not afford to purchase its new shoulder patches, designed by Lt. Clay Keith in 1951 at a cost of 22 cents each. Funds *were* found for creation of a new Investigation Section in 1952, as a response to bribery scandals involving driver's license examiners. Aside from traffic matters, the division was also tasked to investigate all worker's compensation claims throughout the state. A teletype system was installed in 1953, and Florida created a commercial driving school under FHP supervision that same year. A volunteer FHP Auxiliary was created in 1957, in collaboration with the American Legion.

By its 20th anniversary in 1959, the FHP boasted full-time troopers and one six-passenger Cessna airplane. Still, the numbers were inadequate to deal with Florida's postwar population boom. State legislators authorized 600 troopers in 1961, but only 566 were on staff two years later, as civil rights demonstrations created new levels of tension statewide. Unlike some other southern states, Florida won honorable mention in that troubled era, as state troopers interposed themselves between racist local officers and violent members of the KU KLUX KLAN. Fingerprinting of some 40,000 state employees added another burden in 1962, and many troopers worked 12-hour shifts, six days a week, until Governor Haydon Burns established a 40-hour week in January 1966. The same year launched a new FHP training academy in Tallahassee. The first black trooper reported for training on July 4, 1971. The first female trooper was hired in October 1977.

The FHP's public image was tarnished in 1979 by a federal lawsuit alleging racial and sexual discrimination in the ranks. As a result, the state arranged a settlement with the U.S. JUSTICE DEPARTMENT, whereby a consent decree was issued on July 12, 1979, mandating recruitment of more women and ethnic minorities. Ten months later, FHP officers were burdened by the Mariel boatlift, in which some 125,000 Cuban refugees (including many felons and mental patients) arrived without warning on Florida shores. The resultant crime wave, fueled by wholesale importation of illegal DRUGS, has taxed FHP resources to the limit. Troopers also took

time from their normal patrols for riot duty in Miami's "Liberty City" ghetto (May 1981), establishment of a drug-sniffing K-9 UNIT (December 1983), protection of Pope John Paul II on a visit to Miami (1987), and disaster relief during various hurricanes. At the turn of the millennium, the FHP became the 13th state police agency formally accredited in America.

Flynn, William James (1867–1933)

A native of New York City, born November 18, 1867, William Flynn joined the U.S. SECRET SERVICE in 1897 and remained until 1919, spending five years as chief of the agency. Attorney General A. MITCHELL PALMER chose Flynn to head the FBI on June 20, 1919, and he took office the following day. In announcing Flynn's appointment, Palmer dubbed him America's top "anarchist chaser," reporting that "He knows all men of that class. He can pretty well call them by name."

That qualification seemed critical, with a series of supposed anarchist bombings still unsolved from April 1919. Flynn launched a fruitless search for the bombers, claiming they were "connected with Russian Bolshevism, aided by Hun money," but in fact he had no idea who they were. Flynn had better luck as a strikebreaker, though the Bureau had no legal authority to pursue labor unions. Demanding a new purge of "enemy aliens" on August 12, 1919, Flynn told his G-men: "You will also make full investigation of similar activities of citizens of the United States with a view to securing evidence which may be of use in prosecutions under the present existing state or federal laws *or under legislation of that nature which may hereinafter be enacted.*" (Emphasis added) Five months later, in the wake of the notorious Palmer raids, Flynn claimed that his work had averted a revolution in the United States.

Public outcry over those illegal raids and the FBI's sweeping infringement of civil liberties ultimately drove both Flynn and Palmer from office. Attorney General HARRY DAUGHERTY replaced Flynn with WILLIAM J. BURNS on August 22, 1921, as part of President Warren Harding's bid to restore "normalcy." Flynn died in 1933.

See also: ANARCHISM; BOMBINGS AND BOMB SQUADS; STRIKEBREAKING.

Ford, Richard, and Robert A. Von Villas

Richard Ford was a natural actor, starring in several high school stage plays, but upon graduating in 1957 he declined a chance to study at the Pasadena Playhouse in favor of joining the U.S. Army. He served 10 years in uniform, twice wounded and decorated for bravery as a helicopter gunner in Vietnam, before discharge as a sergeant in 1968. Thus accustomed to uniforms and action, he soon joined the LOS ANGELES POLICE DEPARTMENT. In June 1969 he was wounded again, this time by a car thief who disarmed him and used Ford's own pistol to shoot Ford and his partner before they returned fire, killing the gunman.

By the early 1970s Ford was assigned to UNDERCOVER WORK, where colleagues noted that his "pleasant and witty personality kept the unit laughing." He made detective in 1977, then surprised his supervisors a year later with admissions of alcoholism and marital problems. If not removed from his latest ghetto assignment, Ford said, he might end up "shooting a coon." Referred to a psychologist, Ford told his counselor that "something is going on inside me that isn't right." He aired an increasing desire "to kill drug dealers," prompting a diagnosis of "stress overload" with recommendation for transfer to "a less dynamic area."

In retrospect some would say that Ford had merely used his acting skills to work the system, leaving the ghetto for a post in LAPD's relatively peaceful Devonshire Division, nicknamed "Club Dev." Strangely, Ford's first evaluation in the new job ranked his skills as mediocre, prompting him to rage at his commander, "This is bullshit! I'm the best detective in the world!"

Ford's favorite part of Devonshire Division was his new friendship with Robert Von Villas, another decorated Vietnam veteran. Assigned to work JUVENILE CRIME cases, Von Villas moonlighted as a security guard at private homes, shopping malls, concerts, and movie sets. When not so engaged, he dabbled in real estate and sold various merchandise from his car trunk. Von Villas was also well known as a ladies' man, scanning police reports for cases of assaults on women, whom he seduced while serving as a paid bodyguard. One such infraction earned him a two-week suspension in November 1982, and financial losses that December prompted him to tell a female friend, "I'm tired of being an honest cop. If you hear of any job I can do for money, let me know. There isn't any job I wouldn't do for money, including murder."

Richard Ford, meanwhile, had reached a similar conclusion. In November 1982, while on a "hunting trip" to Colorado, Ford bought a crate of submachine guns and silencers, telling friend Bruce Adams that he needed the illegal weapons for a jewel heist. Warning Adams to silence, Ford added, "I've knocked people off before. It wouldn't bother me at all." Days later, Ford introduced Adams to Bob Von Villas, described by Ford as his partner in the upcoming robbery.

On November 18, 1992, Ford and Von Villas purchased wigs and fake beards in Hollywood. Four days later, thus disguised, they robbed a Northridge jewelry store, escaping with gems worth $200,000. Detectives assigned to the case noted that store employees had been threatened with "cop talk" during the holdup. In December 1982 Von Villas bankrolled Adams in an auto shop, paying rent and startup costs with loose diamonds from the Northridge heist. The shop served as cover for a prostitution ring, "Classy Ladies," that brought Ford and Von Villas some $25,000 before they abandoned the trade as too risky.

Another source of income for the two rogue officers was contract murder. On February 23, 1983, they killed Thomas Weed, on the eve of Weed's divorce hearing. Soon after Weed vanished, Bruce Adams saw Von Villas hand Ford $10,000 in cash, explaining the money to Adams as their payoff from a murder contract purchased by Weed's wealthy soon-to-be ex-wife. "Weed's bones are bleaching out in the desert," Ford remarked.

Adams and Von Villas quarreled in May 1983, when Adams refused to pick up a shipment of stolen grenade launchers from the U.S. Marine Corps base at El Toro, California. Von Villas threatened his life, and Adams responded by reporting Von Villas to the Bureau of Alcohol, Tobacco and Firearms (ATF). ATF agents carried the tale to trusted LAPD administrators, whereupon Adams agreed to record future conversations with Ford and Von Villas.

Meanwhile, Von Villas had found a new target for murder. After purchasing a house from exotic dancer Joan Loguerico, to help her in the midst of a bitter divorce, Von Villas persuaded Loguerico to purchase a $100,000 mortgage insurance policy, naming him as beneficiary in case of her death. Soon afterward, Von Villas encouraged Loguerico to "date" a wealthy strip club patron whom she knew as "Dr. Anderson." She fled their first hotel rendezvous, on June 17, 1983, after the "doctor" donned surgical gloves and reached for her face with "something black" in his hand. Loguerico subsequently told Bruce Adams that she thought Von Villas wanted her dead. Adams agreed after she described "Dr. Anderson's" skull-and-crossbones tattoo, identical in all respects to one worn by Richard Ford.

Adams reported the apparent murder plot to ATF and LAPD, prompting acceleration of the sting on Ford and Von Villas. On July 6, 1983, he recorded a conversation with Von Villas, in which the officer pledged $12,500 for Loguerico's death. A subsequent phone call from Ford confirmed the price and was likewise recorded for posterity. Meeting with Ford that night, Adams heard and recorded Ford's plan to drug Loguerico and stage her murder as a random SEX CRIME. It would be simple, Ford said, "like taking candy from a baby." En route to the presumed crime scene, Ford boasted for the hidden microphone, "As for killing assholes, I just do it for kicks. Instead of being depressed, going out and shooting at fuckin' rocks and squirrels, I go down south and shoot niggers. I think it's fun, but I'd rather get paid for it." Moments later, Adams drove Ford into a police trap, where he was arrested. Officers collared Von Villas at home the same night, retrieving 20 stolen diamonds from his briefcase.

On July 12, 1983, Ford and Von Villas were arraigned on charges of attempted murder, attempting to administer a stupefying drug, and carrying concealed weapons. A month later, prosecutors added 10 more charges related to the Northridge jewel robbery. On September 26 Judge Michael Sauer ordered both defendants to stand trial for robbery, conspiracy, and attempted murder. On February 15, 1984, Ford and Von Villas were indicted for Thomas Weed's murder, with additional charges filed against Weed's widow and a fourth conspirator. In June 1994 Weed's widow turned state's evidence against her erstwhile hitmen.

A nine-month preliminary hearing consumed most of 1986, and it was April 1987 before Ford and Von Villas faced trial on their original charges. Prosecutors took five months to present 140 witnesses and 400 exhibits, followed by a two-month defense case. Ford himself spent two weeks on the witness stand, but he and Von Villas failed to sway the jury. On January 7, 1988, the panel convicted both defendants on 13 counts each, including conspiracy to murder Joan Loguerico, attempted murder, robbery, conspiracy to commit robbery, false imprisonment (of three jewelry store employees), and assault with a firearm (in the holdup). Ford was also convicted of attempting to drug Joan Loguerico at their hotel date in June 1983. At sentencing on March 11, Ford received a prison term of 36 years to life, while Von Villas drew 35 years to life.

On April 12, 1988, a peculiar trial opened before Judge Darlene Schempp, in the murder of Thomas Weed. After rejecting a motion to sever the defendants, Judge Schempp empanelled two separate juries to hear the case simultaneously. Ford's jury began deliberations on October 4 and returned a week later, convicting him of first-degree murder and conspiracy to murder, both counts bearing "special circumstances" required for a death sentence. Von Villas received an identical sentence on November 3, 1988. In the penalty phase, Ford's jury deadlocked 11-to-1 in favor of life imprisonment, and that sentence was formally imposed on February 22, 1989. Von Villas heard himself condemned to life without parole on December 15, 1988, a verdict affirmed by the judge on March 8, 1989.

forensic science

Forensic science is the branch of scientific study applied to legal matters, both criminal and civil. It spans such variant disciplines as anthropology, chemistry, engineering, medicine, and physics. In broad terms, it includes analysis of any and all *circumstantial* evidence (as opposed to eyewitness testimony) which has any bearing on the outcome of a criminal or civil trial. Commonly recognized branches of forensic science include ballistics (evidence related to firearms), DNA profiling, fingerprint analysis, odontology (teeth and bite marks), psychology (PROFILING), serology (blood evidence), tool mark analysis, and toxicology (drugs and poisons).

Attorneys and authors of fiction commonly denigrate circumstantial (or "trace") evidence, yet items collected from crime scenes are often more useful than eyewitnesses testimony in divining guilt or innocence. Witness may lie or be mistaken, but fingerprints and DNA profiling can (theoretically) identify one individual among all others living on the planet. A problem arises when unscrupulous police officers plant evidence, as part of a deliberate frame-up, or where unscrupulous practitioners misrepresent their laboratory findings. In the 1990s a rash of scandals surrounded medical examiner RALPH ERDMANN and two criminalists—JOYCE GILCHRIST and FRED SALEM ZAIN—who convicted scores of innocent defendants with false testimony. Conditioned by programs such as TV's *CSI* series and its spin-offs, which often rely on exaggerated or simplistic depictions of crime scene investigations, many average Americans now place almost supernatural faith in forensic science and the all-too-human individuals who present evidence in court.

See also: FINGERPRINTS; FRAME-UPS.

frame-ups

A frame-up is the malicious prosecution of an innocent person for crimes which he or she did not commit. It is distinguished from cases of mistaken identity or other wrongful prosecutions conducted in good faith by the egregious misconduct of police and prosecutors, commonly involving perjured testimony, confessions obtained via "THIRD-DEGREE" TACTICS, concealment of exculpatory evidence, and criminal fabrication of false evidence to convict the accused.

Thankfully, such cases occur more often in fiction than in fact, but they are not uncommon in U.S. history. In 1992 authors Michael Radelet, Hugo Bedau, and Constance Putnam published a survey of 416 defendants wrongfully convicted of capital crimes in America between 1901 and 1989. Many of those cases naturally involved mistaken eyewitness testimony or confusion of forensic evidence in the days before DNA analysis, but at least 154 of the cases (37 percent) revealed clear evidence of framing. While no similar study of noncapital cases has yet been attempted, the implications are disturbing.

A short sampling of 20th-century American frame-ups includes:

- 1896—Chicago's HAYMARKET BOMBING resulted in conviction of eight supposed anarchists, with no evidence linking any defendant to the actual crime.

- 1915—After a young factory employee was murdered in Atlanta, police first arrested a black suspect, then used his testimony to convict Leo Frank, Jewish proprietor of the plant. Frank received a life prison term, but was subsequently lynched. Deathbed testimony received in the 1980s exonerated Frank and named his accuser as the actual killer.

- 1916—On July 22 a bombing claimed 10 lives and wounded 40 victims at a pro-war Preparedness Day parade in San Francisco. Officers of the SAN FRANCISCO POLICE DEPARTMENT framed "radical" unionists Warren Billings and Thomas Mooney for the crime, and both were sentenced to die. Both were exonerated and released in 1939.

- 1920—A similar wave of antiradical hysteria convicted anarchists Nicola Sacco and Bartolomeo Vanzetti of a Massachusetts holdup-murder. Secret FBI reports confirm perjured testimony and false ballistics evidence were used to convict and condemn both men. The defendants were executed in 1927, although members of the real holdup gang had long since been identified. Sacco and Vanzetti were pardoned on the 50th anniversary of their deaths.

- 1933—Members of the Al Capone bootlegging syndicate conspired with FBI agent MELVIN PURVIS to frame rival bootlegger Roger Touhy for a kidnapping that never occurred. Purvis collaborated on the scheme after failing to convict Touhy of another kidnapping. Touhy was exonerated in 1959. Chicago mobsters murdered him 16 days after his release from prison.

- 1933—FBI agents and local authorities suppressed evidence and used perjured testimony to convict defendant Adam Richetti of murder in the notorious KANSAS CITY MASSACRE. Richetti was executed in 1938 for killing a policeman actually shot by an FBI agent.

- 1935—Bruno Hauptmann was condemned in New Jersey for the Lindbergh KIDNAPPING, based on perjured testimony and false evidence. A local reporter subsequently admitted writing one of the "kidnap notes" used to put Hauptmann on death row. Classified FBI files acknowledged the prosecution's use of "fabricated evidence," but

G-men failed to intervene and still claim credit for Hauptmann's conviction.

- 1949—In Florida's notorious Groveland rape case, three black defendants were convicted of raping a white woman (who was actually beaten by her own abusive husband). When the original convictions were overturned on appeal, Sheriff WILLIS McCALL shot two of the defendants "in self-defense," but one survived to describe the murder attempt. The deputy in charge of casting footprints at the alleged rape scene was later caught fabricating footprint casts in another case, using the suspect's shoes. Despite clear evidence of a frame-up, the surviving defendants remained in prison until 1954 and 1962, respectively.

- 1964—Members of Boston's Winter Hill Gang conspired with corrupt FBI agents to frame four innocent defendants for a gangland murder. All four were convicted, on perjured testimony from the actual slayers. Two defendants died in prison, while the other two were finally exonerated and released in 2000.

- 1970—FBI agents and members of the LOS ANGELES POLICE DEPARTMENT framed a local leader of the Black Panther Party, Elmer "Geronimo" Pratt, for a murder committed in 1968. Pratt spent 27 years in prison before he was finally cleared of all charges.

- 1973—Allan Thrower received a life prison term for the ambush slaying of an Ohio police officer, despite evidence that he was in Michigan when the murder occurred. The dead officer's partner, who identified Thrower, was later suspended for committing perjury. A detective also resigned when his false testimony in the case was revealed.

- 1976—Defendant Robert Wilkinson was convicted on five counts of murder in the firebombing of a Philadelphia, Pennsylvania, home. Prior to formal sentencing, a newspaper investigation revealed that his confession was obtained by violence, while seven other prosecution witnesses were beaten or threatened by police prior to giving false testimony. Several officers of the PHILADELPHIA POLICE DEPARTMENT were convicted for their "brutal and unlawful" actions in the case, while Wilkinson received a settlement of $325,000.

- 1981—Charles Persico pled guilty to manslaughter in Los Angeles, to avoid the risk of trial and possible conviction on more serious murder charges. Three years after Persico's parole from prison, in 1987, prosecutors charged Officer WILLIAM FRANCES LEASURE with the same slaying. Leasure pled guilty in 1991. Persico sued the city for

$62 million and ultimately settled for a smaller amount.

See also: ANARCHISM; BOMBING AND BOMB SQUADS; FEDERAL BUREAU OF INVESTIGATION; LYNCHING.

France, Johnny (b. 1940)

A Montana rancher's son, born in 1940, Johnny France enjoyed an unremarkable tour of duty as sheriff of rugged Madison County until July 15, 1984. That afternoon, Kari Swenson, a 23-year-old women's biathlon competitor in training for the Olympic Games, was abducted near Big Sky by two bearded, rifle-toting strangers. The crime was reminiscent of a horror film: 50-year-old self-styled "mountain man" Don Nichols had decided it was time for his son, 19-year-old Dan, to marry. Prospects were slim for an unwashed, penniless hermit, so the Nicholses resorted to KIDNAPPING. After capturing Swenson, the father-son team marched her to their mountain camp, where she was chained to a tree for the night.

A search began next morning, led by Sheriff France. Two would-be rescuers, Alan Goldstein and Jim Schwalbe, found the Nichols camp on July 16 and a shootout ensued. Dan Nichols wounded his reluctant fiancée, perhaps accidentally, while Don murdered Goldstein. Schwalbe fled to get help, while the Nicholses unchained Swenson and left her in camp, themselves retreating deeper into the wilderness. Trackers found Swenson that afternoon, and Sheriff France pledged to catch her kidnappers. "I'm a mountain man, too," he told reporters. "It will take one to catch one."

In fact, it took five months for France to locate the fugitives. He caught them napping on December 13, 1984, and captured both without resistance. Dan received a 20-year term for kidnapping in May 1985. Father Don got 85 years in September 1985, following his conviction on charges of homicide, kidnapping, and aggravated assault. The high-profile arrest did Sheriff France no good, however, as voters denied him reelection in 1986.

Fraternal Order of Police

The world's largest police union, claiming more than 318,000 members in 2005, sprang from humble beginnings in 1915. Two patrolmen with the PITTSBURGH POLICE DEPARTMENT, Delbert Nagle and Martin Toole, conceived the idea in 1915, but cast their brainchild as a fraternal lodge to avoid the antiunion stigma of their time. With 21 other Pittsburgh officers, they met for the first time on May 14, 1915 and founded the FOP's Fort Pitt Lodge No. 1. A message to Mayor Joe Armstrong expressed the FOP's intent "to bring our aggrievances [sic] before the Mayor or Council and have many things adjusted that we are unable to present in any other way."

By 1917 the FOP's message and methods had spread nationwide, with chapters springing up from coast to coast. The concept of unionizing law enforcement officers, even in the guise of a lodge, still met dogged resistance in conservative quarters, and that resistance was toughened by Boston's police strike of 1919. Nonetheless, expansion was inevitable, and today the FOP boasts more than 2,100 lodges nationwide. The self-styled "voice of law enforcement professionals" lobbies in Washington and various state legislatures, while simultaneously seeking other avenues of support for its members. According to the FOP's Web site:

> We are committed to improving the working conditions of law enforcement officers and the safety of those we serve through education, legislation, information, community involvement, and employee representation. No one knows the dangers and the difficulties faced by today's police officers better than another officer, and no one knows police officers better than the FOP.

Frazer-Miller feud

G. A. "Bud" Frazer was the son of a Texas judge, born at Fort Stockton on April 18, 1864. He joined the TEXAS RANGERS at age 16, later serving as a deputy sheriff in Pecos County. Voters in neighboring Reeves County chose Frazer as their sheriff in 1890, and his trouble began when he hired James B. Miller as a deputy.

"Killin' Jim" Miller was an Arkansas native, born at Van Buren on October 23, 1866. Before landing in Texas and donning a badge, he was a drifter, saloon-keeper, and rustler of livestock, who reportedly killed his first man—brother-in-law John Coop—in July 1884. In March 1887 he ambushed and murdered City Marshal Joe Townsend, of Ballinger, Texas, to avenge Townsend's killing of Miller's employer. With that background, it came as no surprise when Miller killed an unarmed Mexican at Fort Stockton in 1891. Miller claimed the dead man had resisted arrest, but Sheriff Frazer believed Miller killed him because the victim knew Miller had stolen two mules. Frazer fired Miller and charged him with theft, but Killin' Jim escaped conviction. He ran against Frazer for the sheriff's job and lost in 1892, then moved across the county line and became town marshal in Pecos. In that post he killed several more Mexican prisoners, each shot while "trying to escape." (Miller boasted to friends, "I have lost my notch stick on Mexicans that I killed out on the border.")

The brooding lawmen's feud escalated on April 12, 1894, when Frazer rode to Pecos and spotted Miller outside a hotel. Frazer fired without warning, wounding Miller in the arm, while Miller's return fire struck a bystander in the hip. Frazer emptied his pistol into Miller's chest, but Killin' Jim was saved by a steel plate worn beneath his clothing (perhaps the first U.S. example of a lawman wearing BODY ARMOR). Defeated for reelection as sheriff in November 1894, Frazer returned to Pecos on December 26 and fought another duel with Miller, this time wounding Miller in the arm and leg. Again, the steel vest stopped two shots to Miller's chest, and Frazer fled before his stunned opponent could recover. Miller finally settled the feud on Sept 14, 1896, when he surprised Frazer in a Toyah, Texas, saloon and blew his head off with a shotgun.

Five years after the fact, Frazer partisan Joe Earp tried to file murder charges against Miller, for Frazer's death, but no indictment was returned, and Miller soon shot Earp from ambush in Coryell County. (Some critics also claimed that Miller poisoned the prosecutor in that case, who died at Memphis, Texas, of supposed food poisoning.) Despite his record, Miller next became a member of the Texas Rangers in 1900, claiming yet another victim in Collingsworth County. Local authorities called that shooting a contract murder, but Miller and accomplice Lawrence Angel were released on pleas of self-defense. He soon left the Rangers, billing himself as a killer for hire at $150 per murder. His known victims over the next few years include two alleged rustlers (summer 1902), two Mexicans (1903), Lubbock attorney James Jarrott (1904), Frank Fore of Fort Worth (1905), and U.S. Deputy Marshal Ben Collins (1906). Miller was indicted for that crime—a revenge killing financed by kin of a fugitive Collins had crippled—but he once again escaped conviction.

Miller was a prime suspect in the February 1908 ambush murder of ex-lawman PAT GARRETT, near Las Cruces, New Mexico, but he presented an alibi and was never charged in that case. Three days short of one year later, on February 26, 1909, Miller claimed his final victim, Oklahoma rancher Gus Bobbitt. Initially hired by three land-hungry neighbors of Bobbitt, Miller escaped to Texas but was extradited to face charges. A lynch mob kidnapped Miller and his three employers on April 19, 1909, hanging all four men in a livery stable at Ada.

freedom rides

The "freedom ride" movement of 1961 was designed to test federal court orders requiring racial desegregation in interstate commerce. The KU KLUX KLAN swiftly mounted opposition, acting in collaboration with racist law enforcement officers.

By the time two busloads of demonstrators left Washington, D.C., on May 4, 1961, FBI headquarters knew from its many INFORMANTS that Alabama Klansmen and police planned a violent reception for the riders. Birmingham police commissioner Eugene "Bull" Connor guaranteed local Klansmen 15 minutes of uninterrupted mayhem when the riders arrived on May 14, decreeing that he wanted the protesters beaten until they "looked like a bulldog got hold of them." Connor also suggested that Klansmen strip their victims of clothing, so that demonstrators could be jailed on charges of indecent exposure.

FBI leaders failed to warn Attorney General ROBERT FRANCIS KENNEDY of the impending violence, but they *did* alert police in Anniston, Alabama, where the riders were scheduled to stop en route to Birmingham. Officers were nowhere to be seen when Klansmen attacked the first bus, beat its passengers, then set the bus afire. When the second bus arrived, Klansmen rushed aboard and beat several more riders, inflicting permanent brain damage on Dr. Walter Bergman. FBI agents watched and took notes as the captured bus rolled on toward Birmingham.

There a racist mob at least 1,000 strong took full advantage of Bull Connor's promise, savaging demonstrators, black bystanders, and journalists before police reluctantly arrived to shoo them off. Connor explained the lapse by claiming that most of his officers spent that Sunday—Mother's Day—at home with their families. "Our people of Birmingham are a peaceful people," he said, "and we never have any trouble unless some people come into our city looking for trouble."

Those riders still able to travel moved on to Montgomery on May 20, 1961. Despite FBI warnings of Klan riot plans, police commissioner Lester Sullivan stationed no officers at the bus depot. Another riot erupted, again with G-men on the sidelines, snapping photographs and taking notes. They made no move to intervene, even when JUSTICE DEPARTMENT observer John Seigenthaler was clubbed unconscious and left bleeding on the sidewalk for 25 minutes. Medical aid was slow in arriving, Commissioner Sullivan later explained, because every "white" ambulance in town had "broken down" at the same moment.

Having failed to prevent the violence in Alabama, FBI agents belatedly arrested four Klansmen involved in the Anniston riot. They and five more were indicted by a federal grand jury on September 1, 1961. Five defendants were convicted in January 1962 and received one year's probation in return for promises to sever all Klan ties. No one was ever prosecuted for the riots in Birmingham or Montgomery.

More than two decades after those riots, in 1983, injured freedom riders Walter Bergman and James Peck sued the FBI for permitting the violence and concealing the role of an FBI informant in the Birmingham attacks. A federal judge found the Bureau liable for injuries suffered by the plaintiffs. On February 17, 1984, Bergman was awarded $45,000 in damages, while Peck received $25,000.

See also: CONNOR, THEOPHILUS EUGENE ("BULL"); FEDERAL BUREAU OF INVESTIGATION.

Freeh, Louis Joseph (b. 1950)

A Jersey City, New Jersey, native, born January 6, 1950, Louis Freeh graduated from Rutgers University in 1971 and received his J.D. from the same institution's law school in 1974. He joined the FBI in 1975, serving first in the New York City field office, then as a supervisor of ORGANIZED CRIME investigations at headquarters in Washington (1980). Freeh left the Bureau to serve as a federal prosecutor in New York (1981–91), then as a federal judge (1991–93).

When FBI director WILLIAM STEELE SESSIONS was dismissed in 1993, President Bill Clinton tapped Freeh to fill the post. Thus began a tumultuous tenure, launched with a staff meeting wherein Freeh urged his aides to "talk straight" and "tell me if I'm full of shit." Despite that plea, subordinates soon realized that Freeh resented criticism. "Freeh killed the messenger," one high-ranking FBI agent told journalist Robert Kessler. "After a while, there were no more messengers." Kessler himself criticized Freeh for "colossal mismanagement" over the next eight years, claiming that he ultimately "left the FBI in a shambles."

One key problem was Freeh's adversarial relationship with President Clinton and Attorney General JANET RENO. Freeh urged appointment of a special prosecutor to investigate charges of Democratic financial scandals during the 1996 election, and he carried the debate to Congress when Reno refused. The clash went public in December 1997, and while Reno described herself as "a great admirer" of Freeh, they were constantly at odds. Clinton declined to give his FBI director a public vote of confidence, and in private (according to columnist Robert Novak) described Freeh "in three unspeakably vulgar words." Freeh dismissed suggestions that he resign, whereupon JUSTICE DEPARTMENT leaders moved to censure him for the FBI's mishandling of the BRANCH DAVIDIAN SIEGE. (Freeh had been a judge when those events occurred, but critics charged him with participating in a subsequent cover-up.) Assistant Attorney General Stephen Colgate finally refused to censure Freeh, on grounds that "I just didn't think it was necessary. Freeh was a small part of it."

Freeh's tenure was burdened with scandal, including exposure of malfeasance at the FBI's laboratory;

the case of RICHARD JEWELL; the unexplained loss of numerous weapons and laptop computers; and the "accidental" misplacement of some 30,000 documents relevant to the trial of Oklahoma City bomber Timothy McVeigh. Overall, the impression was one of mismanagement from top to bottom, with strong suggestions of malicious intent in some cases. Freeh announced his retirement from the FBI on May 1, 2001, effective on June 22. By July 2001 he was installed ("ironically," in Robert Kessler's terms) as senior vice chairman for administration of MBNA, a major credit card company. In 2005 Freeh published a memoir defending his conduct as FBI director, blaming various failures on subordinates and superiors.

Fuhrman, Mark (b. 1952)

Controversial officer Mark Fuhrman was born on February 5, 1952. He joined the U.S. Marine Corps at age 18 and served five years (1970–75), discharged with the rank of sergeant. Fuhrman subsequently joined the LOS ANGELES POLICE DEPARTMENT and rose through the ranks to become a detective. On the night of June 12, 1994, police were summoned to a double-murder scene in the affluent Brentwood district, where Nicole Brown Simpson and a friend, Ron Goldman, had been stabbed to death. Fuhrman was part of the team that went to notify Nicole's ex-husband—celebrity athlete/actor O. J. Simpson—of the crime.

His life would never be the same.

At Simpson's estate, police found blood and other evidence suggesting his guilt in the crime. Fuhrman personally found a bloody glove discarded in the shrubbery behind Simpson's house. Indictments followed, and a lengthy trial ensued, televised worldwide. Defense attorneys sought to obscure persuasive DNA evidence of Simpson's guilt by claiming that police—and Fuhrman in particular—planted the glove and other evidence in Simpson's home. (No motive was suggested for the alleged FRAME-UP, but jurors bought the argument and acquitted Simpson.) During his testimony, Fuhrman was accused of RACISM and unwisely maintained that he had not used the word *nigger* for at least a decade. A journalist's audiotapes proved otherwise, and Fuhrman subsequently pled no contest on a perjury charge. He received probation, paid a $200 fine, and retired from LAPD to a home in Idaho.

Things looked bleak for Fuhrman after Simpson was acquitted. Anthony Pellicano, a private investigator sometimes employed by Fuhrman, told the *Washington Post* on August 22, 1995: "Fuhrman's life is in the toilet. He has no job, no future. People think he's a racist. His life is ruined. And for what? Because he found a key piece of evidence." Fuhrman bounced back, however, and became a best-selling author of true-crime books that have redeemed in large part his reputation as an investigator.

Fuhrman's first book, *Murder in Brentwood* (1997), predictably gave an alternative view of the Simpson case. He followed up with *Murder in Greenwich* (1998), which revitalized a "cold" case in Connecticut and sent a member of the wealthy Kennedy clan to prison for life. Fuhrman's third book, *Murder in Spokane* (2001), examined police errors in a Washington case of SERIAL MURDER. Most recently, Fuhrman's research for *Death and Justice: An Expose of Oklahoma's Death Row Machine* (2003) transformed Fuhrman into a surprise critic of CAPITAL PUNISHMENT.

Fuld, Leonhard Felix (1883–1965)

The son of a wealthy New York City merchant, born in 1883, prolific scholar Leonhard Fuld earned five degrees from Columbia University during 1902–07. For his Ph.D. in administrative law and municipal science,

he prepared a dissertation comparing operations of the NEW YORK CITY POLICE DEPARTMENT with other large forces across the United States and Europe. The end result—titled *Police Administration: A Critical Study of Police Organizations in the U.S. and Abroad*—not only cinched Fuld's doctorate, but qualified for publication in 1909. Among the innovations Fuld proposed were mental/psychological screening of police recruits; strict limits on the use of DEADLY FORCE; elimination of political patronage and cronyism; creation of a professional INTERNAL AFFAIRS unit to supplant interdepartmental spying and blackmail; and special inducements to attract high school graduates or college-educated officers.

While Fuld's recommendations were well received by readers, they had limited impact on NYPD's day-to-day operations, and less still on Fuld's private life. Pursuing a solitary existence that paralleled in some respects the life of Howard Hughes, Fuld died in New Jersey on August 31, 1965. His will left $25 million to a foundation for student nurses, and a smaller sum for officer training at the NEW JERSEY STATE POLICE Academy.

G

Garland, Augustus Hill (1832–1899)

Tennessee native Augustus Garland was born in Tipton County on June 11, 1832. He was educated at St. Mary's College and St. Joseph's College, both in Kentucky, before privately studying law and winning admission to the bar in 1850. Garland thereafter practiced law in Arkansas (1850–61) and served as a presidential elector in 1860. Disappointed by Abraham Lincoln's election to the White House, Garland next surfaced as a delegate to Arkansas's secession convention in early 1861. Throughout the Civil War, he served Dixie as a member of the Confederate Congress (1861–65). Arkansas voters sent him to the U.S. Senate in 1866, but Garland was denied a seat since his state had not been readmitted to the Union. Undismayed by that setback, he won election as governor (1874–77), then campaigned for the Senate once more without opposition, under the South's new one-party system, in 1876. Garland served in the Senate until March 1885, when President Grover Cleveland named him attorney general. Garland assumed office on March 9 and held that post until March 5, 1889. Thereafter, he returned to the private practice of law. Garland collapsed and died while arguing a case before the U.S. SUPREME COURT on January 26, 1899.

Attorney General Augustus Garland (Author's collection)

Garrett, Pat (1850–1908)

Born in Chambers County, Alabama, on June 5, 1850, and raised in Louisiana, Patrick Floyd Garrett left Dixie to become a cowboy and buffalo hunter in 1869. The late 1870s found him in Lincoln County, New Mexico, where feuding between English and Irish immigrant ranchers erupted into the bloody "Lincoln County War." A leading participant in that guerrilla campaign was Henry McCarty, better known to history as William Bonney or "Billy the Kid." McCarty and Garrett were friends, known to acquaintances as "Little Casino" and "Big Casino" for their respective sizes. They parted company in 1880, when Garrett was elected Lincoln County's sheriff on a pledge to end the local feud.

Garrett's posse cornered McCarty and four companions at Stinking Springs on December 23, 1880, killing one fugitive before the other three surrendered. McCarty was tried for murder and sentenced to hang, but he escaped from jail in Lincoln on April 28, 1881, killing two guards in the process. Garrett finally tracked McCarty to the home of a lover, near Fort Sumner and shot him from ambush. (The Kid was unarmed.) Fame generated by that incident and by Garrett's ghost-written autobiography made his name a household word, enshrining him in legend of a sort, but he lived in fear of retaliation by Billy's allies. Garrett subsequently failed at ranching, spent a short time with the TEXAS RANGERS (1884–85), and lost a race for sheriff in Chaves County (1890).

Garrett moved to Texas, served a term as county commissioner in Uvalde (1894–96), then returned to New Mexico for a special manhunting assignment. Judge Albert Fountain and his son had vanished near White Sands, presumably murdered, and Garrett was named Doña Ana County's sheriff to solve the case. He suspected outlaws James Gilliland and Oliver Lee, finally tracking them to a ranch south of Alamagordo on July 13, 1898. In the ensuing shootout, Garrett lost one deputy and suffered a lethal blow to his career when jurors acquitted both suspects at trial.

Rejected for another term as sheriff, Garrett moved on to a job as a customs agent in El Paso, appointed by President THEODORE ROOSEVELT, then tried ranching again with no better luck than before. After reneging on a business deal, Garrett was shot and killed from ambush on February 28, 1908. Suspect Wayne Brazel was acquitted on a plea of self-defense, but most historians name Jim Miller—a contract killer and principal in the FRAZER-MILLER FEUD—as Garrett's actual assassin.

See also: CUSTOMS SERVICE.

Garrity, John J.

Named to lead the CHICAGO POLICE DEPARTMENT in 1918, John Garrity was the fourth chief appointed by Mayor William "Big Bill" Thompson in as many years. Thompson craved a reduction in street crime— not at all the same thing as cleaning up Chicago—and Garrity talked a good game. Known as "Colonel" Garrity to his subordinates, he supervised a new program of vigilance that saw 76,793 persons jailed for violating city ordinances in 1919, while felony arrests increased by 3,000 over those in 1918. Unfortunately, making charges stick was not the department's strong point. Of the 76,793 persons arrested on municipal charges, fewer than 22,000 were finally convicted. Judge Harry Olson complained, "The police arrest thousands and are unable to substantiate charges brought."

That failure prompted a six-month investigation of Garrity's department by rogue aldermen, still in progress when Chicago's worst riot to date erupted in July 1919. The racial clash left 34 persons dead, 14 of them white, and highlighted lax police treatment of such racist gangs as the pernicious Ragen's Colts. In the wake of that outbreak, Mayor Thompson bypassed Garrity and ordered his deputies to submit a plan for reorganization of the entire police department. Perhaps predictably, their effort gave more power to the mayor, while doing little or nothing to reform the CPD.

Matters went from bad to worse with the onset of PROHIBITION and unfettered street warfare between rival bootlegging gangs. In September 1920 alderman Guy Guernsey told reporters, "Chief Garrity should clean up the police department and make the town safe for its citizens or resign his job." The following month, Garrity remained tight-lipped during his appearance before a grand jury probing mob murders, but he could not save himself with silence. Mayor Thompson demanded and received his resignation on November 10, 1920.

Gary, Elbert H. (1846–1927)

Born at Wheaton, Illinois, in 1846, Elbert Gary joined the Union army after graduating from the Illinois Institute, in 1864, but his military service encompassed a mere two months. Quitting the service to teach school, he studied law privately before enrolling at Chicago's Union College of Law in 1866. Gary deferred private practice to serve three years as a court clerk, then joined his brother in a law firm that made them both wealthy. By 1898 he was the president of J. P. Morgan's Federal Steel Company, later U.S. Steel.

By the advent of PROHIBITION in 1920, Gary was rich and respected enough that he needed to spend little time at a desk. Casting about for causes to support, he soon noticed the liquor-fueled crime wave engulfing America, with the onset of ORGANIZED CRIME and pervasive official CORRUPTION. In August 1925 he convened a gathering of the U.S. business elite who shared his concerns for the rising crime rate, and thus was born the National Crime Commission (NCC), an unofficial group with no police powers which nonetheless devoted itself to fighting crime by means of education (some said propaganda). Other members of the commission included onetime Secretary of State Newton Baker, SUPREME COURT Justice Charles Evan Hughes, Illinois ex-governor Frank Lowden, and future president Franklin Roosevelt. Gary declined to lead his own organization, passing the chair to ex-attorney general GEORGE WICKERSHAM, but he retained strong influence over the NCC.

Lacking any judicial authority, the NCC lobbied for new legislation curbing immigration, restricting ownership of pistols in New York and standardizing penalties from crimes in various jurisdictions. Gary died in 1927, with the NCC's work far from finished, and the U.S. Steel company town of Gary, Indiana, was named in his honor.

Gates, Daryl Francis (b. 1926)

Born in Glendale, California, in 1926, Daryl Gates joined the U.S. Navy at age 17, then tried his hand at college after World War II. Poverty got the better of him in 1949, and he left the University of Southern California to join the LOS ANGELES POLICE DEPARTMENT. A standout in his class at the police academy, Gates was quickly drafted to serve as an aide and chauffeur to Chief WILLIAM HENRY PARKER, who soon adopted Gates as a kind of surrogate son. The affection was mutual, Parker aide and future chief EDWARD MICHAEL DAVIS reporting that Gates was "totally smitten" with Parker.

Gates spent seven years as "Parker's boy," while finishing his USC degree at night, then served as chief of operations for Ed Davis. That training predisposed him to pursuit of sweeping DOMESTIC SURVEILLANCE, making Gates (in author Frank Donner's words) "a true believer in the Southern California gospel of countersubversion." He occupied the chief's office on March 28, 1978 and continued the Parker-Davis tradition of unfettered spying by LAPD's Red squad, the Public Disorder Intelligence Division. In 1980 he refused to share details of the PDID's budget with L.A.'s city council, warning that "each council member would naturally become suspect" if INFORMANTS were exposed and murdered. The same year brought further controversy when Gates, in an interview on fatal CHOKE HOLDS, told the *Los Angeles Times,* "We may be finding that in some blacks when it is applied, the veins or arteries do not open up as fast as they do in normal people."

Charges of RACISM multiplied with a rash of police shootings in the L.A. ghetto and revelations that PDID officers had infiltrated a group organized to protest the death of shooting victim EULIA LOVE. Elsewhere, Gates's Criminal Conspiracy Section grilled and harassed left-ist victims of right-wing bombings, while the terrorist

attacks went forever unsolved. In January 1982 city council members rebuked Gates for "crying wolf" in an attempt to pad the LAPD's budget, a complaint renewed two years later in regard to "terrorist" alerts at the Olympic Games.

Gates was finally driven from office after the ROD-NEY KING beating and subsequent riots of 1991, during which he appeared to withhold police from riot-torn areas out of spite toward the black community. Gates countered that charge with claims that LAPD was unprepared for rioting, an assertion that cast doubts upon his leadership. Gates remained in office long enough to deny reports that he was "forced out," then retired from LAPD on June 27, 1992, to become a radio talk-show host.

See also: BOMBINGS AND BOMB SQUADS; RED SQUADS; TERRORISM.

Gaynor, William Jay (1849–1913)

Native New Yorker William Gaynor—born William James in 1849; his middle name was later changed—trained for the priesthood at a Catholic seminary and the Christian Brothers College in St. Louis, then changed his mind and renounced the church at age 20. He chose the law instead, working as a criminal defense attorney in Flatbush, Brooklyn, where he defended countless petty criminals. His libertarian position on CONSENSUAL CRIMES galled officers of the NEW YORK CITY POLICE DEPARTMENT, but Gaynor had enough supporters to propose a race for mayor in 1892. Declining that idea, he instead sought and won election as a judge of the state Supreme Court.

Judge Gaynor's criticism of police carried more weight from the bench than it had when he was a mere attorney. During his tenure as a judge (1893–1909) he championed the right to privacy of every citizen, including the proprietors and customers of gambling dens and brothels. "So long as the house on my block is so decorous and orderly in the windows and on the stoops that I am not able to see a single thing wrong with it," Gaynor declared, "I am willing to go by and leave it alone and I want the police to do the same."

The year 1909 brought a political change of heart for Gaynor. He won that year's mayoral race with support from TAMMANY HALL, whose leaders sought a malleable candidate to briefly pacify civic reformers. Instead of a stooge, however, Tammany got "one of those old-fashioned kind of men, who merely says in plain and peculiarly pungent and interesting English just what is in his mind and lets the consequences take care of themselves." Social critic Albert Jay Nock once said of Gaynor, "No one in my time understood so well the function of a public servant under a republic." In fact, Nock called Gaynor "the last American . . . in public life."

A relentless critic of police malpractice, Gaynor banned NYPD officers from moonlighting as strikebreakers and ordered them to stay out of saloons. His police, Gaynor declared, "do not club boys and defenseless people in this town . . . nor break into houses without warrants, either." The mayor urged citizens to visit him personally with complaints of police malfeasance, an invitation that brought humble working men and racketeers alike to City Hall for private interviews. New York police, while furious at Gaynor's new restrictions, used the hands-off rule as a license to collect bribes from the underworld.

Ten months after his election, while preparing to embark on a European vacation, Gaynor was ambushed and shot in the head by a would-be assassin at Hoboken Pier, in New Jersey. He survived the wound, although the bullet could not be removed. Reformers offered him a gubernatorial nomination in 1910, but Gaynor declined, insisting that his job as mayor of New York was more important. Tammany leaders denied him renomination in 1913, but a citizen's group successfully placed his name on the mayoral ballot. Sadly, Gaynor died before the election, while enjoying a sea cruise on September 10, 1913.

See also: STRIKEBREAKING.

Georgia Bureau of Investigation (GBI)

Law enforcement in the Peach State was a strictly local affair until March 1937, when Governor E. D. Rivers and the state legislature established a Department of Public Safety. That agency, in turn, was divided into a uniformed GEORGIA STATE PATROL and a "plainclothes" unit originally called the Division of Criminal Identification, Detection, Prevention, and Investigation. Three years later, that long-winded handle was officially shortened to the Georgia Bureau of Investigation (GBI). Its original charter authorized the GBI to maintain fingerprint and criminal history information, while investigating crimes on state property or highways and assisting local agencies with their investigations.

Unfortunately, both Governor Rivers and successor Eugene Talmadge were machine politicians and active members of the KU KLUX KLAN whose CORRUPTION and blatant RACISM tarnished the GBI's image. Georgia led the nation in unsolved LYNCHINGS, and Talmadge appointed Detective Sam Roper—a Klan "cyclops" and member of the ATLANTA POLICE DEPARTMENT—to lead the GBI during 1941–43. Some critics found the same mentality in play four decades later, when GBI agents

illegally suppressed evidence of KKK involvement in the Atlanta "child murders," which sent black suspect Wayne Williams to prison for life.

Governor Jimmy Carter did his best to overhaul the GBI in the early 1970s. First, in June 1972, he established the Georgia Crime Information Center, operating as a subdivision of the GBI to facilitate collection, storage, rapid retrieval and dissemination of data related to law enforcement and criminal justice. Carter also introduced the Executive Reorganization Act of 1972, which with subsequent amendments made the GBI an independent agency, separated from the Department of Public Safety in February 1974. As reorganized by Carter, the GBI today consists of three divisions: the Investigative Division, the Division of Forensic Sciences (state crime lab) and the Georgia Crime Information Center. The GBI was also officially renamed Division of Investigation, but official and public protests reversed that change in 1975.

History aside, the modern GBI declares its mission "to provide the highest quality investigative, scientific, and information services and resources to the criminal justice community and others as authorized by law, for the purpose of maintaining law and order and protecting life and property. The Mission will be achieved by a team of skilled and dedicated employees, utilizing innovative programs and state of the art technology."

See also: FINGERPRINTS; FORENSIC SCIENCE.

Georgia State Patrol

Governor E. D. Rivers created the Georgia State Patrol in March 1937, responding to public demands for a statewide agency to deal with traffic accidents and rising crime rates. The first GSP training class met that summer and graduated 80 officers. While most state criminal investigations are conducted by the GEORGIA BUREAU OF INVESTIGATION, GSP troopers pride themselves on using new technology to reduce highway fatalities and otherwise ensure public safety. The GSP's self-described "elite and diverse team" declares that "[t]rust is our hallmark and foundation. Our word is our bond. Truthfulness is what the public expects from us and what we demand of ourselves. We are committed to the highest ethical standards and highest level of performance beyond reproach." Blacks and civil rights workers questioned that commitment at various times, when RACISM and infiltration by the KU KLUX KLAN compromised the GSP's integrity, but such complaints are relatively rare today. "We have the courage and wisdom to be fair," GSP spokesmen proclaim. "We are sensitive to the needs of others and are committed to treat all with dignity and respect."

Gerard, James Watson (b. 1794)

Wealthy Manhattan native James Gerard was born in 1794 and volunteered at age 18 to serve with the Iron Grays, a unit organized to defend New York's coastline from British attack during the War of 1812. After the war (in which he saw no combat), Gerard graduated from Columbia University (1816) and prospered in private legal practice. Despite a busy work schedule, he found time for involvement in various social causes, including ardent opposition to slavery, membership in the Society for Suppression of Pauperism, and sponsorship of the country's first House of Refuge for Juvenile Delinquents.

Despite his readiness for battle against Britain in 1812–14, Gerard remained an avid Anglophile, as revealed in his 1853 comparison of London's police force with the NEW YORK CITY POLICE DEPARTMENT. In London, he wrote, hoodlums "kept within their dins," while New York's streets were thronged with "rowdies walking arm in arm abreast, filled with liquor and deviltry, with segars [sic] in their mouths elevated at an angle of 45 degrees and their hats cocked sideways 30 degrees, cracking their coarse jokes, or singing their ribald songs." To counter that menace, Gerard proposed adoption of distinctive police uniforms to make patrolmen more impressive and more visible on crowded streets.

After private discussions with Gerard and others, Chief GEORGE MATSELL agreed to a police dress code, which his rank-and-file officers adamantly opposed. The additional expense was one problem, offset in part by a $100 yearly wage increase, but officers also resisted on grounds that uniforms would make policemen resemble liveried servants. Protests notwithstanding, though, the uniforms were phased in over time and finally became a point of pride with New York's Finest.

Gettler, Alexander Oscar (1884–1968)

Austrian, born in 1884, Alexander Gettler immigrated to the United States with his family in 1889. They settled in Brooklyn, New York, and Gettler studied at Columbia University, earning a Ph.D. in chemistry at age 28. Six years later, New York City replaced its elected coroner with a more efficient medical examiner, Dr. CHARLES NORRIS, and Gettler joined the staff as a forensic toxicologist. Over the next four decades, until his retirement in 1960, Gettler performed blood tests on more than 100,000 corpses, while inventing new equipment and procedures to determine whether death was caused by drowning, alcohol intoxication, drugs, or poison. He died in 1968, at age 84.

Gibbons, Nelson H.

A college football star and ex-Marine, Nelson "Skip" Gibbons served as a New York state trooper for seven years before he joined the FBI. Assigned to the Detroit field office, Gibbons single-handedly exposed a Russian spy, Kaarlo Tuomi, whose confessions later revealed three more spies in New York and earned the Bureau national accolades in 1963. By that time, however, Gibbons had been hounded from the FBI by J. EDGAR HOOVER, in a classic display of the director's personal malice.

The trouble began in 1958, when Hoover's physician ordered him to lose weight. Determined not to suffer alone, Hoover issued an insurance firm's weight charts to all field offices, insisting that every agent register a "desirable" weight for his height. Physicians ridiculed the plan, one U.S. Navy doctor branding it "irresponsible," but Hoover was adamant. Even after one agent died in the midst of a crash diet, his widow filing suit against the FBI for wrongful death, Hoover clung to his chart as if it were infallible. Agent Gibbons was five pounds over the limit at his 1960 evaluation, and a physician's statement that his weight was "medically proper" failed to impress Hoover. The order came back from Washington: "Lose 5 lbs."

Gibbons next sought a meeting with Hoover. "Although I did not specify a date," he recalled, "I received the stock answer that he would be unavailable." Two weeks later, in September 1960, Gibbons received an "unsatisfactory" personnel rating and a punitive transfer from Detroit to Mobile, Alabama. The travel papers carried an order for Gibbons to be shipped out again in November 1960, this time to Oklahoma City (a tactic of harassment known to G-men as "the Bureau bicycle"). When Gibbons arrived in Oklahoma City, agent-in-charge Wesley Grapp told him, "I'm going to give you ulcers." In January 1961 Gibbons received a three-week suspension without pay for allegedly displaying "an unsatisfactory attitude toward the physical requirements of your position." Further requests for a meeting with Hoover were denied, but Assistant Director John Mohr told Gibbons to expect a 30-day suspension if he had not lost five pounds by February 2, 1961.

When Gibbons and colleague William Turner filed harassment complaints against Agent Grapp, Hoover deemed their complaints "baseless" and transferred both agents—Gibbons to Butte, Montana, and Turner to Knoxville, Tennessee. An FBI hearing in October 1961 failed to resolve the matter, and Gibbons was next transferred to Alaska. Still he refused to quit, but FBI leaders solved the problem in autumn 1962, issuing Gibbons a medical discharge for "nervousness," with a monthly pension of $250 for life.

See also: FEDERAL BUREAU OF INVESTIGATION.

Gilbert, Daniel

Few officers of the CHICAGO POLICE DEPARTMENT have matched Daniel "Tubbo" Gilbert for sheer notoriety. He joined the force as a patrolman on April 6, 1917—the same day America entered World War I—and simultaneously pursued a parallel career in labor union politics, rising at one point to secretary-treasurer of the Baggage & Parcel Driver's Union, Local 725. During one labor conflict, Gilbert was charged with assault; the case was suspended with leave to reinstate, but the file mysteriously vanished from Chicago's criminal court. As it turned out, Gilbert's close association with the Teamsters' Union was only one of his links to ORGANIZED CRIME.

Tubbo Gilbert never met a bribe he didn't like, and PROHIBITION provided the perfect opportunity for him to enrich himself. He initially attached himself to bootlegger Mike "de Pike" Heitler, identified by witnesses as one of 20 officers who stood by, drinking, while a trainload of Heitler's illegal liquor was unloaded at Gresham Station in September 1920. A grand jury questioned Gilbert about that incident, but no charges were filed. Gilbert next cast his lot with the Torrio-Capone liquor syndicate, but he was not averse to squeezing rivals for cash. In 1923 Gilbert seized a truckload of beer owned by Roger Touhy's gang, then released it to Touhy at a price of five dollars per barrel.

Such antics did not interfere with Gilbert's promotion to lieutenant in 1926, or to captain by the decade's end. In 1926 he also forged a close alliance with Thomas Courtney, then sergeant-at-arms for Chicago's city council, later state's attorney for Cook County during 1932–44. When Touhy won his first election as state's attorney, he chose Gilbert to be his chief investigator, a post Gilbert would hold despite recurring scandals until his retirement in 1950.

Through thick and thin, Gilbert remained devoted to the mob. In 1933, with FBI agent MELVIN PURVIS, he assisted the Capone gang's frame-up of Roger Touhy for a gangland kidnapping that never happened. Touhy spent 25 years in prison for that mythical crime before he was finally exonerated (and then murdered) in 1959. In ordering Touhy's release from prison, Judge John Barnes cited Gilbert's personal hatred for Touhy and evidence that Gilbert personally bribed ex-convict Ike Costner to perjure himself at Touhy's trial.

Gilbert himself faced indictment in 1936, for helping the Teamsters fix retail milk prices in Chicago, but Courtney dismissed the charge as political persecution and kept Gilbert on the state payroll. The charge was later dropped, but Gilbert's problems continued. In 1940, while running unsuccessfully for state's attorney, Judge Oscar Nelson accused Gilbert of protecting mob boss Frank Nitti. As evidence, Nelson noted Gilbert's recent vacation in Hot Springs, Arkansas, where he played golf with gold-plated clubs supplied by Nitti. A year later the *Chicago Tribune* obtained financial books for Nitti's gang, listing local payoffs for the month of July 1941. Gilbert was listed, by the nickname "Tub," as a recipient of $4,600 that month. Press reports dubbed him "the millionaire cop," but Gilbert estimated his net worth at a mere $350,000.

Tom Courtney's passing from the political scene left Gilbert unfazed. State's attorney William Touhy (no relation to Roger) kept him on as chief investigator during 1944–48, and successor John Boyle followed suit, despite a promise to fire Gilbert if he (Boyle) was elected. Once in office, Boyle changed his mind, announcing that he would dump Tubbo only if ordered to do so by Mayor Martin Kennelly The order never came, and Gilbert was safe—for a while.

His world was shaken, finally, by Senator ESTES KEFAUVER's televised investigation of gambling and organized crime. An ex-Chicago cop turned private eye, William Drury, offered information on Gilbert to Kefauver, and made the same offer to Republican Party officials when Gilbert got the Democratic nod to run for sheriff of Cook County in 1950. Mayor Kennelly, himself a Democrat, was called upon to endorse Gilbert, but he sabotaged Tubbo with a banquet speech that dubbed Gilbert "Two-Ball Dan," a hopeless cheater on the golf links. Laughter still echoed from that performance when rival John Babb swamped Gilbert by a landslide at the polls, but Gilbert lost his sense of humor before the Kefauver Committee. As noted in the committee's final report:

> A reason for lack of conscientious enforcement of gambling laws [in Chicago] was disclosed by the testimony of Police Captain Dan Gilbert, known as the world's richest cop. . . . Gilbert testified . . . that he had placed bets himself with a well-known Chicago betting commissioner. He admitted this was not legal betting. In explanation he testified, "I have been a gambler at heart." Although agreeing that raids could be initiated by his office on bookies in the city, Gilbert admitted that it had not been done since 1939 despite the fact that practically every bookmaking establishment in the city of Chicago was listed in the recently published hearings before the McFarland subcommittee of the Senate Interstate and Foreign Commerce Committee.

Bill Drury never had a chance to testify for Kefauver. Instead, he was ambushed in the driveway of his home, killed by four shotgun blasts a few hours before he was scheduled to meet the committee. Gilbert fared better, retiring with his fortune to an idle life of high-stakes gin rummy at Fritzel's Restaurant on Randolph Street.

See also: FRAME-UPS; KIDNAPPING.

Gilchrist, Joyce

An African-American native of Oklahoma City, Joyce Gilchrist was drawn to police work while a student at the University of Oklahoma. By 1980, when she earned her degree in forensic chemistry, Gilchrist was already employed in the OKLAHOMA CITY POLICE DEPARTMENT's crime lab, working on 3,000 cases between 1980 and 1993. In 1985 she was named OCPD's "civilian employee of the year."

Gilchrist was a compelling witness at trial, invariably supporting prosecution theories with the kind of scientific evidence certain to impress jurors. Legendary Oklahoma City prosecutor Bob Macy was especially enamored of Gilchrist's technique, and police dubbed her "Black Magic" for her high conviction rate. "It was in reference to a homicide case," Gilchrist later told *60 Minutes II*, "where the defense attorney referred to me in his closing argument as a sorcerer . . . and stated that I seemed to be able to do things with evidence that nobody else was able to do."

And that was the problem.

In 1987 another forensic chemist, John Wilson of Kansas City, wrote an angry letter to the Southwestern Association of Forensic Scientists (SAFS), asserting that Gilchrist offered "scientific opinions from the witness stand which in effect positively identify the defendant based on the slightest bit of circumstantial evidence." Wilson took the unusual step of criticizing a colleague after several Oklahoma defense attorneys asked him to review Gilchrist's testimony from preliminary hearings. Convinced that Gilchrist had presented false evidence in court, Wilson ultimately testified against her in three separate murder cases. Although he "got major heat" for siding with the defense, Wilson told interviewers that he "felt I had an ethical obligation" to do so. "When I read the transcripts and saw what she was saying, I was really shocked. She was positively identifying hair, and there's no way in the world you can do that without DNA."

The SAFS conducted its own investigation and determined that Gilchrist had violated the group's code of ethics, resulting in a formal censure. In 1988 an appellate court overturned Curtis McCarty's murder conviction, based on the fact that Gilchrist gave the court "personal opinions beyond the scope of scientific capabilities." A year later, the same court reversed a second murder conviction, finding that Gilchrist had misrepresented hair and fiber evidence at trial.

Notwithstanding such disclosures, Gilchrist was promoted to supervisor of the OCPD crime lab in 1994 and continued to testify in criminal cases for another five years, until Judge Ralph Thompson rebuked her in August 1999, for giving false testimony in a rape-murder case. (Semen samples excluded defendant Alfred Mitchell as a suspect, but Gilchrist called them "inconclusive.") As a result of that finding and others, police finally removed Gilchrist from the crime lab in March 2000, reassigning her to an administrative post. Seven months later, the Association for Crime Scene Reconstruction expelled Gilchrist. Oklahoma state attorney general Drew Edmondson announced a review of Gilchrist's capital cases on April 25, 2001—the same date that an FBI report blamed her for giving testimony "beyond the limits of forensic science" in at least eight cases. Even more disturbing was the fact that Gilchrist's testimony had sent 23 defendants to death row, 11 of them subsequently executed.

In May 2001, after DNA evidence exonerated Gilchrist victim Jeffrey Price of rape charges (for which he had served 15 years), Governor Frank Keating ordered a sweeping probe of 1,200 cases involving Gilchrist. She was formally fired on September 25, 2001, though her lawyer called Gilchrist "a scapegoat" for other, unnamed offenders. By November 2001 state investigators had flagged 165 cases for further study in depth, and while Drew Edmondson declared himself "personally satisfied that no innocent person was executed" because of Gilchrist, grave doubts remain. No charges have been filed thus far against Gilchrist for perjury or any other criminal offense.

See also: DNA; FEDERAL BUREAU OF INVESTIGATION; FORENSIC SCIENCE.

Gilpin, Henry Dilworth (1801–1860)

British subject Henry Gilpin was born in Lancaster, England, on April 14, 1801. He attended school outside London (1811–16), then immigrated to the United States and graduated from the University of Pennsylvania in 1819. Thereafter, he studied law privately and was admitted to the state bar in 1822. Ten years later, he was named U.S. attorney for the eastern district of Pennsylvania, promoted to serve as solicitor for the TREASURY DEPARTMENT in 1837. President Martin Van Buren named Gilpin attorney general on January 11, 1840, and he held that post until March 5, 1841. Gilpin died in Philadelphia on January 29, 1860.

Girard, Stephen (1750–1831)

Born in 1750, British sea trader Stephen Girard immigrated to North America at age 26 and settled in Philadelphia on the eve of the American Revolution. Expanding his fleet in the wake of that conflict, he became one of the new republic's wealthiest inhabitants, an ardent Patriot who spent his money freely, both in politics and in pursuit of charitable works. In 1810 he saved the Bank of the United States from collapse

Philanthropist Stephen Girard (Author's collection)

with a $1 million investment, then purchased its buildings for cash when Congress denied the bank an operating charter.

At his accidental death in 1831, Girard left a complex and controversial will that lavished money on the city of Philadelphia, including a $500,000 bequest for the PHILADELPHIA POLICE DEPARTMENT to hire new personnel. Girard's relatives bitterly contested the will, fighting it all the way to the U.S. SUPREME COURT, where its terms were upheld in 1844. Philadelphia police administrators thereafter used Girard's bequest to hire 24 new full-time officers and 120 part-time night watchmen. Girard's will made news again in 1968, when the Supreme Court amended its language to strike racial limitations on a boarding school established for "poor, white, male orphans."

Goddard, Calvin Hooker (1891–1955)

Born in 1891, Baltimore native Calvin Goddard trained as a physician at Johns Hopkins University (Class of 1915), specializing in cardiology. He joined the U.S. Army in 1916 and achieved the rank of major during World War I. Goddard left military service in 1920, to serve as assistant director of Johns Hopkins Hospital, but he returned to the army in 1922 with a very different mission, assigned to the Ordinance Reserve. Fueled by a lifelong interest in firearms, his tour of duty at various arsenals and graduate study at the Massachusetts Institute of Technology made Goddard an early expert in the fledgling field of ballistics.

In April 1925 Goddard joined John Fisher, PHILIP O. GRAVELLE, and Charles Waite in founding the New York-based Bureau of Forensic Ballistics, created to provide firearms identification services for police departments lacking their own lab equipment. Together, the team invented a side-by-side comparison microscope permitting examination of bullets and cartridge cases, used to match test samples with evidence collected from crime scenes or victims' bodies.

Goddard's first headline case, in 1927, involved the Massachusetts holdup-murder convictions of anarchists Nicola Sacco and Bartolomeo Vanzetti. Ballistics evidence in that case was confused at best, and one state expert was later accused of falsifying evidence in other cases. Goddard's test allegedly linked one bullet from the shooting to a pistol owned by Sacco, even though the wheelman for an unrelated gang confessed involvement in the crime and named alternate suspects in 1925. No reliable evidence was ever found linking Vanzetti to the murders.

Two years after that case, Goddard examined bullets and cartridges fired in Chicago's notorious St. Valentine's Day Massacre, determining that the killers used two Thompson submachine guns and one shotgun in the slayings. One of the tommy guns was later confiscated from syndicate hit man Fred "Killer" Burke, but he was never tried for the Chicago murders. Still, Chicago's grand jury foreman asked Goddard in 1930 to establish a local ballistics laboratory. Goddard accepted the offer and became director of the new Scientific Crime Detection Laboratory, affiliated with the Northwestern University School of Law outside Chicago. He remained as director of that lab until 1934, when he left to found a private firm. While working in Chicago, during 1932, Goddard also helped the FBI establish its own forensic lab in Washington, D.C.

Recalled to noncombatant military service during World War II, Goddard served as chief historian for the army's Ordinance Division. In 1947 he was transferred to Japan, as assistant chief of the historical section, then as head of Tokyo's Far Eastern Criminal Investigation Laboratory. Ill health drove Goddard back to the United States in 1951, but he remained active as an army historian, with sideline contributions on ordinance and ballistics to the *Encyclopaedia Britannica*. Goddard died in 1955, two days after delivering a ballistics lecture to the American Academy of Forensic Sciences in Los Angeles.

See also: ANARCHISM; FEDERAL BUREAU OF INVESTIGATION.

Gonzales, Alberto R. (b. 1955)

Texas native Alberto Gonzales was born in San Antonio on August 4, 1955. While employed with the Houston law firm of Vinson & Elkins (1982–95) he forged political ties that paved the way for his employment as general counsel to Governor George W. Bush (1995–97), then as Texas secretary of state (1997–99). Gonzales spent a year on the Texas Supreme Court before Bush was elected president of the United States in 2000, whereupon he left for Washington to serve as Bush's White House counsel (2001–05).

In November 2004, with the announcement that JOHN ASHCROFT would not return for a second term as attorney general, Bush nominated Gonzales to fill the JUSTICE DEPARTMENT's top post. That selection sparked immediate controversy, based on legal advice from Gonzales to Bush, suggesting that Bush's invasion of Iraq had "rendered obsolete" the Geneva Convention's "quaint" rules on treatment of military prisoners. That judgment seemed to pave the way for torture of POWs—which indeed occurred at the hands of U.S. troops and CIA interrogators at Iraq's Abu Ghraib prison. In light of those opinions, civil libertarians joined forces to oppose Gonzales's confirmation in January 2005.

Their efforts were wasted as Gonzales coasted to easy confirmation, promising the U.S. Senate that he would respect the Constitution and all treaties governing treatment of prisoners. "The American people expect and deserve a Department of Justice guided by the rule of law," Gonzales declared. "There should be no question regarding the department's commitment to every American. On this principle there can be no compromise." He took office as attorney general on February 4, 2005.

Gonzales, Thomas A. (1878–1956)

Dr. Thomas Gonzales served on the staff of premier New York City medical examiner CHARLES NORRIS, then succeeded Norris as acting medical examiner upon his death in 1935. Two years later, at age 59, Gonzales won a permanent appointment to the post and served until 1954. Ranked as one of the nation's foremost forensic pathologists, Gonzales became so proficient at his craft that he could often solve a case, for all intents and purposes, after viewing a corpse for mere minutes. His testimony sent hundreds of killers to prison, but Gonzales took special pride in exonerating the inno-

cent. In one such case, a real estate agent was charged with murder in the presumed beating death of an elderly man, with whom he had quarreled over rent and the cost of repairs. Gonzales proved that the "victim" had suffered a heart attack in private, creating apparent signs of a struggle as he thrashed about the room while dying. Gonzales survived two years in retirement, then died in 1956.

Gravelle, Philip O. (1877–1955)

Born in 1877, San Francisco native Philip Gravelle moved across country as a young man and settled in New York City, working as a textile designer while taking night classes at Columbia University. His twin passions were cameras and microscopes, a bent that brought him kudos in 1923 as the first U.S. citizen ever to win the London Photomicrographic Society's Barnard Gold Medal. Two years later, in April 1925, Gravelle applied his talents to FORENSIC SCIENCE, joining colleagues John Fisher, CALVIN HOOKER GODDARD and Charles Waite to found the Bureau of Forensic Ballistics. Together, they pioneered new equipment, including a side-by-side comparison microscope, to test ballistics evidence for police departments nationwide. Gravelle's role was to photograph the markings found on various bullets and spent cartridge casings recovered from crime scenes, preserving that evidence for trial. After lending his skill to many notorious cases, from the Massachusetts Sacco-Vanzetti murders to Chicago's St. Valentine's Day massacre, Gravelle died in New Jersey on February 3, 1955.

Gray, L. Patrick, III (b. 1916)

A St. Louis native, born June 18, 1916, Louis Patrick Gray III grew up in Houston, Texas, and studied at Rice University before proceeding to the U.S. Naval Academy at Annapolis, Maryland. He graduated as a commissioned officer, later serving as a submarine commander in World War II and as commander of a submarine flotilla in the Korean War. While still in military service, during 1949, Gray graduated from George Washington University School of Law. After service as assistant to the Joint Chiefs of Staff, he retired from the navy in 1960 to join Richard Nixon's presidential campaign staff. Following Nixon's defeat, Gray practiced law in Connecticut, then rejoined Nixon for the 1968 presidential race. By December 1970 he was assistant attorney general in charge of the JUSTICE DEPARTMENT's Civil Division, where he prosecuted antiwar protesters and defended the FBI against lawsuits filed by female applicants whom Director J. EDGAR HOOVER had rejected.

On May 3, 1972—one day after Hoover's death—President Nixon named Gray to serve as acting FBI director. His first task was a fruitless search for Hoover's secret files. Having failed at that mission, Gray quickly established an unsavory reputation in office. Assistant Director Leonard Walters later told journalist Robert Kessler that "Gray would lie regularly" to the press and his subordinates. He also avoided headquarters whenever possible, earning the nickname "Three-Day Gray" for his abbreviated workweeks and extended tours of distant field offices (costing taxpayers more than $100,000 for air transportation in 11 months).

The positive aspects of Gray's FBI tenure included new initiatives to recruit minority and female agents, but Gray was doomed by the festering Watergate scandal. Secret White House tapes reveal that Nixon first discussed firing Gray on March 7, 1973, after Gray (at his Senate confirmation hearing) admitted destroying documents relevant to the Watergate cover-up. Aide John Ehrlichman remarked on that occasion, "I think we ought to let him hang there. Let him twist slowly, slowly in the wind." Six days later, Nixon said, "Gray should not be the head of the FBI," adding on March 22, "The problem with [Gray] is that he's a little bit stupid." Gray withdrew his name from nomination on April 5, 1973, and formally resigned his post on April 27.

Returning to private practice in Connecticut, Gray discovered that his problems were not finished. In April 1978 he was indicted with FBI officials W. MARK FELT and Edward Miller, on charges of approving illegal break-ins around New York City. Gray denied any knowledge of the crimes and requested a separate trial. Felt and Miller were convicted and fined in November 1980, subsequently pardoned by President Ronald Reagan in March 1981. Federal prosecutors dismissed Gray's charges in December 1980, citing lack of evidence.

See also: FEDERAL BUREAU OF INVESTIGATION.

Great Falls Police Department

The police department of Great Falls, Montana, was created in 1888, when the city was incorporated. City Marshall John Hurly supervised "Chief" George Huy, though in fact they were the only two lawmen in town. Two officers were hired in 1889, patrolling without standard uniforms until the mid-1890s. By 1909 the force included 14 officers, certified upon passing an examination and completing six months of probationary service. Patrol cars were introduced in 1914, followed by two-way radios in 1940. Computers arrived in 1970, and the force had grown to include 78 officers and 65 vehicles by 2004. Its three divisions include Operations, Support Services, and Records.

Greensboro Police Department

John Logan won appointment as Greensboro, North Carolina's first "public officer" to keep the peace in 1829, augmented in March 1830 by creation of a "citizen's patrol" system requiring nocturnal service from all males (except ministers) between the ages of 21 and 45 years. While civilian patrolmen were unpaid, one year's service canceled their poll tax for the same 12 months. Greensboro hired the Lumbley brothers, Jeremiah and Jesse, as part-time night watchmen in 1839, and a new town charter in 1870 empowered commissioners to hire "one or more Constables" who doubled as tax collectors during their 12-month terms. Yet another charter, in July 1889, finally provided for creation of a bona fide police force, with R. M. Reese as the first chief.

As elsewhere in the United States, police work in Greensboro was closely tied to economics and politics. While installation of the town's first telephones (1894) streamlined crime reports and communication with officers on the beat, Greensboro's force remained small, numbering only seven officers in 1902. Headquarters closed at night until 1904. In 1911 the 21-member department worked 12-hour shifts, with no cars or radios. PROHIBITION tested the Greensboro PD, costing two officers' lives and requiring expansion of the force to 45 officers in 1923. The force inaugurated radio communications in 1934, received its first conduct manuals in October 1937, and launched its first in-service training courses during January 1938. By the time America entered World War II, in 1941, Greensboro PD boasted 94 officers, 16 cars, and eight motorcycles.

Postwar Greensboro witnessed the department's first organized vice investigations (1952), intensified firearms training (1953), and creation of a police cadet program (1954). The "direct action" phase of America's Civil Rights movement began in Greensboro with a series of sit-in demonstrations in February 1960, taxing the all-white police force as a violent KU KLUX KLAN swung into action, terrorizing blacks and actively recruiting white lawmen. The same year brought scandal to the force, with exposure of a police burglary ring including one sergeant and two lieutenants. That revelation forced internal reorganization of the department, with strict new rules of accountability for patrolmen and detectives.

In November 1972 Greensboro PD promoted "meter maid" Anne Garcia to serve as the city's first female patrol officer. Chief William Swing added a Community Services Division to the force in May 1975, followed by a Warrant Squad in June 1978. The following year brought tragedy, in November 1979, when Klansmen and neo-Nazis fired on parading members of the Communist Workers' Party, killing five unarmed victims. Despite advance warning, police were suspiciously absent from the shooting scene, and subsequent investigation proved that a civilian police informant helped plan the attack, but his handlers went unpunished, and all-white juries acquitted the killers in a series of high-profile state and federal trials.

Greensboro PD bounced back from that incident to win full accreditation in November 1986, from the Commission on Accreditation for Law Enforcement Agencies. The accreditation process required a complete review of departmental rules and regulations, adoption of new procedures and policies, and publication of a new Departmental Directives Manual. By 1989 the department had 402 sworn officers and 117 civilian personnel, operating on a $21 million budget. Department publicists declare that Greensboro PD is "committed to providing citizens with the highest caliber of police services and are dedicated toward setting the standards of excellence for the next 100 years."

See also: INFORMANTS.

Gregory, Thomas Watt (1861–1933)

Mississippi native Thomas Gregory was born at Crawfordsville on November 6, 1861, and lost his father in the Civil War. He graduated from Southwestern Presbyterian University in 1883 and thereafter was a "special" student at the University of Virginia (1884). Gregory entered the practice of law at Austin, Texas, in 1885 and spent eight years as a regent of the state university. He declined appointment as the Lone Star State's assistant attorney general in 1892, likewise rejecting a state court appointment four years later. In 1904 he was a delegate to the Democratic National Convention in St. Louis and reprised that role in Baltimore, in 1912. On May 20, 1913, President Woodrow Wilson appointed Gregory as a special assistant to Attorney General JAMES CLARK MCREYNOLDS, investigating alleged misconduct by the New York, New Haven, and Hartford Railroad Company. Gregory replaced McReynolds as attorney general on September 3, 1914, and held that post until March 1919.

Unlike McReynolds, Gregory's administration was both active and controversial. He increased the FBI's strength from 122 agents to 225, while boosting the support staff from 39 to 268. At the same time, Bureau strength was further enhanced by Gregory's ill-advised alliance with the vigilante American Protective League (APL) in February 1917. That collaborative effort produced the sweeping "slacker" raids of 1918, generating public outcry against the FBI's abuse of power. Gregory subsequently helped draft the equally controversial Espionage and Sedition Acts, thereby continuing his department's involvement with APL amateur spies throughout World War I. Gregory resigned on March 4, 1919, and subsequently served as a member of Woodrow Wilson's Second Industrial Conference (1919–20). Thereafter he returned to private practice in Austin, where he died on February 26, 1933.

See also: FEDERAL BUREAU OF INVESTIGATION.

Griggs, John William (1849–1927)

Born at Newton, New Jersey, on July 10, 1849, John Griggs graduated from Lafayette College in 1868, then studied law and was admitted to the bar in 1871. He practiced privately in Paterson for five years, then won election to the state assembly (1876–77) and state senate (1882–88). New Jersey voters chose Griggs as their governor in 1895, but he resigned that post to serve as President William McKinley's attorney general from February 1, 1898, to March 29, 1901. Upon leaving the JUSTICE DEPARTMENT, Griggs served on the Permanent Court of Arbitration at The Hague from 1901 to 1912. He died at Paterson, New Jersey, on November 28, 1927.

Grimsley, James Ira (1912–1987)

A Mississippi Gulf Coast native, born in 1912, James Grimsley was a promising amateur boxer in his youth, before going to work in Pascagoula's shipyards. He pursued premed studies at Jackson's Millsaps College, but left school without graduating. Instead, Grimsley used his incomplete education to win election as Jackson County's coroner (1957–60), then as county sheriff (1961–65).

The sheriff's job also incorporated tax collection, but a more lucrative field of income was graft from the operators of Pascagoula's illegal brothels, gambling clubs, and moonshine stills. Harold Jones, one-time chief deputy who left Grimsley's force to join the U.S. Army, told FBI agents, "There was no bag man. Each guy paid off directly to the sheriff." Jones also described Grimsley's penchant for "cutting"—sexually assaulting—women other than his wife. According to Jones's sworn statement: "Worst part about the sheriff is that he'll try to cut every woman he gets alone. Women who come to visit their husbands in jail. . . . Wife of a guy we held on car theft charges. Everytime she came in sheriff would cut her."

A lifelong alcoholic who periodically vanished from Pascagoula to "dry out" in Alabama, Grimsley was also known for the intensity of his RACISM. In September 1962 he led three deputies and 30-odd vigilantes to Oxford, where they joined in the OLE MISS RIOT against black student James Meredith's enrollment at the University of Mississippi. In the wake of that melee, Grimsley organized 600 bigots into a new Jackson County Citizens Emergency Unit, whose purpose was described by Ira Harkey, Jr., editor of the Pascagoula *Chronicle*.

[T]hey outlined their program of civic improvement: to eradicate local "niggerlovers," to boycott all businesses that employed or sold goods to Negroes, to "attend to" persons placed on a list by an "action committee," to train a strongarm squad at weekly maneuvers . . . and in the main and particular to put out of business the Pascagoula daily newspaper, the Chronicle, identified by them as "the leading niggerlover in the State."

In fact, FBI files document the JCCEU's plans "to do away with" Harkey and his newspaper. According to the same FBI files, the central purpose of Grimsley's goon squad was "to secretly go to the University of Mississippi . . . 'to get' or kidnap" Meredith. FBI investigation discouraged that plan, and the JCCEU rapidly lost members, while Sheriff Grimsley slid deeper into drunkenness. Jackson County voters rejected his reelection bid in 1964, and Grimsley lapsed into obscurity. He died in Pascagoula on October 19, 1987, on a street that bore his name, from the combined effects of liver disease and youthful exposure to asbestos.

See also: FEDERAL BUREAU OF INVESTIGATION.

Groome, John C. (1884–1930)

Born in 1884, Philadelphia native John Groome joined the Pennsylvania NATIONAL GUARD as soon as he was old enough, rising through the ranks to command an infantry unit which he led to foreign combat during the Spanish-American War (1898–99). Back in Pennsylvania at war's end, he saw action again in the anthracite coal strike of 1902, ended when President THEODORE ROOSEVELT intervened from Washington. Three years later, Governor Samuel Pennypacker tapped Groome to serve as the first commander of the fledgling PENNSYLVANIA STATE POLICE. Groome accepted the position, on condition that the force would not be composed of political hacks. He built a first-rate professional force before resigning to serve with the U.S. Army in World War I, during which Groome ran a camp for German prisoners of war in France. Back in the States at war's end, Groome served as warden of Pennsylvania's Eastern Penitentiary until he finally retired from public life. He died in 1930, at age 70.

Grosso, Salvador (b. 1935)

Born in 1935, Salvador "Sonny" Grosso was an obscure narcotics investigator for the NEW YORK CITY POLICE DEPARTMENT until 1962, when he cracked the famous "French Connection" heroin case with partner EDWARD EGAN. The publicity resulting from that case spurred both detectives to leave NYPD and enter show business, with Grosso serving as a technical adviser to author Peter Maas on his book *The French Connection*,

and on the subsequent Oscar-winning film of the same title (1971). Grosso played a small part in that movie, and in two other Hollywood productions, *Report to the Commissioner* (1974) and *Cruising* (1980).

While Eddie Egan built a post-NYPD career as an actor, though, Grosso was more comfortable off-camera. Prior to teaming with television executive Larry Jacobson in 1980, Grosso served as technical adviser for two more feature films, *The Godfather* (1972) and *The Seven-Ups* (1973). In 1973 he wrote and co-produced *The Marcus-Nelson Murders*, a pilot for the *Kojak* TV series. Grosso also served as TV's technical adviser on *Kojak* (1973–78), *The Rockford Files* (1974–80), and *Baretta* (1975–78). With Jacobson, as a partner in Grosso-Jacobson Productions (later Grosso Jacobson Entertainment Corp.), he produced TV series, including *Pee Wee's Playhouse* (1986–90), *Diamonds* (1987–89), *True Blue* (1989), and *Top Cops* (1990–93).

Grundy, Felix (1777–1840)

Felix Grundy was born in Berkley County, Virginia (now West Virginia), on September 11, 1777. His family soon moved to Pennsylvania, then to Kentucky, where

Attorney General Felix Grundy (Author's collection)

Grundy was educated at home and at the Bardstown Academy. He studied law privately and was admitted to the Kentucky bar in 1797. From 1799 to 1806 Grundy served in the state legislature, then sat briefly on the state's Supreme Court of Errors and Appeals in 1807. He resigned before year's end and moved to Nashville, Tennessee, where he was elected to Congress (1813–15) and subsequently to the Tennessee state legislature (1819–20). In 1820 Grundy was named commissioner to settle a boundary dispute between Tennessee and Kentucky. Nine years later, Tennessee's governor appointed Grundy to fill a vacancy in the U.S. Senate, and he won election to a full term of his own in 1833. President Martin Van Buren named Grundy attorney general in July 1838, assuming office on September 1. He resigned that post on December 1, 1839, after winning election to another Senate vacancy, but critics questioned his right to seek elective office while serving as attorney general. Grundy resolved the controversy by resigning from the Senate on December 14, 1839, and was reelected the same day. He served one year and five days of his term before dying, in Nashville, on December 19, 1840.

gun control

A hot-button issue throughout the United States, gun control inspires fervent debate wherever the subject is raised. Opposition to gun-control statutes is based on the Constitution's Second Amendment, which states: "A well-regulated militia being necessary to the security of a free State, the right of the people to keep and bear arms shall not be infringed." Pro-gun advocates commonly ignore the reference to a militia—defined by various federal statutes and court rulings as the NATIONAL GUARD—while insisting that "the people's" right to own and carry guns is sacrosanct.

In fact, some 20,000 federal, state, and local statutes presently restrict the use and possession of firearms throughout the United States. All states forbid ex-convicts from owning firearms, and most extend the same ban to registered mental patients. All states impose restrictions on private ownership of various "criminal" or military weapons, ranging from switchblade knives to machine guns and grenade launchers. Most jurisdictions require special permits to carry concealed firearms, and many ban the public carrying of guns outside

of designated hunting seasons. Some cities (such as Las Vegas, Nevada) require registration of handguns. New York's Sullivan Law, among the toughest in the nation, forbids purchase of pistols without a police permit. Other jurisdictions, particularly in the South and West, have adopted so-called Make My Day statutes (named from a line in a Clint Eastwood film, *The Enforcer*), encouraging gun ownership and armed self-defense against criminals or attackers.

Federal gun-control statutes date from 1934, when the National Firearms Act imposed transfer taxes and mandated registration of "gangster" weapons including machine guns, silencers and sawed-off rifles or shotguns. The Gun Control Act of 1968 banned mail-order sale, prohibited sale of pistols to persons under 18 years of age, and expanded federal taxation to "destructive devices" (including grenades, bazookas, flamethrowers, etc.). Another statute passed in 1987 banned civilian purchase of machine guns manufactured after that year, but allowed continued sale of weapons produced earlier. Civilian purchase of armor-piercing "cop-killer" bullets was subsequently banned. Finally, a 10-year ban on semiautomatic "assault weapons," defined by various cosmetic traits, was passed in 1994 and expired in 2004.

Guttenplan, Henry L. (1918–1982)

Born in 1918, Henry Guttenplan graduated from the City College of New York at age 22, then joined the U.S. Navy for a foreign tour of duty in World War II. Discharged in 1944, he joined the NEW YORK CITY POLICE DEPARTMENT as a patrolman and rose steadily through the ranks to become an inspector commanding the department's scientific research office in 1959. That same year, Guttenplan earned his master's degree, again from City College, then began work on his Ph.D., completed in 1965. Guttenplan's doctoral dissertation called for sweeping reorganization of the NYPD's crime lab, ballistics division and bomb squad, together with various changes in duty shifts and detective assignments. Commissioner Howard Leary found the paper persuasive enough that he implemented most of Guttenplan's suggestions. Guttenplan retired from the NYPD in 1967 to teach police science at Pennsylvania State University. He died in 1982.

See also: BOMBING AND BOMB SQUADS.

Hale, David Olin

On July 21, 1968, a bomb exploded at the Tucson, Arizona, home of Detroit mobster Peter Licavoli. One day later, two explosions damaged the nearby home of transplanted New York gangster Joseph Bonnano. Over the next year, Tucson was rocked by 15 more bombings while newspapers carried reports of a "gang war" raging between rival leaders of ORGANIZED CRIME. In fact, as local authorities learned in 1970, the bombing campaign was an FBI COINTELPRO operation planned and carried out by Tucson agent David Hale in a bizarre attempt to foment gangland bloodshed.

As later revealed in sworn courtroom testimony, Hale recruited two local felons to plant the bombs on command. Once, after one of Hale's accomplices was shot while fleeing the scene of an attempted bombing, Hale brought a bomb to his hospital room and asked the wounded man to "crimp a cap onto a fuse" for the next scheduled blast. (Hale's accomplice could not do the job with one hand disabled.) A female college student was found shot to death after boasting to friends that she and Hale had tried to bomb Joe Bonnano's car, but Tucson police ruled her death a suicide.

Agent Hale was suspended from duty when his criminal accomplices went on trial for the bombings in June 1971, and he resigned after a witness named him in court as the plot's mastermind. (After his resignation, FBI spokesmen claimed that Hale was on the verge of being fired for taking cash and gifts from unnamed private citizens.) The bombers were convicted but escaped with a $260 fine, their trial judge ruling that they had been "taken in, misled, led down the primrose path pointed out" by Hale. According to the judge, the bombing plot was solely Hale's idea, "a frolic of his own that has brought embarrassment to all concerned." No state or federal charges were filed against Hale, who moved on to an executive position in private industry. Observers note that transition as evidence that Hale received a favorable recommendation from FBI headquarters.

See also: BOMBING AND BOMB SQUADS; FEDERAL BUREAU OF INVESTIGATION.

Hale, George W. (1855–?)

Massachusetts native George Hale, born in 1855, was a man of many parts. At various times in his youth, Hale tried his hand at mining, ranching, and crewing Mississippi River steamboats, then embarked on a sporadic military career that saw him serve with the U.S. Army during 1879–82 and again in 1886–87. While details on the rest of his life are vague, sources report that Hale joined the police department of Lawrence, Massachusetts, around 1889. Soon afterward, he began work on his comprehensive *Police and Prison Cyclopedia,* researched via questionnaires Hale sent to police chiefs throughout North America, Europe, and parts of Asia. Published in 1892, Hale's work ranks as the first law enforcement encyclopedia, including meticulous details on police assignments and performance worldwide, plus personnel rosters for every police force in U.S. cities with 10,000 or more inhabitants. Hale intended yearly updates of his *Cyclopedia,* but no second edition ever appeared, and further details of his life were unavailable at press time for this volume.

Hall, Jesse Lee (1849–1911)

Known to his lifelong friends as Lee or "Red," Jesse Hall was a native of Lexington, North Carolina, born October 9, 1849. The son of a Confederate army surgeon, Hall moved to Texas at age 20 and taught school in Grayson County for two years, before he switched careers and became city marshal of Sherman, the county seat, in 1871. Two years later, he moved to Denison, as a deputy sheriff, and embarked on a series of raids against local outlaws and rustlers. That campaign included two major gunfights in 1873–74, during one of which Hall was critically wounded after killing his opponent.

Undeterred by the near-miss, Hall joined the TEXAS RANGERS in 1876 and was soon promoted to lieutenant of the unit's "Special Force." Before he married and left the Rangers to try ranching, in February 1880, Hall compiled an enviable record of arrests—and another shootout at Wolfe City in November 1879 that left two Mexican bandits dead and a third gravely wounded. By the time of his retirement as a captain, Hall and his squad had captured more than 400 fugitives, while suppressing the bloody Taylor-Sutton feud.

Hall endured as a rancher for five years, during which time a convalescent boarder on Hall's spread, young Will Porter, gathered material for the tales he would later publish as "O. Henry." Appointed to serve as an Indian agent in 1885, Hall was fired two years later on charges of embezzlement, but the case was later dropped for lack of evidence. He settled next in San Antonio, serving as deputy marshal until his wife left him, taking their children, in 1894. Four years later, Hall raised two volunteer companies to fight in the Spanish-American War, but an old hernia delayed his arrival in the Philippines until 1899, when he obtained a lieutenant's commission and won a promotion to captain for valor in combat. Malaria drove Hall back into civilian life before war's end, whereupon he went to Mexico, variously prospecting for oil and ore, and serving as a goldmine guard. He died at San Antonio on March 17, 1911.

Hamer, Francis Augustus (1884–1955)

A legendary lawman in the Wild West tradition, Frank Hamer was born on the Texas frontier in March 1884. By age 22, when he joined the TEXAS RANGERS, he could throw a knife with deadly accuracy and was widely regarded as one of the best shots in Texas. It was a skill that served him well throughout his life; he killed at least 53 felons (some reports say 65) over the next quarter century.

Hamer's employment with the Texas Rangers was an on-and-off affair. After two years in the saddle, he resigned in 1908 to become marshal in lawless Navasota, cleaning up that town before he moved on to serve as a Harris County "special officer" in 1911. March 1915 found him back with the Rangers, where three years later he was accused of threatening state legislator José Canales. No charges were filed in that case, and Hamer was promoted to the rank of senior captain in 1921. In 1928 Hamer cracked a "reward ring" that murdered innocent persons, passing them off as bank robbers to collect $5,000 rewards offered by the Texas Bankers' Association. That case forced Texas bankers to insert the words "Or Alive" on posters that had previously marked thieves "Wanted Dead."

Hamer had been officially retired for two years when he took on his most famous case, tracking fugitive bandits Clyde Barrow and Bonnie Parker. It took Hamer 102 days to complete his assignment, trailing Bonnie and Clyde with bulldog tenacity, working in concert with Deputy Sheriff Ted Hinton (a grade-school classmate of Clyde's). On learning that Louisiana native Henry Methvyn had recently joined the Barrow gang, Hamer cut a deal with Methvyn's parents: amnesty for Henry on Texas murder charges, in exchange for betraying his friends. The Methvyns kept their bargain on May 23, 1934, luring Bonnie and Clyde into an ambush near Gibsland, where Hamer and five other lawmen fired at least 167 shots into their car and bodies.

Congress awarded Hamer a special citation for killing Bonnie and Clyde. He spent the rest of the 1930s as a "private agent" for various Texas oil companies, engaged in STRIKEBREAKING, then retired once more. Governor Coke Stevenson recalled him to active duty as a Ranger in 1948, briefly investigating charges of election fraud in two counties where CORRUPTION surpassed the accepted norm, but Hamer retired for the last time in 1949. He died with his boots off at Austin on July 10, 1955.

See also: BANK ROBBERY.

Hamilton, Mary

Details are sadly lacking in the life of this pioneering female officer with the NEW YORK CITY POLICE DEPARTMENT. Memorialized as "one of the first" women hired by NYPD, Mary Hamilton began her law enforcement career in 1917, as a volunteer with the Missing Persons unit. She was subsequently sworn in as a full-fledged officer, primarily handling the cases of vanished women and children. That role gradually expanded into SEX CRIMES, where female victims felt uncomfortable with male detectives. In 1924 Hamilton was named director of the new Women's Police Bureau, serving as NYPD's first female field supervisor from a renovated precinct house on West 37th Street. While it is known that

Hamilton served into the 1930s, specific details of her retirement and demise were unavailable at press time for this work.

Hampton, Fred (1948–1969)

An Illinois native, born in 1948, Fred Hampton led a successful NAACP campaign to integrate Chicago public swimming pools in 1966. A year later, he joined the militant Black Panther Party, instantly falling afoul of the CHICAGO POLICE DEPARTMENT and the FBI's ongoing COINTELPRO campaign against black activists. Hampton's FBI file alone spanned 12 volumes and 4,000 pages, rating his inclusion in the Bureau's Agitator Index as a "key militant leader." William O'Neal, a federal AGENT PROVOCATEUR, served as security chief for the Chicago Panthers and as Hampton's personal bodyguard.

On June 4, 1969, FBI agents raided the Chicago Panther office and arrested eight persons, ostensibly while seeking federal fugitives who were not on the premises. A short time later, G-men approached Chicago police with a plan for additional raids, and a series of violent clashes ensued, leaving two policemen and two Panthers dead in July. After the second police raid, on July 30, "mysterious" fires gutted the Panther office. A third raid, on October 21, left the remodeled office in shambles once more. Throughout the series of attacks, police found nothing to support the FBI's claim that Panthers were hoarding illegal weapons.

On November 9, 1969, the FBI learned that Hampton was scheduled for promotion to serve as the Panther Party's national chief of staff. Four days later, another police raid ended with two more officers and two Panthers dead. On November 21 G-men huddled with Illinois State's Attorney Edward Hanrahan, providing more false information from William O'Neal. After that meeting, the Chicago field office told FBI headquarters: "Officials of the Chicago police have advised that the department is currently planning a positive course of action relative to this information."

On the night of December 3, 1969, some unknown person drugged Fred Hampton with a dose of secobarbitol before he went to bed. Hampton was unconscious at 4:45 the next morning, when state and local police stormed his apartment. Panther Mark Clark was killed by the first police gunshot as officers burst through the door. Dying, he triggered the only shot fired from a Panther weapon that morning, a shotgun blast into the floor. Police sprayed the apartment with an estimated 90 shots, including two close-range pistol rounds fired into Fred Hampton's skull. Five other Panthers were wounded, while various tenants of the flat were charged with attempted murder.

Chicago police claimed that they only fired in self-defense, but FBI agent Wesley Swearingen contradicted those statements, later testifying under oath that a member of the Bureau's Racial Squad told him, "We gave [police] a copy of the detailed floor plan . . . so that they could raid the place and kill the whole lot." Chicago agent-in-charge Marlin Johnson cabled FBI headquarters on December 11, requesting a $300 bonus for William O'Neal and stating that "[t]he raid was based on information furnished by the informant. . . . This information was not available from any other source and subsequently proved to be of tremendous value."

O'Neal earned $30,000 from the FBI for his service in the Panther Party, but the raiders ultimately paid much more. Surviving relatives of Clark and Hampton filed a $47.7 million lawsuit against Hanrahan and others in 1970, claiming conspiracy to violate the dead men's civil rights. A grand jury indicted Hanrahan and 13 police officers for conspiracy in August 1971, but the charges were later dismissed. Finally, in November 1982, the defendants settled with a payment of $1.85 million dollars. One attorney in the case described that settlement as "an admission of the conspiracy that existed between the FBI and Hanrahan's men to murder Fred Hampton."

See also: FEDERAL BUREAU OF INVESTIGATION.

Hanssen, Robert (b. 1945)

Born in 1945, Robert Hanssen was the son of a CHICAGO POLICE DEPARTMENT officer who constantly humiliated him while hounding him to become a doctor. Hanssen spent two years in dental school, then dropped out to earn a master's in business administration from Northwestern University (1973) and became a certified public accountant. He subsequently spent two years with Chicago PD's Internal Affairs Division, then joined the FBI in January 1976, spending two years on white-collar crime investigations in Indiana, where his supervisors "thought Bob Hanssen walked on water."

Still unsatisfied, he sought a transfer to New York and pursuit of ESPIONAGE agents, organizing an abortive sting operation to catch Soviet spies. As a colleague described the effort, "He set up this squad . . . and well over half the FBI guys called in from home. They didn't want to work on Sunday, so the Russians got away." Thereafter, Hanssen apparently despised the Bureau and decided to betray it for profit. In 1979 he accepted $20,000 from Russian military intelligence to reveal various FBI secrets, including the identity of double-agent Dmitri Polyakov (executed in 1988).

Hanssen's career as a spy was nearly ruined in 1980, when his wife caught him writing a letter to his Russian bosses and he confessed his illegal activity. In lieu of surrendering to the FBI, however, Hanssen consulted a Catholic priest who urged him to stop spying, seek counseling, and give the Russian money to charity. Hanssen ignored that advice and continued spying into 1981, when he was transferred to FBI headquarters as a supervisory agent. Two years later, he shifted to the Soviet Analytical Unit in Washington, then back to New York as a supervisor in 1985. Aware that G-men did not monitor mail sent to the home of KGB officers, Hanssen wrote to agent Biktor Charkashin in October 1985 and offered to sell more classified material for $100,000. To prove his worth, Hanssen enclosed the names of three KGB agents secretly serving America. Two were later executed, while the third received a 15-year prison term in Russia.

Over the next 15 years Hanssen emerged as one of Russia's most valuable spies in the United States. He betrayed entire espionage networks, while evading detection by his fellow agents. Returned to headquarters as an intelligence analyst in 1987, he burrowed deeper, using his spare time and computer skills to expose high-level secrets of the FBI, the CIA and the National Security Agency. Moscow was delighted, and his coworkers were none the wiser.

G-men had their first clear chance to catch Hanssen in 1990, when brother-in-law Mark Wauck, a Chicago FBI agent, grew suspicious of Hanssen's wealth. Wauck told his superiors that Hanssen kept unusual amounts of money at home, and that he suspected Hanssen of spying for Russia. The FBI did nothing, and Hanssen continued his illicit operations for another decade. He earned a small fortune from Russia but wisely resisted the urge to indulge in extravagant spending. (One deviation from that pattern was his expensive romance with a stripper, whom Hanssen once flew to Hong Kong for an impromptu tour of the FBI legal attaché's office.)

It was finally a Russian double-agent who betrayed Robert Hanssen in 2000, supplying G-men with material furnished by Hanssen since 1985. FINGERPRINTS lifted from the documents identified Hanssen, and he was placed under surveillance from December 2000 through February 5, 2001. At his arrest on February 18, en route to deliver more stolen documents, Hanssen asked the agents who surrounded him, "What took you so long?"

Hanssen confessed his crimes in custody and bargained with prosecutors to escape CAPITAL PUNISHMENT. On July 6, 2001, he pled guilty to 13 counts of espionage, receiving a life prison term without parole on May 9, 2002. A month before his final sentencing, an FBI report claimed Hanssen had provided "valuable aid" in closing some of the Bureau's security loopholes against future spies.

See also: FEDERAL BUREAU OF INVESTIGATION; INTERNAL AFFAIRS.

"Harlem Six"

On April 17, 1964, several children returning home from school upset the contents of a peddler's fruit stand at 128th Street and Lenox, in New York City's Harlem ghetto. While some of the children began replacing the fruit, others laughed and tossed grapefruits to one another on the sidewalk. The peddler called for help, bringing members of the NEW YORK CITY POLICE DEPARTMENT's Tactical Patrol Force to the scene. Author Truman Nelson describes what happened next, based on interviews with witnesses:

> [The police] came in force and fell on the children with drawn guns and flailing clubs, in an attack so fearful and merciless that the people came swarming out of their tenements in horror and shock.
>
> Some young Negroes, teenagers, felt compelled to come between the attackers and their defenseless victims, and became, in turn, the victims. These boys were handcuffed and beaten in the street and then taken to the precinct house, where, handcuffed, they were beaten again, mercilessly and incessantly by cops who exchanged uniform coats for sweatshirts so as to carry on with more comfort and efficiency. The boys were beaten steadily from four in the afternoon until around midnight, taken to the Harlem Hospital to be patched up, taken back and beaten again (handcuffed as usual), with the sweatshirted police working in shifts.

Two adults, 47-year-old Fecundo Acion and 31-year-old Frank Stafford were also arrested for "interfering" with police and dragged to the station for marathon beatings, which cost Stafford one of his eyes. The prisoners were finally released without charges, to nurse their wounds at home, but the matter was not settled yet.

Twelve days after the "Little Fruit Stand Riot," Frank and Margit Sugar were robbed and stabbed in their secondhand store at 125th and Fifth Avenue, in Harlem. Mrs. Sugar died from her wounds, but Frank survived to describe his attackers as black teenagers. Detectives soon arrested Frank Baker and five fellow members of a local karate club, who had been jailed and beaten for interceding in the April 17 police riot. Held for interrogation without counsel present, two of the youths confessed to attacking the Sugars and implicated their friends. Collectively, the defendants were nicknamed the "Harlem Six."

A judge appointed counsel for the indigent accused, and trial on first-degree murder charges proceeded in March 1965. All six defendants were convicted and received long prison terms. Activist-attorneys Conrad Lynn and William Kunstler appealed those convictions on grounds of incompetent counsel, noting that one court-appointed lawyer died in court from acute alcoholism while the trial was in progress. The verdicts were reversed, but on different grounds—specifically, that confessions from defendants Robert Rice and Daniel Hamm were improperly admitted as evidence against their codefendants. New trials were granted, beginning with Rice (serving life) and Hamm (15 to 35 years) in November 1970.

The Lynn-Kunstler team discovered that two key prosecution witnesses had perjured themselves in the first murder trial. Jurors deadlocked on a verdict in the Rice-Hamm trial, on April 18, 1971, and a mistrial was declared. A third trial brought the same result, with jurors deadlocked 7-to-5 for acquittal. With a fourth trial pending, New York prosecutors offered a bargain: In return for guilty pleas on a reduced manslaughter charge, the defendants were released with no further time spent in jail. Lynn and Kunstler, for their part, remained convinced that the case was a FRAME-UP, citing evidence that police had faked FINGERPRINTS from two of the defendants, allegedly found at the crime scene. Lynn later told the press, "It was a sordid case and could have wrecked the lives of six promising young men. There was ample evidence that the real criminals were the ones who did the prosecuting."

See also: POLICE RIOTS.

Harmon, Judson (1846–1927)

Ohio native Judson Harmon was born in Hamilton County on February 3, 1846, and graduated from Denison University (at Granville) in 1866. He completed studies at the Law School of Cincinnati and won admission to the bar in 1869, then entered private practice. He was elected as a judge of common pleas in 1876, then unseated four months later after a failed campaign for the state senate. Harmon returned to the bench two years later, this time on Cincinnati's superior court (1878–87), then returned to private practice. He assumed office as President Grover Cleveland's second attorney general, on June 11, 1895, and held that post until March 5, 1897. Harmon subsequently served as Ohio's governor (1909–13) and made an abortive run for the White House in 1912. He was a delegate to the 1924 Democratic National Convention and died in Cincinnati on February 22, 1927. Although he was a lifelong resident of Ohio, Oklahoma's Harmon County (created in 1909) was named in his honor.

Harrington, Penny E. (b. 1942)

Penny Harrington's police career exemplifies the struggle of women to attain equality in American law enforcement. A Michigan native, born in 1942, she graduated from Michigan State University in 1964 with a degree in criminal justice. Moving to Oregon, Harrington joined the PORTLAND POLICE DEPARTMENT in 1964, despite some initial resistance to hiring a woman. She was assigned to the Women's Protective Unit.

It was progress of a sort, but after years of static assignment with no promotion in sight, Harrington recognized that she was trapped within an "old boy's club." Women were barred from serving as detectives on the Portland force, and seemingly from any meaningful promotion through the ranks. Unwilling to accept discrimination, Harrington filed a series of complaints and lawsuits against her employers, fighting a long war of attrition that won her appointment as PPD's first female detective (1972), sergeant (1972), lieutenant (1977), and captain (1980).

In 1985 Harrington was named to lead Portland PD, the first female police chief of a major American city. Her triumph was soured, however, by an escalation of the same backbiting and political maneuvering that had raised roadblocks throughout her career. Her efforts to promote more women and minorities produced a "breakdown in morale" among white male subordinates and prompted the creation of a special commission to review Harrington's performance. The panel condemned Harrington's "poor management style" and recommended dismissal, a suggestion rubber-stamped by the same mayor who had appointed Harrington just 18 months earlier.

Harrington resigned on July 1, 1986, and filed her last lawsuit for sexual harassment, naming the mayor and Portland PD as defendants. Her claim was finally dismissed, leaving Harrington to chronicle her case and her career in an autobiography, *Triumph of Spirit* (1999). Far from inactive after leaving the police force, Harrington worked for the California State Bar (1988–94), then founded the National Center for Women & Policing in 1995, directing that group until 2001. She also served as a consultant and expert witness in cases of discrimination and sexual harassment from 1999 to 2005, when she planned a well-deserved retirement.

hate crimes

The federal Hate Crimes Statistics Act of 1990 defines these offenses (also called "bias crimes") as "crimes that manifest evidence of prejudice based on race, religion, sexual orientation or ethnicity, including where appropriate the crimes of murder, non-negligent manslaughter, forcible rape, aggravated assault, simple assault, intimidation, arson, and destruction, damage or vandalism of property." No federal hate crime legislation existed at press time for this book, but 24 states and the District of Columbia have comprehensive hate crimes statutes; 20 more have laws excluding sexual orientation as a factor; and seven states (Arkansas, Hawaii, Indiana, Kansas, New Mexico, South Carolina, and Wyoming) have no legislation in place.

The Hate Crimes Statistics Act carries no enforcement provisions, merely requiring the FBI to collect and tabulate statistics voluntarily submitted by other law enforcement agencies around the United States. How well has the statute worked in tracking hate crimes? A detailed study by the Southern Poverty Law Center in 2003 revealed that while voluntary reports of such crimes increased from 2,215 to 12,122 between 1991 and 1999, the system remains "seriously flawed." Donald Green, a hate crimes expert at Yale University, went further, telling the SPLC that "the overall numbers are worthless." Among the many problems found with published FBI hate crime data, the following stand out:

- Hawaiian authorities refuse to participate on grounds that the federal definition of hate crimes is "very broad and subjective."

- Alabama, long a hotbed of Ku Klux Klan activity, reported "zero" hate crimes statewide for years on end and has submitted no reports at all for "five or six years."

- In Kansas only the Wichita Police Department reports hate crimes, and its clerks lag several years behind schedule. As of September 2001, they had not tabulated hate crimes for the years 1999–2000.

- In 1999, 83 percent of all reporting jurisdictions claimed "zero" hate crimes for the year. SPLC investigators found that officials in seven states arbitrarily reported "zero" hate crimes to the FBI on behalf of agencies that filed no reports for themselves.

- A report from the U.S. Justice Department, released in September 2000, found that nearly 6,000 law enforcement agencies had falsely reported "zero" hate crimes, when one or more offenses within their jurisdictions met the federal definition.

See also: Federal Bureau of Investigation.

Hawaii Department of Public Safety

Contrary to popular fiction, engendered by the television program *Hawaii Five-O*, Hawaii has no state police force. Instead, the Department of Public Safety stands pledged "to provide for the safety of the public and state facilities through law enforcement and correctional management." Where other states commonly separate law enforcement and correctional operations, Hawaii merges the two. Its Department of Public Safety includes three divisions: Administrative, Correctional (including state prisons and the Hawaii Paroling Authority), and

Law Enforcement (divided into the Sheriff's Division and a Narcotics Enforcement Division). State officers collaborate with the Honolulu Police Department and other agencies responsible for law enforcement on individual Hawaiian islands.

Haymarket bombing

On May 1, 1886, labor unions in Chicago organized a strike for eight-hour work days. Two days later, a riot erupted outside the McCormick Harvester Plant when officers of the Chicago Police Department attacked striking workers and killed one union activist. On May 4, at a mass rally in Haymarket Square, someone hurled a bomb at advancing police ranks, fatally wounding eight officers and four civilians.

Illinois governor J. P. Altgeld pardoned some of the convicted Haymarket defendants. (Author's collection)

Since several speakers at the rally had been anarchists, the press and prosecutors blamed foreign radicals for the strike and deadly bombing. Police never identified the bomb-thrower, but eight defendants—mostly German immigrants—were charged as conspirators and convicted at trial. Judge Joseph Gary condemned five defendants, while sentencing the other three to 15-year prison terms. One of those condemned, Louis Lingg, killed himself in prison with a smuggled stick of dynamite. After a series of appeals, defendants George Engel, Adolph Fischer, Albert Parsons, and August Spies were hanged. Governor John Altgeld pardoned surviving defendants Samuel Fielden, Oscar Neebe, and Michael Schwab on June 26, 1893. Few historians today believe that any of those convicted were guilty as charged, leaving the case on record as a classic political FRAME-UP.

See also: ANARCHISM; BOMBING AND BOMB SQUADS.

Hays, John Coffee (1817–1883)

A distant relative of President Andrew Jackson's wife, "Jack" Hays was born January 28, 1817, on a plantation near Nashville, Tennessee. His father died when Hays was just 15, leaving him with an uncle who wanted Jack to attend West Point. Hays ran away from home instead, traveling westward, reaching San Antonio soon after the Battle of San Jacinto freed Texas from Mexican rule (1836). He quickly joined a company of TEXAS RANGERS, soon distinguishing himself in combat with Indian raiders and Mexican bandits. Promoted to captain in 1840, Hays still impressed one observer as a "small, boyish looking youngster, not a particle of beard on his face, [a] homely palefaced young man."

The Tex-Mex border was a source of constant turmoil during the years of the Texas Republic (1836–45), and Jack Hays found himself in the thick of the action. In 1844 the Texas Congress named him to command a Ranger company of 40 privates and one lieutenant, but his tenure was already drawing to a close. Hays left the Rangers for the U.S. Army two years later, and emerged as a hero of the Mexican War (1846–48). In June 1848 he visited Washington, D.C., to resign his army commission and lobby for construction of a new road linking El Paso to San Antonio. Congress authorized a 72-man expedition, led by Hays, which mapped the 600-mile route between August and December 1848, but their achievement was soon overshadowed by the California gold rush.

Hays himself moved on to California next, elected as sheriff of San Francisco County in 1850. Three years later, President Franklin Pierce named him surveyor-general of the state, a task climaxed when Hays plotted the future city of Oakland. As Northern California grew too tame, Hays drifted to Nevada, where he fought native tribesmen in the brief Paiute War of 1860. Hays subsequently prospered in California real estate, and died there in 1883.

Healey, Charles

Captain Charles Healey of the CHICAGO POLICE DEPARTMENT's Mounted Squadron was recognized worldwide as an expert on traffic congestion. In 1908 Chief George Shippy named him as liaison to the Windy City's downtown merchants, in a bid to solve the growing problem. Soon, Healey embarked on a tour of Europe's capitals, sponsored by the Association of Commerce, to observe how other big-city police departments kept their traffic flowing. His eventual report was the first of its kind to establish clear-cut rules for urban traffic control.

At the same time, Healey ingratiated himself with Chicago's wealthiest entrepreneurs, a link that made him useful to fledgling mayor William "Big Bill" Thompson in April 1915. Boosted by an endorsement from Nelson Lampert, president of the Fort Dearborn Bank, Healey became the first of Thompson's eight police chiefs. On the day of his appointment, Healey told the press, "As the first and most important step in ridding Chicago of its crime I will close every vicious poolroom in the city. Folktalk of driving the criminal from Chicago is not all that is needed. We have to strike first at the crime factories."

It was tough talk without substance. Healey fell in line at once with Thompson's plan to run Chicago as a "wide open" city, ignoring the 1:00 A.M. closing law for saloons while Thompson restored liquor licenses lifted by his predecessor, Carter Harrison, Jr. Healey demoted and transferred a captain who "harassed" Levee vice dens, while replacing the Morals Squad's staff of detectives with lazy political hacks. Thompson's city comptroller frankly admitted that Big Bill's regime was "trying to make friends. We have to have friends if we are going to build a machine."

Alleged reformer Healey, meanwhile, took the lead in graft collections for the police department. State's Attorney MacLay Hoyne gathered evidence enough to indict Healey and two gamblers in October 1916, on charges of funneling bribes through the Sportsman's Club of America (created in 1915 to help elect Thompson). Big Bill immediately transferred Hoyne's detectives, while telling reporters, "The chief has a clean slate as far as I'm concerned." At trial in October 1917, Healey was defended by famed attorney Clarence Darrow, who painted his client as "old, weary, feeble, and broken . . ." Jurors bought the argument, along with Healey's posture as an old man trembling at death's door, and acquitted him of all charges. Still, it marked the end of a law enforcement career that brought shame to Chicago PD, as Thompson replaced Healey with Chief Herman Schluetter.

Heinrich, Edward Oscar (1881–1953)

Wisconsin native Edward Heinrich was born at Clintonville in April 1881, and earned a degree in chemistry from the University of California. Settling in Tacoma, Washington, he pioneered in the field of FORENSIC SCIENCE and became a favorite expert witness at criminal trials. As his fame spread, Heinrich was lured from Washington to fill other posts—as police chief in Alameda, California (1917–18), and as city manager in Boulder, Colorado (1918–19). After World War I, he lectured at UC Berkeley on his recent discoveries in the field of ballistics.

While Heinrich participated in more than 2,000 criminal cases, his best-known achievement was the solution of a 1923 robbery and mass murder in Oregon. On October 11, bandits stopped a Southern Pacific train in a mountain tunnel near Siskiyou Station, fatally shooting four railroad employees in a fruitless effort to steal $40,000 from the train's baggage car. Dozens of suspects were interrogated, but Heinrich broke the case after examining a pair of overalls abandoned near the scene by one bandit.

Heinrich told police that their man was a left-handed lumberjack approximately 25 years old, with brown hair and a fair complexion, 5 feet 8 inches and 165 pounds, and a man of fastidious habits. Detectives were incredulous until Heinrich explained his conclusions: Strands of hair had been recovered from the overalls, along with Douglas fir needles and fresh pitch from pine trees; furthermore, the garment was worn along the right side only, as where a southpaw might lean against trees while swinging his ax left-handed. If this was not enough, a slip of paper found inside one pocket proved to be a receipt for a registered letter. Further investigation identified the sender as Roy DeAutremont, mailing $50 to brother Hugh in New Mexico on September 14. Authorities visited Paul DeAutremont in Eugene, Oregon, and he confirmed that his three sons were all lumberjacks, Roy being the left-handed one.

Capture of the globe-trotting fugitives was delayed until 1927, but no one questioned Dr. Heinrich's key role in solving the crime. Heinrich continued his work in forensic science for decades after his most famous case, and he died on September 28, 1953.

Held, Richard G.

FBI agent Richard G. Held was stationed in Birmingham, Alabama, during May 1961, when leaders of the BIRMINGHAM POLICE DEPARTMENT collaborated with KU KLUX KLAN members to encourage attacks on integrated "freedom riders." His role (if any) in those events remains unknown today, but Bureau files released under the Freedom of Information Act confirm that G-men kept Klan-affiliated policemen informed of the demonstrators' itinerary, thus facilitating Ku Klux riots in three separate communities. Agents observed and filmed the attacks but did not intervene, even when JUSTICE DEPARTMENT advisor John Seigenthaler was beaten unconscious by Klansmen.

Held became agent-in-charge of the Minneapolis field office in October 1962, Eight years later, he replaced Marlin Johnson as agent-in-charge of Chicago, in the midst of a cover-up surrounding FBI involvement in the death of FRED HAMPTON, local leader of the Black Panther Party. When Hampton's mother sued officers of the CHICAGO POLICE DEPARTMENT for killing her son while he slept, Held was called as a witness to explain the Bureau's role in that event. He testified that all relevant FBI documents had been surrendered to the court, whereupon Mrs. Hampton's attorneys produced several memos obtained from other sources, which the Bureau had concealed. A threat of perjury charges prompted Held to reconsider his position, afterward delivering a cache of 100,000 pages previously "misplaced" by his agents. FBI headquarters imposed no disciplinary action for Held's false testimony under oath, and he remained in command of the Chicago field office for six more years.

Much of that time saw him active outside Illinois, after Director CLARENCE MARION KELLEY sent Held to supervise FBI campaigns against the American Indian Movement (AIM) at South Dakota's Pine Ridge Reservation. Held was present as an "observer-consultant" during the 1973 Wounded Knee siege, where he provided FBI support for vigilante Guardians of the Oglala Nation (GOON) squads accused of harassing assaulting and murdering AIM supporters. On April 24, 1974, Held submitted to headquarters a paper titled *The Use of Special Agents of the FBI in a Paramilitary Law Enforcement Operation in the Indian Country.* Held's report complained that G-men at Pine Ridge were ordered "to aim to wound rather than kill," further protesting that members of the U.S. MARSHALS SERVICE and other agencies present did not "submit to FBI authority." In future confrontations, Held declared, "the FBI will insist on taking charge from the outset and will not countenance any interference on an operational basis with respect to our actions."

Fourteen months after submitting that paper, Held was back at Pine Ridge (with son RICHARD WALLACE HELD), commanding the investigation of a shootout that left two G-men dead. At the time, Bureau documents identified Held as both the agent-in-charge of Chicago and chief of the FBI's Internal Security Section, responsible for "counterintelligence" campaigns in the mold of Director J. EDGAR HOOVER's illegal COINTELPRO operations. Investigation of the Pine Ridge killings ultimately led to acquittal of two admitted shooters on a self-defense plea, while AIM activist Leonard Peltier was imprisoned for life. Agent Held left Pine Ridge on October 16, 1975, but Bureau documents show that he was still involved in the case a year later. In June 1976 he penned another position paper, this one titled *Predication of Investigation of Members and Supporters of AIM,* which read in part:

> The government's right to continue full investigation of AIM and certain affiliated organizations may create relevant danger to a few citizen's [sic] privacy and free expression, but this danger must be weighed against current domestic threats.

A few weeks later, with Held's role in the Hampton shooting under state and federal investigation, Director Kelley promoted Held to the post of associate director, in effect making him the second most powerful FBI official. He avoided disciplinary action when his Chicago agents were censured by the 7th Circuit Court of Appeals for obstructing the judicial process and other misconduct in the Hampton case.

See also: FEDERAL BUREAU OF INVESTIGATION; FREEDOM RIDES.

Held, Richard Wallace

The son of FBI Associate Director RICHARD G. HELD, Richard Wallace Held followed in his father's footsteps as a leader of the Bureau's illegal COINTELPRO operations under Director J. EDGAR HOOVER and pursued a similar course of action for two decades beyond Hoover's death, long after the FBI reportedly abandoned such tactics.

Held's first known involvement in Bureau harassment campaigns occurred in the late 1960s, when he served as chief COINTELPRO agent for the Los Angeles field office. There, Held's primary target was the Black Panther Party, "neutralized" by such tactics as the frameup of party leader Elmer Pratt for a murder he did not commit. (Pratt spent 27 years in prison on that charge. During a 1985 habeas corpus hearing, Held repeatedly testified that he "could not recall" various FBI documents related to the case, including some he personally dictated.) In a lighter vein, Held launched a plot to cause actress Jane Fonda "embarrassment and detract from her status with the general public" by leaking derogatory information to Hollywood gossip columnists.

It was a short drive from Los Angeles to San Diego, where Held was reportedly instrumental in helping local G-men create the Secret Army Organization (SAO), a right-wing terrorist group responsible for several bombings and the attempted murder of a liberal college professor. During the trial of three SAO members for those crimes, testimony from an FBI informant in the ranks revealed that G-men had supplied nearly all of the group's money, firearms, and explosives, hiding a rifle used in the murder attempt officers of the SAN DIEGO POLICE DEPARTMENT.

Between 1973 and 1976 Held, with his father, was active against members of the American Indian Movement (AIM) at South Dakota's Pine Ridge Reservation. In that campaign FBI agents armed and financed a vigilante group, Guardians of the Oglala Nation (GOON) which was accused of 300 assaults and 64 homicides on federal property. (Those crimes were never prosecuted, since the FBI claimed "insufficient manpower" to investigate the charges.) Two FBI agents were killed at Pine Ridge in June 1975, and AIM activist Leonard Peltier was convicted of their murders under circumstances strongly reminiscent of the Pratt case in Los Angeles.

In 1978 Held was transferred to Puerto Rico as agent-in-charge of the San Juan field office. His arrival corresponded with an escalation of COINTELPRO-style attacks on various Puerto Rican nationalist groups and individuals, including numerous illegal WIRETAPS later admitted by Held's agents under oath. The home of independence spokesman Juan Mari Bras was firebombed in 1978; six years later, a former secretary for the San Juan field office testified that FBI agents were responsible for that crime. Held's Puerto Rican tenure climaxed on August 30, 1985, with sweeping raids conducted by some 300 agents, jailing scores of activists on "John Doe" warrants for alleged involvement in a 1983 Connecticut BANK ROBBERY. When Governor Rafael Hernández objected to the paramilitary action, Held's office dismissed the complaint as "lamentable."

From San Juan, Held was next transferred to San Francisco, again as agent-in-charge. More controversy ensued in 1988, when Held ordered his agents to stop using Dr. James Cullen for their yearly physicals. Cullen had been diagnosed HIV-positive and subsequently died of AIDS-related illness. His estate sued the Bureau, charging illegal discrimination, and the U.S. Court of Appeals agreed in July 1995, ruling that Held's office had wrongfully terminated contracts with Dr. Cullen "solely because of his handicap." The court further held that "[i]f the FBI had been legitimately concerned about the risk of transmission, it would have inquired as to the character and effectiveness of the infection-control procedures [at Cullen's office], as it was required to do by the Rehabilitation Act. It made no attempt to do so."

An even more troubling case involved the May 1990 bombing that nearly killed Earth First! activists Judi Bari and Daryl Cherney in Oakland, California. Held's G-men and officers of the OAKLAND POLICE DEPARTMENT charged Bari and Cherney with building the bomb themselves, branding them both "members of a violent terrorist group involved in the manufacture and placing of explosive devices." That charge collapsed in court, while Bari and Cherney survived their wounds to sue the FBI and Oakland PD. Held, named as a defendant, retired from the Bureau on August 1, 1993, then repeated his performance in the Pratt case when he "testified throughout his deposition that he did not remember the details of Plaintiffs' case, and that he did not keep abreast of all of the cases in the San Francisco office." Furthermore, Held maintained under oath that he "did not recall any specific conversations" with various agents concerning the high-profile case. A federal judge released Held from the lawsuit in October 1997, curiously ruling that despite his appointment as agent-in-charge. "there is no evidence that . . . Held had any duty to supervise the daytoday [sic] activities in any given investigations." Four lesser agents ultimately lost the case, ordered with their codefendants from Oakland PD to pay Bari and Cherney $4.4 million in damages.

See also: BOMBING AND BOMB SQUADS; FRAME-UPS; INFORMANTS; TERRORISM.

Helm, Jack (d. 1873)

Nothing is known of Jack Helm's life before 1860, when he surfaced in Texas as a cowboy on the huge cattle ranch owned by Shanghai Pierce. After the Civil War, he became embroiled in the bloody Sutton-Taylor feud as a member of William Sutton's trigger-happy "Regulators." The feud dragged on until William Sutton was ambushed and killed in March 1874.

In the midst of that feud, in July 1869, Helm joined the fledgling Texas State Police, appointed as one of the force's four captains. Law enforcement did not suit him, though, and he was suspended in October 1870, charged with misusing his authority to murder a pair of Taylor supporters, while "taxing" local residents 25 cents apiece to pay his hotel bills. Dismissed for good in December 1870, Helm somehow won election as sheriff of DeWitt County where he continued his role as a feudist until 1873. In April of that year, Helm moved to Albuquerque, New Mexico, feverishly working to perfect an invention to combat boll weevils.

The move did not save him. In July 1873 Helm and several friends from the Sutton clan spied enemy Jim Taylor in Albuquerque, idling in a blacksmith's shop with legendary gunman John Wesley Hardin. At Helm's approach, Hardin produced a shotgun and fired at close range, striking Helm in the chest. Helm was probably dead by the time Taylor emptied a six-shooter into his skull.

Helpern, Milton (1902–1977)

New Yorker Milton Helpern earned a medical degree from Cornell University in 1926, at age 24. After five years in private practice, he teamed with premier New York City medical examiner CHARLES NORRIS and spent the next four decades building a reputation as the American dean of FORENSIC SCIENCE. Helpern replaced Dr. Norris as New York's chief medical examiner in 1954 and held that post until his retirement in 1973. During his tenure with the city, Helpern performed some 80,000 autopsies and co-authored (with Thomas Gonzales and Morgan Vance) a classic text on the subject, *Legal Medicine and Toxicology* (1937). His public statements were sometimes controversial, as when he remarked of the Dallas autopsy performed on President John Kennedy in 1963: "Selecting a hospital pathologist to perform a medico-legal autopsy . . . and evaluate gunshot wounds is like sending a seven-year-old boy who has taken three lessons on the violin over to the New York Philharmonic and expect[ing] him to perform a Tchaikovsky symphony. He knows how to hold the violin and the bow, but he has a long way to go before he can make music." Dr. Helpern died in 1977.

Hennessey, David Peter (d. 1890)

Every group of immigrants to the Unites States has been a mixed bag, insofar as ethics and behavior are concerned. Each race and nationality included good and bad alike, some of the latter dedicated criminals before they ever landed in America. The Mafia, a criminal society transplanted from its native soil in Sicily, reached the United States sometime during the 1870s and flourished to a varying degree in cities spread from coast to coast. New Orleans was a hotbed of Mafia activity by the 1880s, when a bloody feud erupted between rival families, the Matrangas and the Provenzanos. Between 1888 and 1890, the gang war claimed at least 40 lives, as the contenders fought for effective control of the Crescent City's waterfront.

Into the fray stepped David Hennessey, chief of the NEW ORLEANS POLICE DEPARTMENT. No details of his early life are presently available, though most accounts describe the chief as "young" in 1890, living with his widowed mother. Some accounts depict him as an avid anti-Mafia crusader, but others note that Hennessey's crackdown on "Italian crime" fell almost entirely upon the Matranga family, while the Provenzanos went unmolested. On October 15, 1890, gunmen ambushed Hennessey as he was walking home from work, blasting him with shotguns a half-block from his house. He survived for several hours, long enough to blame "the Dagoes" for his shooting, then expired and left the town in raging turmoil.

A grand jury investigated Hennessey's murder, reporting that "the existence of a secret organization known as the Mafia has been established beyond doubt." Nineteen suspects from the Matranga family were indicted as principals or conspirators in the slaying, but their trial was a thinly veiled charade. Crime historian Carl Sifakis reports that "[a] large number of the 60 potential witnesses were intimidated, threatened or bribed and several members of the jury were later found to have taken bribes as well." The outcome was acquittal for 16 defendants, while jurors deadlocked on the other three.

The defendants were returned to jail pending final disposition of their case, while local Mafiosi foolishly held public celebrations of their victory. Two days after the mistrial, on March 14, 1891, a mob of several thousand citizens stormed the jail and hanged two of the suspects from nearby lampposts. Seven more were gunned down by a vigilante firing squad, and two others were riddled with bullets while cowering in the jail's kennel. Strangely, the mob's leaders (described as "60 leading citizens") ordered that mob leaders Antonio and Carlo Matranga should be spared from execution.

The mass lynching threatened diplomatic relations between Italy and the United States, until authorities in Washington authorized payment of $25,000 to relatives of the mob's victims in Sicily. The Mafia survived, in New Orleans and elsewhere, emerging as a major component of U.S. ORGANIZED CRIME during PROHIBITION.

See also: LYNCHINGS.

Hickey, Michael

Historian Richard Lindberg described Michael Hickey as a "venal and dangerous" officer whose tenure with the CHICAGO POLICE DEPARTMENT was marred by perpetual scandal. During an 1868 probe of police CORRUPTION, led by alderman John Comiskey, Captain Hickey was cited for running a bail-bond racket out of the Armory Station, but he escaped discipline. He served as "eyes and ears" for longtime Chief JACOB REHM, thus securing a degree of immunity and Rehm's endorsement to run for superintendent in 1869. (Hickey lost.) Unfazed by that setback, Hickey closed ranks with gambler "King

Mike" McDonald in 1870, crushing McDonald's competition with a series of strategic raids.

Three years later, in July 1873, Hickey was suspended for his personal dealings with brothel madam Lizzie Moore. Moore had reported jewelry stolen from her workplace, and when Hickey "found" it in a Pittsburgh pawn shop, he demanded $430 in cash for its safe return. A department trial board cleared Hickey of involvement in the theft, and Mayor Harvey Colvin named him chief in 1875, when Rehm retired to seek election as city collector. More scandal overtook Hickey in 1876, with newspaper accusations that he had taken bribes from thieves and fences, while enjoying shady real estate transactions with pimp Dan Webster. The city council investigated, but Mayor Monroe Heath refused to fire Hickey. "There is no doubt in my mind," Heath told reporters, "but this attack on the chief of police was originated and came from some leading gamblers or bunko men and was aimed at the entire department with the hope of crippling them."

A year later, in the midst of a bitter railroad strike, Hickey unleashed his troops to punish labor unionists. On July 26, 1877, officers attacked a peaceful Association of Joiners meeting at Turner Hall, killing one man with gunfire and wounding 20 more, clubbing the terrified survivors as they fled. The union won its lawsuit against Hickey, but the chief escaped with a reprimand for the brutal assault. Order was finally restored after President Rutherford Hayes pulled the 22nd Infantry from frontier combat duty to patrol Chicago's streets. A year later, with Hickey's contract up for renewal, the city council voted 22 to 11 against his continued employment.

Hickok, James Butler (1837–1876)

Described by one biographer as "the most dangerous gunman who ever lived," James Hickok was born May 27, 1837, in Troy Grove, Illinois, to a family transplanted from Vermont. His long nose and protruding upper lip earned him the childhood nickname "Duck Bill." It would take a thick mustache and much publicity about his prowess with a gun before "Duck Bill" Hickok won the more respectful sobriquet "Wild Bill."

At age 18, still living in Troy Grove, Hickok got into a fistfight with a teamster who insulted him. Both men fell into a canal, where Hickok wrongly supposed his opponent had drowned. Fearing a murder charge, he fled to "Bleeding Kansas" and joined a free-soil militia opposed to slavery in the territory. In March 1858 he was elected constable of Monticello Township, moving on from there to hunt buffalo and drive freight wagons. The latter job took him to Rock Creek, Nebraska, where he found an instant enemy in 40-year-old David McCanles.

For whatever reason, McCanles hated Hickok on sight, teasing him incessantly, then swearing vengeance when Hickok began courting McCanles's mistress. On July 12, 1861, McCanles appeared at the freight office with his son, cousin James Woods, and a friend named James Gordon. McCanles challenged Hickok to "come out and fight fair," but Hickok lingered in the station, shooting McCanles from ambush as he entered. Woods and Gordon rushed the building next, both wounded by Hickok, then finished off by station operator Horace Wellman and a stable hand, Doc Brink. The judge at their murder trial barred testimony from young Monroe McCanles, and all three defendants were acquitted.

Over time, the Rock Creek slaughter morphed into legend, florid tales depicting Hickok's one-man stand against the nine-member "McCanles gang." One version even claimed that he was shot 11 times, yet still had strength enough to kill his enemies. Further gunplay was delayed by the Civil War, wherein Hickok joined the Union army as a wagon master, later serving as a part-time guide and spy. Tales of his wartime exploits, including frontline action in the 1862 battle at Pea Ridge, Arkansas (where Hickok claimed to have killed 50 Confederate soldiers with 50 shots), remain unsubstantiated today.

His next confirmed killing occurred on July 21, 1865, in Springfield, Missouri. The loser in that showdown was Dave Tutt, a Union veteran and wartime acquaintance of Hickok's, with whom Wild Bill quarreled over women and cards. That episode rebounded against him on Election Day, when Hickok lost his bid to become Springfield's police chief. He moved on from there to try ranching, served as a scout for the Seventh Cavalry in 1867, and lost his second election that same year, running for sheriff in Ellsworth County, Kansas. Undiscouraged, he became a deputy U.S. marshal, pursuing army deserters and rustlers of government livestock through most of 1868. Along the way, Hickok spun fantastic tales to journalist Henry Stanley (of later Stanley and Livingston fame), claiming to have killed 100 men in standup fights. Stanley believed it all and spread the legend nationwide.

Elected sheriff of Ellis County, Kansas in August 1869, Hickok killed a drunken soldier within days of taking office, then shot and killed a teamster in a saloon "riot" on September 27. Local voters were tired of Wild Bill by November 1869, some claiming that he took more than his share of graft, and they replaced him with one of his deputies. Resentful and frequently drunk, Hickok remained in Hays City long enough to shoot two more soldiers, one of them fatally,

Frontier lawman and gunfighter "Wild Bill" Hickok (Author's collection)

on July 17, 1870. Fleeing to Abilene, he became the city's marshal in April 1871, supplementing his $150 monthly salary with one-fourth of all fines collected. He spent most of that income on whiskey and poker, while cowboys ran wild in his town, but Hickok did bestir himself to quell one rash of drunken revelry on October 5, 1871. Confronting a violent, armed drunk named Phil Coe, Hickok gunned him down, wounding two bystanders in the process. Rapid footsteps at his back made him turn and fire again—killing his deputy, Mike Williams.

No charges were filed against Hickok, but he was forced out of office by year's end. He drifted aimlessly during 1872–76, appearing with "Buffalo Bill" Cody's Wild West troupe, and logging an arrest for vagrancy in Cheyenne, Wyoming, his eyesight failing from advanced gonorrhea. Married to an old acquaintance, circus owner Agnes Lake, in March 1876, Hickok soon left her for the gold fields and poker tables of Deadwood, South Dakota. He was murdered there, while playing cards in a saloon, on August 2, 1876. Reports differ as to whether his killer, Jack McCall, was angry over losing $110 to Hickok at poker, or whether he was paid to do the deed by Hickok's enemies in town.

See also: U.S. MARSHALS SERVICE.

Hoar, Ebenezer Rockwood (1816–1895)

Massachusetts native Ebenezer Hoar was born at Concord on February 21, 1816. He earned his B.A. from Harvard in 1835 and received his LL.B. from the same university in 1839. Admitted to the state bar in 1840, Hoar subsequently served as a judge on the court of common pleas (1849–55) and as associate justice on the state supreme court (1859–69). President Ulysses Grant chose Hoar as his second attorney general, holding office from March 11, 1869 to July 8, 1870. Grant nominated Hoar as an associate justice of the U.S. SUPREME COURT in 1869, but the Senate withheld confirmation. Hoar subsequently served as a member of the Joint High Commission, which framed the Treaty of Washington with Great Britain in 1871 (establishing a tribunal to adjudicate Civil War claims surrounding the Confederate warship *Alabama*) and in the U.S. House of Representatives (1873–75). Following completion of his term in Congress, Hoar returned to pri-

Attorney General Ebenezer Hoar (Author's collection)

vate practice in Boston and Concord, where he died on January 31, 1895.

Hogan's Alley

A mock town located at the FBI Academy in Quantico, Virginia, "Hogan's Alley" is used to train agents in simulated street situations. Its facilities include facsimiles of a bank, pharmacy, pool hall, movie theater, post office, restaurant and bar, pawn shop (with concealed gambling casino), and warehouse, plus residential structures including a motel, trailer park, rooming house, and apartments. Some of the buildings are real, containing offices and classrooms, while others are simply false fronts in the manner of a Hollywood movie set. Agents use the facility to practice arrest and pursuit techniques, with other G-men or professional actors cast in the roles of criminals, victims, and bystanders. Most of the facilities in Hogan's Alley are acquired via property seizures conducted by the FBI or the DRUG ENFORCEMENT ADMINISTRATION.

Homeland Security Department

President George W. Bush created the U.S. Department of Homeland Security in June 2002, under Secretary TOM RIDGE, as a response to the terrorist attacks of September 11, 2001. The department's primary task is to coordinate defense of the continental United States and its territories, eliminating bureaucratic rivalries, and minimizing redundant efforts by various agencies. As described on its Internet Web site, the department "leverages resources within federal, state, and local governments, coordinating the transition of multiple agencies and programs into a single, integrated agency focused on protecting the American people and their homeland." Given the involvement of some 87,000 governmental jurisdictions nationwide, the effort sometimes has been awkward and less than efficient.

Major subdivision of Homeland Security include the Office of the Chief Privacy Officer, Office of Civil Rights and Civil Liberties, Office of Counter Narcotics, Office of General Counsel, Office of the Inspector General, Office of Legislative Affairs, Office of National Capital Region Coordination, Office of the Private Sector, Office of Public Affairs, and Office of State and Local Government Coordination and Preparedness. Formerly independent agencies absorbed by Homeland Security include the Federal Emergency Management Agency (FEMA), the U.S. COAST GUARD, the SECRET SERVICE, and U.S. CITIZENSHIP AND IMMIGRATION SERVICES.

Homeland Security's division of Border and Transportation Security includes Customs and Border Protection (absorbing the U.S. BORDER PATROL), Immigration and Customs Enforcement, plus the Transportation and Security Administration. Emergency Preparedness and Response absorbed FEMA to coordinate response in case of terrorist attacks or natural disasters. The Information Analysis and Infrastructure Protection division strives to prevent or mitigate attacks on America's computer infrastructure while disseminating critical information to law enforcement at all levels. The department's Directorate of Science and Technology serves as Homeland Security's primary research and development arm, including the Homeland Security Laboratories, Office of National Laboratories, and Homeland Security Advanced Research Projects Agency. Finally, an Office of Management handles Homeland Security's budget, facilities, property, and equipment.

See also: CUSTOMS SERVICE; TERRORISM.

Honolulu Police Department

Hawaii's largest law enforcement agency, covering the entire island of Oahu, traces its lineage to April 1846, with passage of an Act to Organize the Executive Departments of the Government. That statute empowered a Marshal of the Kingdom to appoint and supervise sheriffs on each of the major islands (Hawaii, Kauai, Maui, and Oahu). By January 1847 Oahu had a police force consisting of two officers and 34 patrolmen. Home rule was overthrown by white intruders in January 1893, followed by annexation as a U.S. territory in August 1898, under a constitution known as the Organic Act. Four county governments were established, each with its own sheriff, in 1905.

Rising crime rates in the 1920s prompted Governor Lawrence Judd to appoint an advisory committee on crime, which recommended creation of a police commission in Honolulu. The Honolulu Police Department was active by 1931, although official authorization was delayed until January 1932. A local businessman, Charles Weber, served briefly as the first chief of police, then resigned in August 1932 to make way for William Gabrielson, lured away from California's highly esteemed BERKELEY POLICE DEPARTMENT. Manpower shortages during World War II prompted creation of the Honolulu Police Reserves to fill gaps in the thin blue line, while Governor Joseph Poindexter ceded Hawaii's government to military rule for the duration. Martial law, coupled with wartime blackouts and curfews, slashed island crime rates throughout the remainder of the war.

An ugly specter of CORRUPTION surfaced in the postwar years, involving payoffs from organized gamblers. Honolulu's police commission sought help from the territorial attorney general and public prosecutor to investigate the charges, afterward suspending a cap-

tain of the Vice Division and various officers. One was convicted at trial and received a 10-year sentence, while several others were acquitted. Chief Gabrielson resigned for "personal reasons," while the commission denied any link between his departure and the bribery scandal. Chief William Hoopai held office for only two years, during 1946–48, but in that time he established the HPD's Plans and Training Bureau, along with a gang-busting Metro Squad.

Hawaii became the 50th American state in August 1959, its tourist economy ballooning with advances in air travel through the 1960s and beyond. That traffic naturally led to an increase in crime, both native and imported, which the HPD was forced to recognize. Strict vice enforcement was initially hampered by U.S. SUPREME COURT rulings on the legal rights of criminal suspects, but HPD adapted with intensive training courses designed to keep its officers on the right side of evolving law. Despite professed sensitivity to social issues and ethnic "minorities," however, HPD did not recruit its first female officers (Mary Beck and Barbara Uphouse) until 1975.

Police Chief Lee Donohue (1998–2004) confronted numerous problems at the dawn of a new millennium, including an exodus of officers to better-paying mainland jobs, which left HPD with 400 vacancies. Even as he sought new recruits, however, scandals hampered the effort. Five officers were convicted of beating a county jail inmate, two others confessed to banking thousands of dollars from illicit moonlighting assignments, and civilian employees in the HPD's vehicle maintenance section were caught accepting kickbacks from a vendor who sold auto parts at highly inflated prices. The nadir of Donohue's administration came when an assistant chief and major pled no contest on theft charges, accused of stealing money earmarked for prisoner meals. In 2003 the department paid $650,000 to Detective Ken Kamakana, resulting from a whistleblower lawsuit that alleged serious misconduct in the department's criminal intelligence unit. Chief Donohue, who suffered a heart attack while demonstrating martial arts to his recruits in 1999, told reporters, "This job is not for the faint of heart."

Hoover, J. Edgar (1895–1972)

The FBI's most famous and longest-serving director, John Edgar Hoover, was born in Washington, D.C., on January 1, 1895. High school classmates dubbed him "speed," for his rapid stride, while his 1913 yearbook called Hoover a "gentleman of dauntless courage and stainless honor." That October he found work at the Library of Congress, four blocks from his home, while skipping college to take night classes at George Wash-

J. Edgar Hoover (Bettmann/Corbis)

ington University Law School. Hoover earned his LL.B in 1916 and his LL.M. in 1917, then passed the bar exam in Washington but never practiced law.

On July 16, 1917, two months after the United States entered World War I, Hoover left his library job for a draft-exempt post as a clerk at the JUSTICE DEPARTMENT, assigned to the Alien Enemy Bureau. He was promoted to "attorney" on June 18, 1918, (still handling no cases), and again on July 1, 1919, to serve as special assistant to Attorney General A. MITCHELL PALMER. That move placed Hoover in charge of the General Intelligence Division, where he organized and supervised Palmer's "Red raids" of 1919–20. The lawless conduct of those sweeps doomed Palmer, but Hoover set a pattern for the future by somehow avoiding blame (and later rewrote history to claim that he "deplored" the raids).

On August 21, 1921, Hoover was promoted again, this time to serve as the Bureau of Investigation's first assistant director under WILLIAM J. BURNS. Questions concerning his evasion of wartime military service were quashed in 1922, when Hoover was commissioned as a reserve officer in the U.S. Army's Military Intelligence Division. (By the time he "retired" in 1942, without ever serving a day in uniform, Hoover held the rank of lieutenant colonel.) Scandals surrounding President Warren Harding's "Ohio Gang" ultimately doomed Burns and Attorney General HARRY DAUGHERTY, but Hoover once again emerged unscathed from the wreckage at Justice, despite his willing participation in various illegal activities. Attorney General HARLAN FISKE STONE named Hoover acting director of the Bureau on May 10, 1924, and confirmed him as full-time director on December 10, a post Hoover held until his death on May 2, 1972.

As the "new broom" at Justice, Hoover fired scores of incompetent agents and corrupt "dollar-a-year men," created the nation's first central fingerprint repository (July 1924), set rigorous standards for FBI investigations and issued the FBI's first *Manual of Investigation* (September 1927), established the first formal training courses for federal agents (January 1928), provided agents with their first handbook of regulations (April 1928), and established the FBI crime lab in Washington, D.C. (November

1932). When federal authority was broadened to include prosecution of BANK ROBBERY, interstate KIDNAPPING and other crimes in 1932–34, Hoover pursued flamboyant "PUBLIC ENEMIES" from coast to coast—and in the process made his name a household word. Friendly journalists supported that publicity campaign, beginning with the first national radio program based on FBI files (*The Lucky Strike Hour*) premiering in October 1932. Despite serious (and sometimes fatal) gaffes, Hoover's G-men emerged from the Great Depression wearing haloes in the eyes of most white, middle-class Americans.

It was, however, a very different story for political dissenters and racial minorities, incessantly subjected to DOMESTIC SURVEILLANCE and harassment by agents who deemed them "subversive." Hoover never deviated from his adolescent conviction that a vast network of "Reds" and anarchists conspired to wreck the U.S. status quo. His RACISM was thinly veiled in public and blatantly displayed to close acquaintances. Hoover once complained that SUPREME COURT rulings on civil rights had "gone into the field where police officers must address [suspects] in courteous language, particularly in the case of Negroes, and instead of saying, 'Boy, come here,' they want to be addressed as 'Mr.'" He viewed all minorities with suspicion and spent the last decade of his life working to "prevent the rise of a 'messiah'" in the black community. His near-pathological racism was revealed in 1949, when President Harry Truman asked the FBI to investigate the attempted murder of (white) labor leader Victor Reuther. Attorney General THOMAS CAMPBELL CLARK returned from Hoover's office to tell Truman: "Edgar says no. He says he's not going to get involved every time some nigger woman gets raped."

That case also highlights another irony of Hoover's reign as FBI director. While demanding absolute obedience from his employees—driving Congress to exempt FBI agents and clerical staff from provisions of the Civil Service system in the name of "national security"— Hoover himself often deceived or defied his superiors. Attorney General Stone appointed Hoover in 1924 on the condition that FBI agents should abandon all political investigations and limit their scrutiny to federal lawbreakers. Hoover agreed, then continued Red-hunting without interruption, as he had under Stone's predecessors. Two decades later, when Attorney General FRANCIS BEVERLEY BIDDLE ordered Hoover to discard his illegal CUSTODIAL DETENTION INDEX, Hoover "obeyed" by renaming it the Security Index, commanding his subordinates to keep the program secret even from the White House.

Like most fallible humans, J. Edgar Hoover was a living study in contradictions: an insubordinate employee who ruled his staff with an iron hand, employing harsh (often capricious) punishment for minor (or imagined)

infractions; a champion of "law and order" who sanctioned thousands of criminal acts, including "BLACK BAG JOBS," illegal WIRETAPS, FRAME-UPS, and ENTRAPMENT by hired AGENTS PROVOCATEURS; a "gangbuster" who hunted rural bandits while dismissing reports of ORGANIZED CRIME as "baloney"; a homophobe who bugged FBI restrooms to catch "queers" in action, yet may have been a closet gay himself (based on reports from field agents, biographers, and longtime private friends). For nearly half a century, his bulldog visage was the figurehead of U.S. law enforcement, yet he stubbornly denied—as his successors do today—that the FBI he built was a national police force.

Thus, it was all the more disturbing for Hoover's admirers when evidence revealed after his death proved that he was corrupt throughout his tenure at the FBI. As director, Hoover illegally employed Bureau agents and technicians to remodel and maintain his home free-of-charge, while ghostwriters in the Crime Records Division prepared books and articles for publication in Hoover's name. His income from book and film royalties alone exceeded $250,000, "donated" to the FBI Recreational Association and other charities that Hoover and his top aides used as private slush funds. With constant companion CLYDE ANDERSON TOLSON, Hoover accepted free vacations and gambling junkets each year (officially labeled "inspection tours"), with wealthy "patriots" paying the tab. Those same friends guaranteed no-loss investments in oil and natural gas, while notorious mobsters funneled cash into the "nonprofit" J. Edgar Hoover Foundation. The *Los Angeles Times* described Hoover's legacy in an editorial dated January 13, 1978:

> It was, as corruption goes, pretty piddling stuff, almost embarrassingly so. The point is that the most powerful law-enforcement official in the world, who would severely discipline or fire underlings for the least infraction of the FBI's rules of personal conduct, could not himself resist the temptation to embezzle from the public purse with routine and unblushing regularity. And because Hoover was corrupt, some of those around him in the upper echelons of the Bureau felt that they too had the right to be corrupt.

Hoover's mental fitness for duty was another question altogether. A hypochondriac who secretly consulted dozens of physicians in Washington and New York City for imaginary ailments, Hoover nurtured an obsessive fear of disease, outfitting his home and office with special "bug lights" designed to "electrocute" germs, and he displayed an "almost demented" reaction to flies in his office. Assistant Director WILLIAM CORNELIUS SULLIVAN was assigned to scour the media for articles on treatments alleged to prolong human life, "no matter how farfetched the claims," while Hoover displayed peculiar fear of letting anyone step on his shadow. By the mid-1960s a private nurse was employed to give Hoover "massive injections of some substance to keep him going." As described by biographer Curt Gentry, Hoover received his shots at 9:00 A.M. each day, thereafter displaying "almost maniacal energy until he crashed after lunch, often napping until it was time to go home." In 1970 *Time* magazine reporter Dean Fischer found that Hoover was mentally confused, noting that he "had difficulty in responding to a question . . . without losing himself in a forest of recollections" from the 1930s.

Hoover's death in May 1972 was officially blamed on "hypertensive cardiovascular disease," but rumors persist that he may have been murdered. (One plot, outlined by ex-FBI agent G. GORDON LIDDY, allegedly included plans by Watergate conspirators to invade Hoover's home and place some toxic substance on his toothbrush.) Be that as it may, Hoover's corpse was protected in death by a massive lead-lined coffin guaranteed to frustrate vandals and the ravages of nature. Two of the young servicemen who carried Hoover's casket to the Capitol rotunda, where he lay in state, suffered hernias on their short journey, while a third collapsed unconscious on the steps outside.

See also: ANARCHISM; FEDERAL BUREAU OF INVESTIGATION; FINGERPRINTS.

Horn, Tom (1860–1903)

Born near Memphis, Missouri, on November 21, 1860, and raised on a rural farm, Tom Horn had no patience with school or the parental discipline that sought to curb his habitual truancy. He fled home at age 15 and reached Arizona sometime in early 1875. Employment followed as a railroad laborer, teamster, and stagecoach driver, before Horn joined the army as a civilian scout in 1876. Nine years later, he succeeded famous chief of scouts Al Sieber and played a major role in the capture of Apache war chief Geronimo.

A crack shot with few scruples where cash was concerned, Horn surfaced in 1887 as a hired gunman in Arizona's Pleasant Valley War, then switched sides to serve as a deputy sheriff in Yavapai County. Horn kept the badge but sought a change of scene in 1888, as a deputy in newly constituted Gila County, but rodeo contests frequently drew him away from his duties. Horn also worked a gold claim outside Tombstone, then sold it in 1890 and joined the PINKERTON Detective Agency.

Reports of his activities over the next five years conflict. Horn claimed that he remained with Pinkerton, working under famed agent JAMES P. MCPARLAND, until 1894, but other sources claim he joined the Wyoming Cattle Growers' Association in 1892 as a "range detective"—also known as a "thief killer." It is unclear whether Horn participated in Wyoming's Power River War of 1891–92. Horn drifted to Colorado in 1894, still tracking rustlers with a bounty on their heads, then returned to Wyoming as a heavily armed "horse-breaker" for the Swan Land and Cattle Company. Rustlers remained a primary target for Horn, executed at an average price of $600 per man, but Horn's employers also added pesky homesteaders and shepherds to the hit list. Horn's technique involved a long-range shooting, after which he cleaned up any evidence around the scene and left his victim with two stones beneath his head. As Horn explained, "That is the way I hang out my sign to collect my money for a job of this kind."

Horn's murderous career was interrupted in 1898–99 by the Spanish-American War. He rejoined the U.S. Army, running pack trains in Cuba, then returned at war's end to his favorite trade in Wyoming. The year 1901 found Horn working for John Coble, on a spread north of Laramie. Coble and his neighbors, the Millers, were feuding with a sheep man in the area, Kels Nickell. On July 18, 1901, a sniper killed Nickell's 14-year-old son and left him on the prairie with two stones beneath his head. The Millers were immediate suspects, but the stony pillow seemed to finger Horn.

Manhunter Joe Lefors tracked Horn to Denver in January 1902 and got him raving drunk, extracting a boozy confession of sorts. According to Lefors, Horn boasted of the Nickell murder—calling it "the best shot that I ever made and the dirtiest trick I ever done." Horn also allegedly laid out his rates, remarking that he had recently earned $1,200 "for three dead men, and one man shot at five times. Killing men is my specialty. I look at it as a business proposition, and I think I have a corner on the market."

Arrested for murder with no physical evidence against him, Horn repudiated his confession at trial, blaming Lefors for ENTRAPMENT and perjury. Two jurors held out for acquittal through five ballots, then switched on the sixth to convict. Horn briefly escaped from jail on August 9, 1903, but he was swiftly recaptured. He was hanged at Cheyenne on November 20, 1903, reportedly swinging on a rope he plaited himself. Controversy still surrounds Horn's case, with some ardent supporters describing his trial as a FRAME-UP.

Houston Police Department

The city of Houston, Texas, was incorporated in June 1837, with G. W. Holland elected as the first constable before year's end. Few actual patrols were performed prior to the Civil War, and no standard rules for officer hiring or conduct were written until 1865.

Police duty in Houston was relatively safe until April 1, 1910, when the force lost its first officer—Chief William Murphy—shot by former patrolman Earl McFarland. (In the absence of witnesses, McFarland was acquitted on a plea of self-defense.) Houston PD purchased its first patrol car the same year, and created a new traffic squad to cope with motor vehicles that suddenly outnumbered horses on the city's streets. Five years later, patrolmen received their first pay raise since 1873, boosting salaries to $65 per month. The city's first female officer, Eva Bacher, joined the force in 1918, promoted three years later to serve as detective on the Police Morale and Safety Squad. Applicant examinations were expanded in 1920 to include the city's first written tests for prospective peace officers.

The 1920s and early '30s were a hectic time for law enforcement in Houston, as everywhere else across the United States PROHIBITION brought a new crime wave and fresh opportunities for CORRUPTION, while Houston installed its first traffic signals (1921), created a Mounted Traffic Squad (1927), and purchased the first patrol-car radio (tuned to KPRC, a local radio station, for emergency bulletins). Two years later, Chief McPhail abolished the job of policewoman on grounds that "a woman on the police force is unnecessary." In their place, McPhail appointed "matrons," a position deemed "more appropriate since it had no arrest powers." In 1930, after two officers died in a shootout with robbers at the Touchy Furniture Store, Houston PD replaced its .38-caliber revolvers with more powerful .44-caliber Smith & Wessons. Thompson submachine guns were added for use against "desperate criminals," while the mayor swore in 425 reserve officers to assist with street patrols.

Houston PD received a federal license for two-way radio broadcasts in 1936, and three years later established a police academy, graduating 50 cadets on August 16. By 1940 the department boasted 466 officers and a budget approaching $1 million. A roving "booster squad" was established in 1951, to strike at high-crime areas in Houston, but the effort sparked complaints of RACISM and EXCESSIVE FORCE from black and Hispanic suspects. A K-9 UNIT was established in March 1960, and the same year saw Houston's Central Intelligence Division created to keep track of "hoodlums." Controversy surrounding local use of DEADLY FORCE resulted from riots at Texas Southern University in May 1967, which left one officer dead and 488 students incarcerated.

Progress continued in the 1970s and '80s, with establishment of a Helicopter Patrol Division (1970), Houston's first SWAT TEAM (1975), a new Internal Affairs Division (1977), and an Automated fingerprint Identification System (1979). In 1989 a new city ordinance required 60 hours of college classwork for entry into the police academy. Houston's first female police chief, Elizabeth Watson, was appointed by Mayor Kathy Whitmire in January 1990.

Predictably, some problems still persist in Houston. In 1994 and 1997 auditors from the controller's office were denied access to the police evidence room during yearly inventories, an obstruction that allowed some 280 boxes of evidence from 8,000 criminal cases to be temporarily "lost." Captain Mark Aguirre, censured for allegedly swearing at subordinates, alleged in June 2002 that Chief C. O. Bradford had committed perjury in testimony at a May grievance hearing. Specifically, Bradford denied ever using profanity toward his subordinates, while other HPD employees disagreed. Sporadic claims of brutality and racial PROFILING also persist.

See also: FINGERPRINTS.

Hudson, Jack Ray, Jr. (b. 1958)

A native of Waxhaw, North Carolina, born in 1958, Jack Hudson, Jr. was an Eagle Scout and science buff whose high school years included stints with the band, football team, and Future Business Leaders of America. He joined the U.S. Marine Corps in 1976, rising to a sergeant's rank by 1991, when he arrived at the marine air station in Yuma, Arizona. A drunk-driving arrest in June 1992 stymied further advancement in the Corps, and Hudson retired in early 1993. He joined the Yuma County Sheriff's Department that August, and won recognition in October 1994 as Rookie of the Year.

Soon after receiving that honor, Hudson was assigned to the Southwest Border Alliance (SBA), a narcotics task force combining local officers with agents of the CUSTOMS SERVICE, BORDER PATROL, and the DRUG ENFORCEMENT ADMINISTRATION (DEA). Hudson managed the squad's inventory, logging in confiscated cash, drugs and guns. His job also included UNDERCOVER WORK with motorcycle gangs, and Hudson underwent a sharp personality change, transformed from a crew-cut, spit-and-polish cop to something very different. He lost weight rapidly, but reassured colleagues that he was simply "working out" to stay in shape. Still, his first six-month performance review showed Hudson doing an "excellent job," and supervision relaxed almost to the point of nonexistence.

By June 1995 something was obviously wrong at SBA headquarters. Money, guns, and drugs vanished from Hudson's evidence vault, prompting his superiors to install a secret surveillance camera. The lens caught Hudson stealing from the lockup on July 4, and a silent alarm brought officers racing to the scene. First to arrive were Yuma Police Department Lt. Dan Elkins, the SBA's commander, Mike Crow from the Arizona Department of Public Safety, and task force surveillance technician Jim Erhardt. Confronted by his superiors, Hudson claimed he was performing routine inventory, then ducked back into the lockup and grabbed a submachine gun.

In a matter of moments, Hudson fatally wounded Crowe and Elkins, then turned the gun on Erhardt, but it jammed. Erhardt, unarmed, fled to a nearby office in search of a weapon. Before he could find one, reinforcements arrived and captured Hudson without further resistance. A search of his car revealed three more guns, a smoke grenade, and $51,834 in cash. A subsequent raid on his home found 43 weapons and various drugs including cocaine, marijuana, and methamphetamines. Tests performed on Hudson in custody revealed both amphetamines and methamphetamines in his blood.

Hudson was held in lieu of $15.5 million bail, charged with first-degree murder, aggravated assault, burglary, and theft. At trial in November 1996, Hudson claimed that he was "forced" to take drugs as part of his undercover mission, and that the chemicals rendered him legally insane. Prosecutors countered with evidence that Hudson was deeply in debt, owing $5,000 in back taxes, while writing 25 bad checks between November 1994 and January 1995. He started stealing from the SBA in February 1995, to make ends meet, sampling various drugs in the process. Jurors convicted Hudson on January 13, 1997, but subsequently voted to spare him from execution, resulting in a term of life imprisonment.

Hughes, Michael

Michael Hughes joined the CHICAGO POLICE DEPARTMENT in 1897 and was twice wounded in shootouts with felons before he won promotion to lieutenant. His performance was recognized in 1920, when Chief CHARLES C. FITZMORRIS promoted Hughes to lead the scandal-ridden detective bureau, simultaneously stripping 75 desk-bound "investigators" from the bloated unit's personnel roster. Fitzmorris gave Hughes a free hand in running the detective bureau, but Hughes must have known that appearance and reality were often at odds in the Windy City.

In 1923 Hughes was invited to a banquet in Chicago, ostensibly convened for Jerry O'Connor, secretary of the Theater Janitors' union. On arrival at the restaurant, however, Hughes discovered that the fete was actually a testimonial for murderous bootlegger Dion O'Bannion, chief rival of "Scarface" Al Capone. A year later, following O'Bannion's murder, rumors circulated that Hughes had helped plan the dinner and that he contributed toward purchase of a diamond-studded watch for O'Bannion. Chief MORGAN COLLINS privately

insisted that Hughes had been "framed" by mobsters who despised him, yet Collins raised no protest when Mayor William Dever fired Hughes from the force.

From the police department, Hughes moved on to head Cook County's highway patrol under Sheriff Charles Graydon, a mob puppet who made no secret of his alliance with organized gamblers. There Hughes remained until 1927, when Mayor "Big Bill" Thompson brought him back from exile to serve as chief of police. His mandate was to curb street crime, crack down on gambling, and solve the rash of recent bombings, whose targets included the home of ex-Chief Fitzmorris. Hughes began by stripping his men of their pet machine guns ("too hard to turn off," he decreed) and creating a Bomb Squad to track mob demolitionists. "You can be sure," he said, "these bombers won't be handled with kid gloves"—but none were caught. As for the much anticipated gambling raids, injunctions issued by corrupt judges kept Hughes from making good on that promise.

Some critics claimed that there was more behind the chief's inaction than simple bad luck. Hughes seemed especially zealous in protecting gambler Larry Mangano, a fact that gained increased significance when journalists revealed that Hughes and Mangano retained the same attorneys. Mayor Thompson, seeking scapegoats while his third and last administration wallowed in CORRUPTION, praised Hughes as "the greatest thief-catcher Chicago had ever seen," then demanded his resignation. Hughes told reporters, "I was forced out and I am as much a friend of Mayor Thompson today as I was the day he appointed me." He had barely left headquarters when media reports began describing Hughes as a "friend and protector of the syndicate."

See also: BOMBING AND BOMB SQUADS.

Hume, James B. (1827–1904)

New York native James Hume was born in 1827 and made his way westward in stages, settling first in Indiana, then moving on to California for the gold rush of 1849–50. Weary of prospecting by 1860, he settled in Placerville and sought a new career in government, serving first as tax collector, then town marshal, and later as undersheriff of El Dorado County. Hume lost his first race for the sheriff's office in 1865, then won election in 1868, but local voters deserted him after one term.

Unemployed for the first time in 20 years, Hume went to work as a detective for the WELLS FARGO express company (though not the first, as sometimes claimed). He took a leave of absence in 1871, serving briefly as a reform warden at Nevada's state prison, then returned to Wells Fargo in the midst of a veritable crime wave.

Between 1870 and 1884, Wells Fargo reported 347 attempted robberies of its gold coaches. During the same period, 240 thieves were arrested by company agents, most of them run to ground by Hume and occasional partner John Thacker. One who nearly escaped was outlaw poet Charles "Black Bart" Bolton, whose fatal slip involved a handkerchief dropped at the scene of one holdup. Hume traced the laundry mark—"F.X.O.7."—through 91 laundries before he finally traced Bolton to a San Francisco hideout and ended his one-man crime spree. Hume retired from Wells Fargo with an unrivaled record of arrests and died peacefully in 1904.

Hunt, Nicholas

Irish immigrant Nicholas Hunt arrived in New York City alone and penniless, at age 14. He made his way cross-country to Chicago, working as a laborer in Hyde Park before he joined the CHICAGO POLICE DEPARTMENT in 1871. By 1890 he was an inspector in the stockyard district, where he ruled the roost by catering to wealthy meat packers and gamblers for more than two decades. His unswerving allegiance to big money, the Republican party and gambling boss Jim O'Leary helped Hunt compile a personal fortune of $250,000, including a block of rental flats on Indiana Avenue.

Hunt's rule of law was simple. He protected meat-packing magnates from troublesome labor unions and turned a blind eye to O'Leary's gambling clubs (except when O'Leary welched on bets by local judges, thus provoking raids). During the 1902 Teamsters' strike, Hunt provided police escorts for company meat wagons in defiance of contrary orders from Chief FRANCIS O'NEILL, arresting 200 strikers on charges that fell through in court. The advent of a Democratic chief, John Collins, saw Hunt suspended in August 1906, but the tide changed again in 1907, and Hunt was reinstated by Republican mayor Fred Busse. The inspector returned to an office packed with roses, courtesy of slaughterhouse millionaire J. Ogden Armour.

Soon after his return to uniform, Hunt joined the United Police, a pressure group of corrupt high-ranking officers created to ensure free-flowing graft. The same group had peddled worthless Mexican land to hapless patrolmen in 1905. Now they compiled an "agitation fund" for lobbying and keeping crooked colleagues out of jail. (In 1909 alone, 72 percent of the United Police treasury was spent on legal fees for officers accused of malfeasance.) In one campaign, Hunt carried a $5,000 bribe to state legislators in Springfield, opposing inclusion of police matrons in revised pension laws.

Thirty officers were later indicted for their roles in the United Police (which dissolved in January 1913), but Hunt slipped through the net, resigning in 1911

before the axe fell. In retirement, he opened a private detective agency with ex-Chief George Shippy. Mayor William Thompson briefly considered Hunt as a candidate for chief in 1918, when Chief Herman Schluetter died in office, but Hunt was passed over in favor of JOHN J. GARRITY.

Hurt, Clarence O. (1897–1975)

Famed lawmen Clarence Hurt was an Illinois native, born in 1897, but his family soon moved to Oklahoma, and the Sooner State became his home. Hurt joined the U.S. Army during World War I, then signed on with the OKLAHOMA CITY POLICE DEPARTMENT as a patrolman in 1919. His primary qualifications were a steady hand with firearms and the ability to drive both cars and motorcycles (rapidly emerging as crucial police equipment). After one year in uniform, Hurt was named secretary to Chief Calvin Linville, but appointment of a new chief in 1921 banished him to traffic enforcement. His first gunfight occurred in 1922, when Hurt lost his partner and killed the two bandits responsible. A short time later, Hurt was briefly detached to serve with the U.S. MARSHALS SERVICE, investigating multiple murders of Native tribesmen on the Osage Indian Reservation. (FBI spokesmen later claimed credit for solving that case, wherein discovery of oil led white land barons to kill and swindle tenants of the reservation.)

By 1927 Hurt was assigned to plainclothes work in Oklahoma City, promoted a year later to supervise the new Auto Theft Bureau. Before year's end he was named assistant police chief, filling that post for two years before his transfer (as a lieutenant) to the Detective Bureau. In 1933 he was promoted yet again, this time to command Oklahoma City PD's night shift. Meanwhile, a wave of bank robberies had enveloped the Midwest, with 59 reported from Oklahoma alone in 1932. Celebrity outlaws such as John Dillinger, "Pretty Boy" Floyd, and "Tri-State Terror" Wilbur Underhill roamed at will, unchallenged by an FBI that had no jurisdiction to pursue them. Hurt was present in Shawnee, Oklahoma, on December 30, 1933, when a party of lawmen fatally wounded Underhill, and his performance in that shootout brought him into favor with the FBI.

Ironically, Hurt had already filed an application with the Bureau, but it was rejected with the observation FBI headquarters saw "nothing in applicant to indicate the possession of any particular constructive imagination." Still, Hurt was good with a gun, and while G-men were not authorized to carry firearms until June 1934, Director J. EDGAR HOOVER began recruiting a crack team of "cowboys" or "hired guns" months in advance. Hurt joined the team, and he was part of the firing squad that killed Dillinger in Chicago, on July 22, 1934. Twenty-one months later, Hurt was part of the 14-man squad that captured bandit Alvin Karpis in New Orleans, giving Hoover credit for the "personal" arrest.

Though "PUBLIC ENEMIES" were suddenly in short supply, Hurt remained with the Bureau until 1955. Upon retirement, he returned to Oklahoma and served as a sheriff for several years. He died in 1975.

See also: BANK ROBBERY.

hypnosis

Hypnosis is defined by the American Psychological Association as "a procedure during which a health professional or researcher suggests that a client, patient, or experimental participant experience changes in sensations, perceptions, thoughts, or behavior." Its traditional application to law enforcement involves recovery or enhancement of memory, eliciting more detailed information from eyewitnesses and victims. In some cases, those memories have supplied the foundation for crimi-

nal charges in cases occurring years earlier, evoking testimony from persons who (allegedly) repressed conscious knowledge of traumatic incidents. More commonly, hypnosis is employed to obtain specific details—personal descriptions, license plate numbers, etc.—which are glimpsed but go unrecognized at conscious levels.

Forensic hypnosis remains a highly controversial subject. Defense attorneys and the expert witnesses employed by them insist that no memory extracted via hypnosis is reliable. They claim that most such memories are either confabulated by the subject (filling memory gaps with fantasy) or else implanted by the hypnotist. That implantation, critics argue, may be inadvertent or deliberate, one phase of a malicious FRAME-UP. Guilty verdicts in several SEX CRIME cases based on repressed memories were overturned on appeal in the 1990s, and some U.S. jurisdictions now exclude testimony from witnesses who have been hypnotized. Many investigators and psychologists, however, still regard hypnosis as a valuable tool, both in criminology and psychotherapy.

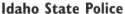

Idaho State Police

Idaho legislators created a Department of Law Enforcement while reorganizing the state's government in early 1919. A short time later, on May 18 of that year, they established a Bureau of Constabulary invested with responsibility for "detecting and investigating crime," with additional duties to "order abatement of public nuisances and to enforce such orders" by court injunctions, "to suppress riots, to prevent affrays," and to punish "wrongs to children and dumb animals" as prescribed by law. And if that was not enough, the bureau was also tasked with organizing all other state, county, and municipal peace officers throughout Idaho.

Immediate problems for the new agency included PROHIBITION enforcement (after January 16, 1920), licensing of motor vehicles, and suppression of "radical" labor unions under Idaho's syndicalism statutes. The bureau's first superintendent regarded leftists as the "most serious problem facing peace officers of the state," and more than half of all his officers in northern Idaho worked full time at harassing the Industrial Workers of the World. IWW members were jailed for simply possessing a union membership card, treated so harshly in confinement that by 1920 the bureau had radical matters "well in hand"—or so its leaders thought, until a statewide railroad strike created chaos during 1922–23.

In August 1922 Republican officials launched a cost-cutting drive to abolish the state constabulary. They succeeded in February 1923, leaving the Department of Law Enforcement at loose ends until March 1929, when escalating highway fatalities prompted creation of a state traffic patrol with 15 sworn officers. Ten years later, in March 1939, the Idaho State Police was created as a regular state agency with full police powers. Its forensic laboratory, established by the Department of Health in 1963 to perform blood and breath alcohol tests, expanded into full-scale criminal investigation by 1972 and was formally transferred to the Department of Law Enforcement in 1988.

Illinois State Police

Illinois had no statewide law enforcement agency before June 24, 1921, when state legislators authorized the Department of Public Works and Buildings to hire a "sufficient number of State Highway Patrol Officers" to enforce provisions of the Motor Vehicle Laws. Formally organized in 1922, the Illinois State Police quickly expanded into PROHIBITION enforcement and investigation of crimes committed outside the jurisdiction of local police departments, responding to riots and natural disasters.

The modern ISP, with some 3,000 sworn officers and civilian support personnel, operates with two major divisions. The Division of Administration handles all fiscal, logistical, personnel, data processing, and communications functions, while conducting operations at the Illinois State Police Academy. The Division of Operations, meanwhile, includes aircraft support and vehicle investigations, underwater search and recovery efforts, K-9 UNITS for tracking and drug detection, investigation of various crimes, apprehension of fugitives, plus public presentations on traffic safety and crime prevention.

See also: DRUGS.

Indianapolis Police Department

Founded in 1821, the city of Indianapolis, Indiana, was policed by an ever-changing combination of night watchmen, town marshals, and sheriff's deputies during its first 33 years. In September 1854 Mayor James McCready organized a 14-man police force under Captain Jefferson Springsteen. The new department's first major task, in summer 1855, was enforcement of a ban on alcoholic beverages. It went badly, sparking a riot that left several citizens wounded by police bullets. As a result of that outbreak (and second thoughts over the cost of running a police force), the department was disbanded on December 17, 1855.

A new 10-man force was organized in early 1856, but political wrangling forced its disbandment by May. Twelve months later, an even smaller force was launched—seven officers under Captain A. D. Rose—but this time it survived. Patrols were strictly nocturnal until 1862, when "day work" was added. By 1865 the IPD included a chief, two lieutenants, 27 patrolmen, two detectives, and 16 "specials." Thirty-five years later, 166 officers were employed to police a population of 170,000. Civilian personnel were added to perform administrative duties in the 1950s, totaling 250 by 2005 (with 1,000 sworn officers in the field).

Mobility and communication came by stages, with a bicycle "Flying Squadron" organized for "hot runs" in 1897, supplanted by motorcycles in 1909 and two patrol cars in 1910 (increased to 60 by 1929). Patrolmen used telephone booths to communicate from the late 1870s until 1897, when a call-box system was installed citywide. In 1929 the IPD became America's second police force with radio-equipped patrol cars, though two-way communication was delayed for another nine years. In the 1990s patrol cars were equipped with mobile data terminals for high-tech communication.

Diversity of a sort caught up with IPD in 1876, when the first black patrolman was hired. Five graced the 71-man force by 1890, but their assignments restricted them to all-black neighborhoods. Fourteen female officers (including two blacks) were hired in 1917, increased to 26 over the next three decades, but only two policewomen were assigned to street patrols in 1947. Twenty-one years after that, IPD became the first U.S. department to place female officers in a squad car, teaming Betty Blankenship and Elizabeth Robinson in Car 47. (Co-ed teaming was still considered too risky—and "tempting" for male officers.)

Despite such advances, IPD remained essentially a white male bastion through World War II and beyond, assailed with persistent charges of RACISM. Indiana harbored the nation's most powerful KU KLUX KLAN organization in the 1920s, with 240,000 members statewide and some 38,000 in Indianapolis. "Grand Dragon" D. C. Stephenson dominated Hoosier politics, his hooded followers including Governor Ed Jackson, Indianapolis mayor John Duvall, and a host of lesser politicians. Duvall appointed Klansmen to the city's Board of Public Safety and as leaders of the fire department. His appointment of Arthur McGee as police inspector was rescinded when black activists revealed McGee's multiple arrests for beating black citizens, but McGee's replacement (Walter White) was also a Klansman.

It finally took a murder conviction to break D. C. Stephenson's grip on Indiana, but complaints of IPD racism endure to the present day. Alleged beating victim Danny Sales led protests outside police headquarters in July 1995, sparking a confrontation that Mayor Stephen Goldsmith termed a "mini-riot," while FBI agents investigated claims that black youths were routinely assaulted by roving teams of police "jump-out boys." Chief James Toler subsequently resigned, complaining that his "hands were tied" in dealing with problem officers. A year later, in August 1996, drunken off-duty cops assaulted several patrons at a local bar, brandishing their weapons while they shouted racial epithets. That scandal prompted Chief Donald Christ to resign "in the best interest of the department as well as the city." Four officers were charged with battery in that incident, three more with violation of departmental rules. The four ringleaders faced trial in October 1997, but a hung jury spared them from conviction. Two later resigned from the force (with back pay), while the others remained in uniform, with a prescription for counseling.

Meanwhile, in December 1997, a joint state and federal task force was organized to investigate charges of CORRUPTION inside the IPD. The move came after Patrolman Myron Powell was charged with murdering a local drug dealer. Convicted pusher Michael Highbaugh, charged as the triggerman in that slaying, told authorities that Powell had stolen drugs and money from street dealers during four of his seven years on the job. Highbaugh pled guilty to murder on February 4, 2000, and received a prison term of life without parole. Jurors convicted Powell on April 28, 2000; he received a 65-year prison term on June 16, 2000. The federal investigation revealed no accomplices on the force.

See also: FEDERAL BUREAU OF INVESTIGATION.

Indiana State Police

Hoosier legislators created the Indiana State Police in 1933, in response to a wave of bank robberies committed by such flamboyant outlaws as John Dillinger and "Baby Face" Nelson. The ISP's first commander, MATTHEW LEACH, was equally flamboyant, adopting public relations techniques that created a longstanding rift between the state police and FBI director J. EDGAR

HOOVER. The ISP fared poorly in its war on bandits, losing all of its high-profile fugitives to quick-trigger G-men, but the force endured and grew into a model of professionalism.

Today the ISP combines highway patrol functions with broader criminal investigations and enforcement duties. Its Laboratory Division operates four FORENSIC SCIENCE labs statewide, devoting an estimated 55 percent of its field services and 80 percent of its analytical services to support of county or municipal law enforcement agencies. The ISP's Criminal Investigation, with 200 sworn officers and 56 civilian personnel, probes major crimes, conducts specialized investigations and provides investigative support for local agencies. A new Bureau of Criminal Investigation was created in November 1997 "for the sole purpose of making the department more efficient and effective in criminal investigative matters." The Gaming Division includes detectives and support personnel assigned to "protect the integrity" of legalized gambling statewide. It includes a Background Investigative Unit (designed to weed out felons or members of ORGANIZED CRIME) and a Riverboat Investigative Unit created to monitor Indiana's floating casinos.

See also: BANK ROBBERY; FEDERAL BUREAU OF INVESTIGATION.

informants

For all the advances made in FORENSIC SCIENCE during recent decades, police at every level still depend on informants—dubbed "squealers," "rats," "snitches," and "stool pigeons" in underworld parlance—to solve a large proportion of their cases. While DNA, ballistics, FINGERPRINTS and such may provide irrefutable proof of guilt or innocence, most juries still prefer descriptions offered by eyewitnesses or criminal accomplices. It seems to matter little that such testimony may be biased, incomplete, or wholly fabricated. Jurors like the human touch.

Authors Harry and Bonaro Overstreet, writing in *The FBI in Our Open Society* (1969), list three broad categories of informants: (1) individuals like Mafia defector Joe Valachi, who turn on their former comrades out of personal fear; (2) persons who become disillusioned with the criminal activities of groups they joined in good faith; and (3) agents who infiltrate suspect organizations on behalf of law enforcement never intending to be a loyal member. Even a cursory review of history, however, highlights several other classes of informants. They include:

- Active criminals who trade favors with authorities, to protect their own illicit enterprises and/or sabotage competitors. A case in point is the Capone gang's 1933 collaboration with Chicago FBI agents to frame rival bootlegger Roger Touhy for a kidnapping that never happened.

- Felons awaiting trial or sentencing, who barter testimony in return for leniency. One such notorious case involves Mafia underboss Sammy "The Bull" Gravano, who escaped prosecution for 19 contract murders by "rolling over" on "Dapper Don" John Gotti.

- Professional informants such as Louis Budenz and Herbert Philbrick, prominent ex-Communists in the 1950s, who profit from the celebrity of their "born-again" virtue, whether they desert religious cults, political extremist groups or criminal syndicates.

- Disgruntled ex-spouses, neighbors, coworkers, and other grudge-bearers who furnish (or fabricate) derogatory information to punish objects of personal spite. Every high-profile case produces numerous false leads and accusations against persons who had no part in the crime.

- AGENTS PROVOCATEURS employed by unscrupulous agencies to boost arrest statistics and/or "neutralize" specific targets by promoting ENTRAPMENT on various charges. Sadly, the FBI has made extensive use of such agents throughout its history, while local law enforcement sometimes follows suit.

- Informants who are pressured or intimidated into giving testimony, which sometimes proves to be false. "THIRD-DEGREE" TACTICS are banned today throughout the United States, although President George W. Bush and his advisers have actively promoted "aggressive questioning" of suspected terrorists, engaging in debates over the precise definition of torture.

Writing two years before exposure of the FBI's COINTELPRO crimes, the Overstreets maintained that "[t]here is nothing to suggest that the use of informants leads to the conviction of innocent persons." Today we know better, official FRAME-UPS serving as an object lesson in the folly of excessive reliance on testimony from tainted sources.

See also: TERRORISM.

intellectual property theft

As defined in current U.S. statutes, intellectual property theft includes the misappropriation of any copyrighted, patented or registered ideas, proposals, working drafts or other specialized, technical, medical or business information. The U.S. JUSTICE DEPARTMENT maintains an Internet Web site established to track such offenses, also listing various federal statutes that define the violations more specifically. Common offenses in this realm include bootlegging of films, videotapes, recorded music or patented computer software; industrial ESPIONAGE involving theft of trade secrets; trademark mimicry or counterfeiting; and false copyright claims applied to items previously copyrighted by others. Such cases have proliferated since the advent of the Internet, with a global cast of pirates making the enforcement of domestic legislation doubly difficult.

Internal Affairs

Until the mid-20th century, most U.S. complaints of police CORRUPTION or brutality were either swept under the rug by politicians and commanding officers, or—in sensational cases that could not be hidden—resulted in special investigations (such as New York City's Lexow Committee) or show trials of individual "bad apples." Routine graft and deployment of EXCESSIVE FORCE, especially against racial minorities or political "subversives," was widely accepted as a way of life in law enforcement. Still, reformers and civil libertarians demanded, "Who watches the watchmen?"

After World War II, major police departments nationwide established special divisions to cope more evenhandedly with disciplinary infractions. The division assigned to police other cops is commonly known as Internal Affairs, though other labels are applied in some jurisdictions. (The FBI's disciplinary unit, belatedly established in October 1976, is called the Office of Professional Responsibility.) Created in some cases to forestall establishment of dreaded CIVILIAN REVIEW BOARDS, The Internal Affairs Division accepts complaints of malpractice from law enforcement personnel or private citizens. Today, some departments even take complaints online, via e-mail through Internet Web sites.

At least in theory, Internal Affairs investigates all complaints of police misconduct, interviewing the officers involved, their alleged victims, and any available witnesses. If complaints are sustained, officers found guilty face a variety of punishments ranging from simple reprimands to dismissal and referral for criminal prosecution. Outsiders frequently complain that departmental disciplinary hearings are closed to the public, and that the outcome of their investigations is frequently kept secret. In Los Angeles, members of the CHRISTOPHER COMMISSION found that officers with multiple brutality complaints were not dismissed by the LOS ANGELES POLICE DEPARTMENT, and the same can probably be said for other agencies, both large and small. In too many cases, a "blue wall of silence" surrounds the workings of Internal Affairs, leaving the unit's success—or failure—shrouded in mystery. Meanwhile, Internal Affairs detectives are widely reviled as "traitors" by the officers whom they are assigned to police.

See also: FEDERAL BUREAU OF INVESTIGATION.

Internal Revenue Service

The IRS dates its history from 1862, when Congress enacted the nation's first income tax to pay Civil War expenses. A Commissioner of Internal Revenue was named to collect those funds, continuing until the act's repeal in 1872. Another federal income tax, imposed in 1894, was ruled unconstitutional by the U.S. SUPREME COURT a year later. That roadblock to taxation was removed by the Sixteenth Amendment, ratified in 1913, granting Congress authority to collect income tax. A new Bureau of Internal Revenue was created to supervise collections, renamed the Internal Revenue Service in the 1950s.

During PROHIBITION, while enforcement of the national ban on liquor fell to agents of the TREASURY DEPARTMENT, IRS agents led by ELMER LINCOLN IREY built tax-evasion cases that imprisoned prominent bootleggers Al Capone (in Chicago), Waxey Gordon (in New Jersey), and Morris Kleinman (in Cleveland). Irey also played a key role in the Lindbergh KIDNAPPING case, though FBI agents falsely claimed credit for that crime's solution. In later years, various IRS commissioners collaborated with the FBI to investigate (or harass) selected targets. FBI director J. EDGAR HOOVER often requested tax audits on "subversive" groups or individuals, a practice emulated by some presidents with their political opponents. In 1970, two years before his death, Hoover severed FBI relations with the IRS in protest against President Richard Nixon's sweeping plan to unite all U.S. intelligence agencies under direct White House control.

In 1975–76 the CHURCH COMMITTEE revealed extensive abuses of power by the IRS in respect to discretionary audits, but also found that most had been initiated by the White House or the FBI. The IRS Restructuring and Reform Act of 1998 inaugurated the agency's most comprehensive modernization in half a century, dividing the IRS into four divisions: Wage and Investment (covering 116 million taxpayers who file individual and joint returns); Small Business/Self-Employed (dealing with 45 million self-employed taxpayers); Large and Mid-Size Business (serving corporations with assets over $10 million); and Tax-Exempt and Government Entities (covering employee benefit plans, government organizations, and tax-exempt charities or social welfare groups). In 2004 the IRS had more than 99,000 employees, operating on a $10.2 million budget.

See also: FEDERAL BUREAU OF INVESTIGATION.

International Association of Chiefs of Police

Founded in 1893 as the National Chiefs of Police Union, the IACP was initially created to apprehend fugitives who fled local jurisdictions in the days before interstate flight was a federal offense. Today its stated mission is "to advance the science and art of police services; to develop and disseminate improved administrative, technical and operational practices and promote their use in police work; to foster police cooperation and the exchange of information and experience among police administrators throughout the world; to bring about recruitment and training in the police profession of qualified persons; and to encourage adherence of all police officers to high professional standards of performance and conduct." Behind those lofty aims the IACP operates as a political lobby on issues deemed critical by its leaders (and ostensibly by police officers nationwide).

J. EDGAR HOOVER's rise to power at FBI headquarters signaled a merger of sorts between his Bureau and the IACP. In 1924 Hoover's Bureau annexed the IACP's National Bureau of Criminal Identification files, established in 1897, followed by absorption of the IACP's uniform crime records reporting system in 1930. Four years later, the two organizations pooled their resources to found the FBI National Academy, offering advanced training to selected police officers throughout the country. FBI assistant director Quinn Tamm served for many years as Hoover's liaison to the IACP, once telling author Sanford Ungar, "We used to control the election of officers. We had a helluva lot of friends around, and we would control the nominating committee." So it was that a personal feud between Hoover and WILLIAM PARKER, chief of the LOS ANGELES POLICE DEPARTMENT, effectively blocked Parker from the IACP's presidency in 1959.

Tamm "betrayed" Hoover in 1961, leaving the FBI to serve as president of the IACP despite his old boss's strenuous objections. Tamm dropped another gauntlet in 1967, with his proclamation that henceforth the IACP—and not Hoover's FBI—would be the official "spokesman for law enforcement in this country." The rift was ultimately healed with Hoover's death in 1972, and the IACP remains a powerful lobbying voice where law-and-order issues are concerned.

Iowa State Patrol

In May 1935 Iowa legislators authorized creation of a 53-member Safety Patrol for state highways. After training at Camp Dodge, the original force of three supervisors and 50 sworn officers launched a system of 12-hour patrol shifts, employing 37 cars and 12 motorcycles. Patrolmen were equipped with AM radio receiv-

ers, but the Des Moines broadcasting station closed each day between 2:00 A.M. and 8:00 A.M. The team lost its first (and thus far, only) member murdered on duty, Patrolman Oran Pape, in 1936.

Slowly but surely, the Iowa Highway Patrol expanded over time. It gained another 72 members in 1937, retired all motorcycles in 1942, and issued new cars to each patrolman the following year. Another 41 officers were hired in 1946, and 77 more in 1953, but the ISP's original base pay of $100 per month would not increase until 1953, when it doubled to $200. For that princely sum, patrolmen worked 10-hour days and six-day weeks, with a guarantee of one Sunday off per month. Two airplanes joined the IHP motor pool in 1956, and radar was added to the arsenal in 1958. State troopers took over the governor's security detail in May 1970, and the first two female troopers were hired in 1975. That same year brought a change of name for the agency at large, rechristened the Iowa State Patrol.

Expansion and refinement continued through the last quarter of the 20th century. The ISP returned to motorcycle patrols in 1979, with purchase of two Kawasaki 1000's, but it lost one of the bikes in a highway crash four days later. A K-9 UNIT was created in 1991, and the force promoted its first female trooper to sergeant in 1995. The ISP conducted its first sting operation, collaborating with federal agencies, to recover $1 million in stolen construction equipment during 2001–02. Still, budget constraints create problems statewide, costing the agency 50 full-time employees since 2000.

Irey, Elmer Lincoln (1888–1948)

Born in 1888, Elmer Irey joined the INTERNAL REVENUE SERVICE at age 26 and soon found a place in the agency's enforcement division. By 1919 he was the chief of that unit, distinguishing himself by pursuit of millionaire bootleggers during PROHIBITION. Those convicted and imprisoned by Irey's crack team included Chicago's "Scarface" Al Capone, New Jersey's Irving Wexler (Aka "Waxey Gordon"), and Morris Kleinman (the "Al Capone of Cleveland"). During Irey's tenure the IRS arrested 15,000 tax evaders and enjoyed a 90-percent conviction rate, far superior to that of the rival FBI.

It was also Irey's suggestion to include obsolete gold certificates in the Lindbergh KIDNAPPING ransom, though FBI director J. EDGAR HOOVER falsely claimed credit for solving that case. After the arrest of suspect Bruno Hauptmann, Charles Lindbergh later told Irey, "If it hadn't been for you fellows being in the case, Hauptmann would not now be on trial and your organization deserves full credit for his apprehension." That compliment is dubious, since Hauptmann was apparently the victim of a frame-up, but Hoover learned of it and harbored a lifelong grudge against both Irey and Lindbergh. Irey's name goes unmentioned in FBI accounts of the case, and the snub enraged him. As colleague Malachi Harney told author Ovid Demaris, "Irey was a good Christian who didn't cuss, but the air would turn blue when the subject of the Lindbergh kidnapping came up."

In pursuit of that feud, Irey used Hoover's own weapons, including leaks to friendly journalists, complaints to his superiors, and testimony in Congress. In 1935 Irey opposed the Bureau's latest name change on grounds that the new FBI label made Hoover's agency sound like the only federal law enforcement agency, instead of one among many. Irey lost that battle, along with his bid to bring the FBI under Civil Service on the eve of World War II, but he won promotion in 1937 to serve as chief coordinator of the TREASURY DEPARTMENT, supervising all of the department's law enforcement programs. Irey remained a thorn in Hoover's side until his retirement in 1941. He died seven years later, at age 60.

See also: FEDERAL BUREAU OF INVESTIGATION; FRAME-UPS.

"jack-in-the-box" teams

Briefly popular in the early 1960s, police "jack-in-the-box" teams were assigned to hide inside various business establishments after closing time, then spring from hiding and strike if burglars appeared. The squads in some cities appeared to shoot first and ask questions later, if at all, engaging in activities that smacked of summary execution. One early unit, established by the DALLAS POLICE DEPARTMENT, drew complaints from the AMERICAN CIVIL LIBERTIES UNION, which noted that its victims were almost always black or Hispanic. Adverse publicity, lawsuits, and court decisions limiting the use of DEADLY FORCE combined to wipe out such units by the end of the 1960s.

Jackson, Robert Houghwout (1892–1954)

Pennsylvania native Robert Jackson was born at Spring Creek on February 13, 1892. He earned an LL.D. from National University and was admitted to the bar in 1913. Jackson subsequently served as president of the Western New York Federation of Bar Associations (1928–39), as a member of the New York State Commission to Investigate the Administration of Justice, as chairman of the National Conference of Bar Associations (1933–34), and as general counsel for the Bureau of Internal Revenue (1934). His service with the U.S. JUSTICE DEPARTMENT included appointments as assistant attorney general in the Tax Division (February 1936), the Antitrust Division (January 1937), and as Solicitor General of the United States (March 1938). President Franklin Roosevelt named Jackson as his third attorney general on January 18, 1940.

Jackson was a weak attorney general, who proved himself subservient to FBI director J. EDGAR HOOVER in various controversial cases. He defended FBI raids on the Abraham Lincoln Brigade (which opposed fascism in the Spanish Civil War), secretly approved the Bureau's CUSTODIAL DETENTION INDEX, and condoned illegal WIRETAPS, telling Hoover of his wish to "have no detailed record kept concerning the cases in which wiretapping would be utilized." Any record of illicit taps, Jackson decreed, "should be kept in Hoover's immediate office, listing the time, places, and cases in which this procedure is utilized." In November 1940 Jackson approved the FBI's covert alliance with the American Legion, creating a nationwide army of civilian INFORMANTS.

Jackson left Justice in July 1941, when Roosevelt appointed him to the U.S. SUPREME COURT. After World War II he served as President Harry Truman's representative in meetings with the "Big Three" powers—England, France, and Russia—to negotiate international prosecution of Nazi war criminals. While remaining on the Supreme Court, Jackson served as chief counsel for the International Military Tribunal at Nuremberg, and later as trustee of George Washington University and Union College. He died in office on October 9, 1954.

See also: FEDERAL BUREAU OF INVESTIGATION; INTERNAL REVENUE SERVICE.

Jackson Police Department

The largest law enforcement agency in Mississippi's former "closed society" has suffered numerous complaints of RACISM throughout its history. All white until the mid-late 1960s, the Jackson PD earned a grim reputation for brutalizing blacks and harassing civil rights activists. In May 1963, one month before the ASSASSINATION of local NAACP leader Medgar Evers by a member of the KU KLUX KLAN, Mayor Allen Thompson bought an armored car—dubbed "Thompson's Tank"—for use against nonviolent protesters. Seven years later, Jackson police and members of the MISSISSIPPI HIGHWAY PATROL lied to FBI agents about their unjustified use of DEADLY FORCE against unarmed black students in the JACKSON STATE COLLEGE SHOOTINGS.

Jackson PD is integrated today, but many problems remain, ranging from budgetary problems in America's poorest state to persistent claims of racism. In the late 1990s, 30 officers and dispatchers age 40 or older sued the department for age discrimination based on a pay system that granted higher-percentage salary increases to workers with five or fewer years on the job. Nearly all workers who qualified for the larger increases were under age 40. Two federal courts rejected the lawsuit before it reached the U.S. SUPREME COURT, where a decision was pending at press time for this volume.

In 2000 Jackson PD received a $4,452,356 federal grant to "enhance community policing" by hiring 67 new officers and reassigning 39 to community details. An audit in 2001 found budgeting "adequate," but identified failures which led the Inspector General to "question grant funds spent of $3,173,594 and identified $2,216 of enhanced revenue." Specifically, new officers were not hired and maintained according to the plan, and Jackson PD "did not remit $2,216 in interest earnings to the Department of Health and Human Services as required."

Jackson State College shooting

The month of May 1970 witnessed nationwide demonstrations against President Richard Nixon's covert military actions in Cambodia. The official reaction was harsh, including deployment of the NATIONAL GUARD at Ohio's Kent State University, where 13 students were shot (four fatally) on May 4, and police shootings of 86 blacks (six fatally) in Augusta, Georgia, on May 11. Demonstrations at Mississippi's Jackson State College included scattered rock- and bottle-throwing on May 13, and tragedy struck the next day, when local police and MISSISSIPPI HIGHWAY PATROL officers opened fire on campus, killing two persons and wounding 12 more.

Both departments involved in the shooting had long histories of RACISM and friendly collaboration with the KU KLUX KLAN, a mindset emphasized when Highway Patrol inspector Lloyd "Goon" Jones radioed a call for ambulances to transport wounded "niggers" from the campus on May 14. Officers involved in the shooting immediately collected their empty shells and reloaded their weapons to make it appear that no shots had been fired—this, despite the casualties and 400 bullet holes in the women's dormitory of Alexander Hall, plus other damage caused by gunfire. When questioned later, every officer present denied firing his weapon, a circumstance that led Mississippi-Louisiana Press Association to pass a resolution condemning the official conspiracy of silence.

FBI investigation of the shooting quickly identified buckshot pellets from Alexander Hall and confirmed that only members of the JACKSON POLICE DEPARTMENT carried shotguns on May 14. Highway patrolmen destroyed their own spent cartridges, but threats of grand jury subpoenas prompted them to surrender several shotgun shells fired by city officers. Confronted with irrefutable evidence, various officers finally admitted firing in response to "sniper fire" from Alexander Hall. FBI director J. EDGAR HOOVER issued a premature statement on May 18, falsely claiming "substantial proof . . . that there was sniper fire on the troops [sic] from the dormitory roof before the troops fired." In fact there was none, as his own agents later confirmed.

The Scranton Commission, appointed by President Nixon to investigate campus unrest nationwide, described the Jackson shooting as "an unreasonable, unjustified overreaction" by police. It also accused Mississippi officers of lying and concealing or destroying vital evidence, concluding that "a significant cause of the deaths and injuries at Jackson State College is the confidence of white officers that if they fire weapons during a black campus disturbance they will face neither stern departmental discipline nor criminal prosecution or convictions."

That expectation was borne out by subsequent events. Although lying to FBI agents carries a maximum penalty of 10 years in prison and a $10,000 fine, G-men deviated from their normal routine of collecting signed statements in the Jackson case, thus exempting all concerned from prosecution. A federal grand jury convened in June 1970 under Judge Harold Cox (who once described black Mississippians as "chimpanzees"), but it returned no indictments after Cox informed the panel that student demonstrators "must expect to be injured or killed." A Hinds County grand jury acknowledged that initial police statements were "absolutely false," but decreed that any indictment of officers for perjury would be "unwarranted, unjustified and political in nature." Instead, the panel indicted a black bystander, 21-year-old Ernest Kyles, for ARSON and inciting a riot. (Those charges were later dropped for lack of evidence.)

Litigation from the Jackson State shootings dragged on for more than a decade. Relatives of slain victims Phillip Gibbs and Early Green sued state and local police for $13.8 million in federal court. At trial, two officers admitted lying to the FBI, and five G-men testified that there was no evidence of any sniper fire on campus, but an all-white jury ruled in favor of the defendants on March 22, 1972. A federal appellate court upheld that verdict in October 1974, strangely finding that there *was* a campus sniper, then decreeing that police "far exceeded the response that was appropriate." Still, "sovereign immunity" exempted Mississippi police from any lawsuit, regardless of their conduct. In January 1982 seven justices of the U.S. SUPREME COURT declined to review the case.

See also: KENT STATE UNIVERSITY SHOOTINGS.

Jacksonville Police Department

Jacksonville, Florida, has been a hotbed of racial violence since Reconstruction and has served since 1920 as state headquarters for the KU KLUX KLAN. In such an atmosphere it comes as no surprise that the police department—lily white until the 1960s—has faced charges of discrimination and EXCESSIVE FORCE against black citizens, while some observers noted police sympathy for the violent KKK. Mayor Haydon Burns set the standard for such behavior during 1949–65, granting parade permits to Klansmen while he ordered the arrest of civil rights protesters, openly courting Klan votes while he displayed a "shuddering distaste for doing anything to promote racial amity."

Police chief Luther Reynolds publicly announced in summer 1960 that Jacksonville was "not ready" for desegregation. When sit-ins began on August 27, Reynolds "went fishing" and most of his officers vanished from sight, leaving mobs of Klansmen to assault demonstrators in a riot dubbed "Axe-handle Saturday." Two dozen whites and 60-odd blacks were arrested that day, while police shot and killed one black motorist. Mayor Burns blamed the mayhem on out-of-town whites, while Reynolds insisted that "all the fellows we arrested were local boys." In any case, white rioters were freed on payment of fines as low as $10, while the stiffest punishment—90 days, after a jailhouse beating by white inmates—was reserved for a black college student who led the sit-ins.

Many observers found it curious, in May 1958, when Burns and Reynolds took the lead in creating a SOUTHERN CONFERENCE ON BOMBING, inviting law enforcement leaders from 22 southern cities to collaborate in solving a wave of TERRORISM that had rocked Dixie with 46 dynamite blasts in the past 15 months. FBI director J. EDGAR HOOVER refused to participate in the

effort, and with leaders such as Birmingham's Eugene "Bull" Connor in the forefront, it may come as no surprise that the short-lived SCB failed to solve a single bombing case.

Today Jacksonville remains a hard-bitten city with clear racial problems and rising crime rates. It boasted 90 murders in 2002, up from 75 in 2001, and the year's crime index was 542.2 (versus the U.S. average of 330.6). In December 2002 a federal jury convicted six defendants, including three former deputy sheriffs, for a local crime spree that included home invasions, KIDNAPPING, armed robbery, and the murder of a Jacksonville businessman. On January 22, 2003, ex-cop Aric Sinclair received a 17-year prison sentence and was fined $108,000. Jason Pough drew a five-year sentence and a $500 fine, while Reginald Bones—convicted on unrelated bank fraud charges—was slapped with 100 hours of community service and fined $11,000. Three civilian accomplices received prison terms ranging from four to 19 years.

See also: BOMBING AND BOMB SQUADS; CONNOR, THEOPHILUS EUGENE ("BULL"); FEDERAL BUREAU OF INVESTIGATION.

Janklow, William John (b. 1939)

A Chicago native, born September 13, 1939, William "Wild Bill" Janklow served in the U.S. Marine Corps after high school (1955–59), then obtained his B.S. from the University of South Dakota, Vermillion, in 1964, followed by an LL.B. from the same school two years later. He was employed as a tribal attorney for the Rosebud Sioux in January 1967, when he was accused of raping his children's 15-year-old babysitter. The alleged victim, a Brulé Lakota girl named Jancinta Eagle Deer, reported the incident to the BUREAU OF INDIAN AFFAIRS POLICE on January 14, claiming that Janklow attacked her while driving her home from his house. BIA authorities recommended prosecution, but the FBI intervened to claim jurisdiction. Minneapolis agent-in-charge RICHARD G. HELD, later revealed as a participant in the Bureau's illegal COINTELPRO campaigns, investigated the case and informed FBI headquarters that there was "insufficient evidence, the allegations were unfounded; we are therefore closing our files on this matter." Janklow left Rosebud (where tribal jurisdiction prevailed), while Jancita Eagle Deer moved to Iowa.

Six years later, while employed as an assistant prosecutor with the state attorney general's office, Janklow had his first public clash with members of the American Indian Movement (AIM). Victorious in that trial, Janklow thereafter billed himself as an "Indian fighter" and campaigned in 1974 to become the state's attorney general. The rape allegations resurfaced, pressed by

AIM attorneys, although FBI files were sealed and the Bureau "refused to cooperate in any way." Nonetheless, with barely a month remaining before the November election, tribal judge Mario Gonzales charged Janklow with "assault with intent to commit rape, and carnal knowledge with a female under 16." Two witnesses testified that Janklow had "brooded" over the rape and offered money to Eagle Deer's grandfather after the incident. Janklow denied all charges and refused to appear in tribal court, thus avoiding prosecution. He won the election and shortly thereafter proclaimed, "The only way to deal with the Indian problem in South Dakota is to put a gun to AIM leaders' heads and pull the trigger."

Aggressive pursuit of AIM "radicals" was a ticket to political success for Janklow, who served four terms as South Dakota's governor (1979–87, 1994–2002). During his first gubernatorial term, author Peter Matthiessen published his study of the FBI's war against AIM, *In the Spirit of Crazy Horse* (1983), which included sharp criticism of Janklow and a review of the Eagle Deer case. Janklow retaliated with a $24 million libel suit, which was dismissed by federal judge Gene Kean (in a decision ratified by the U.S. SUPREME COURT). Despite a promise to pursue the lawsuit "as long as I live," Janklow diverted his energy to a congressional campaign, winning election to the House of Representatives in 2002.

On August 16, 2003, Janklow sped past a stop sign in Flandreau, South Dakota, traveling 71 miles per hour in a 55-mph zone, and struck a motorcyclist who had the right of way. The victim died, and Janklow was charged with second-degree manslaughter on September 1. Ignoring public calls for his immediate resignation, Janklow blamed diabetes for his reckless driving. Jurors disagreed, convicting him of manslaughter on December 8, 2003. Janklow faced a maximum sentence of 10 years in prison, but Judge Rodney Steele imposed a 100-day sentence (with three years' probation) on January 22, 2004. Janklow resigned from Congress the same day.

See also: FEDERAL BUREAU OF INVESTIGATION.

Jewell, Richard (b. 1962)

Shortly before 1:00 A.M. on July 27, 1996, private security guard Richard Jewell noticed an abandoned backpack tucked beneath a bench in Atlanta's Centennial Park. Security was tight in the vicinity, with countless law enforcement officers assigned to prevent acts of TERRORISM during the summer Olympic Games. Jewell reported his find to an agent of the Bureau of Alcohol, Tobacco and Firearms, then remained nearby as that agent opened the pack. Inside was a bomb that exploded moments later—but not before Jewell had escorted more than 100 bystanders to safety.

Early reports hailed Jewell as a hero, but the FBI took a different view, publicly declaring him "the chief suspect in the bombing." Overnight the global news media pounced on Jewell's story, portraying him as a "bizarre character" who bombed the park in a sick bid for personal glory. Bureau psychologists even had a name for such behavior: the "recognition (hero)" syndrome. G-men placed Jewell under 24-hour surveillance, questioned him at length without advising him of his legal rights, and searched his apartment with television crews standing by to broadcast the event worldwide. (Raiders confiscated Jewell's guns, his mother's Tupperware, and a collection of Walt Disney videotapes.) Only weeks later, in October 1996, did JUSTICE DEPARTMENT spokesmen finally exonerate Jewell, shifting their focus to fugitive terrorist Eric Rudolph, linked to antiabortion violence in Alabama and Georgia.

FBI director LOUIS FREEH disciplined two agents for their conduct in the Jewell affair. Agent Don Johnson received a five-day suspension for failure to advise Jewell of his rights during interrogation, while Atlanta agent-in-charge David Johnson (no relation) received a letter of censure. Jewell declined to sue the FBI, but he did file civil actions against several media organizations, collecting more than $2 million. As for the Bureau, five years after the fact Jewell told reporters, "Nobody's ever called me, written me a letter, sent me an e-mail, [or] called any of my attorneys" to apologize for the false accusations.

See also: BOMBING AND BOMB SQUADS; FEDERAL BUREAU OF INVESTIGATION.

Johnson, Reverdy (1796–1896)

Born at Annapolis, Maryland, on May 21, 1796, Reverdy Johnson graduated from St. John's College in 1811, then studied law with his father and won admittance to the Maryland bar in 1815. After six years in private practice, he was elected to serve as a state senator (1821–27). He subsequently won election to the U.S. Senate (1846), but resigned on March 8, 1849, to become attorney general under President Zachary Taylor. Once again, his tenure was brief, ended in this case by the death of President Taylor on July 20, 1850. Johnson resigned two days later, subsequently serving as a member of the Peace Congress in Washington (1861), as a Maryland state legislator (1861–62), as U.S. senator from Maryland (1863–68), and as America's minister to Great Britain

Attorney General Reverdy Johnson (Author's collection)

(1868–69). He died at home, in Annapolis, on February 10, 1876.

Jones, Frank (1856–1893)

A native Texan, born in 1856, Frank Jones exemplified the TEXAS RANGERS of popular legend, fast on the draw and frequently reckless where fine points of law were concerned. Even as a teenage recruit, Jones's superiors could not restrain him from illegally chasing outlaws across the Mexican border, though he once grudgingly promised that he "would not cross into Mexico where there are settlements and [there] would be any danger of stirring up international trouble." In true Ranger style, Jones not only escaped censure, but won promotion to captain.

Jones's tenure with the Rangers included numerous shootouts with badmen. In one case, around 1875, Jones pursued three bandits who had killed his partners, blasting two from their saddles and bringing the third back alive. Some months later, after three more Rangers were killed and Jones was kidnapped, he reportedly disarmed one of his captors and killed five bandits with his

adversary's rifle. In October 1891 Jones led a Crockett County posse after four train robbers, wounding and capturing three before the final suspect shot himself.

Jones ran out of luck on another illicit border crossing in June 1893. Accompanied by four other rangers and a deputy sheriff, Jones rode into a rustler's ambush near Tres Jacales on June 30. Bullets struck Jones in the chest and thigh, killing him within minutes, while his disheartened comrades let the ambushers escape.

Jones, James Wormley (1884–1958)

The son of a Virginia lighthouse keeper, born in 1884, James Jones stopped one year short of completing his bachelor's degree at all-black Virginia Union University. He joined the WASHINGTON, D.C., METROPOLITAN POLICE DEPARTMENT in January 1905, rising through the ranks from patrolman to detective by 1917. With America's entry into World War I, Jones joined the U.S. Army as a captain, commanding Company F of the 368th Infantry. He saw combat in France during 1918 and was back on duty with the Washington police before year's end.

Chief A. BRUCE BIELASKI appointed Jones as the FBI's first black agent on November 19, 1919. The postwar Red scare was already well advanced, tinged with deep strains of RACISM, and Bielaski realized that white agents could not effectively shadow black "radicals." Assigned to UNDERCOVER WORK from the start of his Bureau career, Jones infiltrated the African Blood Brotherhood and Marcus Garvey's Universal Negro Improvement Association (UNIA), signing his reports with the code-number "800." As a trusted UNIA captain, Jones addressed crowds in Harlem, where the *Negro World* observed: "Mr. Jones, who is very light-complexioned, was mistaken by the audience for a white man."

Garvey trusted Jones enough to have him monitor accounts at the UNIA's Harlem restaurant, but Jones was devoted to putting Garvey in prison. He was the first to suggest a MANN ACT prosecution of Garvey for traveling with girlfriend Amy Jacques, but that effort proved fruitless. An old acquaintance recognized Jones as a "former detective" in July 1920, but while Jones retreated briefly to Washington, he remained active in the UNIA. Back on the case full time in August 1921, Jones emerged as a full-blown agent provocateur, stirring up feuds between the UNIA and African Blood Brotherhood, while encouraging disgruntled ex-employees to sue the UNIA for back wages.

In January 1923 Jones was one of seven UNIA members whose affidavits permitted federal prosecutors to charge Marcus Garvey with fraud. Jones filed his last report with the FBI on February 18, 1923, and resigned two months later, though several accounts describe him "encouraging" prosecution witnesses during Garvey's later trial. Jones died in Pittsburgh, Pennsylvania, in 1958.

See also: AGENTS PROVOCATEURS.

"Joyner's Guerrillas"

This covert unit of the Meridian (Mississippi) Police Department was created by Chief Roy Gunn in late 1967, to combat a wave of bombings committed by the KU KLUX KLAN. While Mississippi law enforcement officers have often been accused of RACISM—and rightly so, in some cases—Chief Gunn and Sgt. Lester "Gigolo" Joyner were outraged by KKK TERRORISM around Meridian, including attacks on synagogues and the homes of Jewish residents. Members of the anti-Klan unit led by Joyner (and named in his honor) dressed in black and took their cue from the FBI's illicit COINTELPRO operation, waging a war of harassment against known Klansmen even as they sought evidence for future prosecution. On several occasions, according to journalist Jack Nelson, Joyner's Guerrillas even detonated small explosive charges at the homes of known Klansmen.

The group's primary mission, though, was to recruit INFORMANTS who would put Klan bombers "on the spot" for a reward. Collaborating with FBI agents and leaders of the Jewish community, Joyner's Guerrillas paid brothers Alton and Raymond Roberts (both violent Klansmen) to betray their hooded comrades. Finally, in return for a payoff of $30,000 or more (reports vary), the brothers arranged for nightriders to bomb the home of entrepreneur Meyer Davidson. Joyner's men staked out the house, expecting to ambush and kill Klansmen Danny Joe Hawkins and Thomas Tarrants, but Hawkins surprised them by dropping out of the plot. His replacement, Kathryn Ainsworth, was a local schoolteacher whose public life gave no hint of her nocturnal involvement with the KKK.

Joyner's Guerrillas were waiting when Tarrants and Ainsworth arrived on the night of June 29, 1968. A chaotic gun battle ensued, leaving Ainsworth dead, while Tarrants, Officer Mike Hatcher, and a civilian bystander were gravely wounded. All of the injured survived, and Hatcher had recovered enough from his three chest wounds by mid-July for a confrontation with Tarrants's father. Chief Gunn later told Jack Nelson that Tarrants Sr. was "mouthing off" about the police when Hatcher, a karate expert, "beat the hell out of him."

That incident was the last gasp for Joyner's Guerrillas, and the group soon disbanded as Klan terrorism faded from the Mississippi scene. Thomas Tarrants served a long prison term, while Sgt. Joyner received

various community service awards and was honored by the INTERNATIONAL ASSOCIATION OF CHIEFS OF POLICE. Nelson revealed the bomb plot's machinations, with its overtones of ENTRAPMENT, in a 1970 series of articles for the *Los Angeles Times*.

See also: BOMBING AND BOMB SQUADS; FEDERAL BUREAU OF INVESTIGATION.

Justice Department

While Congress authorized appointment of a U.S. attorney general in 1789, the department that officer presently leads was not created until 1870, in the midst of the chaotic Reconstruction era. Even then, federal prosecutions were so rare that Justice required no detective force of its own for another decade. As responsibilities expanded with passage of the Interstate Commerce Act (1887) and the Sherman Anti-Trust Act (1890), various attorneys general used agents of the Pinkerton Detective Agency on a part-time, case-by-case basis. That relationship was severed in 1892, when Pinkerton's brutal STRIKEBREAKING activities prompted a congressional ban on temporary hiring of agents employed in the private sector. For the next 16 years, Justice borrowed SECRET SERVICE agents from the TREASURY DEPARTMENT, until further abuses led Congress to ban that practice in May 1908. Two months later, Attorney General CHARLES BONAPARTE created a detective force at Justice that became the FBI.

Passage of the MANN ACT (1910) and the DYER ACT (1919) further broadened the Justice Department's authority, but investigations took an increasingly political (and often personal) turn after the Russian Revolution of 1917. Fear of anarchists and the Communist Party drove Attorney General THOMAS GREGORY to create an Alien Enemy Bureau in 1917, closely followed by Attorney General A. MITCHELL PALMER's Red-hunting General Intelligence Division and the sweeping "Red raids" of 1919–20. PROHIBITION and the advent of President Warren Harding's "Ohio Gang" brought unprecedented CORRUPTION to official Washington in 1921. Under Attorney General HARRY DAUGHERTY, Justice was soon nicknamed the "Department of Easy Virtue," populated by political hacks with their hands out for bribes. The Teapot Dome scandal nearly sent Daugherty to prison, while his replacement—hard-line reformer HARLAN FISKE STONE—set out to reform Justice. Stone's choice of J. EDGAR HOOVER as FBI director was based on Hoover's promise (soon proved false) to ban political investigations and pursue only those persons who committed federal crimes.

Over the next 48 years, relations between the FBI and Justice depended chiefly on the latitude that various attorneys general granted Hoover in pursuit of his personal agendas. Between 1925 and 1960 most of Hoover's nominal superiors avoided exercising any serious supervision over the FBI, while a few—including Attorneys General HOMER STILLÉ CUMMINGS and HERBERT BROWNELL, JR.—actively encouraged illegal DOMESTIC SURVEILLANCE techniques. Attorneys general who attempted to restrain the Bureau, such as ROBERT FRANCIS KENNEDY and WILLIAM RAMSEY CLARK, were opposed and publicly reviled by Hoover at every turn, largely defeating their ability to function in office. By the end of Hoover's life, history had come full circle with Justice mired in another morass of corruption under Attorney General JOHN NEWTON MITCHELL and President Richard Nixon.

In the wake of the Watergate scandal that sent Mitchell to prison and drove Nixon from the White House in disgrace, priorities at Justice have been largely dictated by partisan politics. Attorneys General EDWARD HIRSCH LEVI and GRIFFIN BOYETTE BELL emphasized prosecution of ORGANIZED CRIME leaders and restricted FBI surveillance on political groups, while successors WILLIAM FRENCH SMITH, EDWIN MEESE III, and RICHARD LEWIS THORNBURGH took the opposite approach, condemning "subversives" while mobsters and white-collar crimes were largely ignored. Attorney General JANET RENO was widely accused of political motives in protecting President Bill Clinton from various investigations, but the same must be said of attorneys general serving Presidents Ronald Reagan and George H. W. Bush.

Following the catastrophic terrorist attacks of September 11, 2001, President George W. Bush and Attorney General JOHN ASHCROFT announced a "wartime reorganization" of Justice with primary emphasis on homeland security. Ashcroft's "blueprint for change" reassigned 10 percent of the department's headquarters staff to "front line" field offices nationwide, while declaring that nonpolitical cases would take a backseat. "We cannot do everything we once did," Ashcroft told reporters, "because lives now depend on us doing a few things very well." Critics suggested that the shift was not only a response to "9/11," but also a deliberate retreat from cases that held little interest for the Bush

The Department of Justice Building in Washington, D.C., 1935 (Corbis)

White House, including prosecution of corporate and ENVIRONMENTAL CRIMES.

See also: ANARCHISM; FEDERAL BUREAU OF INVESTIGATION; HOMELAND SECURITY DEPARTMENT; PINKERTON, ALLAN J.; TERRORISM.

juvenile crime

In the United States, juvenile crime is broadly defined as any offense committed by persons below the age of 18 years. Treatment of minor offenders differs in accordance with their actual age and the nature of their offenses, most courts agreeing that very young children lack capacity to act with true criminal intent. Still, the variations in juvenile law from one state to another may literally mean the difference between life and death.

America's first juvenile court was established in 1899, to shield minors from the harsh penalties and prison conditions imposed on adult offenders. Every state had separate juvenile courts by 1945, and most states established probation programs for youthful offenders by 1927. In the 1980s conservative politics and public alarm over rising crime rates prompted emphasis on punishment over rehabilitation, with an increasing trend to try juvenile offenders as adults for major felonies. And while the U.S. SUPREME COURT has banned execution of any defendant who commits a murder before age 16 (*Thompson v. Oklahoma*, 1988), various states still set their own rules for which juveniles may be tried as adults.

In Oklahoma, seven-year-olds may be tried as adults if the state proves the defendants knew their acts were wrong. Two states, Nevada and Washington, peg the age of "criminal responsibility" at eight years. Two states, Kansas and Vermont, permit transfer of 10-year-olds to adult criminal court. Five others—Colorado, Georgia, Missouri, Montana, and Washington—draw the line at 12 years. Six permit adult trials for 13-year-olds, including Illinois, Mississippi, New Hampshire, New York, North Carolina, and Wyoming. Another 17 states—Alabama, Arkansas, California, Connecticut, Idaho, Iowa, Kentucky, Louisiana, Massachusetts, Michigan, Minnesota, New Jersey, North Dakota, Ohio, Texas, Utah, and Virginia—permit adult trials for defendants 14 and older. New Mexico allows adult trial for 15-year-olds. The 18 U.S. jurisdictions with no state minimum age for transfer to adult court include Alaska, Arizona, Delaware, the District of Columbia, Florida, Hawaii, Indiana, Maine, Maryland, Nebraska, Oregon, Pennsylvania, Rhode Island, South Carolina, South Dakota, Tennessee, West Virginia, and Wisconsin.

Kansas Bureau of Investigation

Kansas state legislators established the Kansas Bureau of Investigation 1939 "to combat the increasing magnitude and complexity of crime in general and bank robberies in particular." Named in imitation of the FBI, it operates as a division of the state attorney general's office. As initially conceived, the KBI was meant to investigate only those cases handpicked by the attorney general, or where local agencies requested state assistance. A FORENSIC SCIENCE laboratory was later added, and the KBI today assists in training local police officers, while providing crime-trend information, and maintaining state criminal records.

See also: BANK ROBBERY; FEDERAL BUREAU OF INVESTIGATION.

Kansas City massacre

A pivotal event in FBI history occurred on June 17, 1933, as G-men and police transported fugitive Frank "Jelly" Nash from Hot Springs, Arkansas, to Leavenworth federal prison in Kansas. Nash's escorts left their train at Kansas City's Union Station at 7:00 A.M., retrieving two cars for the 30-mile drive to their final destination. Suddenly, gunmen appeared and shooting erupted. When the smoke cleared, Nash was dead, along with three policemen and FBI agent Raymond Caffrey. Two other federal agents were wounded, while a fourth emerged unscathed.

The event was predictably chaotic. Patrolman Mike Fanning, assigned to Union Station that morning, fired at one of the shooters—a "fat man"—and saw him fall. "I don't know if I hit him or whether he fell to escape," Fanning said. "In any event, he got up, fired another volley into the car, and ran toward a light Oldsmobile car, which roared west toward Broadway." Fanning saw three men in the fleeing car, but admitted "there may have been more." Seconds later, he said, "[a] 1933 Chevrolet car with more gunners swooped past [Agent Caffrey's] parked car and riddled it from the rear. I ran into the street, fired two shots into the back of that car, and rushed to the parked Chevrolet. I still didn't know the men in it were officers."

If Fanning's story is true, there were two cars and at least six shooters involved in the ambush. Other witnesses were hopelessly confused. G-men Francis Lackey and Frank Smith disagreed on the number of gunmen, while Agent Reed Vetterli identified one as escaped convict Robert Brady, a known associate of bank robber Harvey Bailey. That meshed with testimony from two other witnesses who named Bailey as one of the shooters. Yet another witness named the getaway driver as Bailey cohort Wilbur Underhill, but FBI reports dismissed that witness as delusional, noting his claims of friendship with ex-president THEODORE ROOSEVELT and various crowned heads of Europe. Witness Lottie West identified one gunman as Oklahoma bandit Charles "Pretty Boy" Floyd, but others disputed her claim, naming the "fat man" in question as a Union Station employee.

Ballistics evidence was problematic. Souvenir hunters snatched up all but a handful of .45-caliber shells, and those were useless without weapons for comparison. Meanwhile, G-men learned that Agent Lackey had fired two shotgun shells loaded with steel ball bearings, inflicting fatal wounds on Nash, Agent Caffrey,

Spectators throng the scene of Kansas City's Union Station massacre on June 17, 1933. (FBI)

and Officer Frank Hermanson. While Bureau head-quarters buried that evidence, analysts found that Officer W. J. Grooms was killed by .45-caliber bullets. Oklahoma police chief Otto Reed had two potentially fatal wounds, one each from .45-caliber and .38-caliber weapons. Agents Lackey and Vetterli were struck by .45-caliber rounds but survived. None of the .38-caliber pistols carried by officers at Union Station were tested against the bullet removed from Chief Reed.

FBI agents traced telephone calls from Frank Nash's wife to Vernon Miller, a sheriff-turned-outlaw who lived in Kansas City with girlfriend Vivian Mathias. Miller was gone when agents raided his home, but FINGER-PRINTS confirmed his presence in the house. Other prints from the dwelling failed to match a list of notorious felons including Bailey, Brady, Underhill, Floyd, and Floyd sidekick Adam Richetti. G-men missed their chance to question Miller when his corpse was found outside Detroit, the product of a gangland torture-execution, on November 29, 1933.

Frustrated, agents arrested Vivian Mathias and held her incommunicado until she named the Union Station murderers as Miller, Floyd, and Richetti. Floyd suffered a shoulder wound, she said, thereby accounting for some bloody rags found at Miller's home. On February 13, 1934 G-men miraculously "found" another finger-print in Miller's basement, identified a month later as Adam Richetti's. Seven months elapsed before Richetti was captured in Ohio, on October 19. Three days later, Chicago agent MELVIN PURVIS led a party that cornered and killed Charles Floyd on a nearby farm.

FBI ballistics experts allegedly matched one of Floyd's .45 automatics to a single shell casing found at Union Station, but his autopsy raised more problems. Specifically, Floyd had no shoulder wound as claimed by Vivian Mathias. Agents picked up Mathias again and obtained a new statement, wherein she "remembered" that the bloody rags had nothing to do with Floyd, after all. Otherwise, she swore, Floyd's wound "was the only part I wasn't telling the truth about in the first statement."

Federal attorneys refused to file charges on such flimsy proof, and Kansas City prosecutor Michael O'Hearn was likewise "inclined to doubt the fact that there is sufficient evidence to convict Richetti," but his superiors disagreed. Richetti was indicted on one murder count, for killing Officer Hermanson—who was actually shot by Agent Lackey. His trial began on June 13, 1935.

The case against Richetti had the earmarks of a classic FRAME-UP. No evidence placed him at the murder scene, but FBI witnesses took up the slack. Reed Vetterli told Bureau headquarters in June 1933, "I am convinced that the man who first opened fire from our right, with a machine gun, is Bob Brady." At trial, he identified the gunman from mug shots as Pretty Boy Floyd. In 1933 Frank Smith reported seeing one machine-gunner and stated unequivocally that he "was unable to obtain any kind of description of him and was unable to see anyone else who did the shooting." Two years later, Smith named the faceless shooter as Verne Miller. Finally, Francis Lackey reported in 1933 that "there were at least four and possibly more men shooting," although he only glimpsed two and was "not sure that he could identify either of these men," seen only in a "hurried glance" and "through a none too clean window." At trial, Lackey not only named Richetti as a Union Station gunman, but falsely denied firing any shots himself.

The verdict was a forgone conclusion. Richetti was convicted of murder on June 17 and sentenced to hang. Progress spared him from the noose, but not from execution: On October 17, 1938, he became the first man to die in Missouri's new gas chamber. Author Robert Unger revealed the truth about Union Station in 1997, including an FBI agent's admission to federal judge William Becker: "Our agent sitting in the back seat pulled the trigger on Nash, and that started it. The machine gunners didn't shoot first. Our guy panicked."

See also: FEDERAL BUREAU OF INVESTIGATION.

Kansas City Police Department

Official law enforcement in Kansas City, Missouri, dates from 1870, when state militia veteran and ex-alderman Thomas Speers was elected town marshal. A friend of such famous frontier lawmen as Wyatt Earp, Bat Masterson, and "Wild Bill" Hickok, Speers managed the wide-open cow town with "nerve and good judgment" sufficient to "command the respect of the rough bordermen and criminals alike." Passage of the city's Metropolitan Police Law created a three-member board of police commissioners in April 1874, whereupon Speers was named chief of police.

He maintained that post for 21 years, demanding proactive police work in an age when most agencies simply reacted to ongoing crimes. Under Speers, "known criminals" were jailed upon arrival in Kansas City, held for display to all officers, then released with a warning against misbehavior. Speers also maintained a rogue's gallery of mug shots and pioneered KCPD's adoption of the BERTILLON SYSTEM for criminal identification. His file of mug shots contained 1,000 photos when Speers was fired in May 1895, for exposing the CORRUPTION of a local judge closely linked to Governor William Stone.

Despite Speers's best efforts, politics and graft inevitably tainted the KCPD. By the advent of PROHIBITION in 1920, Kansas City was known as "Tom's Town," in honor of political boss Tom Pendergast, who collaborated with gangster John Lazia to operate a free-wheeling empire of vice and illegal liquor. "Tom's Town" was a haven for fugitives with cash to spend, on a par with the gangland sanctuaries of Hot Springs, Arkansas, and St. Paul, Minnesota. The KANSAS CITY MASSACRE of 1933 turned unwelcome light on local corruption, but little changed for the better until the televised Kefauver crime hearings of 1950–51.

Police professionalism generally improved under Chief CLARENCE MARION KELLEY (1961–73), although Kelley's history of service as an FBI agent also ensured that KCPD would collaborate with G-men on the Bureau's illegal COINTELPRO campaigns against black militants and leftists. Kelley, in turn, left Kansas City to serve as the FBI's director during 1973–78. Problems continue to the present day, as with any big-city police department. Allegations of RACISM persist despite thorough integration of KCPD, and corruption remains a critical issue in a city well known for its ORGANIZED CRIME "families." On October 7, 2004, a former KCPD sergeant, Robert Maize, pled guilty in federal court, on charges of swindling $30,000 from the U.S. government, for security services he never performed at housing projects run by the Department of Housing and Urban Development.

See also: FEDERAL BUREAU OF INVESTIGATION.

Kansas Highway Patrol

Acting in response to a wave of bank robberies in 1930–33, Kansas governor Alf Landon joined state legislators and the Highway Department attorney Wint Smith to create a force of 10 "motor vehicle inspectors" in 1933. The legislature formally organized the Kansas Highway Patrol four years later, with personnel including a superintendent, assistant superintendent, and 45 troopers assigned primarily to traffic enforcement. Imposition of Civil Service guidelines standardized recruitment in 1941, but political affiliation still counted as late as 1945, when half of all KHP appointees were members of the reigning governor's party, the other half selected from the party that placed second in the most recent gubernatorial race.

The KHP held its first formal training session in May 1938, transferred to Salina's deactivated Schilling Air Force Base in the 1960s. Political recruiting was abandoned after World War II, while a new Protective Services division was launched in the 1950s, providing a single officer to guard the governor. That mission expanded in 1976, with creation of Troop K—the

Capitol Area Security Patrol—assigned to safeguard the state legislature. Female troopers joined the KHP for the first time in 1981.

See also: BANK ROBBERY.

Katzenbach, Nicholas de Belleville (b. 1922)

Philadelphia native Nicholas Katzenbach was born on January 17, 1922. After service with the Army Air Corps in World War II, he earned a B.A. cum laude from Princeton University (1945) and an LL.D. cum laude from Yale University Law School (1947). Katzenbach was a Rhodes scholar at Oxford (1947–49) before gaining admission to the New Jersey bar in 1950. He subsequently served as attorney-adviser to the Air Force Office of General Counsel (1950–52), as an associate law professor at Yale (1952–56), and as a law professor at the University of Chicago (1956–60). His service with the U.S. JUSTICE DEPARTMENT included terms as assistant attorney general in the Office of Legal Counsel (1961–62) and as deputy attorney general (1962–65). President Lyndon Johnson named Katzenbach attorney general on February 11, 1965.

Attorney General Nicholas Katzenbach (Library of Congress)

Even before his appointment as attorney general, Katzenbach clashed repeatedly with FBI director J. EDGAR HOOVER. On March 30, 1964, Katzenbach issued an order restricting FBI BUGGING, requiring specific approval from Justice for each installation of electronic listening devices. Hoover retaliated by leaking derogatory information on Katzenbach to the press and blaming the attorney general's office for years of illegal DOMESTIC SURVEILLANCE conducted by G-men. Katzenbach later told the CHURCH COMMITTEE that Hoover routinely lied to his superiors in periodic briefings and implied that FBI forgers had signed his name to three memos authorizing bugs installed in motel rooms occupied by civil rights leader Martin Luther King, Jr. Finally, Katzenbach told Senate investigators, "My correspondence with Mr. Hoover . . . unavoidably became a bitter one and it persuaded me that I could no longer effectively serve as Attorney General because of Mr. Hoover's obvious resentment of me."

Katzenbach resigned on October 2, 1966, moving on to a post as under secretary of state (1966–69). He served as a New Jersey presidential elector in 1996 and remains an active member of the Council on Foreign Relations.

See also: FEDERAL BUREAU OF INVESTIGATION.

Kefauver, Carey Estes (1903–1963)

Born near Madisonville, Tennessee, on July 26, 1903, Estes Kefauver served five terms in the House of Representatives (1936–49) before he was elected to the U.S. Senate in 1948. Two years later, he made headlines as chairman of the Senate Special Committee to Investigate Organized Crime in Interstate Commerce. The investigation placed Kefauver at odds with FBI director J. EDGAR HOOVER (who described reports of the Mafia as "baloney") and with Attorney General J. HOWARD McGRATH (who publicly denied the existence of a "national crime syndicate").

Kefauver proved both men wrong with a series of nationwide televised hearings that focused chiefly on illegal gambling and the CORRUPTION it spawned. Obstructed by the FBI at every turn, Kefauver turned to Hoover rival HARRY J. ANSLINGER and his FEDERAL BUREAU OF NARCOTICS for support, calling more than 800 witnesses whose ranks included mobsters, politicians, and law enforcement officers. Americans were captivated by their first glimpse of gangsters such as Meyer Lansky, Frank Costello, Moe Dalitz, and Mickey Cohen, but the drama had a down side. After two key witnesses were murdered, Kefauver sought FBI aid once again, but Hoover remained intractable, advising Kefauver: "I regret to advise the Federal Bureau of Investigation is not empowered to perform guard duties."

Kefauver resigned his chairmanship of the crime committee in May 1951, and while he offered various explanations for the move, he failed to mention the recent arrest of a friend and campaign contributor, Nashville gambling boss Herbert Brody. Hoover's G-men collected rumors of a $5,000 bribe from Brody to Kefauver, along with other skeleton's in the senator's closet. (Merle Miller, in his biography of President Lyndon Johnson, called Kefauver "a boozer, a womanizer, and an eager accepter of bribes from any source.")

Despite the potential embarrassment, however, Kefauver still harbored presidential ambitions. He entered the Democratic field in 1952 and 1956, selected in the latter year as Adlai Stevenson's running mate. Hoover promptly furnished Vice President Richard Nixon with Kefauver's FBI file, plus unsubstantiated rumors of Stevenson's homosexuality. Kefauver never occupied the White House, but he remained in the Senate until an aortic aneurysm claimed his life on August 10, 1963. When his safe deposit box was subsequently opened, it revealed $300,000 in stock from various drug companies Kefauver was supposed to regulate.

See also: ORGANIZED CRIME.

Kelley, Clarence Marion (1911–1997)

A Missouri native, born October 24, 1911, Clarence Kelley graduated from the University of Kansas at Lawrence in 1936, then earned his LL.B. from the University of Kansas City School of Law four years later. He joined the FBI in October 1940 and served in various field offices before joining the U.S. Navy (1944–46). Kelley resumed his service with the Bureau in 1946, heading field offices in Kansas City, Birmingham, and Memphis before he retired to serve as chief of the KANSAS CITY POLICE DEPARTMENT in 1963.

Following the death of FBI director J. EDGAR HOOVER and Acting Director L. PATRICK GRAY's resignation in disgrace over the Watergate scandal, President Richard Nixon named Kelley to lead the Bureau in June 1973. Assistant Director Oliver Revell later told author Robert Kessler that Nixon chose Kelley in the belief he would be "malleable," but Kelley "was entirely different from that. He was very amiable, but also very straight. He brought with him the concept of reorganizing the Bureau that today is largely responsible for what we are doing and how we are doing it."

Kelley's innovations included expanding UNDERCOVER WORK, instituting a standard of "quality over quantity" for FBI investigations, and allowing female employees to wear pant suits instead of dresses. Publicly, he condemned Hoover's illegal COINTELPRO campaigns as "clearly wrong and quite indefensible," yet Kelley's own agents pursued an identical course of action against the "New Left," the American Indian Movement (AIM), Puerto Rican nationalists, and other dissident groups. The FBI's case against AIM leaders active in the Wounded Knee siege of 1973 was thrown out of court by Judge Fred Nichol, who detailed the Bureau's illicit tactics and lamented that "the FBI I have revered so long has stooped so low."

Kelley also continued Hoover's illegal practice of using FBI agents and technicians to maintain his home free of charge, a foible that prompted Special Counsel John Dowd to urge Kelley's dismissal in January 1978. A JUSTICE DEPARTMENT report on the scandal claimed that Kelley was "initially unaware" of work performed at his home, but the embarrassment proved too much and Kelley resigned in February 1978. He returned to Kansas City, where he ran a private security firm for several years. Kelley died on August 5, 1997.

See also: FEDERAL BUREAU OF INVESTIGATION.

Kendall, Amos (1789–1869)

A descendant of 17th-century British colonists, Amos Kendall was born in Massachusetts on August 16, 1789. He worked his father's farm to age 16, then entered Dartmouth College with a year's preparation and graduated at the top of his class in 1811. He subsequently studied law and was admitted to Kentucky's bar in 1814. There, he served as Georgetown's postmaster and edited a local newspaper, moving on in 1816 to edit the *Argus of Western America* in Frankfort, Kentucky.

An ardent Democrat, Kendall supported presidential hopeful Andrew Jackson in 1824 and 1828. Successful in his second race for the White House, Jackson rewarded Kendall with appointment as fourth auditor of the U.S. TREASURY DEPARTMENT, then with appointment as Postmaster General in May 1835. Kendall held that post for the remainder of Jackson's presidency (1835–37) and continued under successor Martin Van Buren until May 19, 1840. Some observers suggested that Kendall played a much larger role in Jackson's administration. The Washington *Globe* described him as "one of the most remarkable men in America. He is supposed to be the moving spring of the administration; the thinker, planner, and doer; but it is all in the dark."

Kendall established the federal government's first law enforcement agency, embodied in an Office of Inspection to police the U.S. mail. He also raised a storm of controversy in 1835 by refusing to punish a South Carolina postmaster who let pro-slavery advocates destroy copies of a northern newspaper supporting abolition. A year later, Kendall proposed legislation banning aboli-

Attorney General Amos Kendall (Author's collection)

tionist material from the mail entirely, but his measure was defeated.

After his retirement from the cabinet, Kendall published two short-lived newspapers, *Kendall's Expositor* (1841) and the *Union Democrat* (1842). He also served as a collection agent for claims against the U.S. government (1843) and declined President James Polk's offer of a foreign mission. In 1845 Kendall became associated with Samuel F. B. Morse, as co-owner of Morse's telegraph patents, and prospered greatly from that enterprise. He died in Washington, D.C., on November 12, 1869.

Kennedy, Robert Francis (1925–1968)

Born in Boston on November 20, 1925, a child of vast wealth and political influence, Robert Kennedy served in the U.S. Naval Reserve (1944–46) before earning his B.A. degree from Harvard in 1948. After a short stint as correspondent for the *Boston Post,* he studied law at the University of Virginia and was admitted to the Massachusetts bar in 1951. Kennedy joined the U.S. JUSTICE DEPARTMENT's Criminal Division that same year, later serving as counsel to the Senate Permanent

Subcommittee on Investigations (1953–57) and chief counsel to the Senate Select Committee on Improper Activities in the Labor or Management Field (1957–59). That experience sparked a lifelong crusade against ORGANIZED CRIME, with particular emphasis (some said obsession) on prosecuting Teamsters' Union president James Hoffa.

Kennedy managed his brother John's successful presidential campaign in 1960 and was rewarded in January 1961 with appointment as U.S. attorney general. He clashed immediately with FBI director J. EDGAR HOOVER over civil rights, integration of the Bureau, and investigation of national crime syndicates (which Hoover dismissed as "baloney"). Ironically, while pursuing top mobsters with unrivaled zeal (including frequent use of illegal BUGGING and WIRETAPS), Kennedy also forged a secret alliance with Mafia leaders in a fruitless campaign to murder Cuban dictator Fidel Castro. Hoover kept track of Kennedy's foibles, including various romantic liaisons, and waged a bureaucratic war of nerves with the Kennedy White House until President Kennedy was assassinated on November 22, 1963. Thereafter,

Attorney General Robert Kennedy (Library of Congress)

the FBI director treated Robert Kennedy with absolute disdain, ignoring his directives and consulting directly with President Lyndon Johnson.

Johnson, in turn, had his own personal and political axes to grind with Robert Kennedy. Their mutual contempt prompted Kennedy's dismissal on September 3, 1964, and propelled him into a New York senatorial campaign. Kennedy won election to the U.S. Senate in 1964, using his office as a launching pad to run for president in 1968. While Kennedy's public campaign focused on opposition to the Vietnam War, few doubted that his election would launch a new national drive against organized crime. Some insiders also claimed that Kennedy hoped to identify conspirators responsible for his brother's murder in Dallas. Those hopes were dashed on the night of June 5, 1968, when Kennedy was shot and fatally wounded in Los Angeles, moments after winning the California presidential primary. As in his brother's death, conspiracy theories surround the RFK assassination to this day.

Kent State University shootings

In May 1970 revelation of President Richard Nixon's covert military action in Cambodia sparked demonstrations on college campuses across America. Students at Ohio's Kent State University rioted on May 1 and burned the campus ROTC building on May 2, prompting Governor James Rhodes to mobilize the NATIONAL GUARD. Another demonstration was in progress on May 4, when Guardsmen opened fire with rifles and at least one pistol, killing four unarmed students and wounding nine more.

Nixon described himself as "deeply saddened" by the deaths at Kent State and others in a similar shooting at Mississippi's Jackson State College. FBI agents were assigned to investigate the Ohio shooting, while Nixon appointed a President's Commission on Campus Unrest (better known by the name of its chairman, former Pennsylvania governor William Scranton) to do likewise. G-men submitted 8,000 pages of testimony to the Scranton Commission, while Director J. EDGAR HOOVER complained that the investigation cost $274,100 in overtime pay. (Staff members at Kent State told their congressmen that agents spent much of that time examining classroom lesson plans and probing the political beliefs of various professors.) Long before the investigation was finished, Hoover told White House aide Egil Krogh that "the students invited and got what they deserved."

In fact, Hoover's own agents documented an 11-second burst of undisciplined and indiscriminate gunfire, including at least 54 (and perhaps 60) shots fired by 29 of the 78 Guardsmen present. None of the four

students killed had been demonstrators; they were shot at ranges between 85 and 139 yards from the Guardsmen, two with their backs turned and one while lying prone on the ground. Of the nine students wounded, only one appeared to be a demonstrator, shot while making "an obscene gesture" to the Guardsmen from 20 yards away; the rest were shot at distances of 37 to 250 yards. A JUSTICE DEPARTMENT summary of FBI reports likewise dismissed claims that the Guardsmen believed themselves to be under sniper fire.

At the time of the shootings, the National Guard clearly did not believe they were being fired upon. No Guardsman claims he fell to the ground or took any other evasive action and all available photographs show the Guard at the critical moments in a standing position and not seeking cover. In addition, no Guardsman claims he fired at a sniper or even that he fired in the direction from which he believed the sniper shot. Finally, there is no evidence of the use of any weapons at any time in the weekend prior to the May 4 demonstration.

Furthermore, six Guardsmen (including a captain and two sergeants) also "stated pointedly that the lives of the members of the Guard were not in danger and that it was not a shooting situation." As for the 11 Guardsmen who later expressed mortal fear, the Scranton Report concluded: "We have some reason to believe that the claim by the National Guard that they thought their lives were endangered by the students was fabricated subsequent to the event." A report in the Akron *Beacon Journal* (May 24, 1970) corroborated that claim with a quote from one of the Guardsmen: "The guys have been saying that we got to get together and stick to the same story, that it was our lives or them, a matter of survival. I told them I would tell the truth and couldn't get in trouble that way."

Reactions from Washington were predictably hostile. Vice President Spiro Agnew called the Scranton Report "pabulum for permissivists," while the commander of Ohio's National Guard deemed the FBI's findings "just unbelievable." Even Hoover did not seem to trust his own agents, writing to the *Beacon Journal:* "I can assure you that any comments you may have seen in the news media to the effect that the FBI drew conclusions indicating guilt on the part of National Guardsmen . . . are absolutely and unequivocally false." A local grand jury refused to indict any Guardsmen, instead condemning student "agitators" and professors who encouraged an "overemphasis on dissent." The panel's report found that Guardsmen "fired their weapons in the honest and sincere belief . . . they would suffer serious bodily injury had they not done so."

See also: JACKSON STATE COLLEGE SHOOTINGS.

Kentucky State Police

State legislators created the Kentucky Highway Patrol in 1936, with 40 sworn officers. The force increased to 200 patrolmen by early 1948, when Governor Earl Clements requested creation of a new state police agency to augment law enforcement by county and municipal police. The legislature complied in July 1948, whereupon the Kentucky State Police absorbed men and equipment of its defunct predecessor. A three-week training course was soon established, and the KSP gained its first piece of scientific equipment: a comparison microscope purchased for $1,200.

In the 1950s a merit system was established for the KSP, theoretically safeguarding troopers from political pressure, and "incognito squads" were organized to roam state highways in unmarked cars. A decade later, radar joined the KSP arsenal, and the first black trooper was hired. The 1970s witnessed creation of a drug enforcement unit, employment of the first female trooper, and establishment of LINK—the Law Information Network of Kentucky, marshaling uniform crime information. The 1980s brought Operation Green/Gray Sweep, a large-scale marijuana eradication campaign collaborating with the NATIONAL GUARD, while a new Drug Enforcement/Special Investigations branch merged major crime investigations under a single command. By the dawn of the new millennium, video cameras were installed in all marked patrol cars, a state-of-the art Centralized Laboratory was established, and Operation Green/Gray Sweep evolved into a grander (yet still, largely futile) Governor's Marijuana Strike Task Force.

See also: DRUGS.

Kerner Commission

The National Advisory Commission on Civil Disorders—commonly known by the name of its chairman, Illinois governor Otto Kerner, Jr.—was created by President Lyndon Johnson to investigate the causes of widespread U.S. ghetto riots during 1967's "long hot summer." While FBI director J. EDGAR HOOVER tried to persuade the commission that a communist conspiracy lay behind the riots, Kerner and company disagreed. The commission's report, published in early 1968, was pessimistic in tone, blaming poverty, RACISM, and police applications of EXCESSIVE FORCE for most of the outbreaks. Hoover, for his part, replied that the "communist policy to charge and protest 'police brutality' . . . in racial situations" was part of an "immensely successful" and "continuing smear campaign" against law enforcement. "The net effect," Hoover concluded, "is to provoke and encourage mob action and violence by developing contempt for constituted authority."

Governor Kerner left office in 1968, after another season of ghetto riots appeared to validate his commission's findings. In 1973 he received a federal prison term upon conviction for his role in a racetrack bribery scandal.

Kersta, Lawrence George (b. 1907)

New Jersey native Lawrence Kersta, born December 22, 1907, studied electrical engineering and physics at New York's Columbia University. In 1962–63, while employed by Bell Laboratories, he began experiments with a sound spectrograph invented by Bell technicians in 1944. That study convinced Kersta that spectrographic tracings of human voices—which he dubbed "voiceprints"—could match known subjects to recordings of unknown persons, as with anonymous telephone calls. Excited by the potential applications of his discovery, Kersta left Bell in 1966, patented the term *voiceprint*, and founded his own International Association of Voice Identification (IAVI). His colleagues included Ernest Nash (who helped create the MICHIGAN STATE POLICE crime lab) and Oscar Tosi (a founder of the Michigan State University FORENSIC SCIENCE program).

For the best part of a decade, Kersta, Nash, and Tosi dominated voiceprint technology in the United States, testifying as expert witnesses in many criminal cases. With some 50,000 individual voice samples on file, IAVI claimed 99.6 percent accuracy in matching anonymous recordings to known subjects. Kersta's technology and methods were adopted by the FBI, and are today employed by law enforcement agencies around the world. In 1980 the IAVI was absorbed by the International Association of Identification, previously concerned for the most part with FINGERPRINTS.

kidnapping

America's first "official" ransom kidnapping was the Philadelphia abduction of young Charles Ross in July 1874. Ross was never found, although a burglar in New York made a deathbed confession to the kidnapping five months later. Hundreds of similar cases were reported over the next 57 years, but kidnapping remained a strictly local crime. FBI agents investigated only those cases where victims were kidnapped on government land, as in national parks or on Indian reservations.

Concerted demands for a federal anti-kidnapping statute began in 1931. The prior decade had witnessed 279 reported abductions in 28 states, including five high-profile murders of children and nine successful ransom kidnappings of wealthy businessmen. The final impetus came from New Jersey, where Charles

Lindbergh, Jr. was kidnapped on March 1, 1932. The infant's corpse was found on May 11, followed one month later by passage of the Lindbergh Law, granting the FBI jurisdiction in cases of interstate kidnapping. (A "presumption" of interstate flight allows FBI intervention after seven days.) Congress subsequently amended the Lindbergh Law to authorize CAPITAL PUNISHMENT for kidnappers whose victims suffered "harm," automatically waived if the offenders pled guilty. That amendment was ruled unconstitutional in 1967, on grounds that "harm" was undefined and that the provision extorted confessions in violation of the Fifth Amendment. No U.S. jurisdiction presently imposes the death penalty for kidnapping, unless the abduction victim is murdered.

King, Rodney (b. 1965)

An African American, born in Sacramento, California, on April 2, 1965, "Rodney" Glen King had a long history of criminal behavior behind him when he engaged in a high-speed vehicle chase with officers of the LOS ANGELES POLICE DEPARTMENT on March 3, 1991. Subsequent blood tests confirmed that King was legally drunk and had recently smoked marijuana, but claims that he had also ingested the drug PCP proved false. So, too, was the "Rodney" appended to his name for the first time in erroneous 1991 police reports.

After a protracted chase, King stopped his car and stepped out of the vehicle, allegedly approaching officers with "threatening" gestures and incoherent speech. Two applications of 50,000 volts from a Taser stungun failed to drop him, whereupon officers kicked and struck him a total of 56 times with batons before taking King into custody. (Two companions in his vehicle were unharmed.) Unknown to the 27 officers present during the beating, a civilian neighbor captured the incident on videotape and sold it to various television networks, which in turn broadcast the disturbing footage worldwide.

On March 15, 1991, a local grand jury indicted one LAPD sergeant and three officers for "assault by force likely to produce great bodily injury" and assault "under color of authority"; two officers were also charged with filing false reports on the incident. Defense attorneys secured a change of venue to suburban Simi Valley, a mostly white district where many police officers reside. Three defendants were acquitted on April 29, 1992, while the jury deadlocked on one count against a single officer. That outcome shocked most of America, including President George H. W.

Bush, who declared that the verdict "has left us all with a deep sense of personal frustration and anguish." Wholesale rioting erupted in the Los Angeles ghetto, leaving 26 persons dead, 2,328 injured, and some $900 million in property damage by May 4. City police were widely criticized for their "hands-off" behavior during the riot, suggesting deliberate negligence while black neighborhoods burned.

In the wake of that riot, federal prosecutors filed civil rights charges against the officers already acquitted in state court. Two were acquitted in July 1993, while Sergeant Stacy Koon and Officer Laurence Powell were found guilty as charged, receiving 30-month prison terms on August 4. Critics of the federal prosecution note that King has been arrested several times since 1991 for traffic violations, drug offenses, and crimes of violence.

Kipley, Joseph

Joseph Kipley personified the partisan style of law enforcement that once dominated the CHICAGO POLICE DEPARTMENT. A die-hard Democrat who spent nearly 20 years on the force, Kipley occupied most of the department's top posts at one time or another, including command of the Harrison Street Precinct that produced six chiefs between 1875 and 1907. Unswerving loyalty to Mayor Carter Harrison, Jr. won Kipley his appointment as chief in 1897, and he wasted no time in purging the force of Republicans. The sweep began with General Order No. 14, dismissing 158 officers loyal to the GOP, and continued with General Order No. 32, firing all cops hired between May 1895 and April 1897 (under Republican mayor George Swift and Chief John Badenoch).

That style of police work left Kipley vulnerable to shady deals and bad companions. After banker Edward Dreyer tapped $12,000 from the Policeman's Benevolent Association, Kipley sought to recover the money with a book on the CPD's history, sold by subscription to prominent merchants and philanthropists. The scheme worked well enough to justify a sequel, but Kipley ran into trouble the second time around, when two of his colleagues—Patrolman Walter Magnus and con man Amos Atwell—skipped town with 30 percent of the money and no book to show for it. Under grilling by state legislators, Kipley pled ignorance, describing Atwell as "a successful individual" who managed to dupe him.

Backroom politics finally doomed Kipley's tenure as chief. In 1900, for reasons still unclear, Mayor Harrison urged Kipley to break with his longtime friend Bobby Burke, then secretary of the Democratic County Committee, later a city oil inspector. Stung by the snubs, Burke responded in early 1901 by nominating Chief of Detectives Luke Colleran to fill Kipley's post. The needless feud divided Democratic cops so bitterly that Harrison finally demanded Kipley's resignation. The chief left with no pension, replaced by John Collins.

Kleindienst, Richard Gordon (1923–2000)

A native of Winslow, Arizona, born August 5, 1923, Richard Kleindienst served in the U.S. Air Force (1943–46), received his B.A. from Harvard University in 1947, and graduated from Harvard Law School three years later. He served two years in the Arizona state legislature (1953–54), and subsequently was a member of the Republican National Committee (1956–60, 1962–63). Eleven years of private law practice (1958–69) were briefly interrupted by an unsuccessful gubernatorial race in 1964. President Richard Nixon named Kleindienst deputy attorney general on January 31, 1969, and promoted him to the JUSTICE DEPARTMENT's top office in June 1972, after Attorney General JOHN NEWTON MITCHELL left to manage Nixon's reelection campaign.

The Watergate conspiracy ultimately snared both Kleindienst and his predecessor (who served prison time). Kleindienst chose L. PATRICK GRAY as FBI director to replace the late J. EDGAR HOOVER, but that move only worsened the scandals enveloping Justice. Kleindienst resigned on May 24, 1973, and was subsequently indicted for perjury over his testimony in the Watergate hearings. In 1974 he pled guilty on a reduced charge of "failure to testify fully" concerning Nixon's corrupt relationship with International Telephone and Telegraph (ITT). His prison sentence was suspended, but prosecutors filed new perjury charges in 1981. Kleindienst was acquitted in that case, but his license to practice law was suspended for one year. He died of lung cancer at Prescott, Arizona, on February 3, 2000.

Knapp Commission

Scandals involving CORRUPTION have rocked the NEW YORK CITY POLICE DEPARTMENT at regular intervals since the LEXOW COMMITTEE published its report on rampant bribery in 1894. In 1970 detective FRANK SERPICO blew the whistle on payoffs related to DRUGS, thus inspiring creation of the Knapp Commission (named for chairman Whitman Knapp, a prominent lawyer

and future federal judge. As with past investigations, Knapp obtained detailed testimony from various corrupt policemen, implicating others in their crimes. Jay Kriegel, a close adviser to Mayor John Lindsey, narrowly escaped indictment on a perjury charge, after denying any knowledge of police payoffs. Serpico and partner DAVID DURK revealed that they had briefed Kriegel on the problem in 1967, but Kriegel failed to act, informing them that "he didn't want to upset the police."

While Knapp produced a short-term shakeup at NYPD headquarters, it failed—as demonstrated by renewed investigations in the 1990s—to root out the problem of institutionalized corruption. The commission's chief contribution, finally, was an analysis of corrupt police that divided the subculture into distinct groups.: "grass eaters" and "meat eaters." In NYPD parlance, *grass eaters* are those officers who accept whatever bribes may come their way during the course of normal operations. *Meat eaters,* by contrast, aggressively abuse their powers in pursuit of huge profits, robbing drug dealers and other criminals, extorting payoffs from felons, even serving on occasion as contract killers for hire. The pattern revealed in New York has been duplicated in other departments across the country, notably including the CHICAGO POLICE DEPARTMENT and the LOS ANGELES POLICE DEPARTMENT.

K-9 Units

K-9 Units are those that employ specially trained dogs for some aspect of police work, named with a military-style variation of the adjective "canine." British constables patrolled their beats with dogs as early as the 15th century, though the animals were drafted more for company than any special skills. Tracking dogs, typically bloodhounds, were widely used for pursuit of fugitives and missing persons by their scent during the 19th century, when many rural prisons and a few police departments kept dogs for manhunting. Specific training of attack dogs to apprehend and subdue violent subjects is a more recent development, corresponding with military use of dogs in the two world wars. Today dogs of various breeds are also trained to sniff out specific contraband items, including DRUGS and explosives.

Police dogs are a valuable addition to the modern law enforcement arsenal, but they also come with psychological baggage in tow. Televised images from the 1960s, of racist southern police unleashing attack dogs on black children and peaceable civil rights protesters,

A San Jose police dog named Dino, who is a Belgium Malinois, checks baggage from an American West flight with San Jose police officer Kevin Metcalf on a moving carousel at an airport in San Jose, California, Thursday, July 7, 2005. (Paul Sakuma/Associated Press)

still resonate in many African American communities when K-9 Units are employed. Their value may thus be outweighed, in some cases, by a potential for inflaming already-tense situations. Overall, officers assigned to K-9 Units typically report close bonding with their four-legged partners, often deeply mourning their loss when a police dog is killed in the line of duty. Internet memorials have been established for fallen "K-9s," as for law enforcement officers slain in pursuance of their duty.

Knox, Philander Chase (1853–1921)

Born in Brownsville, Pennsylvania, on May 6, 1853, Philander Knox graduated from Ohio's Mount Union College in 1872. He studied law privately in Pittsburgh and was admitted to the Pennsylvania bar in 1875. President William McKinley named him attorney general on April 5, 1901 and Knox continued in that role under President THEODORE ROOSEVELT, following McKinley's ASSASSINATION, until June 30, 1904. Pennsylvania's governor appointed Knox to fill the U.S. Senate seat vacated by M. S. Quay's death on July 1, 1904, and Knox won election to the Senate in his own right six months later. He resigned from the Senate in 1909 to serve as secretary of state under President William Taft (1909–13), where he drafted legislation creating the Commerce and Labor Departments. Knox died in Washington, D.C., on October 12, 1921.

Koehler, Arthur (1885–1967)

Born in 1885, Arthur Koehler translated a fascination with wood into a career as head of the U.S. Agriculture Department's Forest Service Laboratory in Madison, Wisconsin. During the late 1920s and 1930s, police frequently sought Koehler's expert opinion on wooden bits of evidence from various criminal cases. During 1932–34 Koehler applied himself single-mindedly to the Lindbergh KIDNAPPING case, and thereby helped to perpetrate a great injustice.

Soon after the ransom kidnapping of Charles Lindbergh, Jr., on March 1, 1932, police found a crude homemade ladder and a 3/4-inch chisel outside the Lindbergh home. NORMAN SCHWARZKOPF, SR. commander of the NEW JERSEY STATE POLICE, submitted the ladder to Koehler for study, whereupon Koehler identified its various mismatched woods and launched an epic search for their point of origin. Before he finished, Koehler sent inquiries to 1,598 lumber mills and visited 30 East Coast lumber yards, later claiming that yellow pine cut at the same South Carolina mill that produced one rung of the kidnap ladder had been sent to a New York lumberyard where suspect Bruno Hauptmann

Attorney General Philander Knox (Author's collection)

purchased wood. Granted, Koehler could never prove that Hauptmann bought the planks in question, but that was the least of his failings.

In his original findings, Koehler claimed that no tests could determine the size of chisel used to make the kidnap ladder. An FBI report from May 1932 agreed, stating more specifically that "no conclusion that the chisel [found at Lindberg's home] was used in building the ladder is warranted." Two years later, at Hauptmann's murder trial, Koehler reversed himself, claiming that tool marks on the ladder had been made by a 3/4-inch chisel. Under prosecution coaching, he also claimed that Hauptmann's tool kit contained no 3/4-inch chisel—thus implying that Hauptmann had dropped his outside Lindbergh's house. In fact, however, a suppressed police report uncovered decades later by author Anthony Scaduto reveals that *two* 3/4-inch chisels were found in Hauptmann's garage (and later concealed from the jury).

In respect to the ladder itself, Koehler claimed that one rung was made from wood previously used as attic flooring. Police searched Hauptmann's attic nine times between September 19 and 25, 1934, but found no evidence of missing floorboards. New Jersey state trooper Lewis Bornmann searched the attic twice more on September 26. After his first search, he noted that "nothing of value was found." During a second search that afternoon, however, Bornmann claimed to notice for the first time that a plank of yellow pine was missing from the floor. Koehler arrived on October 10—after Bornmann rented the apartment and barred defense attorneys from the premises—to examine the flooring with Bornmann. Together, they decided that nail holes in the small ladder rung "exactly matched" those in the other floorboards—but they kept the secret to themselves. On December 8, 1934, Koehler "emphatically denied" that any wood from the ladder had been traced to Hauptmann's home. "There is absolutely no truth in the matter at all," he told reporters.

Koehler sang a different tune at Hauptmann's trial, persuading jurors that Hauptmann had torn one plank from his attic, for reasons unknown, ignoring his stockpile of scrap wood, to furnish one rung of the kidnap ladder. That "evidence" and other perjured testimony sent Hauptmann to the electric chair, but FBI agents were not so easily deceived. Their classified report of May 26, 1936, kept secret long after Hauptmann's execution, read in part:

The identification of the wood in the ladder, resulting in the opinion that the wood in the attic of Hauptmann's residence was identical to that of the ladder, was developed subsequent to the withdrawal of the Bureau from an active part in the investigation, and occurred after the New Jersey State Police had rented the Hauptmann residence.

You will also recall that at one stage in the trial of Hauptmann it was indicated that efforts would be made by the defense counsel to subpoena records of this department relative to Arthur Koehler, with the thought in mind that the defense could establish and check that Arthur Koehler's story concerning the wood identification could be proved as having been fabricated by the joint efforts of the New Jersey State Police and the New Jersey Prosecutor's Office in co-operation with Arthur Koehler. However this request was not received by the Bureau from the defense attorneys.

Koehler spent the rest of his life writing and lecturing about his pivotal role in the Lindbergh case. He died in 1967.

See also: FEDERAL BUREAU OF INVESTIGATION.

Kohler, Frederick (1864–1934)

Cleveland native Fred Kohler was born on May 2, 1864. He joined the CLEVELAND POLICE DEPARTMENT as a young man, quickly earning the reputation of an officer who was tough but fair. He also managed to avoid CORRUPTION during his rise through the ranks, prompting reform mayor Thomas Johnson to name him police chief in 1903. Kohler held that post for a decade, during which time he angered some policemen and conservative politicians by releasing certain nonviolent offenders with warnings. Nicknamed "Golden Rule" Kohler for his practical application of merciful Scripture, he could none the less be merciless on racketeers and his corrupt subordinates.

Critics had a field day with Kohler in 1912, upon discovering that he had plagiarized the text of a speech he presented to the INTERNATIONAL ASSOCIATION OF CHIEFS OF POLICE. Still, he hung on as chief for another year, until the revelation of an adulterous love affair prompted Mayor Newton Baker to demand Kohler's resignation. Despite that embarrassment, Kohler won election as Cleveland's mayor in 1921, completing a two-year term before he traded offices to serve as Cuyahoga County's sheriff. Kohler's worst embarrassment was posthumous. After his death on January 21, 1934, $500,000 in unexplained cash was found in his safe deposit box.

Krogman, Wilton Marion (1903–1978)

Born in 1903, Milton Krogman was a U.S. pioneer in the realm of forensic anthropology, reconstructing likenesses of unknown subjects from their skulls and other bones discovered by police across the country. Krogman operated from the University of Pennsylvania Medical School, where he also served as a professor of physical anthropology. While his techniques are now almost taken for granted, Krogman led the way in molding features onto cast-off skulls, determining the race and gender of unidentified corpses. In 1962 he coauthored *The Human Skeleton in Forensic Medicine,* with M. Yasar Iscan. Krogman died in 1978.

Ku Klux Klan

A year after General Robert E. Lee's surrender at Appomattox, six Confederate veterans in Pulaski, Tennessee, organized a social club to pass the time. As former college men, they borrowed the Greek word for *circle* (*kuklos*) from a popular southern fraternity, Kuklos Adelphon, and called their group the Ku Klux Klan. From late-night drinking they progressed to playing cruel "jokes" on former slaves, soon recognizing that the KKK might have political uses in the unsettled South.

"Radical" Reconstruction, imposed by a Republican majority in Congress, frightened and infuriated most white southerners with its demands for black suffrage and treatment of ex-slaves as human beings with full rights of citizenship. In April 1867, racists from all parts of Dixie met in Nashville, Tennessee, to reorganize the KKK along military lines. Led by former slave trader and Confederate cavalry leader Nathan Forrest, the remodeled Klan was a combination vigilante group and terrorist organization, pledged to preserving the South as a "white man's country" under one-party Democratic rule. With members in 12 states —the former Confederacy plus Kentucky—the KKK launched a reign of terror that claimed thousands of lives and left thousands more injured, reversing America's first civil rights movement so effectively that Dixie was "redeemed" for white "home rule" by 1876.

In the process, Klansmen naturally clashed with U.S. troops and peace officers who opposed the KKK's brutal tactics. Victims of ASSASSINATION in the South included congressmen, state legislators, and lesser officials, along with any sheriffs, deputies, or constables who openly defied the Klan. At the same time, racist votes installed Klansmen as sheriffs in various southern counties, invariably followed by more bloodshed, TERRORISM, and unpunished LYNCHINGS. A congressional investigation, federal prosecutions, and selective imposition of martial law finally curbed most Klan units in 1873–74, but the hooded "knights" had already achieved most of their goals, and resurgent violence during the 1876 presidential election sealed the fate of southern blacks for the next 90 years.

William Simmons, a defrocked Presbyterian minister, revived the KKK in 1915. Despite appeals to Dixie's "glorious" history, the order grew slowly until 1920, when race riots combined with a postwar Red scare and renewed advertising efforts to create a recruiting explosion. Over the next five years, an estimated 4 million white Americans joined the KKK nationwide, with northern states like Colorado, Indiana, and Ohio boasting larger memberships than some parts of the South. Aside from blacks and Reds, the new Klan also hated Catholics, Jews, labor unions, and most immigrants. It supported PROHIBITION (at least publicly) and vowed to help local police suppress the crime wave of the Roaring Twenties, crushing bootleg gangs and "radicals" alike.

In such an atmosphere, it came as no surprise that thousands of American policemen joined the KKK. County sheriffs often paid their dues in hopes of gaining votes, while police chiefs from coast to coast swallowed the Klan's propaganda. From Los Angeles and Denver to Indianapolis, Dallas, Birmingham, and Atlanta, Klansmen commanded police departments and filled their ranks. Despite the Klan's "law-and-order" message, however, its members were prone to CORRUPTION and outbursts of sadistic violence. By 1926 a series of scandals caused thousands of members to flee the "Invisible Empire," while voters turned against Klan candidates and hooded terrorists faced criminal charges in several states. Conviction remained problematic, but media exposure of Klan violence and financial chicanery sapped the order's strength.

The 1930s found Klan membership reduced to an estimated 100,000 nationwide, but its reactionary message still appealed to many law enforcement officers. High-ranking members of the DETROIT POLICE DEPARTMENT joined a Klan offshoot, the Black Legion, to harass and murder union organizers. Tampa, Florida's, police chief and some of his officers faced trial for a series of floggings that left one victim dead in 1935. Elsewhere in Florida, a police-Klan alliance stripped citrus workers of their right to organize, while similar violence across the Deep South crushed the Southern Tenant Farmers' Union. In the 1940s Klan-allied governor Eugene Talmadge named a Klansman to head the GEORGIA BUREAU OF INVESTIGATION. Birmingham police commissioner EUGENE "BULL" CONNOR protected Klan terrorists so well that his city was soon nicknamed "Bombingham," with its largest black neighborhood dubbed "Dynamite Hill."

The U.S. SUPREME COURT's rulings against school segregation in 1954–55 launched a "Second Reconstruction" in Dixie, marked by lawsuits, sit-ins, protest marches, and reluctant federal intervention in support of black demands. Initially, most southern police leaders cast their lot with the "respectable" White Citizens' Councils, but moderation failed to stem the tide of racial progress, driving some die-hard lawmen back to the Invisible Empire. Lieutenant George Butler told a reporter that half of

Members of the Ku Klux Klan stage a torchlight demonstration (Florida State Archives)

the DALLAS POLICE DEPARTMENT's officers were Klansmen in 1961. A year later, Klansmen and Mississippi police officers joined ranks to oppose school integration in the OLE MISS RIOT of September 1962. Elsewhere in Mississippi, Klansmen dominated the NESHOBA COUNTY SHERIFF'S DEPARTMENT (participating in a triple murder) and infiltrated the state Highway Patrol. Bull Connor remained intractable as ever, conspiring with Klansmen to stage riots during the integrated FREEDOM RIDES of 1961. ALBERT J. LINGO, appointed to lead the ALABAMA HIGHWAY PATROL in 1963, appeared at Klan rallies where speakers introduced him as "a good friend of ours." Congressional investigators found similar examples from every southern state in 1965–66, but the real surprise came from Illinois, where three Klansmen on the CHICAGO POLICE DEPARTMENT conspired to kill Mayor Richard Daley in 1968.

As in the 1920s, Klan-police violence ultimately backfired on its perpetrators, gaining sympathy for blacks in the media and in Congress, where sensational murders produced landmark civil rights legislation.

Today the Klan is a shadow of its former self, more extreme than ever with ties to the neo-Nazi fringe, but it still holds appeal for some law enforcement officers. In 1979 a police informant helped organize the Klan massacre of five unarmed demonstrators in Greensboro, North Carolina, while his handlers, forewarned of the impending violence, were strangely absent from the scene. Investigation of nocturnal cross-burnings in Polk County, Florida, revealed that two sergeants of the local sheriff's department were "former" Klansmen. Three other officers—in Century, Fort Lauderdale, and Jacksonville—were fired in the 1990s for involvement with the Klan. All sought reinstatement, pleading First Amendment rights, but none prevailed in court.

See also: INFORMANTS.

Kynette, Earlee

Earlee Kynette joined the LOS ANGELES POLICE DEPARTMENT in 1925. A volatile man, fiercely ambitious and equally venal, he would later be described by author

Frank Donner as "one of the most disreputable figures to emerge from the milieu of LAPD corruption." Still, he seemed lucky at first, handpicked by Captain JAMES EDGAR DAVIS for Vice Squad duty on the very day he graduated from the police academy. Soon Kynette was recognized throughout the force as "Davis's dirty-job man."

That job was hazardous at times. Kynette was fired in the early 1930s for extorting bribes from prostitutes, but Davis rehired him when he (Davis) became police chief for the second time in 1933. In fact, Kynette was not only restored to duty, but promoted to serve as the head of the LAPD's Red squad. In that post, he mounted sweeping DOMESTIC SURVEILLANCE against critics, pursuing Davis's instruction that the squad's job was "to check on the activities of . . . criminal political elements . . . attempting to destroy confidence in the police department."

By 1937 those "criminal political elements" included members of the Citizens' Independent Vice Investigating Committee (CIVIC), an unofficial group created to examine LAPD's ties to ORGANIZED CRIME. Kynette's 19-man unit spied on 50 of CIVIC's leading allies—including District Attorney Byron Fitts, two county supervisors, and a newspaper editor—but their main target was CIVIC's lead investigator, Harry Raymond. Before joining CIVIC, Raymond had served as chief of police in San Diego and Venice, California (fired in the latter city for making false arrests). Now in private practice, he seemed unaware as Kynette's spies shadowed him for months, watching his house, installing WIRETAPS on his telephones. On the night of January 13, 1938, Kynette and two other policemen invaded Raymond's garage. Neighbor George Sakalis caught them at it, whereupon they beat him and warned him to

"keep his mouth shut." Next morning, when Raymond started his car, a powerful bomb exploded beneath the hood, leaving him near death with 150 shrapnel wounds.

Chief Davis placed Kynette in charge of the bombing investigation, announcing on January 21 that LAPD had been cleared of suspicion. Kynette suggested that Raymond had planted the bomb himself, but D. A. Fitts was unconvinced. He convened a special grand jury on February 5, calling George Sakalis to describe his brief encounter with Kynette. Most members of the Red Squad refused to testify, including seven officers suspended for declining to explain their whereabouts on January 13–14, 1938. On February 13 the panel indicted Kynette, his lieutenant, and sergeant on various felony charges including attempted murder.

At trial in April 1938, Chief Davis provided rambling, contradictory testimony which the judge dismissed as "a debris of words." "My memory is not sufficiently clear to state that I directly ordered Captain Kynette to keep Raymond under surveillance," said Davis, "but I did not order him to do so." With Sakalis as the state's star witness, Kynette and his lieutenant were convicted, while the sergeant was acquitted. Kynette received a sentence of two years to life in prison. He and the lieutenant were finally fired, though a departmental Board of Rights returned the seven suspended policemen to full duty.

It hardly mattered for the Red squad, forced to disband in the wake of Kynette's trial when L.A.'s city council refused Chief Davis's request for $90,000 to support the team. Davis himself resigned under fire in 1939, perhaps at last regretting his choice of a "dirty-job man."

See also: BOMBING AND BOMB SQUADS; CORRUPTION; RED SQUADS.

L

Ladner, Thomas

A native of Sabine County, Texas, Thomas Ladner caught his first glimpse of the outside world when he was drafted by the U.S. Army in 1967 to fight in Vietnam. Home again in 1971, he found work as town constable in tiny Yellowpine, where a local prosecutor subsequently labeled him a "psychopathic bully." In 1974 Ladner pulled a gun on Hemphill city marshal Andy Helms, to liberate a drunken driver who was one of Ladner's friends. (Helms resigned over the incident, when Mayor Charlie Rice and Sheriff Blan Greer supported Ladner's criminal behavior.) Four years later, after his appointment as Hemphill's chief of police, Ladner earned a reputation for harassing teenage girls, often stopping them on lonely roads outside his jurisdiction, jailing them on false charges and subjecting them to crude interrogations.

Between Ladner and Sheriff Greer, elected in 1965, African Americans were constantly at risk in Sabine County. Ladner and Greer's chief deputy, Billy Ray Horton, were both investigated by the FBI for civil rights violations, with Ladner logging at least three complaints, but witnesses in every case refused to testify, citing fear of reprisals. On the night of December 25, 1987, Ladner and Deputy James Hyden stopped three black men in a pickup with Louisiana license plates. All three were jailed without explanation, later accused of drunk driving and public intoxication. Ladner became enraged when driver Loyal Garner, Jr. asked to telephone his wife, and a vicious beating ensued, during which Ladner broke his blackjack on Garner's head. ("They don't make 'em like they used to," he quipped.) Jailer Clyde King found Garner comatose

the next morning and summoned an ambulance, but it came too late. He died in a hospital at Tyler, 100 miles northwest of Hemphill, on December 27.

Within an hour of Garner's death, a Hemphill ambulance arrived to claim his body, but local justice of the peace Bill Baird refused to surrender the corpse, standing firm when a Sabine County judge called to explain the dead man's injuries as "accidental." Back in Hemphill, Garner's two companions, brothers John and Alton Maxie, were released after paying small fines—and after signing affidavits that described Ladner and his fellow officers as "acting like gentlemen and kindly." Both later recanted those statements, claiming they signed them unread, and evidence suggests the affidavits were typed by State Trooper Bill Bradberry (disciplined in 1979 for falsifying official reports to conceal a partner's misconduct).

Chief Ladner refused to speak with FBI agents, but he made a public statement describing Garner as a belligerent drunk who assaulted Deputy Hyden in jail. Ladner admitted striking Garner once with his blackjack, but claimed he "didn't even get a good lick at him." While they scuffled, Garner fell, "hitting his head against the wall. The next thing I know, they say he's in a coma, and the next thing I know, they say he's dead. I just can't believe it."

Five witnesses described Ladner's beating of Garner before a local grand jury, and even Sheriff Greer admitted he was "disappointed" in Deputy Horton for failing to stop it. On January 5, 1988, the panel indicted Ladner, Hyden, and Billy Horton on two counts each, for beating Garner and then denying him medical treatment. Deputies Horton and Hyden were suspended without pay on January 31; a short time later, Hemphill's city council reluctantly suspended Chief Ladner. On February 8 a coroner's inquest in Tyler found that Garner "died of injuries to his head as a result of homicide." New indictments were issued on March 3, charging all three officers with murder.

When Sabine County prosecutors balked at pursuing the case, Alabama's Southern Poverty Law Center (SPLC) retained U.S. Attorney John Hannah to pursue the Hemphill case under a Texas statute authorizing victims or their families to coordinate prosecution in the face of official negligence. At trial on the assault and neglect charges, Hemphill judge O'Neal Bacon manipulated evidence in favor of the defense, thus securing acquittal of all three defendants by an all-white jury on July 15, 1988. Legal maneuvers delayed the murder trial for another two years, while Hemphill politicians settled out of court with Garner's family for an undisclosed amount.

Hemphill became a powder keg. Arsonists burned Ladner's mobile home, while members of the KU KLUX KLAN marched in support of the defendants. On May 3, 1991, jurors convicted all three officers of murder. The next day, Ladner received a 28-year prison term, while Hyden drew 14 years, and Horton got 10 years. Ladner's appeal was denied on September 21, 1991.

Larson, John A. (1892–1965)

Born in 1892, Dr. John Larson worked as a police officer and teacher before devoting himself to scientific criminology in Berkeley, California. Collaborating with legendary police chief AUGUST VOLLMER, Larson invented the polygraph—a supposed "LIE DETECTOR"—in 1921. Testing hinged upon Larson's R/I (relevant/irrelevant) interrogation technique, which intersperses questions relevant to the crime ("Do you own an axe?") with questions entirely divorced from the case ("Are you 40 years old?"). Larson theorized that innocent persons would display similar reactions to both types of questions, while the guilty would react to relevant questions with elevated pulse rate, higher blood pressure, faster breathing, and increased perspiration.

Expert testimony on the results of polygraph faced a telling challenge in the case of *Frye v. United States* (1923), which disallowed polygraph results as "scientific" evidence, but Larson kept striving to perfect his device. With colleague Leonarde Keeler, Larson refined the polygraph through the 1930s and published a book on the subject, *Lying and Its Detection* (1932), with coauthors Keeler and George Harry. Most published sources credit Keeler with developing the polygraph in common use today. Larson, meanwhile, retired from crime-fighting to practice psychiatry. He died in 1965.

Las Vegas Metropolitan Police Department

Law enforcement in Las Vegas, Nevada, and environs was initially divided between the Clark County Sheriff's Office (CCSO), created in 1909, and a municipal police force organized two years later. The CCSO patrolled rural areas, while the Las Vegas Police Department's jurisdiction was bounded by the city limits. Rapid population growth—from 19 residents in 1900 to 945 in 1910—set the tone for Las Vegas, which endures to this day. Standard big-city problems were exacerbated after 1931 by legalized gambling, an "industry" infested from its earliest days by members of ORGANIZED CRIME.

Chief Robert Malburg assumed command of LVPD in December 1947, when his predecessor committed suicide after six days in office. One month later, Malburg's secretary became the city's first policewoman, though in fact she seldom left her desk. LVPD initiated civil service exams in 1950, expanding to include 91 officers by 1954. The CCSO, meanwhile, patrolled 8,550 square miles—including the famous Las Vegas Strip—with only 52 deputies as of 1957. Antagonism between the two agencies made it a simple matter for suspects to escape, in some cases by simply crossing a street from one jurisdiction to the other.

To remedy that problem, a committee organized in 1968 to plan a merger of the two departments, finally achieved on July 1, 1973. The new Las Vegas Metropolitan Police Department, with jurisdiction spanning Clark County, was led by Sheriff Ralph Lamb; former police chief John Moran designated as the undersheriff. Standardization of uniforms, equipment, and salaries cost taxpayers $763,000, but efficiency was greatly improved and the LVMPD won national accreditation from the Commission on Accreditation for Law Enforcement Agencies in 1989. Nine years later, it was one of only 14 U.S. agencies to boast the "triple crown"—accreditation from the CALEA, the Commission on Accreditation for Corrections, and the Commission on Correctional Healthcare.

Leach, Matthew (1894–1955)

Croatian native Matthew Lichanin, born in 1894, immigrated to the United States with his parents at age 13. The family name was Anglicized to "Leach" on arrival in Pennsylvania in 1907, and the clan moved on to Indiana three years later. Matthew worked in a steel mill, then joined the U.S. Army in 1915, seeing action in Mexico and on the western front in World War I before his return to civilian life. Soon after leaving the army, Leach joined the Gary (Indiana) Police Department as a vice detective. His active role in the American Legion paid off in 1932, when national commander Paul McNutt was elected governor of Indiana. The following year, McNutt named Leach to lead the fledgling INDIANA STATE POLICE.

That same year, 1933, witnessed a rash of Indiana bank robberies committed by a ruthless gang of fugitives from the state prison at Michigan City. Leach, an early advocate of using psychology to catch criminals, adopted a divide-and-conquer strategy for hunting the gang. In his official press releases, Leach named young bandit John Dillinger as the gang's leader, hoping that veteran outlaw Harry Pierpont would get jealous and break up the outfit. Pierpont ignored the jibes, however, leaving Leach to chase the gang through a series of bungled raids that failed to net his prey. In one such raid, conducted outside Leach's jurisdiction in Paris, Illinois, on December 20, 1933, Indiana troopers wound up shooting at each other, killing Officer Eugene Teague with "friendly fire."

Police in Tucson, Arizona, bagged the elusive gang one month later, but Leach could not hold Dillinger, even when others made the catch for him. On March 3, 1934, Dillinger escaped from jail at Crown Point, Indiana, reportedly using a hand-carved wooden gun. FBI agents dominated the manhunt from that moment on, tracking Dillinger for violation of the DYER ACT, while Leach became embroiled in a personal feud with Bureau director J. EDGAR HOOVER. After G-men killed Dillinger in Chicago in July 1934, Leach publicly claimed that an Indiana detective had fired the fatal shots; furthermore, he charged, some $7,000 had been stolen from the bandit's corpse.

Leach's feud with the FBI went from bad to worse in 1937, during a wide-ranging hunt for the trigger-happy Brady gang. Hoover charged that Leach had counseled Indiana citizens to withhold cooperation from federal agents, thus delaying capture of the homicidal fugitives. Donald Stiver, chief of Indiana's Department of Public Safety, demanded Leach's resignation on September 4, 1937. Embittered, Leach spent several years writing a tell-all book that never found a publisher. On June 14, 1955, while returning from an unsuccessful bid to sell his manuscript in New York, Leach died in a car crash on the Pennsylvania Turnpike.

See also: BANK ROBBERY.

Leary, Howard A. (1912–1994)

Born in 1912, Howard Leary joined the PHILADELPHIA POLICE DEPARTMENT as a patrolman in 1940 and earned a law degree in night school while rising through the ranks. He became Philadelphia's police commissioner in 1963, and was lured away three years later by Mayor John Lindsay, to fill the same post in New York City.

Leary obviously meant well, but his status as an outsider barred him from being a truly effective reformer of the scandal-ridden NEW YORK CITY POLICE DEPARTMENT. (One observer compared his appointment to "making the Bishop of Canterbury a Pope.") Leary's innovations included New York's first computerized police dispatch system and a new 911 emergency telephone number, coupled with increased hiring of ethnic minorities, but the Patrolmen's Benevolent Association stymied efforts to create a CIVILIAN REVIEW BOARD with a campaign of racist television ads, and Leary was never able to suppress New York's endemic police CORRUPTION.

After four years of incessant controversy, Leary resigned in September 1970 and embarked on a tour of Europe. Upon returning to the States, he worked first as a security executive with the Abraham & Straus department store, then held a similar position with a private agency, Holmes Protection. Leary spent the final decade of his working life as a professor of criminal justice at New Jersey's Trenton State College (1972–82). He died in 1994.

Leasure, William Ernest (b. 1946)

A native of Wayne, Michigan, born in 1946, William Leasure joined the U.S. Marine Corps at age 20 and served in Vietnam without seeing combat. Discharged without job prospects in 1969, he soon joined the LOS ANGELES POLICE DEPARTMENT, and was assigned in 1970 to Central Traffic, where he spent the bulk of his career.

While most officers view traffic duty as a launching pad to more adventurous and lucrative assignments, Leasure seemed content—not only in his work, but on the night shift, sometimes aggravating supervisors with his slow, painstaking style of writing accident reports. He shunned promotion, claiming to have failed a sergeant's test deliberately. Although married, he dated women whom he stopped for speeding, sometimes those he met at crime scenes, until an enemy inside LAPD alerted his wife in 1972.

Remarried by 1975 to lawyer Betsy Mogul, Leasure boasted a yearly household income exceeding $100,000, and still appeared to live beyond his means. The couple had a $250,000 waterfront condo and boat slip in Long Beach, a three-bedroom rental home in Sun Valley, and their Northridge home, while modest in itself, sat on a huge lot occupied by Leasure's collection of classic Corvettes, ranging from 12 to 17 cars at a time. Unknown to his employers, Leasure also kept a stockpile of 40-odd weapons at home, including illegal machine guns and silencers.

It is unknown precisely when Leasure went bad. The final list of charges filed against him ranged from auto theft to contract murder, and some of the ever-changing

Corvettes in his private fleet were definitely stolen. He also collected shady friends, including con men, bank robbers, and hired assassins. In conversations with his underworld associates and sundry girlfriends, Leasure offered to perform delicate favors . . . for a price.

One acquaintance, Paulette de los Reyes, asked Leasure in June 1976 to eliminate her estranged husband. "Piece of cake," Leasure replied, but his first attempt—a bombing at husband Tony's apartment on October 7—simply wrecked the target's car. Five months later, Paulette's stepfather (and a partner in the family business) was gunned down in his driveway. Years later, triggerman Dennis Winebaugh, also a police officer, would name Bill Leasure as the mastermind of that crime and his getaway driver. A few months after that ASSASSINATION, Tony de los Reyes paid Winebaugh $5,000 to kill Paulette, unaware that she had become Winebaugh's lover. Winebaugh kept the cash but warned Paulette. Tony survived a drive-by shooting in spring 1981, but Winebaugh finally finished the job that September, killing Tony with a close-range shotgun blast.

Another satisfied customer, Art Smith, wearied of ongoing divorce proceedings in 1980, telling a friend, "I know two cops who will kill anybody you want for $50,000." He planned to send them after his wife, Anne Marie, "and make it look like a sex-fiend killing." Instead, she was fatally shot on May 28, 1980, during an apparent holdup at a Highland Park beauty salon. Bill Leasure called in sick on the day of the murder, and the gunmen fled in a distinctive car resembling one owned by a friend of Leasure's, Dennis France (who had his car repainted a new color that same week).

When not engaged in murder, Leasure joined another friend, ex-convict Robert Kuns, to steal and sell at least five luxury yachts. They were caught together on May 29, 1986, while transporting a stolen yacht from San Diego to Richmond, California. Soon after that arrest, Jerry France —brother of Dennis—was jailed for writing bad checks in Long Beach. He quickly struck a deal, naming his brother and "a traffic cop named Bill" as perpetrators of a crime spree in Los Angeles. Confronted with his brother's accusations, Dennis France soon fingered Leasure as the brains behind three homicides and varied lesser crimes. Authorities traced Dennis Winebaugh to Oklahoma City, where a search of his home revealed weapons and incriminating notes in Leasure's handwriting.

The investigation widened. Leasure and patrol partner Ralph Gerard were indicted in February for yacht thefts and insurance fraud, while Betsy Mogul faced perjury charges. Three months later, Art Smith and Paulette de los Reyes were charged with conspiracy to murder their respective spouses, both turning state's evidence against Leasure in a bid for leniency. After 14 months of hearings and appeals, LAPD dismissed Leasure in June 1988 for conduct "totally inconsistent with his role as a police officer." Dennis Winebaugh drew a life sentence for killing Paulette's stepfather, while Paulette's plea bargain let her escape with six years in prison.

Tried on three counts of first-degree murder in spring 1991, Leasure won a mistrial when the jury deadlocked at 10 to 2 in favor of conviction. Retrial was scheduled for Halloween, but Leasure struck a deal with prosecutors on October 30, pleading "no contest" on two reduced charges of second-degree murder, receiving a prison term of 15 years to life.

Lee, Charles (1758–1815)

Born at Leesylvania, Virginia, in 1758, Charles Lee received his bachelor's degree from Princeton University at age 17. He studied law privately in Philadelphia and was admitted to the bar in June 1794. Lee subsequently served as a naval officer and Virginia state legislator, before President George Washington appointed him as the nation's third attorney general, on December 10, 1795. Lee continued in that office under President John Adams, until March 4, 1801. He later declined President Thomas Jefferson's invitation to serve as chief justice of the U.S. SUPREME COURT. Lee died in Fauquier County, Virginia, on June 24, 1815.

Legaré, Hugh Swinton (1797–1843)

A native of Charleston, South Carolina, born January 2, 1797, Hugh Legaré graduated from the College of South Carolina in 1814. He studied law in the United States until 1817, then traveled widely through Europe while continuing his studies there. Upon returning to South Carolina, Legaré was elected to the state legislature (1820–22, 1824–30) and as state attorney general (1830–32). In 1832 he became the U.S. charge d'affaires in Brussels, Belgium. Returning once more to America, he served one term in Congress (1837–39), and was named attorney general by President John Tyler in 1841. Legaré died in office while attending the unveiling ceremony for Boston's Bunker Hill Monument, on June 20, 1843.

Levi, Edward Hirsch (1911–2000)

Born in Chicago on June 26, 1911, Edward Levi received his Ph.D. from the University of Chicago in 1932, followed by a JD from the same school in 1935, and won admission to the bar in 1936. While serving as an assistant professor of law at Chicago University (1936–40), Levi earned a J.S.D. from Yale (1938). His teaching career was interrupted by service with the U.S. Justice Department (1940–45), where he variously filled posts in the Antitrust Division, the Consent Decree Section, the War Division, and the Interdepartmental Committee on Monopolies and Cartels. He returned to his alma mater as a full professor after World War II and became dean of the law school (1950), then provost (1962), and finally president of the university (1968). During the same years, he also served as chief counsel for the House Judiciary Committee's Subcommittee on Monopoly Power (1950), as a member of the White House Central Group on Domestic Affairs (1964), the White House Task Force on Education (1966–67), and the President's Task Force on Priorities in Higher Education (1969–70).

President Gerald Ford named Levi attorney general on February 7, 1975. Five weeks later, Levi testified before the House Subcommittee on Civil and Constitutional Rights, revealing the existence of FBI director J. Edgar Hoover's "Official and Confidential" files containing derogatory information on presidents, cabinet members, and other prominent Americans. Levi had found some of those files, but ex–Assistant Director William Cornelius Sullivan told author David Wise, "He didn't get the gold." A year later, in March 1976, Levi issued new guidelines for FBI "domestic security" investigations which (theoretically) limited the Bureau's power to conduct random fishing expeditions and monitor personal beliefs. The new rules permitted 90-day "preliminary investigations" to determine whether subjects had violated federal statutes, and "full" investigations were barred without substantive proof of criminal activity. (Some critics doubted that the Bureau would abide by those or any other rules.)

Levi left office on January 20, 1977, with the inauguration of President Jimmy Carter. Levi's restrictions on federal snooping survived until the advent of President Ronald Reagan, who campaigned on a vow to "unleash" the FBI. Levi died of Alzheimer's disease on March 7, 2000.

Lexow Committee

Named for its chairman—state senator Clarence Lexow of Rockland County, New York—the Lexow Committee was organized in 1894 to investigate corruption spawned by Tammany Hall within the New York City Police Department. The committee's creation was sparked, in large part, by the efforts of reformer Charles Parkhurst, whose private investigation of Tammany Hall threatened to scuttle con-

solidation of New York's five boroughs under one government.

Key witnesses included NYPD Captain Max Schmittberger, who admitted taking bribes and listed other officers who did the same; Captain Timothy Creedon, who purchased his rank for $15,000 in anticipation of much greater profits; and Captain Alexander "Clubber" Williams, who threatened the committee's counsel while denying any knowledge of graft. The public exposure of widespread bribery and brutality outraged New York voters, who defeated Tammany in 1894's election to install "fusion" candidate William Strong as mayor. Unfortunately, subsequent investigations of NYPD conducted between 1912 and 1992 demonstrated that the subculture of corruption is not easily uprooted.

Liddy, G. Gordon (b. 1930)

Born in 1930, Gordon Liddy earned a law degree from a Jesuit college before joining the FBI in 1957. He was a zealous agent, fond of "black bag jobs" and other covert operations, dubbed "Wild Man" and "Superklutz" by colleagues. Officers of the Kansas City Police Department once arrested Liddy for burglary, but he was released after a phone call to Chief Clarence Marion Kelley (himself a former G-man and future FBI director). Liddy left the Bureau in 1962, served briefly as an assistant district attorney in Poughkeepsie, New York, then joined Richard Nixon's presidential campaign in 1968. His service there won Liddy a place on the White House staff, where top aides made good use of his skills and FBI contacts.

Liddy was a prime mover in various illegal break-ins conducted by Nixon's staff, beginning in 1971, and debated means for removing elderly FBI director J. Edgar Hoover (reportedly including plans to enter Hoover's home and place a toxic substance on his toothbrush). In 1972 Liddy served as general counsel for the Committee to Re-Elect the President (CREEP), directing a series of burglaries and other "dirty tricks" intended to disrupt the Democratic Party. One of Liddy's break-ins, at Democratic National Committee headquarters in June 1972, unleashed the Watergate scandal that drove Nixon from office in 1974.

Prosecutors indicted Liddy for the Watergate break-in and for burglarizing the office of Daniel Ellsberg's psychiatrist. Convicted and slapped with a sentence of 80 months to 20 years, Liddy served 53 months in prison and emerged to become a media celebrity, actor, best-selling author, and right-wing radio pundit. In 1986 a federal court found him liable for $20,499 in back taxes on unreported Watergate bribes. Seven years later, following the tragic Branch Davidian siege in Texas, Liddy condemned FBI agents as "jackbooted thugs" and advised potential suspects on the best means of killing G-men clad in BODY ARMOR: "Head shots! Head shots!"

See also: FEDERAL BUREAU OF INVESTIGATION.

"lie detectors"

From the earliest days of trial by ordeal, humans have sought a foolproof way of separating truth from lies. Triumph eludes us to this day, but science has been drafted to refine the effort, producing a series of devices collectively (and incorrectly) known as "lie detectors" that are widely used by law enforcement agencies throughout the world.

Albert Schneider pioneered the field of scientific lie detectors in the 1890s, with invention of a device meant to chart electrical brain-wave activity correlated to physiological changes wrought by stress. William Mar-

ston refined the technique in 1917, with a machine that measured changes in a subject's systolic blood pressure. In 1921 JOHN LARSON invented the polygraph, which combines blood pressure readings with calibration of a subject's heart rate, respiration rate and electro-dermal activity (sweating). Larson's protégé Leonarde Keeler later refined the polygraph into the device widely employed today, while others continued alternate experiments. Published sources differ as to whether Jacque Bril or Rev. Walter Summers invented the 1930s "pathometer," designed to record emotional reactions during questioning. The early 1960s brought a new method of "lie detection," the psychological stress evaluator (PSE), whose inventors claimed recordings of a human voice alone could reveal if its owner was lying.

Larson's polygraph hit an early snag in court, with the 1923 landmark case of *Frye v. United States*. Accused murderer James Frye appealed his convic-

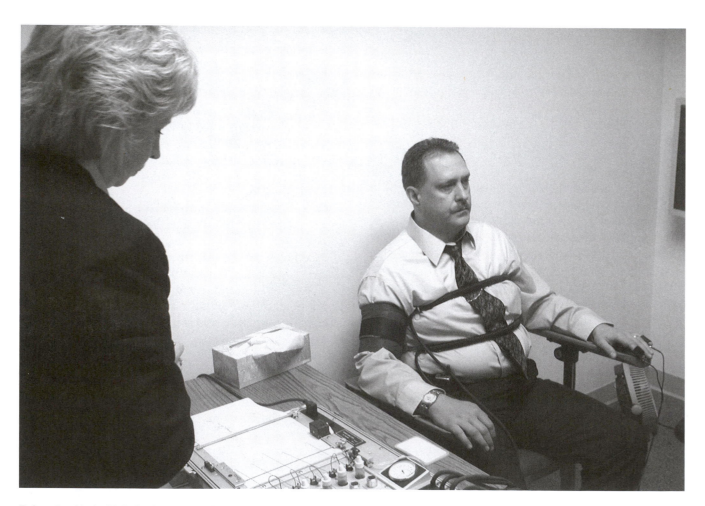

Police Lt. Kathy Tytla looks over a chart from a polygraph examination November 2, 2004, of Detective Derek Burleson. Tytla demonstrated the machine by asking Burleson to lie about which of seven cards he had selected. Using the machine, she was able to determine which card he chose. (Associated Press/The Leavenworth Times)

tion on grounds that the court had barred a polygraph examiner from testifying that he passed a "lie detector" test. A federal appellate court upheld Frye's conviction and established the "Frye Test" for expert testimony, decreeing that such testimony must be "sufficiently established to have gained general acceptance in the particular field in which it belongs." As recently as 1998 the U.S. SUPREME COURT decreed: "There is simply no consensus that polygraph evidence is reliable: The scientific community and the state and federal courts are extremely polarized on the matter."

Most U.S. states still ban polygraph test results from admission as evidence, and with good reason. While some professional polygraph examiners naturally promote their technique as 99-percent reliable (thus hoping to gain more clients), a host of problems surrounds scientific lie-detection, rendering any test results problematic at best. Such factors as the subject's health, state of mind, and chemicals ingested may produce false readings. Polygraphs measure stress, not honesty, and some subjects are frightened by the test itself, while hard-core sociopaths or individuals trained to resist interrogation can "beat the box" at will. Even in ideal conditions, some critics maintain that polygraph results are accurate no more than half the time, a margin of "success" equivalent to flipping coins. Prior to writing this entry, the author sat for two separate polygraph tests with different examiners and found erroneous results in both evaluations—an error factor of 100 percent.

Lincoln, Levi (1749–1820)

America's fourth attorney general was born in Hingham, Massachusetts, on May 15, 1749. He graduated from Harvard University in 1772 and thereafter studied law privately. After the battle of Lexington (1775), Lincoln volunteered to serve with the Massachusetts Minute Men, but legal duties kept him from the battlefield. Instead of facing combat, he served first as a clerk, then probate judge in Worcester County (1775–81). Although elected to the Continental Congress in 1781, Lincoln declined to serve. After the Revolutionary War, he was elected to the Massachusetts House of Representatives (1796), then to the state senate (1797), and finally to Congress (1800). President Thomas Jefferson named him attorney general on March 5, 1801. Lincoln held that post until March 3, 1805, then returned to Massachusetts, where he served on the state council (1806) and as lieutenant governor (1807–08). Lincoln became governor in 1808, with the death of Governor James Sullivan, but voters failed to grant him his own term in 1809. He declined appointment to the U.S.

Attorney General Levi Lincoln (Author's collection)

SUPREME COURT in 1811 and died in Worcester, Massachusetts, on April 14, 1820.

Lingo, Albert J. (1910–1969)

Born January 22, 1910, in Clayton, Alabama, Al Lingo served briefly with the ALABAMA HIGHWAY PATROL in the 1930s, then retired from law enforcement to operate a logging company. During his short stint in uniform, and afterward, he earned a reputation as a brutal racist who was "hell on niggers," prone to confrontation, with a violent temper that prompted him to take tranquilizers "by the handful" in later life. In the 1950s he befriended a fellow resident of Barbour County, George C. Wallace, and Wallace tapped Lingo as his right-hand man upon winning the 1962 gubernatorial primary election. In September of that year, Wallace sent Lingo to Mississippi, where he observed police defiance of federal marshals at the OLE MISS RIOT and reported back to his employer on methods of stalling school integration.

Upon inauguration, Wallace named Lingo to head the Alabama Department of Public Safety, where Lingo soon renamed the highway patrol Alabama State Troopers, affixing Confederate battle flags to the bumpers of each patrol car. The patrol was soon transformed into a mobile strike force for disrupting civil rights demonstrations, armed with clubs, electric cattle prods, and guns which Lingo's troopers did not hesitate to use on unarmed blacks. On the side, Lingo routinely reinstated the suspended driver's licenses of convicted drunk drivers, acting at the governor's personal request to curry favor with poor white voters.

In office Lingo did his best to honor Wallace's campaign promise of "segregation forever." Appearing on the dais at a KU KLUX KLAN rally, Lingo was introduced to the crowd as "a good friend of ours." In spring 1963, with two black students scheduled for court-ordered admission to the University of Alabama, Lingo ordered investigator Ben Allen to "find something on those two niggers" that would bar them from the school. (He failed.) Three months later, in Birmingham, Lingo met privately with leaders of the neo-Nazi National States' Rights Party, urging them to mount violent demonstrations outside local schools, thus giving Wallace an excuse to close the schools before they were desegregated.

Nor was Lingo's part in racial violence limited to an observer's role. After Klansmen bombed a Birmingham church in September 1963, killing four young girls, Lingo first blamed Black Muslims for the crime, then met with state Klan leaders in an effort to deflect blame from the KKK. As FBI agents built a case against the bombers, Lingo jailed three of them on misdemeanor dynamite-possession charges, thereby persuading FBI director J. EDGAR HOOVER to let the case die. In June 1964, after Mississippi Klansmen murdered three civil rights workers, Lingo falsified statements for Governor Wallace that the three victims had been seen alive in Alabama following their disappearance. In August 1965, after longtime friend and Klansman Tom Coleman shot two white ministers in Lowndes County, killing one, Lingo personally drove a Klan bondsman from Montgomery to post Coleman's bail, then took charge of the investigation and refused to share his information with FBI agents or state attorney general Richmond Flowers. (Flowers called Lingo's investigation a whitewash.) The night before Coleman's acquittal on manslaughter charges, the defendant attended Lingo's retirement party.

Although he was leaving the state payroll, Lingo still craved a place in law enforcement. He ran for sheriff of Jefferson County (Birmingham) in 1966, but newly registered black voters ignored his belated attention, rejecting his candidacy on election day. Lingo died in 1969, a symbol of the cruel intolerance that stained Alabama's honor and ensured passage of landmark civil rights legislation in the turbulent 1960s.

Little Rock Police Department

Little Rock, Arkansas, emerged as a national symbol of RACISM in 1957, when Governor Orval Faubus defied federal court orders to maintain school segregation, but the city's history of violence against blacks did not begin in the mid-20th century. Local police failed to prevent or punish public LYNCHINGS in 1892, 1895, and 1913, later signing on as members of the 1920s KU KLUX KLAN whose 7,800 members controlled politics in Little Rock and surrounding Pulaski County. It is no wonder, then, that local racist bombings went unsolved until the terrorists responsible turned their attention to city-owned property in 1959.

Today, despite inescapable echoes of its past, the Little Rock PD presents a very different public face. Its stated goal is "to provide the citizens of Little Rock, Arkansas with a law enforcement system that effectively integrates and utilizes Departmental, civic and community resources to protect life and property, preserve law and order and enforce State Laws and City Ordinances within the framework of the Constitution." To that end, department spokesmen pledge themselves to a six-point program that includes:

- *Recognizing [that] the spirit of the Little Rock Police Department is one of helping people and providing assistance at every opportunity.*
- *Enlightening citizens about public safety issues and striving to gain community support in the suppression of criminal activity.*
- *Realizing that the employees of our Department are the most important part of the organization and constantly striving to help them in their performance and development.*
- *Developing leadership throughout the Department in order to effectively utilize allocated resources for maximum productivity.*
- *Aggressively responding to criminal activity throughout the City of Little Rock in a manner consistent with safeguarding the rights of all citizens.*
- *Consistently demanding the highest degree of integrity and professionalism from all employees.*

See also: TERRORISM.

Lopez, Julius M. (–1996)

Julius M. Lopez starred on the baseball and football teams at Chicago's Loyola University, prior to obtaining his B.A. from that institution. After graduation he remained at Loyola as a coach, then moved on to the University of Chicago, where he was credited (with coach Clark Shaughnessy) with developing football's "T" formation. He joined the FBI in 1936, variously serving in the Birmingham, Chicago, Jackson, Memphis, New Orleans, and Savannah field offices. In Memphis he was named assistant agent-in-charge on October 23, 1941, thus becoming the first Hispanic G-man of command rank under Director J. EDGAR HOOVER. Lopez was subsequently named assistant agent-in-charge of the Indianapolis field office (April 22, 1942) and agent-in-charge of the San Juan, Puerto Rico, field office (April 17, 1943). He retired from the Bureau in 1960 to become director of public safety in Biloxi, Mississippi. Lopez died on July 14, 1996.

See also: FEDERAL BUREAU OF INVESTIGATION.

Los Angeles County Sheriff's Department

Although rated as the world's largest sheriff's department in 2005, with 8,553 sworn officers and 5,815 civilian personnel, the Los Angeles County Sheriff's Department (LASD) had humble beginnings. Organized in April 1850, the department consisted of Sheriff George Burrill and two deputies. Sheriffs were elected annually until 1882, then for two-year terms over the next 12 years, and finally to four-year terms (since 1894). The small department was augmented during 1852 by a 100-member posse dubbed the Los Angeles Rangers, described as "one of the most colorful law enforcement bodies to be organized in California."

Bandits killed Sheriff James Barton and several of his Rangers in January 1857, prompting the arrest of 52 suspects, 11 of whom were hanged. Sheriff William Getman was gunned down by a "maniac" one year later, after serving only seven days in office. October 1871 witnessed an outbreak of anti-Chinese rioting and lynching, quelled by Sheriff James Burns with the arrest of 150 racist vigilantes. Twentieth-century progress included acquisition of the LASD's first automobile (1907), employment of the first female deputy in the U.S. (1912), establishment of a modern fingerprint system (1915), creation of a crime lab and a county-wide teletype system (1928), and an Aero Squadron for airborne patrols (1931).

Eugene Biscailuz set the county service record, with 51 years on the LASD and 26 years as sheriff (1932–58), including establishment of the department's training academy in 1935. Unfortunately, PROHIBITION had thoroughly corrupted the department before Biscailuz took office, and he showed no inclination to clean house. Under his administration, payoffs guaranteed virtual immunity for leaders of ORGANIZED CRIME such as Benjamin "Bugsy" Siegel, Mickey Cohen, and Jack Dragna.

RACISM, likewise, did not vanish from Los Angeles County with the anti-Chinese riots of 1871. Sheriff's deputies led brutal STRIKEBREAKING raids against Mexican celery pickers in 1936. Tension between sheriff's deputies and Hispanic Angelenos was still running high in August 1970, when officers routed Latino antiwar protesters, jailing 60, and killing journalist Rueben Salazar with a badly aimed tear-gas projectile. Four officers were indicted in March 1971, for Salazar's death and the slaying of a second Hispanic victim. Street gangs exacerbate ethnic antagonism, including complaints of EXCESSIVE FORCE against the LASD's Gang Enforcement Team (created in 1988).

In September 1990, five months before the infamous RODNEY KING beating incident, the NAACP filed a class action lawsuit against the LASD (*Thomas v. County of Los Angeles*), seeking injunctive relief and monetary damages for an alleged pattern of brutality, racial harassment, and illegal searches in the mostly Hispanic community of Lynwood. Judge Terry Hatter granted a preliminary injunction in September 1991, commanding all LASD employees to follow the department's established guidelines on searches and use of force, further ordering LASD to submit monthly use-of-force reports to the court. Three months later, county supervisors appointed ex-judge James Kolts to investigate complaints against the LASD. The Kolts Report, issued in July 1992, acknowledged both excessive force and lax internal discipline, concluding that LASD seemed "unable to reform itself." Sheriff Sherman Block agreed to implement Kolts's recommendations for community-based policing and civilian monitoring of the department. The *Thomas* lawsuit climaxed in July 1995, with a jury verdict finding Sheriff Block and two of his top aides liable for various civil rights violations, awarding $611,000 to three plaintiffs. An additional 23 lawsuits were settled in December 1995, with cash payments totaling $7.5 million. Meanwhile, a covert investigation of departmental CORRUPTION ("Operation Big Spender," launched in 1988) saw 19 deputies convicted by December 1993.

LASD's season of scandal produced uneven reforms. Amnesty International monitored the force throughout the latter 1990s, reporting in February 1999 that police shootings had reached a new low of 36 in 1998 (down from 55 the previous year), while force-related lawsuits hit an all-time record low in 1997–98. The same report, however, noted a continuing "failure to impose adequate discipline in some substantiated cases of excessive force." Longstanding complaints of brutality also continued from LASD's Twin Towers county jail, where the sheriff suspended one group of "rogue deputies" for beating a mentally ill prisoner in August 1998, and a second inmate's death while struggling with deputies was ruled a "homicide" produced by "probable positional asphyxia." Department leaders ignored a May 1999 recommendation from the U.S. Commission on Civil Rights, urging creation of a CIVILIAN REVIEW

BOARD, and the term of office for LASD's Special Counsel expired on December 31, 1999, effectively ending external monitoring of departmental conduct.

Los Angeles Police Department

The LAPD is one of the world's largest law enforcement agencies, with more than 9,000 sworn officers and 3,000 civilian personnel policing 467 square miles and some 3.5 million residents. Its rich and controversial history has inspired countless novels, films, and television programs since the 1930s, ranging in viewpoint from the gung-ho propaganda efforts of "JACK" WEBB to the dark tales of James Ellroy.

L.A.'s first peace officers were the Los Angeles Rangers, a volunteer force organized in 1853 and soon supplanted by the unpaid Los Angeles City Guards. Neither team succeeded in curbing the city's reputation as a wide-open haven for violence, gambling, and vice. Professional law enforcement arrived in 1869, with City Marshal William Warren hired to supervise six patrolmen. Warren was murdered by one of his own officers in 1876, followed in rapid succession by 15 different chiefs during 1876–89. Reformer John Glass took office as chief in 1889 and remained for 11 years, pushing LAPD toward new levels of professionalism. The advent of Civil Service in 1903 brought LAPD's strength to 200 officers, but they received no formal training until 1916. Another period of rapid turnover in chiefs saw 16 commanders come and go during 1900–23.

After World War I a virulent Red scare combined with the advent of PROHIBITION to cause serious problems for LAPD. A new RED SQUAD was organized to suppress "radical" activity at any cost, while some local officers joined the resurgent KU KLUX KLAN and many more wallowed in the CORRUPTION spawned by bootlegging and illegal gambling. Illegal DOMESTIC SURVEILLANCE extended to disruption of public meetings, epitomized by Chief R. Lee Heath's proclamation that "I will not allow any man to deny the existence of God down there in the plaza." False arrests and application of "THIRD-DEGREE" TACTICS were routine.

Chief JAMES EDGAR DAVIS (1926–31, 1933–39) was a new broom of sorts, firing one-fifth of the force for bad conduct during his first term in office, but the transformation was scarcely an improvement. Creating a 50-man "gun squad" to confront bootleggers, Davis dismissed any notion of due process with announcements that he planned to "hold court on gunmen in the Los Angeles streets; I want them brought in dead, not alive and will reprimand any officer who shows the least mercy to a criminal." Davis also strengthened the LAPD Red squad to "investigate and control radical activities, strikes, and riots," encouraged by a police commissioner who gave reporters his prescription for handling Reds: "The more the police beat them up and wreck their headquarters, the better. Communists have no Constitutional rights and I won't listen to anyone who defends them."

Such tactics backfired on Davis, literally, in 1938, when Captain EARL KYNETTE conspired to bomb the car of a reformer from the Citizens' Independent Investigating Committee. The victim survived, but Kynette and his civilian accomplice wound up in prison, while Chief Davis soon found it wise to retire. Reform mayor Fletcher Bowron launched his administration by firing 45 high-ranking officers, but new chief Arthur Hohmann could not buck the civic tide, forced to resign in 1941 after he refused to use cops as strikebreakers at Inglewood's North American Aviation plant. World War II left LAPD's ranks depleted, forcing Chief Clemence Horrall to lower his standards and cut normal training in half. The result was displayed during 1943's "Zoot-Suit" riots, wherein rampaging servicemen beat dozens of Mexican Americans, while police followed behind the mobs and jailed their victims.

Chief WILLIAM HENRY PARKER (1950–66) is often compared to FBI director J. EDGAR HOOVER for his impact on LAPD, whipping a lax department into shape and making it the envy of police from coast to coast. Unfortunately, Parker's resemblance to Hoover ran deeper, including a deep strain of RACISM (he once compared black citizens to "monkeys in a zoo"), capricious discipline (short-sleeved summer uniforms were banned because Parker hated tattoos and "hairy arms"), and extreme right-wing political views. Parker endorsed the fanatical John Birch Society, while an estimated 2,000 of his officers became members, and he revived LAPD's moribund Red Squad to mount surveillance on thousands of subjects who had committed no crime. Illegal BUGGING and WIRETAPS flourished under Parker, who in 1954 denounced a legal challenge to his tactics as a communist conspiracy. When neo-Nazis and members of the Ku Klux Klan launched a bombing campaign against liberal churches in L.A., Parker emulated Birmingham's Eugene "Bull" Connor, grilling and blaming the victims.

A persistent myth contends that Parker cleansed Los Angeles of ORGANIZED CRIME, but such is not the case. His bugging of selected gangsters' homes produced reams of intelligence on underworld activities, but none of it would be admissible in court, and it remained for the INTERNAL REVENUE SERVICE to prosecute prominent mobsters Mickey Cohen and Jack Dragna in the 1960s. In the ghetto, meanwhile, Parker's 1955 motto—"To Protect and Serve"—rang hollow for blacks who suffered EXCESSIVE FORCE on a daily basis. When police violence sparked the Watts riot of August 1965, Parker predictably blamed Reds for plotting to destroy L.A.

Chief THOMAS REDDIN (1967–69) had trouble controlling his troops, as witnessed in a 1967 police riot against antiwar protesters, while Chief EDWARD DAVIS (1969–78) seemed intent on retooling LAPD into a paramilitary unit for suppression of minorities and leftists. His community policing initiatives were overshadowed by creation of the department's first SWAT TEAM, advocacy of public hangings, and distribution of spent cartridge casings as souvenirs after a deadly shootout with the Symbionese Liberation Army. Author Frank Donner found LAPD's intelligence service under Davis "unique because of its unabashed right-wing commitment." The Criminal Conspiracy Section went further still, employing AGENTS PROVOCATEURS to disrupt various groups and—according to employee LOUIS E. TACKWOOD—plotting assassinations of selected black and left-wing targets. It is known that LAPD joined the FBI's COINTELPRO program against the Black Panther Party, encouraging members of a rival group (led by a paid police informant) to murder Panthers on sight.

Chief DARYL GATES (1978–92) proved as controversial as Davis, beset by scandals on every side throughout most of his administration. Federal litigation filed in 1978 revealed LAPD's spy network, including infiltration of a group organized to protest the police shooting of EULIA LOVE. City officials settled the federal lawsuit in February 1984, agreeing to payment of $1.8 million in damages. At the same time, LAPD leaders vowed to limit spying to cases based on "a reasonable and articulated suspicion" that the targets are "planning, threatening, attempting or performing a significant disruption of the public order." Fourteen months later, the police commission announced plans to destroy 2 million dossiers illegally compiled on some 55,000 groups and individuals since the 1920s. At least 2,500 active files survived the purge, with surveillance presumably continuing. The RODNEY KING beating and subsequent riots finally drove Gates from office in 1992.

His replacement, WILLIE WILLIAMS, was L.A.'s first black police chief, but he failed to heal the city's racial schism and resigned in 1997 after revelations that he had accepted favors from Las Vegas gamblers. Successor Bernard Parks (1997–2002) faced more scandal, as detectives in LAPD's Rampart Division admitted stealing DRUGS and organizing FRAME-UPS of innocent persons. An FBI investigation of that case produced a federal consent decree, whereby the force consented to a course of supervised reforms. At press time for this volume Chief William Bratton was in charge of rebuilding LAPD's tarnished image and bringing it into compliance with federal guidelines.

See also: ASSASSINATION; BOMBING AND BOMB SQUADS; CONNOR, THEOPHILUS EUGENE "BULL"; FEDERAL BUREAU OF INVESTIGATION; STRIKEBREAKING.

Louima, Abner (1967–)

On August 9, 1997, officers of the NEW YORK CITY POLICE DEPARTMENT (NYPD) arrested 30-year-old Haitian immigrant Abner Louima during a brawl at a Brooklyn nightclub. Officer Justin Volpe, mistakenly believing that Louima had punched him during the barroom altercation, subsequently dragged Louima into a restroom at the 70th Precinct station. There, in the presence of other policemen, Volpe sodomized Louima with a toilet plunger's handle, inflicting damage on Louima's bowels and bladder, which required multiple corrective surgeries.

Investigations by NYPD's INTERNAL AFFAIRS Division and the FBI resulted in charges filed against Volpe and five other officers. Volpe pled guilty in 1999 to violating Louima's civil rights and received a 30-year prison term. Officer Charles Schwarz received a 15-year sentence for holding Louima down during Volpe's attack, and for lying about his role in the crime. Two other officers received five-year terms for obstructing investigations of the assault, but their convictions and Schwarz's were later reversed on appeal, leaving Volpe alone in prison. Louima sued for $155 million in 1998, claiming that NYPD officers created a "blue wall of silence and lies to obstruct justice." Authorities settled the case out of court for $8.75 million, including $7,125,000 from the city and $1,625,000 from the Patrolmen's Benevolent Association. That settlement presently holds the record for a New York City case involving police brutality.

See also: FEDERAL BUREAU OF INVESTIGATION.

Louisiana State Police

Louisiana's first statewide law enforcement agency was a team of Highway Commission inspectors created in 1922, with 16 officers assigned to motorcycle patrol on state highways. By 1928, with 70 uniformed officers on staff, commission activities had expanded beyond mere traffic enforcement and accident reportage, prompting creation of a separate Bureau of Criminal Investigation. Highway patrolmen were authorized to carry firearms in 1932, followed in July 1936 by creation of the Louisiana State Police, merging traffic and criminal duties in one agency.

The LSP's first superintendent, General Louis Guerre, modeled his agency on the FBI led by J. EDGAR HOOVER, creating a state crime lab and police training academy. Decades before the federal "war on DRUGS," Guerre's troopers focused on eradication of narcotics traffic in Louisiana (while ignoring, for the most part, widespread illegal gambling conducted by members of ORGANIZED CRIME). Still, in a rigidly segregated state, where LYNCHINGS were common and the violent KU KLUX KLAN enjoyed near impunity, black citizens often complained that the LSP's motto of "Courtesy, Loyalty, Service" applied to whites only.

State legislators imposed a civil service system in 1940, offering troopers "protection from political considerations," then abolished the Department of State Police two years later, transferring the LSP to a new Department of Public Safety. Governor Earl Long, known for his corrupt ties to gamblers and other crime figures, dismantled civil service in 1948 and returned the LSP to a system of political cronyism spanning the next four years. Long's defeat in 1952 restored civil service, but he rebounded in 1956, winning reelection as governor with a vow that state police would no longer "harass and intimidate citizens"—a reference to casino raids ordered by his successor in office.

State troopers faced an emotional challenge in 1965–66, when they were summoned to curb Klan violence against black demonstrators in Bogalusa. Their presence did not prevent Klansmen from murdering black deputy sheriff O'NEAL MOORE in June 1965, nor did they solve that crime. Instead, the force spent $22,000 on a homemade tank, "Big Bertha," to run interference in civil disturbances. Spurred by a turnout of 60,000 persons for a 1971 "Festival of Life" rock concert, the LSP created a Narcotics Education Unit "to enlighten young people and their parents about the dangers of drug abuse." Increased federal surveillance on drug smugglers in Florida, meanwhile, prompted an increase in contraband traffic through Louisiana in the late 1970s and early 1980s. Efforts to stem that tide were hampered by Reagan-era budget cuts and transfer of troopers to staff a new Charitable Gaming Unit (supervising bingo, raffles, and other fund-raising events). Cutbacks forced closure of two troops, at Leesville and Opelousas, during 1988.

The 1990s brought new duties to the LSP, including regulation of video poker and riverboat gambling, incorporation of a new Automated Fingerprint Identification System, and broader investigation of organized crime. More prosperous years fostered growth, the LSP expanding to 1,000 officers. The agency achieved a longtime goal in November 2003, with receipt of national accreditation from the Commission on Accreditation for Law Enforcement Agencies.

Louisville Metro Police Department

Louisville, Kentucky's, police department was established in June 1806, with five officers retained to enforce all city ordinances and harbor regulations. A sixth officer, designated as a general "Watch," joined the force in December 1810. State legislators abolished the watchman's position in 1856 and decreed that Louisville PD should be remodeled on the pattern of big-city Eastern departments, with a chief commanding 51

subordinates. By 1872 the all-male, all-white force had grown to include 180 officers.

Slow but steady progress followed those beginnings. Chief Jacob Haager introduced the city's first covered patrol wagons in 1898. A generation later, bracing for the rigors of PROHIBITION in 1920, the department established its first rifle team equipped with crude BODY ARMOR. Louisville PD hired its first female officer a year later, followed by its first black patrolmen in 1923. New divisions added over time included the Crime Prevention Bureau (1932), the Vice Squad (1948), a bomb squad, a sex crimes investigation unit (1974), a K-9 UNIT and a SWAT TEAM (both in 1981).

While Mayor George Smith ordered police to keep a short leash on the 1920s KU KLUX KLAN in Louisville, banning public sale of Klan literature and driving public rallies across the river to Jeffersonville, Louisville still experienced its share of the social conflict rampant in the South. Complaints of police RACISM and EXCESSIVE FORCE persisted through the 20th century, prompting demands for a CIVILIAN REVIEW BOARD in early 1999. To that end, local residents founded CAPA—Citizens Against Police Abuse—and held a public meeting on April 22. Their pleas for independent oversight were emphasized three weeks later, when two Louisville officers fatally wounded an unarmed black youth, Desmond Rudolph, striking him with 10 of 22 close-range pistol shots. Protest marches followed, escalating in March 2000, after Rudolph's killers received departmental awards for "exceptional valor." That gaffe prompted Mayor Dave Armstrong to fire Chief Gene Sherrard, claiming Sherrard had "violated the mayor's trust" by granting the awards. Nine police commanders resigned in protest, while 75 patrolmen suffered bouts of "BLUE FLU." Police and CAPA members staged opposing marches on City Hall, while the local *Courier-Journal* ran a series on police brutality. On April 3, 2000, Mayor Armstrong vowed to improve police training and accountability procedures, but he ducked meetings with CAPA leaders and vetoed a civilian-review ordinance passed by Louisville's board of aldermen in May.

Matters went from bad to worse from there, beginning with Greg Smith's June 11 appointment to serve as LPD's chief. The move was a promotion from leadership of the Metro Narcotics detail, but Gene Sherrard's appointment to replace Smith as commander of the drug detail produced howls of indignation from black Louisville. City aldermen overrode Mayor Armstrong's veto of the civilian-review ordinance on June 13, whereupon the FRATERNAL ORDER OF POLICE filed a lawsuit to block its implementation. On September 6, 2000, Louisville PD administrators refused to participate in a statewide survey of racial PROFILING, insisting that they had no problems in that area. Their words rang hollow two weeks later, when a local grand jury deemed black victim Rodney Abernathy's killing by four officers a homicide. A short month later, on October 23, corrections officer Timothy Barnes faced trial on charges of killing a black jail inmate. (Jurors deadlocked in that case, November 9.)

On December 5, 2000, Mayor Armstrong and Chief Smith announced a new policy barring officers from using "race, ethnicity, gender, sexual orientation, religion, socio-economic status, or disability of a person as the sole reason" for traffic stops, searches or arrests—then added that Louisville police would record the race and sex of every driver stopped after January 1, 2001. The new year was eight days old when detectives from the Street Crimes Unit killed another unarmed black youth, 18-year-old Clifford Lewis. More protests ensued, and while the officers avoided charges in that case, Louisville authorities settled out of court in lawsuits filed by surviving relatives of Desmond Rudolph ($200,000) and Rodney Abernathy ($600,000). A local judge ruled Louisville's civilian-review ordinance unconstitutional in May 2002.

Love, Eulia (c. 1940–1979)

A 39-year-old mother of three residing in the black ghetto of South Central Los Angeles, Eulia Love lost her husband to sickle cell anemia in June 1978. His death left her with no income except a $680 monthly Social Security check, one-third of which was used to pay her mortgage. Love applied for state assistance to cover her utility bills while she sought work, but the checks were slow in coming, and she owed the gas company $69 by year's end.

On January 3, 1979, technician John Ramirez came to shut off Love's gas. He described Love as "distraught" and "frothing at the mouth," claiming she struck him with a garden spade. Ramirez fled, reporting the incident to his supervisor and to the LOS ANGELES POLICE DEPARTMENT. In his absence, Love obtained the $22.09 minimum due on her gas bill and sat waiting for another employee to surface. Three company trucks arrived at 4:00 P.M., but supervisor Bill Jones refused to accept the money or even to speak with Love. Love's daughters say she was "irrational" by the time police arrived on the scene, pacing the sidewalk with a kitchen knife in her hand, talking to herself.

Patrolman Lloyd Callaghan and Edward Hopson towered over the 5-foot 4-inch woman who greeted them on the street with angry profanity. Both were veteran officers, Hopson's experience including a tour with the CHICAGO POLICE DEPARTMENT before he moved to L.A. Eyewitnesses later insisted that the patrolmen could have disarmed Love easily, yet they fired 12 shots instead, striking Love eight times. As she lay dying on the sidewalk, Hopson allegedly placed his foot on her neck and said, "Stay down, bitch."

Community reaction to the shooting—one in an ongoing series where LAPD's use of DEADLY FORCE raised troubling questions—was immediate and heated. The *Los Angeles Herald Examiner* ran front-page stories critical of LAPD shooting policies, while Wayne Satz of local television station KABC requested details on several similar cases from Chief EDWARD DAVIS. Davis never replied, but police cruisers soon sprouted bumper stickers reading "Satz Sucks," and Satz was besieged with anonymous telephone death threats.

Callaghan and Hopson were cleared of any wrongdoing at a departmental hearing, which black spokesmen dubbed a whitewash. LAPD's Public Disorder Intelligence Division (PDID) sent two officers to monitor public hearings on the case, and also illegally infiltrated a private group organized to protest the shooting. When the surveillance was finally exposed, Chief DARYL GATES initially denied it, then reversed himself to claim that some unnamed group participating in the protests was a target of PDID investigation. Gates failed to explain why his department also infiltrated and harassed two other groups created to protest LAPD shootings in parallel cases from the late 1970s.

Ludlow massacre

Colorado's bloodiest strike began in September 1913, after thugs employed by the Colorado Fuel and Iron (CF&I) Corporation murdered a union activist. Coal miners abandoned the CF&I's mines on September 23, striking to demand recognition of the United Mine Workers union, improved working conditions, and a pay increase beyond $1.68 per day (paid illegally in scrip redeemable only at high-priced company stores). Company leaders promptly hired the Baldwin-Felts Detective Agency, known for its brutal STRIKEBREAKING techniques, to harass strikers and union organizers in the Colorado coalfields.

The Baldwin-Felts Agency's primary weapon was an armored train equipped with machine guns, dubbed the "Death Special," from which its gunmen fired on encampments of striking miners. The first such attack, directed at a tent colony near Forbes on October 17, left one miner dead and two children badly wounded by gunfire. Governor Elias Ammons deployed NATIONAL GUARD units on October 28, but violence continued to the point where many miners dug pits beneath their tents, as shelter from bullets.

As the strike ran into spring 1914, Governor Ammons grew concerned over the cost of keeping troops in the field. Unwisely, he accepted an offer from CF&I leaders to "keep the peace" by dressing Baldwin-Felts goons in National Guard uniforms. Led by Lieutenant Karl Linderfelt—self-described as "Jesus on horseback"—the new "Guard" began harassing miners in the patented Baldwin-Felts style. After a strikebreaker was killed on March 10, by persons unknown, Linderfelt unleashed his men to destroy the Forbes tent colony, and thereby set the stage for all-out war.

The UMW's largest tent city was located at Ludlow, northwest of Trinidad (and today a ghost town). On April 20, 1914, Linderfelt's guardsmen opened fire without provocation on the Ludlow encampment, disrupting a Greek Easter ceremony. Miners fought back in a battle raging for hours, until union leader Louis Tikas sought to negotiate a truce. Guardsmen lured Tikas from the camp, then executed him with three shots in the back, before storming and burning the Ludlow camp at nightfall. Two women and 11 children died in pits beneath their tents, added to 13 persons shot and killed throughout the day.

As news of the Ludlow massacre spread, armed miners rose in mass to attack the Colorado National Guard, while railway workers and other unions struck in sympathy for their cause. Several southern Colorado towns were occupied by miners' "armies," while a number of coal camps were captured and blasted with dynamite. After 10 days of fighting, President Woodrow Wilson sent federal troops to suppress the violence. UMW leaders failed to win their demands, and the union went unrecognized in Colorado, while none of those responsible for the Ludlow massacre were ever prosecuted. A monument erected to honor the Ludlow victims in 1918 was defaced by unknown vandals in May 2003.

lynching

Lynching is broadly defined as the extralegal execution by a mob of persons who are frequently (but not always) accused of some crime. The practice is allegedly named for Charles Lynch, a justice of the peace in 18th-century Virginia, whose court meted out rough justice to Tories, horse thieves, and other undesirables.

Before the Civil War, lynchings were typically the province of "regulators" or "vigilance committees" operating in regions where normal law enforcement was either nonexistent or deficient in some fundamental sense, unable or unwilling to arrest and prosecute

Thousands of lynchings like this one went unpunished between the Civil War and 1959. (Library of Congress)

210

offenders. Victims in such cases were typically suspected criminals, ranging from murderers and thieves to prostitutes and crooked gamblers. That pattern of lynching continued in various northern and western states through the mid-1880s, then ceased as viable courts and police forces were established in various cattle towns and mining camps.

The *other* kind of American lynching, frankly racist in nature, comprised a kind of TERRORISM exercised by whites against blacks, Hispanics, and Asian. Southern states, with their tradition of KU KLUX KLAN violence, produced the great majority of racist lynchings, but no part of the United States was immune to mob rule. Published statistics on lynching are seldom consistent, but they paint a disturbing picture of anarchy nationwide in the lynching decades. Alabama's Tuskegee Institute recorded 4,708 lynchings between 1882 and 1944, including 3,417 black victims and 1,291 whites. The NAACP, meanwhile, counted 3,224 victims lynched (2,522 black and 702 white) between 1889 and 1918. The worst five states for lynching, based on body counts, were Georgia, Mississippi, Texas, Louisiana, and Alabama.

Police response to lynchings varied as widely as the locale and accusations made against specific victims. Some frontier lawmen, including Wyatt Earp, reportedly stood alone against armed mobs and forced the would-be lynchers to back down. In Dixie armed resistance to lynch mobs was virtually unknown before the 1930s, though conscientious sheriffs sometimes transferred prisoners to other jurisdictions for safekeeping. Too often, though, racist police participated in the violence, stood idly by, or let themselves be "overpowered" after token resistance. Lynchers rarely disguised themselves, and many posed for photographs beside their victims. Prosecutions were rare and convictions unheard of before the last half of the 20th century.

Southern tolerance for lynching was conditioned by a history of slavery and segregation, by racist politicians who freely advocated mob violence, and by voters who persistently reelected brutal or negligent sheriffs. Federal intervention was required to identify lynchers in most cases, and the first significant conviction of southern lynchers (on federal charges) came only in 1967. Two more decades elapsed before state authorities convicted and condemned two Klansmen for a lynching they committed in Mobile, Alabama.

Modern security measures and media scrutiny make police-assisted lynchings a virtual impossibility today, but persistent echoes of the bad old days remain. On May 28, 2003, authorities found 32-year-old Ray Golden hanged from a tree in Belle Glade, Florida. Eleven months later, on April 23, 2004, 55-year-old Roy Veal was found hanged in Donegal, Mississippi. Both men were black, and while police describe both deaths as suicides, rumors of lynching persist, including claims that Golden's hands were bound behind his back. Sadly, the southern history of lynching with police complicity makes any verdict in such cases highly suspect.

MacVeagh, Isaac Wayne (1833–1917)

A native of Phoenixville, Pennsylvania, born April 19, 1833, Isaac MacVeagh was 20 years old when he graduated tenth in his class from Yale College. He subsequently studied law and was admitted to the Pennsylvania bar in 1856. During the Civil War, ill health forced MacVeagh's resignation from the Union Army with the rank of major, but his ongoing service with the Republican party secured an appointment as U.S. minister to Turkey (1870–71). President James Garfield named MacVeagh U.S. attorney general on March 5, 1881, but he resigned on October 24, five weeks after Garfield's ASSASSINATION. MacVeagh later served as U.S. ambassador to Italy (1893–97). He died in Washington, D.C., on January 11, 1917.

Madsen, Christian (1851–1944)

A native of Denmark, born at Schleswig-Holstein on February 25, 1851, Chris Madsen was the son of a professional soldier who followed in his father's footsteps, fighting with the Danish army against Germany at age 14. He later joined the French Foreign Legion, and served in Algeria during 1868–69, then was recalled to fight in the Franco-Prussian War of 1870. Wounded and captured at the Battle of Sedan, Madsen escaped and fought with a guerrilla unit for the duration of the war, then immigrated to America in early 1876.

Upon arrival in New York, Madsen quickly joined the U.S. Cavalry and fought in several Indian skirmishes, joining the burial detail for George Custer's troops at the Little Big Horn. (One newspaper account of Custer's last stand erroneously listed Madsen as a casualty of the battle.) His Indian campaigns continued through the Wounded Knee massacre of 1890, then he resigned from the army in 1891 to become a deputy U.S. marshal operating in the Indian Territory (now Oklahoma). That tenure was interrupted in 1898, when Madsen returned to military service as one of THEODORE ROOSEVELT's "Rough Riders" in the Spanish-American War, but he had already earned fame as one of Oklahoma's stolid "Three Guardsman" (with HENRY THOMAS and WILLIAM TILGHMAN).

On returning from Cuba, Madsen picked up his federal badge and returned to the badlands, serving with sufficient distinction to win appointment as U.S. marshal for Oklahoma in 1911. He resigned that post in 1916 for a fling at show business, assisting in promotion for Bill Tilghman's movie about western outlaws, but law enforcement exerted an irresistible lure. During 1918–22 Madsen served as a special investigator for Oklahoma Governor J. B. A. Robertson, resigning before the state was overrun with nightriding terrorists of the KU KLUX KLAN. Madsen died at Guthrie, Oklahoma, on January 9, 1944.

Maine State Police

Established in July 1921, Maine's State Highway Police included 59 "inspectors" by late August. Most were employed on a seasonal basis, with only a handful working full time. State legislators permitted full-time employment of 60 patrolmen in July 1925, each issued a pistol, a motorcycle, and a law book, working seven days a week and earning four dollars per day. In 1935 the agency's name was shortened to its present title, with funding provided for employment of 40 new officers. A year later, a new State Bureau of Identification was created, under state police control, to maintain all criminal records for Maine.

Further advancements followed on the eve of World War II, with installment of the department's first two-way radios in 1940. A year later, for the first time in two decades, troopers were granted one day off per week. A detective was named for each state police troop in 1955, handling criminal matters aside from the agency's traffic enforcement duties, and a separate Criminal Intelligence Unit was established in 1968, to investigate ORGANIZED CRIME and white-collar crime. Four years later, the State Police became a division of Maine's new Department of Public Safety. The first female trooper, Anna Polvinen, was hired in 1977, while a new program was launched two years later, expanding employment of women and minorities.

Expansion in the last two decades of the 20th century included creation of a Tactical (SWAT) Team in 1980, establishment of a K-9 Corps in 1982, introduction of an Organized Crime Investigative Division and a Division of Internal Affairs in 1984, construction of a crime laboratory in 1986 (nationally accredited in 2000), and establishment of a Bomb Disposal team in 1994. In 2000 Maine State Police leaders adopted "Integrity, Compassion, Fairness and Excellence" as a statement of the agency's core values.

See also: INTERNAL AFFAIRS.

Mann Act

The early 1900s witnessed a nationwide panic concerning "white slavery" in America, defined as the forcible abduction of females into lives of prostitution from which there was no escape. RACISM played a role in the scare, as many such crimes were blamed on Chinese Tong societies and the Sicilian Mafia. In June 1910 Congress passed the White Slave Traffic Act, better known as the Mann Act (after its primary sponsor, Illinois Representative James Mann). The law provides a 10-year maximum prison term and/or fines for anyone convicted of transporting females across state lines "for the purpose of prostitution or for any other immoral purpose."

While congressional debate on the Mann Act made clear its design to crush organized prostitution rings, the law's vague language allowed prosecution of private "immorality" wherever FBI agents were particularly zealous. As practiced during 1910–17, Mann Act enforcement saw G-men polling police chiefs and postmasters to learn which towns hosted brothels. Agents then visited individual bordellos, accompanied by local police and attorneys, to survey the occupants for any

interstate travelers. In the process, FBI headquarters accumulated reams of information on civic CORRUPTION and the private lives of prominent citizens, later useful for blackmail. Suppression of private "immorality" was encouraged in 1917, when the U.S. SUPREME COURT affirmed (in *Caminetti v. U.S.*) that noncommercial sex was also subject to Mann Act restrictions.

Targets of Mann Act prosecutions varied widely through the years. One prominent case involved black boxer Jack Johnson, convicted in 1913 for crossing state lines with his white fiancée. An aide to President Woodrow Wilson proved more fortunate, when Democratic prosecutors sidetracked his case prior to trial. FBI chief WILLIAM J. BURNS told Congress in 1922 that organized vice rings had ceased to exist (untrue), but that his G-men still tracked individuals who crossed state lines in search of private pleasure. Edward Clarke, a high-ranking KU KLUX KLAN official, was fined $5,000 for a Mann Act violation in 1924. (Unlike Jack Johnson, he received no prison time.) Musician Chuck Berry was indicted in 1959 for inviting a 14-year-old Arizona girl (later jailed as a prostitute) to work in his St. Louis jazz club, drawing a three-year jail term and a $10,000 fine. The Mann Act remains in effect today, used most commonly against "outlaw" motorcycle gangs and other groups that transport underage females across state lines to work as prostitutes or strippers.

Martinez, Robert (b. 1934)

Robert Martinez was born in Tampa, Florida, on December 25, 1934, the son of Spanish immigrants who left their homeland to work in Tampa's cigar industry. He was a star athlete in high school and at the University of Tampa, where he earned a B.A. in social sciences in 1957. Martinez next taught school in Tampa until 1962, when he enrolled at the University of Illinois to earn an M.A. in labor and industrial relations. With that degree in hand, he returned to Tampa as a teacher in 1964, then won appointment as executive director of the Hillsborough County Classroom Teachers Association two years later.

A taste for politics prompted Martinez to run for mayor of Tampa in 1974, but voters rejected him, and he left the teachers' union in 1975 to manage an uncle's café. Before year's end, Martinez accepted appointment of the Southwest Florida Water Management District, then rallied support for a successful mayoral campaign in 1978. He served two terms as Tampa's mayor (1979–86), highlighted by a switch from the Democratic party to the right-wing Republican camp, then resigned in 1986 to run for governor. The combination of Hispanic roots and a "conservative" philosophy carried Martinez to victory, and while he won kudos for his efforts to suppress the Florida drug trade, critics lambasted his anti-abortion campaigns, imposition of a stiff service tax, and futile efforts to convict rap singers under state obscenity statutes.

Democratic challenger Lawton Chiles defeated Martinez in 1990, but the ex-governor's right-wing pronouncements impressed President George H. W. Bush enough to win Martinez appointment as the new U.S. "drug czar." He remained in that post until Bill Clinton replaced Bush in January 1993, and while Martinez accomplished little or nothing in terms of blocking drug imports from abroad, he stimulated controversy by calling for mandatory drug testing of all college students. In May 1993 Martinez joined son Alan to create Bob Martinez and Company, a marketing and public affairs consulting agency. More recently, Martinez has appeared as a political pundit on various television programs and served as a government consultant for Tampa's Carlton Fields law firm.

See also: DRUGS.

Maryland State Police

Maryland took its first tentative step toward creation of a statewide police force in 1914, with creation of a motorcycle corps assigned to enforce traffic laws under the state's Commissioner of Motor Vehicles. Confronted with a "crime wave" after World War I, the governor established a training camp for military veterans in 1921, and the following year fielded a force of "motorcycle deputies" with statewide jurisdiction over criminal cases, when asked to assist by county sheriffs. The present-day Maryland State Police was established in 1935, as a separate branch of state government empowered to maintain a training school, enforce criminal laws, and further supervise enforcement of Maryland's conservation statutes. In 1970 the agency merged with the state's Department of Public Safety and Correctional Services. Change came again in 1994, when the Department of Maryland State Police was created as a principal executive department, renamed the Department of State Police one year later.

Maryland's state police presently enforces state criminal and motor vehicle statutes and "safeguards the lives and safety of all persons within the State." It enjoys statewide jurisdiction, outside of incorporated municipalities, and may intrude upon those areas under certain conditions regulated by law. State police officers also enforce Maryland's statutes concerning controlled substances (DRUGS) without regard to local jurisdiction.

Mason, James Young (1799–1859)

James Mason was born near Hicksford (now Emporia), Virginia, on April 18, 1799. He graduated from the University of North Carolina in 1816 and was admitted to the state bar three years later. After four years of hometown private practice, he served in the Virginia state legislature (1823–27), as a state judge, and as a U.S. representative (1831–37). In 1837 Mason was appointed to the federal bench, where he served until President John Tyler named him secretary of the navy in March 1844. A year later, on March 6, 1845, President James Knox Polk appointed Mason to serve as U.S. attorney general, a post he held until September 9, 1846. He then resumed private legal practice until January 1854, when he was named envoy extraordinary and minister plenipotentiary to France by President Franklin Pierce. Mason died while serving in Paris, on October 3, 1859.

Massachusetts State Police

America's oldest state police force was launched in 1865 as Massachusetts State Constabulary, tasked primarily with enforcement the Bay State's laws governing manufacture and sale of alcoholic beverages. Over the next 56 years, the agency changed names three times, becoming the State Detective Force, the District Police, and finally the State Police Patrol (in 1921). Motorcycles were widely employed from 1921 onward, as the force assumed highway patrol tasks along with its previous duties of criminal investigation, but the MSP remains a full-service law enforcement agency. At press time for this volume it employed 2,300 sworn officers and 400 civilian support personnel. In April 2005 the U.S. JUSTICE DEPARTMENT granted the MSP $500,000 to assist in solution of "cold" cases and facilitate identification of missing persons through DNA evidence.

mass murder

The FBI's *Crime Classification Manual* (1992) defines mass murder as the unlawful slaying of four or more persons by one offender during the course of a single event. That rather narrow definition ignores multiple murders committed by pairs or small groups of killers, but it still serves to distinguish mass murder from the repetitive pattern of SERIAL MURDER.

Modern police have no significant defense against mass murder, since few (if any) public warning signs exist before the explosive event. Likewise, detective work is rarely necessary to solve such crimes, since the killer commonly commits suicide or remains to be captured or killed at the scene. Such incidents often evoke public cries for presumed remedies, such as tighter GUN CONTROL and censorship of violent films or video games, but no official action to date has succeeded in preventing deadly outbursts by mentally unbalanced offenders.

Masterson Brothers

After the EARP BROTHERS, no family is more closely associated with Old West law enforcement through history
and legend than the three Masterson Brothers. Ironically,
two of the three were natives of Quebec, Canada. The
oldest, Edward, was born at Henryville in September
1852, followed fourteen months later by William Bartholomew (known as "Bat"). The family moved to Illinois before James arrived in 1855, and while their seven
siblings led peaceable lives, the three brothers were fated
to traffic in violence. As with the Earps, it was sometimes difficult to tell which side of the law the Masterson
Brothers staked out as their own.

Ed and Bat moved to Dodge City, Kansas, in 1872,
soon followed by James, where they worked as railroad contractors and buffalo hunters. Bat drifted to the
Texas panhandle in time to fight Indian raiders at the
Battle of Adobe Walls, in July 1874, then spent several
months as a civilian guide for the U.S. Army. In January
1876, while drinking in a saloon at Mobeetie, Texas,
Bat took offense at a cavalryman's comments toward
Bat's female companion. Pistols blazed, leaving the soldier and the woman dead, while Bat emerged from the
fray with a leg wound that prompted him to carry an
ornate walking stick.

By 1877 Bat was back in Dodge City, running a
saloon. He was pistol-whipped by the town's marshal
that spring while helping a prisoner escape from jail, but
the fracas proved no obstacle to his subsequent employment as a deputy sheriff for Ford County. Brother Ed,
meanwhile, was named deputy marshal for Dodge in
June 1877 and fought his first duel with a drunken
cowboy five months later. (Both men were wounded,
but survived.) Ed was less fortunate in his next gunfight, on April 8, 1878. That time he faced two drunks
who refused to surrender their pistols, killing one and
wounding the other, but his own wounds proved fatal.

James joined Dodge City's police force in June 1878,
patrolling the streets in company with Wyatt Earp.
Together they shot it out with three assailants on July
26, one or the other fatally wounding opponent George
Hoy. (Most accounts credit Earp with Hoy's arm
wound, which festered and claimed his life four weeks
later.) Sheriff Bat gained even more authority in January
1879, with his appointment as a deputy U.S. marshal,
but he strayed from both jobs two months later, for
an interlude as a hired gun in a railroad turf war. That
absenteeism caused Bat to miss his brother's next gunfight, a nonfatal match on June 9, and also prompted
local voters to reject his bid for reelection in November.

Both Bat and James had shelved their badges by early
1881, Bat joining the Earps and "Doc" Holliday in
Tombstone, Arizona, while James emerged as co-owner
of a Dodge City saloon. On April 9 James and his part-

Frontier lawman "Bat" Masterson retired as a sports
writer in New York City. (Author's collection)

ner traded shots with a disgruntled former employee, Al
Updegraff, but no one was wounded. Bat came to join
the feud on April 16 (thus missing the worst of the Earp-
Clanton grudge match in Tombstone), and was ambushed
by Updegraff at the Dodge railway depot. With James
and a friend, Bat returned Updegraff's fire, one of the trio
killing their assailant and thus ending the "war."

The year 1883 found Bat in the midst of another
saloon feud, teamed with the Wyatt Earp, Doc Holliday,
and other gunmen as a member of the misnamed DODGE
CITY PEACE COMMISSION. The group cowed reformers
and salvaged Dodge City's red-light district without
firing a shot, and Bat drifted on from Dodge to work
as a newspaper sports writer, then as a Denver-based
prize fight promoter. James, meanwhile, was embroiled
in another Kansas feud, this time between residents of
Cimarron and Ingalls, to determine which town would
become Gray County's seat. Hired by the folk of Ingalls
as a "special deputy," with BEN TILGHMAN and others,
James embarked on a raid to loot public records from
the Cimarron courthouse on January 14, 1889. Cimarron residents fought back, but the "deputies" were better shots, killing two men and leaving a third gravely

wounded, against two of their own with flesh wounds (and Tilghman with a sprained ankle).

A few weeks later, James moved to Guthrie, Oklahoma, where he served as a deputy sheriff, then won appointment as a deputy U.S. marshal in 1893. In that capacity, on September 1, he joined a posse that ambushed the Bill Doolin gang at Ingalls, Oklahoma. When the smoke cleared, two lawmen were dead, two bandits and five townsfolk wounded, but Masterson emerged from the carnage unscathed. He lived another dozen years in Guthrie, dying peacefully on March 31, 1895.

Bat had long since abandoned his pistols, prospering as a sportsman and journalist. In 1902 he married and settled in New York City, working full time as a sports writer for the *Morning Telegraph*. President THEODORE ROOSEVELT named Masterson a deputy U.S. marshal in 1905, but Bat resigned two years later, when the job interfered with his newspaper deadlines. He died in New York on October 25, 1921.

Mathis, Sylvia E.

Information is curiously sparse on the FBI's first black female agent. A native of Durham, North Carolina, birth date unpublished, Sylvia Mathis earned her LL.B. in May 1975 and was admitted to the North Carolina bar two months later. She joined the Bureau on February 17, 1976, and received her first assignment to the New York City field office. No further data is presently available on what should have been a proud (albeit belated) appointment for the FBI.

See also: FEDERAL BUREAU OF INVESTIGATION.

Matsell, George (1811–1877)

A son of Irish immigrants, born in New York during 1911, George Matsell found his first employment as an apprentice in his father's bookstore, later running his own shop while he studied law. After his appointment to serve as a police magistrate, in 1840, Matsell quickly realized that New York City's antiquated nightwatch system failed to meet the law enforcement needs of a thriving metropolis. Matsell first organized his own troupe of private patrolmen, working the waterfronts by night to prevent crimes and arrest violent felons, then pushed for passage of the Metropolitan Police Act which created the NEW YORK CITY POLICE DEPARTMENT in 1844. Grateful Mayor William Havemeyer named Matsell as the NYPD's first chief, and the force of 800 officers hit the streets in July 1845.

Matsell served as chief for the first 12 years of NYPD's existence, proving himself an energetic administrator, committed to establishing his young department's credibility. Although the force initially lacked uniforms, Matsell approved a copper badge, which most historians agree was responsible for patrolmen being nicknamed "coppers," then "cops." He also campaigned for the establishment of a special river police force, to protect commercial property along the city's many waterways. Matsell retired in 1857, but that passage did not end his ties to New York law enforcement. Fourteen years later, during a period of "radical" disturbances in 1871, Mayor Havemeyer named Matsell superintendent of NYPD, but the aging law man was clearly "past it" (as described by NYPD historians James Lardner and Thomas Reppetto). A few months later, Havemeyer solved the Matsell problem by "kicking him upstairs," to a seat on New York's board of police commissioners. He was elected to one term as president of the board, then retired once more to private legal practice and died in 1877.

McCall, Willis Virgil (1910–1994)

Ex–dairy farmer and federal fruit inspector Willis McCall was elected sheriff of Lake County, Florida, in 1944. Although financially supported by the county's leading gamblers, McCall promised a "good, clean, fearless and conscientious execution of my duties" if elected, and voters took him at his word. Henceforth, he ruled Lake County with an iron hand in the name of white supremacy and union-busting until he was finally removed from office by the governor in 1972.

McCall's first brush with fame in 1945 set the tone for his long-running career. Acting under Florida's wartime "work or fight" statute, he jailed various blacks and "radicals" on trumped up charges, holding them in virtual slavery while he pocketed their fines. Strikers were "vagrants" in Sheriff McCall's eyes, and he invaded their homes without warrants, beating those who "resisted arrest." His brutality toward union organizers was legendary, and he led a boycott against editor Mabel Reese of the *Mount Dora Topic*, who dared to publish exposés on McCall's lawless tactics.

Still, it was Lake County's blacks who felt McCall's heavy hand most frequently. Identified in FBI reports as an active member of the KU KLUX KLAN, McCall spared no efforts in harassing African Americans or those whom he suspected (often erroneously) as blacks trying to "pass for white." In 1949 McCall framed four black defendants on false charges of raping a local white woman, in the notorious Groveland rape case. One suspect was killed by McCall's civilian posse, while two others received death sentences and the fourth (a minor already in jail for vagrancy when the alleged rape occurred) was imprisoned for life. Revelations of "THIRD-DEGREE" TACTICS and fabricated evidence led the

U.S. SUPREME COURT to order a new trial for two Groveland defendants in 1951. While transporting them from prison to the county jail that November, McCall shot the two handcuffed prisoners, killing one and leaving the other gravely wounded. A local grand jury praised McCall for his action, while an elderly U.S. attorney (and friend of McCall's) subverted a federal investigation of presumed civil rights violations.

Sheriff McCall continued in that vein for the remainder of his career. He was a suspect (though never charged) in the December 1951 bombing murder of NAACP leader Harry Moore, at Mims, Florida. Twelve years later, McCall's Tavares office was the only public building in Florida that did not lower its flag to half-mast following President John Kennedy's ASSASSINATION. McCall's explanation: he feared that lowering the flag would damage it, by causing it to flap against the courthouse wall. McCall threw Native American children out of Lake County's schools, lured interracial couples to the woods for beatings by his deputies, and maintained "Colored Only" signs in his waiting room long after they were banned by law. Governor Claude Kirk finally suspended McCall from office in April 1972, after McCall beat and kicked a black prisoner to death in his jail cell. He avoided conviction on second-degree murder charges, but voters were fed up, casting their ballots for a Detroit Yankee to defeat McCall's reelection bid that November. McCall died in April 1994, at age 84, at his home on a street that bore his name.

McCulloch, Hugh (1808–1895)

A son of Scottish immigrants, Hugh McCulloch was born in Maine on December 7, 1808. Although his family was impoverished by losses suffered in the War of 1812, he still spent one year at Bowdoin College and emerged from that minimal training to become a teacher. Switching to the law a short time later, McCulloch moved to Indiana, where he was admitted to the bar, and subsequently rose to manage the state bank. His reputation for financial wizardry prompted Secretary of the Treasury Samuel Chase to pick McCulloch as

Florida Sheriff Willis McCall stands with two unarmed prisoners he shot in November 1950. (Florida State Archives)

comptroller of U.S. currency in 1863. A year later, after Secretaries Chase and William Fessenden resigned, President Abraham Lincoln promoted McCulloch to chair the TREASURY DEPARTMENT.

By that time, America's monetary system was in critical disarray, with bills and coins issued by various states through individual banks, while more than one-third of all currency in circulation was counterfeit. At McCullough's suggestion, President Lincoln created the U.S. SECRET SERVICE in April 1865, to crack down on counterfeiters, and the agency began active service two months later. McCulloch remained as secretary of the treasury under President Andrew Johnson, then retired in 1869. He died on May 24, 1895.

McDonald, William Jesse (1852–1918)

A Mississippi native, born on September 28, 1852, William McDonald moved to Texas with his family at age 14. Two years later, following the LYNCHING of two black murder suspects, U.S. troops arrived to protect the black populace, whereupon 16-year-old McDonald "joined enthusiastically in efforts to resist them." The result was a treason charge, but an all-white jury acquitted McDonald, and he subsequently left for New Orleans, where he graduated from a "commercial college" in 1872 and opened a chain of grocery stores. Commerce soon paled, however, and McDonald sold out his business in 1883, returning to Texas as a cattleman, then deputy sheriff of Hardeman County.

McDonald's success in that post prompted his appointment as a deputy U.S. marshal, riding circuit over a vast territory in northern Texas and southern Kansas, including the area then known as Indian Territory (later Oklahoma). His skill at tracking rustlers and bandits, coupled with an uncommon tendency to bring his captives in alive, moved Texas governor Stephen Hogg to commission McDonald as a captain of the TEXAS RANGERS in January 1891. His legend continued to grow, fostered by incidents such as the time when three gunman attempted to kill him at Quanah, Texas. Facing the three (and a corrupt local sheriff) at close range, McDonald killed one assailant and put the rest to flight, while suffering wounds to his left arm and lung.

So renowned was McDonald by 1905 that he was chosen to serve as bodyguard to THEODORE ROOSEVELT when the president toured the Texas panhandle that year. A year later, in August 1906, McDonald investigated a shootout between black soldiers and white civilians at Brownsville. Advancing himself as a man who "knew Negroes," McDonald persuaded President Roosevelt to ignore reports from U.S. Army investigators and issue dishonorable discharges for three full companies of black infantry. It was, as one admiring

author wrote, "just what Texans expected of a Ranger. Particularly of Captain Bill McDonald!"

That performance prompted Governor Thomas Campbell to commission McDonald as a state revenue agent in 1907. Five years later, McDonald escorted another U.S. president—Woodrow Wilson—on a tour of the Lone Star State. Wilson expressed his appreciation by naming McDonald U.S. marshal for the northern district of Texas. Pneumonia claimed the aging lawman's life on January 15, 1918.

McGranery, James Patrick (1895–1962)

A Philadelphia native, born July 8, 1895, James McGranery served as an observation pilot for the U.S. Army during World War I. He graduated from Temple University Law School in 1928 and won admittance to the Pennsylvania bar that same year. After a period of private practice he served in Congress (1937–43), then joined the U.S. JUSTICE DEPARTMENT as an assistant to the attorney general, assigned to supervise the FBI, CITIZENSHIP AND IMMIGRATION SERVICE, and the Federal Bureau of Prisons. President Harry Truman awarded McGranery the Medal of Merit in 1946 and named him to serve as attorney general in January 1952.

After his prior service under Attorney General TOM CLARK, McGranery had few illusions concerning the FBI's history of illegal "BLACK BAG JOBS." In April 1952 Bureau director J. EDGAR HOOVER submitted a list of "hypothetical situations," seeking McGranery's judgment on cases where "trespass was involved." Specifically, Hoover complained to his putative boss that the present rules "regarding the use of microphones without trespass" were "so highly restrictive" and "instances in which we could install microphones without trespass are so few that we have been stripped of this medium of gathering intelligence." Pleading concerns for "national security," Hoover claimed the Bureau had "a definite obligation to obtain and furnish such intelligence to responsible officials," and that "if we did not do so, we would be derelict in our duties." In Hoover's view, "all possible means, consistent with good judgment" were required to protect America from "subversive elements" and threats of "foreign invasion." He closed by arguing that strict controls on "investigative techniques in the face of such grave responsibilities could be considered detrimental to the best interests of the nation. . . . The Bureau as the responsible agency should be permitted to utilize any reasonable means at its disposal as long as such activity is properly supervised."

There would be no such supervision under McGranery, however. He accepted Hoover's self-serving argument as fact and approved warrantless BUGGING "in any case where elements were at work against the security of the United States." A self-addressed memo penned by Hoover on June 9, 1952, noted that McGranery "would leave it to my judgment as to the steps to take. I told the Attorney General that this authority would only be used in extreme cases and only in cases involving the internal security of the United States."

Two more decades elapsed before Hoover's deception and abuse of power was exposed. As for McGranery, he left office with Truman's administration on January 20, 1953, and died at Palm Beach, Florida, on December 23, 1962.

See also: FEDERAL BUREAU OF INVESTIGATION.

McGrath, James Howard (1903–1966)

Born at Woonsocket, Rhode Island, on November 28, 1903, J. Howard McGrath earned a B.A. in philosophy from Providence College in 1926, followed by an LL.B. from Boston University in 1929. He was admitted to the Rhode Island bar in 1929 and served as city attorney of Central Falls (1930–34), U.S. district attorney for Rhode Island (1934–40), governor of Rhode Island (1941–47), and as a U.S. senator (1947–49). During the latter term, he also served as chairman of the Democratic National Committee, thus playing a prominent role in the 1948 election of President Harry Truman. McGrath's reward, in August 1949, was an appointment to serve as U.S. attorney general.

Author Robert Donovan, in his history of the Truman years (*Conflict and Crisis*, 1977), notes that McGrath "was lazy and it was well known in Washington that he drank too much . . . McGrath seems not to have been aware of much that was going on around him." In short, he allowed FBI director J. EDGAR HOOVER to operate with minimal supervision while engaging in various forms of illegal DOMESTIC SURVEILLANCE. As a result, in October 1951 Hoover took the unusual step of seeking JUSTICE DEPARTMENT guidance on use of BUGGING and WIRETAPS. His memo to McGrath read, in part:

As you are aware, this Bureau has also employed the use of microphone surveillance on a highly restrictive basis, chiefly to obtain intelligence information. The information obtained from microphones . . . is not admissible in evidence. . . .

As you know, in a number of instances it has not been possible to install microphones without trespass. In such instances the information received therefrom is of an intelligence nature. Here again, as in the case of wiretaps, experience has shown that intelligence information highly pertinent to the defense and welfare of this nation is derived through the use of microphones.

Having thus informed his nominal superior that the FBI was guilty of criminal "BLACK BAG JOBS" to obtain inadmissible evidence, Hoover requested McGrath's "definite opinion" on whether the lawless activity should continue "or whether we should cease the use of microphone surveillance in view of the issues being raised." On February 6, 1952, McGrath replied:

The use of microphone surveillance which does not involve a trespass would seem to be permissible under the present state of the law. . . . Such surveillances as involve trespass are in the area of the Fourth Amendment, and evidence so obtained and from the leads so obtained is inadmissible. . . . [P]lease be advised that I cannot authorize the installation of a microphone involving a trespass under existing law.

With that verdict in hand, Hoover restricted (but never ceased) illegal break-ins to install bugging devices. McGrath, meanwhile, made no effort to curtail illegal surveillance authorized directly from Hoover's office. McGrath resigned as attorney general on April 7, 1952, and returned to private legal practice. He died at Narragansett, Rhode Island, on September 2, 1966.

McKellar, Kenneth Douglas (1869–1957)

A veteran U.S. senator from Tennessee, born in 1869 and elected to his first term in 1917, Kenneth McKellar was an outspoken critic of FBI director J. EDGAR HOOVER. In 1933 Hoover refused to appoint several of McKellar's constituents as G-men, whereupon McKellar complained to Attorney General HOMER CUMMINGS. Far from achieving his goal, McKellar was livid when Hoover retaliated by firing three Tennessee natives already employed by the Bureau. Sadly for Hoover, McKellar served as chairman for the Senate Subcommittee on Appropriations, and he was ready for battle when Hoover appeared before the committee in early 1936, requesting nearly twice his previously estimated budget for the year.

McKellar launched his attack with stinging criticism of recent "G-men" films produced in Hollywood, which "virtually advertised the Bureau" on theater marquees. Hoover replied that he had objected to such films "in every instance," but grudgingly admitted that his photo appeared on many of the movie posters. Hoover also denied the existence of any paid publicity agents "in the Bureau of Investigation," while neglecting to mention those who drew salaries directly from the U.S. JUSTICE DEPARTMENT.

Moving on, McKellar criticized FBI performance in a recent series of high-profile KIDNAPPING cases, which Hoover claimed were solved by his agents. Under pressure, the director acknowledged that several had been cleared by local police or with assistance from civilian INFORMANTS. After noting that "PUBLIC ENEMY" Alvin Karpis had escaped three FBI traps in recent weeks, while G-men killed eight other bandits and lost four of their own to enemy fire, McKellar declared, "It seems to me that your Department is just running wild, Mr. Hoover. . . . I just think that, Mr. Hoover, with all the money in your hands you are just extravagant."

The worst embarrassment, however, came when McKellar forced Hoover to admit that he had never made an arrest in his 19 years at Justice. Instead, Hoover countered, he had "made investigations." Biographer Ralph de Toledano observes that Hoover left the Senate chamber "feeling that his manhood had been impugned"—which was doubtless McKellar's intention. In short order, Hoover arranged the "personal" captures of Karpis and bank robber Harry Brunette, thereby employing the very publicity apparatus whose existence he denied to salvage his battered reputation.

Senator McKellar, meanwhile, recommended a $225,000 cut in Hoover's budget request for 1936. FBI supporters raised the specter of a new crime wave if Hoover was denied the cash. The final vote not only approved Hoover's budget request but also raised his salary by $1,000 per year. McKellar, himself the subject of several FBI dossiers, never again opposed Hoover. In 1943 he attended graduation ceremonies at the FBI National Academy and praised "this great instrument that has been built up by the grand man who is your director." McKellar retired from the Senate in 1953 and died at home in Tennessee, in 1957.

See also: FEDERAL BUREAU OF INVESTIGATION.

McKenna, Joseph (1843–1926)

Philadelphia native Joseph McKenna, born August 10, 1843, graduated from California's Collegiate Institute in 1865 and won admittance to the state bar that same year. After a brief period in private practice, he was twice elected as district attorney of Solano County (1866–68), then served in the state legislature (1875–76). After failed congressional campaigns in 1876 and 1878, McKenna won election to the U.S. House of Representatives in 1884 and served four terms (1885–92). He resigned from Congress in 1892 to accept a post on the federal bench, then left that job in turn to serve as U.S. attorney general under President Benjamin Harrison, from March 1897 to January 1898. McKenna left the JUSTICE DEPARTMENT for a seat on the U.S. SUPREME COURT, where he served until his resignation on January 25, 1925. He died in Washington, D.C., on November 21, 1926.

Attorney General Joseph McKenna (Author's collection)

McKenna, Mark Douglas

In the early 1990s Atlanta, Georgia, was plagued by a ring of daring thieves who specialized in burglarizing nightclubs, warehouses, department stores, and supermarkets, disabling the most sophisticated alarm systems, sometimes making off with heavy safes. At one point, the gang was blamed for some 500 robberies. By 1992 they focused on local topless bars, scoring five large hauls within a span of 16 months. Somehow, the burglars always seemed to know which clubs had large amounts of cash on hand, and when it would be easiest to loot the bars. Strip club proprietor Henry Jeffcoat was hit three times, including two burglaries at his Goldrush Club and one at his home, losing nearly $200,000 between September 1991 and January 1993.

After the third robbery, Jeffcoat told an employee, "If they try something again, I'll have a surprise waiting for them." One month later to the day, on February 10, Jeffcoat was murdered at his home in suburban Morrow, Georgia, shot nine times as he parked his car in the garage. Homicide investigators had no leads in the case until March 1, when they received a tip from Tami Hurst, proprietor of a gymnasium in Fayetteville. Hurst told investigators that two of her regular patrons,

Riverdale patrolmen Mark McKenna and James Bastel IV, had confessed to Jeffcoat's murder in her presence, explaining that they only meant to rob him, "but things got out of hand."

Skeptical detectives checked out the tip, discovering that Jeffcoat had employed several off-duty policemen as bouncers, while another employee—one Christopher Grantham—was on probation for illegal possession of explosives. Grantham was another patron of Tami Hurst's gym, where he often worked out with Bastel and McKenna. Riverdale police administrators claimed McKenna was on leave, caring for a sick relative in Ohio, but neighbors reported him at home, wearing a large bandage on his face.

Atlanta police surprised McKenna at home on March 2, arresting him and searching his house. Among the items confiscated was an old police report, with a floor plan of Henry Jeffcoat's home drawn on the back. McKenna explained his bandaged face as the result of an accident, then admitted that Jeffcoat had shot him before Jeffcoat, in turn, was killed by James Bastel. Both officers confessed and named accomplices, in return for waiver of CAPITAL PUNISHMENT. Chris Grantham was captured in Alabama, with 10 more arrests (including eight policemen) logged by week's end. Chief Eldrin Bell of the ATLANTA POLICE DEPARTMENT told reporters, "I'm going to be just as venomous as a snake in handling this. If they are dirty, they can expect no mercy."

Mark McKenna was the first to cut a deal, his statement implicating Fulton County sheriff's deputy William Moclaire as one of Jeffcoat's murderers. McKenna, Bastel, Moclaire, and Chris Grantham were charged with Jeffcoat's murder, while other charges accumulated. On June 3, 1993, Moclaire, Atlanta patrolman Brett Morrill, and strip club bouncer Troy Endres faced trial on multiple counts of burglary and armed robbery. Bastel and McKenna testified for the state, resulting in conviction of all three defendants. Moclaire and Morrill received 25-year prison terms, while Endres drew a 10-year sentence.

More trials followed. On June 16, 1994, Morrill, ex-cop Eric Hagan, and nightclub manager James Kirkland were acquitted on separate burglary charges. McKenna pled guilty to the Jeffcoat murder on May 4, 1995, and received a life sentence on July 13. James Bastel likewise pled guilty in that case, receiving his life term on July 6, 1995. The final wrap-up came on July 27, 1995, when multiple cases were settled: Donald Curtis White, former trainer of drug-sniffing police dogs, pled guilty to armed robbery and drew a five-year sentence; Fulton County prosecutors dismissed burglary charges against Chris Grantham (already serving life for murder); and Mark McKenna received a 10-year sentence for armed robbery, to run concurrently with his life term. Even

then, McKenna seemed confused about his fate. "We were just a bunch of cops working out in a gym," he declared. "Then it all got out of control."

McParland, James P. (1843–1919)

An Irish native, born in 1843, James McParland was 24 years old when he set sail from Liverpool for the United States. Settling in Chicago, he opened a liquor store, only to see it destroyed in the great fire of 1871. Thereafter, he joined the Pinkerton Detective Agency and spent four years on minor cases, before he was assigned to infiltrate an Irish secret society—the Ancient Order of Hibernians, better known as the "Molly Maguires"—in the Pennsylvania coal fields. At the time of McParland's assignment, the blue-collar Hibernians were locked in a bitter struggle with management, including TERRORISM on both sides. When members of the Coal and Iron Police assassinated union leaders, the secret order retaliated in kind, claiming an estimated 50 lives in Schuylkill County alone. McParland infiltrated the Molly Maguires as "James McKenna," collecting sufficient evidence to hang 19 union members, while 40 others were imprisoned.

That success earned McParland a promotion to oversee Pinkerton's western operations, and a cameo appearance in Sir Arthur Conan Doyle's novel *The Valley of Fear*, wherein McParland briefly meets Sherlock Holmes. McParland was aging and largely deskbound by January 1906, when Allan Pinkerton assigned him to investigate the bombing ASSASSINATION of Idaho governor Frank Steunenberg. McParland soon arrested suspect Harry Orchard, caught with dynamite in his hotel room, and he procured a confession from Orchard implicating leaders of the Western Federation of Miners. Three union chiefs were charged with murder in that case, acquitted in a three-month trial at which they were defended by celebrity attorney Clarence Darrow. Orchard, meanwhile, was spared from the gallows as a prosecution INFORMANT. Prosecutor James Hawley's opening statement at the trial identified McParland as "the terror of evildoers throughout the West," but he was never called to testify. McParland subsequently headed Pinkerton's office in Denver, and died in 1919.

See also: PINKERTON, ALLAN J.

McReynolds, James Clark (1862–1946)

Born at Elkton, Kentucky, on February 3, 1862, James McReynolds earned a B.S. from Vanderbilt University in 1882 and graduated from the University of Virginia's law school two years later. Thereafter, he practiced law in Nashville, Tennessee, and served as a professor at Vanderbilt Law School (1900–03).

President THEODORE ROOSEVELT named McReynolds an assistant U.S. attorney general in 1903, and he held the post until 1907. Moving on to private legal practice in New York, McReynolds served the federal government in antitrust cases, principally opposing the Tobacco Trust and illegal combinations in the anthracite coal industry. President Woodrow Wilson named McReynolds as his first attorney general on March 5, 1913, and McReynolds held that post until August 1914, when Wilson promoted him to a seat on the U.S. SUPREME COURT. McReynolds left the court in 1941 and died in Washington, D.C., on August 24, 1946.

Meagher, Michael (1841–1881)

A native of County Cavar, Ireland, born in 1841, Michael Meagher immigrated to the United States with his younger brother, John, and settled first in Illinois. Both brothers served in the Union Army during the Civil War, then moved on to Kansas as stagecoach drivers in the latter 1860s. In 1871 Michael was named city marshal in Wichita, with John serving as his deputy. Over the next three years, as described by Wild West historian Bill O'Neal, Meagher "consistently distinguished himself by making arrests, often in the teeth of drawn guns, without violence and by frequently preventing bloodshed."

In 1874 Meagher struck off for Indian Territory (now Oklahoma), where he worked briefly as a carpenter and teamster before returning to law enforcement as a deputy U.S. marshal. At the same time, he was commissioned as a first lieutenant of an Indian-hunting militia company. Adventure soon paled, however, and Meagher returned to his post as marshal of Wichita, Kansas, in 1875. His first real gunfight, on January 1, 1877, resulted from a drunken stagecoach driver's vow to avenge his arrest for public intoxication. Sober and armed, Sylvester Powell ambushed Meagher on his nightly rounds, wounding the marshal twice before Meagher drew his gun and shot Powell in the heart.

As cattle drives and cowboys made a marshal's life in Wichita too hazardous, Meagher moved to Caldwell, Kansas, and tried his luck at gambling. He soon prospered as a saloon owner, and voters elected him mayor in 1880. A year later, on December 17, 1881, Meagher complained to city marshal John Wilson about the rowdy conduct of a drunken cowboy, one Jim Talbot. Arrested for carrying a pistol, Talbot was fined and sent with Deputy Will Fossett to retrieve the necessary funds. En route to his hotel, three cohorts freed Talbot from custody at gunpoint, firing shots at Marshal Wilson when he tried to intervene. Meagher ran to assist the lawmen, and was struck by one of Talbot's slugs, perforating both lungs. A civilian's bullet killed one of Talbot's friends, while the others escaped, pursued by a lynch mob into the badlands. Meagher died 30 minutes later, at a nearby barbershop.

Means, Gaston B. (d. 1938)

Little is known about the early life of Gaston Means, but his adult escapades were so notorious that it hardly matters. In 1923 the *New York Sun* summarized his achievements as follows:

> *Means has been in the papers for a long time. . . . He was an agent of Germany (in 1916) paid to embarrass British commerce. In 1917 he was accused of the murder of a rich widow, Mrs. Maude A. King, who was killed by a pistol bullet while in North Carolina with . . . Means. He was acquitted of the killing, only to be denounced in another court for filing a forged will which would have put the King estate practically at his disposal. Next we find this fellow an investigator for the Department of Justice. . . .*

Even that synopsis failed to cover all of Means's shady activities. In the early years of World War I he had actually been paid by Germany *and* England, each nation employing him to spy on the other. When not immersed in ESPIONAGE, Means liked to boast that he had been tried and acquitted of every crime known to man. He was appointed as an FBI agent by Director WILLIAM J. BURNS, a close friend who had used Means as a private detective in the past. Though officially paid only seven dollars per day, Means compiled a fortune as a G-man, including a lavish home and a chauffeur-driven Cadillac. As historian Francis Russell later described the situation: "At his disposal were badge, telephone, official stationery, an office, and the complete files of the Bureau of Investigation. That was all he needed."

Operating in the shadow of President Warren Harding's corrupt "Ohio Gang," Means fixed federal cases, sold liquor licenses and pardons to PROHIBITION-era racketeers, and pursued various "special assignments of a confidential nature" for the Harding administration. Many of those "special" tasks involved blackmailing political opponents, as Means later explained to congressional investigators.

> *There is a servant working in this house. If she is a colored servant, go and get a colored detective woman [to] take her out; have this colored detective to entertain her, find out the exact plan of the house, everything they discuss at the table, the family, write it down, make a report. And any information you find that*

is—report what you find . . . and then if it is damaging, why of course it is used. If it is fine, why you cannot use it. It does no damage.

Means eventually grew too flamboyant for his own good, whereupon Attorney General HARRY DAUGHERTY suspended him from duty on February 9, 1922, "until further notice." Director Burns compensated for that embarrassment by hiring Means back as an FBI INFORMANT, but that cut both ways. In October 1923 Means appeared as a key witness before a Senate committee investigating the Teapot Dome scandal, led by Senators Thomas Walsh and Burton Wheeler. He described clandestine FBI surveillance of the senators themselves, including an attempted FRAME-UP of Wheeler on false CORRUPTION charges, but Means himself was soon bound for prison, drawing a two-year term for larceny and conspiracy in a jury-tampering case. Incredibly, Burns kept him on the FBI payroll as a "temporarily suspended" agent, but J. EDGAR HOOVER later corrected that error by firing Means once and for all, in May 1924.

Hoover had not heard the last of Means, however. In 1930 the con man published a book, *The Strange Death of President Harding,* which became a surprise bestseller. Two years later, Means surfaced in the midst of the Lindbergh KIDNAPPING case, to bilk newspaper heiress Evalyn McLean of $100,000 "ransom" and $4,000 in "expenses." Informed of the swindle by McLean's attorney, G-men were present when cronies of Means returned to ask McLean for another $35,000. Means was arrested for embezzlement on May 5, 1932, and was later sentenced to 15 years in prison. He survived six years in confinement, then died in 1938. His last $100,000 score was never recovered.

See also: FEDERAL BUREAU OF INVESTIGATION.

Meese, Edwin, III (b. 1931)

Oakland, California, native Edwin Meese III was born on December 2, 1931. He graduated from Yale University in 1953 and obtained his LL.B. from the University of California, Berkeley, five years later. After admission to the California bar he served as deputy district attorney of Alameda County (1959–67), then joined Governor Ronald Reagan's staff as legal affairs secretary (1967–69) and chief of staff (1969–74). Retired from public service when Reagan left the governor's mansion, Meese became a professor of law at the University of San Diego (1977–81), where he doubled as director of that institution's Center for Criminal Justice Policy and Management.

Reagan's election as president in 1980 brought Meese to Washington, where he initially served as White House counsel (1981–84). In that role he recom-

mended the appointment of Jackie Presser—an eighth-grade dropout and Teamsters' Union official with longstanding ties to ORGANIZED CRIME, under federal investigation for CORRUPTION—as a "senior economic advisor" to Reagan's transition team. Meese's friendship with Presser (also a secret INFORMANT for the FBI) rebounded to his discomfort in January 1984, when Reagan named Meese to replace U.S. Attorney General WILLIAM FRENCH SMITH. Meese's confirmation was delayed for over a year by investigation of his Teamster connections, charges of political patronage, various interest-free loans and investments in a Nevada slot-machine business.

Finally confirmed in February 1985, Meese took office as attorney general on March 25. Barely four months later, the JUSTICE DEPARTMENT abandoned its pending case against Jackie Presser in a move that prompted widespread criticism. Meese appeared on *Good Morning America* to deny any role in that decision, insisting, "It's very clear [that] at no time was there any political influence or undue influence." Others disagreed, and a January 1986 report from the President's Commission on Organized Crime criticized the Reagan administration for its close ties to the Teamsters. Meese immediately called another press conference, declaring, "At no time have I, nor to my knowledge any member of the administration, done anything which was designed to assist or aid anyone involved with organized crime. The fact that people did meet with labor leaders was certainly not designed or intended to in any way interfere with the proper investigation of organized crime."

Seven months after that furor, Meese created a new one by releasing a Justice Department report which blamed pornography for rising rates of SEX CRIME in America. The "evidence" was slim, at best, and skewed from a right-wing religious perspective that produced charges of bias from civil libertarians. Meese resigned as attorney general in August 1988 and moved on to head the private Heritage Foundation, a far-right organization that continued under his leadership when this work went to press. Meese memorialized his days in Washington in a memoir, *With Reagan: The Inside Story,* published in 1992.

Memorial Day massacre

In 1937 the Congress of Industrial Organizations called a strike against the Republic Steel Company and others in Chicago. Republic kept its plant open by hiring armed guards and housing nonunion workers inside the factory, while officers of the CHICAGO POLICE DEPARTMENT protected the "scabs" and disrupted CIO picket lines. On Memorial Day a column of some 2,000 strikers marched on the Republic plant and were confronted by police. Moments later, for reasons still unclear, officers opened fire on the crowd, then pursued the fleeing survivors with nightsticks. When the gunsmoke cleared, 10 strikers lay dead or dying, while another 58 marchers and 16 policemen were injured.

Police spokesmen described the shootings as self-defense against a mob led by "Communists" and "outside agitators," yet none of those killed or wounded by police gunfire was armed. A camera crew from Paramount Pictures filmed the event, then suppressed the footage for fear that it might "incite [a] local riot and perhaps riotous demonstrations." Senate investigators later subpoenaed the film and screened it for journalists, who described "scores of uniformed policemen firing their revolvers pointblank into a dense crowd of men, women, and children, and then pursuing and clubbing the survivors unmercifully as they made frantic efforts to escape." Despite the cinematic evidence, no officers were disciplined for their performance in the bloody police riot.

See also: POLICE RIOTS.

Memphis Police Department

Founded in 1827, the Memphis (Tennessee) Police Department began life as a group of town constables patrolling the city on foot. It was disgraced on April 30, 1866, when uniformed officers led rioting whites on a three-day pogrom against black residents and white Republicans, killing 48 persons, demolishing 90 black-owned homes, 12 schools, and four churches. Twelve years later, a yellow fever epidemic struck Memphis, infecting all 55 of the city's policemen and leaving 10 dead.

Enduring RACISM and CORRUPTION posed twin problems for the Memphis law enforcement during the early 20th century. PROHIBITION-era bootleggers bribed most of the force, and Memphis was christened America's "Murder Capital of the Year" for 1932, with 102 homicides. The police department was integrated by the 1960s, but it seemed to make little difference. In April 1968 the ASSASSINATION of Dr. Martin Luther King, Jr. raised serious questions about MPD procedures, including Public Safety Director Frank Holloman's decision to withdraw police security from Dr. King a few hours before his murder. (Conspiracists noted that Holloman had come to Memphis PD from the FBI, where he had long served King's worst enemy, Director J. EDGAR HOOVER.)

Ten years after King's slaying, Memphis police staged an eight-day strike, climaxing a labor dispute with city leaders. Another decade passed before the department welcomed its first black chief, James Ivy, to police a city still deeply divided along racial lines. The 1990s witnessed new moves toward community policing, with establishment of various "mini-precincts" and a Family Trouble Center designed to cope with domestic violence. Other moves toward a kinder, gentler MPD included creation of a Police Athletic League, boys choir, summer youth camps, and a midnight basketball program.

Miami Police Department

Miami, Florida, hired its first city marshal, demolition expert Young Gray, in 1896. Gray earned $50 per month chasing stray dogs and occasional felons, while wearing multiple hats as Miami's building inspector, sidewalk and street superintendent, sanitation inspector, and tax collector. A new city charter abolished the marshal's office in 1907 and established the Miami Police Department under Chief Frank Hardee. Miami hired its first female officer (Ida Fisher) during World War I, while patrol cars replaced horse-drawn police wagons.

The 1920s brought dual problems to the Miami PD, as PROHIBITION spawned rampant CORRUPTION and a revived KU KLUX KLAN actively recruited white peace officers. Klan TERRORISM against blacks, Jews, Catholics, and labor unions endured through the 1950s, with strong implications of police collaboration. Echoes of that racist heritage resounded in 1980, when the acquittal of a white officer, charged with killing an unarmed black youth, sparked catastrophic riots in the Liberty City ghetto. The same year witnessed a "Cuban crime wave," sparked by the Mariel boatlift that dumped 125,000 new Cuban refugees on Florida shores (including an estimated 10,000 hard-core criminals and mental patients). The 1980s also witnessed a flood of DRUGS from Latin America, primarily cocaine, and hasty recruiting opened Miami PD's ranks to certain unsavory individuals. The worst of them, Miami's notorious "RIVER COPS," earned a reputation for robbing and murdering drug smugglers.

While coping with those problems, Miami PD still managed to improve its professional image, winning accreditation from the Commission of Accreditation for Law Enforcement Agencies (CALEA) in the mid-1990s. Between 1997 and 1999, major crimes in Miami declined by 39 percent. Raul Martinez, the department's first Hispanic chief, took office in 2000 and soon found himself tested by the new demands of President George W. Bush's "War on Terrorism." Still, crime-eradication programs continued to work in Miami, with a further 15-percent decline in major crimes during 2001–02.

Michigan State Police

On April 19, 1917, Michigan governor Albert Sleeper created the Michigan State Troops Permanent Force (also known as the Michigan State Constabulary), with 300 men assigned to serve under Col. Roy Vandercook. Despite its name, the agency was conceived as a temporary force, established to protect the state during World War I. Two years later, in March 1919, a new state law reestablished the Constabulary as the permanent peacetime Michigan State Police. A new state constitution, adopted in 1963, reorganized the State Police once again as one of 20 government departments, with a motto promising "SERVICE through EXCELLENCE, INTEGRITY and COURTESY."

Miller, Richard W.

Richard Miller barely made it through training at the FBI Academy in 1964, emerging as a mediocre agent of slovenly habits, seemingly incapable of submitting proper reports on deadline. Still, he lasted 20 years with the Bureau and was assigned to a foreign counterintelligence team at the San Francisco field office in 1984, when he finally distinguished himself as the first G-man ever arrested for ESPIONAGE.

Fellow agents discovered Miller's illicit activity while they were investigating Russian émigrés Nikolai and Svetlana Ogogodnikov, both of whom worked for the KGB. In the course of their surveillance on the couple, G-men discovered that Richard Miller was having an affair with Svetlana, including occasions when she performed oral sex on him in Miller's car. Recruited as a Russian spy in August 1984, Miller had delivered a classified FBI manual to the Ogogodnikovs, then demanded $15,000 in cash and $50,000 in gold. They refused to meet his price, but by that time it hardly mattered. After failing a polygraph test, Miller admitted his crime. He was fired and then arrested on October 3, 1984, the sequence of events allowing FBI headquarters to report that a "former agent" had been jailed for espionage.

On June 26, 1985, the Ogogodnikovs pled guilty on charges of conspiracy to receive stolen FBI documents. Both agreed to testify against Miller, but convicting the traitorous G-man was no simple task. His first trial ended in a hung jury in November 1985 after Miller claimed his dealings with Svetlana were part of a clumsy attempt on his part to infiltrate the KGB. He was convicted of espionage and conspiracy in a second trial, on June 19, 1986, and received two concurrent life sentences. An appeals court quashed that verdict on April 25, 1989, finding that the trial judge had erred by admitting evidence of Miller's failed polygraph test. A third jury convicted Miller on six counts of espionage in October 1990 and he received a 20-year sentence. That judgment was affirmed on appeal in January 1993.

Miller, William Henry Harrison (1840–1917)

A native of Augusta, New York, born September 6, 1840, William Miller attended country schools and Whitestown Seminary before graduating from Hamilton College at age 21. He studied law privately and was admitted to the Indiana bar in 1865. After several years of private practice in Peru, Indiana, where he doubled as county school examiner, Miller joined the staff of Indiana senator Benjamin Harrison (grandson of President William Henry Harrison, for whom Miller was named). Miller served as Harrison's confidential adviser during the 1888 presidential campaign, and was rewarded with appointment as attorney general on March 5, 1889. He held that post until Harrison left office on March 6, 1893, then retired to private life. Miller died in Indianapolis on May 25, 1917.

Milwaukee Police Department

Upon incorporation as a village in 1834, Milwaukee, Wisconsin, hired its first town marshal. Appointed by the mayor, that lone peace officer quickly found himself unequal to the task of curbing rising crime rates. In September 1855 a new city ordinance established the Milwaukee Police Department, activated on October 4 under Chief William Beck, with six policemen recruited for their size and pugilistic skills. In 1861 the city weathered a major bank riot, followed two months later by a LYNCHING that prompted Chief Beck to resign. (He later returned as chief, during 1863–78 and 1880–82.)

Milwaukee abolished its "spoils" system in 1888, theoretically removing the police and fire departments from undue political influence, but no great city in America truly escaped the taint of patronage and CORRUPTION during those years. Milwaukee PD suffered its greatest single tragedy on November 24, 1917, when two boys found a bomb at a local church and carried it to police headquarters. Nine officers died in the resultant blast, and while anarchists were blamed, the crime remains officially unsolved today.

Milwaukee hired its first black officer (Judson Minor) in October 1924, but another half century elapsed before a woman (Ada Wright) joined the force in April 1975. By 1997 Milwaukee PD reported that 29.7 percent of its officers represented MINORITIES, while 14.7 percent were female. The department is commanded by a Board of Fire and Police Commissioners who establish policy, while the police chief's term is limited by statute.

See also: ANARCHISM; BOMBING AND BOMB SQUADS.

Minneapolis Police Department

Minneapolis, Minnesota, avoided most of the opprobrium cast upon neighboring St. Paul as a gangster's paradise in the 1920s and early 1930s, but PROHIBITION fostered the same CORRUPTION found in every other American city, and the local police department has endured countless complaints of EXCESSIVE FORCE through the years. A local CIVILIAN REVIEW BOARD—the Civilian Police Review Authority (CPRA)—was established in 1990, collecting reports of police brutality against ethnic minorities and other victims. According to the CPRA's files, 54 percent of all such reports in 1994 were filed by persons of color, a percentage that increased to 58 percent in 1995 and 61 percent in 1996. In 1994 Mayor Sharon Belton told reporters, "There was a problem and continues to be a problem of excessive force in this community. I'm not going to deny that. I grew up here."

Even before that admission, Chief Tony Bouza (1980–88) told journalists that the force was "damn brutal, a bunch of thumpers" when he took office. Despite his best efforts, Bouza added, "Police will abuse their power. . . . They feel themselves leashed. They want to be free to 'thump,' free to handle assholes. When someone gives them lip, they want to be able to kick their ass[es], and when you don't let them, they feel shackled. I do not let them 'handle' assholes." And yet, despite that assurance, the brutality complaints continued.

One seeming attempt to resolve that problem, in early 2003, was the appointment of Richard Stanek to serve as Public Safety Commissioner. A 17-year veteran of the Minneapolis PD, Stanek boasted more than 40 letters of commendation in his personnel file, plus various other awards and degrees for specialized training. Still, the local black press claimed that his record also revealed a "history of brutal and racist behavior" that was seemingly "erased from City Hall" in his selection as commissioner. In 1992 black motorist Anthony Freeman claimed Stanek cursed and beat him for running a red light. Under oath, Stanek admitted racist jokes and comments, but denied Freeman's charges and claimed he was unaware of Freeman's race until hours after the incident. (The city settled Freeman's lawsuit out of court.) A year later, Stanek was one of four policemen named as defendants in another black victim's brutality lawsuit, also settled prior to trial. In 1996 a third black victim accused Stanek of beating him in a local nightclub, where Stanek moonlighted as a security guard. That case was also settled quietly, boosting Stanek's city tab above $50,000. While remaining on the force, Stanek also served as a state legislator, helping to defeat a legal ban on racial PROFILING sponsored by Rep. Gregory Gray. Gray later told the press: "Rich Stanek doesn't give a good rip about the civil rights of black people and people of color. It's not so much racism as it is just not giving a damn."

Minneapolis is self-insured, paying damage awards in brutality cases from the police department's budget upon authorization from the city council (which frequently tries to avoid public trials). Total awards paid out in the mid-1990s included $570,000 for 1993; $1,367,680 in 1994 (for 10 separate cases); and $1,390,000 in 1995 (eight cases). Between 1992 and 1996, federal prosecutors investigated 32 brutality cases but prosecuted only six.

Minnesota State Highway Patrol

Minnesota state legislators first raised the possibility of creating a state highway patrol in 1925, but the first bill to accomplish that goal was proposed (and defeated) in 1927. Two years later, a force of 35 officers was finally created as an adjunct to the state Highway Department. Highway Commissioner Charles Babcock chose Hennepin County sheriff Earle Brown as the agency's first chief, and Brown conducted the first training course on his farm, between January 18 and April 1, 1930. Graduates worked 12 hours per day, seven days a week, with one day off per month—all for a monthly salary of $150. Chief Brown left the force in 1932, for an abortive gubernatorial race, but the department survived without him, expanded in 1941 to include 126 officers. Various nontraffic duties were added to the patrol's responsibilities over time, including general law enforcement tasks and security for the state capitol complex and governor's mansion (in 1970). In 1999 Highway Patrol officers inaugurated a specially trained K-9 Corps to sniff out DRUGS hidden in cars stopped for speeding on Minnesota highways.

See also: K-9 UNITS.

minorities in law enforcement

Aside from Indian reservations, American law enforcement has long been dominated by Caucasians. That situation, with racial minorities on the receiving end of "white man's justice," has prompted countless complaints of institutional RACISM, ranging from occasional incidents of EXCESSIVE FORCE, "THIRD-DEGREE" TACTICS and racial PROFILING to the extremes of POLICE RIOTS, deliberate murder, police-assisted LYNCHINGS, and collaboration in acts of racial TERRORISM perpetrated by such groups as the KU KLUX KLAN. Each jurisdiction has individual issues and problems awaiting resolution in the 21st century, but one fact remains: Despite concerted efforts to recruit racial minorities for law enforcement, most large agencies remain under predominantly white control.

Statistics in this field regrettably lag far behind the times, but the Bureau of Justice Statistics—a branch of the U.S. JUSTICE DEPARTMENT—reports the following data for U.S. state police agencies in 1997 (the last year with statistics listed on the BJS Web site as of 2005). Hawaii has no state police, and Illinois failed to provide demographic information to Justice, but among the other 48 departments, none is less than 87 percent white (Wisconsin), and 27 range from 95 to 99 percent white. The average percentage of black officers was 6.9 percent, while Hispanic officers accounted for an average 3.8 percent. Ironically, considering their history of long resistance to civil rights in all forms, the ALABAMA HIGHWAY PATROL and the MISSISSIPPI HIGHWAY PATROL were America's most thoroughly integrated state police agencies, with 30 and 29 percent black personnel, respectively. Eight agencies had no black officers at all, including state police in Idaho, Maine, Montana, New Hampshire, North Dakota, South Dakota, Utah, and Vermont.

Whether minorities avoid law enforcement careers for personal reasons or find themselves barred by subtle forms of de facto segregation—such as the "special" physical examinations once performed on black applicants by the LOS ANGELES POLICE DEPARTMENT—minority suspicion of predominantly white police will doubtless continue until the Thin Blue Line reveals more black and brown faces.

Miranda, Ernesto Arturo (1941–1976)

Few lawbreakers have had a greater influence on U.S. police procedures than Ernesto Miranda, born at Mesa, Arizona, on March 9, 1941. From eighth grade onward, following his mother's death and his father's remarriage, Miranda engaged in various juvenile crimes, leading to a 1954 burglary conviction that sent him to reform school. In 1956, a month after his release from custody, Miranda was jailed in Los Angeles for armed robbery, and while he was acquitted on that charge, a list of unrelated SEX CRIMES sent him back to juvenile detention for 30 months. Released and deported to Arizona at age 18, Miranda joined the army but was dishonorably discharged after 15 months, following multiple criminal charges and abortive psychiatric treatment.

Miranda's first adult conviction, for violation of the DWYER ACT, sent him to federal prison for a year, then he apparently "went straight," working as a common laborer in Phoenix, until he was jailed in March 1963 as a suspected serial rapist. Eyewitness testimony placed his car near the scene of the latest attack, and Miranda confessed after two hours of police interrogation. He wrote his statement on a pad provided by police, each page of which bore a printed warning that the signatory

made his statement "voluntarily and of my own free will, with no threats, coercion or promises of immunity and with full knowledge of my legal rights, understanding any statement I make may be used against me." At trial, in June 1963, Miranda's statement was admitted over the objections of his public defender, resulting in his conviction of charges of rape and kidnapping. Miranda received a sentence of 20 to 30 years on each count.

Arizona's supreme court upheld the verdict, but the U.S. SUPREME COURT subsequently reversed Miranda's confession on grounds that he was not informed of his right to consult an attorney. The court further ruled (in *Miranda v. Arizona*) that police must henceforth inform all prisoners of their right to stand silent at the time they were arrested. While police nationwide bemoaned the ruling, Miranda was retried and convicted once again, after the rape victim identified his voice. Paroled in 1972, he returned to Phoenix and led an uneventful life until January 31, 1976, when he was stabbed to death in a barroom scuffle at age 35.

Mireles, Edmundo, Jr.

Texas native Edmundo Mireles, Jr. joined the FBI in 1979, soon after earning his B.A. in business administration from the University of Maryland. He served first in the Washington, D.C., field office, then was transferred to Miami in 1985. There, on April 11, 1986, he joined other agents in pursuit of fugitives William Matix and Michael Platt, wanted in connection with a series of murders and violent armed robberies. The chase turned into a bloody firefight when Platt and Matix were cornered on a dead-end street, their gunfire killing two G-men and wounding five others. Agent Mireles, with one arm disabled, still managed to kill both gunmen in a fierce exchange of fire. As a result of his actions, Mireles received the FBI's first Medal of Valor and was named Police Officer of the Year by the INTERNATIONAL ASSOCIATION OF CHIEFS OF POLICE. While recuperating from his wounds, Mireles served as an instructor at the FBI Academy, then briefly returned to Miami before he was transferred to the Omaha field office.

See also: FEDERAL BUREAU OF INVESTIGATION.

Mississippi Bureau of Investigation

According to its Internet Web site, the Mississippi Bureau of Investigation (MBI) was created "to investigate, report, and prevent criminal activities; to coordinate activities between federal, state, and local authorities involved in crime prevention and criminal investigations; and other related tasks as may be assigned." Its subdivisions include a Special Operations and Major

Crimes Unit, a Protective Services Unit (for state officials and visiting dignitaries), and a Salvage Inspection Unit. Aside from normal law enforcement and protective duties, the MBI also maintains a Criminal Information Center, responsible for interstate exchanges of data with parallel agencies.

Mississippi Highway Patrol

Founded in 1938, the Mississippi Highway Patrol was primarily directed to enforce traffic laws on state and U.S. highways. Patrolmen—commonly called state troopers—were also expected to assist local police departments with criminal cases (before creation of the MISSISSIPPI BUREAU OF INVESTIGATION) and to cope with statewide emergencies at the governor's request. Between 1954 and 1968, Mississippi's chief "emergency" was concerted suppression of the black civil rights movement, and numerous complaints were filed against the Highway Patrol, alleging harassment or EXCESSIVE FORCE directed at African Americans and white civil rights workers. In July 1964 the FBI identified several highway patrolmen as members of the KU KLUX KLAN, whereupon Governor Paul Johnson allegedly commanded them to quit the KKK or leave their jobs, but the patrol maintained its racist reputation through the remainder of the 1960s. In 1970 state troopers were involved with officers of the JACKSON POLICE DEPARTMENT in the JACKSON STATE COLLEGE SHOOTINGS, but none were disciplined for the illicit use of DEADLY FORCE or their documented attempts to conceal evidence from federal agents. Today state spokesmen assure us that "officers of the patrol exemplify the agency's motto of 'Courtesy, Service and Safety.'" Their goals are to enforce traffic laws "in a fair, impartial and courteous manner," while "enhanc[ing] the public esteem for law enforcement by precept and example of each member of the department."

Missouri State Highway Patrol

Created by the state legislature in 1931, Missouri's highway patrol was authorized to hire 125 uniformed officers, but limited appropriations limited the force to 55 patrolmen and a handful of civilian aides. As suggested by its name, the agency's primary duties included traffic safety enforcement and administration of motor vehicle statutes, but that brief expanded over time to include statewide criminal investigations, laboratory analysis of crime scene evidence, and training of law enforcement officers. In 1992 the department became America's 10th state highway patrol accredited by the Commission on Accreditation for Law Enforcement Agencies (CALEA).

Mitchell, John Newton (1913–1988)

Born in Detroit on September 15, 1913, John Mitchell earned his LL.B. from Fordham University in 1938 and was admitted to the New York bar that same year. After four years in private practice, he joined the U.S. Navy in 1942. After World War II, Mitchell returned to private practice in New York City, where he met Richard Nixon in 1963. They became partners in 1967, and Mitchell played a key role in Nixon's 1968 presidential campaign, rewarded in January 1969 with appointment to serve as attorney general.

Observers recall Mitchell as Nixon's primary confidant, described in one account as "the uniquely intimate counselor to whom Nixon turned on every subject from minor political matters to Supreme Court appointments." Mitchell also appeared to enjoy a close relationship with FBI director J. EDGAR HOOVER, both men sharing Nixon's view of "subversives" and political "enemies." That affinity prompted Mitchell to approve many illegal WIRETAPS and "BLACK BAG JOBS" directed at a wide variety of targets, including White House aides, reporters, Democrats, black militants, and members of various "New Left" organizations. Mitchell was fond of mass "conspiracy" indictments as a means of silencing antiwar protests, and he made no effort to restrain Hoover's illegal COINTELPRO campaigns. On one occasion, when a female reporter asked Hoover if he had any plans to retire, Mitchell warned her, "You're so far off base I'm going to belt you one." When Rep. Hale Boggs accused Hoover of tapping his telephones, Mitchell "categorically" (and falsely) denied that G-men had tapped congressional phones "now or in the past," further demanding that Boggs retract his "slanderous falsehoods" and "apologize to a great American." Hoover, for his part, described Mitchell as "a very able man, a very down-to-earth individual."

Mitchell resigned on March 1, 1972, to head Nixon's Committee to Re-Elect the President (CREEP). He hired G. GORDON LIDDY to coordinate CREEP's "dirty tricks," including a series of burglaries and other crimes that precipitated the Watergate scandal. On May 10, 1973, Mitchell and others were indicted on federal charges of conspiracy, obstructing justice, and lying under oath in their efforts to conceal Nixon's illegal actions. Mitchell was convicted in 1974, receiving a prison term of 20 months to five years, ultimately serving 19 months. He was acquitted in a second case, on charges of accepting a $250,000 bribe to protect millionaire swindler Robert Vesco. The publishing house of Simon & Schuster sued Mitchell in 1981 for failure to deliver a contracted Watergate memoir. Mitchell died in New York City on November 9, 1988. Ex-president Nixon led the funeral procession for his longtime friend and loyal accomplice.

Mitchell, William DeWitt (1874–1955)

A Minnesota native, born at Winona on September 9, 1874, William Mitchell graduated from the University of Minnesota in 1895 and earned his LL.B. from the same institution a year later. After practicing law in St. Paul, he served as a U.S. Army officer in the Spanish-American War and World War I. President Herbert Hoover chose Mitchell as his attorney general in March 1929, and Mitchell held that post until Hoover left office on March 4, 1933.

A "dry" Protestant who favored PROHIBITION, Mitchell resisted expansion of federal authority into other areas of law enforcement traditionally left to the states. In 1932 he publicly opposed passage of the Lindbergh Law that made interstate KIDNAPPING a federal defense. In that case, he told Congress, "You are never going to correct the crime situation in this country by having Washington jump in." FBI director J. EDGAR HOOVER disagreed strenuously, pursuing ever greater jurisdiction (and publicity) for the Bureau despite Mitchell's opposition.

Mitchell retired with the inauguration of President Franklin Roosevelt, in March 1933, and left no visible mark on the U.S. JUSTICE DEPARTMENT. While maintaining a private legal practice in New York City, he also served as chairman of the Committee on Federal Rules of Civil Procedure, and as chief counsel for the joint congressional committee investigating the Japanese raid on Pearl Harbor. Mitchell died at Syosset, New York, on August 24, 1955.

Mitrione, Daniel A., Jr.

The son of a former police chief and CIA agent, Daniel Mitrione, Jr. joined the FBI a few years after his father was kidnapped and murdered by rebels in Uruguay. Assigned to the Miami field office, in 1985 he became the first G-man convicted and sentenced to prison for trafficking in DRUGS.

Mitrione was regarded as a model FBI employee until his arrest, and former colleagues attributed his downfall to the pressures of UNDERCOVER WORK involving cocaine smugglers. According to sworn testimony, Mitrione accepted a Rolex watch and other expensive gifts from one of his INFORMANTS, gradually coming to regard the drug smuggler as "the father he barely knew." Over time, Mitrione accepted cash and other rewards to permit distribution of cocaine in Florida, Pennsylvania, and other states. When his informant finally suggested that they steal drugs from an incoming shipment and sell the contraband themselves, with Mitrione earning $850,000 for his part in the plot, Mitrione agreed. On March 15, 1985, Mitrione pled guilty to possessing and distributing 92 pounds of cocaine, as well as taking

bribes to ignore other shipments. He received a 10-year prison term, but obtained leniency by returning nearly $1 million in illegal assets and agreeing to testify against other conspirators in the case. Mitrione ultimately spent three years in a Catholic monastery normally reserved for discipline of wayward priests.

Others indicted in the same case included Florida drug kingpin Hilmer Sandini, Pennsylvania ringleader Eugene Gesuale, and several Latin American smugglers. One of the small-fry, Vincent Ciraollo of Deerfield Beach, Florida, was accused of trying to kill Sandini with a car bomb. Ciraollo countered with a claim that Agent Mitrione planted the bomb in Sandini's car, while he (Ciraollo) later glimpsed its dangling wires and disarmed the device. No mention of that "rumor" was allowed at Ciraollo's trial, where he received a six-year sentence on drug charges. Years later, after his release from prison, Ciraollo obtained various FBI documents related to his case under the Freedom of Information Act. Included was an "informative note" from the Bureau's Criminal Investigative Division, written two days before Ciraollo's indictment, admitting that Mitrione planted the bomb and describing his act as an "attempted homicide." The document was illegally withheld from Ciraollo's defense counsel, JUSTICE DEPARTMENT spokesmen later claiming that Ciraollo's prosecutors never saw it either, since the note was sent directly from the Miami field office to FBI headquarters. Whatever the truth of the matter, no charges were filed against Mitrione for the attempted murder.

Mitrione, Daniel A., Sr. (–1970)

A former police chief of Richmond, Indiana, and a graduate of the FBI National Academy, Daniel Mitrione, Sr. was dispatched to Brazil in 1960 under the auspices of the U.S. State Department's International Cooperation Agency. During his seven-year tenure in Brazil, torture was widely used by police against "enemies of the state," and those same police—many of them trained by Mitrione—organized clandestine death squads that murdered dozens of persons without any pretense of trial.

Transferred to Uruguay in 1967, Mitrione performed the same function as "police adviser" in that nation, widely regarded by government critics as an instructor in torture techniques and ASSASSINATION. His motto, according to CIA acquaintance Manuel Hevia Coscolluela, was: "The precise pain, in the precise place, in the precise amount, for the desired effect." Nor, reportedly, was Mitrione above murder, telling Hevia that "[a] premature death means a failure by the technician. . . . It's important to know in advance if we can permit ourselves the luxury of the subject's death."

On August 1, 1970, Mitrione was kidnapped from Montevideo by members of the revolutionary Tupamaros movement. In exchange for his safe return, Mitrione's abductors demanded the release by August 9 of various political prisoners held in Uruguay, with aircraft provided for their evacuation to Mexico, Peru, and Algeria. At the same time, numerous documents were released to the press, demonstrating Mitrione's official status and provoking media debate of his activities. The Uruguayan government refused to free any prisoners, and Mitrione was executed on schedule, his corpse recovered from the trunk of an abandoned car.

A massive search for Mitrione's killers failed to locate those responsible, although a Spanish Tupamaros member was finally tried in 1977, receiving a 30-year sentence for complicity in the KIDNAPPING. Meanwhile, Mitrione's reputation received a posthumous makeover, official U.S. statements branding him "a defenseless human being," while celebrity entertainers convened a Las Vegas performance in his honor. Family members hailed Mitrione as "a perfect man" and "a great humanitarian," while White House spokesmen told reporters, "Mr. Mitrione's devoted service to the cause of peaceful progress in an orderly world will remain as an example for free men everywhere."

Manuel Hevia, for his part, recalled a different side of Dan Mitrione, describing a torture class conducted for Uruguayan police officers in the soundproof basement of Mitrione's Montevideo home:

Soon things turned unpleasant. As subjects for the first testing they took beggars, known in Uruguay as bichicomes, from the outskirts of Montevideo, as well as a woman apparently from the frontier area of Brazil. There was no interrogation, only a demonstration of the effects of different voltages on the different parts of the human body, as well as demonstrating the use of a drug which induces vomiting—I don't know why or what for—and another chemical substance. The four of them died.

Mitrione's son subsequently joined the FBI and was convicted in 1985 of trafficking in cocaine. Like his father, he was favored with special treatment, his 10-year prison term reduced to three years in a Catholic monastery.

Montana Highway Patrol

During 1933–34 Montana led the U.S. in traffic fatalities, with a 74 percent increase in highway deaths over the previous year. Stunned by that carnage, state legislators created the Montana Highway Patrol in May 1935, selecting 24 officers from a pool of 1,500 applicants,

authorizing the new team to enforce a battery of 11 traffic statutes. During the agency's first year of operation, highway fatalities dropped 25 percent. General law enforcement functions were added to the patrol's responsibilities over time, and in 1956 Chief Alex Stephenson took the unusual step of adding a uniform shoulder patch with the numerals "3-7-77"—a code of uncertain origin widely used by lynch-law VIGILANCE COMMITTEES of the 19th century. In 1972 the Highway Patrol lost its independence, reorganized as a bureau within the Montana Department of Justice. Four female officers joined the force six years later. A three-year review process climaxed in 1988 with national accreditation, making Montana's force the first U.S. highway patrol so acknowledged. In 2001 the Highway Patrol expanded its brief to include dignitary protection.

Montgomery Police Department

As the original capital of the Confederacy, Montgomery, Alabama, had a reputation to uphold in terms of white supremacy during the Jim Crow era. Although they lacked the fearsome reputation of Birmingham's police under Commissioner EUGENE "BULL" CONNOR, Montgomery's officers were equally zealous in upholding the city's various segregation statutes. A particular sore point with civil rights activists was segregated seating on municipal buses, where local blacks were frequently arrested (and occasionally shot) for taking "white" seats.

At last, in late 1955, Montgomery's blacks launched a boycott of the city buses, led by Dr. Martin Luther King, Jr. Police commissioner Clyde Sellers responded by publicly attending racist rallies, behavior that prompted the *Montgomery Advertiser* to proclaim that "in effect, the Montgomery police force is now an arm of the White Citizens' Council." Sellers subsequently retired, with the boycott still ongoing, but his replacement—L. B. Sullivan—was no improvement. Under Sullivan, police harassed black car-pool drivers, yet seemed unwilling to pursue white thugs who rampaged through the black community. Montgomery briefly replaced "Bombingham" as Alabama's epicenter of racist TERRORISM, and while Sullivan's detectives finally arrested four members of the KU KLUX KLAN (two of whom confessed), the bombers were released in a general amnesty which also saw charges dismissed against boycott participants. Once again, blacks were outraged to see their peaceful and legal behavior equated with criminal acts of violence.

Commissioner Sullivan found a new, novel way of harassing those who criticized his racist policies. When boycott leaders, such as Dr. Martin Luther King, Jr., ran a full-page ad in the *New York Times,* Sullivan filed a libel suit against the signatories and against the paper, citing various minor discrepancies in the ad's text (the precise number of blacks arrested in a given year, etc.). A white local jury was pleased to rule in Sullivan's favor, thereby threatening to bankrupt Dr. King and his movement, but the U.S. SUPREME COURT eventually overturned that verdict in a groundbreaking First Amendment decision (*Sullivan v. New York Times*).

While that case wound its way through the courts, integrated freedom riders rode their buses into Montgomery on May 20, 1961. Six days earlier, KKK members had rioted against the demonstrators in Birmingham, their violence covertly sanctioned by Bull Connor's police, and while no evidence has surfaced of a similar Klan-police bargain in Montgomery, the end result was identical. Protesters were mobbed and beaten at the local bus station, along with newsmen and black bystanders, while police were nowhere to be found. Arriving late on the scene, Commissioner Sullivan watched as John Seigenthaler—a JUSTICE DEPARTMENT observer sent by Attorney General ROBERT KENNEDY—was beaten unconscious by Klansmen. While Seigenthaler lay sprawled on the sidewalk, Sullivan first told reporters that "he hasn't requested" medical aid, then announced that every "white" ambulance in Montgomery had simultaneously broken down. As in Birmingham, no Klansmen were arrested or prosecuted for their part in the riot.

Montgomery P.D. has presumably made great strides toward improvement in the past four decades, but its Internet Web site revealed no substantive material at press time for this volume, and repeated inquiries were met with silence.

See also: FREEDOM RIDES.

Moody, William Henry (1853–1917)

William Moody was born at Newbury, Massachusetts, on December 23, 1853. He graduated from Harvard University in 1876 and studied law privately before winning admission to the Massachusetts bar in 1878. After 12 years of private practice in Haverhill, Massachusetts, he served as city solicitor (1888–90) and as district attorney for the state's Eastern District (1890–95). Chosen to fill a vacancy in Congress during 1896, Moody won three more elections on his own, serving in the House of Representatives until May 1902, when President THEODORE ROOSEVELT named him secretary of the navy. Two years later, in July 1904, Roosevelt transferred Moody to the JUSTICE DEPARTMENT as attorney general. He held that post until December 1906, when he left to fill a seat on the U.S. SUPREME COURT. Ill health forced his retirement from the court on December 16, 1910, and Moody died in Haverhill, Massachusetts, on July 2, 1917.

Moore, O'Neal (?–1965)

Washington Parish, Louisiana, was a hotbed of racial violence in the early 1960s, with Bogalusa—the county seat—boasting the largest per capita KU KLUX KLAN membership of any town in the U.S. Unpunished TERRORISM was so common that local blacks organized an armed resistance group, the Deacons for Defense and Justice, to protect themselves. On June 3, 1964, Sheriff Dorman Crowe responded to pressure from civil rights groups by appointing O'Neal Moore and Creed Rogers as the first black deputies in Washington Parish history.

One year later to the day, on the night of June 3, 1965, Moore and Creed were driving home to Varnado, north of Bogalusa, at the end of their shift, when a pickup truck overtook their patrol car. Gunfire erupted from the truck, killing Moore instantly with a shot to the head; Rogers survived, though wounded in the shoulder and blinded in one eye by shotgun pellets. The gunmen sped away, leaving Rogers to radio for help.

An all-points bulletin was broadcast for the suspect vehicle. One hour after the shooting, Bogalusa resident Ernest Ray McElveen was arrested at Tylertown, Mississippi, 20 miles northeast of Bogalusa. Walthall County's sheriff reported that McElveen's pickup matched the broadcast description, and that he was armed with two pistols, one of them recently fired. McElveen waived extradition on June 4 and returned to Bogalusa, represented by a lawyer who often defended Klan members. Investigators reported that McElveen belonged to several racist groups, including the White Citizens' Council, the neo-Nazi National States' Rights Party, and the United Conservatives (identified as a front group for the Louisiana KKK). A relative of the suspect, D. D. McElveen, was also identified by congressional investigators in 1966 as a member of the Bogalusa Klan's "wrecking crew."

Two days after the Moore-Rogers ambush, on June 6, unknown gunmen fired shots into the home of Doyle Holliday, a white sheriff's deputy assigned to investigate the case. Governor John McKeithen offered a $25,000 reward for information leading to the arrest and conviction of Moore's slayers, but it brought no takers, and Ernest McElveen was soon released by local prosecutors for lack of evidence. A quarter century later, FBI spokesmen announced that they had reopened the case, but no charges had been filed by press time for this volume.

See also: FEDERAL BUREAU OF INVESTIGATION.

Mortensen, Ronald

Daniel Mendoza, a 21-year-old resident of Las Vegas, Nevada, was sitting with friends on the steps of his apartment house at 1:00 A.M. on December 28, 1996, when a dark blue pickup truck pulled to the curb nearby. A passenger rolled down the pickup's window, three times shouting, "Come here!" at Mendoza. When Mendoza failed to move, the stranger fired six pistol shots across the sidewalk, one bullet striking Mendoza in the heart and killing him instantly.

Officers of the LAS VEGAS METROPOLITAN POLICE DEPARTMENT initially suspected a gang-related motive, but Mendoza's friends and family denied any gang involvement. Witnesses described the shooter as a "white boy" who had fired with no apparent provocation. Thirty-six hours after the murder, investigators secured a confession from Christopher Brady, a 24-year-old Las Vegas policeman and son of a retired homicide detective. Brady admitted driving the murder vehicle, but blamed the shooting on his passenger, rookie patrolman Ronald Mortensen. They had been driving aimlessly around town, Brady claimed, celebrating Mortensen's 31st birthday, when Mortensen fired several shots from the pickup. Brady thought that Mortensen had fired into the air, until he heard reports of Mendoza's death the next day.

Officers arrested Mortensen on December 29, when he reported for work on the graveyard shift. Newspaper reports described Mortensen as one of 147 officers recently hired without the customary background checks, to compensate for sudden population growth in Las Vegas. His personnel file included a note recommending against his employment, citing his combative conduct while employed as a private security guard, but LVMPD had ignored the warning in its haste to fill gaps in the ranks.

Chris Brady resigned from the force on January 24, 1997, followed by Mortensen on February 13. At his murder trial, in April 1997, defense attorney Frank Cremen named Brady as an alternate suspect in the shooting, citing complaints of EXCESSIVE FORCE and sexual assault filed by two unrelated civilians in 1995. The alleged rape was never prosecuted, but Brady's victim in the other case received a $10,000 out-of-court settlement for his injuries and unlawful arrest. Jurors rejected Cremen's theory and convicted Mortensen of first-degree murder with use of a deadly weapon on May 14, 1997. One day later, the panel recommended a sentence of life imprisonment without parole.

Mossman, Burt (1867–1956)

Born in 1867, Illinois native Burt Mossman moved westward to New Mexico with his family at age 15. He soon abandoned formal education to work on various cattle ranches, winning promotion to foreman of one spread at age 21, rising to superintendent at age 30 of another ranch that covered some 2 million acres in northern Arizona. Around that same time, he participated in the Pleasant Valley War between cattlemen and the "invaders" who raised sheep, but his specific role in the bloodbath remains obscure. At the outbreak of the Spanish-American War, Mossman joined several other famous frontier characters as a member of THEODORE ROOSEVELT's Rough Riders in Cuba. Back in civilian life by August 1901, he accepted appointment as the first commander of the fledgling ARIZONA RANGERS, but his tenure was brief. Mossman's last case, before retiring in August 1902, was the capture of fugitive murderer Augustine Chacon, proud slayer of 42 victims. Mossman used shady lawmen BURT ALVORD and Billy Stiles to arrange a meeting with Chacon, where the bandit was trapped and held for execution of his previous death sentence. After hanging up his badge, Mossman survived to the ripe old age of 89, dying in 1956.

MOVE bombing

There has seldom been an odder couple in U.S. religious history than the cofounders of the American Christian Movement for Life (MOVE, for short). One half of the team, Donald Glassey, was a white academic in his mid-20s, teaching at the University of Pennsylvania while completing graduate studies in social work. The other, Vincent Leaphart, was a black, middle-aged grade-school dropout whose criminal record included convictions for auto theft and armed robbery. The unlikely duo met sometime in the early 1970s, at a fair-housing demonstration held near the UP campus. By 1972 they were pushing a strange brand of communal religion on the streets of Philadelphia, Leaphart sporting dreadlocks and raging against "The System," boarding converts at Glassey's crumbling mansion on North 33rd Street.

By 1975, when the house sheltered 35 devotees and an equal number of stray animals, Leaphart had changed his name to "John Africa," insisting that all his disciples adopt the "Africa" surname. Glassey was the sole exception, clinging to his identity while he transcribed Leaphart's "deep" thoughts, producing a 300-page volume entitled *The Teachings of John Africa* (later simply retitled *The Book*). In practice, cult members obeyed Leaphart's every whim. Female recruits were expected to bear children for MOVE, instructed by "expert" John Africa in techniques of biting through the umbilical cord and licking their newborns clean. Rigorous calisthenics were also prescribed, offset by "distortion days" when MOVE members binged on junk food.

As MOVE grew, its members courted the media spotlight, staging public demonstrations, compiling an impressive list of misdemeanor arrests and civil complaints, the latter chiefly nuisance violations focused on their squalid headquarters. In 1974 alone, MOVE members were jailed 150 times, always defending themselves in chaotic court proceedings. The *Philadelphia Inquirer* described MOVE's performance at a governor's conference, held in a downtown restaurant: "It was this night that MOVE members demonstrated their most baffling ability: How can they talk continuously, punctuating each phrase with an obscenity, without ever saying anything comprehensible?"

Don Glassey left the cult in 1975, voicing fears of imminent violence with complaints that Leaphart/Africa "wanted absolute control over everyone." Neighbors complained incessantly of cultists roaming at large in the nude, surrounding themselves with stray dogs, flinging trash and human waste from their windows to rot in the streets. The cult responded by erecting a stockade, complete with wooden stage and loudspeakers that bellowed threats and challenges around the clock. One tirade warned the neighborhood that MOVE was working on an atom bomb. In 1976, following a sidewalk scuffle with police, MOVE's amplifiers blared accusations that officers had stormed the house and killed infant "Life Africa." Politicians and reporters who investigated the charge were shown a baby's rotting corpse, lying on a bed of dirt and garbage in a cardboard box. A female defector later told authorities the child died from neglect, a victim of John Africa's ban on medical treatment.

City authorities secured an eviction notice for MOVE in May 1977, but the cult refused to leave, its members brandishing guns and vowing a fight to the death. Mayor FRANK RIZZO told reporters that "MOVE has had its day," but the zealots were still holed up in their fortress in March 1978, when Rizzo ordered a blockade on incoming supplies. Five months later, denouncing the sect as "a bunch of complete idiots," Rizzo prepared to storm the compound. On August 8 MOVE met the assault troops with gunfire, killing Officer James Ramp and wounding three other policemen and four firefighters. Nine cultists were finally sentenced to life for their roles in the shooting, but John Africa slipped through the net. He was captured in New York, three years later, but won acquittal on weapons charges and returned to Philadelphia.

The sect welcomed him, inaugurating 1984 with threats to "take care of you people" on the anniversary of the August 1978 shootout. Mayor Wilson Goode imposed another siege on the cult's compound in April 1984, plotting an assault with aid from aerial surveillance. On Mother's Day, May 12, police launched "Operation Move," evacuating homes within a six-block radius of cult headquarters, then using tear gas and water cannons on the fortress. MOVE members returned fire with automatic weapons, prompting

a pitched battle that raged for hours. Finally, when 10,000 bullets and 650,000 gallons of water failed to rout their targets, police dropped an incendiary bomb from the air at 5:30 P.M. By midnight the raging flames had devoured MOVE central and 60 adjoining homes. Two members of the cult survived, leaving John Africa and 10 others to burn in the wreckage. Five of the dead were children, the youngest barely six years old. In retrospect, the MOVE bombing ranks among the most egregious examples of EXCESSIVE FORCE in U.S. history.

Mueller, Robert Swan, III (b. 1944)

A native of New York City, born on August 7, 1944, Robert Mueller III received a B.S. degree from Princeton University in 1966, then served in the Marine Corps (1967–70) before pursuing further education. He earned an M.A. in international studies from New York University in 1972, and an LL.B. from the University of Virginia in 1973. Thus prepared, he served as a federal prosecutor in San Francisco (1973–76), a U.S. attorney in Boston (1986–87), assistant attorney general (1990–93), chief of the U.S. attorney's homicide section in Washington, D.C., (1996–98), and a U.S. attorney in San Francisco (1998–2001). In July 2001 Mueller was chosen by President George W. Bush to replace LOUIS FREEH as director of the FBI. At his Senate confirmation hearing Mueller declared, "We must tell the truth and let the facts speak for themselves. The truth is what we expect in our investigations of others, and the truth is what we must demand of ourselves when we come under scrutiny."

Officially installed as FBI director on September 4, 2001, Mueller found his campaign to "fix" the scandal-ridden Bureau interrupted one week later by the terrorist attacks of September 11. In the wake of that disaster, the FBI found itself immersed in new controversy. Media sources found G-men active with security forces in Pakistan, while FBI headquarters denied it. Bureau leaders debated the possibility of torturing terrorist suspects for information in "emergency" situations, or perhaps having foreign police do it for them (a plan implemented with White House approval by CIA agents). Incessant "terror alerts" from Mueller and Attorney General JOHN ASHCROFT soon lost their impact when no attacks materialized (and one alert, complete with photos of five alleged terrorists roaming at large in America, was retracted as a "hoax" in January 2003). Civil libertarians worried that Mueller's FBI, granted sweeping new powers of DOMESTIC SURVEILLANCE under the USA PATRIOT ACT, might commit abuses surpassing those of late director J. EDGAR HOOVER. As a case in point, the FBI in 2001 reactivated its "Library Awareness Program," professing to believe that a review of books read by Arab Americans or persons with "Arab-sounding" names may somehow prevent acts of terrorism.

Murphy, Francis William (1890–1949)

A Michigan native, born at Harbor Beach on April 13, 1890, Frank Murphy received his LL.B. from the University of Michigan Law School in 1914 and won admission to the state bar before year's end. He joined the U.S. Army as an officer in World War I, then returned to pursue a political career in civilian life. Murphy served first as assistant U.S. attorney for the Eastern District of Michigan (1919–20), but failed in his 1920 effort to win a congressional seat. After briefly teaching law at the University of Detroit, he became a state judge (1923), then served two terms as mayor of Detroit (1930–33), one term as the first U.S. high commissioner of the Philippines (1935–36), and one term as governor of Michigan (1937–38). Defeated in his bid for reelection, Murphy was named U.S. attorney general by President Franklin Roosevelt on January 2, 1939. He held that office for barely a year, moving on to the U.S. SUPREME COURT in January 1940.

When Murphy reached the JUSTICE DEPARTMENT, FBI director J. EDGAR HOOVER had compiled a secret dossier of derogatory information concerning his political beliefs and private life. We can only speculate on the extent to which that file made Murphy a malleable tool of his nominal subordinate, but after barely two months in office Murphy approved a plan to greatly expand the FBI's DOMESTIC SURVEILLANCE powers, while cutting the State Department out of such cases entirely. Hoover petitioned Murphy on March 16, 1939, to grant the Bureau control over investigations "intended to ascertain the identity of persons engaged in espionage, counter-espionage, and sabotage of a nature not within the specific provisions of prevailing statutes." Under standing policy, Hoover complained, G-men required "specific authorization" from State to pursue such cases. Murphy discussed the matter with President Roosevelt, who in turn issued a directive on June 26, 1939, ending State Department oversight and requiring that "all espionage, counterespionage, and related matters" should henceforth be "controlled and handled" by the FBI or military intelligence units. All other U.S. agencies were ordered to give the FBI "any data, information, or material . . . bearing directly or indirectly" on such matters.

Having won the new authority he coveted, Hoover set out to jealously protect it. On September 6, 1939, he alerted Murphy to the creation of a 50-member "special sabotage squad" within the NEW YORK CITY POLICE DEPARTMENT, expected to gain another 100 officers in the "rather near future." Hoover complained of

publicity surrounding the NYPD squad, sparking fears that "consequently much information in the hands of private citizens concerning sabotage and saboteurs will be transmitted to the New York City Police Department rather than the FBI." Hoover sought a White House "statement or request addressed to all police officials in the United States and instructing them to turn over to the nearest representative of the Federal Bureau of Investigation any information obtained pertaining espionage, counterespionage, sabotage, subversive activities and neutrality regulations." Roosevelt complied with an order commanding all state and local police "promptly to turn over" all such data to FBI headquarters.

Murphy added his own postscript to Roosevelt's order, praising the FBI's professionalism and vowing that "if you want this work done in a reasonable and responsible way it must not turn into a witch hunt. We must do no wrong to any man." Hoover ignored that proviso, but Murphy would not live to witness exposure of the FBI's abuses. He died on July 19, 1949.

Murphy, Patrick V. (1920–   )

Brooklyn, New York, native Patrick Murphy was born in 1920, the son of a sergeant with the NEW YORK CITY POLICE DEPARTMENT, two of whose older brothers were also policemen. He served as a U.S. Navy pilot during World War II, then returned home to enter "the family business" as a patrolman for NYPD. After advancement through the ranks, he left Manhattan in the early 1960s to serve as chief of police in Syracuse, New York. That tour of duty was followed by a stint as deputy chief of NYPD, then Murphy retired in 1965 to accept a post with the U.S. JUSTICE DEPARTMENT in Washington, D.C. There, Attorney General RAMSEY CLARK was so impressed with Murphy that he soon named Murphy to run the capital's police force. Following Richard Nixon's election to the White House, in 1969, Murphy left Washington to serve as police commissioner in Detroit, Michigan.

Still, the lure of his hometown was strong, and in 1970 Murphy accepted Mayor John Lindsay's invitation to take charge of the NYPD. Department historians James Lardner and Thomas Reppetto describe Murphy's three-year tenure as "the most fertile moment in the saga of the NYPD's management from the mid-1940s through the early 1990s." Aside from encouraging the first significant promotions of female officers, Murphy also swam against the tide with efforts to curtail police CORRUPTION, but his methods left something to be desired. As one means of removing temptation, Lardner and Reppetto note, Murphy "all but ma[de] gambling legal by ordering an end to most enforcement of the laws against it." (Arrests were barred unless a citizen formally complained about ongoing gambling in his or her neighborhood, thus minimizing contact between police and gamblers linked to ORGANIZED CRIME.) Unfortunately, ample opportunities for graft remained in the narcotics trade, prostitution, and other avenues of illicit commerce, as illustrated by Detective FRANK SERPICO and the investigations of the KNAPP COMMISSION.

Embarrassed by public revelations of widespread bribery within NYPD, Murphy resigned in 1973 and spent the next 12 years as president of the Washington-based Police Foundation, a law enforcement think tank bankrolled by grants from the Ford Foundation. Retiring from that post in 1985, he next directed the U.S. Conference of Mayors' Police Policy Board until December 1998, when he was named executive director of the Drug Policy Foundation. Assuming that post, Murphy issued a public call for sweeping reforms in America drug laws—a call which has thus far been ignored by the White House and Congress.

Nashville Police Department

The area of modern Nashville, Tennessee, saw its first trading post established in 1717, but no organized settlement existed until 1779. Fort Nashborough was renamed Nashville in 1784 and became Tennessee's state capital in 1843. Local policing was haphazard in the city's early years, and the 1785 murder of Nashville's founder, Col. John Donelson, remains unsolved today. Future president Andrew Jackson served briefly as the city's public prosecutor (1788) before moving on to private practice.

Nashville was devastated by the Civil War, occupied by Union troops in 1862, and it harbored a deep-seated hatred of blacks and Yankees during Reconstruction. Leaders of the "fraternal" KU KLUX KLAN met in Nashville during April 1867, to reorganize their order as a paramilitary terrorist organization. That legacy of violent RACISM continued long after the South was "redeemed" for white-supremacist "home rule," with unpunished LYNCHINGS recorded from Nashville as late as December 1924. The 1920s brought PROHIBITION-era CORRUPTION and a revived KKK, which recruited 3,500 members (10 percent of the state's total) in Nashville. Some of those "white knights" were policemen, and their sympathy for terrorists continued through the civil rights era, with a series of racist bombings officially unsolved in 1960.

Local voters approved a new metropolitan charter in April 1963, whereby Nashville's city government merged with that of Davidson County. Police attention to blacks and "radicals" continued after the reorganization. In 1967 Capt. John Sorace of Nashville P.D.'s Intelligence Unit told congressional investigators that his department had monitored various "subversives" since 1956, with aid from a private organization, the Law Enforcement Intelligence Unit, founded by a high-ranking member of the LOS ANGELES POLICE DEPARTMENT. Today Nashville police confront the full range of challenges and temptations found in any U.S. city of similar size, with a half-million residents inhabiting 533 square miles.

National Center for Analysis of Violent Crime

Established on July 10, 1984, at the FBI National Academy in Quantico, Virginia, the National Center for Analysis of Violent Crime (NCAVC) is an outgrowth of the Bureau's early Behavioral Science Unit (now Investigative Support Services). The unit employs psychological PROFILING in an effort to pinpoint unidentified offenders and maintains the Violent Criminal Apprehension Program (VICAP) computer network to assist local police in tracking unsolved "pattern crimes." The NCAVC's work has been publicized (and greatly exaggerated) in Hollywood productions ranging from *The Silence of the Lambs* to TV's *Profiler* series. In fact, NCAVC staff members do not pursue suspects and rarely visit crime scenes, working primarily in the Profiling and Behavioral Assessment Unit of the Forensic Science Research and Training Center.

See also: FEDERAL BUREAU OF INVESTIGATION; FORENSIC SCIENCE.

National Crime Information Center

Arguably the FBI's most valuable service to state and local police agencies, the National Crime Information Center (NCIC) has been operational since January 1967, providing a nationwide computer linkup for arrest and identity records. An ever-expanding Computerized Criminal History File went online in November 1972, but NCIC's files are not limited to arrest and conviction records; they also include information on stolen vehicles, firearms, securities, and any other property identified by serial numbers. A Missing Person File was added in October 1975, followed by an Unidentified Person File in June 1983, and the two were cross-referenced in February 1984.

Like most other units of the FBI, the NCIC has been shuffled from one division to another throughout its history. It began life as part of the Uniform Crime Records Division, then was transferred five years later to the new Computer Systems Division. In 1992 it was shifted again, to the fledgling Criminal Justice Information Services Division, where a new and improved NCIC 2000 was launched in 1999.

At last report, 99 percent of all NCIC requests were processed for state and local police or other federal agencies outside the FBI, but the system still pays dividends for the Bureau. On July 23, 1970, a computer "hit" enabled Michigan authorities to capture Lawrence Plamendon, a leftist radical listed as one of the FBI's "Ten Most Wanted" Fugitives. A quarter century later, following the catastrophic Oklahoma City bombing of April 19, 1995, terrorist Timothy McVeigh was jailed for driving a car with no license plates and for carrying a concealed pistol. A scan of NCIC records revealed no outstanding warrants, but the system helped G-men locate McVeigh two days later, tracing him to the Noble County jail after independent evidence linked him to the bombing. Without that rapid linkup, McVeigh might have posted bail on local charges and escaped.

National Guard

America's oldest military unit is the National Guard, tracing its roots to the first militia companies organized by English settlers of the Jamestown colony in 1607. Massachusetts raised the first militia regiments in 1636, and from the Pequot War of 1637 onward, militiamen have fought in every American war, from the revolution against Britain to the 21st-century invasion of Iraq. Militia troops made up the majority of combat forces in the Spanish-American War, then were renamed the National Guard in 1903 and formally established as a reserve force of the U.S. Army. National Guard units provided 40 percent of U.S. combat troops during World War I and fielded 75,000 troops or pilots during the Gulf War of 1991.

The Guard's law enforcement function is more limited, since federal law generally bans use of federal troops to act as police within the United States. Exceptions include cases of natural disasters and civil disturbances, when the Guard may be summoned by state governors to augment local police departments. Guardsmen were deployed extensively during the ghetto riots of 1965–68, and during the chaotic Democratic National Convention of 1968, in Chicago. In 1970 an Ohio Guard unit was responsible for the KENT STATE SHOOTINGS that left four persons dead and many others injured, during a campus demonstration against the Vietnam War. President George W. Bush also mobilized National Guard units to police U.S. airports following the TERRORIST attacks of September 11, 2001, before sending them on to the Middle East as part of "Operation Iraqi Freedom."

See also: RIOTS AND RIOT CONTROL; TERRORISM.

National Sheriffs' Association

The National Sheriffs' Association (NSA) was created in 1940 as a nonprofit organization, dedicated (in its own words) to "raising the level of professionalism among sheriffs, their deputies, and others in the field of criminal justice and public safety so that they may perform their jobs in the best possible manner, in service to the people of their communities." In that pursuit, the NSA provides technical resources and information, while doubling as a lobby in Congress on issues of importance to U.S. county SHERIFFS. The NSA is thus analogous to the INTERNATIONAL ASSOCIATION OF CHIEFS OF POLICE. As explained on the NSA's Internet Web site, "We believe that the Office of Sheriff is one of our nation's most vital institutions, and we will never cease in our efforts to both preserve and strengthen it."

Navy Judge Advocate General

In 1775 the Continental Congress enacted Articles of Conduct for members of the service that later became the U.S. Navy. A quarter century later, more sophisticated regulations were adapted from the British Naval Code. No lawyers were employed to administer naval justice until the Civil War, when Secretary of the Navy Gideon Welles enlisted an assistant U.S. attorney from Washington to prosecute complicated courts-martial. Welles dubbed his legal adjutant Solicitor of the Navy Department, and Congress followed up in March 1865 with a statute authorizing presidential appointment of a "Solicitor and Naval Judge Advocate General." Five years later, Congress transferred the post to the JUSTICE DEPARTMENT and renamed its occupant the Naval Solicitor. Yet another federal statute, enacted in 1880, reestablished the billet of Judge Advocate General of the Navy (elevated to the rank of rear admiral in 1918).

In May 1950 Congress mandated that all future judge advocate generals must be attorneys, with at least eight years of service as commissioned officers. The same statute established for the first time a Uniform Code of Military Justice. Modifications of the system continued under successive administrations, climaxed in December 1967 with a law establishing the Judge Advocate General's Corps within the Department of the Navy. Today, the JAG Corps maintains a global network of 730 judge advocates, 30 limited-duty legal officers, 630 enlisted personnel, and some 275 civilian employees. The JAG provides advice to the secretary of the navy on all legal and policy matters involving military justice, administrative or environmental law, ethics, damage claims, and so forth. As described on the unit's Internet Web site, JAG's mission "embraces virtually all aspects of Department of the Navy activities." Unlike the characters on television's popular *JAG* series, however, real-life department personnel seldom (if ever) engage in gunfights, brawls, or high-speed chases, leaving such chores to the Navy's Shore Police.

Neagle, David (–1926)

Boston native David Neagle moved to San Francisco with his parents at an early age. He quit school at 13 to pan for gold, then drifted through the various Wild West professions of bartender, gambler, and gunfighter. In 1880 he was named deputy sheriff under JOHN BEHAN in Tombstone, Arizona, where Neagle managed to avoid involvement in the feud between the EARP BROTHERS and Behan's allies from the Clanton-McLowery gang. After the O.K. CORRAL GUNFIGHT and subsequent Earp exodus from Tombstone, Neagle became city marshal. He subsequently lost a bid for Behan's job as SHERIFF, then returned to San Francisco, where peculiar fame awaited him.

It was the classic story of a woman scorned. Sarah Althea Hill, the mistress of Nevada senator William Sharon, declared herself his wife and produced a marriage certificate to prove it. Sharon denied the claim and sued to stop Hill from using his surname. A district court determined that the marriage license was a forgery, whereupon Hill appealed to the Tenth Circuit Court in San Francisco, Judge Stephen Field presiding. With the case still pending, Sharon died and Hill married her lawyer, David Terry. That union notwithstanding, she still went berserk in court when Judge Field upheld the lower court's ruling. Terry supported his wife, brandishing a Bowie knife, and both were jailed for contempt of court. From their cells, they issued death threats against Field, whereupon U.S. Marshal John Franks named David Neagle a special deputy to guard the judge.

On August 14, 1889, the Terrys confronted Field and Neagle aboard a train passing through California's San Joaquin Valley. David Terry slapped the judge, then reached inside his coat when Neagle ordered him to stop, and Neagle killed him on the spot. Sarah Terry filed murder charges against Neagle and Field, whereupon both were arrested in San Joaquin County. Field was released on his own recognizance, while Neagle spent several days in jail. A federal court then ordered his release on a writ of habeas corpus, but San Joaquin's sheriff appealed to the U.S. SUPREME COURT. That body's landmark ruling established a key guideline of federal authority, finding that Neagle "was acting under the authority of the law of the United States, and was justified in so doing; and that he is not liable to answer in the courts of California on account of his part in that transaction." Although the federal government had no specific constitutional authority to protect judges, the High Court interpreted "law" to mean "any obligation fairly and properly inferable" from the Constitution.

Sarah Hill-Terry subsequently went insane and was committed to California's Stockton State Hospital, where she remained until her death, some 45 years later. David Neagle passed into obscurity and died in 1926, but his legacy lived on, used by President THEODORE ROOSEVELT and other U.S. chief executives to expand federal authority, even in the absence of specific statutes or constitutional provisions.

Nebraska State Patrol

Established in 1937, the State Patrol is Nebraska's only statewide law enforcement agency, assigned to duties that include traffic enforcement and investigations, plus general enforcement of other criminal statutes. Its motto is Pro Bono Publico ("for the good of the public"). State Patrol officers are recognized as sworn deputy sheriffs and operate with full authority in all of Nebraska's 93 counties. Divisions of the NSP include the Air Wing, Carrier Enforcement, Communications, Community Policing, Executive Protection, INTERNAL AFFAIRS, Investigative Services, the K-9 Corps, Legal, Supply and Radio Engineering, Traffic Enforcement, and a Training Academy.

Nelson, John (1791–1860)

A native of Frederick, Maryland, born June 1, 1791, John Nelson graduated from William and Mary College in 1811, then studied law privately and was admitted to the Maryland bar in 1813. He served one term in Congress (1821–23) but declined to stand for reelection. In October 1831 President Andrew Jackson named Nelson U.S. charge d'affaires to the Two Sicilies, a post he held for 12 months. President John Tyler appointed Nelson attorney general in July 1843, and he held that post until March 1845 (also briefly serving as Secretary of State ad interim during 1844). Retired to private life after Tyler left office, Nelson died in Baltimore on January 8, 1860.

Neshoba County Sheriff's Department

Neshoba County, Mississippi, is located 40 miles northwest of Jackson. During the troubled 1960s, when Mississippi's black population struggled to achieve even the most basic civil rights, Neshoba was a die-hard island of resistance in a state already known for its devotion to the cause of white supremacy, and much of that resistance emanated from the sheriff's office in the county seat, at Philadelphia.

For at least 12 years, between 1960 and 1972, the Neshoba sheriff's office was controlled by members of the violent KU KLUX KLAN. Sheriff Ethel Glen "Hop" Barnett was elected sheriff in 1959 and terrorized local blacks throughout his tenure, with help from deputies like Lawrence Rainey. Rainey killed one black man while a member of the Philadelphia (Miss.) Police Department, in October 1957, and later joined his chief in beating a black woman who criticized that unprovoked shooting. Rainey joined the sheriff's department in 1961, and killed a second black victim—prisoner Willie Nash—in May 1962. Evidence from that case reveals that Nash was handcuffed when Rainey, another deputy, and Sheriff Barnett shot him multiple times.

In 1963 Rainey campaigned for sheriff on a promise to "handle the niggers and outsiders" expected to flood the state during Mississippi's "Freedom Summer" in 1964. Voters elected him, and Rainey hired Cecil Price, a like-minded bigot, as his chief deputy. In 1964 Rainey and Price were indicted on federal charges for beating black mechanic Kirk Culbertson and fracturing his skull. Those charges were still pending when FBI agents identified Rainey and Price as prime suspects in the murders of three civil rights workers who vanished on June 21, 1964, after Price arrested them for speeding in Neshoba County. Subsequent investigation revealed that Price—a member of the KKK, as were Sheriffs Rainey and Barnett—had jailed the three activists, then released them after nightfall, only to stop them once more on the highway and deliver them to a Klan murder squad.

Rainey, Price, and Barnett were all among 21 Klansmen initially charged in federal court with conspiracy to violate the victims' civil rights. Trial was delayed until 1967, at which time Price was convicted and sentenced to six years in prison. Rainey was acquitted, while the jury failed to reach a verdict on Barnett. Given the atmosphere in Mississippi at the time, it came as no surprise when Price and Barnett both campaigned for the sheriff's office in 1967, with criminal charges still pending against them. Price reminded voters of how he had worked to "maintain a buffer between our people and the many agitators who have invaded our county," adding: "You can be sure that I will be ready to serve you in the future." Still, voters chose Barnett for a second term, serving as sheriff until 1972. The federal charge against him was dismissed in January 1973.

See also: SHERIFFS.

Ness, Eliot (1903–1957)

Chicago native Eliot Ness was born on April 19, 1903, the fifth child of a middle-class family. He graduated from the University of Chicago in 1925, with degrees in law and business, then studied criminology at night under visiting professor AUGUST VOLLMER, while working days as a retail credit investigator. In 1927 Ness joined the U.S. TREASURY DEPARTMENT's Chicago office, one of 300 PROHIBITION agents assigned to halt the flood of illegal liquor inundating the Windy City.

Pervasive CORRUPTION made enforcement of the liquor laws almost impossible, but Treasury officials

Eliot Ness (Bettmann/Corbis)

embarked on a two-pronged attack against local underworld celebrity Alphonse Capone. While a team of accountants investigated Capone's income tax returns (or lack of same), Eliot Ness was assigned to build a case against "Scarface" Al for Prohibition violations. To that end, Ness screened 50 applicants to pick a 10-man team, dubbed "the Untouchables" for their supposed incorruptibility. (In fact, one member of the team was "touched" by bribes, his name and details of his case later omitted from laudatory accounts of Ness's quest to break the Capone mob.)

Between 1929 and 1932 the Untouchables closed several large distilleries around Chicago, seizing numerous trucks and their liquid cargoes. Illegal WIRETAPS helped Ness predict Capone's movements, and the campaign resulted in several hundred charges based on manufacture of illicit booze—but all were dismissed when Capone pled guilty on income tax charges in 1932. Thus, while Ness enjoys a posthumous reputation as the agent who "got Capone," his team served chiefly as a diversion for the accountants working quietly to trap Big Al with numbers.

Following Capone's imprisonment, Ness was transferred to Ohio, where well-organized bootleggers continued their trade well beyond the repeal of Prohibition in 1933. Published reports credit Ness with destroying some 1,000 stills by November 1935, when Cleveland mayor Harold Burton chose Ness as the city's new public safety director, placing him in charge of the police and fire departments. As in Chicago, corruption spawned by Prohibition and exacerbated by wide-open illegal gambling had brought the CLEVELAND POLICE DEPARTMENT into disrepute. High-ranking officers initially dismissed Ness as a "Boy Scout," but his rapid transfer and dismissal of corrupt policemen quickly changed their minds. While most of the local syndicate's gambling clubs lay outside his jurisdiction, in territory patrolled by a corrupt county sheriff, Ness campaigned against labor RACKETEERING, modernized police procedures, and reduced the town's abysmal record of traffic fatalities until Cleveland ranked as "America's safest city."

Ironically, alcohol and careless driving ended Ness's career in Cleveland. In the predawn hours of March 5, 1942, while returning from a party with his wife and two friends, Ness struck another car and fled the scene. Exposure of his part in the accident, and the fact that Ness had been drinking, ultimately forced his resignation as public safety director. Rejoining federal service, Ness spent the remainder of World War II touring U.S. military bases, working to eradicate venereal disease among the troops.

In May 1944 Ness left government service to serve as the chairman of the Diebold Corporation, a lock manufacturer in Canton, Ohio. He ran for mayor of Cleveland three years later, but suffered an embarrassing defeat and never quite recovered. Forced out of Diebold by business rivals, Ness floundered through a series of failed operations, finally settling in Pennsylvania, on the staff of a languishing paper company. His prospects seemed to improve in early 1957, when a publisher contracted for his memoirs of Chicago, but a heart attack killed Ness on May 16, 1957, before *The Untouchables* was published. He never saw the films or TV series that would make his name a household word, synonymous with incorruptible crime-fighting. Death also spared Ness from the wrath of FBI Director J. EDGAR HOOVER, who deeply resented the T-man's posthumous fame, raging when fictional TV scripts credited Ness with apprehending "PUBLIC ENEMIES" captured or killed by the 1930s FBI.

See also: FEDERAL BUREAU OF INVESTIGATION.

Nevada Highway Patrol

The Nevada Highway Department hired its first state highway patrolman on June 23, 1923, supervised by an inspector of the NEVADA STATE POLICE. Two more patrolmen were on staff by 1934, still overseen by State Police administrators. Not until 1949 did Silver State legislators create the Nevada Highway Patrol, as a division of the state Public Service Commission, thereby merging the State Police with inspectors from the Nevada Department of Taxation. A new Department of Motor Vehicles was created in 1957, receiving administrative jurisdiction over the Highway Patrol. In 1985 that department was renamed the Department of Motor Vehicles and Public Safety, reflecting the Highway Patrol's gradual expansion from mere traffic enforcement to general police activities. Today, with 356 commissioned officers and 177 civilian support personnel, the Nevada Highway Patrol combines traffic enforcement with broader police powers and operation of the state's criminal history repository.

Nevada State Police

Red-baiting governor (later senator) Pat McCarran created the Nevada State Police in 1908, as a hard-line official response to labor unrest in the Silver State's mining industry. Although it began life primarily as a STRIKEBREAKING FORCE, the agency also assumed general statewide law enforcement duties and from 1923 onward supervised the state's tiny Highway Patrol (one officer at its inception, only three by 1934). One dramatic incident in the force's early history, unrelated to labor disputes, was a pitched battle fought between NSP officers and a band of nomadic Indian raiders led by "Shoshone Mike," at High Rock Canyon in February 1911. One officer died in the shootout, along with eight fugitives (including several women and children). The Nevada State Police survived until 1949, when it merged with the newly created NEVADA HIGHWAY PATROL.

Newark Police Department

Police in Newark, New Jersey, have borne a troubling reputation since the early days of PROHIBITION, when mobsters such as Arthur "Dutch Schultz" Flegenheimer and Irving "Waxey Gordon" Wexler ruled the city's bootleg traffic and fostered pervasive CORRUPTION throughout the department. At the same time, black residents of Newark complained that the mostly white force seemed addicted to use of EXCESSIVE FORCE against minorities, a trait that boiled over into catastrophic violence during July 1967.

Newark's ghetto riot of that "long, hot summer" began with the arrest of a black taxi driver, John Smith, who was arrested and severely beaten for the "crime" of passing a double-parked patrol car. False rumors spread that Smith had died in custody, prompting angry blacks to stone the police station where he was held. White officers, their badge numbers concealed by strips of tape, responded with a club-swinging charge that ignited further rage and sparked five days of rioting. When the smoke cleared, 26 persons were dead, at least 725 injured, and nearly 1,500 were in jail. All but two of the dead were blacks, most of them shot by police or members of the New Jersey NATIONAL GUARD, some killed under circumstances that suggested deliberate execution. Those victims included:

- James Sanders, age 16, shot twice in the chest, allegedly while stealing whiskey from a liquor store.
- Teddock Bell, 28, shot by police while standing unarmed outside the tavern where he worked.
- Rufus Council, a 32-year-old laborer, shot in the head while standing outside a restaurant. Witnesses say he had his hands raised, begging the officers who killed him not to shoot.
- Robert Martin, 22, killed by police firing randomly on the street where he lived.
- Cornelius Murray, a 28-year-old father of three, shot on the street where he lived by police who "suddenly came over the rooftops spraying the street below with bullets."
- Isaac Harrison, 74, killed by police while walking from his car to his apartment building.
- Michael Pugh, age 12, shot while dumping his family's garbage behind his apartment house.

- Rebecca Brown, a 29-year-old nurse and mother of four, killed with 41-year-old Eloise Spellman, 53-year-old Hattie Gainer, and 45-year-old Rose Abraham, when police and Guardsmen machine-gunned their apartment buildings.

No officers were disciplined for their actions during the riot, and complaints of violent RACISM persisted 30 years later, including charges filed by one of NPD's own. Samuel Clark was a black sergeant with Newark's police force in 1995, when he was beaten on the street by a white fellow cop. Clark's official complaint resulted in a mild reprimand for his assailant, and Clark ultimately left the department in protest. Publicity surrounding Clark's case prompted other minority officers to contact Newark's Police Complaint Center, while civilian investigators caught Newark's cops engaged in various infractions, ranging from sleeping on the job to killing time with prostitutes. In October 2004 two Newark detectives were indicted on charges of conspiracy, theft, and other charges, exposing a pattern of malfeasance including theft of drugs for resale and FRAME-UPS of innocent defendants.

Against that background, Newark PD announced the appointment of its first Latina motorcycle officer, Elvira Lopez, in 2004, announcing the department's mission "to foster excellence in providing service and protection to the community, while encouraging creative, innovative and proactive policing strategies through a philosophy based on Community Oriented Policing." The department's Web site insists that NPD officers "shall strive to accomplish this mission while upholding constitutional rights and exercising fair and courteous treatment to everyone."

New Hampshire State Police

In July 1869 New Hampshire state legislators passed "an act to create a state police in certain cases," initially consisting of a single constable with the authority to deputize others in any town where local authorities "fail to enforce any law in this state." Particular offenders were the various saloons that operated in defiance of state temperance statutes. As luck would have it, the new plan failed to gain the required support from two-thirds of New Hampshire's voters, whereupon it languished for another 46 years.

On May 1, 1915, a new statute was enacted, appointing a state commissioner of motor vehicles, with authority to hire highway patrolmen. The same law authorized New Hampshire's attorney general to employ investigators "to assist him in the apprehension of criminals." A State Police Commission was appointed in 1931, reporting a statewide crime wave and recommending creation of a new state police force that would absorb the existing Highway Patrol. After six years of debate, a new law was enacted on July 1, 1937, creating a Department of State Police.

New Hampshire's was the 15th U.S. state police force. Further legislation, passed in 1961, created a new Department of Public Safety "to improve the administration of the state government by providing unified direction of related function in the field of public safety, a single highway patrol, consolidating criminal enforcement functions in the division of state police, and making possible . . . the integrated administration and operation of these and other safety functions of the state government." Today spokesmen for the New Hampshire State Police proclaim their organization "dedicated to providing the highest degree of law enforcement service throughout the State of New Hampshire while maintaining the traditions of fairness, professionalism and integrity."

New Haven Police Department

While various forms of protective service have existed in New Haven, Connecticut, since the colony's establishment in 1638, the New Haven Police Department was not organized until August 1861. A six-member board of police commissioners was then created, overseeing a chief of police with one captain, one lieutenant, 14 patrolmen, and 15 supernumeraries (substitutes, or "supers"). A horse-drawn "Black Maria" joined the standard foot patrols in 1873, supported by a system of telephone call boxes in 1882. By 1899 the force had expanded to include 176 officers, with one assigned to a lonely bicycle patrol. A K-9 UNIT and motorcycle patrols were added in 1910, supplemented by patrol cars in the latter 1920s.

The New Haven PD held its first organized training program in 1943, while the same year launched a surreptitious foray into illegal WIRETAPPING. Eavesdropping without warrants expanded in the 1950s, ostensibly to combat ORGANIZED CRIME as exposed by the Kefauver Committee, but later revelations proved that much of the NHPD's DOMESTIC SURVEILLANCE was political in nature. While Mayor Richard Lee (1953–69) cultivated a reformer's reputation and won New Haven "model city" status, Police Chief James Ahern spared no effort or expense in spying on alleged "subversives." The FBI collaborated in much of that illicit surveillance, including a campaign to destroy the local Black Panther Party in 1968–70. Wiretaps suggested that Panthers had murdered a police INFORMANT, one Alex Rackley, and while a handful of convictions were obtained in 1970, subsequent revelations of illegal surveillance won reversal of those verdicts on appeal.

The *New Haven Journal Courier* exposed official spying in January 1977, prompting an investigation by the board of police commissioners and civil litigation by some of the identified targets. Various police officers admitted wiretapping under oath, while Mitchell Moore, chief counsel for the board, described the campaign's full extent as "absolutely mind-boggling." After six years of legal maneuvers, the civil suit gained "class action" status in 1983, with the addition of some 3,000 new plaintiffs. The defendants, including two New Haven mayors, four FBI agents, various policemen, and the Southern New England Telephone Company, ultimately settled out of court for $1.75 million. The FBI, meanwhile, announced that self-investigation had "cleared" its agents of any wrongdoing. New Haven, meanwhile, suffered a serious loss of prestige, transformed overnight from a "model city" to "the Wiretapped City" in newspaper headlines.

New Jersey State Police

New Jersey state legislators first debated the creation of a state police force in 1914, but widespread opposition blocked the establishment of an agency perceived as professional strikebreakers. Another seven years passed before the notion was approved, in March 1921. Four months later, Governor Edward Edwards named HERBERT NORMAN SCHWARZKOPF as first superintendent of the New Jersey State Police. Schwarzkopf screened 1,600 applicants, selecting 116 for the first training class (of which 81 completed the course). The new troopers launched their first patrols on motorcycle and horseback in the midst of a blinding snowstorm on December 5, 1921.

Colonel Schwarzkopf led the New Jersey State Police for 15 years, his military background leaving an indelible imprint on all aspects of the organization, although his legacy was tarnished in 1935 by Schwarzkopf's defense of fabricated evidence in the sensational Lindbergh KIDNAPPING case. While his troopers relied primarily on horses through the 1920s, automobiles permitted 208 officers to patrol 7,000 square miles of rural jurisdiction in the 1930s. A detective bureau, established in 1930, fielded professional investigators for the first time in state history. Three years later, a rash of chicken thefts prompted the force to strike back with a registry of tattooed poultry.

Meanwhile, a Central Bureau of Investigation was created in 1929 (renamed the State Bureau of Investigation in July 1930), responsible for collecting mug shots and FINGERPRINTS of convicted New Jersey offenders. The same year witnessed creation of the Automobile Identification Bureau, to combat car theft, and a Statistical Bureau to keep records of all state arrests, investigations, and other NJSP activities. A License Bureau, added in 1931, processed applications for private detective licenses and registered firearms. While traffic enforcement remained a dominant concern of the NJSP, its Traffic Bureau was not created until January 1939. Six months later, the state police assumed security duties for the visiting king and queen of England.

Although New Jersey has long been a notorious haven for ORGANIZED CRIME, state police leaders refrained from any concerted action on that problem until the late 1960s, with creation of its first Organized Crime Task Force, including an expanded Intelligence Bureau and a new Electronic Surveillance Unit to practice BUGGING and install WIRETAPS. The NJSP's Central Laboratory was established in 1969, to analyze crime-scene evidence, with four regional labs subsequently created. In 1975 the Organized Crime Task Force Bureau acquired a new Corruption Control Unit, specifically targeting bribery of public officials. With the advent of casino gambling four years later, in Atlantic City, more than 100 troopers were detailed to serve the state's new Division of Gaming Enforcement and the Casino Control Commission. In 1981 rising crime rates prompted creation of a new State Police Metro Crime Task Force, consisting of uniformed officers assigned to suppress street crime in urban areas. In 1983 new Missing Persons and Solid/Hazardous Waste Background Investigation Units were created. In the 1990s NJSP leaders consolidated the Narcotics and Organized Crime Bureaus into a new Criminal Enterprise and Racketeering Bureau.

See also: CORRUPTION.

New Mexico Mounted Police

Before New Mexico became a state, its territorial legislature met in February 1905 to establish a territory-wide law enforcement agency patterned on the Royal Canadian Mounted Police. The result, led by Capt. John Fullerton, operated initially from headquarters at the Socorro County courthouse (moved to Santa Fe in 1906). The new force was opposed by a variety of special-interest groups, including jealous—and sometimes corrupt—county SHERIFFS, but it survived New Mexico's transition from territory to state in February 1912.

The first state legislature tried to abolish the NMMP by statute, but when blocked by a gubernatorial veto, lawmakers did the next best thing, cutting off all state appropriations to the force. A seesaw legal fight ensued, leaving the NMMP a "phantom" agency, empowered to enforce state laws, but lacking any funds for salaries, equipment or expenses. A supportive governor employed discretionary funds during 1913–17, keeping some of the original troopers on staff as "special

mounted policemen," then the force was briefly rescued by America's entry into World War I. Border raids by Mexican bandits, coupled with paranoid fears of a full-scale German-Mexican invasion, revived support for the force in the interests of state and national security. Despite an increase in public support, postwar "normalcy" and the pervasive CORRUPTION of PROHIBITION raised new objections to a continuing statewide police force. A statute abolishing the NMMP was passed in late 1920, and the force formally dissolved on February 15, 1921.

New Mexico State Police

After a 16-year experiment with the NEW MEXICO MOUNTED POLICE (1905–21), lawmakers in the Land of Enchantment dispensed with a state police force until 1933, when they created the New Mexico Motor Patrol to enforce traffic laws. The new agency proved a resounding success, generating more than enough income from speeding fines to fund itself. Its authority was broadened in 1935, to include enforcement of all state laws throughout New Mexico. While their early uniforms remain essentially unchanged today (sans riding breeches and boots favored by motorcycle officers), state troopers have increased in number from 30 officers to 525, backed by 490 civilian support personnel. Narcotics enforcement is a primary concern, given the state's shared border with Mexico, and concern over illegal immigrants has heightened since 2001, with the declaration of President George W. Bush's "War on Terrorism."

New Orleans Police Department

New Orleans, Louisiana, has long enjoyed a reputation as the "Big Easy," where anything may be had for a price. Unfortunately, that wide-open reputation has rested in large part on municipal CORRUPTION, including historic malfeasance by members of the New Orleans Police Department. Only at the end of the 20th century were serious attempts made to redeem the department's tarnished reputation.

Organized law enforcement in New Orleans began with French martial law in 1718, failing so abjectly that in 1796 the colonial governor declared: "Crime had reached such proportions by the mid 1790's that a full-time city police force was required." Following the Louisiana Purchase of 1803, a City Watch (Guard Deville) was established, then replaced by more military patrols in 1808. By 1817 the Crescent City employed 46 full-time constables, operating from guard houses in four districts. They, in turn, proved so ineffective that armed VIGILANCE COMMITTEES operated at will throughout the 1820s and early 1830s.

A new mayor overhauled the NOPD in 1852, appointing 12 officers and 345 patrolmen under Chief John Youenes. Most of the force resigned four years later, when ordered to walk their beats unarmed during a riotous city election. The Civil War disrupted efforts to reform the force, and a postwar reorganization in May 1866 failed to cure its problems. On July 30 of that year, policemen joined a mob that rampaged through the city, murdering at least 38 blacks and leaving 146 persons wounded.

ORGANIZED CRIME invaded New Orleans in the 1880s, with two Sicilian Mafia families vying for control of various rackets. Chief DAVID HENNESSY cast his lot with one faction, and the other gunned him down in October 1889. When prosecutors failed to convict the alleged conspirators, a vigilante mob took over and conducted a mass lynching that soured relations between Washington and Italy. Despite that "Mafia purge," the mob neither left New Orleans nor severed its ties with the NOPD. PROHIBITION fostered more rampant corruption, during 1920–33, while syndicate bosses Meyer Lansky and Frank Costello struck a deal with Louisiana "Kingfish" Huey Long, establishing illegal casinos and slot machine parlors in New Orleans under police protection. Mob boss Carlos Marcello ran the city as a private fiefdom through the 1970s, and in the process earned notoriety as a prime suspect in the ASSASSINATION of President John Kennedy.

Other problems with NOPD during the mid-20th century included deep-seated RACISM, with frequent complaints of EXCESSIVE FORCE against blacks, and systematic abuse of female prisoners in custody. Crime historian Hank Messick reports, in his 1970 biography of Meyer Lansky, that NOPD officers enjoyed a practice known as "rape by rank," in which arrested women were routinely violated by policemen in order of rank, with lieutenants following captains, trailed by sergeants, and so on. The NOPD suffered its most tragic losses between December 31, 1972, and January 7, 1973, when deranged sniper Mark Essex embarked on a personal war against white officers, killing five and wounding several more, along with a number of civilians.

Scandal of the worst sort reared its head again in 1990s, with four NOPD officers facing murder charges and 30 others indicted on various other charges. Officer Antoinette Frank was sentenced to death September 1995 for shooting three persons during a restaurant robbery. (The victims included her accomplice, Patrolman Ronald Williams II.) Seven months later, Officer Len Davis drew a death sentence for the contract murder of a female witness in one of his many brutality cases. By that time New Orleans ranked as America's "murder capital," with 421 homicides in 1993 alone. NOPD leaders abolished the Internal Affairs Division in 1995, replacing it with a Public Integrity Division housed outside of police headquarters to provide civilians with "a sense of comfort when filing a complaint." Also established was an "early warning system" to review complaints against cops like Len Davis (whose long history of disciplinary infractions began at the police academy, eight years before his murder indictment). In 1998 the NOPD applied for accreditation from the Commission on Accreditation for Law Enforcement Agencies (CALEA). After a strenuous three-year review of department standards and a revision of the NOPD's operating manual, accreditation was granted in November 2001. In summer 2005, the NOPD was further scandalized when various officers fled the city after Hurricane Katrina, refusing to perform their duties, and were subsequently dismissed.

See also: INTERNAL AFFAIRS; LYNCHINGS.

New York City Police Department

America's largest law enforcement agency was launched in 1625, when Johann Lampo was retained as the first patrolman in New Amsterdam. A squad of roving constables was organized after the colony passed to British control, as New York, but the state's governor did not approve a formal police force until 1844. A year later, in July 1845, the fledgling department of 800 officers began routine street patrols under Chief GEORGE MATSELL.

Policing New York City has never been an easy task, nor one immune to controversy. From the 19th century onward, cyclic exposures and investigations of police CORRUPTION have occurred at approximate 20-year intervals, while complaints of EXCESSIVE FORCE and RACISM have never been in short supply. The catastrophic Draft Riots of 1863—begun as a protest against Civil War conscription, quickly transformed into a pogrom against blacks—tested NYPD to its limits. PROHIBITION refined bribery to an art form as bootlegging gangs evolved into a nationwide network of ORGANIZED CRIME, clearly protected by police paid to ignore speakeasies, gambling dens, and brothels. Sometimes the officers were even more accommodating, as in November 1941, when a team of NYPD detectives accepted $50,000 to stage the "accidental" death of mob informant Abe Reles.

On the racial front, NYPD has seldom been free of controversy. Police shootings of unarmed black citizens sparked race riots in Harlem during 1943, and again in 1964. More recently, Officer Justin Volpe received a 30-year prison term for his August 1997 assault on prisoner ABNER LOUIMA, sodomized with a plunger handle in a Brooklyn precinct house. In February 1999 four undercover officers hit an innocent man, AMADOU DIALLO, with 19 of the 41 bullets they fired at him during a pointless street corner confrontation. In March 2000 narcotics detectives approached Patrick Dorisman, an unarmed security guard, in a misguided attempt to buy drugs, then wound up shooting him to death in the ensuing argument. Timothy Stansbury, a 19-year-old African American, was shot and killed in January 2004 after he "startled" Officer Richard Neri on the roof of a ghetto tenement.

While such incidents spark flares of community outrage, New Yorkers have become almost blasé concerning the periodic exposure of pervasive departmental corruption. Legendary detective FRANK SERPICO shattered the "blue wall of silence" in 1971, after a brush with death at the hands of drug dealers protected by his fellow officers, and other cops eventually shared their stories of bribery with the resulting KNAPP COMMISSION, but matters were even worse in 1993, when Mayor David Dinkins appointed the Mollen Commission to investigate near-identical charges of pervasive malfeasance. According to the Mollen Commission's report: "Today's corruption is not the corruption of Knapp Commission days. Corruption then was largely a corruption of accommodation, of criminals and police officers giving and taking bribes, buying and selling protection. Corruption was, in its essence, consensual. Today's corruption is characterized by brutality, theft, abuse of authority and active police criminality."

The persistence of that corruption was highlighted once again in March 2005, when NYPD detectives Stephen Caracappa and Louis Eppolito were indicted and held without bond on charges that they served as Mafia hitmen, betraying and personally murdering syndicate informers. Charges filed against the two detectives at press time for this volume included eight counts of first-degree murder, two attempted murders, murder conspiracy, obstruction of justice, drug distribution, and money laundering. Prosecutors alleged that Caracappa and Eppolito received $65,000 from the Lucchese crime family for one murder committed in 1992. Defense attorneys insisted that the U.S. JUSTICE DEPARTMENT is "relying on the word of rats" to prosecute the two former detectives. Caracappa and Eppolito were convicted in April 2006 and facing possible life sentences as of this writing.

Despite its manifest shortcomings, NYPD has still compiled an impressive law enforcement record, persevering in the face of persistent budget shortfalls since the 1970s and rising to unprecedented heights of heroism during the terrorist attacks of September 11, 2001. New York City's Transit Police and Housing Police were absorbed by NYPD during 1995, contributing to a force that boasted 40,000 sworn officers and several thousand civilian support personnel by 2004. In recent years, despite a homicide epidemic fueled by crack cocaine, NYPD has scored dramatic successes in the reduction of violent street crime. Much of that success is publicly attributed to COMPSTAT, a computerized database of crime statistics instituted in the 1990s, which enables NYPD to track geographic trends in crime, thereby moving more effectively against a rogue's gallery of miscreants ranging from street beggars to muggers, armed robbers, and drug dealers.

See also: DRUGS; INFORMANTS; TRANSIT POLICE.

New York State Police

A rural holdup-murder in 1913 sparked the movement for creation of a New York state police force, as survivors of victim Sam Howell complained of sparse protection outside incorporated towns and cities. Legislative resistance endured, but a statute establishing the Department of State Police with a $500,000 budget was finally enacted in April 1917. According to that law, unchanged to this day: "It shall be the duty of the State Police to prevent and detect crime and apprehend criminals. They shall also be subject to the call of the Governor and empowered to cooperate with any other department of the State or with local authorities." Military surgeon George Chandler was appointed as the first superintendent, despite his total lack of law enforcement experience.

After a debut policing the 1917 New York State Fair, the NYSP expanded into STRIKEBREAKING during World War I, tried its hand at PROHIBITION enforcement without much success during 1920–33, and assumed highway patrol duties with establishment of a Traffic Bureau in 1937. Still, the force had only 100 officers by 1940, with 35 assigned to assist with FBI investigations of ESPIONAGE and sabotage. Of 1,927 cases investigated by NYSP officers in 1940, 1,636 involved allegations of "subversive activities." ORGANIZED CRIME, though widely entrenched throughout New York State since 1920, received its first concerted attention in November 1957, after state troopers disrupted a meeting of Mafia leaders at Apalachin, New York. The next year, NYSP leaders established a Criminal Intelligence Unit, with 26 agents on staff. Narcotics offenses were mentioned for the first time in a State Police report from 1955, but the department's narcotics enforcement unit was not established until 1968. Three years later, troopers assigned to suppress a riot at Attica state prison killed 10 prison guards and 29 inmates with indiscriminate gunfire.

During the 1990s the NYSP focused primarily on three goals: suppression of the state's rising crime rate, increased cooperation with local law enforcement agencies, and "preparing for the challenges of the rapidly approaching 21st Century." To those ends, in 1993 state police leaders established their first Violent Crime Investigative Teams to work with local police in cases of SERIAL MURDER and other ongoing crimes. In November 1996 the New York State Police Forensic Investigation Center opened to facilitate more rapid analysis of crime-scene evidence.

nonlethal weapons

While the primary goal of armed combat remains the permanent incapacitation of enemies, many other law enforcement situations demand WEAPONS and tactics that do not result in loss of human life or crippling injury. Nonlethal weapons, in the broadest terms, are any instruments designed for use in combat situations which do not *predictably* result in death. There are occasional exceptions to the rule, of course: Asthmatics and the like may suffocate under prolonged exposure to nonlethal gas; electric stun guns may interfere with pacemakers; "flash-bang" concussion grenades may induce a heart attack or cause the subject to fall down with fatal results; rubber bullets and other "baton" rounds may kill in rare cases if they strike a target's skull or chest with sufficient force. In general, though, nonlethal weapons are not expected to kill.

In that context, nonlethal weapons are available in many forms. Their utility likewise varies with the situation and constraints imposed by law or departmental regulations. With those limitations in mind, nonlethal weapons fall into several broad categories, including:

1. *Handheld impact weapons.* The options here include a variety of traditional clubs, blackjacks, and similar weapons. Police make extensive use of various clubs or batons, but their employment is sometimes inflammatory (as in the RODNEY KING case), and they have little value against large groups of adversaries.

2. *Nonpenetrating projectiles.* Typically launched from special guns, the various rubber or wooden bullets, bean-bag projectiles and so forth deliver a painful or stunning blow from a distance, thus preserving a safe interval between combatants. Some concussion grenades also discharge hard rubber pellets or "stingers," for use in confined spaces.

3. *High-pressure liquids.* Although southern police were reviled for turning fire hoses against civil rights protesters in the 1960s, high-pressure hoses and "water cannons" remain a fixture of many police and military riot-control arsenals. Mounted on trucks or armored vehicles, they have seen frequent use against rowdy mobs in Europe and Asia. Serious injury may result in some cases,

due to falls or violent impact with solid objects, but normal damage is limited to drenching and bruises.

4. *Sprays and gases.* Great advances have been made in this field from the early days of bulky tear gas canisters (which still sometimes grow hot enough to set a house on fire). Today a wide variety of nonlethal gases and chemical sprays are available to law enforcement and military personnel. Most are designed to irritate a subject's eyes and/or respiratory system, producing disorientation, temporary blindness, and occasional nausea or unconsciousness.

5. *Electric stun guns.* These weapons operate by transmitting a nonlethal electric charge through the target's body, creating electronic "riffles" that disrupt synaptic pathways and result in temporary incapacitation. High on voltage but low on amperage, they are not designed to kill even with prolonged contact and have no "lethal setting," but they may produce small contact burns. Physical contact is required for all such weapons, many requiring that the gun itself be pressed against an assailant's body, while others (like the Taser) fire barbed darts with slender wires attached to complete the circuit from a distance.

6. *Optical weapons.* As suggested by their name, these weapons interfere with vision to confuse, disorient, or temporarily incapacitate a subject. "Flash-bang" grenades produce a blinding burst of light, coupled with a concussive shock wave, to stun their targets. Pulsing strobe lights use the same principle to disrupt vision. Low-energy lasers may produce temporary blindness, and military technicians have reportedly studied lasers that would make the damage permanent. Obscurants, such as smoke in varied colors, can be used to disorient crowds or individuals, while masking the approach of law enforcement officers.

7. *Acoustic weapons.* As with a target's eyes, the ears may also be assaulted in various ways without inflicting permanent harm. Loud music or similar sound effects are sometimes used as a means of psychological warfare, as when American troops played blaring heavy-metal music outside the besieged headquarters of Manuel Noriega in Panama City. Concussion grenades are designed to stun their targets with a thunderclap of sound. Various levels of high- or low-pitched sound may be used to disperse crowds. Infrasound broadcasts (the nonlinear superposition of two ultrasound beams) are said to produce "intolerable sensa-

tions" including disorientation, nausea and vomiting, and involuntary defecation.

8. *Chemical weapons.* A number of tools are available here, treated separately from the sprays and gases described above. Adhesive agents include a variety of sticky, quick-drying polymer foams that can be removed only with special solvents. Chemical "barriers" consist of dense, rapidly expanding foam or bubbles that inhibit movement and obscure vision, sometimes producing foul odors and/or using dyes to mark subjects for later apprehension. Calmative agents include various sedatives, while hallucinogens confuse and disorient their targets. Lubricants, ranging from simple oil slicks to agents that turn dirt into slippery "chemical mud," impede both attackers and subjects trying to escape. Taggants, while not technically weapons, employ chemical dyes to identify subjects (as in the explosive dye packs sometimes used to foil bank robberies).

9. *"Entanglement munitions."* Rarely used today, and having no significant value against crowds, this category involves use of nets or similar objects to snare and subdue targets. As implied by the title, the nets are fired from various specialized guns, unfurling in midair to drop over the subject. Nets may also be hand thrown, laid as snares, or dropped from aircraft.

See also: RIOTS AND RIOT CONTROL.

Norris, Charles (1867 or 1868–1935)

Born in 1867 or 1868 (reports differ), Charles Norris graduated from New York's Columbia Medical School and continued his studies in Europe, including a valuable internship with German pathologist Eduard von Hofmann. Between 1904 and 1918, he was a professor of pathology at Bellevue Hospital in New York City. In the latter year, he was chosen to serve as the city's first chief medical examiner, replacing the elected (and often unqualified) coroners who previously ruled on cause of death.

Norris and chief assistant Thomas Gonzales were instrumental in developing forensic pathology as a subspecialty of clinical medicine. Supported by toxicologist Alexander Gettler, Norris and Gonzales revolutionized forensic medicine, eliminating the muddled and corrupt system wherein cadavers were often shuffled around New York's five boroughs, generating fees for multiple coroners but yielding no significant medical findings. In 1934 Dr. Norris established a department of forensic medicine at the New York University College of Medicine. He died the following year, leaving Dr. Gonzales in charge of the medical examiner's office until 1954.

See also: FORENSIC SCIENCE.

North Carolina Highway Patrol

As in most other states, North Carolina's state legislature waited for automobile registration and traffic death statistics to suggest the need for an organized highway patrol. Between 1921 and 1929 the number of vehicles registered in North Carolina increased from 150,558 to 503,590, while traffic fatalities reached 690 in 1929. Thus motivated, in 1929 lawmakers created the North Carolina Highway Patrol, established as a division of the State Highway Commission. Ten original officers—including one captain and nine lieutenants—were packed off for training with the Pennsylvania State Police, then returned to serve their home state as instructors.

North Carolina's first Highway Patrol Training School was conducted in May 1929, with 67 cadets selected from a field of 400 applicants. Forty-two completed the course, and 37 of those were sworn in to complete the first roster of highway patrolmen. Starting monthly salaries ranged from $150 (patrolmen) to $200 (commander), but the state slashed wages three times over the next six years, until 1935's patrolmen earned only $87.50 per month. At the same time, new statutes increased the department's size to 67 officers (in 1931), and then 121 (in 1933). Expansion thereafter continued apace, and the modern Highway Patrol—a self-described "semi-military organization"—consists of six sections, each with distinct responsibilities. They include Administrative Services, Communications and Logistics, Inspection and INTERNAL AFFAIRS, Research and Planning, Training, and Zone Operations (the patrol's enforcement arm.)

North Carolina State Bureau of Investigation

While state legislators created the NORTH CAROLINA HIGHWAY PATROL in 1929 to enforce traffic regulations and protect the motorized public, creation of a state-wide police force was delayed until 1937. In that year, a new statute established the State Bureau of Identification and Investigation, directly controlled by the governor, to "secure a more effective administration of criminal laws of the state, to prevent crime, and to procure the speedy apprehension and identification of criminals." Activation of the bureau was further delayed until March 1938, with lawyer and ex–FBI agent Frederick Handy named as the first director. Handy hired his first field agent, Oscar Adkins, four months later, operating in tandem with experts in firearms, questioned documents, and FINGERPRINTS. In 1939 the state legislature renamed its creation the State Bureau of Investigation (SBI), assigning it to a newly created Department of Justice under the state's attorney general. The SBI survives today with eight regional offices statewide, including a forensics laboratory, a Computer Crimes Investigative Unit, and a Diversion & Environmental Crimes Unit.

See also: COMPUTER CRIMES; ENVIRONMENTAL CRIMES.

North Dakota Highway Patrol

In September 1935 North Dakota state legislators authorized creation of a state highway patrol, leaving appointment of its superintendent and his assistant to the state highway commissioner. A 10-man force was funded, but only five patrolmen joined the ranks during 1936. While vested with the full powers of any other peace officer, highway patrolmen (and later women) restricted themselves to traffic duties until 1967, when their duties expanded to include "the enforcement of all criminal laws on highway right-of-ways." Four years later, the Highway Patrol assumed responsibility for North Dakota's statewide Law Enforcement Training Center. In July 1989 it was the state's first police agency to win accreditation from the Commission of Accreditation for Law Enforcement Agencies. The force that started small remains so today, with 135 sworn officers on the payroll in 2003, divided among eight patrol districts.

Oakland Police Department

From the wide-open days of PROHIBITION through the 1940s, Oakland, California's police department was infamous as one of America's most corrupt and brutal law enforcement agencies, where patrolmen rolled drunks on the streets and routinely beat black citizens in front of witnesses. One officer landed in prison following a special investigation by the California state legislature, and reform chief Wyman Vernon wielded the proverbial new broom at headquarters, working apparent miracles before his retirement in 1959.

Vernon's replacement, Edward Toothman, was an 18-year OPD veteran with a diploma from the Northwestern University Traffic Institute when he became chief of police in 1959, and he set exacting standards for new recruits, accepting only eight of 1,049 applicants in 1960. Five years later, OPD spokesmen boasted that 40 percent of all officers on the force had one or more years of college behind them, while 9 percent had earned four-year degrees. The department also led most California agencies in adoption of new technology—and yet, pervasive undertones of RACISM still haunted Oakland P.D., producing repeated complaints of unjustified EXCESSIVE FORCE and DEADLY FORCE employed against nonwhites.

In 1966 those complaints spawned the Black Panther Party, committed to "patrolling the police." Because the Panthers carried weapons (legally), white officers regarded them as dangerous and shooting incidents inevitably followed. During one encounter, party founder Huey Newton was gravely wounded in an incident that left one patrolman dead and another injured. The slain officer had a reputation for abusive behavior, and foren-

sic evidence revealed that the patrolmen were shot with each other's weapons, but Newton was still convicted of manslaughter (subsequently overturned on appeal). A short time later, two Oakland patrolmen, drunk on duty, riddled Panther headquarters with rifle fire.

Black recruits to OPD also complained of racist harassment on the job, but right-wing attitudes at headquarters were not limited to minorities. In October 1965 OPD officers formed a "Berlin Wall" blockade barring antiwar protesters from Oakland, clubbing some and standing idly by while members of the Hells Angels motorcycle gang beat others. John Birch Society literature circulated freely throughout the department and was sometimes distributed from squad cars on the street, prompting author (and ex-FBI agent) William Turner in 1969 to dub OPD a "swagger outfit" with "neolithic" attitudes.

It seems little has changed in the 21st century, as Oakland PD leaders settled a class-action lawsuit filed by a new generation of antiwar protesters in 2004, admitting that officers violated their First Amendment rights during an April 2003 demonstration against the U.S. invasion of Iraq. Eight years before that admission, in November 1996, the AMERICAN CIVIL LIBERTIES UNION reported that Oakland PD's civilian complaint system was "in crisis." According to the ACLU's survey, officers receiving complaints of abuse failed in 95 percent of all cases to mention the existence of Oakland's Civilian Police Review Board, while 37 percent flatly refused to provide telephone numbers for the CPRB to civilian complainants. Deaf citizens had their own share of complaints against Oakland police, prompting an April 1998 settlement with the U.S. JUSTICE

DEPARTMENT requiring classes in improved communication with the deaf during traffic stops and criminal interrogations.

Its many problems notwithstanding, OPD maintains a Web site that describes its mission "to provide competent, effective public safety services to all persons with the highest regard for human dignity through efficient, professional, and ethical law enforcement and crime prevention practices." The department's vision is "to enhance our status as a premier law enforcement agency as championed by our customers and benchmarked by our counterparts." To that end, department leaders declare their "F.I.R.S.T. commitment": Fairness, Integrity, Respect, Service, and Teamwork.

O'Connor, Timothy (1901–?)

Born in 1901, Timothy O'Connor joined the CHICAGO POLICE DEPARTMENT in 1928, when the force was renowned for its CORRUPTION under Mayor William "Big Bill" Thompson and his ally, mob boss Al Capone. Despite pervasive graft, O'Connor managed to retain his personal integrity while rising through the ranks, to become deputy chief of police in the late 1940s. A graduate of the FBI National Academy, he was the perfect candidate to serve as police commissioner in November 1950, when the Kefauver Commission's investigation of ORGANIZED CRIME embarrassed predecessor JOHN PRENDERGAST.

Despite his reputation for scrupulous personal honesty, O'Connor was not chosen to reform the force. Rather, according to CPD historian Richard Lindberg, he was "a figurehead appointee powerless to control the entrenched police bureaucracy," destined to make "a few cosmetic reforms during his tenure in office, [while] the clanking machine of spoils, patronage, and gambling rolled on its merry way." O'Connor's main achievement was "revitalizing" the police crime lab, which had fallen into disrepute since 1938, with many cases left unsolved. At the same time, his rigid austerity program left the department strapped for cash, even as it pleased Mayors Martin Kennelly and Richard Daley by operating under budget. With O'Connor at the helm, desk sergeants were forced to buy their own office supplies, patrolmen sometimes took three hours to answer emergency calls, and the notion of a K-9 UNIT was rejected as "impractical" in December 1957.

Scandal inevitably overtook the figurehead commander, with new revelations of corruption at the CPD's Summerdale Station, in January 1960. O'Connor agreed to outside polygraph testing for 130 suspect officers, prompting Capt. Herman Dorf to resign in protest, then O'Connor himself resigned with a plea of poor health, on January 23. Mayor Daley could not resist a parting shot to the press. "Tim was always telling me how he went home at night and watched TV instead of running around getting into trouble," he told reporters. "I should have asked him why he wasn't running around checking on his policemen at night instead of sitting home and watching TV."

O'Connor's Gunners

In 1926, as Chicago's PROHIBITION-era bootleg wars escalated between Al Capone and various rivals, CHICAGO POLICE DEPARTMENT Chief of Detectives William O'Connor devised a plan to counter the new wave of drive-by shootings. After purchasing a small arsenal of Thompson submachine guns for the force, O'Connor issued a call for volunteers to a new elite "flying squad." Selecting combat veterans of World War I, O'Connor issued his bloodthirsty orders:

Men, the war is on. We have got to show that society, and the Police Department, and not that bunch of dirty rats, are running this town. It is the wish of the people of Chicago that you hunt these criminals down and kill them without mercy. Your cars are equipped with machine guns and you will meet the enemies of society on equal terms. See to it that they do not have you pushing up daisies. Shoot first and shoot to kill. If you kill a notorious feudist, you will get a handsome reward and win promotion. If you meet a car containing bandits, pursue them and fire. When I arrive on the scene my hopes will be fulfilled if you have shot off the top of the car and killed every criminal inside it.

While civil libertarians immediately criticized O'Connor's order for summary execution of suspects, they had nothing to fear. For all the attendant hype, "O'Connor's Gunners" proved themselves harmless, never inflicting a single fatality.

officers killed in the line of duty

Law enforcement in America is dangerous business. Scores of officers die on duty every year, nationwide, revered as heroes in their local communities. Unfortunately, no consensus exists concerning the total number of officers lost on duty throughout U.S. history. Separate Web pages of the American Police Hall of Fame (Titusville, Florida) cite the national total as "nearly 6,000" and "over 7,000" officers slain, while claiming that "a police officer is killed every 57 hours somewhere in the United States." (That figure obviously is not constant from one year to the next.) Meanwhile, the Officer Down Memorial Page (www.odmp.org) cites a much higher figure, claiming 17,899 police officers killed across America since the 1790s. Including accidental deaths (car wrecks, drownings, etc.) and heart attacks with homicides, the ODMP site offers the following statistics for on-duty fatalities through December 2005.

Alabama: 427

Alaska: 41

American Samoa: 2

Arizona: 215

Arkansas: 215

California: 1,408

Colorado: 229

Connecticut: 129

Delaware: 33

District of Columbia: 122

Florida: 645

Georgia: 502

Guam: 10

Hawaii: 46

Idaho: 53

Illinois: 913

Indiana: 343

Iowa: 144

Kansas: 225

Kentucky: 368

Louisiana: 357

Maine: 81

Maryland: 264

Massachusetts: 293

Michigan: 524

Minnesota: 203

Mississippi: 194

Missouri: 602

Montana: 110

Nebraska: 88

Nevada: 76

New Hampshire: 29

New Jersey: 394

New Mexico: 122

New York: 1,354

North Carolina: 395

North Dakota: 46

Northern Mariana Islands: 3

Ohio: 707

Oklahoma: 393

Oregon: 157

Panama Canal Zone: 3

Pennsylvania: 681

Puerto Rico: 322

Railroad agencies: 117

Rhode Island: 41

South Carolina: 268

South Dakota: 47

Tennessee: 457

Texas: 1,359

Tribal agencies: 39

U.S. government: 937

Utah: 106

Vermont: 18

Virgin Islands: 7

Virginia: 365

Washington: 250

West Virginia: 138

Wisconsin: 239

Wyoming: 43

Ohio Highway Patrol

Public support for a statewide law enforcement agency first surfaced in Ohio during 1917, as a response to wartime fears of German subversion, but Buckeye legislators defeated six separate bills to establish a state police force during 1917–31. At last, in 1933, a statute was enacted to create a 60-man Highway Patrol, restricted to traffic enforcement and specifically barred by law from STRIKEBREAKING. The first step toward broader authority began a year later, when OHP officers were trained in criminal identification by members of the small Ohio Bureau of Criminal Investigation. In 1936 the legislature authorized hiring of 80 additional patrolmen, but simultaneous budget cuts stymied that expansion, while a manpower drain during World War II left the Highway Patrol with a skeleton crew. At the same time, the Farm Crimes Act of 1938 granted highway patrol officers their first true authority in nontraffic cases.

A postwar boom in automobile registrations and traffic fatalities brought legislative approval for hiring of 400 new troopers, but a two-year lag in pay raises frustrated recruiters. June 1947 brought new legislation, expanding the OHP's criminal jurisdiction from state highways to any state-owned or leased property. Six years later, a new Department of Highway Safety was created, with the Highway Patrol as one of its two subdivisions, divided into nine districts with a dozen new posts. By the mid-1960s, Highway Patrol officers were engaged in suppression of civil disturbances, including prison riots and campus protests against the Vietnam War. A new statute passed in March 1972, further expanded the OHP's authority in off-highway crimes. Nine years later, yet another law granted OHP officers their first specific powers of search and seizure, on par with other police agencies. The OHP won full accreditation in July 1989, from the Commission on Accreditation for Law Enforcement Agencies, and was reaccredited in July 1994.

O.K. Corral gunfight

In 1880–81 two rival factions fought for control of Cochise County, Arizona. Sheriff JOHN BEHAN earned an estimated $40,000 per year between his legal salary, graft, and illicit diversion of taxes, supported by a gang of rural outlaws led by the Clanton and McLowery families. Meanwhile, gambling and prostitution in Tombstone (the county seat) were dominated by the EARP BROTHERS (including town marshal Virgil Earp and deputy U.S. marshal Wyatt Earp) and dentist-gunman John "Doc" Holliday.

The simmering feud heated up in March 1881, when bandits robbed a stagecoach outside Tombstone, killing two men in the process. Holliday was named as a suspect in that case, briefly jailed in June, but the charges were soon dismissed for lack of evidence. Wyatt Earp, meanwhile, blamed members of the Clanton gang. Unable to find them himself, Earp approached Ike Clanton and promised to give up the $6,000 reward WELLS FARGO had offered for the bandits, if Clanton would deliver them and let Earp take credit for the arrests. Clanton agreed, but he never made good on the deal, since all three suspects were killed in Mexico before he could betray them.

Deprived of his headlines, Wyatt Earp spread the story that Ike Clanton had volunteered to sell out his friends, a slur that infuriated Ike and made him swear vengeance against the Earps. A series of near-miss encounters followed, with members of each faction taunting and threatening the other, until matters came to a head on October 26, 1881. That morning Ike Clanton and Tom McLowery were "buffaloed"—that is, pistol-whipped and arrested—by the Earp Brothers in Tombstone. Ike was fined $25, Morgan Earp offering to pay the tab himself if the Clanton's would agree to a showdown. Later that day, word reached the Earps that five members of the Clanton-McLowery gang had gathered at the O.K. Corral, uttering threats against the Earps. Three Earp Brothers and Holliday (hastily deputized) made their way to the corral, ignoring protests from Sheriff Behan.

The rest is history—or, rather, mythology: 30 seconds of action followed by a century of propaganda, ranging from dime novels to Wyatt Earp's self-serving autobiography, a half-dozen Hollywood films, even an episode of *Star Trek*. Each description of the fight (or massacre) presents a slightly different twist, but it is possible to reconstruct the action from historical accounts.

First, the famous shootout did not occur at the O.K. Corral, but nearby, in an alley adjacent to Camillus Fly's photographic studio. Two members of the Clanton group—Ike and Tom McLowery—were certainly unarmed when the Earps and Holliday arrived, Virgil Earp confusing matters at the start with a shouted order to "Give up your arms or throw up your arms!" Billy Clanton and Frank McLowery may have reached for their guns at that point, but neither had drawn yet, for Virgil then said, "Hold! I don't mean that. I have come to disarm you." Tom McLowery responded by holding open his vest, replying, "I have nothing."

It is still unclear who fired the first shot, but Wyatt Earp is a likely suspect, his bullet striking Frank McLowery in the stomach. Frank staggered away, his pistol still holstered, as the alley exploded in a blaze of gunfire.

Gambler and gunman "Doc" Holliday joined the Earp brothers in their battle with the Clanton-McLowery gang at the O.K. Corral. (Author's collection)

Billy Clanton fired at Wyatt and missed, while Tom McLowery ducked for cover behind his brother's horse, while Billy Claiborne ran for cover in Fly's studio. Billy Clanton was the next to fall, shot in the chest and wrist by Morgan Earp; he slumped against a wall and switched his pistol to his left hand, desperate to stay in the fight. Ike Clanton dodged a shotgun blast from Holliday and followed Billy Claiborne's example, running for cover at Fly's. Meanwhile, the noise from Doc's 10-gauge spooked Frank McLowery's horse, exposing Tom to a charge of buckshot that killed him where he stood.

Frank McLowery had his gun out by then, as Holliday approached him with pistol in hand. They exchanged fire at close range, Doc falling with a bullet in his hip. Billy Clanton, meanwhile, was still firing, striking Virgil Earp in one leg and wounding Morgan in the shoulder. Wyatt and Morgan returned his fire, and Billy Clanton was dying, still pleading for more ammunition, when Camillus Fly removed the empty six-gun from his hand. The two McLowery brothers were already dead.

Tombstone's citizens and newspapers quickly chose sides, the pro-Earp *Epitaph* burying a small report of the shootout on page three, while the dead men lay in state at a local undertaker's parlor, beneath a sign reading: MURDERED ON THE STREETS OF TOMBSTONE. Wyatt and Doc Holliday were ultimately charged with murder, but the case was soon dismissed by a friendly justice of the peace.

The Earp-Clanton feud continued through July 1882, claiming the lives of Virgil Earp (ambushed in Tombstone) and at least five members of the Clanton gang. Public opinion drove Wyatt Earp from Tombstone that summer, while Sheriff Behan resigned before year's end, thereby escaping prosecution for financial irregularities. Ironically, Tombstone's sordid gang war stands immortalized today as a triumph of frontier "law and order" over banditry.

Oklahoma City Police Department

Oklahoma City was established in July 1890, and its founders soon recognized the need for law enforcement. The first police department was a five-man affair, consisting of four local officers and one deputy U.S. marshal. Chief Charles Colcord retired in 1891, followed by five more chiefs during 1891–95. Imposition of statewide PROHIBITION in the early 1900s created new problems and opportunities for CORRUPTION, as the new statute produced "3,000 bootleggers substituting for 30 saloons."

In 1911 a new city charter empowered Oklahoma City's mayor to appoint the police chief, with BILL TILGHMAN chosen first to serve under the new regime.

Paranoia and anti-German hysteria during World War I kept local police busy with pursuit of "subversives," Chief W. B. Nichols collaborating with the FBI to confiscate pro-German books. At the same time, a strict code of conduct for OCPD officers banned such activities as moonlighting and smoking while in uniform. National Prohibition increased the public thirst for illicit alcohol, while the Great Depression brought a rash of BANK ROBBERIES staged by such bandits as Wilbur Underhill and Charles "Pretty Boy" Floyd. The force claimed 228 officers in 1937, including 53 detectives and 17 "special" liquor-raiders, but World War II sapped its strength to the point that entrance requirements were relaxed, and many staff positions were reclassified as civilian jobs.

Postwar prosperity and rising crime rates brought the OCPD back up to full strength, with more than 300 sworn officers in the mid-1950s. At the same time, Oklahoma City itself expanded by 800 percent, from 56 to 480 square miles. The department hired its first full-time training staff in 1962. Nine years later, a Law Enforcement Intern Program was established, fielding unarmed men aged 18–21 as "community service officers." Female officers were slowly integrated into full service during the 1970s, and Officer Shirley Cox scored the first arrest by a policewoman in January 1974. An attack of "BLUE FLU" sidelined all but nine of the OCPD's 559 officers during a four-day strike in 1975, but the issue was soon resolved. At press time for this volume, OCPD employed 1,057 sworn officers and 300 civilian personnel, operating on a yearly budget of nearly $100 million.

Oklahoma Highway Patrol

Rampant BANK ROBBERIES and other violent crimes sparked support for a state police force in Oklahoma during the 1920s, but a state legislature dominated by rural lawmakers stalled action on the proposal until 1935, when a 12-man, six-car unit was created as part of the state tax commission's auto-theft division. Those officers remained subordinate to local police chiefs and SHERIFFS until April 1937, when new legislation established the Oklahoma Highway Patrol under Public Safety Commissioner J. M. Gentry. In that Depression year, a salary offer of $150 per month lured 500 applicants, from whom 140 were chosen for training by instructors borrowed from Maryland and Michigan.

By 1941 Oklahoma had 150 state troopers on duty, but two-thirds of those left the force to fight in World War II, despite a special draft exemption from Gov. Leon Phillips. The OHP recovered quickly in the postwar years, however, and in 1949 became the first U.S. law enforcement agency to employ aircraft for traffic control. Crime-fighting duties expanded throughout the

1950s and 1960s, including suppression of civil disturbances and interdiction of DRUGS. In 1975 the OHP was assigned to protect Oklahoma's governor, lieutenant governor, and the capitol complex in Oklahoma City. The force suffered its darkest day on May 26, 1978, when three troopers were killed in shootouts with two escaped convicts. Seventeen years later, Trooper Charlie Hanger earned hero status by arresting terrorist Timothy McVeigh for driving without a license plate and carrying a concealed weapon. Subsequent investigation linked McVeigh to the Oklahoma City bombing that claimed 168 lives on April 19, 1995, and he was duly executed for that crime.

See also: BOMBING AND BOMB SQUADS.

Oklahoma State Bureau of Investigation

Prior to 1925, the U.S. MARSHALS SERVICE was the only law enforcement agency available to pursue rural felons in Oklahoma, where roving gangs robbed banks and terrorized whole towns with virtual impunity. At last, urged by Governor M. E. Trapp, the state legislature appropriated $78,000 to establish a Bureau of Criminal Identification and Investigation, known today as the OSBI. Within a year of its creation, the unit's three agents reduced statewide bank robbery statistics by 75 percent, arresting some of those responsible and forcing others to try their luck in neighboring states.

Initially established under the state adjutant general's office, the OSBI was transferred in 1939 to the newly created Department of Public Safety. There it remained for 18 years, until another shift placed the agency (with its present name) under direct gubernatorial control. That situation lasted until 1976, when a controversial OSBI investigation of Governor David Hall prompted creation of an independent seven-member commission to supervise the bureau. By law, that commission includes one Oklahoma police chief, one county SHERIFF, one district attorney, and four lay members with no professional ties to law enforcement. All are appointed by the governor to serve staggered seven-year terms. Presently, OSBI investigations may be requested only by the governor, state attorney general, a district attorney, police chief, sheriff, the state's Council on Judicial Complaints, or a legislative committee possessing subpoena powers. In September 2002 the OSBI became Oklahoma's first state agency accredited by the Commission on Accreditation of Law Enforcement Agencies.

See also: BANK ROBBERIES.

Ole Miss riot

In 1962 a federal court ordered the University of Mississippi at Oxford—"Ole Miss"—to accept James Meredith as its first-ever black student. Governor Ross Barnett had exhausted his legal remedies in the fight to exclude Meredith, and the task now fell to a ragtag army of racist police, students, and professional bigots. Mississippi's 82 county SHERIFFS joined Barnett in a pledge of defiance, and spokesmen for the Mississippi Sheriffs Association volunteered to dig up Oxford's streets, as a means of preventing U.S. marshals from delivering Meredith to Ole Miss. When that drastic plan was rejected, the lawmen hatched another plan to block access with their bodies and patrol cars, but that scheme was also abandoned. Meanwhile, white supremacists from the KU KLUX KLAN and various neo-Nazi groups flocked to Oxford, rallying around the banner of resistance raised by former U.S. Army general Edwin Walker.

Meredith arrived on September 30, 1962, escorted by 300 U.S. marshals. That force soon found itself besieged by a mob of several thousand racists who surrounded the administration building, pelting it with stones and gunfire. Police, including members of the MISSISSIPPI HIGHWAY PATROL, gave the rioters advice on vandalizing federal cars, while caravans and busloads of redneck reinforcements were admitted to the campus unimpeded. The U.S. marshals, reinforced by army troops and the NATIONAL GUARD, fought a desperate holding action against rioters who stormed the building on foot, then tried to crash the barricades with a stolen fire truck and bulldozer. When the smoke cleared the next morning, 158 of the 300 marshals were wounded, 58 of them by bullets. At least 130 other persons were injured, with nearly 200 arrested (including Edwin Walker).

Two persons, French journalist Paul Guihard and bystander Ray Gunter, were killed by gunfire during the riot. Gunter's death was an apparent accident, but Guihard was deliberately murdered, shot at point-blank range with a .38-caliber pistol. The weapons carried by all U.S. marshals at Oxford were tested, clearing them in both deaths, but no tests were performed on the .38-caliber weapons worn by many Mississippi officers present on campus. (Such weapons, then as now, were also readily available for sale to civilians.) A local grand jury indicted Chief U.S. Marshal James McShane for causing the riot, but that frivolous charge was finally dismissed in 1964.

Olney, Richard (1835–1917)

Born at Oxford, Massachusetts, on September 15, 1835, Richard Olney graduated from Brown University at age 21 and received his LL.B. from Harvard Law School in 1858. He won admittance to the Massachusetts bar a year later and entered private practice in Boston.

Attorney General Richard Olney (Author's collection)

Olney later served in the state legislature (1873–74), then resumed private practice until President Grover Cleveland named him U.S. attorney general in March 1893. He held that post until June 1895, when he was appointed secretary of state, to replace the late Walter Gresham. Olney remained in charge of the State Department until Cleveland left office in March 1897. Olney's tenure in Washington spawned presidential hopes, but he failed in an attempt to win the Democratic Party's 1904 nomination. Olney died on April 8 or 9, 1917 (published accounts differ).

Omaha Police Department

The city of Omaha, Nebraska, was formally incorporated in February 1857 and hired its first marshal, J. A. Miller, on March 5. The force was expanded to four men in 1866, then to 20 (including one captain and one lieutenant) three years later, but January 1871 brought a reduction to 12 men, with the lieutenant's post abolished. In 1884 Marshal Roger Guthries was convicted and imprisoned for accepting bribes. Three years later, the city marshal's title was formally changed to chief of police, under Webber Seavey (1887–95). Seavey's

leadership was deemed so exemplary that an award still exists in his name, granted periodically to esteemed law enforcement leaders by the INTERNATIONAL ASSOCIATION OF CHIEFS OF POLICE.

Omaha policemen answered calls on horseback, or in buggies and on street cars until 1900, when the first bicycle squad was formed. Horses were phased out entirely by 1909, when the department purchased three automobiles and two motorcycles. Omaha suffered the same wave of CORRUPTION witnessed nationwide during PROHIBITION (1919–33), while a wave of payroll holdups in 1925 inspired creation of a police "money car" service, discontinued in 1932. That year, with the Depression in full swing, 49 of Omaha's 115 officers were laid off indefinitely, while the survivors accepted 12-hour shifts and a salary cut to $30 per month. By 1941 so many civilians held "honorary" OPD badges that the old shield was scrapped in favor of a new design, to prevent vigilantes and felons from posing as sworn officers.

Like other departments nationwide, the OPD has suffered problems with RACISM in its ranks. In September 1919 the all-white force proved unable or unwilling to control a lynch mob that killed Mayor Edward Smith, burned the courthouse, and extracted black inmate Will Brown from his cell, shooting him more than 1,000 times before dismembering his corpse. Two years later, the KU KLUX KLAN established itself in Omaha, working in collaboration with another racist group, the American Fascisti. Some 3,500 of Nebraska's 25,000 Klansmen joined the order in Omaha, including a number of policemen. Thankfully, such problems have been minimized today, under the leadership of Omaha's first black police chief, Thomas Warren.

O'Meara, Stephen (1854–1918)

A Canadian native of Prince Edward Island, born July 26, 1854, Stephen O'Meara immigrated to Massachusetts with his family at age 10. Eight years later, he found work as a reporter for the *Boston Globe* and was promoted to editor in chief by 1891, emerging as the newspaper's new publisher in 1896. In that post, he exerted sufficient influence to gain appointment as the BOSTON POLICE DEPARTMENT's first commissioner in 1906. While promoting high standards of honesty and efficiency, O'Meara remained popular with his troops and quickly established the Boston Social Club as a fraternal body for policemen, simultaneously granting officers a venue for expression of their grievances while sidetracking movements toward a full-fledged police union. The BSC provided no health benefits or other "extras" for Boston police, and friction increased during World War I, when leaders of the rival Policemen's Union claimed that spokesmen for the BSC's grievance committee were fraudulently chosen from the city's several precincts. Still, Commissioner O'Meara seemed ready and able to settle the dispute, when he suddenly died in December 1918. His successor proved intractable, precipitating the infamous Boston police strike of 1919.

O'Neill, Francis (1848–1936)

Christened Daniel and known to friends as Frank, Francis O'Neill was born at Tralibane, Ireland, on August 28, 1848. By age 14 he was a monitor at a school in Bantry, promoted to teacher the following year. O'Neill went to sea aboard an English merchant ship in 1865, survived a shipwreck in the South Pacific, and later settled in Edina, Missouri, as a schoolteacher. There he met his future wife and subsequently married her in Bloomington, Illinois. They moved to Chicago soon after that city's great fire, and O'Neill joined the CHICAGO POLICE DEPARTMENT in 1873. That August, in his first month on the job, he was shot while grappling with a burglar and carried the slug near his spine to the end of his life.

Intelligence and political savvy helped boost O'Neill on a rapid climb through the CPD ranks, from patrolman in the Harrison Street Precinct to become its commander in 1894. Five other captains from Harrison Street went on to lead the force, and O'Neill was no exception, promoted to serve as CPD's superintendent in 1901. According to department legend, he achieved that post through friendship with Kate Doyle, the former governess of Mayor Carter Harrison, and O'Neill's first official move was an announcement that members of the Police Protective Association—a splinter faction of the POLICE BENEVOLENT ASSOCIATION, committed to support for Harrison's chief rival—were subject to dismissal from the force.

That verdict doomed the PPA, but O'Neill was not strictly a tool of the city's machine. Soon after his appointment, he disciplined 12 captains for dereliction of duty and ended the longstanding practice of loaning police badges to wealthy civilians, thus granting them free admission to sporting events. O'Neill likewise refused to deputize untrained "special" officers as strikebreakers in the 1902 stockyard strikes, but his ruling in that instance was undercut by Inspector Nicholas Hunt, commander of the stockyard district for a quarter century, who sent his own patrolmen out to arrest strike leaders and hold them without bail or charges, randomly assaulting pickets and innocent bystanders found near the meatpacking plants. In the face of such corruption, O'Neill remained philosophical, telling reporters, "Every man knows how to manage a woman until he gets married. I had some of those ideas myself until I got to be chief, and then, like the man who gets married, I found out."

O'Neill remained in charge of the CPD until 1905, pleasantly distracted for much of that time by his love—some say obsession—with Irish folk music. While still in uniform, he authored five books on the subject and spent most of his free time playing with a band of fellow countrymen. In 1906 he returned to Ireland for an extended holiday, and he continued recording music until his death in 1936. A plaque was erected on Tralibane Bridge in 1998, celebrating the 150th anniversary of O'Neill's birth, and another monument was planted near his Chicago home in March 2000.

See also: STRIKEBREAKING.

O'Neill, John Patrick (1952–2001)

A native of Atlantic City, New Jersey, born in 1952, John O'Neill was still a teenager when he set his sights on an FBI career. He worked as a Bureau fingerprint clerk after graduating from high school, then served as a tour guide at FBI headquarters while completing course work in forensics at George Washington University. O'Neill became a full-fledged G-man in 1976, assigned to the Baltimore field office. In early 1991 he was appointed chief of the FBI's government fraud unit in Washington, D.C. That July he was transferred again, this time to Chicago as assistant agent-in-charge. There, he established a Fugitive Task Force and supervised cases related to ORGANIZED CRIME. Clearly pleased with his career thus far, O'Neill was fond of telling friends, "I *am* the FBI."

O'Neill returned to Washington in January 1995, promoted to serve as chief of the FBI's Counterterrorism Section, acting as liaison between the FBI and the Central Intelligence Agency. In January 1997 he was transferred again, this time as assistant agent-in-charge of the New York City field office, supervising some 350 agents. The stress of his new position began to tell on O'Neill, producing a series of incidents that damaged his professional reputation. Once he left his palm pilot at Yankee Stadium, filled with contacts for police agencies around the world. A short time later, O'Neill lost his cell phone in a New York taxi. The crowning incident occurred in summer 1999, when he drove with girlfriend Valerie James to the Jersey shore and his car broke down. O'Neill exchanged his vehicle for an FBI car, thus earning a reprimand and losing 15 days' pay for misuse of government property. James later told journalists that the incident preyed on O'Neill's mind. "The last two years of his life," she said, "he got very paranoid. He was convinced that people were out to get him."

The disciplinary action stalled O'Neill's career. Over the next 12 months he applied for promotion three times and was three times refused. In July 2000, while attending an FBI retirement conference in Orlando, Florida, O'Neill left his briefcase filled with official documents in a room with other G-men while he went to make a phone call. Returning to find the case gone, he alerted police, and the bag was recovered with only a pen and a cigarette lighter missing, but the incident produced further criticism. A friend of O'Neill's later told NBC's *Dateline*, "He felt that some people were going to use it—and they did—as a wedge, as a way of painting him in a bad light."

By early 2001 O'Neill seemed convinced that he had reached a dead end with the FBI. His frustration was exacerbated by President George W. Bush, who ordered the Bureau to "back off" its investigation of fugitive terrorist Osama bin Laden's family and his Al-Qaeda organization. In July 2001 O'Neill was offered a post as chief of security for the World Trade Centers in Manhattan, at a starting salary of $300,000 per year. He left the Bureau to assume his new position on August 22, 2001, but maintained his interest in international TERRORISM. On the night of September 10 he told a friend, Jerry Hauer, "We're in for something big. I don't like the way things are lining up in Afghanistan."

The next day, at 8:46 A.M., the first of two airliners hijacked by Al-Qaeda terrorists crashed into the World Trade Center. A second plane struck while O'Neill was en route to the scene, telephoning his son while in transit to say that "he was on his way out to assess the damage." O'Neill entered the crippled structure moments before the Twin Towers collapsed. His corpse was found by searchers a week later.

O'Neill, Kenneth William (1916–1988)

A New York native, born in 1916, Kenneth O'Neill earned a B.S. in chemistry from Fordham University in 1938. Three years later, he joined the NEW YORK CITY POLICE DEPARTMENT, serving as a patrolman and detective before his chemical expertise won him a posting to the department's bomb squad. He was named commander of the squad in 1958 and held that post until 1976, while earning an M.S. in chemistry from Hunter College (1963). During O'Neill's tenure, his elite team of 12 hand-picked officers answered an average of 3,300 bomb threats per year, winning recognition as the country's premier bomb-disposal squad. O'Neill retired from NYPD in 1976 and died in 1988.

See also: BOMBING AND BOMB SQUADS.

O'Neill, William Owen (1860–1898)

Confusion surrounds the birth of William "Buckey" O'Neill on February 2, 1860, with his birthplace listed in various published accounts as Ireland, St. Louis, and Washington, D.C. (During the Civil War, his father served with the 116th Pennsylvania Volunteers.) Some accounts claim that he graduated from Washington's National Law School, before migrating to Arizona Territory at 19. By 1882 he was settled in Prescott as editor of the *Prescott Daily Miner*, later supplanted by a newspaper for stockmen, *Hoof and Horn*. After a short stint as a court reporter, O'Neill was elected probate judge for Yavapai County, then served successively as tax collector, sheriff (three terms), and as mayor of Prescott. He ran for Congress twice, on the Populist ticket, but lost both times to majority candidates.

Tiring of politics, O'Neill switched to mining and prospered first from onyx, then copper. Along the way, he served as captain of the "Prescott Grays" militia, later reorganized with his help as the Arizona NATIONAL GUARD. In 1898, with comrades Alexander Brodie and James McClintock, O'Neill founded the First United States Volunteer Cavalry, later renowned as THEODORE ROOSEVELT's "Rough Riders." He was first among the troop to volunteer for service in the Spanish-American War, and it cost O'Neill his life on July 1, 1898, when he died in the battle for Cuba's Kettle Hill. He was buried at Arlington National Cemetery on May 1, 1899, and a bronze statue was erected in his honor in Prescott on July 3, 1907.

Orangeburg massacre

In February 1968 black students from South Carolina State University in Orangeburg launched a series of protests against a whites-only bowling alley located near campus. The vehicle of protest was a Black Awareness Coordinating Committee (BACC), founded by 22-year-old Cleveland Sellers, Jr. On the night of February 5 students built a bonfire near the bowling alley, which was doused by firefighters after a piece of timber fell and struck an officer of the SOUTH CAROLINA HIGHWAY PATROL. Five minutes later, officers opened fire on the unarmed protesters, killing three and wounding 27 as they fled.

Official statements claimed that the shooting occurred "only after an extended period of sniper fire from the campus and not until an officer had been felled during his efforts to protect life and property," yet no weapons were found on the campus and the one policeman injured had been hurt by accident. FBI agents joined agents of the SOUTH CAROLINA STATE LAW ENFORCEMENT DIVISION (SLED) in a search of the scene and found several .22-caliber bullets embedded in the wall of a nearby railroad warehouse, but ballistics tests could not reveal when they were fired. Examination of the scene *did* prove the slugs originated from a point more than 100 feet away from where the demonstrators had been shot.

The conduct of G-men involved in the Orangeburg case was suspect, at best. Agent Nelson Phillips, a Georgia native with 11 years in South Carolina, was unusually close to the officers involved. In fact, he had helped train them in riot control techniques (see RIOTS AND RIOT CONTROL) and was present at the shooting (though he later falsely denied it to JUSTICE DEPARTMENT attorneys). At least two other FBI agents also witnessed the shooting but claimed they were elsewhere when questioned by investigators from the Civil Rights Division. Those same agents told Col. Frank Thompson, commander of the state highway patrol, that they thought his men had "acted with restraint," while SLED spokesmen announced that G-men would "support the patrol's account of what happened." Relations between the FBI and SLED were so cordial, in fact, that officers involved in the shooting would speak with no one else, flatly refusing interviews with Justice Department investigators.

Attorney General RAMSEY CLARK was admittedly "distressed" by the FBI's obstructionist tactics. "It was a shame," he later said, "that we probably had quite a bit of trouble with a number of FBI agents as to what they said at different times and we had trouble getting all the interviews we wanted. We also had a terribly difficult time finding out where the FBI people were on the night of February 8—where they were, what they were doing, whether they were eyewitnesses." Governor Robert McNair, meanwhile, emerged from a closed-door meeting with G-men to declare that the FBI's final report would be "very interesting and very surprising" to police critics. State spokesmen hinted at a black conspiracy and tried to pin it on "outside agitator" Cleveland Sellers (a South Carolina native born at Denmark, 20 miles south of Orangeburg). Sellers was charged with "inciting a riot," but the state granted an "indefinite delay" in January 1970 and he never faced trial.

In their statements to FBI agents, nine police officers admitting firing on the demonstrators. Lt. Jesse Spell—soon promoted to captain—declared, "I ordered my squad to fire their weapons to stop the mob," yet none of the admitted shooters could recall a verbal order and most of their 30 victims were shot in the back, while running away. A federal grand jury indicted the nine policemen on December 19, 1968, for violating civil rights by means of summary punishment "under color of law." Their trial commenced at Florence in May 1969.

That proceeding was marked by a curious clash between FBI agents, as two testified for the defense and another from the Bureau's laboratory was called to rebut the statements of his fellow G-men. Agents Nelson Phillips and William Danielson swore they heard "small arms fire" from the crowd of demonstrators before police started shooting. Danielson also described Cleveland Sellers "walking around" and "talking to groups," though he admitted, "I never heard him say one word because there was a lot of noise." Phillips described (but could not produce) "a little vial that you have around the laboratory," which was allegedly thrown at police during the demonstration. He said it contained "a yellow substance," which "we sent . . . to our lab and the lab report showed it was highly explosive." Agent Robert Zimmers, dispatched from the Washington lab, contradicted Phillips and Daniels on the source of alleged gunfire, while making no reference to the alleged "explosive." After brief deliberation, jurors acquitted the officers on all counts.

Oregon State Police

In 1930 Oregon governor Julius Meier appointed a five-man committee to organize a state police force, based on study of the Royal Canadian Mounted Police, the TEXAS RANGERS, and state police organizations in several other states. Major General SMEDLEY BUTLER of the U.S. Marine Corps served as the committee's adviser. In March 1931 state legislators approved creation of the Oregon State Police, beginning operations on August 1. The new agency combined law enforcement functions previously performed by the state highway commission, the Ohio secretary of state, the Fish and Game Commission, the state fire marshal, and the PROHIBITION commissioner. In short, the OSP was charged with enforcement of all criminal statutes throughout Oregon, with 95 sworn officers performing rural patrols and assisting local police as required.

The OSP's first superintendent, Charles Pray, was an ex-FBI agent who had also served as a state parole officer. His department, Pray announced, would provide "dignified and courteous law enforcement service devoted to the needs of the public." Assisted by Capt. Harry Niles of the PORTLAND POLICE DEPARTMENT, Pray built the force from scratch and remained at its helm until July 1, 1947. In its first six months of operation, the OSP made 415 arrests, issued 181 traffic citations, detected 200 liquor violations, and collected fines totaling $16,986.60. A new statute, passed in 1939, authorized creation of a crime lab to process forensic evidence, located at the University of Oregon Medical School in Portland. Two years later, a State Bureau of Identification and Investigation was established at OSP headquarters, maintaining the state's master records of FINGERPRINTS and criminal mug shots.

In 1993 state legislators merged the state fire marshal's office, Oregon Emergency Management, the Law Enforcement Data System, and Oregon Boxing and Wrestling Commission under state police control. The

OSP presently has four divisions—Criminal Investigation, Forensic Services, Gaming Enforcement, and Public Safety & Security. The Criminal Investigation Division has seven subsections: ARSON/Explosives, Major Crimes, Investigative Reports, Drug Enforcement, Homicide Investigation and Tracking System (HITS), Missing Children, and Sex Offender Registration. Gaming Enforcement supervises lotteries and casinos established on Native American tribal lands.

See also: DRUGS.

organized crime

While any crime involving two or more participants may be "organized," the term is commonly applied to *syndicated* crime, wherein gangs of "families" of professional criminals engaged in RACKETEERING and other illicit activities. Organized crime as we know it in the United States today began with PROHIBITION (1919–33) and the coalition of various regional bootlegging gangs. A national crime syndicate grew out of organizational meetings held in Cleveland (1928), Atlantic City (1929), Chicago (1932), and New York City (1934), all apparently conducted without police or FBI scrutiny. Indeed, for the first 38 years of his tenure as FBI director, J. EDGAR HOOVER publicly denied the existence of a Mafia or any other nationwide crime syndicate in America, dismissing such claims as "baloney."

Still, it should not be supposed that federal authorities were entirely ignorant of the problem. Officers of the TREASURY DEPARTMENT and its INTERNAL REVENUE SERVICE sent various high-ranking mobsters to prison for income tax evasion in the 1930s, and pursued those who continued bootlegging after Prohibition's repeal. The FEDERAL BUREAU OF NARCOTICS also campaigned against underworld traffic in DRUGS, though some would later say that chief HARRY ANSLINGER went overboard in his zeal for combating "reefer madness." Even Hoover quietly acknowledged the power of regional gangs, launching a 1946 investigation of Chicago's Capone gang (dubbed CAPGA), which was soon torpedoed by Attorney General TOM CLARK.

Eleven years later, officers of the NEW YORK STATE POLICE disrupted a meeting of Mafia leaders at Apalachin, New York, prompting an embarrassed Hoover to create a new "Top Hoodlum Program." Overnight, each FBI field office was ordered to initiate illegal surveillance on ten "top hoodlums"—no more, no less—and report any findings to Hoover. Still, no prosecutions resulted, and Hoover was embarrassed once again in 1963, when mob INFORMANT Joe Valachi publicly detailed the history and workings of the U.S. Mafia. Scrambling to save face, Hoover published a *Reader's Digest* article proclaiming that "La Cosa Nostra, the

secret, murderous underworld combine about which you have been reading in the newspaper, is no secret to the FBI." From that day forward, Bureau reports would refer to La Cosa Nostra ("Our Thing," in Italian)—or to "LCN"—as if the Mob was composed only of Italians, and Hoover had discovered it himself.

President John Kennedy and his brother, Attorney General ROBERT KENNEDY, declared public war on the Mob during 1961–63, but JFK's ASSASSINATION left the campaign in peril. Federal prosecutions declined precipitately under Presidents Lyndon Johnson and Richard Nixon, then resumed after Hoover's death (in 1972) and Nixon's forced resignation (1974).

While many state and federal laws have addressed the problem of organized crime in some way, beginning with the often-abused MANN ACT of 1910, modern prosecutions rely on three federal statutes passed in 1970 and periodically updated since that time by Congress. Those laws include:

- The Organized Crime Control Act, prohibiting the creation of management of any illegal gambling organization by five or more people, operating for more than 30 days and earning $2,000 or more in

Meyer Lansky was a major architect of America's modern crime syndicate. (Library of Congress)

a single day. The statute also established a federal WITNESS SECURITY PROGRAM to facilitate prosecution of mobsters.

- The Comprehensive Drug Abuse Prevention and Control Act, which includes a ban on "continuing criminal enterprise," defined by the JUSTICE DEPARTMENT as "a group of individuals with an identified hierarchy, or comparable structure, engaged in significant criminal activity."

- The Racketeer Influenced and Corrupt Organizations Act, which defines racketeering and punishes various commonplace underworld activities, including loan sharking and any acts of violence committed in furtherance of organized criminal activity.

By the early 1990s FBI spokesmen and friendly journalists commonly described "La Cosa Nostra" as dead or dying in America, but those premature verdicts went largely unnoticed in the murky realm of organized crime. While certain aging and notorious mobsters indeed went to prison, the near-exclusive focus on Italian criminals—and later nonwhites, in the field of DRUGS—prompted critics to complain that law enforcement agencies had a serious blind spot where Caucasian mobsters and white-collar crime were concerned. Continuing scandals and ever-increasing drug consumption nationwide suggest that the critics are correct.

Otto, John (b. 1938)

Born in St. Paul, Minnesota, on December 18, 1938, John Otto served two years in the U.S. Marine Corps after high school, then earned a B.S. degree from St. Cloud State College in 1960. While pursuing graduate studies in educational administration, he served with the Ramsey County Sheriff's Department and the Arden Hills Police Department (both in Minnesota). Otto later moved to California and joined the OAKLAND POLICE DEPARTMENT in 1963, then moved on to the FBI in 1964. After service in Texas and New Jersey, Otto was transferred to FBI headquarters in March 1971, filling various posts there through December 1974. In January 1975 he was named agent-in-charge of the Portland, Oregon, field office, later holding the same position in Minneapolis (1977) and Chicago (1978).

Recalled at headquarters in August 1979, Otto remained there for the remainder of his career. He served as acting FBI director between May 26, 1987 (when Director WILLIAM WEBSTER resigned to lead the Central Intelligence Agency) and November 2, 1987 (when WILLIAM SESSIONS assumed control of the Bureau). In April 1990 Sessions gave Otto the FBI's first Medal of Meritorious Achievement for "extraordinary and exceptional meritorious service in a duty of *extreme* challenge and *great* responsibility." (Emphasis in the original.) Otto retired soon after claiming the award, to become a security agent for Delta Airlines.

See also: FEDERAL BUREAU OF INVESTIGATION.

Outlaw Exterminators Inc.

The VIGILANCE COMMITTEE known as Outlaw Exterminators Inc. was a small group active in Arizona, during the mid-1870s. Its alleged leader, Clay Calhoun, doubled as deputy U.S. marshal in Tombstone, but he was apparently dissatisfied with his own official performance and that of the courts. The band, consisting of five or six men, presumably exterminated outlaws, though it failed to rate mention in a tabulation of U.S. vigilante groups compiled by Richard Maxwell Brown for the National Commission on the Causes and Prevention of Violence, in 1969. The only identified victim is John Allman, a renegade who shot and killed eight men and raped two adolescent girls during 1877. Calhoun tracked Allman to an Indian cliff dwelling and shot him to death, reportedly firing four shots from his mouth to his groin "in perfect alignment." While the killing is generally credited to the Outlaw Exterminators, Calhoun could just as easily have justified it in his official capacity as a federal officer.

P

Palmer, A. Mitchell (1872–1936)

A Pennsylvania Quaker, born on May 4, 1872, Alexander Mitchell Palmer graduated from Swarthmore College in 1891 and studied law at George Washington University, winning admittance to the Pennsylvania bar in 1893. After a period in private practice, he served three terms in Congress (1909–15), where he declared himself a "radical friend" of organized labor. Palmer lost a race for the U.S. Senate (1914), then became a federal judge in April 1915, but resigned from the bench four months later, on September 1. In 1917 President Woodrow Wilson offered to make Palmer his secretary of war, but Palmer refused on ground of religious pacifism. Instead, he became Alien Property Custodian (1917–19), proving so belligerent in that post that acquaintances dubbed him "the fighting Quaker."

Wilson promoted Palmer to attorney general in March 1919, whereupon Palmer reversed his "radical" support for labor unions and suppressed half a dozen major strikes. In April 1919 suspected anarchists mailed a bomb to Palmer's home. That charge failed to explode, but the bombers tried again on June 2, detonating explosives that wrecked Palmer's house in Washington and killed two unidentified men at the scene. Soon after that incident, Wilson cautioned Palmer in a cabinet meeting, "Palmer, do not let this country see red!"

Palmer promptly named WILLIAM FLYNN, whom he dubbed America's top "radical chaser," to lead the FBI in pursuit of supposed subversives. A month later, on August 1, 1919, he created a new Red-hunting General Intelligence Division within the JUSTICE DEPART-MENT, led by young J. EDGAR HOOVER. Together, the trio planned a series of mass arrests memorialized as the "Palmer raids," which rounded up suspected anarchists and Communists in November 1919 and January 1920. Several thousand persons were arrested in the first dragnet, 249 of them later deported as "enemy aliens," while the rest were released without charges. The second sweep jailed at least 10,000 suspects, of whom only 556 were finally deported.

Public outrage at the raids doomed Palmer's presidential hopes in 1920. He spent the rest of his career defending himself in federal court (April 1920), before the House Rules Committee (June 1920), and finally before the Senate Judiciary Committee (January to March 1921). Still defiant as his star waned, Palmer told the Senate:

I apologize for nothing the Department of Justice has done in this matter. I glory in it. I point with pride and enthusiasm to the results of that work; and if, as I said before, some of my agents out in the field . . . were a little rough or unkind, or short or curt, with these alien agitators whom they observed seeking to destroy their homes, their religion and their country, I think it might well be overlooked in the general good to the country which has come from it. That is all I have to say.

Palmer resigned two days after delivering that speech, on March 5, 1921. He served as a delegate to the Democratic National Convention in 1932, but public office had slipped beyond his grasp. He died in Washington on May 11, 1936.

See also: ANARCHISM.

PAL programs

A nationwide network of Police Athletic (or Activities) Leagues—PAL for short—operate with coordination from national headquarters in Jupiter, Florida. That office describes PAL as "a youth crime prevention program that utilizes educational, athletic and recreational activities to create trust and understanding between police officers and youth. It is based on the conviction that young people—if they are reached early enough—can develop strong positive attitudes towards police officers in their journey through life toward the goal of maturity and good citizenship." PAL traces its roots to the early 1900s, when Capt. John Sweeney of the NEW YORK CITY POLICE DEPARTMENT first offered rebellious inner-city youths an opportunity to interact with police in gymnasiums, rather than in violent back-alley confrontations. In the late 1930s, six PAL chapters on the Eastern Seaboard organized the National Association of Police Athletic/Activities Leagues to pool resources and promote athletic competition between cities. At press time for this work, an estimated 80,000 volunteers maintained 350 PAL chapters serving 350 cities and 1,700 civic facilities throughout the United States and the U.S. Virgin Islands, interacting yearly with some 2 million minors each year. PAL headquarters describes its goals as "reducing juvenile crime and drug use through less idle time and exposure to criminal opportunity," while "enhanc[ing] the concept of 'community policing' by exposing children to career opportunities in law enforcement and promoting the recruitment of minority officers."

Parker, Ellis (1873–1940)

Born in 1873, Ellis Parker served for more than two decades as chief of detectives in Burlington County, New Jersey, earning a reputation as the "cornfield Sherlock Holmes" for his solution of baffling crimes. His most famous success, in 1920, was the "pickled corpse case," wherein a missing bank messenger was found more than a week after his disappearance, dressed in sopping wet clothes and buried in a shallow grave. A medical examiner declared that the victim had been dead no more than 48 hours, thus "clearing" the prime suspects, whose alibis were solid for the past two days. Parker disagreed and sent a sample of the water from the victim's clothing to a laboratory for analysis. Those tests revealed high levels of tannic acid, a preservative found in certain local streams, which would have made the "pickled" corpse seem fresh as long as 10 days after death. With their alibis demolished—and the messenger's missing cash recovered from the grave of one suspect's mother—the killers confessed and were later executed.

Parker's reputation—350 cases solved, including 118 of 124 murders he investigated—prompted Charles Lindbergh to enlist his help in March 1932, soon after Lindbergh's infant son was kidnapped and presumably murdered. Three years elapsed before suspect Bruno Hautpmann was arrested in New York, but Parker thought him innocent—in part, because a newsman, Russell Hopstatter, confessed to Parker that he (Hopstatter) had planted false evidence in Hauptmann's home. In the wake of Hauptmann's conviction and death sentence, Parker assisted Governor Harold Hoffman in his review of the case. For reasons still unclear, Parker became convinced that the real kidnapper was Paul Wendel, a 50-year-old New Jersey attorney, disbarred over a perjury conviction, who was wanted on fraud charges in 1935. With son Ellis, Jr., Parker kidnapped Wendel and drove him to New York, where he extracted a 25-page confession to the Lindbergh kidnapping. Announcement of the "break" won Hauptmann a brief stay of execution, but Wendel recanted his statement in police custody, accusing the Parkers of kidnapping and torture.

While Hauptmann ultimately kept his belated appointment with the electric chair, Ellis Parker was indicted under the new Lindbergh Law, which made interstate KIDNAPPING a federal crime. Convicted in June 1937, he received a six-year term and was dispatched to the penitentiary at Lewisburgh, Pennsylvania, where he died in 1940, his mind and reputation in shambles.

Parker, Isaac Charles (1838–1896)

America's most famous (or infamous) "hanging judge" was born near Barnesville, Ohio, on October 15, 1838. After graduating from the Barnesville Classical Institute, he studied law and was admitted to the bar in 1859, then settled in St. Joseph, Missouri, where his uncle was a partner in a legal firm. By 1861 Parker was practicing alone, and April of that year saw him elected to serve as St. Joseph's city attorney. After three years in that office, he won election as county prosecutor (1864), then as a judge (1868). Parker resigned from the bench to seek a congressional seat in 1870, and was elected that November to the House of Representatives. Defeated in his bid for a third term, in 1874, Parker applied for a federal judgeship. In March 1875 President Ulysses Grant nominated him to serve as U.S. district judge for the western district of Arkansas (now Oklahoma).

Arriving in Fort Smith on May 4, 1875, Parker found himself at the heart of a territory overrun by renegades and outlaws. A backlog of felons stood waiting for trial, held over from the corrupt administration of Parker's predecessor, Judge William Story. In his and killed six inmates trying to escape the Fort Smith jail. His judgments were not absolutely merciless, however. "Queen of the Outlaws" Belle Starr, convicted of rustling in Parker's court, received only a one-year sentence, while 98-year-old swindler John Overton escaped with Parker's admonition to "go home and sin no more."

Time and progress ultimately overtook the hanging judge. In 1889 the U.S. SUPREME COURT ruled that federal prisoners sentenced to death could appeal their verdicts. Of 46 defendants who appealed from Parker's court, 30 won reversals of their death sentences, a circumstance which prompted Parker to complain that "appellate courts exist mainly to stab the trial judge in the back." In 1891 Washington ordered Parker to end public executions. Five years later, a new statute removed the Indian Territory from his jurisdiction, effective September 1, 1896. By that time, overwork and the advance of Bright's disease combined to sap Parker's energy. He died on November 17, 1896, leaving a message for his critics: "I never hanged a man. The law hanged him. I was only its instrument."

See also: CAPITAL PUNISHMENT.

"Hanging Judge" Isaac Parker (Author's collection)

first eight weeks as judge, Parker tried 91 defendants, including 18 charged with murder. Of those, Parker convicted 15; eight received life prison terms, while seven were condemned. One of those scheduled to hang was shot while trying to escape. The other six were duly executed on September 3, 1875, before an audience of some 5,000 spectators.

While many critics blasted Parker for his harsh approach to justice, some denouncing him as a sadist, Parker clung stolidly to a simple motto: "Do equal and exact justice. Permit no innocent man to be punished, but let no guilty man escape." To that end, he appointed 200 deputy U.S. marshals (many of whom were killed by fugitives) and constructed a gallows large enough to hang 12 condemned inmates at once. During his two decades as judge, Parker tried 13,490 cases, of which 9,454 resulted in guilty pleas or convictions. Of those cases, 344 involved capital crimes. In all, Parker condemned 168 men and four women, 88 of whom (all men) were ultimately executed. Sixty of those were hanged by executioner George Maledon, who also shot

Parker, William Henry (1902–1966)

South Dakota native William Parker was born in 1902, working various jobs (including that of hotel detective) before he migrated to Los Angeles in 1923. There, while driving taxis for a living, he enrolled in night classes at Los Angeles College of Law. By the time Parker obtained his LL.B., in 1930, he already had three years on the job with the LOS ANGELES POLICE DEPARTMENT, starting as a rookie patrolman in August 1927. Young lawyers had little hope of surviving in Depression-era L.A., but Parker won promotion to sergeant with LAPD in 1930, and any thought of private legal practice was forgotten.

By 1941 Parker was a captain in charge of LAPD's Accident Investigation Bureau, but he took a break from law enforcement to join the U.S. Army and served 26 months in the European theater, returning with a military captain's rank and a Purple Heart for wounds suffered during the D-day landings of June 1944. French authorities also graced Parker with a Croix de Guerre for his role in the liberation of Paris, while Italy awarded him the Star of Solidarity for service in Sardinia. Those decorations served him well, and in 1950, five years after his return from Europe, Parker was named chief of police.

Parker brought stability of a sort to the force, remaining 16 years in office where the average tenure of his predecessors had been 18 months, but he remained a study in contrasts. Parker was a lifelong alcoholic, who nonetheless demanded strict discipline from his subordinates. He ordered harassment and beatings for out-of-town gangsters, proclaiming that L.A. "has no organized crime," yet ignored the thriving operations of mobster Mickey Cohen and Jack Dragna's Mafia "family." When local black ministers accused Parker of RACISM in 1962, he denounced them for using a "big-lie technique" to smear his department; three years later, he publicly compared residents of the Watts ghetto to "monkeys in a zoo."

Much of Parker's vaunted professionalism was style over substance. Throughout his tenure, short-sleeved summer uniforms were banned because of Parker's personal aversion to "hairy arms and tattoos." At the same time, however, he encouraged LAPD officers to absorb the John Birch Society's extremist message and ordered illegal DOMESTIC SURVEILLANCE of various groups and individuals regarded as "subversive." Parker's Organized Crime Intelligence Division, under future chief DARYL GATES, spent most of its time probing the sex lives of prominent locals and state politicians, ever alert for blackmail opportunities. In the ghettos and barrios, meanwhile, heavy-handed repression was the order of the day, outliving Parker and reaping unexpected consequences in the RODNEY KING trial and similar cases.

While Parker's politics and personal approach to law enforcement mirrored those of FBI Director J. EDGAR HOOVER, the two men were bitter enemies throughout Parker's tenure as chief of LAPD. Hoover pulled strings behind the scenes to prevent Parker's election as head of the INTERNATIONAL ASSOCIATION OF CHIEFS OF POLICE, and LAPD officers were barred from study at the FBI National Academy as long as Parker led the force.

Parker's political extremism and racist comments prompted calls for his replacement after the Watts riots of August 1965. Predictably, Parker refused to step down, but cardiac surgery forced him to take a leave of absence in spring 1966. On July 16 of that year, he attended a Marine Corps testimonial banquet held in his honor, and collapsed seconds after accepting a plaque that named him one of America's best police chiefs. Parker was dead before he reached the hospital, but his legacy lived on for decades afterward, enshrined in LAPD policy and the television programs produced by "JACK" WEBB.

See also: ORGANIZED CRIME.

Parkhurst, Charles H. (1842–1933)

Charles Parkhurst never donned a police uniform, but he still had a profound impact on 19th-century law enforcement in New York City. Little is known of his early life, beyond the fact that he was born in 1842 and gravitated to the fundamentalist ministry, leaving the pastorate of a Massachusetts Congregationalist church in 1880 to tackle sin in New York City. There Parkhurst apparently switched sects, becoming pastor of New York's prestigious Madison Square Presbyterian Church. Still, he remained a virtual unknown outside his vestry and immediate social circle until 1891, when he assumed the presidency of the church-run Society to Prevent Crime (SPC).

Obsessed with cleansing the city of vice in all forms, Parkhurst quickly changed the SPC's modus operandi from demands that various specific dives be closed to a general call for dismantling the links of CORRUPTION between politicians, police, and the rulers of crime in New York. In February 1892, Parkhurst called a Sunday-morning press conference at his church and delivered a scathing attack from the pulpit on NYPD and its political masters. Police spokesmen demanded evidence to support Parkhurst's charges, and the minister set off to collect it himself.

A stranger to the seamy underworld of gambling and prostitution, Parkhurst undertook a one-night fishing expedition in March 1892, touring some of New York's worst hangouts with squeaky clean parishioner John "Sunshine" Irving and private detective Charles Gardner. At one stop on their journey, Gardner engaged

Charles Parkhurst (Author's collection)

in a game of nude leapfrog with hookers, which later inspired a popular honky-tonk ditty:

> *Dr. Parkhurst on the floor*
> *Playing leapfrog with a whore*
> *Ta-ra-ra-boon-de-ay!*

The jingle was inaccurate—Parkhurst himself was never "on the floor" with prostitutes, but its tone accurately captured the feeling of most New York politicians toward Parkhurst's crusade. Senator Clarence Lexow told reporters that Parkhurst "considers himself the uncrowned king of New York." Governor THEODORE ROOSEVELT went further yet, branding Parkhurst a "dishonest lunatic." Still, the charges issued in Parkhurst's second antivice sermon, on March 13, sparked a grand jury investigation and subsequent empanelment of a special commission—ironically chaired by Senator Lexow. The LEXOW COMMISSION's hearings revealed numerous examples of corruption, and NYPD Chief WILLIAM DEVERY was driven from office. Propelled by public outrage, a new "fusion" government broke Tammany Hall's grip on local politics, but the reforms were short-lived. Corrupt control was soon reasserted, and Parkhurst witnessed a new age of even more pervasive corruption, with the advent of PROHIBITION's "noble experiment," before his death in 1933.

Peist, William J. (b. 1948)

Born in 1948, native New Yorker William Peist initially aspired to be a famous chef. He studied toward that end and won awards for his pastry creations, but the kitchen's glamour paled by 1974, when he joined the NEW YORK CITY POLICE DEPARTMENT. Budget constraints resulted in Peist being cut from the NYPD's ranks after nine months of service, in June 1975, but the department rehired him in October 1979.

Unknown to his fellow officers, the born-again William Peist was a secret "shoo-fly" for INTERNAL AFFAIRS, ever alert for indiscretions by his colleagues. He might have continued on that course indefinitely, but for an off-duty auto accident that cost him a leg and fostered bitterness when his appeals for line-of-duty compensation were denied. Between his accident and that decision, Peist had been moved to desk work with the NYPD's Intelligence Division, assigned to monitor ORGANIZED CRIME in New York. As a means of revenge against the department, Peist spent three years (1987–90) leaking confidential information to members of the Gambino Mafia family, thereby assisting "Teflon Don" John Gotti in defeating 17 state and federal cases against himself and other family members. The information provided included location of "bugs," dates of

impending indictments, plus names and addresses of jurors in various trials.

FBI agents were finally alerted to Peist's double life through a WIRETAP on Gotti's telephones. Initial mention of a "mole" with a "cousin" named Pete led G-men to Peter Mavis, a gambler heavily in debt to bookie George Helbig and underboss Salvatore "Sammy the Bull" Gravano. In time, the agents learned that Mavis had recruited Peist and used his inside information as a means of wiping out his (Mavis's) debts to the mob. Family associates Helbig and Joe "Butch" Corrao were the intermediaries who received Peist's information and paid him accordingly. In October 1991, Gravano turned FBI informant to save himself from multiple murder prosecutions, and his testimony convicted Peist on charges of racketeering and obstructing justice.

See also: FEDERAL BUREAU OF INVESTIGATION; INFORMANTS.

Petrosino, Joseph (1860–1909)

A native of Sicily, born in 1860, Giuseppe Petrosino immigrated to the United States with his family at age six. His parents settled in New York City, where Giuseppe—his given name Americanized to "Joseph"—completed grade school, then became a city street cleaner. He joined the NEW YORK CITY POLICE DEPARTMENT in October 1883, assigned to Little Italy, and during several years on foot patrol employed his knowledge of the Mafia to arrest various "Black Hand" extortionists. Petrosino's superiors promoted him to sergeant in 1895 and placed him in command of a special "Italian Squad," expanded to include 50 officers by 1896.

Despite an impressive record of arrests, convictions, and deportations in New York—often based on information obtained via "THIRD-DEGREE" TACTICS—Petrosino remained convinced that the root of America's Mafia problem lay in his ancestral homeland. NYPD leaders approved his plan to visit Sicily for consultation with Italian authorities, and Petrosino departed in February 1909. His mission was supposed to be kept secret, but police commissioner Theodore Bingham leaked word of Petrosino's trip to the *New York Herald*. Petrosino was thus expected when he arrived in Palermo. On March 12, 1909, an unknown gunman ambushed and killed Petrosino in that city's Piazza Marina. Persistent rumors name the triggerman as Mafia boss Don Vito Cascio Ferro, who had earlier fled New York City to avoid arrest by Petrosino's Italian Squad. The crime remains officially unsolved today, while Petrosino has achieved near-legendary status as an early opponent of ORGANIZED CRIME in America.

Peyer, Craig Alan (b. 1950)

Craig Peyer was, from all appearances, a model cop. In 13 years with the CALIFORNIA HIGHWAY PATROL he had compiled a spotless record, while his gift for gab elevated him to a post as the CHP's unofficial spokesman on topics related to highway safety. By the time it was revealed that Peyer's supervisor had ignored a series of complaints about his treatment of young women, it was already too late: The "model cop" was jailed on charges of murdering a 20-year-old college coed.

A Minnesota native, born in 1950, Peyer joined the U.S. Air Force after high school and served in Thailand. He joined the CHP in 1973, and the new job worked an immediate change in his personality. Wife Deborah, filing for divorce in July 1978, complained that when Peyer donned his uniform, "His head swelled. He became Mister Macho. The badge was a way to flirt." At home he was abusive, sometimes violent, though his superiors apparently remained oblivious. His standard "flirting" technique involved late-night traffic stops of female motorists along the lonely stretch of Interstate 15 that was his beat. When one angry mother complained about Peyer forcing her daughter off the highway, Sgt. John McDonald explained the move as an "escort" to "an area safely away from the high-speed freeway traffic," granting Peyer a commendation for his "excellent tactics."

On December 28, 1986, San Diego police received a missing-person report on 20-year-old Cara Knott. Her car was found abandoned on Mercy Road, off I-15, with bloodstains on the driver's door. Soon afterward, searchers found her strangled body broken on jagged rocks, 65 feet below a highway overpass. Lab tests revealed that some of the blood on Knott's boots was Type A, while hers was Type O. Three half-empty beer cans, still cold, were found beneath the bridge, some bearing FINGERPRINTS. Technicians also collected several "foreign" fibers from Knott's clothing, for comparison against future suspects.

When Knott's murder hit the airwaves on December 29, CHP leaders chose Craig Peyer to appear on television, offering safety tips for drivers at risk. "Don't get into anyone else's car," he cautioned, "because you're at their mercy. You could be raped if you're a woman—if you're a man, robbed—all the way down to being killed." "If stopped by an apparent police officer," Peyer warned, "Make sure they are in a black-and-white and have a badge on."

While the search for Knott's killer continued, a sheriff's deputy reported seeing Peyer with scratches on his face, the night of December 27. CHP administrators suspended him with pay on January 5, 1987, and detectives searched his squad car two days later, finding a length of rope in the trunk, concealed beneath the spare tire. When questioned about "those young honeys" he

had "escorted" to Mercy Road on prior occasions, Peyer confessed himself "a bullshitter," but denied any wrongdoing. Officially charged with Knott's murder on January 16, Peyer was held in lieu of $1 million bond. Stripped of his badge on May 28, 1987, Peyer faced trial in January 1988. Tire tracks, fibers from his uniform, and rare Type A blood linked Peyer to the murder scene, while threads from Knott's clothing were found on his boots and gunbelt. To clinch the case, prosecutors offered a parade of women Peyer had menaced on the night shift, but jurors still deadlocked on February 25, resulting in a mistrial.

Peyer's second murder trial began on May 17, 1988, with 120 witnesses testifying for the state. Jurors convicted him of first-degree murder on June 23, whereupon he received a prison term of 25 years to life. Judge Richard Huffman also criticized Peyer's superiors for ignoring multiple complaints from female motorists. "They led inexorably to this tragedy," he said, "as surely as the sun came up this morning." Peyer, still hopeful for parole, remains philosophical in prison. "God must want me in here for a reason," he says.

Philadelphia Police Department

Hans Block established the first patrol system in Philadelphia, Pennsylvania, during 1663. A systematic "town watch" was maintained during 1700–51, when the state legislature established the city's first paid force of wardens and constables, alternating foot patrols with stationary duty in "watch boxes." A "police marshal" with authority over the city and outlying districts was appointed in 1850, succeeded by consolidation of authority spanning 129 square miles in 1854. Philadelphia hired its first black patrolman in 1881, though the department remained overwhelmingly white. Matrons without police powers were added to the payroll in 1886.

Philadelphia experienced the same 19th-century hysteria surrounding anarchists and "radicals" that swept America at large, prompting brutal police repression of labor unions and dissent in general. In 1902 Mayor Samuel Ashbridge boasted that "suppression of seditious utterances has been brought about by the vigorous action of the Police Bureau. The city is freer of the objectionable class of people than any other large city in the country." Six years later, four officers won commendations for leading a cavalry charge against peaceful hunger strikers (dubbed the "Broad Street riot"). In October 1909 police leaders refused a speaking permit to anarchist Emma Goldman, then reversed their ruling on condition that she submit her speech in advance for official approval. When Goldman refused, the meeting was raided.

PROHIBITION brought ORGANIZED CRIME and extensive CORRUPTION to Philadelphia, with a thriving Mafia "family" generally unmolested by police (where it was not actively protected) until the early 1970s. Meanwhile, police continued their suppression of "radicals," including a POLICE RIOT on May Day 1932 that sent 12 marchers to the hospital and 17 more to jail on fabricated charges of "resisting arrest" and "attacking police." Observers from the AMERICAN CIVIL LIBERTIES UNION described police on the scene as acting "with a brutality that broke all records in that city." Between 1929 and 1937, records of the PPD RED SQUAD reveal that police mounted surveillance on more than 6,000 "radical" meetings. In April 1940 police officers joined investigators from the House Committee on Un-American Activities to raid the local Communist Party office, carting off two truckloads of documents (later returned when a federal court ruled the raid illegal). By 1950 PPD's Intelligence Unit was working closely with the FBI "to investigate subversive activities."

Liberal police superintendent Howard Leary established the department's Civil Defense Squad (CDS) in 1964, to cope humanely with civil rights protests, but his efforts were ultimately fruitless. Two years later, successor FRANK RIZZO—who reviled Leary as a "gutless bastard" and vowed to "make Attila the Hun look like a faggot"—converted the CDS into an instrument of right-wing DOMESTIC SURVEILLANCE, infiltrating scores of law-abiding groups throughout the city. As police superintendent, and later as mayor, Rizzo energetically persecuted liberals and minorities, secretly condoning EXCESSIVE FORCE that finally landed the city in federal court. As a rationale for his police-state tactics, Rizzo cast himself as a last-ditch defender of American ideals (while urging his campaign supporters to "vote white"). In June 1966 CDS commander Harry Fox told the U.S. Senate, "It frustrates and alarms us to see the cancer of subversive thought spread into our youth with its contamination and certain death."

To counteract that "disease," Philadelphia police eagerly joined in the FBI's illegal COINTELPRO operations. Bureau files from 1967–68 document a pattern of false arrests used to "neutralize" black militants, coupled with a bloody attack on high school antiwar protesters (November 1967), fabrication of "bomb conspiracy" charges against the Students for a Democratic Society (1969), and a raid on the Black Panther Party, wherein those arrested were forced to parade nude before media cameras. (As in other Philadelphia FRAME-UPS, charges of an "ASSASSINATION conspiracy" filed against the Panthers were later dismissed.)

In August 1979 the U.S. JUSTICE DEPARTMENT filed civil litigation against Mayor Rizzo and 18 other city officials, charging them with concealing a pattern of systematic police brutality and "THIRD-DEGREE" TACTICS that "shocked the conscience." Rizzo dismissed the charges as "hogwash," but mayoral successor William

Green agreed to destroy the PPD's "subversive" files in early 1980. One year later, a federal investigation of police CORRUPTION convicted 29 officers—including three lieutenants, one captain, a chief inspector and a former deputy commissioner—on charges including bribery, extortion, and racketeering.

By 1980 some 42 percent of Philadelphia's population was nonwhite, but the police department still had much to learn about community relations, as displayed in the catastrophic MOVE BOMBING of 1985. One year later, in July 1986, five members of an elite narcotics squad faced federal indictments for RACKETEERING and extorting $400,000 from local drug dealers. Such scandals are almost routine in the City of Brotherly Love, but the PPD's Internet Web site maintains that: "Each member of the department is proud of the continuing respect given to the ideals of Honor-Integrity-Service that are the hallmarks of the Philadelphia Police Department."

Phoenix Police Department

Phoenix, Arizona, was incorporated as a city in February 1881, followed shortly by election of Henry Fargias as the first city marshal, serving until 1887. A horse-drawn patrol wagon supplemented foot patrols in the early 1900s, when the city covered only three square miles, and the Phoenix PD maintained an admirable safety record until February 1925, when it lost its first officer slain in the line of duty. Phoenix had doubled in size by 1933, when Ruth Meicher joined the force as its first police matron. The department was reorganized in 1950 with four divisions—Detectives, Patrol, Traffic, and Service. Today, Phoenix PD patrols 469 square miles and some 1.2 million residents, employing 2,600 sworn officers and 700-plus civilian support personnel.

Pickert, Heinrich A. (1886–1949)

Born in 1886, Heinrich Pickert served heroically with the U.S. Army in World War I, winning a personal citation from General John Pershing and subsequently serving as commander of the Order of the Purple Heart. Upon returning to his native Michigan, Pickert assumed command of that state's NATIONAL GUARD, simultaneously rising through the ranks of the new and ultraconservative American Legion, while he cultivated a close friendship with Harry Bennett, chief of security for the Ford Motor Company. Personal inclination and a nose for profit made Pickert a dedicated Red-hunter in those postwar years, dedicated to the service of Detroit's automobile magnates, who viewed any labor union as an army of the Communist International.

In 1929 President Herbert Hoover placed Pickert in charge of the U.S. CUSTOMS SERVICE, a post he retained until becoming Detroit's police commissioner in 1933. His return to Detroit came at an auspicious moment, as members of the United Auto Workers launched a series of sit-down strikes. Pickert instantly expanded and unleashed the DETROIT POLICE DEPARTMENT's Special Investigations Bureau (SIB), a longstanding RED SQUAD created to infiltrate unions and collaborate with private security forces in STRIKEBREAKING. Ford's "security" force, for example, consisted primarily of Mafia thugs and members of the pro-Hitler German American Bund, but Pickert was not to be outdone. He encouraged his officers to join the Black Legion, a violent spin-off of the KU KLUX KLAN, whose members donned black hoods and robes to bomb, whip, and murder union organizers. Persuasive evidence suggests that Pickert himself joined the group, perhaps later regretting it, and one report notes that he "frantically promoted all those police officers who could compromise him."

Exposure of the Black Legion's TERRORISM in 1937 nearly toppled Pickert from his pedestal, but he briefly dodged the bullet and clung to his job while others around him were prosecuted. Subsequent investigation disclosed that his department was not only burdened with fascists, but also riddled with CORRUPTION, spawned by local ORGANIZED CRIME operations and their link to the booming auto industry. By the time Pickert retired in 1939, the AMERICAN CIVIL LIBERTIES UNION ranked DPD's performance "very poor," reporting that "perhaps the most flagrant violation of the civil rights of Detroiters occur at the hands of the Special Squad organized by Commissioner Pickert, commonly called the Red Squad." Pickert survived a decade in retirement, dying in 1949.

Pierrepont, Edwards

A native of New Haven, Connecticut, born March 4, 1817, Edwards Pierrepont graduated from Yale University and New Haven Law School, winning admittance to the bar in 1840. He practiced law in Ohio for five years, then moved to New York City, where he later served as a state judge (1857–60). In 1862 Pierrepont was appointed to a military commission hearing cases of civilian prisoners held by the Union Army. He subsequently served as U.S. attorney for the Southern District of New York (1869–70), and was named U.S. attorney general by President Ulysses Grant in April 1875. Pierrepont resigned that post in May 1876, becoming minister plenipotentiary to Great Britain (1876–77). Upon his return from England, he settled in New York City and died there on March 6, 1892.

Pinkerton, Allan J. (1819–1884)

America's most famous private investigator was born in Scotland on July or August 1819 (reports vary), the

Allan Pinkerton, America's most famous private detective (Author's collection)

son of a Glasgow policeman. Allan Pinkerton initially shunned his father's trade and apprenticed himself to a barrel-maker, then attached himself to the radical Chartist movement that sought universal suffrage and equal rights for Britain's working class. Ironically, Pinkerton's father was badly injured in a Chartist riot, and Allan himself fled Scotland in 1842 to avoid arrest. Upon arrival in the United States, he settled first at Dundee, Illinois, and resumed his barrel-making trade.

One day, while collecting wood for barrel staves, Pinkerton spied a gang of counterfeiters and reported them to local police, returning to participate in the arrest. That moment of celebrity, combined with Pinkerton's habitual travel around the county, persuaded locals to recruit him as a deputy sheriff. The badge fit well enough that Pinkerton soon joined the CHICAGO POLICE DEPARTMENT, becoming the force's first detective in 1850, advancing four years later to serve as a Cook County deputy SHERIFF and "special agent" of the local postal service. Meanwhile, in 1852, Pinkerton also found time to organize and lead his own elite team of private investigators, available to the highest bidder.

Over the next three decades, the Pinkerton Detective Agency tackled a wide variety of cases. One of its earliest assignments, for the Illinois Central Railroad, involved solution and prevention of TRAIN ROBBERIES. That contract placed Pinkerton in touch with future Union general George McClellan (the railroad's president) and president-to-be Abraham Lincoln (the company's lawyer). With the outbreak of the Civil War, Pinkerton and his detectives served double duty as bodyguards for President Lincoln, and as Union intelligence agents, operating on both sides of the Mason-Dixon Line. Pinkerton foiled the first attempt to murder Lincoln, en route to his 1861 inauguration, and later cracked a ring of Confederate spies operating in Washington, D.C. (He did not, as reported by some authors, lead the U.S. SECRET SERVICE.)

The postwar years brought new challenges, both for Pinkerton's acumen and his ethics. Pursuit of the train-robbing Reno brothers climaxed with their execution by an Indiana mob, whereupon Pinkerton publicly advocated lynching of outlaws. Likewise, questions were raised about his agency's techniques in pursuit of

Missouri's James-Younger gang, specifically the bombing (see BOMBING AND BOMB SQUADS) of a rural home that killed a sibling of the quick-trigger James brothers and left their mother maimed for life. By the 1870s, much of Pinkerton's energy was expended on STRIKEBREAKING and infiltration of "radical" labor unions. Agent JAMES MCPARLAND penetrated a union of Irish coal miners in Pennsylvania, nicknamed the "Molly Maguires," and collected evidence that sent several members to the gallows for acts of TERRORISM. Ironically, some critics still insist that Pinkerton detectives were responsible for the 1886 HAYMARKET BOMBING and subsequent frame-up of various anarchists who were hanged or imprisoned on charges of murdering Chicago policemen.

Whether those claims were true or not, most historians agree that some Pinkerton operatives were not averse to bending the rules of procedure, or even staging crimes in order to create more business for the agency. Their zeal in the defense of management during the U.S. labor wars frequently placed Pinkerton detectives on the wrong side of the law.

Allan Pinkerton died in Chicago on July 1, 1884, leaving sons Robert and William to manage his empire. The agency's logo—a staring eye, accompanied by the slogan "We never sleep"—provides the derivation for the slang term *private eye*.

Pinkney, William (1764–1822)

William Pinkney was born at Annapolis, Maryland, on March 17, 1764. He studied medicine but never practiced, shifting instead to the law. Admitted to the Maryland bar in 1786, he served as a member of the U.S. Constitutional Convention two years later (where he opposed ratification). Pinkney also served in the Maryland state legislature (1788–92) and as a member of the state executive council (1792–95). He was elected to the Second Congress, but resigned in November 1791, after eight months of service, when his eligibility was challenged.

President George Washington named Pinkney as one of the U.S. commissioners to London under Jay's Treaty (1796), and President James Monroe sent him back to England on a similar mission in 1806–11. Between those foreign tours of duty, Pinkney served as Maryland's attorney general (1805). Upon Pinkney's return to the United States in December 1911, President James Madison named him U.S. attorney general, a post he held until February 1814. From Washington, Pinkney moved on to combat service in the War of 1812, and was wounded in August 1814. He returned to Congress in 1815–16, then served as U.S. minister to Russia (with a special mission to Naples) in 1816–18. Pinkney's

Outlaw Jesse James (Author's collection)

Attorney General William Pinkney (Author's collection)

career climaxed with election to the U.S. Senate in 1819, and he died in office on February 25, 1822.

Pistone, Joseph D. (b. 1939)

Pennsylvania native Joseph Pistone joined the FBI in July 1969 and spent his first 18 months assigned to the Jacksonville, Florida, field office. His legendary UNDER-COVER WORK began in 1971, when he was transferred to Alexandria, Virginia, and from there to New York City in 1974. Two years later, posing as jewel thief "Donnie Brasco," Pistone became the first G-man in history to penetrate the Mafia. Working his way into the Joseph Bonnano crime family (though never inducted as a "made" member), Pistone remained undercover until January 1981, collecting sufficient evidence for some 200 indictments and more than 100 felony convictions. Pistone received the U.S. attorney general's Distinguished Service Award in January 1983 and remained with the Bureau for three more years, playing a peripheral role in FBI penetration of the Bandidos motorcycle gang. Persistent death threats finally prompted Pistone to leave the FBI in 1986 and take his family into hiding. Two years later, he published an account of his

greatest case—*Donnie Brasco: My Undercover Life in the Mafia.* A film was made of the book in 1997, starring Johnny Depp, but Pistone staunchly repudiates the scenes that show his character assuming the personality and ethics of a mobster.

Pitts, Earl Edwin

Earl Pitts joined the FBI in 1983 and four years later began a career as a double-agent, spying for the Russian KGB. His betrayal was a deliberate choice, initiated in July 1987 when Pitts wrote a letter to the Soviet mission to the United Nations, offering his services as a spy. At the time, he was assigned to counterintelligence operations in the New York City field office, later transferred to the Bureau's Legal Counsel Division in Washington, D.C. KGB officers paid Pitts a total of $224,000 for various documents including a list of FBI INFORMANTS who provided data on the Soviet Union.

Pitts's career in ESPIONAGE stalled in December 1991, when the USSR abandoned communism and subsequently disintegrated. FBI headquarters obtained cooperation from Pitts's original Russian contact, and while Pitts was transferred to a post at the FBI Academy, where he could do no further damage, a "false flag" sting operation was mounted against him. A former contact, now collaborating with the Bureau, approached Pitts with an offer to resume spying for the new Russian Foreign Intelligence Service. Pitts agreed and accepted $15,000 in cash. He was arrested on December 18, 1996, charged with conspiracy to commit espionage, attempted espionage, communication of classified information, and conveyance without authority of government property. Pitts pled guilty in February 1997, calling a psychiatrist to testify that anger had pushed him "beyond his limits." Judge T. S. Ellis III dismissed the argument and slapped Pitts with a 27-year prison term, three years longer than the prosecution had requested.

See also: FEDERAL BUREAU OF INVESTIGATION.

Pittsburgh Police Department

The city of Pittsburgh, Pennsylvania, was incorporated with a population of 9,000 in 1816. Law enforcement was haphazard over the next four decades, until a small police force (one chief and nine patrolmen) was established in 1857. From those humble beginnings, the Pittsburgh P.D. has grown into an agency with 900 sworn officers, policing a city of 335,000 full-time residents.

Along the way, Pittsburgh P.D. confronted the full range of challenges and difficulties confronted by police departments in other U.S. cities: RACISM and endemic

CORRUPTION, the rise of ORGANIZED CRIME during and after PROHIBITION, aggressive recruiting by the 1920s KU KLUX KLAN, street gangs, and an influx of DRUGS in the later 20th century. Sadly, the force earned a reputation for EXCESSIVE FORCE and false arrests, which in the 1980s drew scrutiny from the U.S. JUSTICE DEPARTMENT and the AMERICAN CIVIL LIBERTIES UNION. Notorious incidents included the cases of two women beaten by officers when they stopped to watch police manhandling a stranger on the street; a disabled woman strip-searched in front of her children during a routine traffic stop; a Baptist minister beaten and arrested in his home while listening to gospel music; and a kidney dialysis patient beaten after he told a Pittsburgh traffic cop, "I'll see you in court."

The ACLU and NAACP sued the Pittsburgh P.D. over its abusive practices in March 1996, citing complaints from 65 individual victims. (Pittsburgh ACLU director Witold Walczak was alerted to the problem when he asked a patrolman for directions and was answered with a string of obscenities.) The lawsuit prompted a 10-month federal investigation, which found that department commanders encouraged excessive force. Those findings produced a consent decree, accepted by the city, that provides for computer monitoring of all civilian abuse complaints, mandates reports from officers each time they employ physical force, and requires employment of an independent auditor to monitor compliance. By the time federal oversight was lifted in September 2002, Pittsburgh ranked among America's 10 safest cities, but some critics still claim that nothing has changed. In June 2003 two members of the Pittsburgh school board told reporters that incidents of casual brutality were still ongoing.

Plummer, Henry (1832 or 1837–1864)

One of the Old West's most colorful characters, Henry Plummer was actually a native of Maine, born in either 1832 or 1837 (published versions differ). While his father, older brother, and brother-in-law were sea captains, expecting Henry to follow their lead, he had other ideas. In 1852 he sailed to Panama, then crossed the isthmus by mule train and caught another ship bound for San Francisco, intent on making his fortune in the California gold fields. Instead, he bought half-interest in a bakery, then banked enough money to finance a prospecting jaunt to Nevada City, a mining camp 150 miles north of San Francisco.

There Plummer bought a ranch and mining claim, but in 1854 he swapped his interests for control of another bakery. By 1856 he was well known and well enough respected to win election as SHERIFF of Nevada City, described in some accounts as the third-largest

settlement in California. Easily reelected in 1857, Plummer found trouble soon after the ballots were counted, when miner John Vedder accused him of bedding Vedder's wife. A duel resulted, ending Vedder's life, and while Plummer received a 10-year prison sentence for the killing, a diagnosis of tuberculosis earned him a pardon in August 1859.

Back in Nevada City, Plummer squandered his bakery's earnings on whiskey and hookers, soon joining a gang of highway bandits to supplement his dwindling income via stagecoach robbery. Arrested after one holdup, he won acquittal based on lack of evidence. His next scrape was another murder charge, resulting from an October 1861 duel with one William Riley for the favors of a barroom hostess. Plummer bribed a jailer to release him in that case and fled to Oregon, then Washington and Idaho, where he reportedly killed two more men. After the last killing, of Idaho bartender Patrick Ford, Plummer narrowly avoided LYNCHING.

Gravitating to Montana and another gold rush during 1863, Plummer settled at Bannock and charmed the locals into naming him sheriff, all the while collecting another bandit gang on the sly. Ironically dubbed the "Innocents," Plummer's crew soon outgrew him, its members becoming so numerous that secret handshakes were required for personal identification. While citizens of Bannock apparently did not suspect Plummer's perfidy, they recognized his inability to stem the local crime wave and replaced him with a butcher in the next election. In the meantime, Plummer had wangled appointment as a deputy U.S. marshal for eastern Idaho Territory, but he still resented his loss at the polls and promptly went gunning for his successor. Friends intervened to avert bloodshed, but Plummer's time was running out. By December 1863, a VIGILANCE COMMITTEE was organized and proceeded to hang some two dozen real or suspected outlaws, ex-sheriff Plummer among them. After his execution in 1864, stories spread blaming Plummer for 15 murders, while the "Innocents" were credited with more than 100. The true tally may never be known.

Police Benevolent Association

Founded in the late 19th century, the PBA is America's largest police union, representing officers from most of the major departments nationwide. The group is subdivided by rank, so that larger departments may include representatives from the Captain's Benevolent Association, Lieutenant's Benevolent Association, Sergeant's Benevolent Association, or Patrolman's Benevolent Association. The union provides defense attorneys in the event that members are accused of criminal activity or face civil litigation arising from their on-duty performance, and the PBA also lobbies for higher wages, improved working conditions, and various other demands typical of any labor union. PBA spokesmen also campaign to protect the image of American police, as when they called for a boycott of Bruce Springsteen's recording "41 Shots," inspired by the death of innocent shooting victim AMADOU DIALLO in New York City.

Critics sometimes accuse the PBA and its various branches of acting in a high-handed manner. A typical piece from the *Village Voice* ("Rogue Union," December 7, 1993) called the New York City PBA "an arrogant, insular, and wealthy institution that stands above the law and beyond scrutiny." The article went on to ask, rhetorically, "Where is the $63 million a year in tax funds and union dues [collected by the PBA] going?" Author Russ Baker found the 20,000-member Patrolmen's Benevolent Association in New York "as it did last year [1992] when a PBA rally turned into a drunken riot, with thousands of police officers storming the steps of City Hall and blocking traffic on the Brooklyn Bridge." Baker further alleged that FBI WIRETAPS on members of ORGANIZED CRIME have revealed bribes paid to PBA leaders, that one prominent PBA spokesman suffered from "a gambling addiction," that political contacts aided PBA leaders in obtaining lucrative state and federal contracts, and that the union actively opposes any serious investigations of police CORRUPTION or EXCESSIVE FORCE.

police divisions

American police departments vary widely in their organizational structures and nomenclatures for various departments, but certain similarities emerge from a review of various departments that publicize their internal structure. Nearly all recognize a clear distinction between their Uniform (or Patrol) Division and the corresponding Detective (or Criminal Investigative) Division. Most large departments also feature a Support Services Division and an Administrative Division. Broadly speaking—and with a near-infinite range of local variations—tasks assigned to the three main police divisions break down as follows:

The Uniformed Division performs all normal patrol functions, including traffic enforcement and accident investigations. Depending on local situations and requirements, uniformed officers may also be assigned to beach patrols, service on various mass-transit carriers, gang-control operations, school security duties, animal control, vehicle safety inspections, street crime interdiction (sporadic "stop-and-frisk" operations), security at various public events, and "special" operations such as hostage rescue or riot control. Uniformed officers are generally the first to respond at any crime scene, but in most jurisdictions they play no significant role in subsequent investigation of serious offenses.

Detectives are generally (though not always) distinguished from uniform officers by wearing "plain clothes." In some departments elevation to detective status also means a higher salary, but other forces—notably the LOS ANGELES POLICE DEPARTMENT—transfer officers between divisions without pay raises or elevation in rank. As suggested by the name, detectives are expected to "detect"—i.e., investigate and solve crimes, while apprehending the offenders. Various departments of the average Detective Division include such titles as Robbery and Homicide (sometimes lumped together as Major Crimes), Vice (typically gambling and commercial sex offenses), Sex Crimes (rape and pedophilia, versus prostitution), Intelligence (again, often divided between criminal and political surveillance), Narcotics, Domestic Violence, White-collar Crime, Organized Crime, and Missing Persons.

Support Services (or Operations), where it exists as a separate police division, generally deals with tasks including communications, detention of suspects in custody, storage and transmission of records, preservation of evidence (or "property"), INTERNAL AFFAIRS investigations, plus maintenance of police buildings and vehicles. The Administrative Division is commonly responsible for hiring and training personnel, passing judgment in disciplinary cases, coordinating departmental public relations, handling most legal affairs, and coordinating official involvement in such community programs as CRIME STOPPERS, D.A.R.E. and PAL. In small departments, fewer (if any) divisions exist, while administrative tasks fall on the shoulders of one or two high-ranking individuals.

police riots

While modern police are trained to cope with crowds and various civil disturbances, their response to such events—in the past and during recent times—is not always conducted "by the book." In fact, as human beings subject to personal anger and the influence of mob mentality, officers sometimes behave in a chaotic and undisciplined fashion which fits the legal definition of a riot.

The term *police riot* was popularized during 1968, following globally televised scenes of Chicago police beating antiwar protesters, reporters, and hapless bystanders during the Democratic National Convention. Author Rodney Stark's two-year study of that and similar incidents revealed that such outbursts were not especially uncommon, either in the 1960s or at any other time in U.S. history. Stark defined police riots as follows:

An event is a police riot when roving bands of policemen set upon nonprovocative persons and/or property in an excessively violent manner. When only one small group of policemen sets upon citizens and/or property in a single location it may be useful to call this a police attack. A police riot is any such event involving two or more attacks. [Emphasis in original]

Stark goes on to add that "[n]onprovocative persons are those who represent no significant threat to life, physical safety or property" before the police assault begins. Peaceful participants in a lawful public demonstration would thus be deemed "nonprovocative," regardless of their message, chants or placards, and so forth. Stark further explains that "[o]ne clear indicator that a police attack or riot has occurred is when persons are assaulted by the police and abandoned without being arrested, in other than a situation where arrest is impossible. . . . A second indicator . . . is when police destroy or damage property without filing a report attributing this action to the necessities of duty."

Under those guidelines, even a casual review of history reveals no end of police riots throughout the United States, sometimes with deadly consequences. Incidents covered in this volume include the JACKSON STATE COLLEGE SHOOTINGS, the MEMORIAL DAY MASSACRE, and the ORANGEBURG MASSACRE—all of which resulted in multiple fatalities inflicted on unarmed civilians by undisciplined police. While the U.S. JUSTICE DEPARTMENT is legally responsible for investigating and prosecuting such cases, it has never secured a conviction against any officer in a police riot situation. Likewise, no specific case of local prosecution or departmental disciplinary action arising from a police riot could be located at press time for this volume.

Portland Police Department (Maine)

The town of Falmouth, Maine, was leveled three times between 1675 and 1775—twice by Indian raiders and once by British naval artillery during the Revolutionary War. Still, its residents persevered and ultimately flourished in the Atlantic shipping trade, renaming their town Portland in 1786. Early law enforcement followed the usual New England pattern, beginning with night watchmen and expanding over time to meet the needs of a growing community. SMUGGLING became problematic under the Embargo Act (1807–10), restricting trade with Europe, but Portland survived that challenge and the War of 1812 to serve briefly as Maine's first state capital (1820–32).

Mayor Neal Dow, elected on a strict temperance platform, campaigned successfully in 1851 for passage of the "Maine Law," banning any sale of alcohol except for "medicinal, mechanical and manufacturing purposes." Thus Maine pioneered the U.S. trend in PRO-HIBITION, half a century before the 18th Amendment to the U.S. Constitution outlawed liquor nationwide. Unhappy drinkers responded with the Portland Rum Riot of June 2, 1855, but the statewide ban on booze endured—with all its attendant problems and CORRUPTION—until the Maine Law was repealed in October 1934, nearly a year after the end of national prohibition. Meanwhile, Independence Day fireworks sparked a catastrophic blaze that leveled most of downtown Portland on July 4, 1866, leaving more than 10,000 residents homeless.

Despite its many setbacks, Portland emerged as Maine's largest city in the 20th century, boasting more than 64,000 citizens in 2000. That growth, accompanied by a thriving tourist industry, introduced the full gamut of urban problems, from DRUGS and street crime to concerns about TERRORISM and homeland security. Thus far, the Portland P.D. has proved equal to the challenge.

Portland Police Department (Oregon)

Law enforcement was no simple task in 19th-century Portland, Oregon, where bartenders and hotel proprietors routinely "shanghaied" male patrons, drugging them and selling them into slavery aboard sailing ships bound for the Far East. Still, police persevered, and by the early 1900s Portland had redeemed its reputation, remodeled in large part by teetotalling lumber baron Simon Bensen.

That beatific image was tarnished in the 1920s, when PROHIBITION and the KU KLUX KLAN arrived simultaneously, treating Portland to a new era of CORRUPTION and bigotry. Oregon boasted 50,000 Klan members, with nearly half that number in Portland alone, and a 1923 report by the *Portland Telegram* found the police department "full to the brink with Klansmen." Still, there were so few blacks and Jews to terrorize that the knights and their brothers in blue had to console themselves with a campaign to outlaw Catholic schools. A special "Black Patrol" of strong-arm Klansmen helped police harass "radical" unionists, but time and public disaffection with the Klan's own moral bankruptcy eventually brought the troubling era to an end.

Today Portland and Oregon at large are known as a bastion of free-thinking independence, targeted by Attorney General JOHN ASHCROFT in the early 21st century for passage of legislation approving marijuana prescriptions and physician-assisted suicide. (The state responded with a national "Back Off John" campaign and outlasted Ashcroft, who resigned in early 2005.) Portland P.D., for its part, in 1990 declared its vision to create "a city free from crime and the fear of crime, where people and police work together to improve their neighborhoods." That goal has yet to be achieved in full, but the department remains committed to a list of core values including "integrity, compassion, accountability, respect, excellence and service."

Porvenir massacre

RACISM was rampant along the Tex-Mex border in the paranoid years of World War I. Texans were inflamed by Pancho Villa's border raids and by the infamous Zimmerman Telegram, hinting at an alliance between Mexico and Kaiser Wilhelm's Germany. Rangers and racist vigilantes alike terrorized Mexicans on both sides of the border, with estimates of the Latino body count ranging from 500 to 5,000. In the midst of that carnage, few incidents rivaled the Porvenir massacre of December 1917.

On Christmas Day a band of 40 to 50 bandits raided Brite's store, outside the small village of Porvenir, in the Big Bend district of Texas. While they were looting the store, a stagecoach unexpectedly arrived and the raiders opened fire, killing the driver and two Mexican passengers. From Brite's, they rode on to besiege a nearby farmhouse, but armed settlers repelled the gang, inflicting heavy losses.

It was a victory of sorts, but not enough to satisfy J. M. Fox, a captain of the TEXAS RANGERS who despised Hispanics. Assigned to investigate the raid, Fox heard reports that Chicanos in Porvenir were sporting shoes of the same kind stolen from Brite's store. A Mexican in new shoes was cause for dire suspicion in those days, and Fox swiftly organized a posse consisting of eight fellow Rangers and four Anglo civilians. Boozing all the way to Porvenir, they were in a killing mood by the time they arrived, torturing some two dozen villagers "for information," finally choosing 15 at random and gunning them down in cold blood. When reports of the massacre spread, Fox described the killings as self-defense, claiming that his men had come under fire from bandits while making arrests.

The truth came out in 1919 before a Texas state legislative committee investigating allegations of wholesale civil rights violations by the Texas Rangers. No charges were filed in the Porvenir case, but Fox and his eight fellow gunmen were sacked from the Rangers. Widespread CORRUPTION and brutality continued for years afterward, until 1924 when Governor Miriam Ferguson fired the whole force en masse and started over from scratch, putting state law enforcement on a professional basis for the first time in living memory.

Postal Inspection Service

Postmaster General Benjamin Franklin appointed the first American postal inspector—then called a "surveyor"—in 1772, four years before the colonies declared their independence from Britain. The title was formally changed to "special agent" in 1801, with an Office of Instructions and Mail Depredations established as the investigative branch of the U.S. Post Office Department in 1830. A quarter century later, in 1853, there were still only 18 special agents nationwide, assigned to specific territories where they reported on conditions of stagecoaches, steamboats, railroads, and other mail conveyances.

In 1872 Congress passed a federal mail fraud statute to curb swindles flourishing in the wake of the Civil War. A chief postal inspector was appointed in 1880, with his subordinate special agents rechristened "inspectors." Postal inspectors solved the last known U.S. stagecoach robbery in 1916, and spent three years tracking the D'Autremont brothers, America's most lethal train robbers, during 1923–26. The first of five Postal Inspection Service crime laboratories was established in 1940.

Postal inspectors' duties have expanded greatly since the end of World War II. In 1957 Congress transferred responsibility for Post Office audits from the Bureau of Finance to the Chief Postal Inspector (a circumstance that left some critics wondering if a fox had been assigned to guard the henhouse). Formally renamed the Postal Inspection Service in 1971, the unit gained a uniformed Security Force that same year, while adding women to its ranks for the first time. The Child Protection Act of 1984 expanded federal efforts against child pornography, including prosecution of those who send or receive contraband materials by mail. Three years later, postal inspectors cracked a pervasive network of white-collar crime on Wall Street, including insider trading and a huge check-kiting ring. In 1991 the service exposed a global art fraud ring that sold fake paintings allegedly produced by artists, including Salvador Dalí and Pablo Picasso.

Those achievements have not immunized the Postal Inspection Service from public criticism, however. A notorious postal inspector in New York, ANTHONY COMSTOCK, used his office and authority to carry out a personal crusade against "obscenity" (including literature on birth control) between 1871 and 1915. More recently, conspiracist Alex Constantine accused the U.S. Postal Service of collaborating with the Central Intelligence Agency in mind-control experiments, producing a rash of MASS MURDERS by postal employees across the U.S. (By 1995, "going postal" was a slang description for random, irrational violence.) Ronald Roose, a self-described Postal Service whistleblower and spokesman for the "Postal Justice Project," posts Internet broadsides accusing postal inspectors of persecuting him through "harassment, electronic weapons, [and] chemical assaults." Roose describes postal inspectors as "enforcers" who "carry out the dirty work of the postal service" via "shiftless and reprehensible" tactics. Among the alleged harassment techniques used against him, Roose charges that postal inspectors and other department employees have threatened his life, threatened to burn his home, poisoned his cats, mailed him unsolicited pornography, tapped his telephone, "messed with" his belongings at work, and coerced neighbors into joining the war of nerves at his home. At press time for this volume, postal inspectors had no comment concerning those charges.

Prendergast, John C. (1886–?)

John Prendergast was 15 years old in 1901, when his father, an officer of the CHICAGO POLICE DEPARTMENT, was murdered by a burglar. That day he vowed to join the force as soon as possible, a pledge to himself which he honored in 1907. In 1924 Prendergast wangled an appointment as secretary to police chief Morgan Collins (1923–27), and that association paid off with his promotion to captain in charge of a South Side precinct. Advancement had its risks during the PROHIBITION era, and Prendergast was indicted for liquor violations in 1928. Instead of firing him, his corrupt superiors gave Prendergast a year's leave of absence, and the charges were dismissed upon his return, with Prendergast promoted to command CPD's uniformed division.

Chicago PD historian Richard Lindberg calls Prendergast "a firm believer in the status quo," and that deliberate blindness to CORRUPTION served him well. In December 1945 he was chosen to replace scandal-haunted JAMES ALLMAN as chief of police. After barely a week in office, Prendergast confronted the city's most sensational murder since the Leopold-Loeb case of 1925, with the abduction and gruesome slaying of six-year-old Susan Degnan. Coincidence broke that case and two others, resulting in a life sentence for teenage serial killer WILLIAM HEIRENS, but some observers of that case (then and today) denounced the outcome as a frame-up. Meanwhile, when faced with the usual charges of graft among his subordinates, Prendergast relied on bluster: "Back up the charges, and I will do something about them!"

Finally, with the advent of the Kefauver hearings on ORGANIZED CRIME, Prendergast could postpone the inevitable no longer. He resigned in lieu of testifying publicly, replaced by TIMOTHY O'CONNOR. Few Chicagoans were deceived by Mayor Martin Kennelly's parting comment, claiming that "[a]fter 44 years Prendergast goes out with an unblemished record and the respect of most people."

See also: FRAME-UPS.

profiling

As defined in law enforcement circles, profiling includes any attempt to identify an unknown offender or predict his/her actions based on precedents, physical evidence, or psychological analysis. All aspects of profiling remain controversial, their value touted (sometimes in extravagant and insupportable terms) by proponents and questioned (when not actively condemned) by critics. The three types of profiling relevant to law enforcement include:

Geographic profiling—Analysis of evidence collected from a series of related crime scenes may, at least in theory, help police locate the perpetrator's base of operations. For example, if a dozen women have been raped by the same offender in a particular city, plotting the crime scenes on a map may reveal a pattern in the rapist's attacks—and, by extension, suggest either where he may strike next or where he lives (presumably a central area with no attacks reported). Sophisticated software now exists to facilitate geographic profiling, and Canadian authorities have been voluble in singing its praises.

Psychological profiling—Based in equal parts on statistical precedents and specific crime-scene evidence, this tactic may permit an educated guess as to the serial offender's age, race, gender, employment, or marital status, and so on. In the one and only documented case where such methods produced an arrest, Dr. James Brussell predicted that New York City's "Mad Bomber" of the 1950s was a male immigrant, unmarried and living with a female relative, who would be wearing a double-breasted suit (with the coat buttoned!) at the time of his arrest. When profiling goes awry, however, it is worse than useless, pointing detectives completely away from their subject. A case in point is the 1970s "Skid Row Slasher" murders in Los Angeles, wherein psychologists profiled a tall, emaciated white offender with a physical deformity. The actual killer, when captured, proved to be a stocky African American.

Racial profiling—The most inflammatory form of profiling seeks to identify offenders based on probability that certain crimes in certain areas are most frequently committed by members of a particular race. Thus, some police jurisdictions have adopted policies of randomly stopping black motorists to search their cars for DRUGS, accosting Hispanics to demand proof of U.S. citizenship, and so forth. Innocent persons naturally resent being treated as prospective criminals, especially by officers who may be rude or domineering, and many also resent the tacit implication that other races (generally Caucasians) should be exempt from harassment. Proponents of racial profiling maintain that statistics support their policies—most drug dealers in certain regions *are* black, for example—but civil rights groups and most courts today stand in opposition to the practice.

Prohibition

America has long enjoyed a love-hate relationship with alcoholic beverages. Condemned by religionists and eagerly consumed by members of the populace at large (including certain ministers who railed against drunkards on Sunday), liquor and its purveyors generally avoided direct political attacks until the early 19th century, when an organized "temperance" movement arose in the land. (The title itself was a misnomer, since most of the zealots sought abolition of booze, not "temperate" drinking.) Orators traveled throughout the nation, asking Americans to pledge abstinence from alcohol, and a million complied by 1838. Maine took the next step, as the first state to ban booze outright in 1851, and 13 other states followed suit over the next four years.

Still, the zealots were not satisfied. In 1913 some 5,000 prohibitionists marched through Washington, D.C., presenting Congress with a petition calling for a constitutional amendment to ban beer and liquor. An amendment—the Eighteenth—was duly passed by Congress and sent to the states for ratification. Voters in 36 states approved the amendment by January 16, 1919, and it was scheduled to take effect one year later. Since the amendment contained no enforcement provisions, Congress passed the Volstead Act, imposing criminal penalties for the manufacture, sale, or possession of intoxicating beverages.

America went "dry" at 12:01 A.M. on January 16, 1920, and the first liquor robbery occurred moments later, as gunmen stole whiskey valued at $100,000 from a Chicago railroad yard. Almost immediately, the United States descended into an unprecedented national crime wave, mocking pious descriptions of Prohibition as a "noble experiment." In every state and major city, gangs of bootleggers stole, imported or manufactured huge volumes of liquor and beer, bribing police and politicians to ignore their crimes, while fighting bloody turf wars for control of prime sales territories. In Detroit alone, illegal saloons—dubbed "speakeasies" and "blind pigs"—outnumbered previous legal saloons 10 to one. Chicago's Al Capone was the most flamboyant "beer baron" of the era, but others were equally successful, equally ruthless. By 1927 regional gangs were involved in peace talks and economic negotiations that spawned America's modern-day ORGANIZED CRIME syndicate.

Prohibition was an obvious failure, but many politicians—particularly those dependent on the votes of Christian fundamentalists—refused to acknowledge the obvious. Presidential candidate Alfred Smith opposed Prohibition in 1924 and 1928, but he was defeated both times by conservative voters who feared both his "wet" politics and his Catholic religion. Finally, with the nation mired in the Great Depression, Franklin Roosevelt campaigned successfully for president on a pledge to repeal Prohibition. A Twenty-First amendment, repealing the Eighteenth, took effect in December 1933, and while the United States was legally "wet" once again, the legacy of Prohibition lingers to this day, embodied in a pervasive crime syndicate that taints every aspect of national life.

Providence Police Department

Founded in 1636, the settlement that grew into modern-day Providence, Rhode Island, survived in its early days by turning Caribbean molasses into rum, a part of the historic "triangular trade" that included shipment of black slaves from Africa to the West Indies. The city charter of 1832 established Providence's municipal government, including a small police department on the pattern of other New England cities in that era. By that time, textile mills dominated the local economy, staffed by cheap immigrant labor, and local police were required to perform all the usual functions of STRIKEBREAKING and social control over troublesome minorities. The city's first black patrolman, Alfred Lima, Sr., was not hired until 1947, well after most metropolitan departments north of the Mason-Dixon Line had integrated their ranks. Recruitment of the first female minority officers, Tonya King and Barbara Texeira, was further delayed until 1987.

Today Providence P.D. patrols Rhode Island's largest city and ranks as the state's largest law enforcement agency. It's motto, "Always Vigilant," is reflected in an Internet Web site that promises that Providence P.D. is "always working to better serve, and provide safety and service for everyone who lives, works, or visits the City of Providence."

"public enemies"

While the term *public enemy* appeared in print from time to time during the 1920s, the concept was only formalized in 1930, by the Chicago Crime Commission. Angered by the St. Valentine's Day massacre of 1929, but lacking any actual police powers, the commission responded by publishing a list of 22 local mobsters whom it declared enemies of civilized society. The original list included, in order of notoriety: "Scarface" Al

Capone, Anthony "Mops" Volpe, Ralph Capone, Frank Rio, "Machine Gun" Jack McGurn, James "Bomber" Belcastro, Rocco Fanelli, Lawrence Mangano, Jack Zuta, Jack "Greasy Thumb" Guzik, Frank Diamond, George "Bugs" Moran, Joe Aiello, Edward "Spike" O'Donnell, "Polack Joe" Saltis, Frank McErlane, Vincent McErlane, William Neimoth, Danny Stanton, Myles O'Donnell, Frank Lane, William "Klondike" O'Donnell, George "Red" Barker, William "Three Finger Jack" White, Joseph "Peppy" Genero, Leo Mongoven, and James "Fur" Sammons.

Placement on the list had no significance in terms of indictment for specific crimes. Indeed, given Chicago's climate of pervasive CORRUPTION, those on the list were more likely to be murdered by gangland rivals than prosecuted in court. New names were added as members of the original list were killed or imprisoned. The repeal of PROHIBITION also brought a shift in the identity of "Public Enemies," away from bootleggers (although the survivors continued in ORGANIZED CRIME), toward violent practitioners of bank robbery and KIDNAPPING. Accordingly, when Illinois state authorities issued a list of 21 "Public Enemies" on December 28, 1933, 12 of those named were members of John Dillinger's traveling holdup gang. Contrary to public perceptions, the FBI did not create its own public enemies list, but Director J. EDGAR HOOVER capitalized on lists published by others, sometimes denouncing those listed as "public rats." Another quarter century elapsed before the Bureau created its own list of "TEN MOST WANTED" FUGITIVES in 1950.

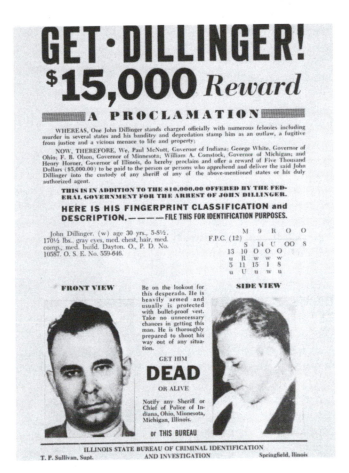

"Public enemy" John Dillinger represented a new breed of transient outlaws in the Great Depression. (FBI)

Al Capone was the first "public enemy" designated by Chicago's Crime Commission. (Library of Congress)

Puerto Rico Police Department

The United States seized Puerto Rico from Spain in 1898, one of several far-flung possessions captured during the Spanish-American War. Since that time, the Caribbean island—although dubbed a commonwealth—has been a de facto U.S. possession, governed from Washington although denied statehood, its citizens barred from voting in U.S. presidential elections. That subject status has produced significant unrest and sporadic waves of TERRORISM since World War II, suppressed by a combination of the FBI (including its illegal COINTELPRO operations) and the native Puerto Rico Police Department.

From its inception in the late 19th century, the PRPD has been shaken by cyclical CORRUPTION scandals and charges of brutality, recently including alleged persecution of its own officers. A longstanding ban on gay police or any association between police officers and known homosexuals was stricken down by federal court rulings in 1998, while PRPD leaders were ordered to pay legal fees for the complaining officers. Department leaders appealed that verdict, but lost their case a second time in 2001. Between August 2001 and January 2002, FBI agents jailed 60-plus officers on charges of protecting drug smugglers and dealers throughout Puerto Rico. Dual investigations—dubbed "Operation Lost Honor" and "Operation Blue Shame"—also bagged a judge and two prosecutors, caught on tape accepting bribes from attorneys and bail bondsmen. Political analyst Marco Rigau told a radio audience in January 2002, "This situation here is very serious. The information about more corruption just keeps on coming so much, I don't know where to start." At last report, more than 40 percent of all cocaine sold in the United States reached North America through Puerto Rico, largely unobstructed by the PRPD's 19,000 officers.

Purvis, Melvin Horace, Jr. (1903–1960)

The son of an affluent southern planter, Melvin Purvis, Jr. was born at Timmonsville, South Carolina, on October 24, 1903. He graduated from the University of South Carolina with an LL.B. in 1925 and spent the next two years in private practice, before joining the FBI under curious circumstances. Although two years below the minimum age set by Director J. EDGAR HOOVER for prospective G-men, Purvis was accepted after Hoover received a phone call from South Carolina's senior U.S. senator and New Deal champion Ed "Cotton" Smith (thus disproving Hoover's lifelong claim that the Bureau was immune to political patronage after he took charge in 1924).

Purvis enjoyed rapid advancement through the FBI ranks, ensconced by 1932 as agent-in-charge of the Chicago field office. His startling rise, surpassed only by that of CLYDE TOLSON, owed more to personal friendship with Hoover than any outstanding performance by Purvis, as evidenced by their correspondence during 1927–34. Initially in awe of Hoover, Purvis addressed him with all due respect until Hoover penned an order to "stop using MISTER" in written salutations. Henceforth, Purvis addressed his boss as "Dear Chairman" or "Dear Jayee" (after Hoover's initials). Hoover's jocular letters to Purvis include observations on one JUSTICE DEPARTMENT attorney's "mental halitosis" and suggestions that Hoover secretary Helen Gandy carried a torch for Purvis. If Purvis turned up for 1932's Halloween Ball, Hoover suggested, Ms. Gandy might be persuaded to greet him in a "cellophane gown." Author Anthony Summers deemed the letters evidence of "a homosexual courtship"; Assistant Director CARTHA DELOACH, by contrast, found them "clearly part of the bantering between two bachelors interested in women." In either case, the warm relationship would not endure.

Purvis might have passed his FBI career as an executive nonentity, but for a geographic coincidence. His Chicago assignment placed him at the heart of bandit country in the Great Depression, and Purvis was involved in pursuit of the era's most notorious "PUBLIC ENEMIES." Unfortunately for the Bureau's reputation and his own, he had a tendency to bungle manhunts or veer to the other extreme and plot FRAME-UPS of innocent defendants.

An early example of Purvis's ineptitude was seen in the search for outlaw Frank Nash, a Leavenworth escapee who had joined the Barker-Karpis gang. Purvis hired an American Indian ex-convict, one War Eagle, as the primary informant on the case, with humiliating results. War Eagle not only fingered the wrong man, but he also loaned Purvis a stolen car for use in the abortive raid. It was small consolation to Purvis when other G-men captured Nash in June 1933, then died with him in the KANSAS CITY MASSACRE while returning Nash to prison.

Purvis saw a chance to redeem himself that same month, when brewer William Hamm, Jr. was kidnapped from St. Paul, Minnesota, and ransomed for $100,000. Hamm's abductors were members of the Barker-Karpis gang, but Purvis fixed his sights on Chicago bootlegger Roger Touhy and three associates, arrested with automatic weapons on July 19, 1933, following an auto accident in Wisconsin. There was no clear reason to suspect the Touhy gang of snatching Hamm, but they were wanted in Chicago for the alleged ransom KIDNAPPING of career criminal Jerome Factor (later proved to be a gangland hoax).

It was enough for Purvis. He pushed for indictments under the new Lindbergh Law that made interstate kidnapping a federal crime. In the absence of evidence, Purvis fell back on "THIRD-DEGREE" TACTICS and perjured testimony to make his case. Touhy later described a series of beatings administered by G-men in jail, and while his complaint might be dismissed as self-serving, Purvis provided his own description of how the FBI handled prisoners. "The escaped prisoner was 'invited' to accompany the special agent to the federal building," Purvis wrote, "and sometimes these invitations were engraved on the minds [sic] of the escape[e] in a very definite manner and they were accepted." Nor were innocent witnesses safe from such treatment. In the Hamm case, prospective defense witness Edward Meany was told by agents, "If you go to St. Paul to testify for Touhy you'll be sorry—and maybe you won't come back."

It was all in vain, despite claims by Purvis that "We have an ironclad case." Touhy and his codefendants were acquitted of Hamm's kidnapping on November 28, 1933. Instead of being freed, however, they were delivered to Chicago authorities for trial in the fabricated Factor abduction. Purvis worked long and hard for the prosecution in that case, but the first jury failed to convict. Finally, with a new cast of witnesses (who later recanted their false testimony), prosecutors finally convicted Touhy and three others, sending them to prison for 99 years. Hoover cheered the frame-up as "a credit to the entire Bureau," ranking Touhy among "the most vicious and dangerous criminals in the history of American crime."

Another quarter century would pass before a federal judge exposed the FBI's malfeasance in Touhy's case. Meanwhile, Purvis had found a new target in the person of bank robber John Dillinger. Chicago was the center of Dillinger's violent world, and Purvis recognized the stakes involved in catching him, dead or alive. If there were any doubts, Hoover dispelled them in a letter dated April 3, 1934, advising Purvis: "Well, son, keep a stiff upper lip and get Dillinger for me, and the world is yours."

Purvis had his chance three weeks later, when tips placed Dillinger's gang at a lodge near Rhinelander, Wisconsin. Bypassing local police, Purvis led an FBI team to raid the lodge on April 22, but the outcome was a grim fiasco. G-men shot three innocent civilians, killing one, and lost one of their own while every member of Dillinger's crew escaped. Purvis further compounded his embarrassment on May 29, 1934, with a premature announcement of Dillinger's death.

Hoover's relationship with Purvis changed dramatically after the Wisconsin shootout. The director's "Dear Mel" letters were supplanted by terse notes addressed to "Dear Mr. Purvis." On June 4 Hoover chastised Purvis for failure to implement some unspecified order, fuming that "You have absolutely no right to ignore instructions." Twelve days later, when Purvis went golfing and missed a call from Washington, Hoover cabled that "There is no reason why the Agent in Charge should not leave word where he can be reached at any time." Agent SAMUEL COWLEY was dispatched from Bureau headquarters to supervise the Dillinger manhunt, undermining Chicago's star G-man to the point that subordinates dubbed him "Nervous Purvis."

Purvis redeemed himself, after a fashion, when Dillinger was killed in Chicago on July 22, 1934. Hoover had long since forgotten his promise to give Purvis "the world," but he managed a private note to Melvin's father, noting that Purvis "conducted himself with the simple modesty that is so characteristic of his makeup. . . . He had been one of my closest and dearest friends." Hoover soon regretted that mild praise, however, when Purvis bagged Kansas City Massacre suspect Charles "Pretty Boy" Floyd, in October 1934. In the wake of that shooting, Hoover moved to dispel "lurid" stories

that Purvis "personally interviewed Floyd" as the bandit lay dying. "As a matter of fact," Hoover told reporters, "Mr. Purvis never spoke one word to Floyd."

With or without conversation, Floyd's slaying put Purvis back on the media fast track. Eleven weeks later, he arrested Arthur "Dock" Barker in Chicago, then captured Barker-Karpis gangster Volney Davis on June 1, 1935. New indictments were filed in the Hamm kidnapping—against the right suspects, this time—and in the January 1934 abduction of banker Edward Bremer. Conviction on Lindbergh charges sent most of the gang up for life.

It was too much for Hoover. Never one to share the limelight gladly, Hoover sent a "Dear Sir" note to Purvis in March 1935, accusing Purvis of public drunkenness. Purvis denounced the charge as an "unmitigated and unadulterated lie," his protest undercut by newspaper accounts of Purvis brandishing his pistol in a Cincinnati store, botching a call to headquarters, then staggering off to his car. Friends of Purvis believe Hoover planted the story himself, but the damage was done. Hounded by reports of poor performance, Purvis left the FBI in summer 1935. Hoover swiftly expunged him from the official record, and no mention of Purvis appeared in *The FBI Story,* published with Hoover's collaboration in 1956.

Purvis moved to San Francisco and published a memoir, *American Agent,* in 1936, thereafter lending his famous face to promotion of various products. He introduced a radio series, *Top Secrets of the FBI,* and served as chairman for the Post Toasties "Junior G-Man Club." A more ambitious move toward Hollywood was blocked by Hoover, who offered active-duty G-men as consultants "free of charge" on gangster films, while warning studio bosses that he would "look with displeasure, as a personal matter" on anyone who hired Purvis.

Purvis returned to South Carolina and legal practice in 1938, then served as an army intelligence officer in World War II. His nomination as a federal judge was blocked by Hoover's negative reports in 1952, and Purvis suffered another black eye when the Touhy frame-up was exposed in 1959. Purvis died from a self-inflicted gunshot on February 29, 1960. A coroner deemed the shooting accidental, but stubborn rumors of suicide persist.

Pusser, Buford Hayse (1937–1974)

A native of McNairy County, Tennessee, born December 12, 1937, Buford Pusser joined the army after high school, but received an early discharge after he was diagnosed with asthma. That illness notwithstanding, he moved to Chicago and worked for a time as professional wrestler "Buford the Bull." In early 1961, newly married, Pusser returned to McNairy County and his first law enforcement job, as Adamsville's chief of police. In 1964 he was elected county SHERIFF, on a promise to clean up the gambling, vice, and bootlegging that were pervasive in McNairy County.

That crusade placed Pusser in conflict with an ORGANIZED CRIME syndicate operating along the Tennessee-Mississippi border, protected heretofore by a blend of CORRUPTION and violence. Pusser's crusade against illicit brothels, gambling clubs, and moonshine stills produced a string of headline news reports and two shootouts in which he killed armed fugitives. Best known for the small log he carried in place of a nightstick, Pusser also armed himself with various other weapons, but they failed him on August 12, 1967, when gunmen ambushed him on a rural highway, killing his wife and leaving Pusser gravely wounded.

That incident and its attendant publicity produced the first in a series of Hollywood films, wherein various actors portrayed Pusser as a swaggering superhero, making the Tennessee lawman a literal legend in his own time. On August 21, 1974, while driving home to Adamsville from a Memphis press conference, Pusser crashed his Corvette sports car into a highway embankment and died instantly. Speculation persists that the crash was "arranged" by his enemies, but no suspects were arrested in that case, or in the murder of his wife. The Hollywood version of Pusser survives in the films *Walking Tall* (1973), *Walking Tall Part II* (1975), *Final Chapter: Walking Tall* (1977), and in a short-lived *Walking Tall* television series (1981). When the legend was revived in *Walking Tall* (2004), producers changed the hero's name to "Chris Vaughn" and transplanted his story to rural Washington State. Fittingly, the last film starred "The Rock," a pro wrestler-turned-actor.

Putnam, Mark Steven (b. 1959)

Born at Coventry, Connecticut, on July 4, 1959, Mark Putnam majored in criminology at the University of Tampa, where he also led the school's soccer team to a championship in 1982. In October 1986 he graduated from the FBI Academy and was assigned to the two-man resident agency in Pikeville, Kentucky. His wife, then pregnant with their second child, hated the town on sight, but Putnam ignored her demands that he seek a transfer. Instead, he threw himself into the job with gusto, seeking ways to impress his superiors and win promotion.

His golden opportunity arrived with a series of local BANK ROBBERIES. The prime suspect, an ex-convict, rented rooms in Pikeville from Ken and Susan Smith, a young divorced couple who still lived together. Putnam sought help from the Smiths and soon embarked on an adulterous affair with Susan, a drug-addicted eighth-grade dropout. Putnam paid Susan $5,000 for testimony against her tenant, keeping her on the Bureau payroll even after the defendant was convicted in January 1988. Intent on marrying Putnam, Smith first confronted his wife, and when that failed to wreck the marriage she stopped using contraceptives in December 1988.

By that time, Putnam was recognized as a rising star within the FBI, solving another bank robbery and shutting down a stolen auto "chop shop." In early 1989 he dropped Susan Smith as an informant, then staged a series of bomb threats against himself, requesting a transfer to Florida for his family's safety. In March 1989 Putnam told Smith of his impending departure, and she countered with news that she was pregnant. Putnam offered to "take care of" Smith, but moved to Miami without settling their business. Back in Pikeville to testify in the chop-shop case, Putnam strangled Smith on June 8, 1989, and planted her corpse in a shallow grave.

Smith's family waited eight days to report her missing, then demanded an investigation of Putnam. Putnam declined requests for a polygraph test in February 1990, while denying any link to Smith's disappearance, but he failed a polygraph exam on May 18, 1990, and confessed the slaying four days later. After resigning from the FBI, he struck a plea bargain with state authorities, leading police to Smith's grave on June 4 in exchange for reduced charges of first-degree manslaughter. On June 12 Putnam received his prearranged sentence of 16 years, to be served in a federal prison. To date, he remains the only FBI agent convicted of criminal homicide.

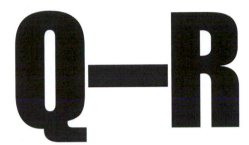

"quality over quantity"

Compilation of statistics was an FBI obsession under Director J. EDGAR HOOVER (1924–72). Indeed, statistics were the very lifeblood of the Bureau, since Hoover based the FBI's reputation and his yearly budgetary requests on ever-increasing numbers of arrests, cases investigated (as opposed to *solved*), hours of "voluntary" overtime worked without pay by his agents, and so forth. If some tabulations—including the yearly number of fugitives captured and stolen cars recovered—involved taking credit for actions performed by local police, so be it.

Director CLARENCE KELLEY sought to change that image and create a more proactive FBI in 1975, with his demand for "quality over quantity" in federal investigations. Abandoning the Hoover system, wherein agents were assigned to case squads (bank robbery, counterintelligence, etc.) and waited in their offices for complaints to arrive, Kelley ordered his troops to select targets in advance—e.g., a corrupt politician or member of ORGANIZED CRIME—and actively pursue that subject through UNDERCOVER WORK, "sting" operations, and the like. The concept was formalized in 1977, with specific Bureau goals enumerated in a series of National Priority Programs.

racism

America's history has been marred from its earliest days with bitter, often deadly conflicts between people of different races. Too often, nonwhites were the victims of discrimination codified by law, enforced by police departments whose officers were white and often brutal toward minorities. Historically, police departments in the South—and nationwide, during the 1920s—have been infiltrated by (or willingly collaborated with) violent white-supremacist groups such as the KU KLUX KLAN. White LYNCHINGS of blacks were rarely punished, and police sometimes participated in the killings, either by surrendering their prisoners or actively participating in the mobs. As recently as 1964, officers of the NESHOBA COUNTY (Mississippi) SHERIFF'S DEPARTMENT conspired with the KKK to lynch three civil rights workers. Six years later, George Wallace won his second term as Alabama's governor by campaigning against integration of the ALABAMA HIGHWAY PATROL.

Today, while legislation and court rulings have attempted to place nonwhites on a more equal footing, most of the larger U.S. law enforcement agencies are still dominated by whites, some of whom maintain (and sometimes articulate) right-wing attitudes unsympathetic to minorities. Such attitudes may translate on the street into EXCESSIVE FORCE or unjustified use of DEADLY FORCE against nonwhites. Since the mid-1960s, such incidents have sparked RIOTS in ghettos across the country, and while a 1967 presidential commission named police racism as the cause of most such outbreaks, many police officers shared the view of FBI Director J. EDGAR HOOVER that any manifestation of nonwhite dissatisfaction sprang from a "Communist conspiracy." Incidents such as the RODNEY KING beating and torture of ABNER LOUIMA are generally explained as the work of "bad apples," but nonwhite officers in many police departments still complain of racial discrimination by their superiors and harassment by their white colleagues.

Even the FBI—once denounced by the Klan as the "Federal Bureau of Integration"—is not immune to such claims. In September 1988 a federal court found the Bureau guilty of "systematic discrimination" against Hispanic employees and ordered a change in promotion procedures. Two years later, in August 1990, Director WILLIAM SESSIONS settled a lawsuit by ex-agent Donald Rochon, alleging racial harassment by his superiors in three different field offices. In addition to Rochon's financial payoff, Sessions disciplined 11 subordinates for either harassing Rochon or ignoring his complaints. In 1991–92, 230 members of BADGE (Black Agents Don't Get Equality) spent a year in tense negotiations with Sessions, climaxed by the director's agreement to place 19 blacks in supervisory posts and take other steps to improve their prospects. In the face of those actions, angry white G-men dubbed their director "Con-Sessions."

racketeering

While the terms *racket* and *racketeer* have been widely used throughout America since the days of PROHIBITION, in reference to such gangsters as Al Capone and Meyer Lansky, they were not legally defined until 1970, with passage of the federal Racketeer Influenced and Corrupt Organizations (RICO) Act. The definition contained in that statute includes "any act or threat involving murder, kidnapping, gambling, arson, robbery, bribery, extortion, dealing in obscene matter, or dealing in a controlled substance or listed chemical . . . which is chargeable under State law and punishable by imprisonment for more than one year." Also included on the list of racketeering activities are the following federal offenses: bribery; counterfeit currency; theft from interstate shipments or interstate traffic in stolen property; embezzlement from pension or welfare funds, loansharking, mail, or wire fraud; interstate transmission of gambling information or paraphernalia; traffic in obscene matter; sexual exploitation of children; "white slavery;" infringement of various copyright laws; murder for hire; various frauds involving financial institutions; and any tampering with witnesses or victims in a legal case.

Under the law, "racketeers" are not always recognized members of ORGANIZED CRIME, nor are they restricted to any particular ethnic group (such as the Italian Mafia). The statute defines as an enterprise "any individual, partnership, corporation, association, or other legal entity, and any union or group of individuals associated in fact although not a legal entity." In recent years, racketeering charges have been filed (or considered) against nonsyndicate perpetrators of various white-collar crimes, as well as certain terrorists and religious or political extremists whose activities include the crimes listed above.

radar/lidar law enforcement applications

Radar—from *ra*dio *d*etecting *a*nd *r*anging—was initially developed as a military tool and later used in civilian capacities, primarily for tracking aircraft on their approach to airports. It is used in the same way by U.S. CUSTOMS SERVICE agents and members of the DRUG ENFORCEMENT ADMINISTRATION to track smugglers approaching America's borders with narcotics and other contraband. The police application most familiar to the average citizen, however, is probably the use of radar to monitor ground traffic speeds and apprehend drivers who exceed the maximum posted speed limit.

In essence, radar uses radio waves to detect and monitor various objects. Its original and simplest function is to determine distance between two objects by emitting a concentrated radio wave and recording the echoes of any objects that block its passage. Since radio waves move through air at a constant speed, radar devices calculate the distance between the transmitter and its target based on how long it takes the "bounced" signal to return. Radar can also measure an object's speed by means of a phenomenon called "Doppler shift." When a radar transmitter and its target are both stationary, the echo has the same wave frequency as the original signal. When the target is moving, however, wave patterns change. Objects moving away from the transmitter "stretch" the waves, while objects approaching the transmitter "compress" the waves, increasing the frequency. Based on the frequency changes, a radar gun calculates how quickly the target (normally but not necessarily a vehicle) is moving toward or away from the transmitter. Further calculations allow for movement of the radar gun itself, as when mounted inside a police car. If the cruiser is traveling at 50 miles per hour and the target is moving away from it at 30 miles per hour, then the target must be traveling at 80 miles per hour. (If both vehicles hold a constant speed there is no deviation in the pattern.)

A newer variation of this tracking system is lidar, for *li*ght *d*etecting *a*nd *r*anging. As suggested by its name, lidar guns use concentrated infrared light (laser) beams in place of radio waves. Calculations are performed on the same basis as with radar, but using the speed of light rather than the speed of sound. In place of constant oscillating radio waves, the lidar gun emits rapid-fire pulses of light to track moving objects over a protracted distance. Many police departments use hand-held or dashboard-mounted lidar guns, but the devices may also be mounted beside highways, continuously operating to monitor the speed of each passing vehicle. Such stationary emplacements frequently include high-speed cameras, employed to snap pictures of the license plates (and sometimes drivers' faces) any time a passing car registers excessive speed. Speeders may thus be traced through computer data banks and receive their citations by mail, without involving officers in time-consuming (and often hazardous) traffic stops.

Lawbreakers normally outdo law enforcement agencies in adopting new technology, and while police initially had the edge in using radar and lidar devices, there is today no shortage of high-tech instruments designed to frustrate their efforts. The simplest evasion devices are radar detectors, basic radio receivers tuned to police frequencies which (the speeder hopes) will pick up radar signals in time to slow down and avoid a citation. Simple detectors are most effective when traffic officers leave their guns constantly turned on without sighting a particular target, thus beaming detectable signals throughout their patrol shift. The detector is useless, though, if an officer turns off his gun until a target is sighted. In that case the driver's warning comes too late, since his or her speed has already been recorded.

More sophisticated radar-jamming devices are also available, operating on the same principle used for years by military aircraft to avoid detection by their enemies. Jammers, unlike simple radar detectors, are not passive devices. They register incoming waves, then transmit their own signal, replicating the original radar gun's signal but mixing it up with additional radio noise, thus preventing an accurate reading. Many American jurisdictions have outlawed radar detectors and jammers, making their possession a separate offense. In those areas, police are often equipped with "VG2" devices—simple high-powered radio receivers tuned to the signal frequency commonly used by radar detectors and jammers. Ironically, a driver with an active radar detector in the car may be stopped and cited for illegal possession, even if he or she was not speeding at the time.

Scofflaws have likewise kept pace with lidar technology. Many modern radar detectors use a light-sensitive panel to register beams from police lidar guns, but their effectiveness is limited since lidar guns are best used over short distances and focus strictly on a single target. Thus, again, by the time a detector alerts the speeding driver, he or she has already been "painted" by the lidar beam with the illicit speed recorded. Some dedicated speeders try to defeat lidar by decreasing the reflectivity of their vehicles. Black paint may be helpful, since it absorbs more light and reflects less than other hues, while certain plastic covers reduce the reflective properties of metal license plates. At best, however, such tricks buy the speeder a few seconds to slow down between the time his or her car is sighted and the speed is registered by the lidar gun. Lidar jammers are more effective, equipped with their own light-emitting diodes (LEDs) that blind a lidar gun to reflected light.

The prevalence of radar guns in modern traffic enforcement has fostered a number of myths. It is not true, for instance, that inclement weather disables radar guns, although their sensitivity may be diminished somewhat by extremely heavy rain, snow, or dust storms. Radar and lidar do not "prefer" one type or color of vehicle—e.g., red sports cars—over any other (although, as a psychological matter, it may be true that drivers of bright-colored sports cars are more likely to speed and/or draw attention to themselves). Likewise, with the exception of black paint (discussed above), no particular color of vehicle makes detection by lidar less likely—and color has no effect whatsoever on radar. By the same token, radar and lidar guns are not infallible. Their readings may be challenged and occasionally proved inaccurate. Various publications detail means of fighting radar/lidar citations in court, and further discussion of the subject may be found at www.CopRadar.com.

radio codes

While codes used for communication via police radios vary somewhat from one jurisdiction to the next, the following codes (except where identified for a specific state) have widely entered general usage.

AC   aircraft crash

ADW   assault with a deadly weapon

AID   Accident Investigation Detail

BO   out of order

BT/Bravo Tango   bomb threat

CP   complaining party

CPD   city/county property damaged

CRT   information

CVC   California Vehicle Code

DB   dead body

Deuce   drunk driving

DMV   vehicle registration

DOA   dead on arrival

ETA   estimated time of arrival

GOA   gone on arrival

GTA   grand theft, auto

HBD   has been drinking

J   juvenile

NCIC   National Crime Information Center

PAB   Police Administration Building

PC   penal code/person complaining

PR   person reporting

QT   location secret

UTL   unable to locate

VIN   Vehicle Identification Number

W   female

Code A   no rain expected

Code B   rain expected

Code 1   answer on radio

Code 2   proceed immediately without siren

Code 3   proceed with siren and flashing lights

Code 4   no further assistance needed

Code 4A   no further assistance needed, but suspect is not in custody

Code 5   uniformed officers stay away

Code 6   out of car to investigate

Code 6A   out of car to investigate, assistance may be needed

Code 6C   suspect is wanted and may be dangerous

Code 7   out for a meal

Code 8   fire alarm

Code 9   jail break

Code 10   request clear frequency

Code 12   false alarm

Code 13   major disaster activation

Code 14   resume normal operations

Code 20   notify news media to respond

Code 30   burglar alarm ringing

Code 33   Emergency! All units stand by

Code 99   Emergency!

Code 100   in position to intercept

187   homicide

207   kidnapping

207A   kidnapping attempt

211   armed robbery

217   assault with intent to murder

220/261A   attempted rape

240   assault

242   battery

245   assault with a deadly weapon

261   rape

288   lewd conduct

311/314   indecent exposure

390   drunk

390D   drunk unconscious

415   disturbance

415C   disturbance, children involved

415E   disturbance, loud music or party

415F   disturbance, family

415G   disturbance, gang

417   person with a gun

459   burglary

459A   burglar alarm ringing

470   forgery

480   hit-and-run (felony)

481   hit-and-run (misdemeanor)

484/488   petty theft

484PS   purse snatch

487   grand theft

502   drunk driving

503   auto theft

504   tampering with a vehicle

505   reckless driving

507   public nuisance

586   illegal parking

586E   vehicle blocking driveway

594   malicious mischief

595   runaway car

647   lewd conduct

901   ambulance call/accident, injuries unknown

901A   ambulance call/attempted suicide

901H   ambulance call/dead body

901K   ambulance has been dispatched

901L   ambulance call/narcotics overdose

901N   ambulance requested

901S   ambulance call/shooting

901T   ambulance call/traffic accident

901Y   request ambulance if needed

902   accident

902H   en route to hospital

902M   medical aid requested

902T   traffic accident, noninjury

903   aircraft crash

903L   low-flying aircraft

904A   fire alarm

904B   brush fire/boat fire

904C   car fire

904F   forest fire

904G	grass fire		920F	found child
904I	illegal burning		920J	missing juvenile
904S	structure fire		921	prowler
905B	animal bite		921P	Peeping Tom
905N	noisy animal		922	illegal peddling
905S	stray animal		924	station detail
905B	vicious animal		925	suspicious person
906K	rescue dispatched		926	request tow truck
906N	rescue requested		926A	tow truck dispatched
907	minor disturbance		927	investigate unknown trouble
907A	loud radio or TV		927A	person pulled from telephone
907B	ball game in street		927D	investigate possible dead body
907K	paramedics dispatched		928	found property
907N	paramedics requested		929	investigate person down
907Y	Are paramedics needed?		930	see man regarding a complaint
908	begging		931	see woman regarding a complaint
909	traffic congestion		932	woman or child abuse/open door
909B	road blockade		933	open window
909F	flares needed		949	gasoline spill
909T	traffic hazard		950	burning permit
910	Can you handle?		951	request fire investigator
911	advise party		952	report conciliations
911B	contact informant/contact officer		953	check smoke report
912	Are we clear?		954	arrived at scene
913	You are clear.		955/57	fire under control
914	request detectives		956	available for assignment
914A	attempted suicide		960X	car stop/dangerous suspects
914C	request coroner		961	take a report/car stop
914D	request doctor		962	subject is armed and dangerous
914F	request fire department		966	sniper
914H	heart attack		967	outlaw motorcyclists
914N	concerned party notified		975	Can your suspect hear your radio?
914S	suicide		981	frequency is clear
915	dumping rubbish		982	Are we being received?
916	holding suspect		983/996	explosion
917A	abandoned vehicle		995	labor trouble
917P	hold vehicle for fingerprints		996A	unexploded bomb
918A	escaped mental patient		998	officer involved in shooting
918V	violent mental patient		999	officer needs help, urgent
919	keep the peace		10-1	you are being received poorly/change location
920	missing adult		10-2	you are being received clearly
920A	found adult		10-3	stop transmitting/change channels
920C	missing child		10-4	OK/message acknowledged

10-5	relay	10-47	emergency road repairs needed
10-6	station is busy, standby unless urgent	10-48	traffic sign needs repair
10-7	out of service, radio off	10-49	traffic light out
10-8	in service	10-50	accident
10-9	repeat last message	10-51	wrecker needed
10-10	out of service, radio on	10-52	ambulance needed
10-10	fight in progress	10-53	road blocked
10-11	transmitting too fast	10-54	livestock on highway
10-12	stand by	10-55	intoxicated driver
10-13	advise of weather and road conditions	10-56	intoxicated pedestrian
10-14	report of prowler	10-57	hit-and-run
10-15	en route to jail with prisoner	10-59	direct traffic
10-16	pick up prisoner	10-60	squad car in vicinity
10-17	pick up papers	10-61	personnel in area
10-18	complete assignment quickly	10-62	reply to message
10-19	go to your station	10-63	prepare to make written copy
10-20	What is your location?	10-64	message for personal delivery
10-21	telephone your station	10-65	net message assignment
10-22	disregard/cancel last message	10-66	message cancellation
10-23	stand by	10-67	clear to read net message
10-24	assignment completed	10-68	dispatch information
10-25	report in person	10-69	message received
10-26	detaining subject	10-70	fire alarm
10-27	check computer for warrants	10-71	advise nature of fire
10-28	vehicle registration information	10-72	report on progress of fire
10-29	check and advise if vehicle or subject is wanted	10-73	smoke report
10-30	subject has no record, no wants	10-74	negative
10-31	crime in progress	10-76	en route
10-32	subject is wanted*	10-76J1	en route with prisoner
10-32	man with gun*	10-76J2	en route with female prisoner
10-33	emergency traffic in the air	10-77	estimated time of arrival
10-34	riot	10-78	need assistance
10-35	backup needed	10-79	notify coroner
10-36	correct time	10-80	vacation check
10-37	investigate suspicious auto	10-82	reserve lodging
10-38	stopping suspicious auto	10-83	door check
10-39	message delivered	10-84	will be late
10-39	urgent—use lights and siren	10-85	traffic check
10-40	silent run—no lights or siren	10-86	report to station
10-41	ending tour of duty	10-87	meet an officer
10-44	request permission to leave patrol car	10-87	pick up checks for distribution
10-45	animal carcass	10-88	advise of present phone number
10-46	assist motorist	10-89	car to car

10-90	bank alarm
10-91	unnecessary use of radio
10-92	frequency check
10-93	blockade
10-94	drag racing
10-95	test radio
10-96	mental subject
10-97	arriving at assigned detail
10-98	assigned detail complete
10-98	prison/jail break
10-99	Emergency!
10-99	records indicate wanted or stolen
11-6	illegal discharge of firearms
11-7	prowler
11-8	person down
11-10	take a report
11-12	dead animal
11-12	injured animal
11-14	animal bite
11-15	ball game in street
11-17	wires down
11-24	abandoned vehicle
11-25	female motorist needs assistance
11-27	subject has record but no wants
11-28	rush vehicle information
11-30	incomplete phone call
11-31	person calling for help
11-40	advise if ambulance needed
11-41	request ambulance
11-42	ambulance not required
11-43	doctor required
11-44	possible fatality
11-45	attempted suicide
11-46	death report
11-47	injured person
11-48	provide transportation
11-50	field interrogation
11-51	security check
11-70	fire alarm
11-71	fire report
11-78	paramedics dispatched
11-79	traffic accident, ambulance dispatched
11-80	traffic accident, serious injury

11-81	traffic accident, minor injury
11-82	traffic accident, property damaged
11-83	traffic accident, no details
11-84	direct traffic
11-85	send tow truck
11-86	special detail/bomb threat
11-87	assist other unit/bomb found
11-88	assist motorist
11-98	meet an officer
11-99	officer needs help
5150	mental case
10851	grand theft, auto
10852	tampering with vehicle
20001	hit-and-run, felony
20002	hit-and-run, misdemeanor
20007	hit-and-run, unattended vehicle
21958	drunk pedestrian on roadway
22350	speeding
22500	illegal parking
23101	drunk driving, injury involved
23102	drunk driver
23105	driver under influence of narcotics
23109	cars racing
23110	persons throwing objects at vehicles

*Differs among departments

Raleigh Police Department

Planned and constructed in 1792 as the capital of North Carolina, Raleigh grew slowly at first, with the business of government its primary focus. Physically unscathed by the Civil War, it gradually evolved into the retail center of eastern North Carolina, with a solid tourist trade on the side. Police work in Raleigh, as in other southern cities during the late 19th and early 20th centuries, involved a combination of traditional crime-fighting and enforcement of the Jim Crow segregation codes that publicly divided black from white.

The advent of national PROHIBITION, in 1920, tempted Raleigh police and civilians alike into new paths of CORRUPTION spawned by bootlegging and the parallel rise of ORGANIZED CRIME. Local leaders of a newly revived KU KLUX KLAN sought to "clean up" the town by aggressively recruiting members from the Raleigh P.D. One who joined the fold was Detective Joe Wiggins, exposed as a Klansman during his September 1924 court appearance in a criminal case. That same year, Klan leaders demanded the resignation of Chief

A. E. Glenn, and allegedly handpicked his replacement, one J. Winder Bryan. The taint of Ku Kluxism lingered through the 1960s, when congressional investigators found more Klansmen in North Carolina than in any other state, but Raleigh avoided most of the violence that scarred other fronts in the long struggle for black equality.

The modern Raleigh P.D. won accreditation from CALEA (the Commission on Accreditation for Law Enforcement Agencies) in 1992, and again in 1997. Publicly committed to a policy of "serving and protecting better than ever before," the department promotes itself as characterized by "transformation, innovation and results." Its stated values include "preservation of life and safety, compassion, fairness, integrity, commitment, accountability, high-caliber service, [and] innovative leadership."

Randolph, Edmund Jennings (1753–1813)

A native of Williamsburg, Virginia, born August 10, 1753, Edmund Randolph attended the College of William and Mary and studied law in his father's office, prior to the outbreak of the American Revolution. During and after that conflict he served as aide-de-camp for General George Washington (1775), as a delegate to the Virginia state constitutional convention (1776), as attorney general of Virginia (1776–82), and as a member of the Continental Congress (1779–82). While serving as governor of Virginia (1786–88), Randolph also attended the U.S. Constitutional Convention (1787). He spent one term as a state legislator (1788) before President Washington named him the first U.S. attorney general in September 1789. Randolph held that post until January 1794, when he became secretary of state. He resigned on August 19, 1795, pursuant to charges of misconduct filed by the French government (later dismissed as false). He subsequently served as Aaron Burr's defense counsel, when Burr was charged with treason. Randolph died in Virginia on September 12, 1813. Randolph County, Illinois, is named in his honor.

range detectives

Range detectives were those individuals employed by ranchers in the 19th and early 20th centuries to hunt and eliminate rustlers of livestock. They enjoyed no special status as peace officers, but their connection to wealthy land barons and corporations often conferred upon them an immunity which bona fide police might envy. Many of the so-called detectives were no more than hired killers, paid by the head for each alleged rustler they eliminated. Some operated alone, like the famous (or infamous) TOM HORN, while others joined

paramilitary bands to purge a district of "undesirables," as in Wyoming's Johnson County War of the 1890s. On occasion, range detectives were employed by legitimate agencies such as Pinkerton's or WELLS FARGO, and some also spent time as sworn peace officers, but the majority were simply "regulators," hired for their ability with guns and willingness to kill on order, without regard to statutory law.

See also: PINKERTON, ALLAN J.

Reddin, Thomas (1916–2004)

Tom Reddin was born on June 25, 1916, and joined the LOS ANGELES POLICE DEPARTMENT at age 25, on the eve of World War II. While future LAPD chief WILLIAM HENRY PARKER was in military service, storming the beaches of Italy and France, Reddin worked to advance himself within the department. In February 1967 he was named to replace Parker as chief of police, and Reddin faced his first media crisis four months later, following a POLICE RIOT in Century City. Some 15,000 antiwar protesters gathered outside the Century Plaza Hotel, where President Lyndon Johnson was scheduled to address supporters at a lavish banquet, and police attacked the demonstrators without any semblance of restraint, clubbing most and ramming some with motorcycles. Reddin subsequently defended those actions as necessary and proper.

Reddin also encouraged LAPD's illegal DOMESTIC SURVEILLANCE operations against political dissidents and racial minorities—this even though he had reviewed his own intelligence file within days of becoming chief, later remarking that "The notions [it contained] were almost laughable, and most of them were wrong." At the same time, Reddin expanded DARYL GATES's Metropolitan Division—the "shake, rattle and roll boys"— from 50 to 220 officers, operating on standing orders to "roust anything strange that moves on the streets." In August 1968, LAPD faced new accusations of brutality and murder, after officers attacked a crowd of African Americans gathered for the annual Watts Festival, killing three and wounding 35 more.

Reddin announced his resignation from LAPD in April 1969, effective May 2, and left to become a television commentator for local station KTLA. His new $500,000 three-year contract represented a sixfold increase over Reddin's salary as chief of police. Reddin died on December 4, 2004, at age 88.

Red squads

As suggested by the name, police "Red squads" historically have been created to investigate, arrest, and/or harass various left-wing radicals collectively dubbed "Reds." In the 19th century, such units concerned themselves primarily with anarchists and labor unions, sometimes diverted from legitimate law-enforcement functions to perform as strikebreakers for wealthy commercial interests. Following the Russian Revolution of 1917, local police and federal agencies often focused more narrowly on the Communist Party and affiliated organizations, but wherever they operated, Red squads also found time to spy on various racial and ethnic minority groups.

Throughout U.S. history, Red squads have been responsible for some of the worst police excesses and legal transgressions on record. The FBI's original Red squad—dubbed the General Intelligence Division (GID)—helped Attorney General A. MITCHELL PALMER conduct sweeping "Red raids" in 1919–20, arresting thousands of innocent persons for every legitimate "enemy alien" captured and deported. Although repeatedly ordered to destroy the GID's files, Director J. EDGAR HOOVER continued illegal DOMESTIC SURVEILLANCE and harassment until his death in 1972, most notoriously in the FBI's wide-ranging COINTELPRO campaigns. Police departments across the nation collaborated with the FBI or followed the Bureau's example independently, spying on countless individuals and groups whose only crime was peaceful dissent against the status quo. In the process, Red squad officers frequently broke the law themselves, with unauthorized BUGGING and WIRETAPS, ENTRAPMENT, and FRAME-UPS, as well as POLICE RIOTS targeting various alleged "subversives."

Criminal activity and RACISM aside, the Red squads were frequently misled by their reliance on information obtained from extremist groups (e.g., the AMERICAN PROTECTIVE LEAGUE and KU KLUX KLAN) or from dishonest INFORMANTS. The latter, often compensated in direct proportion to the sensational quality of their reports, frequently served as AGENTS PROVOCATEURS, encouraging members of otherwise peaceable groups to commit violent acts, sometimes providing the weapons or explosives used from police sources.

During the final decades of the 20th century, media exposure and civil litigation filed by the AMERICAN CIVIL LIBERTIES UNION prompted Congress and state legislators to ban most typical Red squad activities across the board. Unfortunately, the terrorist attacks of September 2001 and subsequent passage of the USA PATRIOT ACT created an atmosphere in which many tactics from the "bad old days" are both encouraged and legitimized by statute.

See also: ANARCHISM; STRIKEBREAKING; TERRORISM.

Rehm, Jacob (1828–1915)

The life of Jacob Rehm, three-time chief of the CHICAGO POLICE DEPARTMENT, illustrates the adage that Chicago was "a city built on beer." A son of German immigrants, born in 1828, Rehm ran a brewery for many years, while active in the Republican Party, allied with German-American politicians and newspaper publishers. His first term as chief of police was brief (1858–59), but Rehm returned in 1861 as deputy superintendent with full power over appointments. That post let him handpick Chicago's "finest" from the office of his brewery, ensuring that CORRUPTION was perpetuated citywide.

During his second and third terms as Chicago's top cop (1866–70, 1874–75), Rehm was simultaneously active as a principal in the nationwide "Whiskey Ring" that defrauded the U.S. government of millions in tax revenue by falsifying whiskey production records. Agents of the TREASURY DEPARTMENT traced the fraud to Rehm and his cronies, conducting a series of high-profile arrests in May 1875. Rehm found it necessary to resign, then turned state's evidence against his cronies in Chicago, New Orleans, and St. Louis, bargaining for a maximum six-month sentence and a wrist-slap $20,000 fine. His handpicked successor as chief of police was Capt. Michael Hickey, described by CPD historian Richard Lindberg as a "venal and dangerous" officer. Cited in 1868 for running an illicit bail-bond racket from his post at the Armory Station, Hickey avoided punishment and survived to run the force as Rehm's eyes and ears during 1874–78.

Nor did retirement and a guilty plea to fraud remove Rehm from the roll of police puppet master in Chicago. As a civilian of great influence, he lobbied successfully to dismantle Chicago's police commission, replacing that body with a city marshal empowered to appoint men of "suitable" character as "special police." Behind the scenes, Rehm held the power to approve all transfers of police captains, lieutenants, and sergeants until 1895, when Civil Service finally began the long, slow task of reforming the CPD. Rehm lived on until 1915, serving at various times as Cook County's treasurer and Lincoln Park board commissioner. In 1931 Chicago's city council named a park—Rehm Arbor—in his honor.

Reiss, Albert John, Jr. (b. 1922)

Wisconsin native Albert Reiss was born in 1922 and received his B.A. from the University of Milwaukee in 1944, proceeding from there to the University of Chicago, where he earned his Ph.D. in sociology (1949). While briefly employed as a teacher at Tennessee's Vanderbilt University, Reiss devoted himself more specifically to the study of criminology. Teaching appointments at universities in various states ultimately brought him to Yale, where he settled and remained for the rest of his professional career.

Reiss's numerous publications include *Beyond the Law* (with Michael Tonry); *Crime and Communities; Data Sources on White-Collar Law-Breaking* (with Albert Biderman); *Indicators of Crime and Criminal Justice; Studies in Crime and Law Enforcement in Major Metropolitan Areas;* and *Understanding and Preventing Violence.* His groundbreaking volume *The Police and the Public* (1973) stands as the first scientific survey of EXCESSIVE FORCE by urban police, researched during a series of 1971 ride-along excursions Reiss conducted in Boston, Chicago, and Washington, D.C. Reiss observed that abusive treatment was suffered by 22.6 per 1,000 Caucasian individuals confronted by police, and by 41.9 percent per 1,000 blacks.

Reno, Janet (b. 1938)

A Miami native, born on July 21, 1938, Janet Reno graduated from Cornell University in 1960, with B.A. in chemistry, and earned her LL.B. from Harvard Law School three years later. In 1971 she was named staff director of the Judiciary Committee of the Florida House of Representatives. Two years later, Reno joined the Dade County state's attorney's office, then left public service in 1976 to join a private law firm. In November 1978 Governor Reubin Askew named Reno to fill a vacancy as state's attorney for Dade County. She was reelected to that office five times, working to reform the juvenile justice system and establish the Miami Drug Court. President Bill Clinton chose Reno as the nation's first female attorney general, and she assumed control of the JUSTICE DEPARTMENT on March 12, 1993.

Reno arrived in Washington at an inauspicious moment, with FBI director WILLIAM SESSIONS accused of professional misconduct and the BRANCH DAVIDIAN SIEGE already under way at Waco, Texas. In April 1993 she approved the Bureau's plan to rout the barricaded cultists with tear gas, an effort that ended tragically with close to 80 persons dead. (In 1996 a House report branded Reno's approval of the FBI attack plan "premature, wrong, and highly irresponsible.") Reno seemed to enjoy a good relationship with new FBI director LOUIS FREEH until the Bureau and Congress began investigating charges of Clinton financial corruption during the 1994 midterm elections. Thereafter, Reno and Freeh were often at odds, with some of their clashes played out in the media. Reno was widely criticized for protecting her boss in the White House, and while some of those charges are well documented, her defensive behavior never matched the obstructionism practiced by attorneys general under Presidents Richard Nixon, Ronald Reagan, and George H. W. Bush.

Reno left office with the inauguration of President George W. Bush in January 2001 and returned to her home in Miami. She lost Florida's Democratic gubernatorial primary in September 2002. The onset of Parkinson's disease rendered her political future uncertain, but it failed to detract from her 2003 induction into the Florida Women's Hall of Fame.

Rhode Island State Police

In April 1925 Rhode Island state legislators authorized a state police force patterned on the Pennsylvania State Police, consisting of a superintendent (answering directly to the governor), one captain, one lieutenant, and 21 officers. Its founding statute permitted the force to suppress rural RIOTS, but barred riot duty inside established cities without express orders from the governor or a request from city authorities. Local police were required by law to accept state police prisoners, and were subject to fines for refusing. Governor Aram Pothier named Everitte Chaffee as first superintendent of the RISP, with a five-year term established by statute.

A former colonel in the U.S. Army, Chaffee organized the RISP along military lines and preferred army veterans as his first recruits, in the interest of discipline. Six hundred men applied for positions on the force, that number whittled down to 23 by a screening board composed of five ex-army officers. Training began in May 1925, and the RISP lost its first trooper one month later, when one of the new recruits crashed his motorcycle. By July Chaffee's men had launched coordinated raids against statewide gambling rings, but an advance tip to the gamblers left the raiders empty-handed. Chaffee rebounded with tighter security and a "Trojan horse" tactic, hiding officers inside a produce wagon to surprise unsuspecting targets. Enforcement of the PROHIBITION ban on liquor proved more problematic, though RISP officers successfully stormed Block Island, closing several speakeasies in summer 1925. Chaffee's vigilance and the department's small size minimized CORRUPTION in the bootleg era, but on balance, Rhode Island was as "wet" as any other U.S. state.

From those humble beginnings, the RISP has grown into a force recognized for both its professionalism and its sense of style. Although its uniforms remain unchanged from 1925, in 2002 the RISP was voted America's "best-dressed" state police agency. Its mission statement calls upon all officers "to fulfill the law enforcement needs of the people with the highest degree of fairness, professionalism and integrity, and protect the inherent rights of the people to live in freedom and safety."

Richardson, Elliot Lee (1920–1999)

Born in Boston on July 20, 1920, Elliot Richardson graduated cum laude from Harvard in 1941, then served in the U.S. Army during World War II. Upon return to civilian life, he graduated cum laude from Harvard Law School (1947), then served as law clerk for U.S. SUPREME COURT justice Felix Frankfurter. Richardson's private practice in Boston was interrupted by service as an aide to the Senate Armed Services Committee (1953–54), assistant secretary of health, education, and welfare for legislation (1957–59), and acting secretary of health, education and welfare (April–July 1958). Richardson subsequently served as U.S. attorney for Massachusetts (1959–61) and special assistant to the U.S. attorney general (1961). He was elected lieutenant governor of Massachusetts in 1964, followed by a term as state attorney general (1966–69). President Richard Nixon named him under secretary of state in January 1969, followed by promotion to secretary of health, education, and welfare in June 1970. Richardson served Nixon as secretary of defense between January and May 1973, then assumed command of the JUSTICE DEPARTMENT as attorney general on May 25, 1973.

Richardson's tenure at Justice was brief. Predecessor RICHARD KLEINDIENST had been snared in the Watergate scandal, but Richardson refused to follow that example. On the day of his appointment as attorney general, he named Archibald Cox as special prosecutor to investigate Nixon's web of conspiracy. That move caused immediate tension between Richardson and the White House, but he sought to proceed despite obstruction from Nixon and chief of staff Alexander Haig. Under pressure to fire Cox, Richardson himself resigned on October 23, 1973. He later served President Gerald Ford as ambassador to Great Britain (1975–76) and secretary of commerce (1976–77). In 1984 Richardson lost his bid for a U.S. Senate seat from Massachusetts. He received a Presidential Medal of Freedom in 1999 and died in Boston of a stroke on the last day of that year.

Richmond Police Department

As the capital of the Confederacy, Richmond, Virginia, was saddled with a reputation for intransigent RACISM long after the Civil War. That specter reared its head again in 1920, when the revived KU KLUX KLAN recruited 2,000 members in Richmond and some 20,000 statewide. Richmond's leaders were impressed with the Klan's hateful message, Police Chief Charles Sherry proclaiming that he had never heard more patriotic speeches than those delivered by KKK Imperial Wizard William Simmons. At least 25 of Sherry's officers joined the Klan, along with 20-odd firemen, several Common Council members, the Commissioner of Revenue, and one-third of Richmond's aldermen.

Klanism and police resistance to desegregation remained a persistent problem through the 1960s, but the Richmond P.D. has evolved into a modern force with 650 sworn officers and 130 civilian employees. Its mission statement—"We Engage the Community, We Solve Problems"—was validated at the turn of the 21st century, when Richmond's Community Assisted Public Safety initiative won national honors as the top community policing program among U.S. cities of 100,000 to 250,000 residents.

Ridge, Thomas Joseph (b. 1945)

A native of Munhall, Pennsylvania, born on August 26, 1945, Tom Ridge graduated with honors from Harvard University in 1967. Drafted by the U.S. Army during his first year at Dickinson School of Law, Ridge served in Vietnam and won a Bronze Star for valor in combat. Returning to civilian life, he completed law school and entered private practice, then opted for a career in Republican politics, serving first as assistant district attorney in Erie County. Ridge was elected to Congress in 1983 and served until 1995, subsequently winning election for two terms as Pennsylvania's governor (1995–2001). Ridge's second term was interrupted in October 2001, when President George W. Bush chose him to lead the new HOMELAND SECURITY DEPARTMENT.

Ridge projected confidence in that office, despite a long series of headline setbacks in various federal security programs adopted after the terrorist attacks of September 11, 2001. His three-year tenure was marked by a nonstop series of "terror alerts," none of which resulted either in attacks or apprehension of alleged foreign terrorists. Ridge announced his resignation from the post on December 1, 2004, effective February 1, 2005, and listed "personal reasons, namely to devote more time to his family," as his reason for leaving Homeland Security. Seventeen months later, on May 10, 2005, Ridge admitted that he had "often disagreed" with Bush regime officials on the timing of color-coded "threat assessments" broadcast nationwide. Specifically, Ridge told reporters that he wished to "debunk the myth" that his former agency had been responsible for the seesaw public warnings issued during 2002–04. "More often than not," Ridge said, "we were the least inclined to raise it. Sometimes we disagreed with the intelligence assessment. Sometimes we thought even if the intelligence was good, you don't necessarily put the country on [alert]. . . . There were times when some people were really aggressive about raising it, and we said, 'For that?'" In response to Ridge's public statement, Homeland Security spokesman Brian Roehrkasse told USA Today that "improvements and adjustments" in the warning system would be announced "within the next few months." None had been aired at press time for this book.

See also: TERRORISM.

Rios, Ariel (1954–1982)

New Haven, Connecticut, native Ariel Rios was born in 1954. He graduated from Manhattan's John Jay College of Criminal Justice at age 22 and spent the next two years working for local law enforcement agencies, before he joined the Bureau of Alcohol, Tobacco and Firearms in December 1978. His Hispanic background made Rios ideal for UNDERCOVER WORK, and he was transferred to Florida in early 1982, when President Ronald Reagan declared a federal "war on drugs." Although BATF is not normally concerned with narcotics cases, the Reagan administration's initial effort—later described by one COAST GUARD officer as "an intellectual fraud"—demanded assistance from any available agents.

On December 2, 1982, Rios and his partner, Agent Alexander D'Atri, arranged to meet a group of cocaine dealers at a Miami hotel. The meeting initially went smoothly, then one of the suspects spied other agents closing in and drew a pistol, shooting Agent Rios in the face. When the smoke cleared, Rios was dead, D'Atri was badly wounded, and the drug dealers were either dead or in handcuffs. A federal building at 1200 Pennsylvania Avenue, in Washington, D.C., was named in honor of Rios. Its tenants at press time for this work included the ENVIRONMENTAL PROTECTION AGENCY.

riots and riot control

United States is a riotous country. Some incidents of mob violence, including the Boston Massacre and Boston Tea Party, are enshrined as seminal events in our early history, while others are roundly condemned as examples of bigotry or political extremism run amok. Over the past 250 years, police have responded to riots with widely divergent tactics and levels of competence, succeeding in some cases and failing absolutely in others. There have even been occasions when police themselves joined in riots, usually to attack nonwhite minorities, and various examples of undisciplined behavior have been classified by scholars as POLICE RIOTS.

Tactics of riot control have ranged historically from free-swinging baton charges and point-blank gunfire to employment of various tools including tear gas, high-pressure hoses, attack dogs, rubber bullets, and armored vehicles. Nets have been used to capture rioters, while indelible dyes are sometimes used to mark a mob's ringleaders for later arrest. Generally, modern police avoid use of DEADLY FORCE unless their lives are threatened, but wholesale shooting into relatively peaceful crowds has also been witnessed in recent times—including the ORANGEBURG MASSACRE (1968), the KENT STATE UNIVERSITY SHOOTINGS (1970), and the JACKSON STATE COLLEGE SHOOTINGS (1970). In times past, such violent and sometimes deadly methods were also employed for STRIKEBREAKING, as in the MEMORIAL DAY MASSACRE of 1937.

Even in situations where the use of deadly force on rioters is authorized, questions may still arise concerning its advisability. Those questions multiply in situations where predominantly white police confront nonwhite rioters, as during the "long, hot summers" of 1965–67. During those years, three specific riots claimed 104 lives in Los Angeles (35), Detroit (43), and Newark, New Jersey (26). In each case, when the smoke cleared, the vast majority of riot dead proved to be unarmed blacks gunned down by police or members of the NATIONAL GUARD, either for theft, curfew violations, or on vague "suspicion" of some illegal activity. All but four of the dead in L.A. were shot by authorities (including one slain policeman), while authorities killed 31 in Detroit (including one fireman) and 21 in Newark. Ironically, the death toll in those riots was later cited by various racists and right-wing politicians to suggest a black conspiracy against police.

"River Cops"

Southern Florida suffered a drastic increase in violent crime during the 1980s, as an unprecedented influx of illegal DRUGS—especially cocaine—flooded the U.S. market from South America. Miami was among the hardest-hit cities, producing the nation's highest urban murder rate in 1985. At the same time, emergency police recruiting and corresponding relaxation of standards filled the MIAMI POLICE DEPARTMENT's ranks with individuals who apparently joined the force specifically to commit crimes with impunity. During the latter 1980s, more than 100 Miami officers were arrested, suspended, or otherwise punished for various disciplinary infractions.

The worst among those "bad apples" were a 19-man team of officers known as the "River Cops," who robbed narcotics dealers and ransomed or resold their drugs. The group earned its media nickname from a particular incident on July 29, 1985, when officers raided a drug boat, the *Mary C*, moored at a berth on the Miami River. Six men were offloading $12 million worth of cocaine when the raiders struck at 2:00 A.M., shouting, "Kill them! Kill them!" Fearing rival mobsters, the smugglers leaped overboard, where three of them drowned.

Homicide investigators naturally suspected drug dealers of carrying out the attack, but a marina night watchman informed them that the culprits were policemen. Fifteen "River Cops" were finally arrested and convicted at trial on various charges, drawing prison terms up to 35 years. A wider FBI investigation of the case resulted in disciplinary charges against 80 more officers, several of whom were dismissed from the force. Investigators subsequently estimated that the "River Cops" earned between $100,000 and $2 million each from their illicit raids. The team's ringleader, Officer Armando Garcia, escaped from the United States and remains at large today (although, contrary to some published reports, he is not listed as one of the FBI's "TEN MOST WANTED" FUGITIVES).

Rizzo, Frank Lazarro (1920–1991)

Philadelphia native Frank Rizzo was born on October 23, 1920, to a longtime police family. After high school, he served briefly in the U.S. Navy, then spent three years working in a steel mill before he joined the PHILADELPHIA POLICE DEPARTMENT in 1943. He quickly earned a reputation as the "Cisco Kid," for his love of action and his fearless conduct during raids on brothels, gambling dens, and strip clubs citywide. Strangely, that gang-busting reputation failed to produce any significant moves against local ORGANIZED CRIME when Rizzo was named police commissioner in 1967. Indeed, the Philadelphia underworld prospered under his four-year regime, while "radicals" and racial minorities suffered illegal DOMESTIC SURVEILLANCE and frequent EXCESSIVE FORCE at the hands of police. Known and revered in the mostly white ranks as "a cop's cop," Rizzo once left a black-tie dinner in 1969, thrusting a nightstick underneath his cummerbund, to lead "my men, my army" in suppressing a ghetto RIOT.

Rizzo's flamboyance and far-right political views served him well when he ran for mayor as a "law and order" Democrat in 1971. Vowing to "make Attila the Hun look like a faggot" if elected, Rizzo swept the field that November and continued his heavy-handed approach to "justice" throughout two terms as mayor. In the process he stood accused by the U.S. JUSTICE DEPARTMENT of condoning "widespread and severe" police brutality and organizing a secret police squad to spy on his political opponents. In August 1979 he was among 19 Philadelphia officials slapped with federal charges of civil rights violations. A federal judge dismissed the charges two months later, opining that Washington had no authority to prosecute the case.

It remained for Philadelphia's city charter to depose Rizzo, with a provision barring any mayor from serving a third consecutive term. (Rizzo had tried and failed to have the provision repealed.) When he ran for mayor again, in 1983, Rizzo lost the Democratic primary to Wilson Goode, an African American, who won the subsequent general election. Switching parties to the GOP, Rizzo ran for mayor again in 1987 and was once again defeated. A heart attack claimed his life on July 16, 1991, in the midst of his fifth mayoral campaign.

Rodney, Caesar Augustus (1772–1824)

Caesar Rodney was born at Dover, Delaware, on January 4, 1772. He graduated from the University of Pennsylvania in 1789, then studied law in Philadelphia and was admitted to the bar in 1793. After three years in private practice, he won election to the Delaware state legislature, serving there from 1796 to 1802. Rodney next served in Congress (1803–05), but declined to seek a second term. President Thomas Jefferson named him attorney general in January 1807, and Rodney retained that post under President James Madison until December 5, 1811. During the War of 1812 Rodney commanded a volunteer company in defense of Baltimore. He subsequently served on Delaware's Committee of Safety (1813), in the Delaware state senate (1815–16), once again in Congress (1821–22), and in the U.S. Senate (1822–23). In 1823 he was named minister plenipotentiary to Argentina, where he died (in Buenos Aires) on June 10, 1824.

Rogers, William Pierce (1913–2001)

A native of Norfolk, New York, born on June 23, 1913, William Rogers graduated from Colgate University in 1934 and received his LL.B. from Cornell Law School three years later. He practiced law in New York City during 1937–38, then served as assistant district attorney for New York County (1938–42). During World War II, Rogers joined the U.S. Navy as a lieutenant commander, then returned to the New York County D.A.'s office in 1946–47. He subsequently served as chief counsel for the Senate War Investigating Committee (1947–48) and the Senate Permanent Subcommittee on Investigations (1950–52), then returned to private practice.

Under President Dwight Eisenhower, Rogers initially served as a deputy to Attorney General HERBERT BROWNELL, JR. and in that capacity issued a 1955 order curtailing illegal leakage of FBI files to the Red-hunting Senate Internal Security Subcommittee (SISS). Rogers required that G-men limit their assistance to "public source" material, but Director J. EDGAR HOOVER was not so easily foiled. Days later, Hoover inaugurated an "informal" liaison with the SISS, whereby trusted aides were privately briefed in defiance of Rogers and without his knowledge.

Rogers replaced Brownell as attorney general on November 8, 1957, and held that post until President John Kennedy was inaugurated in January 1961. Like Brownell before him, Rogers granted Hoover virtual autonomy to choose his targets and pursue them by any means he deemed fitting. In fairness to Rogers, he apparently knew little or nothing of the FBI's illegal WIRETAPS and "BLACK BAG JOBS" during his tenure, since Hoover decided on his own that Brownell's May 1954 approval of wiretaps in national security cases actually covered "both Security and Criminal matters." With that problem thus resolved, Hoover reported that he enjoyed a "very close" relationship with Rogers, often dining with his nominal superior and joining Rogers for Christmas vacations in Florida.

Years later, journalists revealed that Hoover sabotaged Rogers's nomination to the U.S. SUPREME COURT in 1969, persuading President Richard Nixon to choose Warren Burger instead. Rogers served Nixon as secretary of state from January 1969 to September 1973, when heat from the worsening Watergate scandal prompted him to resign, taking with him a Presidential Medal of Freedom. Rogers died from congestive heart failure on January 2, 2001, in Bethesda, Maryland.

Roosevelt, Theodore (1858–1919)

Born in New York City on October 27, 1858, Theodore Roosevelt graduated from Harvard University in 1880, then studied law before winning election to the state legislature in 1882. A year later, he unsuccessfully sought appointment as speaker of the statehouse, but settled for a post on a commission organized to investigate the NEW YORK CITY POLICE DEPARTMENT in 1884. Two years later, voters rejected Roosevelt's bid to become New York's mayor, but his family's affluence and influence assured him of further public service. In 1889 he became the first U.S. Civil Service commissioner, charged with maintaining civil service standards within NYPD, and before year's end he was named one of four New York police commissioners.

Most sources agree that Roosevelt was devoted to wiping out police CORRUPTION in New York, working tirelessly to liberate NYPD from the clutches of TAMMANY HALL. His marginal success was terminated in 1897, when state Republican leaders arranged his appointment as assistant secretary of the navy. A year later, with the outbreak of the Spanish-American War, Roosevelt joined the U.S. Army and led his "Rough Rider" battalion to somewhat exaggerated glory in Cuba. Those exploits ensured his election as New York's governor in 1899, but political enemies still schemed against him, seeking to bury Roosevelt in the vice presidency under President William McKinley. The

plan backfired in September 1901, when McKinley's ASSASSINATION at the hands of anarchist Leon Czolgosz placed Roosevelt in the Oval Office.

As president (1901–09), Roosevelt inaugurated the Progressive era, dismantling corrupt monopolies and promoting unprecedented measures to preserve national parks. He also signed the Food and Drug Act of 1906, imposing the first federal controls on narcotics. The same year saw Roosevelt win the Nobel Peace Prize for his role in negotiating an end to the Russo-Japanese War in 1905. Near the end of his second term in office, Roosevelt approved creation of an unnamed JUSTICE DEPARTMENT detective force, which subsequently grew into the FBI.

Although Roosevelt declined to run for a third term as president in 1908, he subsequently grew dissatisfied with the performance of handpicked successor William Howard Taft and organized the Progressive (or "Bull Moose") Party to make another White House bid in 1912. During that campaign, on October 12, he was

New York Police Commissioner (later President) Theodore Roosevelt (Author's collection)

shot by would-be assassin John Schrank while delivering a speech in Milwaukee, but Roosevelt completed his address before seeking medical attention. While he won more votes than Taft in November, Roosevelt lost the election to Democrat Woodrow Wilson and retired from politics, declining the Progressive Party's nomination in 1916. He died at Oyster Bay, New York, on January 6, 1919.

See also: ANARCHISM; FEDERAL BUREAU OF INVESTIGATION.

Rothmiller, Mike

Mike Rothmiller completed two years of college before joining the LOS ANGELES POLICE DEPARTMENT in 1972. After six years on the force, he was recruited to serve with the department's elite Organized Crime Intelligence Division (OCID), then led by Captain (later Chief) DARYL GATES, but the experience soon disillusioned Rothmiller. His first clue to the OCID's true nature came when the officers who recruited him asked Rothmiller, "How do you feel about niggers?"

In fact, as Rothmiller quickly discovered, the OCID had little or nothing to do with arresting members of ORGANIZED CRIME. To this day Rothmiller insists that the unit "never arrested one mobster" during his five-year tenure. Instead, OCID conducted widespread illegal surveillance on various groups and persons including politicians, journalists, and celebrities, whose private lives were explored with an eye toward extortion for LAPD's benefit. Targets later named by Rothmiller included California governor Jerry Brown, state attorney general John Van de Kamp, congressmen Mervyn Dymally and Edward Roybal, state senator Art Torres, and L.A. city councilman Richard Alatorre. In the case of Brown and Van de Kamp, Capt. Gates and his spies apparently hoped to prove both men were homosexuals, thus making them vulnerable to blackmail.

In August 1982, after Rothmiller looked too closely at OCID's apparent links to the Central Intelligence Agency and illicit foreign arms sales, an attempt was made on his life. He survived the burst of machine-gun fire from a motorcycle-riding assassin, whereupon Rothmiller's superiors urged him to keep silent about the incident and his inside knowledge of OCID. Rothmiller remained with the force for another 16 months, then retired and ultimately told all in an exposé (*L.A. Secret Police*) that found a spot on the *New York Times* best-seller list. By the time that book was published, in 1992, Daryl Gates was moving toward retirement in the wake of the RODNEY KING beating scandal, and OCID's illegal files had allegedly been purged (though some were later found intact, at a detective's home). Today Mike Rothmiller is a successful television host,

producer, and screenwriter, still residing in Southern California.

roundsmen

Some of the earliest police officers employed in colonial America were "roundsmen"—literally men who made the rounds in early settlements, usually after nightfall, to ensure that no emergencies were overlooked. Frequently unpaid and never formally trained, roundsmen often performed their tasks on a rotating basis, permitting (or requiring) all able-bodied men in a community to take their turns. Some communities required roundsmen to issue periodic calls—the classic "Twelve o'clock and all is well!"—while others simply demanded that they stay awake and walk their beats as dictated. In time, the system of unarmed nightly patrols proved inadequate for peacekeeping in growing cities, whereupon the roundsmen were replaced by full-time, more or less professional police.

Rowley, Coleen (b. 1954)

Iowa native Coleen Rowley was born in 1954 and earned her LL.B. from the University of Iowa in 1980. She then joined the FBI and was initially assigned to ORGANIZED CRIME cases in the New York City field office. By 2001 she was settled in Minneapolis, a mother of four, employed as legal counsel to the Bureau and frequently quoted as a spokesperson for the local field office. Despite that semi-public role, Rowley kept a low profile for the most part—until May 2001, when she penned an explosive 13-page letter to Director ROBERT MUELLER, with copies addressed to members of the Senate Intelligence Committee.

In sum, Rowley's letter charged that officials at FBI headquarters had erected "roadblocks" to a Minneapolis investigation of Zacarias Moussaoui, subsequently identified as a conspirator in the tragic terrorist attacks of September 11, 2001, and thereby allowed the attacks to proceed at a cost of some 3,500 American lives. Moussaoui was arrested by Minneapolis G-men in August 2001, while training at a Minnesota flight school, but headquarters refused to authorize a search warrant for his apartment, and he was subsequently released. Frustrated agents who bypassed Washington to seek information on Moussaoui from the Central Intelligence Agency were reprimanded for their efforts, and Rowley further claimed that Director Mueller had attempted to conceal those facts from Congress and the media. Among her charges, the following stand out:

It is obvious, from my firsthand knowledge of the events and the detailed documentation that exists, that the agents in Minneapolis who were closest to the action and in the best position to gauge the situation locally, did fully appreciate the terrorist risk/danger posed by Moussaoui and his possible co-conspirators even prior to September 11th. I think it's very hard for the FBI to offer the "20-20 hindsight" justification for its failure to act!

Even after the attacks had begun, the [FBI supervisor] in question was still attempting to block the search of Moussaoui's computer, characterizing the World Trade Center attacks as a mere coincidence with prior suspicions about Moussaoui.

The fact is that key FBI personnel whose job it was to assist and coordinate with field division agents on terrorism investigations and the obtaining and use of [classified search warrants] continued to almost inexplicably throw up roadblocks and undermine Minneapolis' by-now desperate efforts.

When, in a desperate 11th-hour measure to bypass the FBI [headquarters] roadblock, the Minneapolis division [notified] the CIA's Counter Terrorism Center, FBI [headquarters] personnel actually chastised the Minneapolis agents for making the direct notification without their approval!

Although I agree that it's very doubtful that the full scope of the tragedy could have been prevented, it's at least possible we could have gotten lucky and uncovered one or two more of the terrorists in flight training prior to Sept. 11, just as Moussaoui was discovered, after making contact with his flight instructors.

I know I shouldn't be flippant about this, but jokes were actually made that the key FBI personnel had to be spies or moles, like Robert Hanssen, who were actually working for Osama bin Laden to have so undercut Minneapolis' efforts.

Unable to conceal Rowley's complaints, Director Mueller admitted that the FBI would need a "different approach" to fighting TERRORISM in the future. Senator Charles Grassley was more critical, telling reporters, "The FBI for too long has discouraged agents from using anything besides outdated tactics from the era of chasing Bonnie and Clyde."

Rowley repeated her charges before the Senate in June 2002. "Mistakes are inevitable," she said, "but a distinction should be drawn between those mistakes made when trying to do the right thing and those mistakes . . . due to selfish motives." While many proclaimed her a hero, others questioned Rowley's loyalty to the FBI. Charles George, president of the SOCIETY OF FORMER SPECIAL AGENTS OF THE FBI, deemed Rowley's comments "unthinkable" and compared her actions to G-man ROBERT HANSSEN, convicted of spying for Russia. The editors of *Time* magazine disagreed, nam-

ing Rowley and two corporate whistleblowers as that journal's "Persons of the Year" for 2002.

See also: FEDERAL BUREAU OF INVESTIGATION.

Ruckelshaus, William D. (b. 1932)

An Indiana native, born on July 24, 1932, William Ruckelshaus graduated from Princeton University and Harvard Law School. In 1966 he was elected to the Indiana state legislature and became House majority leader, prompting an unsuccessful run for the U.S. Senate in 1968. President Richard Nixon named him assistant attorney general in charge of the JUSTICE DEPARTMENT's Civil Rights Division, then tapped Ruckelshaus as the new ENVIRONMENTAL PROTECTION AGENCY's (EPA) first administrator in December 1970. He held that post until April 27, 1973, when he replaced LOUIS PATRICK GRAY as acting director of the FBI.

Bureau historian Robert Kessler reports that Ruckelshaus "had little interest" in the FBI and permitted Acting Associate Director W. MARK FELT to make most of the administrative decisions until Felt retired on June 22, 1973. Ruckelshaus left the Bureau 17 days later, replaced by Director CLARENCE MARION KELLEY, and moved on to become Nixon's deputy attorney general under ELLIOT RICHARDSON. Pressured by Nixon to fire Watergate prosecutor Archibald Cox, both Ruckelshaus and Richardson resigned their Justice posts in the "Saturday Night Massacre" on October 20, 1973.

Ruckelshaus thereafter retired to private law practice in Washington, D.C., but returned to lead the EPA once more under President Ronald Reagan, from May 1983 to January 1985. Since breaking with the Reagan administration, Ruckelshaus has been an associate of Seattle's largest law firm and chief executive officer of the nation's second-largest waste handler, Houston-based Browning-Ferris Industries. He serves on the boards of various other corporations and social policy think tanks in Washington.

Rush, Richard (1780–1859)

America's youngest attorney general was born in Philadelphia on August 29, 1780, the son of a physician who signed the Declaration of Independence. He enrolled at Princeton University in 1793 and graduated four years later, at age 17. Admitted to the Pennsylvania bar three years later, Rush served as the state's attorney general in 1811. He declined President James Madison's offer to head the U.S. TREASURY DEPARTMENT in 1813, but accepted nomination as attorney general in February 1814. Rush held that post until October 1817, briefly doubling (in March 1817) as President James Monroe's secretary of state. His subsequent duties included service as the U.S. minister to England (1817–25) and secretary of the treasury under President John Quincy Adams (1825–29). Rush sought the vice presidency in 1828, with President Adams, but they lost that race to Andrew Jackson and John Calhoun. President James Polk subsequently named Rush the U.S. minister to France (1847–49). Rush died in Philadelphia on July 30, 1859.

Russell, William F.

The very model of a corrupt urban policeman, Capt. William Russell commanded the "Bloody Maxwell" precinct of the CHICAGO POLICE DEPARTMENT in 1920–21, when graft spawned by PROHIBITION swamped the department and members of the Genna bootleg mob paid his patrolmen $15 per week to ignore liquor traffic. Russell's weekly take was closer to $500, and when the scandal broke in 1921, he escaped serious punishment with the wrist-slap of a transfer by Chief CHARLES FITZMORRIS.

Seven years later, at the height of Chicago's bootleg wars and with new police CORRUPTION scandals breaking, Mayor William "Big Bill" Thompson chose Russell to lead the department. Appointed in July 1928, Russell reluctantly transferred 339 crooked cops (none were fired or prosecuted), then created a "flying squad" to chase burglars and a quick-trigger "major crime bureau" under Capt. JOHN STEGE. That unit got its first major workout on February 14, 1929, with the bloody St. Valentine's Day massacre on North Clark Street. Official embarrassment was aggravated by the fact that two of the Capone mob's assassins came disguised as policemen that morning—and some historians still believe they *were* patrolmen, working for Capone.

Russell's detectives solved the crime after a fashion, tracing one of the murder weapons to its original vendor, then to hired assassin Fred "Killer" Burke (who was never charged with the murders). Meanwhile, Russell made a show of furious activity, withdrawing patrolmen from private and unpaid security details to form raiding squads, appointing a privately funded "blue-ribbon" commission to study police department organization. Another gangland murder—the June 1930 shooting of journalist Alfred "Jake" Lingle—finally doomed Russell's career. After the slaying, Russell praised Lingle as a man who "led a clean and honorable life and was deserving of all the confidence placed in him." Sadly, for the chief, investigation soon revealed that he shared a $78,000 bank account with Lingle, from which bribes had been paid to various high-ranking Chicago policemen. Mayor Thompson finally dismissed Russell in early 1931, replacing him with JOHN ALCOCK.

Rynning, Thomas H. (1866–1941)

A native of Beloit, Wisconsin, born in 1866 and orphaned as a child, Thomas Rynning struck off on his own at age 12 and made his way westward, working as a cowboy and a teamster before he joined the U.S. Cavalry in 1885. Stationed in Arizona, he participated in the government's final campaigns against Apache "renegades," then left military service to join "Buffalo Bill" Cody's traveling Wild West show in 1891. Seven years later, he rejoined the army and saw action in the Spanish-American War as one of THEODORE ROOSEVELT's "Rough Riders."

Back in civilian life at war's end, Rynning returned to Arizona and was named a captain in the ARIZONA RANGERS during 1902. He resigned on March 20, 1907, to accept appointment as superintendent of Yuma Territorial Prison, a post he maintained until March 1, 1912. Most sources skip from that point to Rynning's death in 1941, but an interview recorded by the Arizona Historical Society indicates that Rynning returned to service with the Arizona Rangers and participated in the infamous July 1917 deportation of 1,187 copper miners who had struck for higher wages and improved safety conditions. Walter Douglas, grandson of Bisbee's leading copper magnate, described the event as follows:

There was a fellow by the name of Jim Rynning [sic]— he was . . . a colonel in the Arizona Rangers—and they came down . . . with my dad and Colonel Greenway and the rest of the people around there and they decided the only thing to do. . . . They couldn't shoot them on the property or anything, so they thought, well they didn't belong there, they were all out-of-towners, so they would just gather them up, round them up, and ship them out. So they called in all the deputies in Cochise County and made them lieutenants or something to run the posse, and they got the ranchers all around in San Pedro Valley and Sulphur Springs and all that, brought in cowboys, and . . . the Mercantile Company supplied them all with rifles and stuff. They proceeded one early morning to round up all of these guys and drive them down Bisbee Road to Warren to put them in the ballpark because it had a 10-foot wooden fence around it. Then they went down there and they talked them and they says, "If you're going to come to work, all right, but if you're going to just cause a lot of trouble we're going to have to put you out of town, and we don't want you to come back." So then they backed a cattle train in on that siding by the ballpark, loaded them all in, and put in water and food and everything else and sent them to Columbus, New Mexico. And when they got them over there they put the train on the siding and took the engine and caboose off and brought it back and they deported twelve hundred and some people. . . . [O]f course they brought suit against the company, they brought suit against my dad. They threatened him with jail and everything because he violated their civil rights and enslaved them, they said, because they didn't give them any food and water. Federal investigators came out and they had court hearings in El Paso and in Bisbee and they proved that they had been fed and watered and everything else was given to them, even the transportation. (laughter)

Unmentioned in that jocular account is the fact that many of the deported miners—mostly German-Americans and members of the "radical" Industrial Workers of the World—were detained illegally in Columbus for several months.

S

St. Augustine Police Department

St. Augustine, Florida, is America's oldest city, settled by Spanish troops in 1565, and the site of an early MASS MURDER, wherein those same troops slaughtered some 900 French Protestants (also in 1565). Sir Francis Drake sacked and burned the town in 1586, but its settlers rebuilt and endured. During the 17th century, St. Augustine earned the reputation of a lawless no-man's land, a haven for pirates and other fugitives from justice. British forces burned the town again in 1702, but the Spaniards hung on until 1763, trading St. Augustine to Britain in exchange for Cuba. After the United States annexed Florida, in 1819, St. Augustine became a major slave-trading center.

While that traffic ended with the Civil War, St. Augustine remained a hotbed of white-supremacist sentiment for another century, every aspect of daily life rigidly segregated by race. In 1964, as the city prepared for its quadricentennial celebration, civil rights activists led by Dr. Martin Luther King, Jr. launched a series of protest demonstrations, seeking to break down the local color bar. Local police, under Chief Virgil Stuart, issued ill-advised shoot-to-kill orders against demonstrators, while Sheriff LAWRENCE DAVIS openly recruited members of the KU KLUX KLAN as "special deputies." Weeks of night-riding and RIOTS ensued, prompting Dr. King to call St. Augustine "the most lawless community I have ever seen." Passage of a new civil rights law in July 1964 forced concessions from local white leaders, but resentment simmered for years afterward, on both sides.

The modern St. Augustine Police Department operates (at least in theory) on a different standard. Its mission statement calls upon all officers "to enforce laws, provide a safe and secure environment, and respond to the changing needs of the community in order to promote a positive and peaceful quality of life for citizens and visitors within the Nations Oldest City." Department commanders, in their own words, hope "to demonstrate excellence in professional police service by promoting continued education of officers and citizens, demonstrating the highest ethical and moral standards, and adapting to ever-changing community needs."

St. Louis Police Department

St. Louis, Missouri, created a unique police force in 1808, one year before the town was formally incorporated. Members of the four-man force received no pay, but all male residents above age 18 were required to serve four months as a policeman, under penalty of a one-dollar fine if they refused. The system endured until 1818, when population growth required addition of two more officers (including one-armed Gabe Warner) as night watchmen. At the same time, Captain Mackey Wherry was employed for $400 per year as the city's first police commander. In 1826 the force expanded to 26 officers—one captain and 25 lieutenants—whose duties included ringing the church bells at night.

Massive immigration in the 1840s prompted corresponding growth in the police department, with one captain, one lieutenant, and 48 patrolmen on the night watch, while one lieutenant and seven officers were deemed sufficient for daylight patrols. A "black Maria" wagon joined the force in 1850, as geographic expansion made foot patrols more difficult. A police board appointed by the governor assumed control of city law enforcement in 1861, appointing James McDonough as the first official police chief. (He served three terms, twice interrupted by impulsive resignations.) Political machinations dogged the force, resulting in the resignation or removal of all board members within their first six months of service.

Outbreaks of river piracy after the Civil War prompted formation of a local steamboat detective squad in 1866, joined the following year by a mounted patrol to pursue highwaymen. The city's first police telephone system was installed in 1881, transmitting messages via Morse code. By the time the 1904 World's Fair opened, St. Louis ranked as the fourth-largest American city, with rampant crime befitting its size. PROHIBITION brought new difficulties and CORRUPTION in the 1920s, while 46 officers were killed on duty during 1920–30. During the same period, the SLPD inaugurated a Traffic Division (1923), introduced ballistics testing (1928), and established a four-week new police academy (1929).

Other advances lagged behind technology. Female officers had no powers of arrest until 1951, and the city's first K-9 UNIT was established seven years later. Officers did not win the 40-hour work week until 1963, and their patrol cars lacked air-conditioning until 1968. Budget cuts in the 1980s reduced manpower at a time when demands for police response were increasing, prompting SLPD leaders to respond with campaigns such as CAT (*c*ombat *a*uto *t*heft), SCAT (*s*treet *c*orner *a*pprehension *t*eam), and WAR (*w*e *a*re *r*esponsible)—the latter a drug-education program for local schools. Today, the SLPD employs more than 1,400 sworn officers, all looking "to the past with pride and to the future with anticipation and promise."

St. Paul Police Department

St. Paul, Minnesota, has endured crime problems since the date of its foundation. Initially a sprawling river town and frontier trade center, it quickly became what civic leaders now refer to as "a violent town of violent men." Alexander Marshall was appointed as the first town constable in 1851, but he soon gave up the hopeless job. Three years later, with St. Paul's incorporation as a city, William Miller was named to lead a new four-man police department, aided at times by a 40-man VIGILANCE COMMITTEE. Cessation of river traffic during the Civil War plunged St. Paul into an economic depression, during which three-fourths of the police department joined the Union Army. The force was then disbanded entirely, replaced by a force of 200 vigilantes.

The war's end restored prosperity, and a new 12-man police force was created, under Chief Michael Cummings. Still, vice flourished in St. Paul, despite

the earnest efforts of reformers. Police were part of the problem, in fact, as demonstrated clearly during PROHIBITION and the lawless years that followed. By the early 1920s, St. Paul enjoyed a reputation as a wide-open town where fugitives from justice could rest peacefully—as long as they registered with local police captains and paid the appropriate "rent." Some officers and local politicians went further than turning a blind eye to crime, assisting in the execution of two high-profile KIDNAPPINGS that finally drew FBI attention to St. Paul in 1934. While a local grand jury attempted to whitewash the city—described in one graphic account as a place where "gangsters can fuck in the street"—federal prosecutors convicted several prominent locals and sent them to prison.

The Depression-era sweep brought reform of a sort, but other problems endured in St. Paul. Persistent complaints of police RACISM and use of EXCESSIVE FORCE against blacks climaxed in spring 2001 with a series of meetings between police leaders and the local NAACP chapter, supervised by agents of the U.S. JUSTICE DEPARTMENT. The net results included an official promise to abstain from racial PROFILING of suspects, accelerated recruitment of nonwhite officers, and creation of a new Police Civilian INTERNAL AFFAIRS Review Commission to investigate abuse complaints.

See also: FEDERAL BUREAU OF INVESTIGATION.

Salt Lake City Police Department

Organized by Mormon pioneers in 1847, the Salt Lake City Police Department began as a small frontier force, committed to defense of the community against outlaws and Indian raiders, survived Utah's brief guerrilla war with the U.S. government in Washington, and has evolved into a 21st-century law enforcement agency with 650 employees. Specialized units include a Motor Squad (for traffic enforcement), a Crisis Intervention (SWAT) Team, a Public Order Unit (for riot control), and a K-9 UNIT with dogs trained for various functions, including crowd control, corpse retrieval, and detection of DRUGS.

San Diego Police Department

The town of San Diego, California, was governed by martial law from 1845 until 1850, when state legislators established a five-man city council including Marshal Agostin Haraszthy, who supervised a team of roving constables. The city's first jail, built for $5,000 by the son of San Diego's city council president, bankrupted the town and still let its first prisoner escape four hours after his arrest, by digging through the soft wall with a jackknife. A metal cage was soon added, thus making the jail "escape-proof," and a succession of city marshals maintained local order until May 1889, when the San Diego Police Department was established under chief Joseph Coyne.

Thereafter, the SDPD expanded and matured after the fashion of other departments nationwide. Patrolmen served 12-hour shifts until 1895, when tours of duty were cut to eight hours. The force hired its first detective in 1907 and gained its first motorcycle officer two years later. The city's first traffic signal, manually operated by a policeman, was installed in 1920. Patrol cars joined the force during PROHIBITION and were fitted with two-way radios in 1934. The SDPD crime lab was established in 1939, and the department recruited its first civilian reserves in 1942, to compensate for a wartime personnel shortage.

As elsewhere in California (and the nation at large), San Diego's police force harbored more than its share of extreme right-wing sentiment. In 1912, two members of a "radical" labor union, the Industrial Workers of the World, were beaten to death by city police, hundreds more assaulted and jailed before a court ordered the department to permit public meetings. A decade later, San Diego harbored some 2,000 members of the revived KU KLUX KLAN, including a significant contingent on the force. Matters went from bad to worse in the 1960s, when San Diego's RED SQUAD, dubbed the Investigative Support Unit (ISU) collaborated with the FBI's illegal COINTELPRO operations. That collaboration included harassment of the Black Panther Party and criminal involvement with a right-wing TERRORIST group, the Secret Army Organization (SAO), led on behalf of FBI headquarters by agent provocateurs Howard Godfrey.

Fueled with intelligence on local leftists from the Bureau and the ISU, SAO commandos launched a wave of terror that included vandalism, bombings and attempted murder of a liberal college professor. (FBI agents concealed the weapon in that case and protected the sniper.) In December 1969, when SAO commandos invaded and demolished the office of a local leftist newspaper, the *Street Journal,* their number included ISU officer John Paul Murray. Later, when the paper signed a lease for new premises with landlord Bill Reeves, ISU Sergeant Jack Pearson asked Reeves to cancel the contract as "a personal favor." After Reeves refused, he was jailed on false murder charges, held just long enough for officers to ransack his home in a vengeful search for "evidence" of nonexistent crime.

Researcher Frank Donner describes the SDPD as "perennially apathetic" in the face of apolitical crimes, an assessment validated in part by its handling of the SERIAL MURDERS committed by San Diego resident Carroll Edward Cole between 1970 and 1980. Cole killed at least five women in San Diego, including his second wife (strangled and dumped in the closet of their home), but local detectives clung to flimsy pronouncements of "natural death" in each case, even after Cole confessed his crimes and went to Nevada's death row in 1985. Black and Hispanic residents of San Diego also file persistent claims of RACISM and EXCESSIVE FORCE related to their contacts with local police. Some recent cases include:

January 1999—U.S. Navy veteran Rodney Mitchell was assaulted by police officers outside a San Diego fast-food restaurant, while discussing a complaint with an SDPD sergeant. His resultant federal lawsuit (still unresolved) seeks damages for false arrest and injuries sustained in the beating.

April 2002—A civilian's videotape caught Yolanda Fajardo Perez, a 54-year-old Mexican-American housewife, as she was tackled from behind and slammed to the ground by an officer weighing 250 pounds. She sustained a concussion and other injuries in the assault, occurring after police manhandled a suicidal teenager in the San Diego barrio. Mrs. Perez complained of that violent conduct and was then assaulted in turn.

April 2005—An SDPD sergeant assigned to the security detail at Petco Park was charged with molesting two underage girls. Trial was pending when this volume went to press; charges are two counts of child molestation, two counts of "annoying or molesting" a minor, two counts of contributing to the delinquency of a minor, and one count of sexual battery. If convicted, the officer faces 11 years in state prison.

See also: AGENTS PROVOCATEURS; FEDERAL BUREAU OF INVESTIGATION.

San Francisco Police Department

Most Americans know San Francisco, California's, police department chiefly from its Hollywood depictions in Clint Eastwood's "Dirty Harry" films and the *Streets of San Francisco* television series (1972–77). Reality is rather different for the San Francisco Police Department, which dates its modern incarnation from the post-earthquake days of 1906. In the wake of that disaster, San Francisco added 700 men to its small scandal-ridden force, hired for the first time on the basis of impartial test scores. Four chiefs served the department between 1907 and 1911, including William Biggy (1907–08), whose November 1908 murder remains unsolved today. Chief David White, recruited from the ranks of the Pacific Gas & Electric Company in June

1911, demoted and transferred six captains accused of CORRUPTION, pressing on from there to clean up the city's notorious Barbary Coast red-light district.

The early 20th century brought San Francisco its first automobiles, and the SFPD created its Traffic Division in 1909, adding patrol cars six years later. The Preparedness Day bombing (see BOMBING AND BOMB SQUADS) of July 1916 claimed 10 lives and left 40 wounded, "solved" by a police FRAME-UP that sent labor leaders Tom Mooney and Warren Billings to prison on false murder charges. (They were released in 1938, 18 years after SFPD detective Draper Hand confessed to fabricating evidence against them.) PROHIBITION brought new problems with corruption, while the KU KLUX KLAN recruited 3,500 members in San Francisco, including a substantial number of policemen. It was no surprise, therefore, when officers failed to prevent the LYNCHING of three alleged cop-killers, dragged from jail and hanged by a mob on December 7, 1920.

Technology caught up with the SFPD a decade later, beginning with installation of radios in Traffic Division patrol cars. A 90-member "flying squad" of motorcycle officers was introduced at the same time (1930), while mounted units assumed STRIKEBREAKING chores on the San Francisco docks. One of their charges, on July 5, 1930, left two longshoremen dead and many others injured as they fled the SFPD's cavalry. Strikers were also first to catch a whiff of tear gas in San Francisco, while the first aircraft of SFPD's Aviation Police Unit spied on the scene from above. World War II siphoned off more than half the department's manpower, requiring employment of civilian auxiliaries to fill the void, preparing for a Japanese invasion that never materialized.

The postwar era brought problems aplenty, including an obsession with alleged "subversives" that funneled disproportionate amounts of police money and manpower into right-wing political action. By 1960 more officers were assigned to DOMESTIC SURVEILLANCE than to investigation of ORGANIZED CRIME. "Operation S" (for *saturation*) was launched in 1956, resulting in a first-year total of some 20,000 persons stopped and questioned on the streets. Only 1,000 of those were arrested, and while city leaders praised the operation's success, its increasing focus on nonwhite neighborhoods increased tension between minorities and the SFPD. On May 13, 1960, student demonstrations against the House Committee on Un-American Activities sparked a POLICE RIOT, replete with examples of EXCESSIVE FORCE documented by local newspapers. Chief THOMAS J. CAHILL made no apologies for his men, maintaining that police were meant to be the guardians of public conscience and morality. In 1964 the SFPD closed various topless bars for "outraging public decency," until

court orders halted the process. Two years later, Cahill founded a two-man Special Obscenity Squad to police local bookstores and theaters.

Police RACISM has long been a sore point in San Francisco, despite attempts to relieve the problem. In January 1967 Chief Cahill ordered some of his officers to attend a meeting sponsored by the National Conference of Christians and Jews, but Frisco's finest shouted so many racial epithets and anti-Semitic slurs from the audience that an observer from the CALIFORNIA HIGHWAY PATROL told Deputy Chief Al Nelder, "You have a bunch of hoodlums in uniform." That performance followed a September 1966 riot in the Hunter's Point ghetto, sparked by the fatal police shooting of an unarmed black teenager. During that three-day upheaval, white officers posted a photo of the KKK's imperial wizard on a headquarters bulletin board, captioned "Our Hero," and chalked "Take a nigger to lunch today!" on the side of a police bus headed for the riot zone. Another police riot left antiwar protesters bloodied on Nob Hill, in January 1968. The following year, officers collaborating with the FBI's illegal COINTELPRO program raided Black Panther Party headquarters and confiscated pamphlets from the Students for a Democratic Society (destroying all but a handful retained for distribution to veteran's groups nationwide).

On other fronts, the turbulent 1960s witnessed creation of an SFPD Underwater Rescue Unit (1961), a K-9 UNIT (1962), and a long-delayed Bureau of Complaint, Inspection and Welfare (1965). The department's Tactical Division, organized in 1967 to handle emergency and undercover tasks, has expanded over time to include a SWAT TEAM, several Park Units, and a bomb squad. Chief Charles Gain (1976–79) strove to create the image of a kinder, gentler SFPD with baby-blue patrol cars, but his effort foundered in May 1979, when gay San Franciscans rioted over a jury's lenient manslaughter conviction against Dan White, confessed assassin of Mayor George Moscone and gay city supervisor Harvey Milk. Gain's response to that outbreak led the Police Officers' Association to conduct a formal "no confidence" vote on the chief in June 1979, wherein 10,811 negative votes were cast, versus 22 supporting Gain. Mayor Dianne Feinstein thereafter replaced Gain with Cornelius Murphy.

A new series of scandals rocked the SFPD in the early 21st century. On November 20, 2002, three drunken off-duty officers approached Jade Santoro and Adam Snyder outside a local bar, demanding that Santoro surrender the fajitas he was eating. When Santoro refused, the officers beat him, prompting Snyder to call 911 for emergency help. Spokesmen for the AMERICAN CIVIL LIBERTIES UNION contend that the subsequent investigation "was suspect from the start," perhaps because one of the officers accused was the son of Assistant Chief Alex Fagan, Sr. "Lost" evidence, mishandled interviews, and other suggestions of a department cover-up prompted the Office of Citizen Complaints to charge that top-ranking San Francisco officers "routinely obstructed and delayed" investigation of the case. Days later, the San Francisco Controller's office completed a "best practices" review of SFPD's accountability mechanisms and found them woefully inadequate. On February 28, 2003, Chief Earl Sanders, Assistant Chief Alex Fagan, and eight other officers were indicted on charges of conspiring to obstruct justice. Charges against Sanders and Fagan, Sr. were dismissed a month later, while eight others still faced charges. The three patrolmen involved in the original brawl faced charges of assault and battery.

See also: FEDERAL BUREAU OF INVESTIGATION.

Sargent, John Garibaldi (1860–1939)

Born at Ludlow, Vermont, on October 12, 1860, John Sargent earned his B.A. from Tufts College in 1887, then studied law privately and won admittance to the state bar three years later. After a period in private practice, he served as state's attorney for Windsor County (until 1900), as state secretary for civil and military affairs (1900–02), and as state attorney general (1908–12). During the latter term, Sargent also earned a master's degree (in 1912). President Calvin Coolidge named him attorney general in March 1925, and while Sargent held that post until March 1929, poor health and a dislike of Washington, D.C., severely limited his personal role in the JUSTICE DEPARTMENT.

As a consequence, Sargent generally left J. EDGAR HOOVER to run the FBI as he pleased, without supervision. (In the words of Hoover biographer Athan Theoharis, Sargent "saw even less evil than [Harlan] Stone had seen before him.") In matters of protocol, Hoover dealt primarily with William Donovan, head of the department's Antitrust Division, who likewise did little or nothing to curb FBI abuses. Years later, in a press interview, Hoover listed Sargent as one of his all-time favorite attorneys general. Following retirement from federal service, Sargent served as chairman of the Vermont Commission on Uniform State Laws. He died at Ludlow on March 3, 1939.

Savage, Edward Hartwell, Jr. (1812–1893)

A third-generation descendant of Scottish immigrants, Edward Savage, Jr. was born at East Alstead, New Hampshire, in 1812. His father left for Europe soon after Edward's birth, and when his mother died shortly thereafter, Edward was adopted by a maternal aunt whose husband had deserted from the British army during the American Revolution. Still fearing arrest, Edward's uncle lived a nomadic fugitive's life in the New Hampshire wilds, thus providing Edward with a peculiar and adventurous childhood.

Savage moved to Boston in 1843 and joined the BOSTON POLICE DEPARTMENT seven years later, at age 38. He was promoted to captain in 1854, and to deputy chief in 1861. Along the way, he published his first book, *Boston Police Recollections,* and also displayed a fondness for writing poetry. His second volume on local police history—*Police Records and Recollections, or Boston by Daylight and Gaslight for Two Hundred and Forty Years*—was published in 1866. Four years later, Savage was named chief of police, a post which he filled admirably until his retirement in 1878. During his tenure, the Boston P.D. was such a model of efficiency that representatives from London's Scotland Yard were sent to study Savage's administrative methods. Upon retirement, Savage served as Boston's first probation officer, remaining in that post until his death in 1893.

Saxbe, William Bart (1916–)

Born at Mechanicsburg, Ohio, on June 24, 1916, William Saxbe earned his B.A. from Ohio State University in 1940, followed by a period of military service during 1940–45. After World War II he returned to Ohio State University, earning his LL.B. and admission to Ohio's state bar in 1948. Those studied were prolonged by Saxbe's service in the state legislature (1947–54), which in turn were interrupted by a recall to active military duty during the Korean War (1951–52). Two years of private practice ended with his election as Ohio's attorney general in 1956, a post Saxbe held until 1968. That year saw his election to the U.S. Senate, where he remained until President Richard Nixon named him attorney general in January 1974.

Saxbe was the last of Nixon's four attorneys general and the only one not driven from office by Watergate scandals. He outlasted Nixon, in fact, then resigned on February 1, 1975, to become ambassador to India (1975–77). Following completion of those foreign duties, he returned to private legal practice in Ohio.

Schaefer, Gerard John (1946–1995)

A Wisconsin native, born on March 26, 1946, Gerard Schaefer described his childhood in a broken home as "turbulent and conflictual." He consulted psychiatrists in college, during 1966, relating early incidents of masochism and bondage coupled with a morbid death fetish. Married in 1968, he was divorced two years later, his wife claiming "extreme cruelty." Schaefer recuperated from the break-up with a tour of Europe and North Africa, then returned to the United States with a dream of entering law enforcement.

On his first attempt, Schaefer applied to the Broward County (Florida) Sheriff's Department, but he failed psychological tests and was rejected. Undeterred by that result, the tiny Wilton Manors Police Department hired him anyway, handing Schaefer a commendation for a drug bust in March 1972. One month later, on April 20, he was fired. Explanations for the rapid turnaround vary: Chief Bernard Scott claimed Schaefer "didn't have an ounce of common sense," while FBI agent Robert Ressler described Schaefer's penchant for stalking female motorists he stopped for speeding. Whatever the cause of his dismissal, Schaefer found a new post in June 1972 with the Martin County Sheriff's Department. He was on the job less than a month before he made a "dumb mistake" that would cost him his badge and his freedom.

On July 21, 1972, Schaefer picked up two teenage hitchhikers, Pamela Wells and Nancy Trotter, on the highway near a local beach. After telling them (falsely) that hitchhiking was illegal in Martin County, Schaefer offered them a ride to the beach on July 22. That morning, he drove them instead to remote Hutchinson Island, where he bound both girls at gunpoint, threatened them with sale as "white slaves," and left them balanced on tree roots with nooses tied around their necks. Schaefer went to roll call for his daily shift, but the girls escaped in his absence and flagged down a passing police car. They had no trouble identifying their assailant, since Schaefer had told them his name.

Upon discovering the empty nooses, Schaefer telephoned Sheriff Richard Crowder to report that he had "overdone his job," trying to scare the girls out of thumbing dangerous rides. Crowder fired him on the spot, charging Schaefer with false imprisonment and two counts of aggravated assault. He pled guilty on one assault charge in November 1972 and received a one-year jail term from Judge D. C. Smith, who called Schaefer a "thoughtless fool." Schaefer began serving his time on January 15, 1973.

Still, the most shocking revelations were yet to come. On September 27, 1972, while Schaefer was free on $15,000 bond, 17-year-old Susan Place and 16-year-old Georgia Jessup had vanished from Fort Lauderdale. Last seen with a man who called himself "Gerry Shepherd," they had gone to "play guitar" at the beach but never returned. Place's mother had recorded "Shepherd's" license number, but it was March 25, 1973, before sluggish investigators matched it to Schaefer's car. Schaefer denied any contact with Place or Jessup, standing firm on denial after their skeletons were found on Hutchinson Island on April 1, 1973. A search of

Florida policeman Gerard Schaefer was also a sadistic serial killer. (Author's collection)

Schaefer's home on April 7 revealed a stash of women's jewelry, 100-plus pages of writing and sketches depicting slaughter of young women, newspaper clippings about two women missing since 1969, and I.D. belonging to vanished hitchhikers Collette Goodenough and Barbara Wilcox, missing since January 8, 1973. (Their skeletal remains were found in early 1977, but cause of death was undetermined, and no murder charges were filed.)

The news clippings referred to Carmen Hallock, last seen alive in February 1969, and Leigh Bonadies, a neighbor of Schaefer's at the time she vanished in September 1969. Items of jewelry belonging to both women were found in Schaefer's hoard, along with a gold-filled tooth identified by Hallock's dentist, but no charges were filed in either case. More jewelry linked Schaefer to the October 1972 disappearance of 14-year-old Mary Briscolina, who disappeared with 13-year-old Elsie Farmer. Their bones were found in October 1973, but cause of death was once again unknown, and Schaefer escaped prosecution.

The list of suspected victims grew over time, with Schaefer penning a series of letters from jail that claimed

80 to 110 victims on three continents, but he faced charges only in the Place-Jessup murders. Indicted on May 18, 1973, he was convicted on two counts of first-degree murder in October 1973, drawing concurrent terms of life imprisonment. A long series of 20 appeals were rejected by various courts, before Schaefer was stabbed to death by a fellow inmate on December 3, 1995. Freed at last from the threat of libel litigation, ex-FBI agent Bill Hagerty described Schaefer to journalists: "He was one of the sickest. If I had a list of the top five, which would include all of the serial killers I have interviewed throughout the country, he would definitely be in the top five."

See also: FEDERAL BUREAU OF INVESTIGATION.

Schindler, Raymond Campbell (1883–1959)

Raymond Schindler was born in 1883 at Mexico, New York, 20 miles north of Syracuse. His family later moved to Milwaukee, where he finished high school and worked as a salesman before trying his luck as a gold miner in California. Failing at that, he arrived penniless in San Francisco on April 19, 1906—one day after the city's catastrophic earthquake. Schindler soon found work as an insurance investigator, and his work in that capacity won him a job with the WILLIAM J. BURNS Detective Agency, investigating local CORRUPTION on a U.S. government contract. In 1910 Schindler was promoted to run the Burns office in New York, which led to his investigation of the 1911 Marie Smith murder case in Asbury Park, New Jersey.

Smith, a 10-year-old girl, was raped, bludgeoned, and strangled on her way home from school, her corpse discarded in some roadside shrubbery. Police suspected Thomas Williams, a black man with a rap sheet and a flimsy alibi, but Sheriff Clarence Hatrick hired Schindler to review the hasty investigation. Schindler began by examining Smith's neighbors and discovered that one of them, recent immigrant Frank Heideman, had fled Germany after being charged with child molestation. One of Schindler's operatives, posing as a wealthy fellow German, befriended Heideman and soon became his roommate. Through elaborate machinations, including the staged "murder" of an ersatz hobo by Schindler's agent, Heideman was duped into confessing Smith's murder, and he ultimately died in the electric chair, while Thomas Williams was exonerated.

Schindler left the Burns Agency to lead his own detective firm in 1912, running a one-man sting operation that sent several corrupt Atlantic City politicians to prison on bribery charges. Two decades later, in the Bahamas, he helped clear suspect Freddie de Marigny in the still-unsolved murder of Sir Harry Oakes. Three years after that case made headlines, in 1946, Schindler joined the "Court of Last Resort," created by novelist Erle Stanley Gardner to investigate crimes wherein indigent or unpopular defendants stood wrongly accused. The group rescued several innocent persons from prison or imminent death, and some of its cases were dramatized on television in the early 1950s. Schindler died at North Tarrytown, New York, on July 1, 1959.

Schneider, Albert (1863–1928)

Born in 1863, Albert Schneider earned his M.D. from Chicago's College of Physicians and Surgeons in 1887, then garnered various other scientific degrees before completing his Ph.D. at Columbia University, in New York, in 1897. While Schneider spent the remainder of his life in academia—variously teaching at Northwestern University, the University of Nebraska, the University of California (Berkeley), and the University of the Pacific (Stockton, California)—he also pursued a deep interest in crime and criminology.

A veritable genius of microscopy, Dr. Schneider established some of the earliest standards for FORENSIC SCIENCE, specifically the collection of microscopic crime-scene evidence and its presentation at trial. In 1916, while teaching at Berkeley, he pioneered the use of a vacuum cleaner to collect dust samples from a suspect's clothes, thereafter matching them to the crime scene. The same year also saw him working closely with Chief AUGUST VOLLMER of the BERKELEY POLICE DEPARTMENT, coauthoring an article on Berkeley's new police academy for the *Journal of the American Institute of Criminal Law and Criminology*.

In another forensic vein, Schneider ranked among the first scientists to study human brain waves and the physiological changes produced by stress. From that study, he produced an early "lie detector" that attempted to match errant brain waves to the stress produced by lying during a police interrogation. The device was far from foolproof, but it still served as a predecessor of the modern (and intensely controversial) polygraph. Ironically, a cerebral hemorrhage claimed Schneider's life in Portland, Oregon, on November 5, 1928.

See also: "LIE DETECTORS."

Schwarzkopf, Herbert Norman, Sr. (1895–1958)

A New Jersey native, born on August 28, 1895, Norman Schwarzkopf, Sr. graduated from West Point and served with the U.S. Army during World War I. In July 1921 he was tapped to lead the newly created NEW JERSEY STATE POLICE, and while some published accounts claim that Schwarzkopf had "specialized in police organization" prior to gaining that post (with a colonel's rank), his sole "law enforcement" experience prior to appointment was a stint as a floorwalker at Bamberger's department store in Newark. Like FBI Director J. EDGAR HOOVER, Schwarzkopf had never made an arrest nor investigated a crime before he assumed responsibility for statewide law enforcement in New Jersey.

Nonetheless, he won kudos for his military-style organization of the NJSP, and was serving his fourth term in office when the case of a lifetime surprised him in 1932. On March 1 of that year, the infant son of celebrity aviator Charles Lindbergh was kidnapped from the family home in Hopewell, snatched from the upstairs bedroom where a crudely written note demanded $100,000 ransom. Schwarzkopf took charge of the case, determined to solve it without help from Hoover's G-men, and the ransom was paid on April 2. Six weeks later, on May 12, a child's decomposed corpse was found near the Lindbergh home, at a place already searched by police, and while the boy's pediatrician refused to identify the corpse, Schwarzkopf announced that Charles Lindbergh, Jr. was dead.

Another 27 months elapsed before suspect Bruno Richard Hauptmann was arrested in New York in Sep-

Three interesting facsimiles of handwriting which seem to add another link to the chain of evidence which is being built up against Bruno Richard Hauptmann. At the top is Hauptmann's own lettered signature on an auto registration card and below is the ransom note that is one of the items of evidence in the Lindbergh kidnapping case. (Bettmann/Corbis)

tember 1934 and extradited for trial in New Jersey. Jurors convicted Hauptmann of murder on February 13, 1935, and he died in the electric chair on April 3, 1936, but brooding doubts surround Schwarzkopf's solution of the case. Some evidence was clearly fabricated—a newspaper reporter confessed to writing the phone number of a critical witness inside Hauptmann's closet—and various "witnesses" changed their stories radically between 1932 and 1935, probably in hopes of collecting reward money offered for conviction of the kidnapper. Schwarzkopf himself labeled one witness, New York cabbie Joseph Perrone, "a totally unreliable witness," yet he raised no objection to the prosecution's use of Perrone at trial. After Hauptmann's conviction, Schwarzkopf warned the FBI that any other ransom bills retrieved from public circulation should be secretly destroyed, to bury any further hint of Hauptmann's innocence.

Soon after Hauptmann's 1936 execution, Governor Harold Hoffman dismissed Schwarzkopf from the NJSP. Schwarzkopf moved on to head a New Jersey bus line and briefly narrated radio's *Gang Busters* series, then returned to active military service during World War II. In 1942 he was posted to Iran, reorganizing that nation's police after Iran became an Allied protectorate. The postwar years saw him assigned to Italy and Germany, retiring to civilian life with the rank of major general. In 1951 Schwarzkopf was named administrative director of New Jersey's Department of Law and Public Safety, ironically serving once more under ex-governor Hoffman. In 1954 Schwarzkopf repaid Hoffman for his 1936 dismissal, charging Hoffman with financial irregularities. Hoffman left his post and died of a heart attack six weeks later, leaving a note in which he confessed embezzling $300,000. Schwarzkopf died four years later, on November 25, 1958. His son, Norman, Jr., commanded U.S. troops in the Gulf War of 1990–91.

See also: FEDERAL BUREAU OF INVESTIGATION; KIDNAPPING.

Screws, M. Claude

On January 30, 1943, Sheriff M. Claude Screws of Baker County, Georgia, ordered two deputies—Frank Edward Jones and Jim Bob Kelley—to help him arrest a black suspect, one Robert Hall, on charges of stealing a truck tire. The officers found Hall at home and transported him in handcuffs to the county jail in Newton. On arrival at the jail, the officers removed Hall from their car and then began to beat him with their fists and blackjacks, in full view of several witnesses. Sworn testimony indicated that the beating continued for at least 15 minutes, perhaps as long as half an hour. Hall subsequently died at a local hospital.

Evidence emerged that Sheriff Screws had a longstanding grudge against Hall and had threatened to "get" him. Publicity surrounding the case forced county prosecutors to file murder charges against the three officers, but an all-white jury promptly acquitted them. The U.S. JUSTICE DEPARTMENT then indicted the trio under provisions of the 1866 Civil Rights Act, for conspiring to violate Hall's civil rights "under color of law." They were convicted and sentenced to prison on that charge, but appealed the verdict to the U.S. SUPREME COURT in 1944.

Speaking for the court's majority in May 1945, Justice William Douglas denounced Hall's murder as "a shocking and revolting episode in law enforcement," then overturned the convictions on grounds that federal law required "willful intent" to violate civil rights. Since Screws, Jones, and Kelley simply wanted to *murder* Hall, without conspiring to abridge specific rights (such as voting), they were not deemed liable under federal law. A second trial resulted in acquittal of all three defendants, and Screws capitalized on his newfound celebrity to win a seat in the Georgia state senate.

For years afterward, FBI Director J. EDGAR HOOVER used the Supreme Court's ruling in *Screws v. United States* as an excuse to avoid investigations of cases involving police RACISM and EXCESSIVE FORCE. Conditions for African Americans remained grim in "Bad Baker" County, where Sheriff L. Warren Johnson imitated his predecessor's criminal behavior through the civil rights era of the 1950s and early 1960s.

See also: FEDERAL BUREAU OF INVESTIGATION.

Seabury Commission

In August 1930 New York governor Franklin Roosevelt appointed a commission to investigate pervasive rumors of CORRUPTION within the low-level magistrate's courts of New York City. As chairman of the commission, Roosevelt named Samuel Seabury, a prominent attorney and former judge who had presided at the second murder trial of Lt. CHARLES BECKER in 1914. During autumn 1930 the Seabury Commission questioned more than 1,000 witnesses, including judges, attorneys, bail bondsmen, police, and former defendants, their accumulated testimony revealing a bizarre and shocking vision of justice run amok.

Seabury discovered that false arrests were routine in New York, with FRAME-UPS conducted for profit by corrupt police and witnesses bribed to commit perjury. Many of the victims were innocent working-class women, jailed on false prostitution charges, either as a means of extorting de facto ransom payments or on behalf of husbands seeking grounds for a divorce. Street thugs admitted lying under oath to convict blameless defendants, and Seabury exposed several vice cops who had six-figure bank accounts, inexplicable with respect to their $3,000 annual salaries. The commission reported that 51 young women had been falsely sentenced to terms at the Bedford state prison, whereupon New York's Appellate Division stepped in to dismiss several corrupt judges. Various lower-ranking cogs in the conspiracy were likewise fired and prosecuted for their crimes. Some historians suspect that Seabury's probe also prompted the still-unsolved disappearance of Judge Joseph Force Crater in 1930.

Seabury's revelations were so sensational and disturbing that in 1931 a joint resolution of the state legislature gave him free rein to investigate New York City's government at large. Mayor Jimmy Walker agreed to finance the investigation, but soon regretted his promise, as Seabury focused on the mayor's own underworld connections. As a new cast of witnesses shoveled the dirt on Manhattan's flamboyant chief executive, detailing his love of the high life and numerous links to ORGANIZED CRIME, Walker reneged on his funding, prompting an order from the Appellate Division that compelled him to fund the commission. Seabury's final report, delivered to Governor Roosevelt in summer 1932, accused Walker of "malfeasance, misfeasance and nonfeasance" in office. The findings came at a bad time for FDR, already involved in a race for the White House, and Walker was forced to resign in September 1932. He departed on a three-year tour of Europe with a plaintive quip: "This fellow Seabury would convict the twelve apostles if he could."

Sealy, Lloyd George (1917–1985)

Native New Yorker Lloyd Sealy was born in Manhattan on January 4, 1917, and raised in the Prospect Heights section of Brooklyn, the son of black immigrants from Barbados. After graduating from Thomas Jefferson High School—where his mostly white classmates elected him student body president—Sealy joined the NEW YORK CITY POLICE DEPARTMENT in November 1942. Working the streets full-time, he still managed to earn a B.A. in sociology from Brooklyn College in 1946, followed by an LL.B. from Brooklyn Law School six years later.

Education helped Sealy advance within NYPD, but he still faced glaring obstacles, with RACISM chief among them. Despite subtle (and not-so-subtle) discrimination within the department, Sealy earned promotion to sergeant in 1951, lieutenant in 1959, and became NYPD's third-ever black captain in 1962. During the "long, hot summer" of 1964, he advanced to command a precinct in Harlem. While black community leaders praised his promotions, many young militants damned Sealy as a sell-out "Uncle Tom." Still, he played a key role in averting and suppressing riots during that turbulent era, rewarded in 1966 with promotion to serve as the first black assistant chief inspector and first black commander of the Brooklyn North patrol district (encompassing 11 precincts).

While Sealy never served as chief, he retired from NYPD in 1969 with honors to spare, stepping into an associate professorship at Manhattan's John Jay College of Criminal Justice—where, once again, he was the first black staffer in the school's four-year history. In 1973 Sealy advanced to serve as director of John Jay's Criminal Justice Education department, managing a $1.5 million budget. He died on the job and on campus, in the John Jay library, stricken by a heart attack on his 68th birthday.

Seattle Police Department

Seattle, Washington's, police department was established in 1886. Three decades later, on February 6, 1919, Seattle was the scene of America's first general strike, called by local unionists in an effort to win higher pay and better hours. Mayor Ole Hanson and his police chief viewed the strike as a "revolutionary conspiracy," fortifying City Hall while police and 1,000 special deputies were ordered to shoot on sight any person creating a public disturbance. In fact, the unions committed no crimes and the strike soon collapsed on its own, but the Seattle P.D. spent months afterward pursuing alleged radicals, arresting many, once raiding the city's Socialist Party headquarters.

Full-scale DOMESTIC SURVEILLANCE in Seattle dates from that era, expanding dramatically during the 1930s, then declining before it received a boost in 1956, with creation of a new Subversive Activities Unit. In the 1960s the SAU merged with a "criminal intelligence squad" whose duties were also largely political. FBI agents collaborated with the Seattle P.D. on aspects of the Bureau's illegal COINTELPRO campaign, climaxed by the January 1970 ambush slaying of Larry Ward, a black Vietnam War veteran who was hired by an FBI agent provocateurs to bomb a local business establishment. Seattle police commanders denied responsibility for that case of ENTRAPMENT, but the scandal roused city council members to investigate the department's antiradical activities.

Seattle's chief of police grudgingly acknowledged illegal surveillance, but assured the city council in 1974 that he had purged all political files on some 730 subjects. Unconvinced, the AMERICAN CIVIL LIBERTIES UNION and other organizations joined ranks in September 1976 to create a Coalition on Government Spying, launching a campaign to ban political surveillance in Seattle. Eleven months later, 36 individuals and six groups filed civil litigation under Washington state law, demanding access to their police dossiers. Seattle P.D. stalled for time, then finally admitted in pretrial hearings that files existed on 18 of the plaintiffs—and at least 152 other targets. Lieutenant V. L. Bartley tried to hide some of the files, shipping them off to friendly cops in California, but the move cost him his job, while a judge ordered return of the purloined material. When finally disclosed, the Seattle files—like many held by the FBI—consisted largely of misinformation, rumor, and malicious innuendo, revealing no hint of any criminal activity.

On January 1, 1980, a new Seattle city ordinance banned political spying outright, further specifying that no person should "become the subject of the collection of information on account of a lawful exercise of a constitutional right or civil liberty." Furthermore, the Seattle P.D. was barred from collecting any "restrictive information" pertaining to religious or political beliefs and activities, except in relation to criminal investigations or protection of visiting dignitaries.

Seattle has come a long way from that era, earning national accreditation in 2003 from the Commission on Accreditation of Law Enforcement Agencies. Today the Seattle P.D. employs 1,200 sworn officers and 700 civilian support personnel. Its mission statement comprises a vow to "prevent crime, enforce the law and support quality public safety by delivering respectful, professional, and dependable police services."

See also: AGENTS PROVOCATEURS.

Seavey, Webber S. (1841–?)

A native of Maine, born in 1841, Webber Seavey moved to Wisconsin in 1857 and found work as a woodcutter. Two years later, he tried his luck at gold mining in Colorado, then joined the Union Army at the outbreak of the Civil War in 1861. At war's end, Seavey spent seven years working aboard Mississippi riverboats, then served as a lawman in Santa Barbara, California, during 1874–79. From there, ever seeking new horizons, Seavey spent six years as a trader in the South Pacific. Finally, in 1887, he made his way to Omaha, Nebraska, and was named chief of the OMAHA POLICE DEPARTMENT.

After five years in that post, and following protracted consultations with his peers, Seavey conceived the notion of a union for the chief administrators of urban police departments throughout North America. A year later, at Chicago's World Columbian Exposition, Seavey met with leaders of other U.S. and Canadian police departments to found the National Police Chiefs Union, renamed the INTERNATIONAL ASSOCIATION OF CHIEFS OF POLICE in 1902. Appropriately, Seavey was

President Bush and instructor Brian Mowry, right, watch Secret Service dog trainer Samuel Schrader and his dog Robby check suitcases for explosives, during a Secret Service training exercise at the James J. Rowley Training Center in Beltsville, Maryland. (Ron Edmunds/AP)

elected as the group's first president, working to make it "the greatest stroke which has ever been made in this country against crime."

Secret Service

The U.S. Secret Service was created as an arm of the TREASURY DEPARTMENT in July 1865, under Chief William Wood, to suppress counterfeit currency. Two years later, its duties were expanded to include "detecting persons perpetrating frauds against the government"— a catch-all category that included smugglers, moonshiners, mail thieves, and terrorists associated with the early KU KLUX KLAN. Executive protection by the Secret Ser-

vice began in 1894, when agents were assigned to guard President Grover Cleveland on an informal, part-time basis. Congress formalized presidential protection in 1901, following the ASSASSINATION of William McKinley by the anarchist Leon Czolgosz, and the Secret Service assumed full-time executive protection chores the following year.

Expansion of Secret Service duties has continued over time. In 1915 President Woodrow Wilson directed the service to investigate ESPIONAGE (later transferred to the FEDERAL BUREAU OF INVESTIGATION). Protection of the president expanded in 1917 to include members of his immediate family, and to former presidents in 1961. The Secret Service suffered its worst black eye in November 1963, with revelations that members of the presidential detail were out drinking in Dallas the night before President John Kennedy's assassination there. (A special act of Congress promptly extended service protection to Kennedy's widow and her children for two years.) The slaying of presidential candidate ROBERT KENNEDY in 1968 moved Congress to expand protection once again, this time including all major presidential and vice presidential candidates and nominees during election years. Three years later, protection was extended further still, to cover foreign diplomatic missions and visiting heads of state.

The changing face of crime brought new responsibilities to the Secret Service in the closing decades of the 20th century. In 1984 new legislation authorized Secret Service investigation of credit card, computer, and identity fraud. Six years later, the service received concurrent jurisdiction with the JUSTICE DEPARTMENT in cases of fraud against federally insured financial institutions. In the late 1990s Secret Service agents were assigned to investigate telemarketing fraud and identity theft, while collaborating with agents from the Bureau of Alcohol, Tobacco and Firearms, the DRUG ENFORCEMENT ADMINISTRATION, the FBI, U.S. Postal inspectors, CUSTOMS SERVICE, and the U.S. MARSHALS SERVICE on a Child Abduction and Serial Killer Unit. With creation of the HOMELAND SECURITY DEPARTMENT in 2002, the Secret Service was formally transferred from Treasury to serve the new agency, effective March 1, 2003.

See also: ANARCHISM; TERRORISM.

Securities and Exchange Commission

The "Black Tuesday" stock market crash of October 29, 1929, plunged the United States into its worst depression, prompting demands for federal investigation of the shady deals and stock manipulations that precipitated the disaster. After due consideration, Congress passed the Securities Act of 1933 and the Securities Exchange Act of 1934 to restore investor confidence in U.S. stocks, while providing government oversight of the stock market. The instrument of that supervision was a new Securities and Exchange Commission (SEC), led by Joseph Kennedy (a PROHIBITION-era bootlegger, future ambassador to England, and father of 1960s president John Kennedy).

The SEC's primary mission is to protect investors while maintaining the integrity of the U.S. securities market, while enforcing various federal statutes enacted to proscribe white-collar crimes related to the trade in stocks and bonds. Each year, the SEC initiates hundreds of investigations nationwide, filing an average 400 to 500 civil enforcement actions against com-

panies and individuals who violate the securities laws. Common infractions of those statutes include accounting fraud, insider trading (illegal use of privileged information to personal advantage), and providing false information about stocks and/or the companies that issue them.

The modern SEC consists of five commissioners appointed by the president, supervising four divisions and with a staff of some 3,100 persons. Its four major departments include the Division of Corporation Finance (overseeing corporate disclosure of important information to the investing public), the Division of Investment Management (regulating the $15 trillion investment management industry and administering federal statutes that govern investment companies), the Division of Market Regulation (establishing and maintaining standards for fair, orderly, and efficient markets), and the Division of Enforcement (investigating suspected violations and recommending action where appropriate).

SEC enforcement actions may be filed either in federal courts or internally, before an administrative law judge. In civil actions, the SEC files complaints of specific misconduct and seeks various sanctions or remedial actions, which may include audits, injunctions, or court-ordered repayment of illegal profits (called "disgorgement"). Individuals who violate those orders are then subject to fines and/or imprisonment for contempt of court. In cases in which corporate criminality extends beyond manipulation or misrepresentation of securities, the JUSTICE DEPARTMENT may step in to seek criminal penalties.

sedition

Sedition is broadly defined as subversion of an established government, generally distinguished from treason in that (a) sedition may occur in peacetime, while treason requires active collaboration with "enemies," and (b) under many statutes, sedition requires no overt act beyond expressions of opinion or desire.

America's first Sedition Act, passed by Congress in 1798 with a built-in expiration date of March 3, 1801, penalized "any persons [who] shall unlawfully combine or conspire together, with intent to oppose any measure or measures of the government of the United States . . . or to impede the operation of any law of the United States, or to intimidate or prevent any person holding a place or office in or under the government of the United States, from undertaking, performing or executing his trust or duty." Ignoring the First Amendment to the U.S. Constitution, Congress imposed criminal penalties on "any person [who] shall write, print, utter, or publish . . . any false, scandalous and malicious writing . . . against the government of the United States, or either house of the Congress of the United States, or the President of the United States, with intent to defame the said government . . . or to bring them, or either of them, into contempt or disrepute; or to excite against them . . . the hatred of the good people of the United States, or to excite any unlawful combinations . . . for opposing or resisting any law of the United States, or any act of the President of the United States."

In short, for the prescribed three-year period, it was illegal to criticize the U.S. government. A similar statute was passed in 1861, intended to suppress support for the Confederacy during the Civil War, and yet another in May 1918, after America's entry into World War I. That statute punished "Whoever, when the United States is at war, shall willfully make or convey false reports or false statements with intent to interfere with the operation or success of the military or naval forces of the United States, or to promote the success of its enemies, or shall willfully make or convey false reports, or false statements . . . or incite insubordination, disloyalty, mutiny, or refusal of duty, in the military or naval forces of the United States, or shall willfully obstruct . . . the recruiting or enlistment service of the United States." Those prosecuted and sentenced to long prison terms included conscientious objectors to military service, critics of the wartime draft, and even presidential candidate Norman Thomas, a Socialist who blamed the war on wealthy industrialists.

Since 1919 sedition charges have required at least some vestige of an overt attempt to topple the elected government, and those charges have generally failed before trial juries. So it was in World War II when members of the pro-Nazi Christian Front were indicted for sedition, only to have the charges later dismissed. For decades later, another group of white supremacists faced trial in 1988 for plotting to overthrow the federal government (complete with a published declaration of war) and conspiring to finance their putsch via BANK ROBBERY. The evidence of conspiracy was persuasive, but an all-white jury in Arkansas still acquitted the defendants on all charges.

serial murder

The FBI's *Crime Classification Manual* (1992) defines serial murder as a *series* of three or more homicides committed by the same offender, each at a different time and place, with an emotional "cooling off" period between the crimes. That definition makes no allowance for killers such as John Wayne Gacy or Jeffery Dahmer, who murdered and concealed all their victims in one location, nor would it appear to include those cases like the California "Hillside Strangler" slayings, where two or more killers collaborate in a series of murders. Some critics also question the requirement for three victims to complete a "series," noting that the FBI manual has no place in its taxonomy for killers who are captured after claiming their second victim (but who meet the "serial" profile in all other respects).

A better definition of serial murder—quietly adopted in the 1990s even by some FBI spokesmen—was published by the National Institute of Justice in 1988. It described serial killing as "a series of two or more murders, committed as separate events, usually, but not always, committed by one offender acting alone. The crimes may occur over a period of time ranging from hours to years. Quite often the motive is psychological, and the offender's behavior and the physical evidence observed at the crime scenes will reflect sadistic, sexual overtones."

Regardless of its definition, serial murder ranks among the most difficult crimes for modern detectives to solve. FORENSIC SCIENCE may link an offender to his or her victims, but only after a suspect is known. Psychological PROFILING is often employed as an investigative tool in serial murders, but despite some extravagant claims published by retired profilers, it has yet to produce the arrest of a single serial killer. More often, it seems, the killers are trapped by their own arrogance or carelessness, and their arrest frequently astounds neighbors, who recall the suspect as "a nice, quiet person."

See also: FEDERAL BUREAU OF INVESTIGATION.

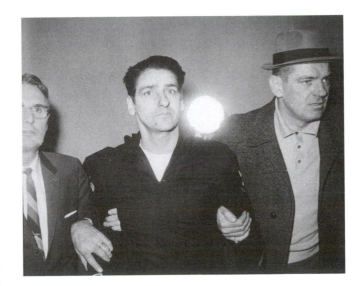

Alleged "Boston Strangler" Albert DeSalvo was posthumously exonerated by DNA evidence. (Author's collection)

Serpico, Frank (b. 1936)

The son of Italian immigrants, born in Brooklyn on April 14, 1936, Francisco Vincent Serpico joined the U.S. Army at age 18 and served in postwar Korea. Upon returning to civilian life, he attended college while working part-time as a private investigator, then joined the NEW YORK CITY POLICE DEPARTMENT in September 1959. From his first day on the beat, in March 1960, Serpico encountered first-hand evidence of the CORRUPTION that pervaded NYPD at all levels. He remained personally untainted, a legendary "clean" cop, while his inquiries and complaints about endemic payoffs fell on deaf ears within the department. Assigned to plainclothes UNDERCOVER WORK, Serpico was shot and nearly killed in a drug sting operation on February 3, 1971, under circumstances suggesting that corrupt NYPD officers may have tried to silence him forever.

Upon recovering, Serpico testified before the KNAPP COMMISSION and collaborated with the *New York Times* on a series of articles detailing police corruption. Author Peter Maas told Serpico's story in a best-selling true-crime book, which was subsequently filmed, earning an Oscar nomination for actor Al Pacino's portrayal of Serpico. The real-life hero remained with NYPD until 1972, when he resigned and went to live in Europe for a decade. In the 1980s he returned to New York State as a born-again Renaissance man, fluent in several languages and deeply immersed in the study of "animal and human behavior, alternative medicine, music, art, literature and philosophy among other disciplines." In 1997 he testified before the New York City Council, concerning proposed legislation to create an Independent Audit Board to review accusations of police corruption and brutality. His latest project, according to his Internet Web site, is "a production company that focuses on projects that progress strong concepts of ethics."

Sessions, William Steele (b. 1930)

Born at Fort Smith, Arkansas, on May 27, 1930, William Sessions was raised in Kansas City and served in the Air Force during 1951–55. He graduated from Baylor Law School (Waco, Texas) in 1958 and spent 11 years in private practice, then joined the U.S. JUSTICE DEPARTMENT's Criminal Division as chief of the Government Operations Section in September 1969. In August 1971 Sessions became the U.S. attorney for western Texas. President Gerald Ford nominated him to the federal bench in 1974, and Sessions served with various federal courts throughout Texas until President Ronald Reagan named him FBI director in July 1987. Sessions was confirmed two months later and took office on November 2, 1987.

Veteran aides recommended that Sessions spend time at FBI headquarters learning his job, but the new director preferred travel—a total of 126 trips with his wife, at Bureau expense, over the next six years. Some of his quirks—like wearing his FBI badge on the lapel of his suit or interrupting Bureau briefings to sing jingles from TV commercials—were curious at best. G-men noted that Sessions "just babbled" when he spoke, stringing non sequiturs together in a form of "gibberish" Bureau insiders soon dubbed "Sessions-speak." Some FBI veterans also thought him weak in dealing with personnel problems, calling him "Con-Sessions" after he settled class-action lawsuits for discrimination filed against the Bureau by black and Hispanic agents.

Other problems were more serious, beginning with Sessions's appropriation of FBI vehicles and resources for private use (including work done on his home, in the tradition of late director J. EDGAR HOOVER). Alice Sessions took advantage of her husband's position, demanding passes for herself to "secure" areas at FBI headquarters, interfering with Bureau security procedures, and so forth. A longtime Sessions aide, Sarah Munford, also basked in the director's reflected power, flashing FBI credentials to beat speeding tickets, violating various state and federal laws with seeming impunity.

Attorney General WILLIAM BARR received two letters complaining of Sessions's abuses in June 1992. One came from Washington journalist Robert Kessler, posing a series of questions about recent incidents; the other, anonymous but purportedly written by an active-duty agent, detailed the director's practice of masking personal travel as "FBI business." Both letters were delivered to the Bureau's Office of Professional Responsibility (OPR), precipitating an investigation that made national headlines in October 1992. A month later, seemingly oblivious, Sessions flew his wife to Atlantic City in the FBI's Sabreliner jet for a ballet performance, with their tickets "comped" by gambling bosses at the Sands Hotel and Casino. President George H. W. Bush, though briefed on the problem with a recommendation that he fire Sessions, did nothing. Barr settled for a stinging memo, penned on January 15, 1993: "Given that you are a former U.S. attorney and federal judge, and that you are currently director of the premier federal law enforcement agency, I must conclude that there is no excuse for your conduct."

Refusing to step down voluntarily, Sessions blamed aides and subordinates for his own misconduct, noting that FBI counsel had "approved" his many trips on the FBI's tab. The OPR published a critical report on Sessions one day before President Bill Clinton was inaugurated, but even then relief took another six months. Clinton fired Sessions on July 19, 1993, and replaced him with Director LOUIS FREEH.

See also: FEDERAL BUREAU OF INVESTIGATION.

sex crimes

Sex crimes rank among the most controversial and misunderstood subjects confronted on a daily basis by modern law enforcement. Before the 1970s, the list included such crimes as forcible rape and pedophilia with CONSENSUAL CRIMES, including voluntary homosexual activity between adults, and in some states even voluntary oral sex within a marriage. Bestiality is also criminalized in most U.S. jurisdictions, although it is no longer a capital offense. (Several defendants in colonial America were executed for having sex with animals, including one Connecticut man who allegedly sired piglets resembling himself!)

Today, U.S. SUPREME COURT rulings have eliminated most legal restrictions on sexual activity between consenting adults, including the sodomy statutes inflicted on gays in some states. Statutory rape—involving sex between an adult and a minor, often with the age disparity specified by law—remains a criminal offense in most states, but its prosecution is highly selective, often dependent on the whims of family members involved in the case. Other sex crimes still on the statute books today include forcible rape (by various names), pedophilia, and incest. A 1972 Supreme Court ruling barred imposition of CAPITAL PUNISHMENT for rape, noting that the penalty had been invoked most often in southern states, against black defendants accused of molesting white women.

Some modern critics question whether the "sex crime" label is appropriate in any case, maintaining that rape and similar offenses are frequently motivated by anger, sadism, a desire for power, and so forth. Their slogan—"Rape is a crime of violence, not sex"—attempts to remove from the victim any undeserved stigma of shame or contribution to the act, but at the same time it appears to miss a vital point.

For many years, psychologists have recognized that a wide range of crimes, from vandalism and burglary to SERIAL MURDER, may be sexually motivated. The offenders in such cases may have no "normal" sexual contact with victims, yet the acts they perform—setting fires, invading homes, even wrecking trains in one bizarre case—provide a twisted form of sexual release which they cannot achieve in any other way. That being true and uncontested in the psychiatric literature, it seems naïve to claim that rape and pedophilia are "never" sex crimes.

Shanahan, Edwin C. (1898–1925)

A Chicago native, born in 1898, Edwin Shanahan served in the U.S. Army during World War I, then joined the FBI in February 1920, assigned to the Chicago field office. On October 11, 1925, while trying to arrest car thief Martin Durkin for DWYER ACT violations, Shanahan was shot and killed, thus becoming the first G-man slain on duty. The resulting manhunt was intense, Director J. EDGAR HOOVER informing his aides, "We've got to get Durkin. If one man from the Bureau is killed, and the killer is permitted to get away, our agents will never be safe. We can't let him get away with it."

The search went national after Durkin shot two Chicago policemen, killing one, then fled the Windy City for parts unknown. FBI agents tracked him to California, then back through Arizona and New Mexico, into Texas. A sheriff stopped Durkin in El Paso, driving a stolen car with a pistol on the seat, but Durkin claimed to be a California lawman. Released to fetch his mythical credentials from a nearby hotel, Durkin fled into the desert with a girlfriend, dumping his car in the wasteland. A farmer gave the couple a ride to Girvin, Texas, and later recalled their plans to catch a train at Alpine. G-men identified the train, bound from San Antonio to St. Louis, and collared Durkin when he disembarked on January 20, 1926.

In custody, Durkin admitted shooting Shanahan, but it was not a federal crime to kill a G-man in those days, so Illinois authorities tried Durkin and sentenced him to 35 years in prison. A federal judge added 15 years for Dwyer Act violations. Durkin was paroled from Illinois in August 1945 and moved to federal prison, where he remained until July 1954. Agent Shanahan's son joined the FBI in 1948 and served for 28 years, the same length of time his father's killer spent in prison.

Shanklin, James Gordon (1910–1988)

Kentucky native James Shanklin was born in 1910 and earned his LL.B. from Vanderbilt University prior to joining the FBI at age 33. In April 1963, after 20 years of service in various posts around the United States, he was appointed agent-in-charge of the Bureau's Dallas field office. Seven months later, Shanklin found himself caught up in the chaos surrounding President John Kennedy's ASSASSINATION—and critics maintain that he played a key role in an FBI cover-up of evidence.

The trouble began on November 1, when Agent James Hosty, Jr. drove to nearby Irving, Texas, seeking one Lee Harvey Oswald. Oswald had defected from the United States to Soviet Russia in 1960, renouncing his citizenship, then returned to America in 1963 with a Russian wife (the daughter of a KGB officer), and settled in New Orleans, where he engaged in agitation for the pro-Castro Fair Play for Cuba Committee. The New Orleans FBI notified Dallas when Oswald moved to Irving, but Hosty came too late to Oswald's last known address. Landlady Ruth Paine and Oswald's wife, Marina, informed Hosty that Lee had found work in Dallas. Neither knew the address of his rooming house, but they promised to get it. When Hosty called back on November 5, Paine had yet to obtain the address.

Sometime within the next three days—published accounts and memories vary—an agitated man entered the Dallas FBI office, demanding to speak with Hosty. Secretary Nanny Fenner reported that Hosty was out, whereupon the visitor left a note for Hosty on her desk. Fenner read the two-paragraph, handwritten message, signed "Lee Harvey Oswald." Later, she would recall only a threat to Hosty, warning him that if he bothered Marina Oswald again, husband Lee would "either blow up the Dallas Police Department or the FBI office." Hosty received the note that afternoon, later recalling that "it didn't appear to be of any serious import." Elaborating, he explained, "It appeared to be an innocuous type of complaint. . . . I looked at it. It didn't seem to have any need for action at that time, so I put it in my workbox."

Approximately two weeks later, on November 22, President Kennedy was shot and killed while riding in a motorcade through downtown Dallas. At 3:00 P.M., Agent Shanklin telephoned Washington and informed Director J. EDGAR HOOVER that Lee Oswald had been jailed, not for killing Kennedy, but for the murder of a Dallas policeman. Agent Hosty, meanwhile, sat in on Oswald's first police interrogation, afterward telling Lt. Jack Revill, "We knew that Lee Harvey Oswald was capable of assassinating the president of the United States, but we didn't dream he would do it." Returning to the FBI office from police headquarters, Hosty found Shanklin waiting with the Oswald note, retrieved from Hosty's desk. Shanklin demanded a full report of the events in writing, before Hosty left for the day.

At 3:15 A.M. on November 24, Shanklin woke Hoover to report an anonymous phone call, received by the Dallas field office. The caller had warned that Oswald would be murdered later that day, during his transfer from DPD headquarters to a secret lockup elsewhere. On Hoover's orders, Shanklin next alerted Dallas police chief Jesse Curry, learning that police had received the same warning. Curry expressed no concern, assuring Shanklin that Oswald would be safe during his transfer—yet small-time gangster Jack Ruby managed to enter the headquarters basement and shoot Oswald at 12:21 P.M. Oswald died at Parkland Hospital some 90 minutes later.

Shortly after Oswald's death, Shanklin confronted Hosty once again and ordered him to destroy the Oswald note. When Hosty began to shred it in his presence, Shanklin said, "No, get it out of here. I don't even want it in this office. Get rid of it." Hosty subsequently flushed it down the men's room toilet, while Hoover and company concealed the entire incident from President Lyndon Johnson and the Warren Commission. Assistant FBI director WILLIAM SULLIVAN later told author Curt Gentry, "Hoover ordered the destruction of the note. I can't prove this, but I have no doubts about it." Shanklin personally denied any knowledge

of the Oswald note until 1975. Four years later, after interviewing both agents, the House Select Committee on Assassinations "regarded the incident of the note as a serious impeachment of Shanklin's and Hosty's credibility." Shanklin died in 1988.

See also: FEDERAL BUREAU OF INVESTIGATION.

sheriffs

Each state in the U.S. is subdivided into smaller governmental units commonly known as counties (or "boroughs" in Alaska, "parishes" in Louisiana). Nationwide, a total of 3,086 counties exist, for an average of 62 per state. In most of those counties—except where voters have elected to merge county and city governments, as in Las Vegas, Nevada, and Nashville, Tennessee—the principal law enforcement officer is known as a sheriff. That term derives from the Old English "shire reeve," the chief law-enforcer in old-time British counties.

Most U.S. sheriffs are elected, making their jobs both legal and political. In order to retain his office, an elected sheriff must find ways to please the very voters he polices—a task made doubly difficult in times past, when many sheriffs doubled as their county's tax collector. While duties may vary by jurisdiction, most sheriffs patrol a county at large (assisted by deputies), while leaving urban problems to the police departments maintained by various incorporated towns and cities. They also typically maintain the county jail, provide security in county courts, and otherwise comport themselves as normal peace officers.

Town-county rivalries are not uncommon in police work, and they may become extremely bitter. For many years, relations between the LOS ANGELES POLICE DEPARTMENT and the LOS ANGELES COUNTY SHERIFF'S DEPARTMENT were so strained that the agencies refused to communicate. FBI agents assigned to investigate local BANK ROBBERIES created two separate squads, one to deal with each force and thus avoid accusations of "taking sides." Likewise, the 1960s found JAMES CLARK (the staunchly segregationist sheriff of Dallas County, Alabama) constantly embroiled in conflict with Selma police chief Wilson Baker over tactics for handling civil rights demonstrations. However, few conflicts between county and city police degenerate to the level seen in Tombstone, Arizona, during 1881, when feuding between the EARP BROTHERS and outlaws allied with Sheriff JOHN BEHAN culminated in the infamous O.K. CORRAL GUNFIGHT.

Siringo, Charles Angelo (1855–1928)

Details are sparse concerning the early life of Texas native Charles Siringo. Born in 1855, he began work as a cowboy around age 13, and reportedly joined in the search for New Mexico gunman Billy the Kid four years later. Siringo failed to bag his man that time, leaving the posse after he lost most of his money gambling, and subsequently spent two years as a grocer in Kansas City. He joined the Pinkerton Detective Agency soon after the HAYMARKET BOMBING of 1886, lending a hand to the investigation and arrest of local anarchists (which most historians now regard as a FRAME-UP of innocent men).

Buoyed by that "success," Siringo spent the next 21 years on ALLAN J. PINKERTON's payroll, pursuing a rogue's gallery of malefactors that ranged from corrupt union leaders to the roving bandits of Butch Cassidy's "Wild Bunch." In 1887, posing as a fugitive from murder charges, Siringo uncovered a plot by Colorado insurgents to murder three Pagosa Springs commissioners, resulting in 16 indictments. Five years later, he infiltrated a miner's union at Coeur d'Alene, Idaho, collecting evidence of endemic CORRUPTION that sent 18 suspects to prison. In Nebraska he captured Ernest Bush, a teenage serial killer-for-profit. Siringo subsequently pursued Butch Cassidy's gang over some 25,000 miles or rugged territory, but the gang's leaders eluded him and fled to South America.

Siringo left the Pinkerton Agency in 1907, retiring to a ranch in New Mexico, but he soon tired of daily chores and joined the Chicago-based WILLIAM J. BURNS Detective Agency. After six years with Burns, Siringo got bored again, and enlisted with the New Mexico Rangers. Around the same time, he published his memoirs, *Cowboy Detective* (1912), which proved highly critical of Pinkerton activities. Pinkerton lawyers sought and secured deletions from the manuscript, enraging Siringo to the point that he self-published a second book in 1915, titled *Two Evil Isms: Pinkertonism and Anarchism*. Siringo died in Hollywood, California, on October 19, 1928. Four decades later, he was featured briefly in a film—*Butch Cassidy and the Sundance Kid*—which showed him only from a distance, face obscured, as he had led much of his life.

See also: ANARCHISM.

skyjacking

Widely regarded as a modern crime, committed principally by terrorists, the hijacking of aircraft—later dubbed "skyjacking"—actually dates from February 1931. The first U.S. incident was recorded in November 1958, when Cuban rebels diverted an airliner from Miami to Havana. The first American plane seized by skyjackers was rerouted to Cuba by gunman Antulio Ramirez Ortiz on May 1, 1961. A federal grand jury indicted Ramirez in August 1961, but it took over a decade for FBI agents to catch him, finally tracing him to Miami in November 1975.

The "golden age" of skyjacking occurred during 1968–79, with 370 incidents reported worldwide for an average of one seizure every 12 days. The United States suffered 144 skyjackings during that era, with 78 aircraft diverted to Cuba and 66 held hostage inside the country. A federal statute on aircraft piracy gave the FBI primary jurisdiction over skyjackings, but the Bureau's performance was mixed: Agents arrested 27 skyjackers during the 12 years in questions, while 69 escaped and remain fugitives. (The other 48 either surrendered voluntarily or were captured by local police.) In cases where G-men employed DEADLY FORCE, they left nine persons dead and seven wounded. Those killed included a crewman and three innocent passengers; the injured included two crew members and an FBI agent.

Skyjacking incidents dropped off dramatically in the 1980s, as new security measures made smuggling of weapons aboard commercial aircraft more difficult. Still, loopholes in security remained, and one of them—a regulation permitting small knives aboard U.S. flights—backfired catastrophically on September 11, 2001. That morning, 19 Muslim extremists boarded four planes lifting off from East Coast airports for various destinations. Armed only with simple box cutters, the flight-trained terrorists killed or overpowered crew members and seized control of the jets. Two subsequently crashed into New York City's World Trade Center, claiming more than 3,000 lives, while a third plunged into the Pentagon and killed 189 persons. The fourth flight, presumably intended for another Washington target, crashed in Pennsylvania with loss of all 44 persons aboard.

See also: FEDERAL BUREAU OF INVESTIGATION; TERRORISM.

Slaughter, John Horton (1841–1922)

A Louisiana native, born in Sabine Parish on October 2, 1841, John Slaughter was barely three months old when his family moved to the Republic of Texas and founded a cattle ranch. During the Civil War, Slaughter joined the TEXAS RANGERS as an Indian fighter and continued in that role sporadically until 1878, when he moved to Arizona. During the Lincoln County War, while employed by legendary cattleman John Chisum, Slaughter was briefly jailed for killing a rustler, one Barney Gallagher, but all charges were subsequently dismissed. Two years later, Slaughter led a raid into Mexico to retrieve stolen livestock, and fought a pitched battle with Mexican bandits.

Cochise County voters chose Slaughter as their sheriff in 1886, and his tenure included several gunfights with local outlaws, as well as several interrupted LYNCHINGS.

Slaughter retired as sheriff in 1890, to operate a cattle ranch, though he received a deputy sheriff's commission in 1895 and kept it until his death. Marginal law enforcement duties did not prevent Slaughter's election to the territorial legislature in 1906, but he left politics after one term to operate a pair of butcher shops in Bisbee. At the same time, Slaughter dabbled in banking and devoted much of his free time to poker. He died at home on February 15, 1922.

See also: SHERIFFS.

slave patrols

Before the Civil War, civilian groups were established in all slaveholding states, to patrol by night and intercept any slaves found wandering at large without their masters. Some jurisdictions mandated participation in the patrols by all white male adults, on a rotating basis, so that all shared the burden of defending Dixie's slave-based economy. Slave patrols were generally authorized to arrest and interrogate (i.e., torture) any slave found abroad after nightfall, and to invade private property where necessary to perform their duty of recapturing supposed runaways. In jurisdictions where professional slave patrols were employed, their members were often crude racists of violent disposition, described by one observer as "the worst men above ground." Their night-riding regimen and brutal tactics survived the war and the Thirteenth Amendment's ban on slavery, revived during the Reconstruction era by the KU KLUX KLAN.

Smith, Stephen Richard

Stephen Smith was a study in contradictions, a gung-ho policeman who loved guns but seemingly hated authority—at least when he was called upon to follow regulations. In his three and a half years with the San Antonio (Texas) Police Department, Smith compiled seven complaints of EXCESSIVE FORCE, but the charges brought only official wrist-slaps. In fact, he was something of a hero on the force, having killed an armed robber in 1982, but officially sanctioned violence was only the tip of the iceberg with Smith.

In December 1982 a part-time handyman named Terrell Folsom was shot and killed by persons unknown, allegedly while breaking into a parked car, and Folsom's mother heard that Smith had bragged of the murder to friends. She informed police, but was unsatisfied with their response. "They swept it under the carpet," she later complained. "They covered it up, is what they did."

Smith remained on the street, patrolling a tough neighborhood and dispensing rough justice as he saw fit. Eugene Sibrian was trying to break up a fight between his two sons when Smith arrived on the scene. "He was

angry, real angry," Sibrian recalled. "He came to me and said, 'I told you to get lost.' He walked from the porch to the fence and grabbed me from the shoulders and threw me against the fence." Sibrian filed a brutality complaint, and his home soon came under sniper fire, a bullet striking son Michael Sibrian in the head and leaving him partially paralyzed. Eugene suspected Smith, but could not prove his case.

Another local resident who earned Smith's wrath was Edward de la Garza, an employee of the San Antonio Power Company who reported Smith's wife for sleeping on the job. A short time later, de la Garza's home was peppered with gunfire, and while no one was injured in that attack, others were not so lucky. Adolfo Queyar was killed by a sniper's bullet during a party at his home, and Clarence Kane, Jr.—a bartender at Smith's favorite hangout—was fatally wounded on the street, on March 28, 1985. A year later, in March 1986, Smith faced brutality charges for beating a shoplifting suspect and brawling with bystanders who tried to intervene. Suspended from duty after his indictment, Smith raged at his superiors for their "lack of support" and planned a campaign of retaliatory mayhem. Deputy Chief Robert Heuck's home was sprayed with gunfire in 1983, while a firebomb damaged Chief Heuck's residence in 1985. Anonymous letters were also mailed to the press and various public officials, accusing department leaders of child molestation and other crimes.

Smith quarreled with his wife on August 17, 1986, and she sought help from a mutual friend, Patrolman Farrell Tucker. Smith's wife informed Tucker that Smith planned to kill Bexar County's district attorney, along with several high-ranking members of the San Antonio PD. Next morning, Tucker reported those threats to his superiors and agreed to wear a microphone to his next meeting with Smith. In fact, the recorder malfunctioned, but it hardly mattered. While talking in Smith's car, Smith drew a pistol and threatened Tucker's life, resulting in a struggle wherein Smith was shot and killed. Police initially doubted Tucker's story—he had lied to superiors about a previous shooting, and a psychiatrist had recommended his dismissal—but Smith's death was finally logged as self-defense. A search of Smith's home revealed 100,000 rounds of ammunition and 29 guns, including a rifle linked to the Queyar and Kane homicides.

Smith, Thomas J. (1830–1870)

A native of New York City, Thomas Smith was born in 1830. Some reports claim that he joined the NEW YORK CITY POLICE DEPARTMENT, but no records of that service remain. By age 24, he had traveled westward, working for the Union Pacific Railroad in Nebraska and Wyoming. In 1868 he led a riot in Bear River City,

Wyoming, to liberate a friend unjustly held in jail, and Smith was badly wounded in the melee. That experience, perhaps ironically, persuaded him to quit his railroad job and become a peace officer, serving in several "end-of-the-track" railroad towns before his June 1870 appointment as chief of police in Abilene, Kansas.

Smith lasted only four months in that post, before he joined in the pursuit of fugitive John Shea, charged with murder in the shooting of a neighbor. Smith and Deputy J. H. McConnell confronted Shea and a friend, Moses Miles, at Shea's farm outside Abilene on November 2, 1870. As Smith read the warrant for Shea's arrest, Shea drew a gun and shot him in the chest. Smith returned fire, then grappled with Shea while Miles shot it out with Deputy McConnell, forcing McConnell to flee. Though wounded himself, Miles then grabbed an axe and finished Smith with hacking blows to the neck.

Smith, Tom

Little is known of Tom Smith's early life, besides the fact that he was born in Texas. As an adult, he served as a peace officer in both Texas and Oklahoma, once holding a commission as a deputy U.S. marshal, but Smith eventually retired his badge to serve as a mercenary RANGE DETECTIVE for the Wyoming Stock Grower's Association. In that capacity, he killed an unknown number of alleged rustlers, and was once indicted for murder (saved from trial by the association's powerful political connections).

In early 1892, as Wyoming cattle barons braced themselves for the impending Johnson County War, Smith was dispatched to Texas on a search for gunmen, offering a salary of five dollars per day, plus $50 for each enemy killed and a $3,000 insurance policy. Smith recruited 26 Texans on those terms, and subsequently led them into battle, spurred by visions of a $100,000 "extermination fund" offered for the deaths of 70 local homesteaders. On April 9, 1892, Smith's "Regulators" fought a pitched battle with settlers at the KC Ranch, where they were defeated and most of Smith's men were arrested. Authorities released Smith in summer 1893, and he returned to Texas, where he quarreled with a black man on the Gainesville train and died in an exchange of pistol fire.

Smith, William French (1917–1990)

A native of Wilton, New Hampshire, born August 26, 1917, William Smith graduated summa cum laude from the University of California at Los Angeles in 1939. He earned an LL.B. from Harvard Law School three years later, followed by service as a lieutenant in the U.S. Naval Reserve (1942–46). In 1946 he joined an

L.A. law firm that counted actor Ronald Reagan among its wealthiest clients. During Reagan's 1980 presidential campaign, Smith introduced Reagan to William Donovan, a New Jersey contractor with ties to ORGANIZED CRIME who gave the campaign $200,000 and thus secured nomination as secretary of labor. Smith, in turn, was rewarded in January 1981 with appointment as attorney general.

Reagan's emotional "law-and-order" campaign included vows to "unleash" the FBI and permit unfettered DOMESTIC SURVEILLANCE of alleged "subversive" elements in the United States. To that end, in March 1983 Smith rescinded the guidelines earlier established by Attorney General EDWARD LEVI, requiring that "national security" investigations of groups or individuals should require some evidence of criminal activity and furthermore must be reviewed by the attorney general "at least annually," with a verdict "in writing" as to whether or not the investigation should continue. Smith scrapped those rules across the board, permitting the FBI to initiate "domestic security/terrorism" probes whenever "facts or circumstances reasonably indicate that two or more persons are engaged in an enterprise [to further] political or social goals wholly or in part through activities that involve force or violence and a violation of the criminal law of the United States." Surveillance was thus extended to those who merely "advocate criminal activity or indicate an apparent intent to engage in crime," while oversight by the attorney general was henceforth purely discretionary.

In practice, Smith's guidelines revived the essence of President Richard Nixon's campaigns against political "enemies," and many of those slated for surveillance were critics of Reagan's illegal activities in Central America (including the Iran-contra scandal). While groups such as the Committee in Solidarity with the People of El Salvador and various Puerto Rican nationalist organizations were subjected to harassment indistinguishable from the FBI's COINTELPRO campaigns of 1956–71, anti-abortion terrorists were completely ignored, based on pronouncements from Bureau headquarters that their bombings and murders "do not constitute domestic terrorism."

On other fronts, Smith moved to eliminate the Ethics in Government Act, the Foreign Corrupt Practices Act and major portions of the Freedom of Information Act. He echoed Reagan by proclaiming a "vigorous" war on crime and DRUGS, but simultaneously slashed the budgets of various federal law enforcement agencies and reshuffled FBI priorities to emphasize "violent crime" over organized crime. Critics ranging from the U.S. COAST GUARD to the AMERICAN CIVIL LIBERTIES UNION denounced the Reagan-Smith crime war as "fraudulent," noting the president's enduring ties to leaders of the corrupt Teamsters' Union, but Smith was unfazed by such criticism. In January 1982, ignoring the protests of FBI director WILLIAM WEBSTER, Smith ordered the Bureau to share jurisdiction in narcotics cases with the DRUG ENFORCEMENT ADMINISTRATION. Later, in June 1984, he inaugurated the Drug Demand Reduction Program in support of First Lady Nancy Reagan's wholly ineffective "Just Say No" campaign. (At the same time, White House aides and leaders of the "contra" terrorist organization were smuggling cocaine into the U.S. and using the proceeds to finance Reagan's illegal proxy war in Nicaragua.) Poor health compelled Smith's resignation on February 25, 1985, whereupon he was replaced by EDWIN MEESE III. Smith died on October 29, 1990.

See also: FEDERAL BUREAU OF INVESTIGATION; TERRORISM.

Smith Act

The Alien Registration Act, most commonly known by the name of Virginia congressman Howard Smith (who wrote its SEDITION provisions), was enacted by Congress on June 28, 1940. It provided a maximum five-year prison term (later increased to 20 years) for anyone who "knowingly or willfully advocates, abets, advises or teaches the duty, necessity, desirability or propriety of violently overthrowing" the U.S. government or the government of any particular state. Although regarded by FBI leaders as a tool for jailing Communists and other leftists, the law was initially used against fascists and Nazi sympathizers during World War II. The first group of 26 defendants, indicted in July 1942, were acquitted when the JUSTICE DEPARTMENT failed to prove that they had plotted revolution. A second batch of 30 defendants was indicted in 1944, but charges were dropped after a chaotic trial that climaxed with the judge's death.

Following V-J Day and onset of the cold war, FBI director J. EDGAR HOOVER prepared a 1,350-page history of the Communist Party (with 546 "exhibits"), presented to Attorney General TOM CLARK in an effort to spur Smith Act prosecution of party leaders. At the same time, in February 1948, the House Committee on Un-American Activities contacted Clark, demanding to know why no indictments had yet been filed under the law. A federal grand jury in New York subsequently indicted 12 members of the party's national board on June 29, 1948, but Clark sealed the indictments for a month and announced them on July 20, after five of the 12 were arrested in New York City. Hoover freely admitted that the arrests were "a political move . . . timed to break just before the [Henry] Wallace for President convention in Philadelphia," and complained that more Reds had not been charged.

Prosecution of defendant William Foster was deferred due to illness, while the other 11 defendants faced trial in New York on January 17, 1949. Key prosecution witnesses were professional ex-Communist Louis Budenz and Herbert Philbrick, an FBI INFORMANT who broke cover at the trial to testify against his former comrades. All defendants were convicted on October 14, with 10 receiving the maximum sentence from Judge Harold Medina. (The lone exception was a decorated war veteran whose medals won him a reduced sentence.) Their convictions (and the Smith Act's dubious constitutionality) were upheld by the U.S. SUPREME COURT in 1951.

That finding on appeal was Hoover's signal to begin a round of "second echelon" roundups and prosecutions against lower-ranking party officers. Over the next three years 126 Communist Party members were indicted for Smith Act violations, with 93 convicted at trial. Hoover's enthusiasm for the roundups paled in 1954, when he realized that continued exposure of hired informants in court jeopardized "the highly essential intelligence coverage which this Bureau must maintain in the internal security field." Effectively choosing secrecy over prosecution of alleged subversives, Hoover recommended that future prosecutions be limited to prominent party leaders.

The Supreme Court changed its view on Smith Act prosecutions in October 1955, accepting one of the "second echelon" cases for review on a writ of certiorari. The final decision in 1957, effectively overturning all but the original dozen convictions, held that mere advocacy of revolution without supporting action should not be prosecuted. A Justice Department ruling, dated March 15, 1956, agreed that any future indictments must include "an actual plan for violent revolution" instead of mere theory. No further Smith Act charges were filed, though the law remains in effect and is used by G-men to justify DOMESTIC SURVEILLANCE in some cases. An attempt to prosecute neo-Nazi activists for sedition in April 1988 resulted in the acquittal of all defendants.

See also: FEDERAL BUREAU OF INVESTIGATION.

smuggling

Smuggling—the illegal traffic items banned by law or otherwise subjected to statutory controls—has been a mainstay of America's "underground economy" from the earliest days. In colonial times, merchants engaged in wholesale smuggling of various items to avoid taxation from Britain, while others dealt freely in loot transported by Caribbean pirates. PROHIBITION brought new refinement to smuggling during 1920–33, as bootleggers imported banned liquor along every U.S. coastline and both international borders. As in the past, that illicit traffic magnified CORRUPTION among police officers and CUSTOMS SERVICE agents, while enriching the smugglers and laying the groundwork for modern ORGANIZED CRIME. More recently, smuggling has thrived in the United States both internally (as with stolen cars and untaxed cigarettes transported between states) and across international borders (with commodities including DRUGS, weapons, and millions of illegal immigrants). While a new wave of concern with homeland security threatened to close America's borders after the terrorist attacks of September 11, 2001, little has been accomplished to stem the tide of foreign contraband and undocumented aliens. Frustration with that failure has inspired organizations such as 2005's "Minutemen" to patrol the Mexican border in search of trespassers.

See also: HOMELAND SECURITY DEPARTMENT.

Society of Former Special Agents of the FBI

Created in June 1937 as a social organization for retired G-men, the Society of Former Special Agents of the FBI (SFSA) committed an immediate faux pas by choosing early Bureau chief A. BRUCE BIELASKI as its first president. Stung by the perceived insult, Director J. EDGAR HOOVER harbored a silent grudge against the society for three decades, refusing to address its annual conventions until 1968, despite yearly invitations to speak.

The SFSA's original constitution offered membership to "men of good moral character . . . who served with due fidelity their oaths of office and with loyalty to the service and to their fellow agents." Retired female agents were also (theoretically) eligible to join, but Hoover hired none during his administration of the Bureau (1924–72), and there appears to be no record of a woman joining the society before his death.

The Bielaski indiscretion was not Hoover's only quarrel with the SFSA. He also objected to admission of retired G-men who left the Bureau under a cloud of his personal disfavor, but that stumbling block was removed by institution of a "double blackball" system, wherein candidates for membership were screened both by the SFSA's members and by FBI headquarters, to weed out targets of Hoover's malice.

Hoover's final qualm—that ex-agents used their former FBI affiliation to launch lucrative second careers—was never resolved. Indeed, a major function of the SFSA has always been easing its members into profitable nonretirement. *The Grapevine,* a society newsletter published since April 1938, proudly reported in its issue of July 18, 1969, that the society had lately helped 39 members find jobs with an average yearly income of $19,750. Others fared better still, including the seven ex-agents found in Congress during 1970 (with Senator Thomas Dodd the best known). Elsewhere, the FBI was well represented in the security and "labor relations" departments of various banks, heavy industry, casinos, the Mormon church, and on the staff of reclusive billionaire Howard Hughes. President Richard Nixon chose two former G-men, Robert

Lee and Randolph Thrower, to head the Federal Communications Commission and the INTERNAL REVENUE SERVICE, investigating and harassing Nixon's many "enemies." Lloyd Wright, a former agent turned Los Angeles attorney, also counted Nixon among his clients. George Wackenhut spent only three years in the FBI before resigning to create his own security team, hired by Florida governor Claude Kirk in the 1960s as what some critics called "a private Gestapo." Another security firm led by ex-FBI agents, Dale Simpson & Associates of Dallas, served various major oil companies. One of their agents, Vincent Gillen, was caught spying on consumer advocate Ralph Nader in 1966.

Despite the long cold-shoulder treatment from FBI headquarters, the SFSA still revered Hoover and all he stood for. Members sold thousands of Hoover's ghost-written books, along with miniature bronze busts of the director. In 1955 a group of ex-agents created the private American Security Council, using "the largest private files on Communism in the country" to screen employees for such mega-clients as Sears Roebuck and General Electric. The SFSA attacked Hoover's critics wherever they appeared, and member Norman Ollestad was expelled in 1967 for publishing a book that criticized the FBI. As late as October 1992, when the society's headquarters moved from New York City to Quantico, Virginia, (home of the FBI Academy), spokesmen still objected to media descriptions of the "old" vs. "new" FBI, suggesting that for some loyal veterans at least, the Bureau is incapable of change.

See also: FEDERAL BUREAU OF INVESTIGATION.

Sorola, Manuel (1880–1957)

A Texas native, born near San Antonio on December 4, 1880, Manuel Sorola studied at Alamo Business College before pursuing diverse careers as a bookkeeper, an insurance agent, and a private investigator for various railroads throughout the Southwest. He joined the FBI as a "special employee" on April 27, 1916, valued for his fluency in Spanish and his knowledge of Mexican politics at a time when guerrilla fighters led by Pancho Villa staged sporadic raids across the U.S. border. Sorola was elevated to full agent's status on July 1, 1922, thereafter serving with field offices in El Paso, Los Angeles, New Orleans, Oklahoma City, Phoenix, and San Antonio. He was placed on "limited duty" in 1938, but continued to serve as a Bureau liaison to the LOS ANGELES POLICE DEPARTMENT until his retirement on January 31, 1949. Sorola died on November 29, 1957.

See also: FEDERAL BUREAU OF INVESTIGATION.

South Carolina Highway Patrol

The South Carolina Highway Patrol was created in 1930 to enforce a battery of new legislation regulating use of automobiles. The original force consisted of one captain, one assistant captain, seven lieutenants, 49 patrolmen, and 11 license inspectors. Patrolmen received no formal training until 1932, when the first three-month course convened at Fort Jackson, a U.S. Army base. The SCHP grew steadily thereafter, gaining a fingerprint expert in 1934 and boasting a total of 90 employees three years later.

Like most other American police agencies, the SCHP faced a critical manpower shortage during World War II, while gasoline rationing sharply restricted patrols. The postwar era witnessed a rapid increase in the number of registered motor vehicles, with a corresponding rise in traffic accidents. Expanding to police a new generation of drivers, the SCHP saw its training program streamlined to eight weeks, while patrol cars were equipped with two-way radios in 1947. In 1953 it was severed from the state highway department to become a separate division of state government.

The SCHP's duties are not limited to traffic enforcement. Since 1972 all new recruits have trained at the South Carolina Criminal Justice Academy, completing a 20-week course. The first eight female SCHP officers were trained and placed on patrol in 1977. A new Department of Public Safety was created in 1993, with the SCHP attached "to promote efficiency and cost effectiveness." At press time for this volume the SCHP employed more than 900 officers, including an Aggressive Criminal Enforcement (ACE) Team assigned to drug interdiction and capture of felony suspects. The department's Multidisciplinary Accident Investigation Team (MAIT) specializes in forensics, vehicle dynamics, and highway engineering to determine causes and responsibility in complex accidents.

South Carolina State Law Enforcement Division (SLED)

SLED is the primary investigative arm of South Carolina's state government, conducting various investigations on behalf of the governor and state attorney general, while providing technical assistance on request to local police. It is not a first-response agency, and generally enters local cases only when its help is sought or when the governor dictates.

One such case, in 1968, was the infamous ORANGE-BURG MASSACRE, wherein members of the SOUTH CAROLINA HIGHWAY PATROL shot 30 unarmed civil rights demonstrators, killing two, then claimed the shooting was done in response to sniper fire. Investigative reporters Jack Nelson and Jack Bass, in their survey of that incident (1970), contend that SLED officers collaborated with FBI agents to misrepresent evidence from the crime scene, supporting a spurious tale of gunshots fired in self-defense when no proof of any sniper fire existed. At the trial of several officers involved in the shooting, where

all were acquitted by white jurors, FBI agents publicly contradicted one another concerning the "evidence" of scattered bullet holes found in a nearby building, which could never be traced to a sniper's weapon nor even reliably dated to match the February 1968 incident.

See also: FEDERAL BUREAU OF INVESTIGATION.

South Dakota Highway Patrol

In 1935 increasing motor vehicle traffic prompted South Dakota governor Tom Berry to create a 10-man "Courtesy Patrol" within the state's Department of Justice. Affectionately dubbed "knights of the road," those purple-coated officers were issued patrol cars (dubbed "milk wagons") with tow chains, first-aid kits, and cans of gasoline to assist motorists on some 6,000 miles of paved and gravel highways. When state legislators abolished the Department of Justice in 1937, the Courtesy Patrol dissolved and was replaced by a new Motor Patrol, attached to the state's Highway Department. Walter Goetz, chief of the Aberdeen Police Department, won appointment as the new unit's first superintendent and served until 1956.

Under Goetz, the Motor Patrol gradually increased from eight to 40 officers, adding two-way radios to its patrol cars in 1948. Despite manpower shortages incurred during World War II, the department maintained its patrols and performed disaster-relief duties through a series of blizzards and floods in 1949–52. Emphasis shifted to accident prevention in 1953, as South Dakota issued its first formal drivers' licenses and 179 motorists died in highway collisions. Three years later, ex-FBI agent Jasper Kibbe replaced Chief Goetz as head of the patrol. While Kibbe's tenure was brief (1956–59), he increased the SDHP's patrol force to 52 officers.

Through the 1960s, the SDHP performed parallel functions including traffic patrol, motor carrier enforcement, disaster relief, and riot control during various strikes. Superintendent Cullen With (1961–65) created the ranks of sergeant and lieutenant, approved an operations manual, and launched the SDHP's first firearms qualification program. State legislators inaugurated a new Motor Vehicle Inspection Program in 1967, while the patrol continued service during floods, blizzards, and protest demonstrations by the American Indian Movement (the latter prompting creation of an Initial Response Unit—now called the ALPHA TEAM—in 1974). Budget cuts in the 1970s reduced the SDHP to 142 sworn officers, but the force has rebounded slightly since then, including 157 officers at press time for this volume.

Southern Conference on Bombing

The U.S. SUPREME COURT's school desegregation orders of 1954–55 produced a wave of racist TERRORISM in the South unprecedented since the days of Reconstruction following the Civil War. Between January 1957 and May 1958 a series of 46 bombings struck various southern targets, including schools, churches, synagogues, and homes owned by African Americans. Most such crimes were traceable to factions of the KU KLUX KLAN or other white-supremacist groups, but the rare cases of arrest usually led to acquittals by all-white juries.

The Southern Conference on Bombing (SCB) was founded in response to those crimes, on May 3, 1958. Police officials from 21 southern cities gathered in Jacksonville, Florida, at the invitation of Mayor Haydon Burns, to compile dossiers on likely bombing suspects and offer rewards that finally totaled $55,700 for information leading to arrests. The FBI refused to participate, but a former G-man employed by the Anti-Defamation League of B'nai B'rith, Milton Ellerin, compiled a list of prominent racists likely to plot terrorist bombings. Conference participant EUGENE "BULL" CONNOR—the Klan-allied public safety commissioner of Birmingham, Alabama, whose police had failed to solve 30-odd bombings since 1949—was embarrassed to find his own name on the list.

Agents of the SCB reportedly infiltrated several racist groups, but no arrests resulted from their efforts. Indeed, while some participants were doubtless sincere in their wish to halt the bombings, the inclusion of Klan-friendly members like Connor and Jacksonville's Mayor Burns (who favored Klansmen with parade permits while jailing black demonstrators) prompted suggestions that the SCB may have been created as a publicity gesture, rather than a serious attempt to curb racist terrorism. The group passed from existence without fanfare, sometime in late 1958 or early 1959.

See also: BOMBING AND BOMB SQUADS; FEDERAL BUREAU OF INVESTIGATION.

Special Unit Senator

Special Unit Senator was a task force created within the LOS ANGELES POLICE DEPARTMENT in June 1968 to investigate all aspects of Senator ROBERT KENNEDY'S ASSASSINATION. Directed by Chief of Detectives Robert Houghton, SUS was publicly described as an "independent" task force, although its 66 sworn and civilian personnel were all drawn from LAPD. Collaborating with the FBI and U.S. JUSTICE DEPARTMENT, as well as the SECRET SERVICE and the LOS ANGELES COUNTY SHERIFF'S DEPARTMENT, Special Unit Senator concluded that Kennedy was killed by lone gunman Sirhan Sirhan, acting without accomplices. The unit disbanded in July 1969, but scrutiny of its work and findings continues to the present day, as critics question many crucial points of evidence. Conspiracists note major discrepancies in eyewitness testimony, the number of bullets retrieved from the crime scene, and the fact that records subsequently disclosed indicate that LAPD matched bullets from the assassination to a pistol Sirhan never owned. That controversy was only exacerbated in 1971, when Chief Houghton's memoir of the case revealed that one leading SUS detective had also been a part-time employee of the Central Intelligence Agency.

See also: FEDERAL BUREAU OF INVESTIGATION.

Speed, James (1812–1887)

Born in Louisville, Kentucky, on March 11, 1812, James Speed graduated from St. Joseph's College, then studied law at Transylvania University and won admittance to the Kentucky bar in 1833. After 13 years of private practice, he served two terms in the state legislature (1847, 1861–63). President Abraham Lincoln named Speed U.S. attorney general in December 1864, and Speed held that post under successor Andrew Johnson until July 1866. He then returned to private practice in Kentucky, and failed to capture the Republican vice presidential nomination in 1868. His congressional campaign in 1870 was likewise unsuccessful. Speed died in Louisville on June 25, 1887.

Attorney General James Speed (Author's collection)

Attorney General Henry Stanbery (Author's collection)

Stanbery, Henry (1803–1881)

Born in New York City on February 20, 1803, Henry Stanbery moved to Ohio with his family at age 11. He graduated from Pennsylvania's Washington College in 1819, then studied law privately before winning admittance to the Ohio state bar in 1824. Ohio's legislature chose him as the state's first attorney general in 1846, a post he held until 1851. President Andrew Johnson named Stanbery U.S. attorney general in July 1866, but he resigned in May 1868 to defend Johnson (successfully) at his impeachment trial before the U.S. Senate. Johnson subsequently nominated Stanbery to a seat on the U.S. SUPREME COURT, but the Senate refused to confirm him. Stanbery died in New York City on June 26, 1881.

Standley, Jeremiah M. (1845–1908)

Missouri native Jeremiah "Doc" Standley was born in Andrew County on August 20, 1845, then moved to California with his parents in 1853. The Standleys settled in Ukiah, raising cattle, and Jeremiah earned his lifelong nickname for nursing sick steers. A solitary rancher by age 16, Standley switched professions three years later to become sheriff's deputy in Mendocino County. His reputation as a lawman was secured in 1874, after Standley first captured the slayers of a local woman, then protected them from LYNCHING prior to trial. Elected SHERIFF in 1882, Standley served for another decade and established a record of sorts, by capturing bandits responsible for 13 of his county's 17 stagecoach robberies during 1887–92.

After retiring as sheriff in Mendocino County, Doc Standley joined the Alaska gold rush, but he ultimately called it quits on mining and served in Nome as a deputy sheriff. Returning to California in 1902, Standley applied for the warden's post at Folsom Prison, but he failed to get the job. Rejection sent him back to Alaska, where he was badly injured in a fall at home in 1908. Although his family undertook the journey homeward to Ukiah, Standley died en route, in Oregon, on July 8, 1908.

Stanton, Edwin McMasters (1814–1869)

Steubenville, Ohio, native Edwin Stanton was born on December 19, 1814. He attended Kenyon College in

Attorney General Edwin Stanton (Author's collection)

his home state, then studied law privately and commenced practice at Cadiz, Ohio—though he did not earn his LL.B. until 1867 from Yale University. Meanwhile, Stanton served as a county prosecutor (1837–39) and as reporter of decisions for the state supreme court (1842–45). After a period of private practice in Washington, D.C., Stanton was appointed by California's governor (1858) to defend U.S. claims in various land disputes with Mexico.

Lame-duck President James Buchanan named Stanton attorney general in December 1860, but Stanton left that post with Abraham Lincoln's inauguration in March 1861. Ten months later, he returned to the cabinet as Lincoln's secretary of war. Stanton was allegedly a target of the same conspirators who murdered President Lincoln and wounded Secretary of State William Seward on April 14, 1865, but he escaped unscathed and some conspiracists today call him the mastermind behind Lincoln's ASSASSINATION. He retained his cabinet post until suspended by President Andrew Johnson on August 12, 1867. The Senate reinstated Stanton on January 14, 1868, but he resigned four months later. President Ulysses Grant nominated Stanton to the U.S. SUPREME COURT in 1869, and while the Senate confirmed him on December 20, Stanton died four days later, without occupying his seat.

Stege, John P.

A PROHIBITION-era legend of the CHICAGO POLICE DEPARTMENT, John Stege remains enigmatic today, his role in crime fighting debated by historians whose 20/20 hindsight somehow leads them to surprising contradictory conclusions. Stege was Chicago's deputy chief of police, in charge of the detective division, when mob gunmen murdered prosecutor William McSwiggin in April 1926. Stege failed to solve that crime, and many others, but he never failed to greet the press with earthy comments on the bootleggers who ran Chicago from behind the scenes. A year after McSwiggin's murder, on the eve of another violent municipal election in April 1927, Stege made a show of equipping his men with submachine guns, training them to fire the weapons in Grant Park. He was fired that same year, for allegedly falsifying patrolmen's applications, but the superior court quashed that charge, and Stege returned from political exile to resume his old position.

In February 1929 Stege was assigned to investigate the St. Valentine's Day massacre—but first he had to be recalled from Florida, where he had been vacationing in close proximity to prime suspect Al Capone. Despite that seeming indiscretion, he appeared to take the job seriously, tracing the murder weapons and linking one of them to a known contract killer (never charged in the case), but Stege's chief contribution to gangbusting was a series of empty threats against Capone and friends, including a vow to have Capone arrested every time he showed his face on a Chicago street. (Chastised for adopting a "communist" stance on law enforcement, Stege replied, "I hope Capone goes to Russia.")

The June 1930 murder of *Chicago Tribune* reporter Alfred "Jake" Lingle embarrassed Stege and the department at large, when rival journalists revealed Lingle's ties to the mob—and to high-ranking policemen. Stege and Chief William Russell (who shared a bloated bank account with Lingle) resigned under fire while that case went unsolved, but Stege rebounded once again, still clinging to his captain's rank as the corrupt regime of Mayor William Thompson passed into history. Before his own 1932 ASSASSINATION in Florida, Mayor Anton Cermak used Stege to lead gambling raids, and in December 1933 Stege organized a special 40-man squad to pursue bandit John Dillinger. (They missed him repeatedly, arresting or killing various look-alikes in the process.) Asked whether he would kill his quarry on sight, Stege solemnly replied, "I'd even give John Dillinger a chance to surrender."

Stein, Robert J. (1912–1994)

A Russian native, born in 1912, Robert Stein immigrated to the United States with his family before the Bolshevik revolution of 1917 and settled in Brooklyn, New York. As an adult, he studied medicine at Austria's University of Innsbruck, receiving his M.D. in 1950, then completed graduate studies in pathology at Northwestern University, in Evanston, Illinois. From there, it was a short step to employment as a forensic pathologist in Chicago. When Cook County finally abandoned its coroner's office, long a tool of political patronage, Stein was retained on personal merit as a medical examiner. In 1976 he won promotion to serve as the county's chief medical examiner, a post which he held for 17 years.

During his tenure, Stein supervised investigations of some 20,000 deaths around Chicago and environs. His famous cases included the 1978 exploration of serial killer John Wayne Gacy's crawl-space graveyard and a 1979 airplane crash at O'Hare International Airport that claimed 279 lives. With so many investigations ongoing at any one time, controversy was inevitable. One such case involved the January 1976 rape-murder of Lisa Cabassa. Dr. Stein opined that two assailants were involved, assuming that one man could not have controlled the struggling victim, and police used that opinion to build their case against suspects Michael Evans and Paul Terry (both later exonerated when DNA evidence proved their innocence and linked the murder to a single offender). Twelve years later, Stein issued a verdict of SUICIDE in the death of police captain Michael O'Mara—a finding hotly disputed by O'Mara's family and their attorney. Asked later whether he had any doubts about the O'Mara diagnosis, Dr. Stein replied: "Well, the very fact that I put pending further investigation, perhaps there was. But if the information that I got, the information was they have nobody in custody, they have no suspects, nothing like that, so I just made it suicide." Dr. Vincent DiMaio, chief medical examiner for Bexar County, Texas, subsequently declared O'Mara's death a homicide.

Stein died in 1994, soon after his retirement. In addition to his long career as a pathologist, he was remembered as a founding member of the Medical Council on Handgun Violence. The Cook County Institute of Forensic Medicine, completed under his supervision in 1983, was renamed the Robert J. Stein Institute of Forensic Medicine in February 1994.

See also: FORENSIC SCIENCE.

Steward, LeRoy T.

Before his appointment as Chicago's police chief, LeRoy Steward served as the city's postmaster, bringing military discipline to a branch of government scandalized by political patronage and flagrant abuses. On the side, while erecting new carrier stations and renumbering the Windy City's streets for more efficient delivery, he also directed reclamation of the boggy shallows where Grant Park stands today. In 1909 he was Mayor Fred Busse's second choice for chief of the CHICAGO POLICE DEPARTMENT, but front-runner Bernard Mullaney declined the post and thus cleared the way for Steward's appointment.

Steward served for less than two years, during 1909–11, but he still managed to institute a number of reforms, beginning with reduction of patrolmen's labor to a 40-hour week. He also launched the CPD's first formal training school, at Shakespeare Station, in October 1910, drilling officers on police techniques and Chicago's municipal code. Steward told reporters, "We are going to inculcate in the minds of the police new sentiment with reference to their duties. It is a fact that the making of an arrest is a small part of the average patrolman's duties. We wish to avoid making an arrest if the peace can be conserved by intelligent handling of a situation by the patrolman on the beat."

With that in mind, Steward still attempted to crack down on vice, ordering immediate arrest of prostitutes caught soliciting in the Levee district. Simultaneously, he transferred—but did not fire or prosecute—the entire staff of the graft-ridden 22nd Street Station, in an effort to dismantle the district's pervasive CORRUPTION. "I could never place my hand on the patrolman, detectives, or officers who were responsible," Steward admitted.

"I did not think that all the men were unreliable, but those who did the fixing were so thoroughly entrenched that it was impossible to find out who they were." His zeal for cleaning house ultimately doomed Steward at headquarters, and he left office in 1911. CPD historian Richard Lindberg observes that Steward's brief administration was "a glimmer of hope in a city oblivious to the broad social changes of the Progressive Era. But unfortunately, that's all it was—a glimmer."

Stone, Harlan Fiske (1872–1946)

A Chesterfield, New Hampshire, native, born on October 11, 1872, Harlan Stone earned his B.S. from Amherst College in 1894, followed by an LL.B. from Columbia Law School in 1898. Admitted to the New York bar, he entered private practice and also lectured at Columbia Law School (1899–1902), then joined the staff as a professor (1902–05) and dean (1910–23). President Calvin Coolidge named Stone attorney general in April 1924 to clean up the scandal-ridden JUSTICE DEPARTMENT shamed by predecessor HARRY DAUGHERTY. Stone served less than a year at Justice, but he made a fateful and enduring decision on May 10, 1924, when he chose J. EDGAR HOOVER to lead the FBI. Various sources have reported (and mythologized) their first conversation as follows:

Stone: Young man, I want you as Acting Director of the Bureau of Investigation.

Hoover: I'll take the job, Mr. Stone, on certain conditions.

Stone: What are they?

Hoover: The Bureau must be divorced from politics and not be a catch-all for political hacks. Appointments must be based on merit. Second, promotions will be made on proved ability and the Bureau will be responsible only to the Attorney General.

Stone: I wouldn't give it to you under any other conditions. That's all. Good day.

True or false, Stone clearly intended to end the FBI's long-running investigation of political beliefs and its harassment of so-called radicals. On May 13, 1924, he sent Hoover a six-point memo detailing policy changes which Stone required of his new director. Five dealt with personnel matters, but the first was most telling in light of Hoover's Red-hunting background: "The activities of the Bureau are to be limited strictly to investigations of violation of law, under my direction or under the direction of an Assistant Attorney General regularly conducting the work of the Department of Justice."

Hoover pretended to agree, and weeks later he assured Senate investigators that "[i]nstructions have been sent to officers in the field to limit their investigations . . . to violations of the statutes." When the AMERICAN CIVIL LIBERTIES UNION complained to Stone that FBI DOMESTIC SURVEILLANCE of dissidents continued unabated, Hoover called the report "untrue and misleading." A "small portion" of the FBI's work involved "ultra-radicals," Hoover admitted, but he vowed that inquiries "are made [only] when there is an indication of a possible violation of a federal statute."

It was a blatant lie, but Stone trusted his new subordinate beyond reason, and his own days at Justice were numbered. Stone confirmed Hoover as full-time FBI director on December 10, 1924, and three months later Stone was gone, resigning in March 1925 to fill a vacancy on the U.S. SUPREME COURT. After 16 years as an associate justice, he was elevated to Chief Justice in 1941 and held that post until his death on April 22, 1946. Author Curt Gentry notes that Hoover "deified" Stone and kept a portrait of his benefactor in his office at FBI headquarters for the remainder of his life.

Stoudenmire, Dallas (1845–1882)

An Alabama native, born on December 11, 1845, Dallas Stoudenmire was already a notorious gunman, with at least two kills to his credit, when residents of El Paso, Texas, hired him to serve as their city marshal on April 10, 1881. Four days later, following a racial altercation between Anglos and Mexicans that left Constable Gus Krempkau dead, Stoudenmire killed three of the combatants in a wild melee worthy of Hollywood. Three days after that fracas, on April 17, ex-marshal Bill Johnson tried to shoot Stoudenmire from ambush, but Stoudenmire killed him, emerging from the battle with a flesh wound in one heel. Yet another ambush, this one staged by local thug Joe King on December 16, 1881, likewise failed to drop Stoudenmire.

El Paso residents were initially thrilled with their two-gun marshal, but they soon grew disillusioned with Stoudenmire's heavy drinking and his habit of "hurrahing" the town—firing pistols aimlessly, at random—while drunk. June 1882 found Stoudenmire replaced by Jim Gillett, and while he retired to run the Globe Restaurant in El Paso, his penchant for shooting scrapes continued. Stoudenmire was arrested on July 29, 1882, after a skirmish that produced no casualties, but a feud with the Manning brothers—Doc, Frank, and Jim—ultimately claimed his life eight weeks later, on September 18.

strikebreaking

Historically, strikebreaking in America has been accomplished by either or both of two means: dismissing union workers and replacing them with nonunion ("scab")

employees, or disrupting and harassing unions to the point of bankruptcy and disbandment. While police have no part in the former effort, they have frequently participated in the latter on behalf of management.

Throughout the 19th century and the first half of the 20th, various American industries and wealthy agricultural interests relied on state and local police to crush labor unions nationwide. The unions were typically portrayed as "radical" or "communistic," sometimes—at least in the South—branded with the additional sin of "race-mixing" for their recruitment of white and minority workers together. Typical law enforcement responses included disruption of public meetings on various grounds, incessant arrests of union organizers on trivial or fabricated charges, FRAME-UPS (as in the HAYMARKET BOMBING), and employment of EXCESSIVE FORCE or "THIRD-DEGREE" TACTICS against union members. POLICE RIOTS were not uncommon, in response to picket lines and sit-downs. In some cases, as when police joined forces with the KU KLUX KLAN to crush the 1930s Southern Tenant Farmers' Union, the authorities have permitted (or participated in) acts of TERRORISM against unions. Unjustified DEADLY FORCE was also used on various occasions, as in the infamous LUDLOW MASSACRE of 1914 and the MEMORIAL DAY MASSACRE of 1937.

Violent strikebreaking was commonly accomplished by collaboration between police, private detective agencies such as those run by WILLIAM BURNS or ALLAN J. PINKERTON, and hired members of ORGANIZED CRIME. There is no doubt that many law enforcement leaders saw disruption of the early unions as part of their duty to preserve social order, although the tactics they employed to that end were in fact more destructive to public order than the strikes themselves. Federal agencies, including the young FBI under Chief William Burns, also participated in strikebreaking, and maintained long-running DOMESTIC SURVEILLANCE on various labor unions under Director J. EDGAR HOOVER.

See also: FEDERAL BUREAU OF INVESTIGATION.

suicide

Law enforcement ranks among the most stressful of all occupations, coupling long hours, personal alienation, and daily risk of death or injury with frequent observations of suffering crime and accident victims. While all major urban police departments now provide psychological counseling programs, many officers shun treatment from fear of being branded "weak" or "crazy" by their peers. That situation is exacerbated when individual officers are caught up in various scandals involving sex, CORRUPTION, and the like. Accordingly, it should be no surprise that suicides among police exceed those of most other professions.

While no definitive statistics are presently available, the National Police Suicide Foundation estimates that suicide rates double or triple the line-of-duty deaths reported for American police and emergency workers each year. In 2000 the INTERNATIONAL ASSOCIATION OF CHIEFS OF POLICE estimated that 300 officers kill themselves each year. Studies of individual states and departments have produced widely disparate results. In 2001 a study of Wyoming peace officers announced a suicide rate of 203 per 100,000—versus a national average of 12 per 100,000 U.S. citizens at large. At the same time, a survey of the NEW YORK CITY POLICE DEPARTMENT claimed a suicide rate of 29 per 100,000, but contradictory reports from Cornell University in 2002 claimed that NYPD officers kill themselves at a rate of 15 per 100,000—versus 19 per 100,000 for Big Apple civilians. The Cornell researchers dubbed NYPD's alleged suicide epidemic an "urban myth," without minimizing the scope of the problem. Psychologists agree that most police suicides presently arise from alcoholism, marital problems, or a combination of both.

Sullivan, William Cornelius (1912–1977)

A Bolton, Massachusetts, native, born May 12, 1912, William Sullivan earned a B.A. from American University in Washington, then taught school in his hometown before moving on to graduate studies in Boston. He later joined the INTERNAL REVENUE SERVICE, then transferred to the FBI on August 4, 1941, serving at six different field offices over the next three years. In June 1944 Sullivan moved to FBI headquarters and supervised foreign operations of the Special Intelligence Service for the remainder of World War II.

Sullivan, nicknamed "Crazy Bill" within the FBI, was assigned to Phoenix in August 1953, then recalled to headquarters 10 months later as an inspector with the Domestic Intelligence Division (where he became assistant director in June 1961). In 1956 he wrote the monograph that launched the FBI's first illegal COINTELPRO campaign against the Communist Party. Briefly detailed to the Crime Records Division in 1962, he was the principal ghost writer for Director J. EDGAR HOOVER's latest book, *A Study in Communism*. In his post at Domestic Intelligence (Division 5) Sullivan ran the intelligence side of the JFK ASSASSINATION case, the 1968 investigation of Dr. Martin Luther King's murder, and most of the Bureau's COINTELPRO operations against black militants, the "New Left," and the KU KLUX KLAN. He was a key figure at headquarters, regarded by many observers as Hoover's heir apparent to command the Bureau.

That vision began to unravel on October 12, 1970, when Sullivan told a gathering of newspaper editors that the Communist Party was "not in any way causing or directing or controlling the unrest we suffer today." Afterward, he claimed that Hoover raged at him in private, "How do you expect me to get my appropriations if you keep downgrading the Party?" Increasingly fed up with FBI politics, Sullivan wrote the first of several "honest memos" to Hoover in June 1971, recommending prompt reduction in the number of FBI legal attachés abroad, cutback in unproductive investigations, and relegation of foreign work to other agencies. A conference of FBI executives, held on June 18, 1971, warned Hoover that Sullivan seemed "more on the side of the CIA, State Department and Military Intelligence Agencies than the FBI." Two weeks later, Hoover promoted W. MARK FELT over Sullivan, with orders to watch Sullivan "very carefully." When White House operative G. GORDON LIDDY spoke to Sullivan on August 2, 1971, he found Sullivan "very insecure in his position, almost frightened."

On August 28 Sullivan wrote a letter to Hoover outlining their recent points of disagreement, assuring Hoover "that those of us who disagree with you *are trying to help you and not hurt you.*" (Emphasis in the original.) A three-hour meeting on August 31 failed to resolve their disputes, and four days later Hoover requested Sullivan's resignation. Sullivan went on leave but declined to retire. When they met again on September 30, Hoover allegedly called Sullivan "a Judas." Sullivan recalled his own reply: "I'm not a Judas, Mr. Hoover, and you certainly aren't Jesus Christ." Fired on the spot for insubordination, Sullivan spent the next five days typing a long letter to Hoover, including detailed criticism on such points as "Concealment of Truth," "Senator Joseph McCarthy and Yourself," "Leaks of Sensitive Material," and "FBI and Politics." Sullivan recommended that Hoover "sit down quietly . . . and work on a plan to reform, reorganize and modernize the Bureau." Failing that, he wrote:

Mr. Hoover, if for reasons of your own you cannot or will not do this may I gently suggest that you retire for your own good, that of the Bureau, the intelligence community and law enforcement. More than once I told you never to retire; to stay on to the last, that you would live longer being active. It looks now that I may have been wrong. For if you cannot do what is suggested above you really ought to retire and be given recognition due you after such a long and remarkable career in government.

While Hoover fumed over that "betrayal," Sullivan leaked various stories to major newspapers, magazines, and television networks, critical of Hoover's tenure at the FBI. He went public for the first time on January 10, 1972, remarking to the *Los Angeles Times* about Hoover's "fossilized" bureaucracy. Shortly after Hoover's death in May 1972, Attorney General RICHARD KLEINDIENST named Sullivan to head a new Office of Narcotics Intelligence, a post he held until January 1973. Retired to a New Hampshire farm, Sullivan revisited Washington to testify before the CHURCH COMMITTEE in 1975. Sullivan's plans to testify before the House Select Committee on Assassinations ended on November 9, 1977, when he was shot and killed in New Hampshire. Authorities named the shooter as a policeman's son and called Sullivan's death a hunting accident.

See also: FEDERAL BUREAU OF INVESTIGATION.

Supreme Court of the United States

America's highest court is the only judicial body specifically established by the Constitution, thus the oldest in existence. It consists of nine judges (or "justices"), with a chief justice presiding. The court does not hear criminal cases per se, its original jurisdiction being restricted to cases directly involving the U.S. government or disputes between states, but many other cases find their way to the court through appeals. Members of the court are appointed by the president (with Senate confirmation) for life terms, which supposedly render them immune to political pressure, but the appointment process itself has become so freighted with politico-religious "litmus tests" that few observers seriously expect appointment of impartial judges.

With its sweeping jurisdiction on appellate cases, the Supreme Court has naturally had a great and lasting influence on American law enforcement. Its shifting composition also guarantees that decisions rendered today may be reversed by contradictory opinions in the future—as when the court approved racial segregation in 1896 (*Plessy v. Ferguson*), then banned it as unconstitutional in 1954 (*Brown v. Board of Education*). Over the past century, various Supreme Court rulings have modified American law on CAPITAL PUNISHMENT, search and seizure, application of federal civil rights statutes, criminal confessions, BUGGING and WIRETAPS, DOMESTIC SURVEILLANCE, "THIRD-DEGREE" TACTICS, infiltration of "subversive" groups, and a host of other issues that affect the daily operations of police nationwide. Since the "liberal" 1960s, many officers profess to feel themselves "handcuffed" by Supreme Court guidelines that require search warrants, ban various types of electronic surveillance, and demand that persons placed under arrest be informed of their basic legal rights. Spokesmen for the AMERICAN CIVIL LIBERTIES UNION and similar

Chief Justice Earl Warren's Supreme Court vastly expanded civil rights protections in the 1950s and 1960s. (Library of Congress)

groups reply that police should not be allowed to "cut corners" in the course of criminal investigations, much less extract confessions by coercion or otherwise ride roughshod over the rights that every American citizen derives from the U.S. Constitution.

Sutherland, Edwin Hardin (1883–1950)

The son of a college professor, born at Gibbon, Nebraska, on August 13, 1883, Edwin Sutherland earned his B.A. in history from Nebraska's Grand Island College in 1904. Moving on to South Dakota, he taught Greek and Latin at Sioux Falls College, while planning to obtain his Ph.D. in history. Upon learning that a course in sociology was required for that course of study, Sutherland completed one at the University of Chicago in 1906, then fell in love with the subject and promptly changed his major. By the time he earned his doctorate in 1939 (also from University of Chicago), Sutherland had published two books in the field: *The Unemployed and Public Agencies* (1914) and *Criminology* (1920).

Sutherland's fascination with criminology continued as he progressed through a series of professorships at universities in Illinois and Minnesota, finishing his career at the University of Indiana (1935–50). In 1939 he was elected as the 29th president of the American Sociological Society, and delivered his groundbreaking paper on "white-collar criminality" to the society's annual meeting that December. Today, although he wrote on many subjects related to criminology, Sutherland is best remembered for coining the popular term *white-collar crime*. His book on the subject, *White Collar Crime,* was released in 1949, joining his other volumes that included *The Professional Thief* and *On Analyzing Crime.* A stroke claimed Sutherland's life on October 11, 1950.

SWAT teams

The first U.S. police SWAT team—Special Weapons and Tactics—was organized and named by leaders of the LOS ANGELES POLICE DEPARTMENT in early 1974, and the unit was tested in May of that year against the radical Symbionese Liberation Army in a shootout that left five SLA members dead beneath the smoking rubble of their hideout. With that example in mind, law enforcement agencies across the country soon followed L.A.'s example by creating their own SWAT teams.

As the name suggests, SWAT officers are trained in "special" paramilitary tactics, using "special" weapons that include (where feasible) state-of-the-art equipment and WEAPONS. Typical SWAT missions include hostage rescue, raids on fortified or barricaded targets (drug labs, gang headquarters, etc.), arrests of dangerous fugitives, and countersniper assignments. Many agencies attempt to soften SWAT's image with less aggressive-sounding names—e.g., the FBI's Hostage Rescue Team—but wherever they operate, SWAT teams remain the last resort of officers under the gun. A SWAT team for animals was also proposed in 2005, after Los Angeles game wardens shot an escaped Bengal tiger. The new squad, if created, would be trained to sedate exotic and dangerous animals without killing them.

See also: FEDERAL BUREAU OF INVESTIGATION.

Sylvester, Richard (d. 1915)

Details are sadly lacking for the early life of a man now revered in some quarters as the "father of police professionalism." After studying law and serving briefly as a member of the Ute Indian Commission, Richard Sylvester joined the Washington, D.C., Police Department as chief clerk. In 1894 he wrote the department's official history, a task impressive enough to win him promotion to major and superintendent four years later, in July 1898. As commander in chief of the force—and later, as president of the INTERNATIONAL ASSOCIATION OF CHIEFS OF POLICE (1901–15), Sylvester advocated the "citizen-soldier" model of law enforcement, spawning (at least indirectly) the paramilitary aspects of police work still used today.

Continuing his early interest in police history, Sylvester published a new work in 1910, titled *A History of the "Sweat Box" and the "Third Degree,"* wherein he chronicled and condemned the extraction of suspect confessions by force. Under Sylvester's leadership, the IACP passed a unanimous resolution rejecting "THIRD-DEGREE" TACTICS—though sadly, their use remained routine among police departments, large and small, throughout the 1920s and the Great Depression, continuing in some quarters (such as the PHILADELPHIA POLICE DEPARTMENT under FRANK LAZARRO RIZZO) well into recent times.

Sylvester fought nonstop to improve the image of U.S. law enforcement, including public condemnation of the *Keystone Kops* and other slapstick comedies, but his own image took an unexpected beating in the early years of World War I, when he collided with activists promoting women's suffrage in Washington. Sylvester unwisely withheld police protection from one suffragette parade involving 8,000 marchers, warning participants of a hostile civilian reception, then suffered criticism when a near-riot erupted. Press condemnation of his seeming apathy prompted Sylvester to resign as chief in April 1915, and he simultaneously left his post as leader of the IACP. He died before year's end, remembered posthumously more for his achievements than the climactic debacle that ended his career.

Tackwood, Louis E.

An African-American resident of Southern California, Louis Tackwood was hired in 1969 to serve as an informant for LOS ANGELES POLICE DEPARTMENT's Criminal Conspiracy Section (CCS), acting in collaboration with the FBI. He was assigned to infiltrate the Black Panther Party and report on its activities, while disrupting the group by any means available, frustrating its proposed alliances with other "New Left" organizations, and entrapping Panthers in various criminal acts. Tackwood's first assignment was to spark a shooting war between the Panthers and Ron Karenga's United Slaves, an effort that claimed several lives within a year.

When not fomenting murder in the streets, Tackwood disrupted Panther alliances with the Students for a Democratic Society and joined police in framing party members for murders they did not commit. One such victim, Elmer ("Geronimo") Pratt, served more than a quarter century in prison before he was finally vindicated and released. During the same period, Tackwood also had contact with Donald DeFreeze, a black prison inmate and alleged subject of government mind control experiments who later formed the Symbionese Liberation Army.

Tackwood describes his final CCS-FBI mission, before he went public in 1971, as a plot "to kill George Jackson," a Panther Party spokesman serving time in San Quentin Prison. Tackwood was not the triggerman, but he allegedly participated in an official conspiracy to slay Jackson during a staged prison break, occurring on August 21, 1971. According to Tackwood, "It was a plot, see, between the CCS and the guards. The guards hate him, they hate his guts.

He's accused of killing a guard, remember that. And they hate him, at least some of them do. They harass him at all times, give him all the hell they can, illegally. Then they kill him. Poor old George." Tackwood blew the whistle on his employers in autumn 1971, with sworn courtroom testimony and a published memoir, *The Glass House Tapes*. He subsequently passed a polygraph test, administered by former FBI agent Chris Gugas, suggesting (if not absolutely proving) that his tale was true.

See also: FEDERAL BUREAU OF INVESTIGATION; INFORMANTS.

Taft, Alphonso (1810–1891)

Vermont native Alphonso Taft was born at Townshend on November 5, 1810. He graduated from Yale in 1833, then worked as a tutor (1833–37) while privately studying law. Taft was admitted to the Connecticut bar in 1838, then moved to Cincinnati, Ohio, in 1839, where he spent three years on the city council. He lost a congressional race in 1856, but was appointed to a seat on Cincinnati's superior court in 1866, holding that post until 1872. (During that service, Taft earned an LL.B. from Yale, in 1867.) President Ulysses Grant named Taft secretary of war in March 1876, then transferred him to lead the JUSTICE DEPARTMENT as attorney general two months later. Taft left Washington with the rest of Grant's cabinet in March 1877 and resumed private practice of law. He subsequently entered diplomatic service, acting as the U.S. minister to Austria (1882) and Russia (1884–85). Taft died in San Diego, California, on May 21, 1891.

Attorney General Alphonso Taft (Author's collection)

Tamm, Quinn (1910–1986)

A Seattle native, born in 1910, Quinn Tamm was the younger brother of FBI assistant director Edward Tamm. He likewise joined the Bureau in 1934, soon after graduating from the University of Virginia, and in 1938 became the youngest G-man promoted to inspector by Director J. EDGAR HOOVER. After 17 years in command of the FBI's Identification Division, Tamm was promoted to serve as assistant director of the Training and Inspection Division. In that post, and later as chief of the FBI's crime laboratory, Tamm served double duty as Hoover's liaison with the INTERNATIONAL ASSOCIATION OF CHIEFS OF POLICE (IACP). As later described by FBI historian Curt Gentry, it was Tamm's job to rig IACP elections so that only officers approved by Hoover rose to lead the association. His primary "triumph," in 1959, was blocking the election of Chief WILLIAM PARKER, from the LOS ANGELES POLICE DEPARTMENT, who had waged a long and bitter feud with Hoover.

Tamm remained in Hoover's good graces until 1961, when he resigned from the FBI to become executive director of the IACP. Hoover opposed the move, but this time his best efforts failed to prevent it. Tamm responded to the challenge in 1962, at the IACP's annual convention, when he declared that the IACP should be "the dominant voice in law enforcement." While he never mentioned Hoover's name, Tamm left no doubt that he was targeting the FBI chief with his bid to make the IACP "the spokesman for law enforcement in this country." Seven years later, Tamm challenged Hoover more directly, warning that a recent plan to "centralize police training in the hands of the director of the FBI could become the first step toward a national police." The feud continued until Hoover's death in May 1972. Tamm served the IACP until January 1975, then retired and died at his home in Washington, D.C., on January 23, 1986.

See also: FEDERAL BUREAU OF INVESTIGATION.

Tammany Hall

Tammany Hall is the popular name given to a Democratic political machine that ruled New York City politics from 1854 until the election of Mayor Fiorello La Guardia 80 years later. Its origins date from 1786, when the Tammany Society of New York City was founded as a social and fraternal organization, increasingly politicized over the next 12 years until it emerged as the chief vehicle of Jeffersonian ideals in New York. Tammany's bonds to the Democratic Party tightened through the early 19th century, and it emerged as the controlling factor in local ward politics under President Andrew Jackson. William ("Boss") Tweed and his cronies in the notorious Tweed Ring ruled Tammany from 1858 to 1871, their flagrant CORRUPTION extending even to appointment and promotion of officers in the NEW YORK CITY POLICE DEPARTMENT. Under leaders John Kelly (1872–86), Richard Croker (1886–1902), and Charles Murphy (1902–24), Tammany forged enduring bonds with ORGANIZED CRIME to buy or coerce votes in crucial elections, paying off with cash, political patronage and immunity from arrest. That protection was especially vital during PROHIBITION, when bootlegging profits filled political coffers in New York and nationwide. Tammany Hall suffered a dual setback in 1932, when corrupt Mayor James Walker was forced out of office and rival Franklin Roosevelt was elected president of the United States, while repeal of Prohibition dried up much of the society's illicit income in 1933. Despite its waning influence under the New Deal and World War II, Tammany enjoyed a minor renaissance under boss Carmine DeSapio (1949–61). Its final defeat was administered by Eleanor Roosevelt, who blamed DeSapio for defeating her son (Franklin Roosevelt, Jr.) in his 1954 campaign to become New York's attorney general. With wealthy friends, Mrs. Roosevelt created the New York Committee for Democratic Voters, opposing DeSapio and Tammany Hall, and the society dissolved in the mid-1960s.

Tampa Police Department

Incorporated in 1855, the city of Tampa, Florida, hired its first city marshal that same year. Over the next two decades, his duties expanded from basic law enforcement to establishment of a nocturnal patrol and recording brands on butchered cattle. A local ordinance created the Tampa Police Department in 1886, replacing the city marshal with a chief of police and five subordinates (an assistant chief, a sergeant, and three mounted officers). Two detectives were hired before year's end, to investigate various crimes.

The 20th century brought changes to Tampa, including the 1913 recruitment of a police identification officer trained in the BERTILLON SYSTEM of bodily measurements. Patrol cars joined the force two years later, ultimately followed by creation of an Auto Theft Bureau in 1936. PROHIBITION brought the same CORRUPTION seen in other cities across the United States, but a more sinister problem in Tampa was the KU KLUX KLAN's extensive infiltration of the Tampa P.D. From 1920 onward, police and Klansmen closed ranks in brutal STRIKEBREAKING campaigns that frustrated unionization of local citrus workers, while ORGANIZED CRIME was ignored. (Gamblers won an estimated $1 million per month in Tampa during 1929 alone.) By 1935 Chief R. G. Titsworth and most of his all-white policemen were recognized Klan members. That November they collaborated in the murder of liberal activist Joseph Shoemaker and the near-fatal flogging of two other socialists. Titsworth and four others received prison terms in that case, but the verdicts were overturned on appeal, prompting Governor Cone to tell reporters, "I'm ashamed of Florida myself."

Little changed in the aftermath of the Shoemaker case, where right-wing politics and union-busting was concerned. Tampa's police force, like so many others in Dixie, fought racial integration through the 1960s, abandoning entrenched RACISM with obvious reluctance. On the crime-fighting front, a Criminal Intelligence Unit was established in 1962, to maintain "special files and investigations." In 1968 Tampa P.D.'s training academy was certified by the State Minimum Standards Training Commission. A bomb squad of sorts was created in 1971, with employment of a lone explosives specialist, joined by several others in 1973. The departments first INTERNAL AFFAIRS Unit was belatedly established in 1974, to investigate complaints of EXCESSIVE FORCE. Tampa's first Tactical Response (or SWAT) Team was

launched in 1977, merging with a new Hostage Negotiation Team two years later.

The closing years of the 20th century demanded more innovations in Tampa. In 1981 the department launched its Special Anti-Crime Squad (later Street Anti-Crime Squad) to address "street level and special crime problems." Mobility was enhanced with the purchase of "special purpose vehicles" resembling golf carts. Tampa P.D.'s first K-9 UNIT was fielded in 1982, followed quickly by a dive team. An increase in DRUG traffic prompted creation of Tampa's QUAD Squads (*Qu*ick Uniformed *A*ttack on *D*rugs) in 1989. Ten years later, a Sexual Predator Identification and Notification program was initiated, to comply with new Florida statutes.

Taney, Roger Brooks (1777–1864)

A native of Calvert County, Maryland, born on March 17, 1777, Roger Taney graduated from Dickinson College in 1795, then studied law privately and won admittance to the bar in 1799. That same year witnessed his

Attorney General Roger Taney later served as chief justice of the U.S. Supreme Court. (Author's collection)

election to the Maryland House of Delegates for a 12-month term, followed by five years in the state senate (1816–20). In 1827 Taney was elected state attorney general, a post he held until President Andrew Jackson named him U.S. attorney general in July 1831. Taney left that post in September 1833 to become Jackson's secretary of the treasury. In 1835 Jackson nominated Taney as Chief Justice of the U.S. SUPREME COURT, and the Senate confirmed him. Taney retained his seat on the court until his death on October 12, 1864. His most momentous—and infamous—decision was rendered in the *Dred Scott* case (1857), wherein he defined black slaves as chattel property, unable to escape their masters by fleeing to states where slavery was banned by law.

Taylor, Creed (1820–1906)

A relative of General (later President) Zachary Taylor, Creed Taylor was born in Alabama on April 20, 1820, and moved to Texas with his family at age four. As a precocious 15-year-old scout and soldier in the Texas revolution against Mexico, Taylor fought in defense of the Gonzales "come and take it cannon," at the battle of Concepción, in the "Grass Fight," and in the siege of Bexar. January 1836 found him with Texan forces at San Patricio, followed by detachment as a courier until he joined Col. James Neill for the Goliad campaign. After the Alamo defeat, Taylor led his family to safety beyond reach of Gen. Santa Anna's army, then returned in time to fight in the climactic battle at San Jacinto on April 20, 1836.

Taylor's exploits continued in the new Republic of Texas, as a member of the TEXAS RANGERS, including front-line service against Indian raiders at Plum Creek (1840) and Bandera Pass (1841). Wounded by Mexican invaders at Salado Creek in 1842, Taylor recovered fully in time for service as a private with the Texas Mounted Rangers during the Mexican War (1846–48). His engagements in that conflict included the battles of Palo Alto, Resaca de la Palma, Monterrey, and Buena Vista. Strangely, given his record, Taylor refrained from joining the Confederate Army until February 1864, then served with distinction for the last year of the Civil War, under Col. John Ford's command. With that conflict behind him, Taylor acted as a patriarch of sorts in the Sutton-Taylor feud that created bloody strife throughout DeWitt County, Texas, during 1867–75.

One contribution of Taylor's to Texas history, now largely forgotten, was his creation (with fellow Texas Ranger WILLIAM "BIG FOOT" WALLACE) of the legend of El Muerto, a South Texas version of the Headless Horseman. The story dates from 1850, when a rustler named Vidal stole several horses owned by Taylor. Recruiting Wallace to help him, Taylor tracked Vidal's

gang to a remote camp, where the Rangers ambushed and slaughtered their targets. That done, they beheaded Vidal and bound his headless corpse to his horse, cruelly releasing the animal with its rotting burden to roam the hills and desert wastes until it died, bearing a grim example of "Texas justice" on its back. For years afterward, cowboys reported encounters with El Muerto, the headless rider whose appearance foretold personal disaster.

In old age, Taylor dictated his memoirs to author James DeShields, but he never saw them in print. Taylor died on December 26, 1906, while his autobiography was not released (as *Tall Men with Long Rifles*) until 1935. A year later, the Texas Centennial Commission erected a marker in Taylor's honor at his grave in Noxville.

"Ten Most Wanted" fugitives

Late in 1949 a feature writer for the International News Service asked the FBI to name the "toughest guys" whom G-men were pursuing at the moment. The resultant story proved so popular and generated so much positive publicity that Director J. EDGAR HOOVER inaugurated the Bureau's "Ten Most Wanted" program a few weeks later, on March 14, 1950. Since then, nearly 500 fugitives have graced the roster, all but 30 of them located by the collaborative efforts of watchful citizens and various law enforcement agencies.

Criteria for the selection of a "Top Ten" fugitive is specialized, befitting designation as among the worst of several hundred thousand criminals at large on any given day. First, the candidate must either have a lengthy history of conflict with the law or else be counted as a special danger to society because of recent actions. Sheer ferocity is not enough, however. It must also

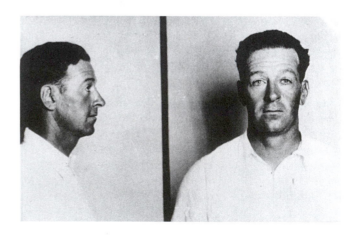

Thomas Holden was the FBI's first "Top Ten" fugitive. (FBI)

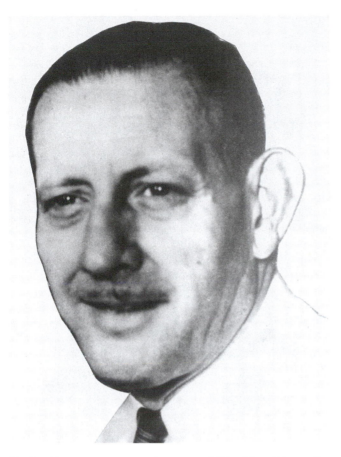

Morley King was no. 2 on the original "Ten Most Wanted" list. (FBI)

Omar Pinson was the fifth fugitive on the FBI's original "Top Ten" list in 1950. (FBI)

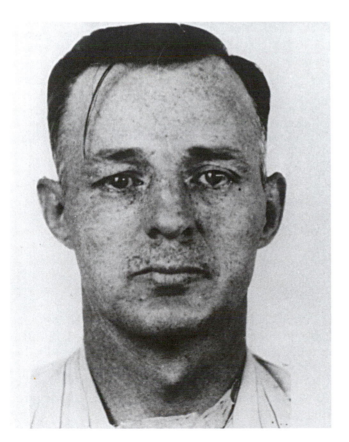

Lee Downs ranked sixth on the first FBI "Most Wanted" list. (FBI)

Orba Jackson placed seventh on the FBI's first "Top Ten" list, in 1950. (FBI)

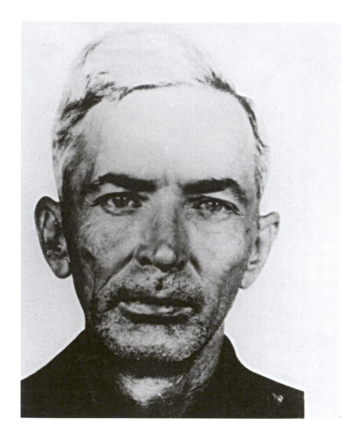

Glen Wright was no. 8 on J. Edgar Hoover's first "Ten Most Wanted" list. (FBI)

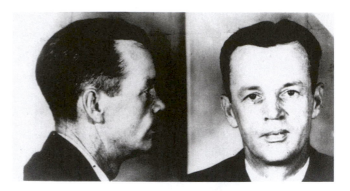

Henry Shelton was the penultimate fugitive on the FBI's first "Ten Most Wanted" list. (FBI)

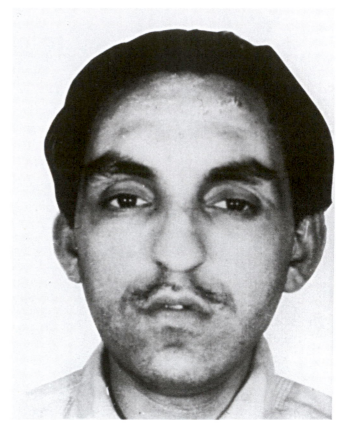

Morris Guralnick completed the first FBI "Most Wanted" list in 1950. (FBI)

be determined that publicity afforded by the program will be useful in apprehending the subject. Thus, the Symbionese Liberation Army abductors of heiress Patty Hearst were not listed in 1974, since they generated ample headlines on their own. Terrorist kingpin Osama bin Laden, by contrast, was listed two years *before* the disastrous attacks of September 11, 2001, and remains on the list today, despite offerings of a multimillion-dollar reward for his capture. Since many of those listed are fugitives from local charges (murder, rape, etc.), a federal count of unlawful flight to avoid prosecution (or confinement, in the case of escaped convicts) is often added to legitimize FBI pursuit.

As noted earlier, not every Top Ten fugitive is apprehended. Fourteen have been found dead, their names removed from the list once identification of their remains was confirmed. Fifteen others have been dropped after federal charges were dismissed, either because the fugitive is presumed dead or capture is deemed so unlikely that space must be cleared for another candidate. Fugitive cop-killer Donald Webb holds the record for evading manhunters to date, listed in May 1981 and still at large today. Billy Bryant, by contrast, was captured two hours after his "Most Wanted" listing was announced

in 1969. Seven fugitives have been arrested prior to public announcement of their Top Ten listing, but they are still considered official members of the FBI's dishonor roll.

Its title notwithstanding, the Ten Most Wanted list has been expanded several times to include more than 10 fugitives. Of 13 such "special additions," seven were leftist radicals listed in September and October 1970, nearly doubling the Top Ten list to include 16 fugitives. That inflation said more about Hoover's obsession with the "Red menace" than any real danger to society at large, and "special" 11th fugitives have been listed only twice since Hoover's death (serial killer Alton Coleman in 1984, and World Trade Center bomber Ramzi Yousef in 1993). Six other fugitives have been listed twice, in different years, for separate offenses.

Many other state and federal agencies now emulate the FBI by posting lists of their "most wanted" fugitives, sometimes including 15 or 20 names on various rosters. In the past decade, public interest in government lists of "PUBLIC ENEMIES" has faded to a large extent, and even the FBI itself no longer reliably advertises the listing or capture of Top Ten fugitives on its own Internet Web site.

See also: FEDERAL BUREAU OF INVESTIGATION.

Tennessee Bureau of Investigation

Creation of the TBI was spurred by a notorious murder case from Greene County, Tennessee, in 1949. Two years later, *Greenville Sun* publisher John Jones, Sr. led a campaign to establish a statewide law enforcement agency. Media agitation prompted state legislators to approve the plan, creating the Tennessee Bureau of Criminal Identification in March 1951. Over the next 29 years, the TBCI served as the "plainclothes" division of Tennessee's Department of Safety, assisting local police departments and conducting criminal investigations that exceeded local jurisdiction. On March 27, 1980, the unit was officially transformed into an independent agency, renamed the Tennessee Bureau of Investigation. Over the past quarter century, the TBI has earned a reputation for professionalism, recognized in its dual accreditation by the Commission on Accreditation for Law Enforcement Agencies and the American Society of Crime Lab Directors/Laboratory Accreditation Board. Its mission statement vows "that guilt shall not escape, nor innocence suffer."

Tennessee Highway Patrol

In 1929 Tennessee state legislators created a State Police Force patterned on the TEXAS RANGERS, followed closely by Governor Henry Horton's creation of a subsidiary Highway Patrol. The state police would not endure, but the Highway Patrol survives today, transferred in 1939 to a newly created Department of Public Safety.

Tennessee issued its first official drivers' licenses in 1937, with 521,571 motorists licensed by year's end. Today, with more than 4 million licensed drivers and nearly 6 million registered vehicles statewide, THP officers patrol 87,000 miles of state and federal highways.

Aside from traffic enforcement and accident investigations, the force also serves to interdict drug traffic on Tennessee highways. Other duties include school bus safety inspections, auto theft investigations, plus enforcement of all commercial vehicle laws and regulations. The THP also maintains a RIOT squad in each of its eight districts, ready to respond in crisis situations.

terrorism

No two sources agree precisely on a definition of terrorism, but most concur that terroristic acts include the use or threat of violence to influence government policies and/or intimidate identifiable segments of a region's population (ethnic or religious minorities, political parties, etc.) in pursuance of political or social objectives. In the United States acts of terrorism date from the Colonial era to modern times, including crimes committed by foreign nationals, extremists of both left and right, assorted labor unions, white-supremacists, members of ORGANIZED CRIME, and sometimes law enforcement officers themselves.

The FBI's response to terrorism nationwide has varied since the term entered common usage in the 1960s. Throughout that decade and the next, Bureau spokesmen commonly branded as "terrorists" any group or individual targeted for DOMESTIC SURVEILLANCE or "neutralization" under various illegal COINTELPRO programs. Frequently, FBI charges of violent behavior were either spurious (as when leveled at the Southern Christian Leadership Conference in 1967–68) or else the product of criminal acts by paid INFORMANTS and AGENTS PROVOCATEURS. At the same time, FBI headquarters actively sponsored certain right-wing terrorist groups, including the Secret Army Organization and various factions of the KU KLUX KLAN. That picture changed in the 1980s and 1990s, as G-men were confronted with real threats from abroad and from domestic groups including neo-Nazis and the "patriot militia" movement.

Following the catastrophic incidents of September 11, 2001, the FBI shuffled its declared priorities to make the foremost goal protection of America from future terrorist attacks. Attorney General JOHN ASHCROFT instantly called for new authority to pursue suspected terrorists, embodied in provisions of the USA PATRIOT ACT. FBI director ROBERT MUELLER likewise declared the Bureau in need of more money, equipment, and agents to cope with the threat, while President George W. Bush created the HOMELAND SECURITY DEPARTMENT to coordinate the activities of several dozen federal agencies.

The FBI was not included in that shakeup, but its post-"9/11" activities still drew criticism from some quarters. Within two weeks of the September attacks,

Muslims and Arab-Americans across the United States complained of harassment by federal agents, including arrests and detentions without warrants, coercive interviews, and surveillance that verged on outright intimidation. The offices of Muslim charities were raided in search of evidence linking them to terrorist leaders, and Ashcroft (echoing the words of A. MITCHELL PALMER in 1919–20) urged his men to be "relentless" in their pursuit of "enemy aliens." At the same time, state and local authorities throughout the country complained that the FBI refused to share information on the continuing terrorist manhunt, thereby preventing any meaningful cooperation toward the common goal of national security. By December 31, 2001, FBI spokesmen cited "more than 150 U.S. terrorist investigations" in progress—none of them finally resulting in arrests or convictions. In late November 2002 G-men blamed shoddy immigration records for their failure to locate 4,344 of 5,046 illegal aliens from Middle Eastern countries, known to be residing in the United States.

Despite the flurry of post-9/11 activity, it is clear that the FBI and Central Intelligence Agency fumbled their antiterrorist duties before the attacks. A 450-page report, issued by the Senate Intelligence Committee in December 2002, revealed that a year before 9/11 FBI agents intercepted telephone calls from one of the hijackers (then living in California) to a terrorist facility in the Middle East. No action was taken in that case, and FBI headquarters likewise ignored warnings from an Arizona G-man that suspected terrorists were training at U.S. flight schools. A CIA-FBI rivalry dating from the days of late FBI director J. EDGAR HOOVER reared its head again in 2000, when CIA agents learned that two Al-Qaeda terrorists had entered the country—and then withheld that information from the Bureau. FBI whistle-blower COLEEN ROWLEY also revealed that agents in Minneapolis arrested one of the 9/11 plotters months in advance of the raids, but were forced to release him when headquarters refused to authorize a search of his home and computer.

As if to compensate for those failures, the FBI followed 9/11 with a series of media "terrorist warnings," none of which proved to be valid. Among those were the following:

October 2001—Director ROBERT S. MUELLER warned U.S. authorities and civilians to "be on the highest alert" for possible attacks over the next week, based on undisclosed information that was "deemed credible," but which was "not specific as to intended targets or as to intended methods."

November 2001—After a warning that terrorists "might attack West Coast bridges," FBI spokes-

men belatedly acknowledged that the "raw intelligence" behind the alert "was not credible."

December 2001—Mueller issued another "general alert" for terrorist attacks. When none occurred, local officials across the United States denounced the continuing alarms as "needless provocations of public anxiety" which "contained so little information or specific guidance for how people should act that they are useless at best, disruptive at worst." One day after those complaints were aired (on December 11), FBI headquarters reported another vague threat suggesting that unknown persons "may retaliate against a Texas school for the U.S. bombing in Afghanistan." Again, no such attacks occurred.

May 2002—FBI leaders warned of "a possible terrorist threat to the Orlando, Florida water supply." Local authorities told reporters on May 21 that the threat "was so vague that officials did not know what contaminants to check for." In fact, none were found.

July 2002—Admitting that their lead was "very vague," FBI spokesmen issued a national warning that "people with ties to terrorist groups are downloading images of U.S. stadiums from the Internet." The alleged terrorists engaged in that legal activity remain unidentified today.

October 2002—Vague as ever, FBI headquarters issued a nationwide alert about "a possible attack soon against transportation systems, particularly railroads." No such attacks occurred.

November 2002—"Despite a lack of specific credible evidence," the Bureau warned Americans that unnamed members of Al-Qaeda were "likely to attempt a 'spectacular' attack intended to inflict large-scale casualties and damage the U.S. economy." Days later, the Bureau reported "unconfirmed information from intelligence sources overseas that hospitals in four U.S. cities could be the targets of a terrorist threat." No cities were named, and no attacks followed.

December 2002—The FBI broadcast photos of four alleged Muslim terrorists said to be at large in the United States and seeking targets. On January 2, 2003, a Pakistani jeweler in Lahore, Mohammed Asghar, identified himself as the man depicted in one photo. By January 7 G-men had called off their search, ruefully confessing that the latest alarm was a hoax "fabricated by an informant."

The result of such attention to terrorism was dramatic. Between September 11 and November 30, 2001, the number of criminal cases recommended for prosecution by FBI agents dropped 76 percent across the U.S. According to JUSTICE DEPARTMENT records, only 263 "ordinary" cases (including narcotics, bank robbery, organized crime, and white-collar crime) were slated for prosecution in the last half of September 2001, versus more than 1,400 cases for the same two-week period in 1999 and 2000. That boon to criminals was balanced, Director Mueller claimed in December 2002, by the fact that "nearly 100 terrorist attacks, some intended to take place on U.S. soil, have been thwarted" since 9/11. None of those cases was further described, and some inkling of the FBI's methods is provided by James Moore, a retired agent for the Bureau of Alcohol, Tobacco and Firearms:

FBI "achievements" in the field of terrorism generally fall into two categories: cases they "adopt" without disclosing that the most critical aspects of the case were actually accomplished by other agencies, and instances where the "accomplishment" is described as "preventing a terrorist act." The latter, translated into what the FBI actually did, consists of having a tip and interviewing the alleged would-be terrorists—informing them that "we know what you're planning" and warning of the consequences, should they choose to carry out the reported plot. Receiving tips is no accomplishment—considering the $3.5 million the FBI paid to informers in 1975 and their mandate, which makes it every police agency's duty to report such rumors to the FBI. "Resolving" the situation through aggressive questioning and dire warning is something any officer could do. Result: No one knows whether there really was a plot, so no one goes to jail.

Even so, a federal commission chaired by former Virginia governor James Gilmore voiced concerns in December 2002 that the FBI might become "a kind of secret police" if its agents continued long-term pursuit of terrorists while also maintaining their normal law enforcement duties. The panel recommended creation of a new National Counter Terrorism Center to "separate the intelligence collection function from the law enforcement function to avoid the impression that the U.S. is establishing a kind of 'secret police.'" Attorney General Ashcroft and Director Mueller predictably opposed any surrender of their new powers under the USA Patriot Act. Recent failures and cutbacks notwithstanding, Ashcroft voiced his belief "that the FBI is well suited to serve as the domestic intelligence and terrorism-prevention agency in the United States," while Mueller deemed the Bureau "uniquely positioned" to perform all jobs at once. It remains to be seen if that faith is well founded.

See also: FEDERAL BUREAU OF INVESTIGATION.

Texas Highway Patrol

In 1927 Texas state legislators created a License and Weight Section within the state's Highway Department. Two years later, the Texas Highway Patrol was organized under License and Weight, to enforce various traffic regulations statewide. In 1935 the Texas Department of Public Safety (DPS) was organized, with the Highway Patrol and TEXAS RANGERS as its nucleus. Subsequent legislation, enacted during 1937–51, gave the DPS a variety of duties, including driver licensing, motor vehicle inspections, and maintenance of vehicle accident records. In 1968 uniformed patrol services were placed under the DPS Traffic Law Enforcement Division, while criminal cases were left to the Criminal Law Enforcement Division. Today the Traffic Law Enforcement Division includes the following branches: the Highway Patrol Service, Driver License Service, License and Weight Service, Motor Vehicle Inspection Service, Breath Test Program, Safety Education Service, and field support operations (including communications and aircraft).

Texas Rangers

Between 1821 and 1823 an estimated 700 citizens of the United States migrated to the Mexican province that is presently the state of Texas. In 1823 the city of Austin established a defensive force of Texas Rangers—so-called because they ranged widely throughout the territory, pursuing bandits and hostile Indians. In 1835 white Texans rebelled against Mexican rule and established a mobile force of 168 Texas Rangers who skirmished Indians while Sam Houston's army fought the troops of General Santa Anna. In December 1836, following establishment of the Texas Republic, legislators established a battalion of 280 mounted riflemen to defend the frontier. Other battalions were later established for various counties, fighting numerous battles with hostile tribesmen through 1845, when Texas joined the Union.

That merger was relatively brief, severed in 1861, when slave-owning Texans voted to secede and join the Confederate States of America. Various Ranger units fought against Union troops in the Civil War (1861–65), then found themselves recast as State Police during Reconstruction (1865–73), when they proved completely ineffective against white terrorist groups including the KU KLUX KLAN, Knights of the White Camellia, and others. After the restoration of all-white "home rule," in May 1874, Governor Richard Coke organized six companies of Texas Rangers, each including 75 men, collectively known as the Frontier Battalion. Serving as a quasi-military force, the Frontier Battalion enforced criminal laws while simultaneously waging war on "outside enemies"—defined as Indians and Mexicans. The Frontier Battalion was formally disbanded in 1901, while the Rangers were reorganized into four companies of 20 men each, assigned to civilian law enforcement duties.

The 20th century presented Texas Rangers with a host of dramatic new challenges, including the Mexican Revolution and Pancho Villa's cross-border raids, World War I, PROHIBITION, and lucrative oil booms. Through much of century's first 20 years, the Rangers maintained a reputation for rough-riding RACISM, exemplified by the PORVENIR MASSACRE of 1918. Governor Miriam Ferguson blamed CORRUPTION for her decision to disband the force in 1925, replacing the old force with 2,300 "special" Rangers (some of whom, ironically, were convicted felons). In August 1935 state legislators created the Texas Department of Public Safety (DPS), absorbing the Rangers and the TEXAS HIGHWAY PATROL as separate divisions, which continue to the present day.

The modern Texas Rangers, with 118 sworn officers and 22 civilian personnel at press time for this volume, are assigned to "suppress all criminal activity in any given area, when it is apparent that the local officials are unwilling or unable to maintain law and order." Additional duties include investigation of ORGANIZED CRIME in Texas, executive protection of elected officials at public functions, investigation of alleged misconduct by other DPS officials, and to provide forensic artwork or hypnosis as investigative tools. September 2000 saw the creation of an Unsolved Crimes Investigation Team, including nine Rangers to investigate current and "cold" murder cases.

"third-degree" tactics

While its origins are long forgotten, the problem of "third-degree" tactics—aggressive interrogation, commonly including violence—remains a serious concern for modern law enforcement. Third-degree brutality differs from ordinary street-level displays of EXCESSIVE FORCE, and even from some cases of deliberate torture (e.g., ABNER LOUIMA), in that its purpose is the extraction of evidence or confessions from suspected criminals. FRAME-UPS sometimes include coerced confessions, but even officers who honestly believe their subject is guilty may elicit false admissions under duress, thereby convicting innocent persons while the guilty escape. While such tactics were once routinely used by police nationwide, progressive court rulings jeopardized convictions obtain in such cases from the 1960s onward. Still, problems continue—as in the revelations of systematic third-degree tactics employed by the PHILADELPHIA POLICE DEPARTMENT through the 1980s—and even

in cases where brutality is clearly proven, the officers involved are rarely prosecuted.

Thomas, Henry Andrew (1850–1912)

Georgia native "Heck" Thomas was born at Oxford on January 6, 1850. His parents hoped he would become a minister, but Thomas ran away from home to join the Confederate Army as a courier for General Stonewall Jackson. Ten years later, married with a family, he moved to Texas during 1871 and found work as a railroad guard. By 1879 Thomas had advanced to serve as chief agent for the Texas Express Company, but he soon left that office to pursue election as Fort Worth's chief of police. Narrowly defeated in that contest, he joined the private Fort Worth Detective Association and soon captured a pair of long-sought fugitives. That exploit earned Thomas appointment as a deputy U.S. marshal, with a transfer to serve under "hanging judge" ISAAC PARKER in Indian Territory (now Oklahoma).

Those were hazardous times for lawmen in the badlands, with 15 officers killed during Thomas's tenure. His wife abandoned him, returning to Georgia with their children in search of a divorce attorney, while Thomas stayed on in pursuit of outlaws. He shot and killed two homicidal fugitives near Dexter, Texas, in September 1885, and was badly wounded himself in another gunfight during June 1888. While recuperating from those injuries, Thomas met his second wife and launched another family, interrupted by his long search for the elusive Dalton and Doolin gangs. In 1893, he was assigned with William Tilghman to tame the town of Perry, Oklahoma, known as "Hell's Half-Acre" for its 110 saloons and 25,000 rowdy residents. Over the next three years, Thomas arrested more than 300 fugitives, winning recognition—with Tilghman and CHRISTIAN MADSEN—as one of Oklahoma's "Three Guardsmen." He was present at outlaw Bill Doolin's killing, near Lawson, in August 1896, but missed his chance to capture "Dynamite Dick" Clifton three months later, at Sapulpa.

In 1902 Thomas accepted appointment as police chief of Lawton, Oklahoma, and served for seven years, until poor health compelled his resignation in 1909. He died in Lawton on August 11, 1912.

See also: TILGHMAN, WILLIAM MATTHEW, JR.

Thompson, Ben (1842–1884)

Ben Thompson was born in England on November 11, 1842, immigrating to Texas with his family at age nine. They settled in Austin, where Thompson acquired some education, then worked as a newspaper printer, while engaging in some teenage gunfights. At age 15, in October 1858, he was fined $100 for wounding a black man on the street, and the following year he shot two hunting companions in an argument over some ducks. In 1860 he joined a posse pursuing the Indian raiders who kidnapped five children, and Thompson's shot dropped the leader of the renegades, permitting the captives to escape.

After that escapade, Thompson moved to New Orleans and worked in a book bindery, where he shot an intruder and was briefly held in jail. Back in Austin when the Civil War began, he joined the Confederate Army and served in Texas for the duration, including an incident at Laredo in 1864, where he killed two Mexicans during a poker game. At war's end in 1865, Thompson remained belligerent, engaging in a shootout with Union occupation troops in Austin that left two Yankees dead and sent Thompson briefly back to jail. After bribing two guards to release him, Thompson fled to Mexico and joined Emperor Maximilian's army at Matamoros. He killed a Mexican policeman there in 1866, but his uniform protected Thompson, and he managed to escape from Mexico before Maximilian was executed.

Making his way in Texas as an itinerant gambler, Thompson drifted from one scrape to another—helping his brother evade a murder charge, fighting a duel with his brother-in-law, serving two years of a four-year prison sentence after he threatened to murder a judge in Austin. Released in 1870, he traveled on to Kansas, where brother Billy murdered Sheriff C. B. Whitney at Ellsworth in 1873. Ben helped his sibling escape once again, then stayed long enough to fight another duel with enemies that August.

The deadly pattern continued as Thompson drifted on to Dodge City in 1878, there befriending Bat Masterson and persuading the lawman to help him extricate brother Billy from another drunken shooting incident in Nebraska. A year later, Thompson stopped in Leadville, Colorado, long enough to participate in the Grant County railroad war of 1879, then used the proceeds of his mercenary stint to open a string of gambling houses in Austin, Texas. Defeated in his first bid to become Austin's city marshal, Thompson tried again in 1881 and was elected. By all accounts, he served with distinction, but only briefly, resigning in 1882 after he killed rival gambler Jack Harris at San Antonio in July 1882. Drinking heavily from that point onward, Thompson went from bad to worse, killed by gunmen on May 11, 1884, in the same Variety Theater where he had slain Jack Harris two years earlier.

See also: MASTERSON BROTHERS.

Thornburgh, Richard Lewis (b. 1932)

A Pennsylvania native, born in Pittsburgh on July 16, 1932, Richard Thornburgh earned an engineering degree from Yale University in 1954, followed by an LL.B. from the University of Pittsburgh in 1957. After 12 years of private practice, he served as U.S. attorney for western Pennsylvania (1969–75), then as assistant U.S. attorney general (1975–77) and as governor of Pennsylvania (1979–87). In his first tour of duty with the U.S. JUSTICE DEPARTMENT, Thornburgh established the department's Public Integrity Section, designed to spearhead prosecution of corrupt politicians. President Ronald Reagan named Thornburgh his third attorney general in August 1988, and Thornburgh remained in that post under successor George H. W. Bush.

Despite his early stance against political CORRUPTION, Thornburgh assisted Presidents Reagan and Bush in their efforts to derail prosecution of conspirators in the Iran-contra scandal, including a failed attempt to dismiss charges filed against defendant Oliver North. Thornburgh treated FBI director WILLIAM SESSIONS with complete disdain, often refusing to accept his calls, but he was willing to expand the Bureau's foreign operations in defiance of international law. On June 12, 1989, Thornburgh authorized G-men to arrest suspected terrorists, drug traffickers, and other fugitives abroad without consulting courts or police in the nations where they reside—an order having no legal effect outside the United States, which might be treated as an act of war by foreign regimes. Thornburgh resigned from Justice in August 1991, later serving as undersecretary-general of the United Nations (1992–93) before returning to private legal practice.

See also: FEDERAL BUREAU OF INVESTIGATION.

Tilghman, William Matthew, Jr. (1854–1924)

Bill Tilghman was born at Fort Dodge, Iowa, on July 4, 1854, and moved to Kansas with his family two years later. By age 16 he was a well-known buffalo hunter, doubling as an army scout until he was appointed deputy SHERIFF of Ford County in 1877. That service was terminated the following year, with two arrests for theft, but Tilghman went straight after a fashion, dividing his time between cattle ranching and running two Dodge City saloons. He subsequently served as marshal of Dodge (1884–86), then hired himself out as a gunman in two of the Jayhawker State's county-seat wars.

In the first conflict, between Coronado and Leoti to become the seat of Wichita County, Tilghman killed his first known victim in a saloon battle fought at nearby Farmer City, on his 34th birthday. Six months later, Tilghman joined James Masterson and others as a "special deputy" of Ingalls, Kansas, in that town's battle against Cimarron, to become the seat of Gray County. Tilghman led a raid on the Cimarron courthouse, on January 14, 1889, that left two men dead and several others wounded. (Tilghman escaped with a sprained ankle.)

Tiring of the wild life, in 1889 Tilghman settled at Perry, Oklahoma, where he soon became a deputy sheriff. In 1892 he was named a deputy U.S. marshal, operating from Chandler, Oklahoma. During 1894–95 he captured three members of the Bill Doolin outlaw gang, including precocious gun moll Jennie "Little Britches" Stevens. Tilghman subsequently served as Lincoln County's sheriff, then won election to Oklahoma's state senate in 1910, but resigned the following year to become police chief of Oklahoma City. PROHIBITION brought Tilghman out of retirement in August 1924, when residents of Cromwell hired him to curb local lawlessness. Two months later, on November 1, Tilghman was fatally wounded while trying to arrest a drunken agent of the TREASURY DEPARTMENT, Wiley Lynn.

See also: MASTERSON BROTHERS.

Tolson, Clyde Anderson (1900–1975)

A Missouri native, born near Laredo on May 22, 1900, Clyde Tolson moved to Iowa as a youth and spent a year (1917) at Cedar Rapids Business College. Somehow avoiding the draft during World War I, he settled in Washington, D.C., during 1918 and enrolled in night classes at George Washington University while working days at the War Department. In 1920 Tolson was appointed confidential secretary to Secretary of War Newton Baker. Tolson finally earned his LL.B. in October 1927 and joined the FBI six months later, on April 2, 1928. On his application, Tolson warned that he was only passing through the Bureau, planning to quit as soon as he had enough money to start a law practice in Cedar Rapids. Director J. EDGAR HOOVER was reportedly amused, telling an aide, "Hire him, if he measures up after the examination and investigation. He will make us a good man."

In fact, he did much more. Within the last six months of 1928 Tolson was stationed in Washington, then transferred to Boston, and finally was recalled to FBI headquarters as chief clerk. On July 31, 1929, Hoover placed him in charge of the Buffalo, New York, field office, then brought him back to Washington as an inspector. On August 16, 1930, Tolson was named assistant director for Personnel and Administration. Less than a year later, Hoover created the new post of assistant to the director (later associate director) for Tolson, thus making him the FBI's number-two man within two short years of joining the Bureau.

Tolson's meteoric rise, coupled with his lifelong bachelorhood and inseparability from Hoover, nurtured rumors that the two men were homosexual lovers. While never definitely proven, the stories were common currency among G-men nationwide and were also widely taken as "common knowledge" among outsiders ranging from gossip columnists to leaders of ORGANIZED CRIME. Whatever the true nature of their personal relationship, from 1928 onward the two men followed a lock-step course through life, even vacationing together on "inspection tours" of race tracks and lavish hotels (all "comped" by wealthy benefactors, many with underworld connections).

Tolson's power grew with that of Hoover and the FBI. In 1936, after Senate critics challenged Hoover's prowess as a lawman, the director staged "personal arrests" of federal fugitives for himself and Tolson: Hoover "captured" bandit Alvin Karpis, while Tolson followed a small army of G-men to clap handcuffs on kidnapper Harry Brunette. Tolson also followed Hoover's lead in 1939, by accepting a commission as a lieutenant commander in the U.S. Naval Reserve (though he had no duties and never spent a day on active duty during World War II).

Tolson's health began to fail in the 1960s, with strokes in 1966–67 leaving him partially disabled. Although he survived and remained on the job, his mental capacity was reduced to the point where he no longer caught all of Hoover's mistakes, and he could not restrain his old friend's erratic fits of rage. Following Hoover's death

J. Edgar Hoover (r) and Clyde A. Tolson (Corbis)

on May 2, 1972, Tolson spent one day as acting FBI director, then ceded his post to L. PATRICK GRAY. Tolson retired from the Bureau on May 16, 1972, and lived in Hoover's former home (which he inherited) until his death on April 14, 1975.

Toma, David (b. 1933)

David Toma was born, the youngest of 12 children in a New Jersey family, in March 1933. His mother was a missionary who often took David along on her visits to jails, where she prayed for the inmates. A gifted high school athlete, Toma joined the U.S. Marine Corps in 1953 and became a service boxing champion, then signed a minor league baseball contract after his return to civilian life. When he failed to make the majors, Toma joined the NEWARK POLICE DEPARTMENT, where a gift for disguises and role-playing made him a natural for UNDERCOVER WORK in vice, gambling, and narcotics. While making thousands of arrests, Toma pursued a second career in public speaking, warning his community about the dangers of DRUGS and street gangs.

In the early 1970s, Toma's street exploits transformed him into a police celebrity, in the mold of EDWARD EGAN, Dennis Farina, and others. ABC television aired a television movie on his life, *Toma*, in 1973, and produced an action series of the same title during 1973–74. While that effort failed to catch fire in the ratings, it was retooled as *Baretta* and ran for six more seasons with Robert Blake in the title role. Toma, meanwhile, retired from police work to pursue a full-time career on the lecture circuit, traveling nationwide with his warnings against substance abuse, delivering an estimated 15,000 speeches as of press time for this volume. His awards for public service include four honorary doctorates, a Humanitarian Award from Columbus Hospital (in Newark), an American Patriots and Humanitarian Award from the International Association of Martial Arts, a "World's Greatest Cop" award from the POLICE BENEVOLENT ASSOCIATION, and a Four Chaplains Award from Vietnam Veterans of America (2004).

Toothman, Edward M.

Edward Toothman joined the OAKLAND POLICE DEPARTMENT as a patrolman in 1941, subsequently advancing through the ranks while he earned a "traffic specialist" certificate from the Northwestern University Traffic Institute. In 1959 he was chosen to replace Chief Wyman Vernon, retiring on the crest of a reform wave that ostensibly had cured Oakland P.D.'s reputation as a force prone to brutality and riddled with CORRUPTION. Toothman sought to maintain that image, but his relentless personal honesty (which earned him the nickname

"The Fang") spilled over into community relations, as when the puritanical chief arbitrarily banned an issue of *Playboy* magazine from Oakland newsstands.

Politically, Toothman fell somewhere to the right of the John Birch Society, showing the same rigidity in his dealings with "radicals" that he displayed in every other aspect of his life. When antiwar protests began in early 1965, Toothman ordered his RED SQUAD to infiltrate the Vietnam Day Committee and report on its local activities. Committee leaders met with Toothman that autumn, seeking permission for a march across Oakland from Berkeley to demonstrate outside an Oakland army base, but Toothman barred access to "his" city, erecting a "Berlin Wall" of uniformed officers on the Bay Bridge to block marchers on October 15–16, 1965. (Only peace demonstrators were barred, however; the police allowed Hell's Angels to pass through the human barricade and assault protesters without official interference.) Afterward, in January 1966, Toothman told interviewer William Turner that the Berkeley students "were antagonistic, unyielding and had no leadership." He termed their proposed demonstration an "impractical" and "arbitrary imposition upon the community," designed (in his view) to provoke riots "more bloody than Watts."

Around the same time, Toothman turned deaf ears to calls for institution of a CIVILIAN REVIEW BOARD to handle complaints of EXCESSIVE FORCE by his officers. That autumn, when protesters picketed his home in an all-white suburb, Chief Toothman summoned 75 officers equipped with gas masks to drive them from the neighborhood. Three months later, Toothman retired prematurely, informing colleagues that he was fed up with civil rights and other protests plaguing Oakland. Departing for Seattle, he listed his old home for sale with a "Caucasians only" clause in the realty contract.

Toothman's reputation preceded him to Seattle, where civic leaders tapped him as interim chief of police during August and September 1970. Behind the scenes, Toothman led a special investigative task force created by King County prosecutor Christopher Bayley and the INTERNATIONAL ASSOCIATION OF CHIEFS OF POLICE, created to root out police corruption in Seattle. Bayley indicted 19 public officials for profiting from illegal gambling, prostitution, bribery, extortion, and blackmail, but most of those charges were later dismissed. Meanwhile, Toothman's task force prepared dual reports near year's end. One report, aired for public consumption, described a limited network of graft involving a few "bad apples" on the force. Privately, in a letter addressed to May Wes Uhlman on September 14, 1970, Toothman wrote: "The information accumulated by the Investigative Task Force indicated that payoffs and the acceptance of bribes and gratuities among certain members of the Seattle Police Department was a practice that had existed for many years." It encompassed the entire Vice Division (where crooked cops netted $70,000 in bribes every year), and was apparently coordinated from the top by Assistant Chief of Police M. E. "Buzz" Cook.

Toucey, Isaac (1792–1869)

Newton, Massachusetts, native Isaac Toucey was born November 15, 1792. He pursued a classical education, then studied law and won admittance to the Connecticut bar in 1818. After four years in private practice, he was appointed Hartford County's prosecutor in 1822 and held that post for 13 years. He subsequently served in Congress (1835–39), then returned to his prosecutor's post in Hartford County (1842–44), and served as Connecticut's governor (1846–47). President James Polk named Toucey U.S. attorney general in June 1848, serving until Polk's administration left office in March 1849. Back in Connecticut, Toucey served once more as a state senator (1850), then was elected to the U.S. Senate (1852–57), and served President James Buchanan as secretary of the navy (1857–61). He died in Hartford, Connecticut, on July 30, 1869.

train robbery

America's first recorded train robbery was committed by Confederate guerrillas at Centralia, Missouri, on September 27, 1864. The raiders escaped with an estimated $6,000, their success encouraging some members of the troupe—Missouri's James and Younger brothers—to continue the practice as civilians, after the cease-fire. They were slow off the mark, however, and the dubious honor of first serial train robbers in the United States goes to Indiana's Reno Brothers, raiding during 1866–68.

Since no federal laws covered robbery at the time, and roving bandit gangs moved freely across state lines, railroads and express companies employed private detectives to pursue and punish train robbers. The firm of WELLS FARGO had been engaged in private law enforcement since 1852, and it was soon joined by the Pinkerton Detective Agency in a guerrilla war of sorts against some of America's most notorious outlaws. While no definitive tabulation exists, train robberies were common events through 1901, when state and private agents finally broke up Butch Cassidy's "Wild Bunch."

Congress passed the Train Robbery Act in 1902, making it a federal crime to board any train with intent to commit robbery or murder. Holdups persisted for a time, with 71 recorded during 1902–05, but by 1907

William Pinkerton felt confident enough to dub train robbers an "almost extinct species." The last known U.S. train robbery was committed in 1937 by bungling outlaws Harry Donaldson and Henry Loftus, who killed one railroad employee in Texas before they were overpowered and disarmed by passengers.

See also: PINKERTON, ALLAN J.

transit police

Transit police are officers specifically employed to prevent or investigate crimes committed on or around urban rapid-transit systems (trains and subways). New York City pioneered the field in 1932, when recruits from the NEW YORK CITY POLICE DEPARTMENT's hiring list were employed as "station supervisors" for the city subway system. A year later, in November 1933, six officers were sworn in as New York State Railway Police and assigned to unarmed patrol on various trains. In 1935 another 20 "station supervisors, class B" were hired, invested with limited powers of arrest. Another 160 joined the force in 1937, supervised by one captain, one inspector, and three lieutenants from the NYPD.

When New York City took over control of the privately run subway lines in 1940, the Transit Police force nearly doubled in size, while falling for the first time under civil service guidelines. Full peace officer status was granted to transit patrolmen in 1947, and the Transit Police Department was formally severed from NYPD eight years later, commanded by former NYPD lieutenant Thomas O'Rourke. Growth continued, with 2,272 officers employed in 1966, increasing to 3,600 by 1975 and 4,500 in 1994 (making Transit P.D. the sixth-largest police department in America). History came full-circle a year later, when the Transit Police Department merged once again with the NYPD.

Treasury Department

From 1789 to the present day, the U.S. government has often used taxation as a means of restricting various commodities—including liquor, DRUGS, and firearms—which it did not ban outright. At the same time, ever-evolving legislation has been passed by Congress to collect federal taxes and prevent counterfeiting of U.S. currency. All of those law enforcement functions, at one time or another in history, have fallen to the U.S. Treasury Department. The CUSTOMS SERVICE and COAST GUARD were initially created as units of Treasury, along with the INTERNAL REVENUE SERVICE (including the Bureau of Alcohol, Tobacco and Firearms), the DRUG ENFORCEMENT ADMINISTRATION, and the U.S. SECRET SERVICE (whose duties include executive protection). Treasury played the leading role in PROHIBITION

Two police officers watch as a portable explosives detector analyzes for trace samples of explosive material after they swabbed a rider's bag at the Grand Central stop in New York after New York City's police department rolled out another antiterrorism device designed to stop bombers from attacking the city's subway system. (Kathy Willens/AP)

enforcement during 1920–33, and continued pursuit of modern bootleggers until those functions were finally transferred to the JUSTICE DEPARTMENT in the 1990s. Other transfers followed the terrorist attacks of September 11, 2001, as various Treasury units were detached for inclusion in the new HOMELAND SECURITY DEPARTMENT. Today Treasury's law enforcement functions are chiefly directed toward exposure and prosecution of federal tax evaders.

See also: TERRORISM.

Tunney, Thomas (1873–)

Born in 1873, Thomas Tunney joined the NEW YORK CITY POLICE DEPARTMENT during THEODORE ROOSEVELT's tenure as commissioner and soon advanced to service on the Black Hand Squad under Lt. JOSEPH PETROSINO. Tunney remained in that post after Petrosino was murdered in Italy, rising to the rank of cap-

tain. On August 1, 1914, he was chosen to lead NYPD's fledgling Neutrality and Bomb Squad, directing 34 detectives in pursuit of presumed anarchists, saboteurs, and agents of combatant nations. Following the ASSASSINATION of Italy's king by anarchist Gaetano Brescia, Tunney declared (but never proved) that the crime was planned by a group of Italian anarchists headquartered on Elizabeth Street in New York's "Little Italy." His response was infiltration, but the officer he chose did not speak Italian, and in fact behaved so suspiciously that he was forced to leave the group under suspicion of acting as a police informant. Tunney's only victory against the "Brescia Group" occurred in March 1915, when disguised officers captured two members on their second attempt to bomb St. Patrick's Cathedral.

Tunney's workload increased exponentially with America's entry into World War I in 1917. Surveillance then expanded to include all manner of "radicals" and "war resisters," ranging from the Industrial Workers of the World to the National Civil Liberties Bureau (later the AMERICAN CIVIL LIBERTIES UNION). That work won Tunney a promotion to inspector, but he soon left the force (with 20 members of his squad) to join the U.S. Army as a captain. There his work remained the same but on a wider front, as Tunney and his team toured the nation, helping to establish "special service" squads in various police departments coast to coast. Upon return-ing to the NYPD at war's end in 1919, Tunney fell victim to political rivalries and found himself demoted from inspector to captain, placed in charge of the pickpocket squad. Recognizing the effective end of his career, he soon resigned to lead his own private detective agency. A cousin, Gene Tunney, subsequently won the world heavyweight boxing championship in 1926.

See also: ANARCHISM.

Ulasewicz, Anthony T. (1918–1998)

Born in 1918, Anthony Ulasewicz joined the NEW YORK CITY POLICE DEPARTMENT and worked his way up through the ranks to serve with the department's "elite" Bureau of Special Services (BOSS) in the turbulent 1960s. In that era, BOSS not only collaborated with the FBI's illegal COINTELPRO operations but exceeded them in many cases, infiltrating various minority and "radical" groups with an eye toward disrupting their activities and practicing ENTRAPMENT. One such case, involving Ulasewicz, was the 1965 indictment of Black Liberation Front members for allegedly plotting to blow up the Statue of Liberty. Trial testimony revealed that most of the "planning" was done by NYPD AGENTS PROVOCATEURS, and the defendants were duly acquitted.

With that background, Ulasewicz soon made the transition from NYPD to the seamy side of big-city private investigations. He was thus engaged in May 1969, when former BOSS colleague John Caulfield introduced Ulasewicz to White House staffer John Ehrlichman. President Richard Nixon, inaugurated only four months earlier, was already obsessed with punishing his political "enemies" and preparing himself for his 1972 reelection campaign. Ulasewicz happily joined the team as a specialist in "BLACK BAG JOBS," willing to bend or break the law on behalf of the highest bidder. Ehrlichman paid him $22,000 per year, siphoned from Republican Party campaign travel funds, and assigned him to various "special" tasks, including a background investigation on presidential impersonator Richard M. Dixon, research on alleged bar-hopping by Speaker of the House Carl Albert, and the tragic Chappaquiddick car crash involving Senator Edward Kennedy and Mary Jo Kopechne.

Ulasewicz reached his pinnacle as a GOP spy in 1972, with creation of CREEP (Committee to Re-Elect the President). Following the Watergate burglary of June 1972, Ulasewicz served as Nixon's bagman, delivering an estimated $75,000 in hush money to various conspirators in that case, while simultaneously planning other "dirty tricks." He also "cased" the Brookings Institution with an eye toward ARSON after White House adviser Charles Colson suggested the place should be burned for its link to release of the Pentagon Papers. Senate investigation of the Watergate break-in soon revealed Ulasewicz's role in the conspiracy, and agents of the INTERNAL REVENUE SERVICE found that he had not declared his GOP income for 1971–72. Indicted for filing fraudulent tax returns, he received a wrist-slap sentence of one year's unsupervised parole. Ulasewicz died in 1998.

undercover work

Undercover operations are distinguished from the use of paid civilian INFORMANTS by involving sworn law enforcement officers who adopt false identities ("covers" or "legends") to penetrate suspected criminal groups and gather evidence from the inside. Most large police departments engage in some degree of undercover work, though infiltration of specific groups may be hampered by racial and religious factors, or by a group's requirement that new members commit certain criminal acts. Among U.S. law enforcement agencies currently practicing such operations, only the FBI has published guidelines for its agents and courted widespread publicity for its achievement in the field.

Undercover operations mounted during the FBI's early history (1917–24) were generally limited to a handful of black agents who penetrated "subversive" black organizations. Director J. EDGAR HOOVER discontinued the practice during his tenure (1924–72), eschewing any plan that violated the Bureau's straitlaced dress code or placed G-men at risk of potential CORRUPTION. (The sole exception was a small team of agents dubbed "The Beards," who grew long hair and infiltrated "New Left" groups near the end of Hoover's life.)

FBI policy changed dramatically after Hoover's death, as subsequent directors relied heavily on undercover operations for "stings" against ORGANIZED CRIME, corrupt politicians, and white-collar crime. Between 1980 and 2000 the Bureau scored numerous indictments and convictions in various operations with code-names such as "Abscam," "Brilab," "Dragon Chase," "Gold Pill," "Greylord," "Lost Trust," and "Silver Shovel." Targets of those stings included venal congressmen, unethical physicians, Mafia leaders, corrupt labor unions, drug dealers, child pornographers, and the like. Agent JOSEPH PISTONE scored a landmark victory as the first FBI agent to penetrate a U.S. Mafia family, sending many of its leaders to prison.

On the downside, undercover operations frequently smack of ENTRAPMENT, and lawsuits have resulted from several campaigns (such as "Operation Recoup," wherein more than 250 good-faith purchasers bought stolen cars). By December 31, 1981, FBI sting operations had already resulted in 29 lawsuits against the JUSTICE DEPARTMENT, with damage claims logged at $424.3 million. To remedy that situation, Attorney General BENJAMIN RICHARD CIVILETTI divided undercover operations into two broad categories labeled Group I (including "sensitive" cases requiring supervision by the FBI's Undercover Operations Review Committee) and Group II (wherein authority for launching sting operations was granted to the agents-in-charge of various field offices).

Group I operations included any investigation of a foreign government, any public official, the news media, or any political-religious organizations; any "domestic security" investigations; any case where agents might break the law (excluding purchase of stolen property or concealing their identities); any case requiring an agent to pose as a lawyer, doctor, journalist, or clergyman; any investigation requiring agents to attend meetings between suspects and their lawyers; and any operation with a risk of significant financial loss to any person. Civiletti also established three general guidelines for undercover activity:

1. Operations are permissible whenever reasonable suspicion of criminal activity exists.

2. Targeted individuals must clearly understand the illegal nature of their own actions.

3. Undercover operations must be "modeled on the real world," rather than fabricating some improbable scenario unlikely to occur without impetus from the FBI.

Those guidelines failed to satisfy the Oregon Supreme Court, which in August 2000 issued a judgment requiring all law enforcement agents to obey a list of ethical rules established by Oregon statute—including a ban on "dishonesty, fraud, deceit or misrepresentation." Henceforth, FBI agents in Washington were barred from adopting "covers" to purchase DRUGS or otherwise trap their targets in criminal activity. Interim U.S. Attorney Mike Mosman called that verdict "a terrible problem" for G-men, calling it "the single greatest challenge" of his career. Defense attorney John Hingson III was more philosophical. "They went rumbling for a fight," he told reporters in July 2001, "and they got kicked."

USA PATRIOT Act

The United States has a long tradition of passing federal legislation in response to crises, including the MANN ACT of 1910 (attacking "white slavery"), the Lindbergh Law of 1932 (aimed at KIDNAPPING), the National Firearms Act of 1934 (intended to disarm gangsters), the SMITH ACT of 1940 (targeting the Communist Party), and others. It was probably inevitable, then, that the catastrophic al-Qaeda attacks of September 11, 2001, should produce legislation seeking to prevent future acts of TERRORISM. Critics, however, charge that the law enacted by Congress and signed by President George W. Bush on October 26, 2001, is a step—or a leap—toward erosion of basic American civil rights.

The law's authors titled it the *Uniting and Strengthening America by Providing Appropriate Tools Required to Intercept and Obstruct Terrorism* (USA PATRIOT) Act. Its major provisions include:

- *Expansion of WIRETAPS and warrants.* Requirements for secret warrants under the Foreign Intelligence Surveillance Act of 1978 are broadened and loosely redefined.

- *Expansion of government authority to search computers.* Requirements for showing "probable cause"—evidence of a criminal act—are eliminated. Henceforth, agents need only claim that information is "relevant" to an ongoing criminal investigation.

- *Exposing confidential records.* The FBI is granted broad new powers to review medical, mental health, financial, and educational records without court orders or producing any evidence of criminal activity.

- *Reviving CIA DOMESTIC SURVEILLANCE.* The Central Intelligence Agency is empowered to designate priority targets for surveillance within the United States, thus violating that agency's original charter restrictions to foreign intelligence collection.

- *Detention of foreign suspects.* The U.S. attorney general is empowered to arrest and detain suspected foreign terrorists for seven days without filing criminal or immigration charges.

- *Designation of terrorist groups.* The attorney general and secretary of state are empowered in their sole discretion to identify "terrorist" organizations and to bar any noncitizen member of those groups from entering the country. Resident aliens holding membership in designated groups may be deported.

- *Secret searches.* Federal agents may obtain warrants and search private property without informing the owner(s).

- *Biological agents and toxins.* Civilian possession is restricted to quantities "justified by a peaceful purpose" (such as medical research). Any possession by nonresident aliens from "countries that support terrorism" is banned.

- *Removing legal barriers between foreign intelligence gathering and domestic criminal investigations.* Henceforth, at their sole discretion, domestic law enforcement agencies are free to share any information gathered during routine criminal investigations (including unverified testimony offered before grand juries) with agencies engaged in foreign intelligence work.

- *Banking provisions.* Banking secrecy regulations are revised to prevent foreign account holders from concealing their identity. Depositors in foreign "shell" banks (existing only on paper) are barred from opening parallel accounts in U.S. banks. American banks are required to monitor transfers from foreign accounts and are penalized for dealing with foreign banks alleged to have "terrorist" ties (as defined by the attorney general or secretary of state).

- *Border surveillance.* The number of border-watching agents from the CUSTOMS SERVICE, BORDER PATROL and the CITIZENSHIP AND IMMIGRATION SERVICE will be tripled.

- *Defining "domestic terrorism."* Domestic terrorism is defined as including any effort "to intimidate or coerce a civilian population" or "to influence the policy of a government by intimidation or coercion." Critics note that the broad definition could be applied to any sociopolitical demonstration, since no specific acts of criminal violence are required.

As administered by Attorney General Ashcroft, the USA PATRIOT Act sparked a series of lawsuits. Mass detention of Muslim immigrants who registered with immigration authorities as required by post-"9/11" regulations have prompted class-action litigation by the AMERICAN CIVIL LIBERTIES UNION and other groups (still unresolved at this writing in 2005). The FBI and other law enforcement agencies can now access library records, including stored electronic data and communications. It seems certain that various other provisions of the law will face challenges in court as long as it remains in force.

U.S. Marshals Service

Established under the Judiciary Act of 1789, the U.S. Marshals Service ranks as America's oldest federal law enforcement agency. The statute mandated appointment of marshals in each U.S. judicial district, to execute and enforce court orders (including execution of condemned prisoners). President George Washington appointed the first 13 marshals on September 24, 1789, and their duties quickly expanded, including pursuit of counterfeiters (until the SECRET SERVICE assumed that task in 1865) and calculation of the U.S. census (until 1870). The service made its first foray into political repression in 1798, after Congress passed a Sedition Act, banning "false, scandalous, and malicious writing" about the federal government.

Controversial and dangerous duties continued for U.S. marshals in the 19th century. Between 1850 and 1861, marshals were expected to enforce the Fugitive Slave Act, pursuing runaway slaves in "free" states and returning them to their white masters. During the Civil War, they chased rebel spies and confiscated northern property used to support the Confederacy. Between 1865 and 1900, U.S. marshals patrolled the "Wild West," battling a cast of desperadoes that included Ned Christie, Bill Doolin, and the Dalton gang. Creation of the JUSTICE DEPARTMENT in 1870 placed marshals under supervision of the attorney general. Two years later, they began assisting the INTERNAL REVENUE SERVICE agents (who lacked police powers) in the arrest of liquor bootleggers. In October 1881 U.S. Marshal Virgil Earp deputized brothers Wyatt and Morgan to battle the Clanton gang at Tombstone, Arizona's O.K. CORRAL. From 1890 onward, marshals were assigned to protect federal judges under order of the U.S. SUPREME COURT.

The 20th century brought new responsibilities and challenges to the Marshals Service. In 1910 revolutionary turmoil in Mexico saw marshals assigned as border guards to block guerrilla raids flowing in both directions. During World War I, marshals competed with the fledgling FBI to capture German spies and saboteurs. Pursuit of bootleggers continued during PROHIBITION, and marshals were also assigned as bailiffs in federal courts between 1920 and 1960. While FBI Director J. EDGAR HOOVER dodged responsibility for civil rights enforcement whenever possible, U.S. marshals frequently took up the slack, guarding black students who entered formerly all-white schools under federal court orders. One such occasion, the OLE MISS RIOT of September 1962 resulted in a pitched battle between U.S. marshals and armed members of the KU KLUX KLAN, supported by racist Mississippi lawmen.

Since 1971 U.S. marshals have administered the federal WITNESS SECURITY PROGRAM, established under the Organized Crime Control Act of 1970. The same year (1971) witnessed creation of a Special Operations Group (or SWAT TEAM), trained in response to critical emergencies. One of the SOG's early missions, in 1973, involved patrols at Wounded Knee, South Dakota, during a federal siege of activists from the American Indian Movement (AIM). That incident found marshals at odds with FBI agents, who financed and armed a militant anti-AIM organization—Guardians of the Oglala Nation, or GOON—on the local reservation. In 1979 the service assumed responsibility for apprehension of federal fugitives, organizing a Fugitive Investigation Strike Team (FIST) in 1981. Three years later, the service also gained responsibility for managing and disposing of properties seized and forfeited by federal defendants nationwide.

See also: EARP BROTHERS; FEDERAL BUREAU OF INVESTIGATION; O.K. CORRAL GUNFIGHT.

Utah Highway Patrol

In 1923 Utah legislators empowered the State Road Commission to patrol state highways and enforce traffic laws. Two years later, the State Road Patrol Force still had only two officers, supervised by civil engineer R. W. Groo. Three additional patrolmen were hired during 1927–28, outfitted with the state's first official uniform in the latter year. State legislators finally passed a Uniform Act Regulating Traffic on Highways in 1931, the same year Patrolman George VanWagenen became the first highway patrolman killed on duty. In 1933 the State Road Patrol Force was officially renamed the Utah Highway Patrol, boasting 30 sworn officers by July 1934. A year later, the Patrol was formally invested with statewide police powers.

Legislation to create a Utah Police School was defeated in 1939, but highway patrol leaders still managed to coordinate a two-week training program, open to all Utah peace officers. Two years later, the UHP was severed from the state Highway Department, henceforth directed personally by the governor. Manpower losses during World War II prompted enlistment of 350 civilian "deputies" in 1942 to guard government property at strategic locations. Patrol cars were equipped with two-way radios in 1944, and the Utah Highway Patrol Civil Service Commission was launched in 1945, with troopers working 60-hour weeks.

The postwar era brought expansion and new technological advancements. Utah's Department of Public Safety was created in 1951, with the Highway Patrol transferred to become a division of the new agency. A 10-man riot squad was established the same year, after the first of several inmate RIOTS at Utah's state prison. A year later, highway patrolmen responded to "Indian uprisings" in San Juan County. Radar patrols began in 1955, and the UHP's riot squad saw more prison action in 1957. The patrol purchased its first aircraft in 1961 and established a statewide police teletype network three years later. Executive protection for the governor was added to the UHP's list of duties in 1965.

In 1980, four decades after the first legislative attempt, the Utah Police Academy was finally constructed. Troopers were allowed to grow mustaches during 1981, and one year later took honors as America's "best dressed" law enforcement agency. In 1984 the UHP received a special U.S. Senate "Award of Achievement" for administration of its Utah/Arizona port of entry. (Three years later, troopers were eliminated from state ports of entry, replaced by "special function officers.") In 1993 the UHP adopted six organizational values, representing the six points of its standard badge: integrity, service, knowledge, professionalism, teamwork, and courage.

Utah State Bureau of Investigation

In 1974, confronted with an alarming rise in substance abuse and traffic in controlled substances, Utah state legislators created the Utah Narcotics and Liquor Law Enforcement Division within the Department of Public Safety. Thirty agents staffed the unit, pursuing liquor bootleggers as well as shipments of illegal DRUGS. The unit has survived several name changes, becoming the Utah Division of Investigations in 1985, the Criminal Investigation Bureau in 1996, and the State Bureau of Investigation in 2000. It was officially disbanded in 2004, its personnel absorbed by the UTAH HIGHWAY PATROL, with criminal investigators assigned to various UHP sections statewide.

Valentine, Lewis Joseph (1882–1946)

Born in 1882, Lewis Valentine was the son of a New York fruit vendor who emigrated from Ireland. He briefly considered the priesthood, then quit high school to work on behalf of his poor family until he joined the NEW YORK CITY POLICE DEPARTMENT in 1903. A decade passed before he earned his sergeant's stripes, prompting NYPD historians to describe Valentine as "just another plodding cop" who made his way through life without distinction. That changed in 1914, when Valentine requested transfer from the hectic Tenderloin district to a quieter precinct, where he could study full-time for his lieutenant's test. Political connections secured the move, and Valentine soon had his new rank—along with a "rabbi" to guide his career.

Inspector Daniel "Honest Dan" Costigan recruited Valentine for a new confidential investigations team, assigning him to track corrupt policemen at a time when NYPD had no INTERNAL AFFAIRS department. Valentine excelled in his work as a "shoofly," but it won him no friends, and retribution was inevitable once Costigan retired from the force in 1918. Valentine soon found himself exiled to Brooklyn as a relief desk lieutenant, filling brief vacancies in the borough's various precincts while vengeful superiors three times rejected his applications for promotion to captain. At last, after eight years of ostracism, Valentine won his captain's bars under new Commissioner George McLaughlin in 1926. Another rapid-fire promotion followed, to deputy inspector, as McLaughlin placed Valentine in charge of his own top-secret raiding team.

Drawing his troops directly from NYPD's POLICE ACADEMY, equipping them with false identities, Valentine launched a whirlwind series of raids against gambling clubs owned by Arnold "The Brain" Rothstein and other top criminals. McLaughlin's departure saw Valentine stripped of his squad and demoted to captain by Commissioner Grover Whalen. Valentine endured another term of exile, until his 1931 testimony in the SEABURY COMMISSION investigation helped topple Mayor Jimmy Walker. In 1933 Mayor Fiorello La Guardia named Valentine deputy police commissioner under John O'Ryan. One year later, after O'Ryan proposed police beatings to cow striking taxi drivers in New York, La Guardia promoted Valentine to replace his recent boss.

Valentine's elevation was the worst possible news for "bad apples" among New York's "finest." During his first six years as commissioner, he fired 300 officers, formally reprimanded another 3,000, and levied fines against 8,000. Civilian transgressors fared no better, as Valentine urged his men who faced suspected killers to "draw quickly and shoot accurately." He forbid EXCESSIVE FORCE against political protesters, but declared that "with . . . criminals, racketeers, and gangsters, the sky is the limit," promising promotions to officers who "kick these gorillas around." Civil libertarians decried Valentine's "mark 'em and muss 'em up" prescription for crime-fighting, and dark suspicions of "THIRD-DEGREE" TACTICS flourished after Valentine barred reporters from crime scenes.

Protests notwithstanding, Valentine's approach toward apprehending felons produced a dramatic decrease in New York's crime statistics. He remained as commissioner until 1945, when the mayoral election of William O'Dwyer prompted Valentine to retire. From NYPD headquarters, he moved on to join NEW JERSEY STATE POLICE commander NORMAN SCHWARTZKOPF, SR. as a narrator for radio's *Gangbusters* series, then accepted Gen. Douglas MacArthur's 1946 request to supervise reform of occupied Japan's police and fire departments. Back in the United States with that imposing task completed, Valentine returned to radio announcing, sat on the editorial board of *True Police Cases* magazine, and served as chief investigator for New York's Election Fraud Bureau. Liver disease claimed his life on December 16, 1946.

Vermont State Police

Until 1947, law enforcement in Vermont rested primarily in the hands of county SHERIFFS and municipal police. A Department of Motor Vehicles Highway Patrol was established in 1936, but its motorcycle officers were restricted to enforcing traffic laws and investigating accidents on state highways. State legislators considered creation of a Department of Public Safety (DPS) in 1937, but budgetary constraints and opposition from jealous county sheriffs stalled the move for another decade. At last, in 1947, the disappearance of an 18-year-old Bennington College student—still unsolved, despite involvement of the FBI—prompted creation of the new DPS under Commissioner Merritt Edson, a former Marine Corps major general who won the Congressional Medal of Honor in World War II.

Though authorized to hire 55 patrolmen and seven civilians, the Vermont State Police began life in July 1947 with 27 officers transferred from the Highway Patrol. The first VSP headquarters, established at Redstone in February 1948, suffered flooding that spring which swamped the basement photo laboratory and forced personnel to work in rubber boots. A starting fleet of 28 patrol cars was purchased for $14,742, and the first state police radio system was established in September 1948. One year later, the VSP gained a new Fire Prevention Division and an Identification and Records Division. William Baumann replaced Commissioner Edson in July 1951, qualified at age 31 as the youngest state police commissioner in the United States.

Year-round tourism, an influx of new industry, and rapid expansion of illegal DRUGS created new challenges for the VSP in the 1960s. State legislators launched a Drug Abuse Control Program, which combined elements of education and enforcement. Narcotics investigations conducted by the VSP increased dramatically from 56 in 1968 to 374 in 1970. That same year (1970) saw the VSP expand to include 193 sworn officers and 85 civilian personnel. Still, the department did not hire its first two female patrol officers until 1977, increasing to a total of 20 female troopers at press time for this volume.

Brisk turnover at the top saw the department led by six different commissioners between 1977 and 1986, until Commissioner A. James Walton, Jr. (1986–2003) restored stability at headquarters. During Walton's tenure, the VSP was chosen to administer a federal drug control and systems improvement grant and underwent sweeping administrative reorganization, while adopting new technology for communication, DNA analysis, and infrared testing of intoxicated drivers.

See also: FEDERAL BUREAU OF INVESTIGATION.

VICAP

While Hollywood has wildly exaggerated the role played by FBI agents in pursuing and capturing serial killers, the Bureau *does* play a part in tracking such predators. The "chase" is typically a mental exercise of profiling unknown subjects, with most of the work done in basement quarters at the FBI Academy in Quantico, Virginia, by members of the Bureau's Investigative Support Unit (formerly Behavioral Science). Accurate PROFILING requires input from detectives working on the case, wherever they may be, and that information is collected through VICAP—the Violent Criminal Apprehension Program.

VICAP was the brainchild of retired Los Angeles police commander Pierce Brooks, a veteran of SERIAL MURDER investigations dating from the 1950s who recognized the glaring lack of any information network geared to track nomadic killers on the move. In Brooks's day, the only method of pursuing such cases was exhaustive study of long-distance news reports or steady correspondence with other (sometimes hostile) law enforcement agencies. Computers offered the obvious solution, and Brooks told anyone who would listen of his plans for a nationwide network designed to collect and compare details of unsolved crimes, thus charting patterns that might otherwise be missed.

Retained by the FBI in 1981, Brooks and former Seattle detective Robert Keppel began hammering out VICAP's framework, drafting an investigative questionnaire for local officers, but they still had far to go in terms of winning over the Washington bureaucracy. Best-selling author Ann Rule beat the drum for VICAP with a series of editorials in 1982, joining Brooks and others to plead the FBI's case in July 1983 Senate hearings. A year later, in July 1984, President Ronald Reagan announced the creation of a National Center for Analysis of Violent Crime, charged with the primary goal of tracking repeat killers. The VICAP computer network, based at the FBI Academy, went online in May 1985, accepting reports of murders, missing persons, and discarded corpses from across the nation.

Unlike fictional G-men and -women, members of the VICAP team and ISU are paid to analyze crimes rather than to conduct active field investigations. With fewer than a dozen full-time agents, ISU is not equipped for staging manhunts, crashing into suspect hideouts, or gunning down desperate killers. On the rare occasions when VICAP agents *do* visit a crime scene, their function is purely advisory, reviewing local task force operations and suggesting more efficient means of handling information. The national program's success or failure ultimately hinges on cooperation from local agencies, where jealousy, resentment, or simple fatigue sometimes conspire to frustrate VICAP.

Six months of operation was enough to highlight VICAP's problems in the field. Overworked police considered the 44-page federal questionnaire too cumbersome and time-consuming. If a killer picked off 10 or 15 victims and the FBI required a separate questionnaire for each, some locals opted to ignore the federal team and spare themselves a case of writer's cramp. The current VICAP forms are two-thirds shorter than their predecessors, but reduced paperwork has not solved all the Bureau's problems in coordinating manhunts. For many local officers, the FBI is still J. EDGAR HOOVER once removed, a headline-grabbing agency more interested in claiming credit for cases solved by local police than helping out the average working cop. Some Bureau spokesmen are still too quick to shoot from the lip—as when an agent in Atlanta blamed anonymous black parents for the deaths of several murdered children—and many police departments still view the feds as rank interlopers, their very presence a tacit indictment of local methods.

A VICAP case where everything apparently worked out as planned occurred in Wilmington, Delaware, where five prostitutes were tortured to death between November 1987 and October 1988. FBI profilers reviewed the case evidence, sketching a portrait of a suspect who was white, a local resident employed in the construction trade, age 25 to 35, fascinated with police work, and using a van for transport and disposal of his victims. Fiber samples taken from bodies narrowed down the range of carpeting inside the van, and VICAP agents recommended a decoy operation to lure the killer with policewomen disguised as hookers. One such decoy managed to obtain some carpet fibers and a license number for the "creepy" trick whose mannerisms set alarm bells ringing in her mind, and surveillance was established on suspect Steven Pennell. A 31-year-old white man, Pennell was a professional electrician with two college semesters of criminology behind him. His applications to local police departments had all been rejected, but he clearly fit the VICAP profile as a "police buff." Scientific analysis of hairs, fibers, and bloodstains from his van convinced a jury of Pennell's guilt in two murders, and he was executed by lethal injection on March 14, 1992.

VICAP spokesmen often cite Pennell's case as proof positive of their success in profiling killers, but Delaware authorities—while grateful for the FBI's help—are more reserved. The fiber evidence was critical, they grant, but it had no connection to the suspect profile, which local investigators now describe as "mostly general stuff." The decoy operation was standard police work, they say, and would have caught Pennell regardless of his occupation, race, or age.

Sour grapes? A touch of jealousy, perhaps? In any case, while many frontline homicide investigators readily acknowledge VICAP's value in connecting far-flung crimes, some still insist that the program has yet to prove itself capable of identifying a specific predator and bringing him (or her) to justice.

ViCLAS

ViCLAS—the Violent Crime Analysis Linkage System—was the brainchild of Canada's first criminal profiler, Sergeant Ron MacKay. Assigned to the General Investigative Section of the Royal Canadian Mounted Police (RCMP) in North Vancouver, MacKay envisioned a system that would improve on the FBI's VICAP program for linking unsolved homicides and sexual assaults across the country. When MacKay conceived his idea in August 1990, the RCMP already maintained a Major Case File at headquarters in Ottawa, but most local police departments refused to submit the voluminous paperwork required for case submissions. MacKay and colleague Keith Davidson sought to remedy that problem with computers, recruiting two students at Ottawa's Algonquin College—Paul Leury and John Ripley—to write the necessary software programs.

Although actively employed from 1992, ViCLAS was formally unveiled on December 16, 1993, with a press conference held at the Ontario Provincial Police Academy outside Toronto. Present for the system's public launch were various RCMP leaders, together with officers from 23 Canadian law enforcement agencies, the FBI, New York and New Jersey State Police, and members of Iowa's Sex Crimes Analysis Section. Administration of ViCLAS was assigned to a new Canadian Association of Violent Crime Analysts (CAVCA).

Like VICAP, the ViCLAS program requires submission of detailed questionnaires from field investigators. Submission forms consist of a 36-page booklet with 245 questions (cut from an original 262 in 1995) or a shorter eight-page form with 83 questions. Within 18 months of its launch, ViCLAS had drawn 57 links among 584 unsolved cases on file. By the end of 1995, the system permitted MacKay to estimate that Canada hosted 12 to 20 active serial killers at large. While some resistance lingers, voluntary ViCLAS submissions increased from 124 cases in 1992 (the year before its formal launch) to 120,362 cases by September 2001.

Since its inception, interest in ViCLAS has spread rapidly around the world. Authorities in Austria and the Netherlands committed to its use on February 9, 1995, four days before MacKay presented the system at an international conference in China. Since then, ViCLAS has been adopted in Australia, Sweden, and several U.S. states. FBI agent Mike Cryan, assigned to the VICAP program at Quantico, Virginia, described ViCLAS as "the Cadillac system in the world," and VICAP pioneer David Cavanaugh (at Harvard University) was equally impressed. "The Canadians," Cavanaugh said, "have done to automated case linkage what the Japanese did with assembly line auto production. They have taken a good American idea and transformed it into the best in the world." On December 13, 1995, summarizing police failures in the case of Ontario sex-slayers Paul Bernardo and Karla Homolka, Justice Archie Campbell recommended that ViCLAS submissions should be mandatory throughout the province. He wrote:

> Experience shows that it is not enough merely to encourage ViCLAS reporting by means of the standard policies and procedures of individual forces. Encouragement is not enough. Unless the entry of information into ViCLAS is centrally mandated and enforced throughout Ontario, and its operation supported through training and strong reinforcement of the reporting requirement, its power to link predatory serial crimes is greatly weakened.

Despite such widespread praise and multiple requests from its own analysts, FBI headquarters remains stubbornly opposed to adoption of ViCLAS in place of VICAP. Given the bureau's history and elitist attitudes, that resistance is unlikely to subside in the near future.

vigilance committees

Vigilance (or vigilante) committees are defined as extralegal groups that engage in private punishment of lawbreakers. Historically, in the United States, they have existed for the most part in frontier regions where courts and law enforcement agencies were not established, but they have also operated in jurisdictions where police were considered (by the vigilantes) as either too corrupt or inefficient to curb rampant crime. The same justification has been claimed by a variety of criminal and terrorist groups—notably the violent KU

KLUX KLAN—which indulge in LYNCHINGS and similar activities motivated by politics or RACISM.

The first acknowledged U.S. vigilance committee operated around Piedmont, South Carolina, during 1767–69, executing at least 16 persons. In 1969 historian Richard Maxwell Brown surveyed vigilante groups for the National Commission on the Causes and Prevention of Violence, reporting that 369 such groups were active in 33 states between 1767 and 1902, executing a minimum of 728 alleged criminals. Those executions, however, include only those publicly announced by the vigilantes or reported by newspapers, and the actual tally was probably much higher.

Virginia State Police

While Virginia state legislators mandated licensing and registration of automobiles in 1906, no officers were hired to enforce that statute for the next five years. In 1911 Louis Blankenship was named the state's first "inspector," without police powers, while Edwin Bosher exercised limited police powers for the state Highway Department. Another eight years passed before a new battery of Automobile Acts invested the state commissioner of motor vehicles and his assistants with the full power of county SHERIFFS. Finally, in 1922, the embryonic Virginia State Police was founded as the Highway Department's Enforcement Division, with eight inspectors on staff. One year later, the legislature created a new Division of Motor Vehicles, transferring all traffic enforcement authority to the new agency, while a motorcycle patrol force was organized under commander J. H. Hayes.

Expansion followed the proliferation of Virginia state highways and automobiles. May 1930 witnessed the first imposition of physical and mental examinations for prospective highway patrolmen. Two years later, the department was empowered to enforce state criminal laws, as well as traffic codes. The department's first extended training school convened that same year, with 60 candidates vying for 25 positions. In November 1938 highway patrolmen were officially renamed "state troopers," and a Bureau of Criminal Investigations was launched as Virginia's "little FBI," investigating major crimes and auto thefts, as well as screening applicants for state police positions.

World War II drained department manpower, leaving only 109 of 248 officers on active duty. New legislation expanded the VSP's authorized strength to 403 in 1946, but that target goal was not attained until 1960, one year after troopers won the right to a five-day work week. The VSP's first K-9 UNIT was organized in 1961, to cope with public demonstrations by civil rights activists and the violent KU KLUX KLAN. Still, it was 1969 before the force hired its first black officer (Reginald Boyd), and the first female trooper (Cheryl Nottingham) was not recruited until 1976. Meanwhile, a new Criminal Intelligence Unit, organized in 1973, assumed responsibility for ARSON investigations and research on ORGANIZED CRIME. The Division of Investigation, launched with 109 officers in 1974, was replaced five years later by a new Bureau of Criminal Investigation (BCI), including five divisions: Administrative Services, Arson Investigation, Criminal Intelligence, General Investigation, and Special Investigation.

The Virginia State Police won accreditation from the National Commission of Accreditation for Law Enforcement Agencies in 1986, renewed successively in 1991, 1996, and 2001. Its Auto Theft Unit and Fugitive Unit were created in 1988. Three years later, the BCI was streamlined into three divisions—General Investigations, Special Investigations, and Support Services. Virginia's lax GUN CONTROL laws made the state a frequent source of firearms used by outside criminals from Washington, D.C., to New York City, prompting belated creation of a Firearms Investigative Unit to track illegal weapons sales in 1992. By the end of the 20th century, the VSP included 1,494 sworn officers (332 assigned to the BCI), and 636 civilian personnel.

See also: FEDERAL BUREAU OF INVESTIGATION.

Vollmer, August (1876–1955)

The son of German immigrants, born in New Orleans in 1876, August Vollmer ended his formal education in sixth grade, with a subsequent course in bookkeeping, typing, and shorthand at New Orleans Academy. His family moved to Berkeley, California, in 1891, and Vollmer joined a friend to run a coal and feed store, while serving with the city's volunteer fire department. With the outbreak of the Spanish-American War in 1898, he volunteered for military service and was twice decorated for valor during combat in the Philippines. Back in civilian life, he worked as a Berkeley mail carrier, then won election as city marshal in 1905, on a platform calling for reorganization of the city's police department along military lines. Vollmer held that post (renamed chief of police in 1909) until 1932, and in the process revolutionized American police work.

Vollmer took office at a crucial moment for the BERKELEY POLICE DEPARTMENT. The force was a corrupt and brutal unit, so ineffectual that street gang violence in West Berkeley had forced the Southern Pacific Railroad to abandon its local depot. Instead of hiring more sluggers—the kind of policemen Vollmer labeled "dumbbells"—he publicly denounced both EXCESSIVE FORCE and CAPITAL PUNISHMENT, calling instead for a concerted attack on the sociological roots of crime. In 1908 Vollmer opened the Berkeley Police School, serving as its chief instructor, expanding over time until 1930s recruits spent 312 hours in the classroom. Vollmer's tactical innovations included use of bicycles, then automobiles, to make his patrolmen more mobile, linked to headquarters by two-way radios. He also pioneered in use of FINGERPRINTS, handwriting classification, and use of "LIE DETECTORS" to screen criminal suspects, while leading the nation in employment of female officers. When recruiting, Vollmer gave priority to college graduates and he himself taught summer sessions in police science at the University of California from 1916 to 1932.

Vollmer's approach to crime-fighting was outlined in a 1919 article for *Police Journal*, "The Policeman as a Social Worker." He encouraged his officers to intervene in the lives of civilians on their beats, especially where juveniles might be diverted from a life of crime. For detection of felons already at large, Vollmer established the nation's first professional crime lab in 1916, and developed modus operandi files as a form of early PROFILING. Vollmer's reputation prompted supervisors of the LOS ANGELES POLICE DEPARTMENT to "borrow" him for a year, during 1923–24, and while Vollmer did his best for LAPD—founding the department's POLICE ACADEMY, establishing a modern motor pool and commissioning five new precinct houses, schooling his men in Constitutional ethics—LAPD in the 1920s was essentially beyond redemption.

By 1932, when he retired from the Berkeley PD, Vollmer had been hired as a consultant by civic leaders in Chicago, Dallas, and Havana, Cuba. Twenty-five of his former subordinates also served as police chiefs in various towns nationwide, while Vollmer himself headed President Herbert Hoover's Commission on Law Enforcement. In retirement, Vollmer served as professor of police administration in the department he had established at UC Berkeley. He also distilled a lifetime of study into one volume, *The Criminal*, published in 1949. In the early 1950s, Vollmer was diagnosed with throat cancer (from a lifetime of smoking) and the onset of Parkinson's disease. After willing his body to the University of California's medical center, he committed suicide on November 4, 1955.

Waldo, Rhinelander (1877–1927)

Born in 1877, Rhinelander Waldo graduated from West Point at age 24 and was dispatched immediately as a captain of the U.S. Army to pursue anti-American guerrillas in the Philippines. Five years later, back in civilian life, he was named deputy police commissioner for New York City, but Waldo resigned in 1907 to head a special police force maintained by the Catskill watershed system. He subsequently served as New York City's fire commissioner, then one appointment as police commissioner.

NYPD historians James Lardner and Thomas Reppetto describe Waldo as "the most hapless" commissioner in the department's history. He collected volumes on international police techniques, but seemed to grasp little or none of the wisdom they contained. Under his predecessor, police raids on "orderly" vice dens had been banned unless civilian neighbors filed official charges, yet the drumbeat of complaints from Rev. CHARLES PARKHURST continued, prompting Waldo to establish new raiding teams. Unfortunately, he chose Lt. CHARLES BECKER to command one of the squads, and Becker's subsequent murder conviction prompted Waldo's dismissal in 1913. He later served as a colonel in the U.S. Army during World War I, then dabbled unsuccessfully in politics. Waldo died in 1927 at age 50.

Walker, J. P. (1917–1976)

Born in 1917, Mississippi native J. P. Walker grew into the living, breathing cliché of a southern lawman, from his girth and habitual use of initials to his virulent RACISM and reckless violence. Walker joined the U.S. Army in June 1936, then deserted on February 1, 1938, after receiving a one-month brig sentence for failure to use prophylaxis during sexual intercourse. Instead of hiding out, however, he rejoined the army in New Orleans, under a false name, and was home on leave from that second enlistment when military police arrested him in Picayune, Mississippi. Walker received a general discharge after his second court-martial on April 10, 1941, but strangely remained in the service on his second enlistment until June 23, 1942, when he was released on medical grounds. Army physicians blamed a cyst on his tailbone, while suppressing their diagnosis of Walker as a "constitutional psychopathic state" with an "inadequate personality."

Home again in Pearl River County, where his father served as SHERIFF, Walker worked as a mechanic, then joined the NATIONAL GUARD in 1950 and served in Korea, finally winning an honorable discharge (for family hardship) in 1951. He opened an auto body shop in Picayune, then spent four years (1952–56) as a deputy sheriff, resigning shortly after Osborne Moody defeated him in the race to become county sheriff and tax collector. Law enforcement colleagues from that period recall Walker as being tough on prisoners, especially blacks, and some report that he (like Pascagoula Sheriff IRA GRIMSLEY) sexually assaulted female inmates of the county jail. By 1959 Walker was tired of working on cars and announced his intent to run once more for sheriff, on a platform of "keeping the niggers down."

His big break came in April 1959, when black suspect Mack Parker was jailed in Poplarville on charges of raping a white woman two months earlier. On April 25 Walker led a gang that removed Parker from jail, with the apparent connivance of his keepers, and drove him across the state line into Louisiana. There Parker was shot and thrown into a river near Bogalusa, where his body was found on May 4. FBI agents investigated the LYNCHING and identified 23 alleged participants, naming Walker as the probable triggerman. Still, local prosecutors refused to file murder charges, and a federal grand jury declined even to question Walker, reporting in January 1960 that they could not indict the lynchers "on the basis of the evidence presented."

Outgoing Sheriff Moody, barred by law from succeeding himself in office, opined that Walker led the mob "partly as an act of racial prejudice and partly as an election ploy." In Mississippi, racial murder was considered evidence of character in those days, and it nearly swept Walker into office. In the August primary, he tied with competitor Bill Owen for votes cast, then narrowly lost in a run-off election. County voters were more generous in 1963, electing Walker sheriff by a landslide. His wife replaced him in 1967, instantly hiring Walker back as a deputy, and Walker was elected sheriff once again in 1971. (His reelection was not hampered by reports that he had tried to frame a rock band, the American Indians, by planting DRUGS in their luggage, nor by his attempt to kill curious newsmen with his squad car when they asked about the frame-up.) State laws were altered in 1975, allowing Walker to succeed himself, but he lost that year's election to his brother-in-law and died a short time later, in early 1976.

See also: FEDERAL BUREAU OF INVESTIGATION; FRAME-UPS; SHERIFFS.

Wall of Honor

Many police departments throughout the United States and around the world maintain a "Wall of Honor" commemorating officers killed in the line of duty. In 1991 President George H. W. Bush dedicated the National Law Enforcement Officers Memorial on Judiciary Square, in Washington, D.C. Designed by architect Davis Buckely, the monument stands on three acres of park land, with dual "paths of remembrance" and blue-gray marble walls bearing the names of some 17,000 officers slain since the first known line-of-duty death in 1792. Each path is guarded by bronze statues of a lioness guarding her cubs, sculpted by artist Raymond Kaskey. The memorial's thematic inscription reads: "In Valor There is Hope."

Wallace, William Alexander Anderson (1817–1899)

Legendary Texan William "Bigfoot" Wallace was born at Lexington, Virginia, on April 3, 1817, a descendant of Scottish freedom fighter William "Braveheart" Wal-

lace. His family migrated to the United States soon after the American Revolution and remained close to the scene of frontier conflict ever after. Wallace lost a brother and cousin in Texas, at the Goliad massacre of 1836, but his pledge of revenge was delayed by Texan victory in the revolt against Mexico.

Wallace tried ranching near LaGrange, Texas, in 1838, but he found the stationary life distasteful. Some sources claim he helped plot and build the new Texas capital at Austin in 1840, while others contend that he stayed in town only long enough to grow sick of the crowds. He fought in the Battle of Plum Creek that same year, then soon found himself in San Antonio, where he was briefly accused of burglarizing a neighbor's home. Fourteen-inch footprints left by the thief exonerated Wallace, pointing to an Indian culprit nicknamed "Bigfoot," but the sobriquet stuck to Wallace as well.

In 1842 Wallace helped repel Mexican General Adrian Woll's invasion of Texas, then volunteered for the retaliatory Somerwell and Mier expeditions south of the Rio Grande. Captured on the latter raid, he was spared from execution but spent time in Perote Prison before his parole to Texas. Undeterred by defeat and captivity, Wallace fought in the Mexican War (1846–48), then led a troop of TEXAS RANGERS in the 1850s, chasing outlaws and hostile Indians along the Tex-Mex border. His expertise at tracking also made Bigfoot a favorite of slave traders, who hired him to stalk runaways and retrieve them before they could reach freedom in Mexico. Wallace avoided front-line combat in the Civil War, but spent the duration guarding the Texas borderlands against Comanches.

Never married, Wallace retired in due course to a tiny village named Bigfoot, in Frio County. Publication of his biography (written by John Duval) in 1870 enshrined Wallace as a permanent Texas folk hero. He died on January 7, 1899, and was buried at Devine, exhumed one month later for reburial at Austin's State Cemetery.

Walling, George Washington (1823–1891)

New Jersey native George Walling attended village schools as a child, then worked packet boats on the Hudson River and Long Island Sound, including a tour on a U.S. revenue cutter (forerunner of the COAST GUARD). In 1847 a well-connected friend resigned his post on the NEW YORK CITY POLICE DEPARTMENT and nominated Walling to replace him, a switch accomplished with assistance from a corrupt alderman. Walling joined the force in December 1847, assigned to the Third Ward, which included City Hall.

In 1856 Walling was one of 300 mutinous officers who left the municipal police force (controlled by

Mayor Fernando Wood) to create a rival metropolitan force. Walling led the team that arrested Mayor Wood in his office, but that failed to resolve the dispute, and for several weeks New York City boasted *two* police forces, as likely to brawl with each other on sight as to jail common felons. Promoted to captain, Walling emerged on the winning side of New York's police feud and was chosen in 1858 to lead NYPD's first 24-man detective force. Five years later, he led the counterattack against lynch-happy mobs during the 1863 draft RIOTS. At one point, separated from his men, Walling met a crowd of rioters breaking into a gun shop. Rushing forward with only his baton, he clubbed the gang's leader, killing him instantly and putting the others to flight.

Named police commissioner in 1875, Walling served for a decade before he finally retired, after 38 years with NYPD. His memoirs, published in 1887, popularized the term *third-degree* for violent extraction of confessions, supported by Walling's admission that "I believe in any method of proving crime against a criminal." Walling died in 1891, leaving future generations of New York's "finest" to follow his example.

Wambaugh, Joseph Aloysius, Jr. (b. 1937)

A native of East Pittsburgh, Pennsylvania, born on January 22, 1937, Joseph Wambaugh received his B.A. from California State College in 1960 and joined the LOS ANGELES POLICE DEPARTMENT that same year. He subsequently earned a master's degree (1968), while rising to the rank of detective with the LAPD. Drawing upon his own experience and tales related by his fellow cops, Wambaugh produced four best-selling books—*The New Centurions* (1970), *The Blue Knight* (1972), *The Onion Field* (1973), and *The Choirboys* (1975)—while still employed with the police department. He then retired to write full-time in 1975, enjoying a long and lucrative career. At press time for this volume, his other books (all bestsellers) included *The Black Marble* (1977), *The Glitter Dome* (1981), *The Delta Star* (1983), *Lines and Shadows* (1984), *The Secrets of Harry Bright* (1985), *Echoes in the Darkness* (1987), *The Blooding* (1989), *The Golden Orange* (1990), *Fugitive Nights* (1992), *Finnegan's Week* (1993), *Floaters* (1996), and *Fire Lover* (2002).

Ward, Benjamin (1926–2002)

Born in 1926, Benjamin Ward was the 10th of 11 children born to a poor black family in Brooklyn, New York. Six of his siblings died in childhood, and Ward later recalled that "everybody around me was poor." He graduated from Brooklyn High School of Automotive Trades in 1944, then spent two years in the

U.S. Army. Back in civilian life, Ward drifted through various jobs until June 1951, when he scored the third-highest mark among 78,000 applicants on an entrance test for the NEW YORK CITY POLICE DEPARTMENT.

Upon completion of his NYPD training, Ward became the first black officer assigned to the 80th Precinct. While confronting RACISM and felons by day, he continued his studies at night, earning his A.A. in police science (1958) and a B.A. in sociology (1961) from Brooklyn College, followed by an LL.B. from Brooklyn Law School (1965). In 1968 Ward was named deputy police commissioner, followed by another promotion to traffic commissioner in 1973. Two years later, Ward was named to head the New York City Department of Corrections, followed in 1979 by a brief appointment to lead the city's Housing Authority, then was chosen commissioner of the state prison system (1979–83). In that post, he launched a drive to bar KU KLUX KLAN members from serving as prison guards, but the courts ultimately ruled against him. In January 1984, confronted by charges of police brutality in Harlem, Mayor Ed Koch chose Ward as New York's first black police commissioner.

Ward's first step toward remediation of the problem was creation of a new Community Patrol Officers Program, wherein special teams consisting of a sergeant and 10–12 officers were assigned to facilitate police-community relations in 64 of New York's 75 precincts. During his five years as commissioner, Ward also added 2,000 officers to the NYPD's ranks, while increasing educational requirements for recruits and fast-tracking promotion of nonwhite officers. In 1988 he sparked controversy by comparing the civilian Guardian Angels to "lynch mobs" and "vigilantes who roam the city in wolf packs." In October of that year, Ward transferred 49 policemen from a precinct in Queens, following complaints of racial harassment from black officers.

Poor health forced Ward's retirement in 1989, but he remained active as an instructor at Brooklyn Law School and John Jay College of Criminal Justice. To those who claimed his advancement at NYPD was due primarily to race, he replied, "I've been smart as hell, and that smartness has been more important than my blackness. Many people make the mistake of thinking that black people are liberal because they are black. I'm very, very liberal when it comes to race relations; but when it comes to law enforcement, I am very, very conservative." Ward died in June 2002 at age 75.

"War on Drugs"

While federal, state, and local authorities have interrupted traffic in various proscribed DRUGS since the late 1900s, the U.S. "War on Drugs" was only formally declared in January 1982 by President Ronald Reagan. Reagan assigned Vice President George H. W. Bush to lead the crusade, while Attorney General WILLIAM SMITH assigned the FBI and the DRUG ENFORCEMENT ADMINISTRATION to joint jurisdiction in federal drug cases. (G-men had formerly avoided narcotics enforcement, leaving it primarily to the TREASURY DEPARTMENT.)

The new "war" was a curious effort from the start, with Reagan slashing funds for drug enforcement even as he announced the sweeping campaign. Despite the president's professed determination to make America drug-free, he cut the FBI's budget by 6 percent and the DEA's by 12 percent, forcing dismissal of 211 agents and 223 support personnel. Senator Joseph Biden noted the cutbacks, coupled with an astounding 60 percent drop in criminal cases prosecuted by the JUSTICE DEPARTMENT under Reagan, and demanded an investigation by the General Accounting Office, but Reagan and Attorney General Smith refused to cooperate by providing necessary documents. By March 1982 some COAST GUARD officers in Florida had branded the drug war "an intellectual fraud."

Eighteen years later, in August 2001, Attorney General JOHN ASHCROFT proclaimed victory in the drug war, noting that 30,000 defendants had been charged with federal drug offenses in 1999. That figure more than doubled the arrest total for 1986, and 91 percent of those convicted at trial were charged with trafficking (versus simple possession). Critics responded to Ashcroft's victory proclamation by noting that 10 percent or less of all drugs entering America were captured by authorities. Debate over that issue vanished three weeks later, with the 9/11 terrorist attacks. Overnight, TERRORISM became the Justice Department's primary target, with public statements announcing a drastic cutback in prosecution of "ordinary" crimes. Premature celebrations notwithstanding, the War on Drugs is far from won—and some critics insist it should never have been waged at all, since most drug offenses involve CONSENSUAL CRIMES.

Washburn, Elmer

Richard Lindberg, unofficial historian of the CHICAGO POLICE DEPARTMENT, described Chief Elmer Washburn as "a man of ripe experience in public affairs but sadly lacking in his perceptions." During his brief command (1872–73), Washburn tried to run a tight ship, enforcing Sunday closing laws and vowing to the public that his officers would ardently uphold all statutes, but the CPD's endemic CORRUPTION and political patronage proved too much for a lone reformer. Washburn's special enemies were German-Irish brewers and the city's many gamblers, whose establishments he raided with a special zeal. Washburn and Mayor Joseph Medill soon

found themselves locked in political combat with the "Committee of Seventy," created in September 1872, for control of the city's police commission. Washburn's opponents insisted that no vice raids should be conducted without prior notice to the commission—a circumstance which invariably resulted in the targets being warned, facilitating their escape. Washburn finally surrendered and resigned, replaced by longtime brewer and two-time former chief JACOB REHM.

Washington, D.C., Metropolitan Police Department

In 1790 Maryland and Virginia ceded portions of their respective states to create the District of Columbia. Constables from both states policed the district until 1802, when Washington, D.C., was chartered as a city with authority to establish patrols and enforce its own laws. Until 1861 the nation's capital made do with an auxiliary watch, consisting of one captain and 15 patrolmen. Outbreak of the Civil War prompted creation of the Metropolitan Police Department—modeled on London's Metropolitan Police and the NEW YORK CITY POLICE DEPARTMENT—which endures to the present day.

Formally established in August 1861, under Superintendent William Webb, Washington's police force started with 10 sergeants and an authorized maximum of 150 patrolmen. No badges or equipment were supplied for the police, who worked 12-hour shifts, seven days per week. Two decades passed before the first matrons were hired, in 1881, forming the basis for a later Women's Bureau handling all cases involving juveniles and female adults. A police "School of Instruction"—forerunner of the present Training Division—was belatedly established in 1919, processing 22 recruits at a time through a 30-day training course.

Policing the nation's capital has involved some unique challenges, including investigation of two presidential ASSASSINATIONS in 1865 (Abraham Lincoln) and 1881 (James Garfield), plus failed attempts on the lives of President Harry Truman, President Ronald Reagan, and Councilman (later mayor) Marion Barry, Jr. Today the Metropolitan Police Department includes 3,600 sworn officers and more than 600 civilian employees. It patrols the city at large, while security for various government buildings falls to officers of the CAPITOL POLICE and the U.S. SECRET SERVICE. At last report, the force leads all other U.S. police departments in its percentage of nonwhite female officers (22.7 percent).

Washington State Patrol

Washington state legislators authorized creation of a highway police force on June 8, 1921, with the first six motorcycle patrolmen commissioned on September 1. While officers were issued badges, cap emblems, and pistols, some worked without standard uniforms until 1924. Nine years later, the state's Highway Patrol Division was officially renamed the Washington State Patrol, invested with full police powers and reporting directly to the governor. Communications remained haphazard until 1933, when the first police radio (in Vancouver) replaced a motley system of transmitting orders via mail, by telephone, or through county SHERIFFS.

Traffic safety duties of the WSP expanded during World War II, with creation of a Motor Vehicle Inspection Division and a Weight Division in 1943. The same year witnessed installation of two-way radios in all patrol cars, followed by inauguration of the first full-time training center in 1947. The WSP's Investigative Assistance Division was established in 1973, including a Narcotics Section, an Organized Crime Intelligence Unit, a Missing Children Clearinghouse, and a Clandestine Laboratory Response Team to raid illicit drug factories. One year later, the Identification and Criminal History Section was established, followed by two full-service crime labs (in Seattle and Spokane) in 1975. The year 1975 also witnessed recruitment of the WSP's first female patrol officers.

The WSP earned international recognition in 1991 for its development of an innovative mobile computer network, which linked laptop computers in patrol cars with satellite and land-based radio communication technology. Four years later, in April 1995, Chief Annette Sandberg became the first woman named to head a state law enforcement agency in the United States. July 1995 witnessed the transfer of the state fire marshal's Office to the WSP's Fire Protection Services unit.

See also: ORGANIZED CRIME.

weapons

Unlike police in England, the majority of sworn officers in the United States are habitually armed. Firearms are standard equipment for police throughout the nation, and most are now also equipped with a variety of weapons commonly classified as nonlethal—though, in fact, *all* weapons may inflict fatal injuries, depending on the circumstances of their application.

The earliest American police weapons were clubs, and many officers today still carry various impact weapons designed to give them an edge in hand-to-hand combat. Full-sized batons, often called nightsticks or billy clubs, are the classic example, although their deployment in street confrontations was downplayed in the 1970s, following various publicized POLICE RIOTS against civil rights marchers and antiwar protesters. Officers assigned to plainclothes or UNDERCOVER WORK

often carry smaller impact weapons, commonly called saps or blackjacks, and collapsible batons are now available, combining easy concealment with extension of an officer's reach in crisis situations. Batons are generally termed nonlethal weapons, but like any other club, they may produce fatalities if used incorrectly or with EXCESSIVE FORCE.

Handguns are today the most common police weapons, available in a variety of styles. Six-shot revolvers were popularized in the mid-19th century and remained the standard sidearm of most American police (outside of military service) until the 1980s, when a trend toward semiautomatic pistols swept the country. Some departments still require their officers to carry revolvers, but a majority now prefer the semiautomatic models for their higher ammunition capacity, swifter reloading, and rapid rate of fire. Long guns—those designed to be aimed and fired from the shoulder—are frequently carried in patrol cars as backup weapons, where the support of a shotgun or rifle may be critical in life-or-death confrontations. Special units such as SWAT TEAMS also train and carry a variety of specialized sniper rifles (for precise long-distance shooting) and full-automatic weapons such as submachine guns.

Various chemical and pyrotechnic devices are used by police to subdue individuals without serious injury, to incapacitate or flush out barricaded subjects, and for purposes of crowd control. The pyrotechnics include so-called flash-bang grenades, whose blinding light and stunning noise (sometimes augmented with hard-rubber shrapnel) are designed specifically to render targets helpless in close spaces. Common tear gas has been supplemented during recent years with other compounds including military CS gas, chemical Mace, and pepper spray, all of which interfere with a target's ability to see and breathe. None are designed to be lethal, but asphyxiation is at least a long-shot possibility whenever gas is used. Likewise, Boston police were forced to reevaluate delivery of pepper spray via pellets fired from guns after a college student was struck in the eye and killed during Game 1 of the 2004 World Series.

Electroshock weapons were first employed by American police in the 1960s, earning a foul reputation after Alabama sheriff JAMES G. CLARK, JR. and others used cattle prods against black civil rights demonstrators. Today many police officers and jailers carry "nonlethal" stun guns, including models that require direct contact with targets and others (like the Taser), which fire darts attached to thin wires and subdue their subjects from a distance. While stun guns are advertised as "safe," civil rights organizations report "more then 70" deaths in the United States and Canada between June 2001 and December 2004. Questions also arise concerning *who* should be shocked with stun guns, and under what circumstances. Recent notorious cases include police stunnings of a six-year-old boy who cut himself with glass in Miami; a 13-year-old girl who threw a book in an Arizona library; a 15-year-old girl involved in a Florida school-bus argument; and a disoriented 75-year-old woman shocked by a policewoman in South Carolina.

Webb, Gregory Jon

As police chief of Lyons, Nebraska, 30 miles northwest of Omaha, Gregory Webb was a figure commanding substantial respect. A 36-year-old bachelor, he had no shortage of female companionship, and first among his lady friends was Marie Anton, a 34-year-old neighbor who lived in the same apartment house. By December 1986, however, their relationship had soured, with Anton complaining about Webb's many lovers.

The quarrel boiled over on December 15, leaving Anton dead from two gunshots. Chief Webb had fled town by the time her corpse was discovered, and investigation led to his indictment for first-degree murder. Apprehension was problematic, since Webb had escaped to Central America, but he returned to the United States in March 1987 and settled in Volusia County, Florida, working construction jobs under various pseudonyms.

Webb had nearly stopped looking over his shoulder by February 1993, when he was profiled on the television program *Unsolved Mysteries*. A Florida neighbor recognized his photo on TV and called police, who arrested Webb at his Daytona Beach work site on February 23. Returned to Nebraska for trial, Webb was held without bond, citing alcoholic amnesia as a defense. He had no memory of killing Anton, Webb insisted, having blacked out from a night of heavy drinking with his sometime mistress and awakened to find her dead on the floor. On March 3, 1994, Webb pled no contest on reduced charges of manslaughter and tampering with evidence (for trying to conceal Anton's body). On May 5 he received a 19-year prison term.

Webb, John Randolph ("Jack") (1920–1982)

A native of Santa Monica, California, born on April 2, 1920, Jack Webb was abandoned by his father prior to birth, raised by his mother and grandmother in abject poverty. A victim of severe childhood asthma, he survived to become an adult chain-smoker who ranked for decades as the LOS ANGELES POLICE DEPARTMENT's chief civilian cheer leader in Hollywood. Starting his entertainment career as a radio disc jockey, Webb graduated to a small role in the film *He Walked by Night* (1948), which propelled him into the role of LAPD Sgt. Joe Friday on radio's *Dragnet* series, premiering in June 1949. Two years later, with the series bound for TV screens,

Webb sought to make a feature film titled *711* (Sgt. Friday's badge number), but LAPD Chief WILLIAM HENRY PARKER balked at the numeral's gambling connotations and insisted on a change of title to *Badge 714*. Webb happily complied, although the film was finally released as *Dragnet* (1954).

Meanwhile, Webb's TV series of the same title ran from December 1951 through September 1959, each episode lavishly praising all divisions of the LAPD for their sterling professionalism and incorruptibility. Chief Parker basked in the free publicity, while Webb moved on to produce and star in various B films unrelated to police work during 1955–61. A box office failure, Webb returned to television in 1963 as head of production for Warner Brothers, but was fired when his revisions on the successful series *77 Sunset Strip* led to its cancellation. After two years of unemployment, Webb returned in 1967 with a made-for-TV *Dragnet* feature, followed by a revamped version of the series, which ran for three and a half seasons. When that run was cancelled, Webb produced another LAPD-based series, *Adam-12*, which continued *Dragnet*'s tradition of inflating LAPD's reputation beyond recognition. A massive heart attack claimed Webb's life on December 23, 1982.

Webster, William H. (b. 1924)

A native of St. Louis, Missouri, born March 26, 1924, William Webster served with the U.S. Navy in World War II, then received his B.A. from Amherst College in 1947 and earned his J.D. from Washington University Law School two years later. He thereafter practiced law in St. Louis for two decades (1949–69), with an interval of navy duty during the Korean War and brief service as a federal prosecutor (1960–61). President Richard Nixon named Webster to the federal bench in 1970, then elevated him to the 8th Circuit Court of Appeals in 1973, where he remained until President Ronald Reagan chose him to lead the FBI. Webster formally replaced Director CLARENCE KELLEY on February 23, 1978.

Webster's tenure as director was marked by some dramatic changes in FBI procedures. He emphasized diversity in hiring, greatly increasing the number of minority and female agents employed by the Bureau. Webster also expanded the FBI's range of UNDERCOVER WORK, emphasizing pursuit of white-collar crime and ORGANIZED CRIME until President Reagan sharply curtailed those activities. Under Webster, use of court-ordered WIRETAPS more than tripled, rising from 326 (in 1977–80) to 733 (in 1983–84). He once boasted to journalist Robert Kessler that since J. EDGAR HOOVER's death in 1972 there had not been "a single proven case of a violation of constitutional rights" by FBI agents, but Webster and Kessler—who calls the director "a legend"—both ignored the Bureau's persecution of Puerto Rican nationalists and the American Indian Movement (the latter instance producing outspoken condemnation of illegal FBI tactics from a federal judge in 1973). Likewise, at the time Webster spoke to Kessler, his G-men were pursuing an identical campaign against various critics of President Reagan's foreign policy in Central America, mimicking in all respects the illegal COINTELPRO operations of 1956–72.

Reagan, in fact, admired Webster enough to name him director of the Central Intelligence Agency in 1987. Webster left the FBI on May 26 and spent four years in his new post, retiring in May 1991. A decade later, in August 2001, Attorney General JOHN ASHCROFT named Webster chairman of a commission to study security policies for sensitive and classified information held by the FBI. The commission's report found fault with FBI headquarters, declaring that "before the Bureau can remedy deficiencies in particular security programs, it must recognize structural deficiencies in the way it approaches security and institutional or cultural biases that make it difficult for the FBI to accept security as a core function."

Wells, Alice Stebbin

No birth date is available for Kansas native Alice Wells, but certain other details of her early life remain. She apparently moved from Kansas to New York City after graduating from high school, and in Brooklyn she worked as a minister's aide. After two years at Connecticut's Hartford Theological Seminary, Wells toured the United States as a religious orator, breaking ground in Maine and Oklahoma as each state's first female pastor. Settling at last in Los Angeles, she lectured on the virtues of "applied Christianity" in law enforcement, and sought to prove her point by joining the LOS ANGELES POLICE DEPARTMENT.

Official resistance was immediate and determined. American police departments had long employed "matrons" to handle female prisoners and juveniles, but they traditionally combined the duties of custodians and social workers, without any true police powers. In 1893 Mary Owens, widow of a slain patrolman, was first to receive the rank of "policeman" with full arrest powers, as a member of the CHICAGO POLICE DEPARTMENT. Twelve years later, in Portland, Oregon, Lola Baldwin received equal powers and was placed in command of social workers assigned to the city's Lewis and Clark Exposition, subsequently leading Portland's Department of Public Safety for the Protection of Young Girls and Women in 1908. Both Owens and Wells are described in various sources as America's "first police-

woman," yet others bestow that title on Alice Stebbin Wells (while commonly misspelling her middle name as Stebbins.)

Wells gathered signatures of 100 prominent citizens supporting her LAPD candidacy, and she was formally sworn in on September 12, 1910. Although she had full arrest powers—and made 13 arrests during her first year on the force—Wells was never permitted to carry a gun, and her $75 monthly pay was on par with jail matrons and janitors, well below that for male officers. Unlike policemen, she was also denied use of her badge as a free streetcar pass when transporting prisoners to jail, but she scored a true American first with issuance of a badge reading "Policewoman."

Soon after her appointment, Wells launched a crusade to recruit more women for law enforcement, lecturing nationwide in her spare time, while launching the first police training program for women at UCLA. In 1915 Wells was instrumental in founding the International Association of Policewomen, organized to create a broad base of support for females in police work. Wells retired from LAPD sometime in the 1920s. No source available at press time for this volume offered a precise date for her departure from the force, or for her death.

Wells Fargo

The discovery of gold at Sutter's mill in January 1848 touched off the California gold rush, bringing thousands of prospectors from all parts of the United States and various foreign countries to try their luck with pick or pan. It also lured a small army of bandits, prostitutes, swindlers, and gamblers to the Golden State, intent on cashing in without necessity of any manual labor. Security was paramount, especially for larger mining firms, and eastern bankers wasted no time in filling the need.

Henry Wells and William Fargo organized the American Express Company in 1850, then pooled their resources in March 1852 to create the new Wells Fargo banking and express company. The first Wells Fargo office opened four months later, in San Francisco, multiplying to 55 offices in western states by autumn 1855. Wells Fargo shipped anything, anywhere, but it was best known for its gold and payroll shipments in the West. By 1866 the company monopolized stage lines west of Missouri, maintaining its custom-made coaches in service until 1918. At the same time, Wells Fargo employed its own detective force to guard precious shipments or, failing that, to pursue and punish those who robbed them.

The bandits were persistent, attempting 347 holdups of Wells Fargo stages between 1870 and 1884. A total of 246 highwaymen were captured and convicted during that same period, most of them run to ground by legendary detectives James Hume and John Thacker. In addition to coaches, transportation of shipments by rail forced Wells Fargo to cope with the threat of TRAIN ROBBERY. Missouri's Dalton gang robbed so many trains in the 1880s that Wells Fargo detective FRED DODGE organized a special "Dalton posse" to pursue them, but citizens of Coffeyville, Kansas, beat him to the kill in 1892.

Railroad baron Edward Harriman gained control of Wells Fargo in 1904, expanding the company to 10,000 U.S. offices by the start of World War I. The company remained in banking and armored transport throughout the 20th century and continues its original function as Loomis Fargo today. Risks remain in the trade, with individual robberies costing Wells Fargo an estimated $42 million between 1969 and 1997. Robberies of federally insured banks are no longer privately investigated, but rather fall within the jurisdiction of the FBI.

West Virginia State Police

West Virginia's state police force was the fourth statewide law enforcement agency organized in America, after those of Pennsylvania (1905), Michigan, and New York (both in 1917). Fear of coal-field "radicals" prompted Governor John Cornwell to advocate the department's foundation, approved by state legislators in June 1919, with a manpower ceiling of 134 sworn officers and two civilian personnel. The department's first superintendent was Jackson Arnold, a grand-nephew of Confederate general Thomas "Stonewall" Jackson.

Hiring state troopers was one thing, but keeping them in service was another. By December 1919 121 officers had been hired, serving a four-month probationary term designed to weed out "types undesirable to the public and men derogative to the best interest of the department." In fact, 141 officers were fired during 1922, followed by 180 more rejects in 1923–24. The dismissal of 94 troopers in 1926 was ranked as a triumph of sorts, the 42 percent turnover ranking as the department's lowest yet. Of 157 officers serving in 1928, only 11 remained from the original contingent hired nine years earlier.

Poor discipline was most evident in West Virginia's labor wars, where the state police became a de facto STRIKEBREAKING force on behalf of mine owners, pitted against the United Mine Workers and smaller dissident factions. Abuse of strikers was so common that 35 of the 100 troopers assigned to bloody Mingo County were discharged within a 10-month period. Indeed, the force came close to foundering in its first year, when journalist Kyle McCormick revealed that every new recruit was presently assigned to infiltrating labor unions, thereby ignoring the rest of their duties statewide.

PROHIBITION distracted some state police from surveillance of strikers, but liquor patrols failed to make a dent in the state's bootlegging syndicates. The Great Depression slashed appropriations for the WVSP, with the result that June 1930 found only 159 officers on the payroll, while 288 were authorized. Despite that shortfall in manpower, responsibilities increased, with transfer of traffic regulation duties from the state road commission to the state police in September 1929. Systematic road patrols began in April 1934, employing 42 motorcycles and 16 patrol cars. America's entry into World War II sapped further strength from the force, as 78 troopers left service to fight overseas.

Hiring problems continued in the postwar era. State legislators authorized a personnel increase from 200 to 357 officers in the 1950s, but only 277 were employed at the close of 1958. Meanwhile, highway patrols were emphasized to curb West Virginia's staggering toll of traffic fatalities—735 in 1950–51, peaking with an all-time high of 587 in 1967. Criminal enforcement, especially involving DRUGS, was also emphasized from the 1960s onward. Major James Baisden's Criminal Intelligence/Narcotics and Dangerous Drugs Division was founded in June 1972, logging 3,442 arrests by July 1977, when it merged with the Criminal Investigation Bureau to create a new Criminal Investigation and Prevention Section. The CIB also includes a Laboratory Section (performing duties related to FORENSIC SCIENCE) and a Records Section (serving as West Virginia's central repository for FINGERPRINTS and criminal records).

Whitehurst, Frederic (b. 1948)

Born in 1948, Fred Whitehurst earned four Bronze Stars for bravery in the Vietnam War and displayed special valor on the night he stopped four fellow U.S. soldiers from torturing and raping a female villager. Back in civilian life, he earned a Ph.D. in chemistry and joined the FBI in 1982. Four years later, he was assigned to the Bureau's Laboratory Division and spent the next decade as an explosives residue analyst in the Materials Analysis Unit.

Whitehurst encountered problems at the lab almost from the moment he was assigned to supervisor Terry Rudolph for training. It soon became apparent that Rudolph and others cut corners in their work, skipping various tests required or "suggested" by FBI lab protocols, and that they often phrased reports in terms favoring the prosecution. Whitehurst was pressured to do likewise and complained repeatedly, without result. Finally, at the 1989 federal trial of defendant Steve Psinakis (accused of shipping explosives to the Philippines in an effort to topple dictator Ferdinand Marcos), Whitehurst aired his concerns to the defense. Psinakis's attorney first suspected that Whitehurst was "some kind of weirdo," then embraced the G-man as an expert witness. Psinakis was acquitted, whereupon his prosecutors complained to the JUSTICE DEPARTMENT, expressing "serious questions" about "the FBI laboratory's procedures."

Still, slipshod work continued at the lab despite that episode and Whitehurst's ongoing complaints. In February 1993 he met twice with FBI director WILLIAM STEELE SESSIONS, who promised a full investigation by the Bureau's Office of Professional Responsibility (OPR). When nothing came of that, Whitehurst contacted the National Whistleblower Center (NWC) in Washington, sitting for interviews with the group's attorneys in October and December 1993. NWC lawyer Stephen Kohn wrote to FBI headquarters in February 1994, demanding a full investigation of Whitehurst's charges, while Whitehurst personally voiced his complaints to the OPR. Attorneys for the FBI's Office of General Counsel interviewed Whitehurst in May 1994, reporting back to Justice that all of Whitehurst's complaints had been fully investigated and resolved except for charges he leveled against Terry Rudolph.

The falsity of that claim was revealed in 1995, when Whitehurst was subpoenaed as a defense witness in the second trial of defendants charged in the 1993 World Trade Center bombing (see BOMBING AND BOMB SQUADS). Judge Lance Ito refused to permit a similar appearance at the O. J. Simpson murder trial, but Whitehurst's allegations went public in September 1995, with his appearance on ABC-TV's *Prime Time Live*. That broadcast named lab supervisor Roger Martz as "one of the agents who pressured Whitehurst to go along with allegedly altered test results." Lab spokesmen refused to be interviewed on camera, but they faxed ABC a statement claiming the Bureau had thoroughly investigated Whitehurst's "concerns about forensic protocols and procedures" and "reviewed more than 250 cases involving work previously done by the Laboratory." The end result of that investigation: "To date, the FBI has found no evidence of tampering, evidence fabrication or failure to report exculpatory evidence."

In fact, ABC's broadcast triggered the first real investigation so far, conducted over the next 18 months by the inspector general's office. A 517-page draft report was submitted to the Justice Department in January 1997, but its contents were withheld in a seeming effort to avoid further problems with the upcoming trial of Oklahoma City bomber Timothy McVeigh. Whitehurst filed suit to compel publication in March 1997, supported by the NWC and the National Association of Defense Lawyers. Only then was a publication date fixed for April 15, 1997, with the McVeigh trial already in progress.

As a result of the inspector general's findings, Agents Roger Martz and David Williams were removed from their posts at the FBI lab, while two others criticized in the report—James Thurman and Michael Malone—had already retired. Whitehurst was penalized at the same time, suspended and placed on administrative leave in a move that violated terms of the 1989 Whistleblower Protection Act. He sued the FBI again and won his case on February 26, 1998, when the Bureau agreed to pay him $1,166,000 for illegal retaliation. Two weeks later, the FBI settled a second lawsuit filed by Whitehurst under the Privacy Act. While most such claims are settled for $5,000 or less, the Bureau agreed to pay Whitehurst $300,000 ($258,500 in legal fees plus the equivalent of salary and pension benefits he would have earned if employed by the FBI to retirement age). As part of the March settlement, FBI officials also promised to release 180,000 pages of lab reports prepared by analysts whom Whitehurst had publicly criticized.

Whitney, Chauncey Belden (1842–1873)

New York native Chauncey "Cap" Whitney was born in 1842 and fought for the Union Army in the Civil War. Two years later, in 1867, he was among the first settlers in the new railhead town Ellsworth, Kansas. Chosen to serve as Ellsworth's first constable, Whitney built the town's jail. In 1868, following local raids by Cheyenne tribal warriors, he joined the 50 "scouts" of Gen. George Forsyth and narrowly avoided death in the battle of Beecher Island. The following year he served as first lieutenant in a state militia company, manning a blockhouse near Ellsworth against further Indian attacks.

From military service, Whitney returned to civilian law enforcement in Ellsworth, serving over the next four years as city marshal, deputy sheriff, and finally sheriff of Ellsworth County. On August 15, 1873, he intervened in a gambling dispute between "Happy Jack" Morco and Billy Thompson, the trigger-happy brother of sometime lawman BEN THOMPSON. Thompson, drunk as usual, shot Whitney in the confused altercation, and Whitney died from his wounds three days later.

Wickersham, George Woodward (1858–1936)

A Pittsburgh, Pennsylvania, native, born on September 19, 1858, George Wickersham earned his LL.B. from the University of Pennsylvania's law department in 1880. Admitted to the Philadelphia bar before graduation, he practiced there until 1882, then moved to New York City and joined a prestigious law firm. President William Taft named Wickersham U.S. attorney general in March 1909, and he retained that post until Taft left office in March 1913.

Under Wickersham, the fledgling FBI grew rapidly, more than doubling in size from 44 agents to 168. Most of that growth was occasioned by passage of the DYER ACT in 1910, making G-men responsible for investigation of interstate car thefts. After leaving the JUSTICE DEPARTMENT, Wickersham resumed private law practice until 1917, when President Woodrow Wilson sent him to Cuba as a member of the War Trade Board. Twelve years later, President Herbert Hoover named Wickersham to chair the National Commission on Law Observance and Enforcement (better known as the Wickersham Commission). As the first federal investigators of nationwide law enforcement, Wickersham's panel examined problems ranging from PROHIBITION violations to police "THIRD-DEGREE" TACTICS. Its final report was issued in 1931, and Wickersham died in New York five years later, on January 25, 1936.

See also: FEDERAL BUREAU OF INVESTIGATION.

Williams, Alexander S. (1839–1910)

Alexander Williams was born in Nova Scotia during 1839, and spent several years as a ship's carpenter before joining the NEW YORK CITY POLICE DEPARTMENT in 1866. After two years on a Brooklyn beat, he was transferred to Broadway, home turf of the city's most notorious street gangs. Legend has it that after two days on his new beat, Williams deliberately picked a fight with two of Broadway's toughest hoodlums and bludgeoned them senseless, then beat half a dozen of their friends who tried to intervene. Over the next four years, according to Williams, he averaged one bloody brawl per day on the street, always emerging victorious. NYPD historians James Lardner and Thomas Reppetto dismiss those tales as self-serving fiction, but the reputation stuck for "Clubber" Williams, who once declared that "there is more law in the end of a policeman's night stick than a Supreme Court decision."

It should not be assumed that Clubber's reputation for beating hoodlums meant he was an honest cop, however. Rumors of CORRUPTION dogged him incessantly, keeping pace with complaints of brutality. Lardner and Reppetto report that Williams faced disciplinary charges "hundreds of times," beating some cases and settling the rest with small fines. Apparently, none of his superiors at NYPD headquarters ever considered firing Williams. On the contrary, in 1871 they promoted him to captain, commanding the notorious 21st Precinct's Gas House District. Three years later, Commissioner RHINELANDER WALDO convened a trial board on Williams, citing charges that he had received expensive gifts from brothel keepers, but Clubber kept his badge

and his command. In 1876 Williams was transferred to the West 29th Street station, widely known as "Satan's Circus." He soon gave it another nickname, remarking to a friend, "I've had nothing but chuck steak for a long time, and now I'm going to get a little of the tenderloin."

Williams later claimed that he had been misquoted, simply proposing a steak dinner, but the Tenderloin nickname stuck to his precinct, and Clubber kept cashing in on the local vice trade. Evidence uncovered by Rev. CHARLES H. PARKHURST and the LEXOW COMMITTEE finally forced Commissioner THEODORE ROOSEVELT to demand Clubber's resignation in May 1895, but it hardly mattered. From a yearly salary of $3,500, Williams had somehow banked $1 million for his premature retirement, while his new yacht was berthed at a $30,000 private dock in Connecticut, site of his summer retreat. Williams enjoyed his ill-gotten gains for another 15 years, until his death in 1910.

Williams, George Henry (1823–1910)

A native of New Lebanon, New York, George Williams was born on March 23, 1823. He completed academic preparatory studies, then studied law privately and won admittance to the New York bar at age 21. Soon thereafter, Williams moved to Iowa and commenced legal practice at Ft. Madison. Six years later, voters chose him as judge of the Iowa's First Judicial District, a post Williams held until 1852. He subsequently served as chief justice for the Territory of Oregon (1853–57), as a member of the Oregon Constitutional Convention (1858), and as a U.S. senator from Oregon (1865–71). Oregon voters failed to grant Williams a second Senate term, but President Ulysses Grant named him attorney general in December 1871, and he held that post until April 1875. Grant nominated Williams as chief justice of the U.S. SUPREME COURT in 1873, but his name was withdrawn prior to Senate confirmation. Williams later served as mayor of Portland, Oregon (1902–05), and died there on April 4, 1910.

Williams, Willie L. (b. 1943)

The first black chief of the LOS ANGELES POLICE DEPARTMENT was a Philadelphia butcher's son, born in 1943. His early life was racked with illness, including three occasions prior to age 18 when he received last rites from priests. Still, Willie Williams survived to join the unarmed Philadelphia Park Guards, later absorbed by the PHILADELPHIA POLICE DEPARTMENT in 1972. Thus Williams became a patrolman, later rising through the ranks as sergeant, captain, and finally police commissioner (after voters deposed the regime of right-wing

Mayor FRANK LAZARRO RIZZO). With an emphasis on community policing, Williams worked to redeem the image of a department soiled by longstanding complaints of CORRUPTION, RACISM, and EXCESSIVE FORCE.

His apparent success in that task made Williams a natural choice for Los Angeles Mayor TOM BRADLEY, when he sought a replacement for LAPD Chief DARYL GATES in the wake of RIOTS sparked by the police beating of RODNEY KING. Williams replaced Gates in July 1992, meeting immediate resistance from within LAPD, not only for his race but for the fact that he was the first-ever chief appointed from outside the department. Despite high hopes, the new police administration was mired in controversy. In September 1995 the *Los Angeles Times* revealed that Chief Williams had accepted five free trips to Las Vegas, sponsored by hotel-casino owners, during 1992–94. Williams retaliated with a $10 million lawsuit against the city for invasion of privacy, then dropped it in October when the city council ordered an investigation of the leak to journalists. Whatever his relationship with Nevada gamblers, the junkets presented an appearance of impropriety, and on March 10, 1997, the Los Angeles Police Commission recommended that Williams be denied a second five-year term as chief. Ironically, he was replaced by Bernard Parks, a deputy chief whom Williams had passed over for promotion, based on Parks's alleged obstruction of internal reforms.

When Williams left office in L.A., a *Times* poll revealed that 66 percent of citizens surveyed approved of his performance (versus 56 percent in June 1996), while 52 percent believed the city's streets were safer than in 1992. In fact, statistics showed that violent crime in Los Angeles decreased by 20 percent during Williams's tenure, while civilian complaints against officers fell from 1,300 in 1991 to 602 in 1995.

Wilmington Police Department

In 1738, nearly four decades before America declared its independence from Great Britain, residents of Wilmington, Delaware, trusted their safety to a pair of constables selected by the town council to patrol during daylight hours, while separate night watch stood guard after sundown. By the early 19th century, Wilmington had outgrown the colonial "watch and ward" system, establishing a formal police force that grew to include 30-odd officers by 1873.

Job security was unknown in those days, when the prevailing "spoils system" allowed the mayor to fire the whole force on a whim, but 1891 brought a first step toward professionalism with passage of the Metropolitan Police Act. Henceforth, officers were hired on merit, rather than political connections, and dismissal

required a hearing to show cause. Two years later, the department hired its first matrons, employed as sworn officers but limited to work with female prisoners.

The 20th century brought new challenges, highlighting a need for specialization. The arrival of automobiles prompted creation of a Traffic Division in 1914, followed a year later by a Detective Division and an Identification Unit (to photograph and fingerprint all prisoners). In 1916 Wilmington P.D. opened its Police School of Instruction, modeled on the NEW YORK CITY POLICE DEPARTMENT's training academy. PROHIBITION's advent touched off a national crime wave, prompting creation in 1922 of a squad armed with high-powered rifles and submachine guns, trained to battle racketeers and suppress RIOTS. In 1924 the Wilmington P.D. hired its first black patrolman, Lockmore Purnell, who also ranked as Delaware's first black peace officer. Six decades later, in 1992, Samuel Pratcher became Wilmington's first black police chief.

Today the Wilmington P.D. includes 289 officers, deployed on foot, in prowl cars, and on bicycles. The department maintains an exemplary safety record, with its last line-of-duty death recorded in 1946. As the 21st century dawned, the force joined some 350 other departments nationwide by winning accreditation from the Commission on Accreditation for Law Enforcement Agencies.

See also: FINGERPRINTS.

Wilson, Frank J. (1887–1970)

Born in 1887, Frank Wilson studied accounting in college and joined the INTERNAL REVENUE SERVICE's fledgling Intelligence Unit as an investigator when it was founded in 1920. He worked on many tax-evasion cases over the next decade, before ELMER LINCOLN IREY tapped him in 1930 to lead a special team of IRS agents pursuing Chicago crime boss Al Capone. Assisted by a 1927 SUPREME COURT ruling that made illegal income subject to federal taxation, Wilson set out to penetrate the many layers of fronts and middlemen who shielded Capone from any apparent income. Wilson broke the case by discovering a cash receipts ledger, which linked Capone directly to profits from an illicit casino, and other evidence was soon collected, supporting Capone's indictment on 23 counts of tax evasion. Jurors convicted Capone on three counts, resulting in an 11-year prison term and a $50,000 fine.

Wilson's pursuit of Capone has been greatly distorted over time, with help from Hollywood. Most television and movie productions credit Capone's conviction to ELIOT NESS, although Brian De Palma's big-screen version of *The Untouchables* (1987) included an IRS agent named Oscar Wallace (portrayed by Charles Martin

Smith), who analyzes Capone's ledger and cracks its code before he is murdered by gunman Frank Nitti. In fact, Wilson's team had little or no contact with Ness and his PROHIBITION agents, working quietly behind the scenes (and well beyond the line of fire) while Ness and company raided breweries.

Wilson's next brush with fame came in 1935, when he was called upon to identify U.S. gold certificates found at the home of alleged Lindbergh kidnapper Bruno Richard Hauptmann. Wilson's perusal of the bills proved they were ransom money, thereby helping to seal Hauptmann's fate, but he otherwise had no significant involvement in construction of what proved to be a frame-up, concocted by Charles Lindbergh and leaders of the NEW JERSEY STATE POLICE under NORMAN SCHWARZKOPF, SR.

Regardless of Hauptmann's guilt or innocence and the means used to convict him, association with a second headline-grabbing case propelled Frank Wilson to the pinnacle of his career, with his appointment to lead the U.S. SECRET SERVICE in 1937. Wilson held that post until 1946, and prior to his retirement from law enforcement he was credited with making great strides against counterfeiters of American currency. Upon leaving the TREASURY DEPARTMENT, Wilson retired from public life. He died in 1970.

See also: KIDNAPPING.

Wilson, Orland Winfield (b. 1900)

O. W. Wilson was born in 1900 at Veblen, South Dakota, and moved to California with his family as a teenager. He dreamed of becoming a civil engineer and joined the BERKELEY POLICE DEPARTMENT in 1921 to earn money for his further education. Wilson's plans changed, however, when Chief AUGUST VOLLMER took a personal interest in his career and began to tutor him in police procedures. Wilson changed his plans and earned a B.A. in criminology from UC Berkeley in 1924. The following year, with Wilson's endorsement, he became the police chief of Fullerton, California, then moved on to run the force in Wichita, Kansas.

Wilson spent 11 years in Wichita, where one mayor described him as "too damned efficient," then he returned to California in 1939, serving as dean of Berkeley's criminology department until 1960. That year brought a plea from Mayor Richard Daley, beseeching Wilson to take charge of the scandal-ridden CHICAGO POLICE DEPARTMENT. His arrival in Chicago was a shock to some policemen, 3,000 of whom threatened to picket city hall with demands for his removal, but Wilson stayed on to reform the department in spite of fierce opposition. CPD historian Richard Lindberg describes Wilson as "both reformer and martinet," a stern but

fair commander whose policy of promotions based on merit (rather than political connections) was "the bane of the Chicago Police Department."

Wilson's reforms included appointment of CPD's first female captain, psychological testing for all applicants and trainees, racial integration of the ranks, and the department's first-ever college cadet program. Progress came with a price tag, however, and some locals were shocked to see the CPD's budget grow from $72 million in 1960 to $186 million in 1961. Still, Wilson weathered the storms of protest and remained at the department's helm until 1967, achieving some dramatic results. At his departure, the *Kansas City Star* applauded Wilson for taking a "rinky-dink police department—sloppy, corrupt, and clownish and fashioning it into a respected major leaguer." Lindberg attributes his success to the fact that CPD was "at long last ready for reform"—but only to a point. By Lindberg's own admission, Wilson left the department "in the hands of lesser men," and many on the force soon fell back into their old ways, prompting new scandals within a year of Wilson's departure.

wiretaps

Wiretapping—the interception of messages transmitted by wire—has been used by police and criminals alike virtually from the day of the telegraph's invention in 1837. The first telephones, in 1876, were also easy prey for eavesdroppers who sought to gain advantage by listening to private conversations. PROHIBITION agent ELIOT NESS tapped the phones of mobster Al Capone in 1930 to obtain information on banned liquor shipments and the location of outlaw distilleries. Countless other examples could likewise be cited of early wiretapping, with mixed results.

Congress made its first effort to regulate wiretapping in June 1934 with passage of the Federal Communications Act. Section 605 banned "interception and divulgence" of any communication "transmitted by wire," but since it failed to specifically mention federal agents, FBI director J. EDGAR HOOVER felt free to continue wiretapping in defiance of the law. The U.S. SUPREME COURT closed that loophole in December 1937 with its ruling in *Nardone v. U.S.* that G-men were included in the statutory ban. Another door was slammed shut in December 1939, when the court banned use at trial of any evidence derived in any way from illegal taps (dubbed "fruit of the poisonous tree"). In response to those rulings, Attorney General ROBERT JACKSON publicly declared, "Wire tapping, entrapment, or the use of any other improper, illegal, or unethical tactics will not be tolerated by the Bureau." Hoover, meanwhile, continued to do as he pleased, albeit with a bit more caution.

In May 1940 President Franklin Roosevelt issued a secret directive to Hoover, stating that he was "convinced that the Supreme Court never intended any dictum . . . to apply to grave matters involving the defense of the nation." Acting without legal authority, FDR approved FBI use of "listening devices" to intercept "conversation or other communications of persons suspected of subversive activities against the Government of the United States, including suspected spies." Wiretaps required direct approval of the attorney general "after investigation of the need in each case," and Roosevelt added: "You are requested furthermore to limit these investigations so conducted to a minimum and to limit them insofar as possible to aliens."

Attorney General Jackson met privately with Hoover on May 28, 1940, to discuss the process further. Hoover's memo of their meeting reports that Jackson said "he would have no detailed record kept concerning the cases in which wiretapping would be utilized. It was agreeable to him that I would maintain a memorandum book in my immediate office, listing the time, places, and cases in which this procedure is to be utilized." The "memorandum book" soon grew into a massive file, revealed after Hoover's death, listing the names of 13,500 persons and groups wiretapped by G-men between 1941 and 1971.

Roosevelt's order approving "national security" wiretaps carried no legal weight with the courts, and evidence thus obtained was still inadmissible. Hoover tried to disguise the source, describing wiretaps as "confidential sources" in various FBI reports, but disclosure of the Bureau's illegal techniques still jeopardized cases at trial. The *Amerasia* case was thrown out of court in 1945, with probable Axis spies released, when illicit Bureau wiretaps were exposed. President Harry Truman expanded use of taps to root out "subversive activities" in July 1946, but federal judges still insisted on observance of the law, dismissing ESPIONAGE charges filed against Judith Coplon in 1949 when more FBI wiretaps were revealed.

Attorney General ROBERT KENNEDY and President Richard Nixon both encouraged illegal wiretapping of alleged subversives and political "enemies" during 1961–63 and 1969–72, but the FBI's tapping was not limited to such personal requests. Revelations before the CHURCH COMMITTEE (1975–76) hinted at the scope of illegal wiretaps under the Bureau's COINTELPRO campaigns, when FBI spokesmen admitted tapping the telephones of 2,305 "subversives" between 1960 and 1974. (Statistics for 1956–59 were strangely "unavailable.")

The Foreign Intelligence Surveillance Act of 1978 created a special secret court to review and authorize wiretap and BUGGING requests in cases allegedly dealing with espionage or foreign TERRORISM. The 11-judge panel examines requests for electronic surveillance and (theoretically) grants warrants on the merits of each case. Those powers were expanded dramatically with passage of the USA PATRIOT ACT in 2001, and the ramifications of that expansion have yet to be tested in court.

See also: FEDERAL BUREAU OF INVESTIGATION.

Wirt, William (1772–1834)

Born at Bladensburg, Maryland, on November 8, 1772, William Wirt was educated in private schools and worked as a tutor before studying law. He was admitted to the bar at age 20 and practiced privately for eight years, prior to becoming clerk of the Virginia state legislature in 1800. Two years later, Wirt became chancellor for the Eastern District of Virginia, then served as U.S. district attorney for Virginia (1816–17) and as prosecutor at the treason trial of Aaron Burr (1817). President James Monroe named Wirt U.S. attorney general in November 1817, and Wirt retained that post under President John Quincy Adams, until Adams left office in March 1829. Thereafter, Wirt moved to Baltimore

Attorney General William Wirt (Author's collection)

and practiced law there until his death, on February 18, 1834.

Wisconsin State Patrol

In September 1939 Wisconsin state legislators created a new Motor Vehicle Department, complete with an executive division consisting of 46 "inspectors," assigned to enforce the state's vehicle code and regulate motor carriers. That unit was the nucleus of the modern-day Wisconsin State Patrol, including 400 uniformed troopers and 112 inspectors. The WSP's patrol cars received their first two-way radios in 1943, easing communication even as World War II drained manpower from the highways. No formal training was supplied to Wisconsin state troopers before 1955, when the WSP opened its POLICE ACADEMY at Fort McCoy. Today that facility provides diverse training for officers from various federal, state, and local law enforcement agencies.

witch trials

Acting on the Old Testament injunction that "Thou shalt not suffer a witch to live" (Exodus 22:18), colonists in 17th-century America conducted a series of inquisitions to rid their settlements of alleged magic practitioners. Between 1647 and 1691, witch trials were conducted in Connecticut (33 cases), Massachusetts (28), Virginia (10), Maryland (6), New York, and Pennsylvania (1 case each). Beyond the influence of British settlers, three witch trials were also convened by Spanish authorities in the region of modern-day New Mexico. The last Spanish case, wherein Governor Juan Francisco de Treviqo jailed 47 prominent Santa Fe residents and had them beaten before their release, was almost certainly political. Other witchcraft charges arose from eccentric behavior, mental illness, and personal spite.

The witch craze of 1692 eclipsed any previous New World outbreak. Massachusetts authorities charged at least 77 persons with witchcraft and "examined" at least 113 others, in proceedings that ranged from verbal interrogation to life-threatening torture. Six of those accused confessed in court, presumably to save themselves from execution. One suspect, Giles Corey, was crushed to death when he refused to confess, during an "examination" that included "pressing" with heavy stones. Of those brought to trial, at least 28 were condemned, but sources vary on the number actually hanged. (No witches were burned in New England, despite fictional portrayals to the contrary.) Salem was not the only Massachusetts town involved in witch-hunting, but it remains the most notorious. Connecticut's witch hunts of 1692 were mild by comparison to those in Massachusetts: Of six defendants charged, five were acquitted and the sixth was reprieved after conviction. Overall, three-fourths of those condemned for witchcraft were women.

Acquittals were the order of the day at subsequent witch trials, held between 1693 and 1724. Fourteen of the period's 20 trials were held in Virginia, with no defendants convicted. A Maryland witch escaped criminal charges but was fined 100 pounds of tobacco after a neighbor sued her for hexing him. Winifred Benham was acquitted of witchcraft charges at Hartford, Connecticut, in 1697, but local church leaders excommunicated her nonetheless.

Witness Security Program (WITSEC)

The federal Witness Security Program (WITSEC) was created under Title V of the Organized Crime Control Act of 1970, empowering the U.S. Attorney General to protect witnesses in "whatever manner deemed most useful under the special circumstances of each case." That vague wording gave the U.S. JUSTICE DEPARTMENT wide latitude in handling of federal witnesses, but no specific operational details. After a brief period of bureaucratic indecision, responsibility for WITSEC was handed to the U.S. MARSHALS SERVICE, which maintains the program to this day. The roster of protected persons rapidly expanded after 1984, with passage of the Comprehensive Crime Control Act, authorizing federal protection for certain relatives and/or associates of federal witnesses.

Since its creation, WITSEC has sequestered, relocated, and provided new identities for more than 7,500 witnesses and 9,500 relatives. U.S. marshals report an 89 percent overall conviction rate obtained with testimony from protected witnesses, and further boast that no WITSEC participant has ever been harmed while under active protection. (Several *have* been killed, however, after slipping out of custody or giving up their anonymity to resume former associations.)

Final selection of WITSEC candidates is made by the attorney general, based on recommendations from federal prosecutors nationwide. Witnesses in state trials may also be guarded, if a state attorney general persuades the JUSTICE DEPARTMENT such action is warranted. Following a pre-admittance briefing, if a witness agrees to enter WITSEC, he or she is typically removed at once from danger, to a secure facility guarded by deputy U.S. marshals. New identities are then provided with "authentic" documentation, commonly including housing, job training and employment at government expense. Twenty-four-hour protection is furnished in high-threat environments, as when a witness must surface for hearings and trials.

Unfortunately, as illustrated in the Hollywood comedy *My Blue Heaven* (1990) and recurring media headlines, not all protected individuals "go straight" in WITSEC. Justice Department spokesmen acknowledge a 17-percent recidivism rate for WITSEC participants, while some independent researchers claim the actual figure is closer to 60 percent. If a witness is arrested while in WITSEC, federal agents attempt to coordinate security with local law enforcement agencies—and failing that, may recommend the witness's return to custody as a full-time prisoner.

See also: ORGANIZED CRIME.

women in law enforcement

Law enforcement, by its dangerous and violent nature, was long considered "man's work" in the United States, as in most nations abroad. Size, physical strength, and a propensity for violence were typically the qualities most valued in police recruits. Gradually, various U.S. police departments recognized the need for female employees to deal with cases involving women. These "matrons" were rarely entrusted with powers of arrest, but rather served as escorts for female and juvenile suspects or victims, often asking questions or performing searches that were deemed indecorous for male officers. Admission of women to the ranks of patrol officers, ultimately followed by detective assignments and elevation to command ranks, came more slowly in some jurisdictions than others.

Federal guidelines were no help, since women lacked the vote until 1920 and federal law enforcement agencies likewise excluded females for the most part. The FBI's first female operatives were ALASKA DAVIDSON (hired in 1922, confined to investigation of MANN ACT cases) and Jessie Duckstein (promoted to full agent status in November 1923, after two years as a typist for Chief WILLIAM J. BURNS). Neither lasted long after J. EDGAR HOOVER became the Bureau's director in May 1924: He demanded Duckstein's resignation on May 26, followed by Davidson's on June 10. Details are sparse, but it seems likely that one or the other was the anonymous female employee described by Athan Theoharis in *The Boss* (1988), sacked for breaking silence on illegal surveillance techniques when called to testify before the U.S. Senate.

The only G-woman appointed by Hoover, Lenore Houston, entered the FBI as a "special employee" in January 1924 and was promoted to full agent status that November. She served in the Philadelphia field office until August 1927, when she was transferred to Washington, D.C. Things went badly for Houston at FBI headquarters, culminating in her resignation in October 1928 and her commitment to a mental institution in 1930, reportedly delusional and threatening to shoot Hoover if she was ever released. No further female agents were hired until November 1972, six months after Hoover's death.

While no comprehensive statistics on male-female demographics are available for U.S. law enforcement, the JUSTICE DEPARTMENT's Bureau of Justice Statistics did survey 49 state police agencies in 1997, receiving data from 48. (Illinois failed to respond.) According to the BJS, no department was less than 87 percent male (Wisconsin). Of the remaining 47 agencies, 26 ranged from 95 to 99 percent male. Throughout the nation, female officers have filed complaints of sexual discrimination and harassment, including several (rare) instances of sexual assault or life-threatening abandonment by male colleagues who refused to answer distress calls. Such behavior is presently illegal under various federal and state statutes, which permit litigation to resolve grievances and impose criminal penalties for the most egregious sexist behavior.

See also: FEDERAL BUREAU OF INVESTIGATION.

Wood, William P. (1824–1903)

Born in 1824, William Wood distinguished himself as a leader of U.S. guerrilla forces in the Mexican War (1846–48), then plunged headlong into Republican politics when that party was formed in 1856. With the inauguration of President Abraham Lincoln in 1861, Wood's friendship with EDWARD STANTON—Lincoln's secretary of war, later attorney general—paid off in the form of appointment to serve as warden of Washington's Old Capitol Prison. In addition to that charge, he was employed by Lincoln and Stanton to investigate swindlers targeting the federal government.

By war's end, America was awash in counterfeit money, much of it printed in Dixie to destabilize the Union economy. In July 1965 Secretary of the Treasury Hugh McCulloch created the U.S. SECRET SERVICE to pursue counterfeiters, subsequently expanding its duties (in 1867) to include arrests of persons defrauding the government and insurrectionists such as the KU KLUX KLAN. Wood was chosen as the unit's first director, dispatching two-man teams to 15 major cities in the early days of his tenure.

Historical opinions vary widely as to Wood's success and methods. The Secret Service, on its Web site, reports that Wood "was very successful in his first year, closing more than 200 counterfeiting plants." That yearly arrest rate continued throughout his tenure, with Wood explaining his success as follows: "Because my raids were made without military escort and I did not ask the assistance of state officers, I surprised the professional counterfeiter. It was also my purpose to convince such characters that it would no longer be healthy for them to ply their vocation without being handled roughly, a fact they soon discovered." With those tactics in mind, crime historians Alan Axelrod and Charles Phillips report that "[f]rom a constitutional standpoint, Wood's methods were routinely scandalous. He frequently detained suspects for days at a time until he got the information he needed—usually the location of engraving plates." Overall, the authors judge, Wood "was unscrupulous and unethical and freely transgressed the Constitution."

Wood's last campaign was an attempt to break up a New York City gang led by William Brockaway, widely renowned as "King of the Counterfeiters." Brockaway did not restrict himself to currency, but also forged government bonds, palming off some on the Wall Street investment firm of Jay Cooke and Company. Outraged, the firm offered a large reward for Brockaway's conviction and recovery of his plates, which provided Wood with extra incentive. Wood captured the plates but failed to nab Brockaway, whereupon Jay Cooke withheld its bounty. Furious, Wood filed a lawsuit that embarrassed the Secret Service and Secretary McCulloch. The controversy cost Wood his job in 1869, and he retired from public life, dying in 1903.

Woodriffe, Edwin R., Jr. (1941–1969)

A Brooklyn, New York, native, born on January 22, 1941, Edwin Woodriffe, Jr. earned a B.S. degree from Fordham University and worked as a criminal investigator for the U.S. TREASURY DEPARTMENT before joining the FBI in May 1967. As a G-man he worked briefly in Cleveland before he was transferred to the Washington, D.C., field office in February 1968. On January 8, 1969, Woodriffe and partner Anthony Palmisano were fatally wounded while trying to capture Billy Austin Bryant, an escaped convict sought for multiple counts of bank robbery. Bryant was immediately named as one of the Bureau's "TEN MOST WANTED" FUGITIVES, captured later the same day. Convicted of double murder on October 27, 1969, Bryant received two consecutive life sentences. Woodriffe, meanwhile, entered history as the first black FBI agent killed on duty.

See also: FEDERAL BUREAU OF INVESTIGATION.

Woods, Arthur (1870–1942)

Widely regarded as one of the NEW YORK CITY POLICE DEPARTMENT's best commissioners, Arthur Woods was born in 1870 and graduated from Harvard University, thereafter teaching at an upper-class prep school. His entry into law enforcement was unexpected, occurring in 1906, when Commissioner Theodore Bingham petitioned the state legislature for a fourth deputy directorship commanding NYPD's detective division. Lawmakers approved the post, and Woods became its first occupant, applying himself to the job with customary vigor. He promoted all detective sergeants to lieutenant and created "Squad Number One," the world's first mobile unit assigned exclusively to homicide investigations.

Two years later, when Bingham resigned during one of New York's periodic political shakeups, Woods bowed to tradition and resigned from NYPD. Five years elapsed before Mayor John Mitchel called him back, this time to serve as commissioner, and Woods returned with a new list of innovative ideas for improving the department. One involved recruiting Boy Scouts to "cooperate with the police department in the suppression of vice." Scout leaders eagerly agreed to "do whatever they could to keep the law and prevent others from breaking it," but political satirists seized on the notion to lampoon Woods, often depicting him as a uniformed Boy Scout in newspaper cartoons.

Ribbing aside, Woods did his best to reform a department mired in CORRUPTION and shackled by political ties to TAMMANY HALL, but for all his good intentions, New Yorkers had a limited tolerance for do-gooders. Tammany's man defeated Mitchel in the mayoral election of 1917, and Woods was soon replaced by a more pliable commissioner. Woods continued to lecture on police reform, however, and in 1918 published *Policeman and Public*, describing an ideal police force strictly pledged to service of the common good. In 1919, Woods served as President Herbert Hoover's secretary of war, subsequently acting as chairman of the Rockefeller Center's education board. He died in 1942.

Wooldridge, Clifton Rodman (b. 1850)

Born in 1850, Clifton Wooldridge left no traces of his early life, before he joined the CHICAGO POLICE DEPARTMENT in 1888. His promotion to detective one year later was presumably occasioned by a combination of his personal crime-fighting style and the pervasive political patronage that riddled the department. No one advanced that quickly in CPD (or any other large urban police force) without benefit of a "rabbi" guiding his career, but once installed in the detective bureau, Wooldridge quickly proved his worth. Before leaving the force in 1910, Wooldridge made 19,500 arrests and single-handedly shut down 100 brothels. In the process, he was wounded 23 times by felons attempting to flee from his clutches. Wooldridge also anticipated Joseph Wambaugh by writing a series of popular books while he was still in the department, beginning with 1901's *Hands up in the World of Crime!*

See also: WAMBAUGH, JOSEPH ALOYSIUS, JR.

Wyoming Highway Patrol

The Wyoming Highway Patrol has had only 10 directors since its creation in 1933. That enviable record stands at odds with some state police agencies, where politics and personality clashes have turned the chief's office into a virtual revolving door. Tasked with the relatively simple mission to "make Wyoming highways safe," the patrol focuses primarily on traffic enforcement and accident investigations, although its officers are fully empowered to make arrests when they observe criminal activity. At full strength, the WHP includes 190 uniformed officers and a parallel support staff of civilian personnel. Patrol officers cover 6,500 miles of state highways and investigate an average of 6,000 auto accidents each year.

X-Files

Millions of persons who know nothing else about the FBI believe today that its files contain vast stores of information on unidentified flying objects (UFOs) and visitors from outer space. They owe that perception to a popular TV series, *The X-Files* (1993–2002), which portrayed the efforts of two stalwart agents to breach an intergalactic conspiracy of silence. Long before the pilot for that drama aired, in July 1966 a writer for another television program asked Bureau headquarters for help in tracing a source of UFO information. Director J. EDGAR HOOVER replied for the record, that "the investigation of unidentified flying objects is not, and never has been, a matter within the investigative jurisdiction of the FBI."

Hoover's response may have been legally correct, yet files retrieved under the Freedom of Information Act reveal that his answer, as in so many other cases, was less than candid.

While UFO reports date back to biblical times, the first modern report—which also coined the term *flying saucers*—was logged by pilot Kenneth Arnold over Washington State on June 24, 1947. Two weeks later, on July 9, Brigadier General George Schulgen of the Army Air Corps asked the FBI to investigate recent UFO reports, specifically to determine if they were part of a plot by Communists or Red sympathizers "to cause hysteria and fear of a Russian secret weapon." Assistant Director CLYDE ANDERSON TOLSON opined, "I think we should do this." Hoover agreed with a proviso, writing: "I would do it, but first we must have access to all disks recovered. For example, in the La. case the Army grabbed it and would not let us have it

for cursory examination." (The case referred to was a UFO hoax perpetrated at Shreveport, Louisiana, on July 7, 1947.)

By the time of Gen. Schulgen's request for help, Hoover had already learned of the now-famous incident at Roswell, New Mexico, on July 8, 1947. Initially reported as a "capture" of an alien craft, the story was revised one day later to announce the crash-landing of a weather balloon. An "urgent" FBI memo from Texas, however, contradicted the official Air Force version of events, noting that while the Roswell wreckage "resembles a high altitude balloon with a radar reflector," FBI "telephonic communication . . . [with] Wright [F]ield has not borne out this belief." Rather, G-men reported, unidentified material was "being transported to Wright Field by special plane for examination."

On July 30, 1947, a message from headquarters ordered all Bureau field offices to "investigate each instance which is brought to your attention of a sighting of a flying disc in order to ascertain whether or not it is a bona fide sighting, an imaginary one, or a prank. . . . The bureau should be notified immediately by teletype of all reported sightings, and the results of your inquiries." Over the next two months, G-men filed some two dozen reports of UFO sightings around the United States, including two reports from Portland, Oregon, made by a navy pilot and the chief of police. Many of the memos bear the heading "Security Matter—X."

The FBI's pursuit of UFOs hit a snag on September 3, 1947, when an Air Force lieutenant colonel gave the San Francisco field office a copy of a letter signed by the assistant chief of staff for intelligence, Lt. Gen. Stratemeyer, explaining to various Air Force commanders that "whereas the Air Defense Command Air Forces would interview responsible observers," the FBI "would investigate incidents of discs being found by civilians on the ground." Thus, Stratemeyer hoped "to relieve the numbered Air Forces of the task of tracking down all the many instances which turned out to be ash can covers, toilet seats and whatnot." Predictably furious, Hoover decreed on October 1 that "All future reports connected with flying discs should be referred to the Air Force, and no investigative action should be taken by Bureau agents."

That resolve on Hoover's part held fast until February 20, 1948, when a letter from headquarters to the San Francisco field office instructed agents to collect any UFO reports filed by witnesses and furnish them to the Air Force, in addition to which the FBI would "receive any information which the Air Forces volunteer." A few reports were exchanged between April and July 1948, but the Bureau's UFO probe remained largely dormant until January 10, 1949, with the receipt of an "Internal Security—X" alert from the Knoxville field office, reporting that saucers had been seen over the nuclear research facility at Oak Ridge, Tennessee. Three week's later, San Antonio's agent-in-charge filed a report on "Protection of Vital Installations," after "balls of fire" were sighted near Kirtland Air Force Base and the Los Alamos nuclear test site.

On March 25, 1949, FBI headquarters issued a letter to all field offices, reading in part: "For your confidential information, a reliable and confidential source has advised the Bureau that flying discs are believed to be man-made missiles rather than natural phenomenon [sic]. It has also been determined that for approximately the past four years the USSR has been engaged in experimentation on an unknown type of flying disc." That "confidential" letter somehow found its way to FBI-friendly journalist Walter Winchell, who announced on April 3 that UFO's were "definitely" Russian aircraft. Air Force spokesmen requested an FBI investigation to

identify Winchell's source, but Hoover refused on April 26, perhaps fearing that he would be named as the leak.

That near-miss discouraged further UFO investigations until March 1950, when Washington agent-in-charge Guy Hottell reported that "an investigator for the Air Force" had admitted recovery of three crashed saucers in New Mexico, containing nine corpses of three-foot-tall aliens. Hot on the heels of that shocker, the *New York Times* of April 4 reported that UFOs were actually experimental U.S. warplanes.

Hoover remained aloof from that debate and ignored the matter until October 1950, when he ordered the Los Angeles field office to "discreetly determine from appropriate sources" whether Frank Scully, author of *Behind Flying Saucers*, had been "actively engaged in Communist activities since the late nineteen thirties." Despite three urgent messages from Hoover, FBI files later released to public scrutiny contain no answer to that query.

Two months later, on December 8, 1950, an "urgent" message from the Richmond, Virginia, field office warned Hoover that agents of Army Intelligence "have been put on immediate high alert for any data whatsoever concerning flying saucers." The FBI provided no assistance in that quest, and only one UFO report was logged at headquarters over the next nine months, concerning a September 1951 sighting by pilots and radar operators at Fort Monmouth, New Jersey. Reports of UFO activity trickled in from various field offices over the next 16 years, including a North Carolina sighting made by an FBI employee on April 9, 1956, but the last known FBI report on UFOs dates from January 18, 1967, when a resident of Chesapeake, Virginia, reported being "taken onto [a] craft which he recalls as being made of a glass-like substance and being transparent." The see-through UFO was "manned by several individuals who appeared to be undersized creatures similar to members of the human race, probably not more than 4 feet tall." G-men scrutinized the witness, reporting that "Bureau indices did not disclose any information which could be identified with Mr. [name deleted]."

Younger, Evelle Jansen (1918–1989)

A native of Stamford, Nebraska, born on June 19, 1918, Evelle Younger joined the FBI after graduating from law school and served in the New York City field office, were he participated in "trash cover" surveillance of labor leader Harry Bridges, a special target of harassment by Director J. EDGAR HOOVER. With America's entry into World War II, Younger joined the U.S. Army, but reports persist that he was actually a counterintelligence agent for the Office of Strategic Services in the Far East. After returning to civilian life, Younger served as a municipal judge in Los Angeles (1953–58), but resigned after the Ethics Committee of the Conference of California Judges criticized his appearance in Chevrolet commercials on a local public service television program, *Traffic Court*. (He had also appeared in commercials for another program, *Armchair Detective*, during 1948–49).

Undeterred by that wrist-slap, Younger campaigned for a seat of L.A.'s superior court and unseated a long-serving incumbent in November 1958. He retained that post until he was elected to serve as district attorney of Los Angeles, in 1964. His tenure in that office included prosecution of Sirhan Sirhan for the June 1968 ASSASSINATION of Senator ROBERT FRANCIS KENNEDY, a case that led some critics to accuse Younger of participation in a cover-up. Specifically, at Sirhan's murder trial, Younger ignored discrepancies between autopsy evidence (revealing that Kennedy was shot at point-blank range) and eyewitness testimony (placing Sirhan's gun at least three feet away from Kennedy, on the wrong side of his body). Questioned about that issue, Younger said, "If somebody says one inch and somebody else says two inches, that's a discrepancy. But the jury didn't think it was a significant discrepancy, and neither did I." When Younger opened his files on the Kennedy case to public scrutiny in 1969, researchers learned that members of the LOS ANGELES POLICE DEPARTMENT had performed ballistics tests and "matches" on the wrong pistol.

Younger campaigned successfully to become California's attorney general in 1970, and voters granted him a second term in 1974. Four years later, Younger failed in a bid to capture the governor's mansion. He died of heart disease in Beverly Hills on May 4, 1989.

Z

Zain, Fred Salem (1951–2002)

Born in 1951, Fred Zain began his tenure at the West Virginia crime lab in 1977, swiftly earning a reputation as a serologist (blood expert) who could solve the most difficult cases, assuring prosecutors of convictions with a solid scientific basis. The district attorneys who revered him—one described Zain as "a god"—presumably were unaware that he faked test results and testified falsely in numerous cases, sometimes reporting positive results for tests his lab could not perform, because it lacked the necessary gear.

In 1985 FBI lab director James Greer informed Zain's boss that Zain had lied about his credentials to obtain his West Virginia job, concealing his failure of basic courses in serology and biochemical methods of testing bloodstains. The supervisor failed to act, supporting Zain even after two coworkers complained about Zain's unethical methods. Zain's public reputation finally began unraveling in 1991, after alleged rapist Glen Woodall (convicted chiefly on Zain's testimony in 1987) was exonerated by DNA evidence.

Zain, meanwhile, had left West Virginia in 1989 and settled in Bexar County, Texas—coincidentally the scene of numerous false autopsy reports filed by pathologist RALPH ERDMANN—where he served as chief of physical evidence for the county's medical examiner. Alerted by headlines from West Virginia, Texas prosecutors charged Zain with perjury and jury tampering, but the charge was dismissed on grounds that the statute of limitations had expired. Soon thereafter, in 1994, Zain was indicted for perjury in Marion County, West Virginia, for lying under oath at the 1991 trial of rape defendant Paul Walker. (Incredibly, West Virginia authorities continued to use Zain's testimony even after he left their state.) One count of that indictment was dismissed before trial; jurors acquitted Zain of a second charge and deadlocked on a third (that he lied under oath concerning fees he received for a murder trial). Another West Virginia grand jury, in Kanawha County, indicted Zain in March 1998, but Judge Andrew MacQueen dismissed the charges nine months later on grounds that the state government could not be a legal victim of fraud. The state supreme court reversed that ruling in 1999, and Zain also faced a new trial in Texas, but poor health postponed those proceedings. Cancer claimed Zain's life on December 3, 2002.

See also: FEDERAL BUREAU OF INVESTIGATION.

Zarcovich, Martin (1896–1969)

A sergeant with the East Chicago (Indiana) Police Department, born in 1896, Martin Zarcovich managed to keep his badge despite a 1930 conviction for smuggling liquor during PROHIBITION. He was notorious for his corrupt association with various underworld figures, including brothel madam Anna Sage (née Cumpanas), who operated in East Chicago from 1919 to 1927. Her financial and romantic dealings with Zarcovich ended the sergeant's marriage, and their illicit liaison continued after Sage moved her operation to Chicago. There, in early 1934, Sage recognized one of her customers as fugitive John Dillinger, America's top-ranking "public enemy."

By that time, Sage faced deportation to her native Romania as an undesirable alien. Plotting with Zarcovich, she devised a plan to betray Dillinger (alias "Jimmy Lawrence") to the FBI in return for cash rewards and Bureau intercession with U.S. immigration officials. Agent MELVIN PURVIS welcomed the offer, some published sources claiming that he agreed with Zarcovich's plan to kill Dillinger on sight, rather than trying to take him alive.

When Zarcovich met Purvis, he (Zarcovich) was already responsible for one lethal shootout involving Dillinger. According to crime historian William Helmer, East Chicago officers Lloyd Malvihill and Martin O'Brien threatened to expose "Zarc's" illegal activities in May 1934, whereupon he arranged for them to roust a couple of "suspicious characters" on the night of May 24. Confronted by Dillinger and bandit Homer Van Meter, the officers died in a blaze of machine-gun fire, while Zarcovich's secrets were preserved. Two months later, Zarcovich allegedly engineered Dillinger's death to keep the outlaw from telling tales of police corruption to G-men.

Zarcovich and East Chicago police captain Tim O'Neil were present when Purvis ambushed Dillinger outside Chicago's Biograph Theater on July 22, 1934 (though officers of the CHICAGO POLICE DEPARTMENT were not informed of the plan). Dillinger was killed as he emerged from the theater with Sage, but confusion still surrounds his killer's identity. Contradictory FBI statements named two different agents as Dillinger's slayer, while Director J. EDGAR HOOVER reportedly blamed Zarcovich, criticizing Purvis in an interview with newsman Russell Girardin for letting Zarcovich and O'Neill join the ambush party.

Other accounts claim Zarcovich himself delivered the coup de grâce, while Dillinger lay wounded, then rifled Dillinger's pockets and stole several thousand dollars.

Zarcovich and O'Neil split a $5,000 reward for their role in Dillinger's capture, and while both testified for Anna Sage at her deportation hearing, it did not help. Sage was deported on April 29, 1936, with a last kiss from Zarcovich at dockside. Zarcovich was later demoted for refusing to discuss the Dillinger case with Indiana's governor, but it proved a minor setback. He was subsequently named chief of detectives and served as East Chicago's police chief from 1947 to 1952. Upon retiring, Zarcovich became a probation officer. He died in East Chicago on October 30, 1969.

See also: FEDERAL BUREAU OF INVESTIGATION; CITIZENSHIP AND IMMIGRATION SERVICE; "PUBLIC ENEMIES."

Z-Coverage

Initiated by J. EDGAR HOOVER in 1940, the FBI's "Z-Coverage" program involved interception and reading of all mail addressed to the German, Italian, and Japanese embassies in Washington, D.C. Later, following America's entry into World War II, scrutiny was extended to the Axis-friendly embassies of Spain, Portugal, and Vichy France, plus the Soviet Union (by then a U.S. ally). In a parallel operation, Hoover also arranged for various international telegraph companies to delay transmission of messages sent from the United States to those seven nations for 24 hours, until they could be copied by G-men and agents of U.S. Army Intelligence. The Z-Coverage program ended in 1945, but illegal FBI "mail covers" on other targets continued at least until 1972, under auspices of the Bureau's COINTELPRO network.

See also: FEDERAL BUREAU OF INVESTIGATION.

Zeiss, George

George Zeiss joined the FBI in 1942 and was assigned before year's end to the FBI Academy's teaching staff, where he remained until his retirement in 1977. Zeiss was best known as an internationally famous trick-shot artist, whose stunts included firing a pistol at the thin edge of a playing card and cutting it in half; using the reflection in a diamond ring to aim at targets behind him; and firing at the sharp edge of an axe, splitting the bullet to strike a pair of targets farther downrange.

Aside from marksmanship, Zeiss also instructed FBI trainees in other forms of self-defense, but his activities were not confined to the academy in Quantico, Virginia. In 1959 he served as a technical adviser and bit player in the film version of Don Whitehead's book *The FBI Story*. Nine years later, Zeiss was sent to retrieve fugitive James Earl Ray, the alleged killer of Dr. Martin Luther King, Jr., from British custody in London. After retiring from the Bureau, Zeiss joined the Wackenhut Corporation, a private security firm founded by former G-men whose clients included billionaire Howard Hughes.

Appendix: Police Academies in the United States

Education of police officers has long been a controversial subject in the United States. Early lawmen were chosen primarily for their brawn, bravery, and marksmanship—all serious prerequisites for hunting desperate characters. Formal education was not so highly prized, and big-city police departments languishing in the grip of political bosses often found themselves riddled with cronyism. Another obstacle was the belief of many old-line administrators that "book smarts" somehow compromised an officer's ability to function in the field. (The CHICAGO POLICE DEPARTMENT) rejected future FBI agent Robert Ressler in the 1950s on grounds that he was "too educated.") As recently as 1966, one small New Jersey town fired its entire police force and advertised for replacements who fit the city-owned uniforms.

Still, thanks to the efforts of law enforcement pioneers like AUGUST VOLLMER, higher education for police has become a priority in America. No major department today accepts recruits without a high school diploma, and college education is preferred (if not required) for advancement through the ranks. Additionally, every state and major city today maintains police academies to train fledgling officers in a wide range of subjects including arrest procedures, civil rights, criminal law, emergency driving techniques, ethics, firearms safety, FORENSIC SCIENCE applications, search and seizure guidelines, self-defense, and so forth. At press time for this volume, the following police training centers were operational in America:

ALABAMA

ALABAMA ADVANCED CRIMINAL JUSTICE ACADEMY
740 Mildred Street NE
Montgomery, AL 36104

ALABAMA CANINE TRAINING CENTER
29 Rice Valley Road
Tuscaloosa, AL 35406

ALABAMA PEACE OFFICERS STANDARDS &
  TRAINING COMMISSION
472 Lawrence Street, Suite 202
Montgomery, AL 36104

BIRMINGHAM POLICE ACADEMY
401-6th Avenue South
Birmingham, AL 35205

CRIMINAL JUSTICE TRAINING CENTER
349 Avenue "C"
Craig Field
Selma, AL 36701

HUNTSVILLE POLICE ACADEMY
2033 Airport Road, SW #B
Huntsville, AL 35801

MOBILE POLICE ACADEMY
1251 Virginia Street
Mobile, AL 36604

NORTHEAST ALABAMA POLICE ACADEMY
Room 220, Brewer Hall
Jacksonville, AL 36265

UNIVERSITY OF ALABAMA LAW ENFORCEMENT
  ACADEMY
P.O. Box 870388
Tuscaloosa, AL 35487

ALASKA

ALASKA DEPARTMENT OF SAFETY TRAINING
  ACADEMY

877 Sawmill Creek Road
Sitka, AK 99835

ALASKA POLICE STANDARDS COUNCIL
450 Whittier Street
Juneau, AK 99811

PUBLIC SAFETY
450 Whittier Street
P.O. Box 111200
Juneau, AK 99811-1200

ARIZONA

ARIZONA LAW ENFORCEMENT TRAINING
ACADEMY
5601 West Trails End Road
Tucson, AZ 85745

ARIZONA PEACE OFFICER STANDARD TRAINING
BOARD
P.O. Box 6638
Phoenix, AZ 85005

ARIZONA WESTERN COLLEGE LAW ENFORCEMENT
TRAINING ACADEMY
P.O. Box 929
Yuma, AZ 85366

CENTRAL ARIZONA REGIONAL LAW OFFICER
TRAINING ACADEMY
8470 North Overfield Road
Coolidge, AZ 85228

COCHISE COLLEGE TRAINING ACADEMY
P.O. Box 4076
Douglas, AZ 85607

FEDERAL LAW ENFORCEMENT TRAINING CENTER
Building 4310/3rd Floor
Davis Montham AFB, AZ 85707

NAVAJO LAW ENFORCEMENT TRAINING ACADEMY
Navajo Department of Law Enforcement
Ganado, AZ 86505

PHOENIX POLICE DEPARTMENT OFFICE OF
ADMINISTRATION
620 West Washington Street
Phoenix, AZ 85003

PIMA COUNTY SHERIFFS TRAINING ACADEMY
P.O. Box 910
Tucson, AZ 85702

TUCSON POLICE ACADEMY
3200 North Silverbell Road
Tucson, AZ 85745

YAVAPAI COLLEGE/POLICE ACADEMY
1100 East Sheldon Street
Prescott, AZ 86301

ARKANSAS

ARKANSAS LAW ENFORCEMENT TRAINING
ACADEMY
P.O. Box 3106
Camden, AR 71701

ARKANSAS STATE POLICE TRAINING SECTION
P.O. Box 5901
Little Rock, AR 72215

CALIFORNIA

ALAMEDA COUNTY SHERIFFS DEPARTMENT
REGIONAL TRAINING CENTER
6289 Madigan Road
Dublin, CA 94568

ALLAN HANCOCK COLLEGE/POLICE ACADEMY
1300 South College Drive
Santa Maria, CA 93454

CALIFORNIA HIGHWAY PATROL TRAINING ACADEMY
3500 Reed Avenue
West Sacramento, CA 95605

CALIFORNIA DEPARTMENT OF FORESTRY/LAW
ENFORCEMENT
4501 State Highway 104
Ione, CA 95640

CENTRAL COAST COUNTY POLICE ACADEMY
5055 Santa Theresa Boulevard
Gilroy, CA 95020

COMMISSION ON PEACE OFFICER STANDARDS &
TRAINING
1601 Alhambra Boulevard
Sacramento, CA 95816

CSU-LONG BEACH/CENTER FOR CRIMINAL JUSTICE
1250 N. Bellflower Boulevard
Long Beach, CA 90840

EL CAMINO COLLEGE SOUTH BAY POLICE ACADEMY
16007 Crenshaw Boulevard
Torrance, CA 90506

LONG BEACH POLICE DEPARTMENT ACADEMY
7380 East Carson Street
Long Beach, CA 90808

LOS ANGELES COUNTY SHERIFF'S ACADEMY
11515 South Colima Road
Whittier, CA 90604

LOS ANGELES POLICE DEPARTMENT TRAINING
DIVISION
1880 North Academy Drive
Los Angeles, CA 90012

NAPA VALLEY COLLEGE POLICE ACADEMY
2277 Napa Vallejo Highway
Napa, CA 94558

OAKLAND POLICE DEPARTMENT ACADEMY
455 Seventh Street
Oakland, CA 94607

ORANGE COUNTY SHERIFF'S ACADEMY
11561 Salinzae Drive
Garden Grove, CA 92643

RICHARD A. MCGEE CORRECTIONAL TRAINING
CENTER
9850 Twin Cities Road
Galt, CA 95632

RIVERSIDE COMMUNITY COLLEGE ACADEMY OF
JUSTICE
1500 Castellano Road
Riverside, CA 92509

SACRAMENTO PUBLIC SAFETY CENTER
570 Bercut Drive, Suite A
Sacramento, CA 95814

SAN BERNARDINO COUNTY SHERIFF' DEPARTMENT
TRAINING ACADEMY
P.O. Box 1456
San Bernardino, CA 92402

SAN BERNARDINO VALLEY COLLEGE EXTENDED
FORMAT BASIC ACADEMY
701 South Mt. Vernon Avenue
San Bernardino, CA 92410

SAN DIEGO LAW ENFORCEMENT TRAINING
CENTER
10440 Black Mountain Road
San Diego, CA 92126

SAN DIEGO REGIONAL TRAINING CENTER
15575 Jimmy Durante Boulevard
Del Mar, CA 92014

SAN FRANCISCO POLICE ACADEMY
350 Amber Drive
San Francisco, CA 94131

SOUTH BAY REGIONAL PUBLIC SAFETY TRAINING
CONSORTIUM
3095 Yerba Buena Road
San Jose, CA 95135

SOUTHWESTERN COLLEGE BASIC ACADEMY
900 Otay Lakes Road, Room 560J
Chula Vista, CA 91910

STATE CENTER PEACE OFFICERS TRAINING
FACILITY
Fresno City College
1101 East University Avenue
Fresno, CA 93741

SUNNYVALE PUBLIC SAFETY
700 All American Way South
Sunnyvale, CA 94086

TULARE-KINGS COUNTY PEACE OFFICER ACADEMY
915 South Mooney Boulevard
Visalia, CA 93277

VENTURA COUNTY TRAINING ACADEMY
425 Durley Avenue
Camarillo, CA 93010

COLORADO

AIMS COLLEGE BASIC PEACE OFFICER ACADEMY
P.O. Box 69
Greeley, CO 80632

ARAPAHOE COUNTY SHERIFFS OFFICE TRAINING
ACADEMY
7305 South Potomac Street, Suite 151
Englewood, CO 80112

ARAPAHOE COMMUNITY COLLEGE LAW
ENFORCEMENT ACADEMY
2500 West College Drive
Littleton, CO 80160-9002

AURORA POLICE ACADEMY
800 Telluride Street
Aurora, CO 80011

BOULDER POLICE ACADEMY
1805 33rd Street
Boulder, CO 80301

COLORADO MOUNTAIN COLLEGE LAW
ENFORCEMENT ACADEMY
3000 County Road 114
Glenwood Springs, CO 81601

COLORADO NORTHWEST COMMUNITY COLLEGE
ACADEMY
500 Kennedy Drive
Rangely, CO 81648

COLORADO SPRINGS POLICE TRAINING ACADEMY
705 South Nevada Avenue
Colorado Springs, CO 80903

COLORADO STATE PATROL ACADEMY
15055 South Golden Road
Golden, CO 80401

COMMUNITY COLLEGE OF AURORA POLICE
ACADEMY
16000 East CentreTech Parkway
Aurora, CO 80011

DELTA-MONTROSE VOCATIONAL TECHNICAL
CENTER CRIMINAL JUSTICE POLICE ACADEMY
1765 U.S. Highway 50
Delta, CO 81416

DENVER POLICE ACADEMY
8895 Montview Boulevard, Building #58
Denver, CO 80220

DIVISION OF WILDLIFE ACADEMY
6060 Broadway
Denver, CO 80216

JEFFERSON COUNTY SHERIFF'S DEPARTMENT
TRAINING UNIT
200 Jefferson County Parkway
Golden, CO 80401

LAKEWOOD POLICE ACADEMY
455 South Allison Parkway
Lakewood, CO 80226

MORGAN COMMUNITY COLLEGE ACADEMY
17800 Road 20
Fort Morgan, CO 80701

NORTHEAST COLORADO REGIONAL POLICE
ACADEMY
Northeastern Junior College
100 College Avenue
Sterling, CO 80751

PIKE'S PEAK LAW ENFORCEMENT ACADEMY
5675 S Academy Boulevard, Box 17
Colorado Springs, CO 80906

PUEBLO POLICE TRAINING ACADEMY
130 Central Main Street
Pueblo, CO 81003

SOUTHERN COLORADO LAW ENFORCEMENT
TRAINING ACADEMY
600 Prospect
Trinidad, CO 81082

CONNECTICUT

MUNICIPAL POLICE TRAINING COUNCIL
285 Preston Avenue
Meriden, CT 06450

DELAWARE

DELAWARE POLICE ACADEMY
110 South French Street, Suite 300
Wilmington, DE 19801

DELAWARE STATE POLICE ACADEMY
P.O. Box 430
Dover, DE 19903

NEW CASTLE COUNTY POLICE ACADEMY
3601 North Dupont Highway
New Castle, DE 19720

UNIVERSITY OF DELAWARE LAW ENFORCEMENT
TRAINING PROGRAM
2800 Pennsylvania Avenue
Wilmington, DE 19806

WILMINGTON DEPARTMENT OF POLICE/83RD
POLICE ACADEMY
300 North Walnut Street
Wilmington, DE 19801

FLORIDA

DEPARTMENT OF LAW ENFORCEMENT TRAINING
CENTER
Route 1, Box 3249
Havana, FL 32333

FLORIDA DEPARTMENT OF LAW ENFORCEMENT
DIVISION OF CRIMINAL JUSTICE STANDARD &
TRAINING COUNCIL
P.O. Box 1489
Tallahassee, FL 32302-1489

FLORIDA DEPARTMENT OF CORRECTIONS
ACADEMY
5880 Lundberg Road
Vero Beach, FL 32966

FLORIDA HIGHWAY PATROL TRAINING ACADEMY
2908 Ridgeway Street
Tallahassee, FL 32310-2908

GULF COAST COMMUNITY COLLEGE
Criminal Justice Training Academy
5230 West Highway 98
Panama City, FL 32401

HILLSBOROUGH COMMUNITY COLLEGE LAW
ENFORCEMENT ACADEMY
P.O. Box 5096
Tampa, FL 33675-5096

KISSIMMEE POLICE ACADEMY
501 Simpson Road
Kissimmee, FL 34744

LAW ENFORCEMENT ACADEMY
P.O. Box 1489
Tallahassee, FL 32302

LEE COUNTY HIGH TECH CENTER, CENTRAL SOUTH-
  WEST FLORIDA CRIMINAL JUSTICE ACADEMY
3800 Michigan Avenue
Fort Myers, FL 33916

LIVELY LAW ENFORCEMENT ACADEMY
Route 1, Box 3250
Havana, FL 32333

MIAMI POLICE ACADEMY
400 NW 2nd Avenue
Miami, FL 33128

NORTH FLORIDA JUNIOR COLLEGE CRIMINAL
  JUSTICE ACADEMY
1000 Turner Davis Drive
Madison, FL 32340

SARASOTA CRIMINAL JUSTICE ACADEMY
4748 Beneva Road
Sarasota, FL 34233

SOUTH FLORIDA COMMUNITY COLLEGE CRIMINAL
  JUSTICE ACADEMY
600 West College Drive
Avon Park, FL 33825

WITHLACOOCHEE TECHNICAL INSTITUTE
  CRIMINAL JUSTICE ACADEMY
1202 West Main Street
Inverness, FL 34450

GEORGIA

ABAC REGIONAL POLICE ACADEMY
49-2802 Moore Highway
Tifton, GA 31794

ARMSTRONG STATE COLLEGE REGIONAL CRIMINAL
  JUSTICE TRAINING CENTER
11935 Abercorn Street
Savannah, GA 31419

ATLANTA POLICE ACADEMY
180 Southside Industrial Parkway SE
Atlanta, GA 30354

CENTRAL SAVANNAH RIVER AREA LAW
  ENFORCEMENT TRAINING CENTER
2092 Greenland Road
Blythe, GA 30805

COLUMBUS COLLEGE REGIONAL LAW
  ENFORCEMENT TRAINING CENTER
4225 University Avenue
Columbus, GA 31907

DEKALB POLICE ACADEMY
2484 Bruce Street
Lithonia, GA 30058

FEDERAL LAW ENFORCEMENT TRAINING CENTER
Building 94
Glynco, GA 31524

GEORGIA DEPARTMENT OF NATURAL RESOURCES
  LAW ENFORCEMENT TRAINING
1000 Indian Springs Drive
Forsyth, GA 31029

GEORGIA POLICE ACADEMY
1000 Indian Springs Drive
Forsyth, GA 31029

GEORGIA PUBLIC SAFETY TRAINING CENTER
1000 Indian Springs Drive
Forsyth, GA 31029

GEORGIA STATE PATROL TRAINING DIVISION
P.O. Box 1456
Atlanta, GA 30371

GWINNETT COUNTY POLICE ACADEMY
P.O. Box 602
Lawrenceville, GA 30246

LAW ENFORCEMENT TRAINING CENTER
3300 Macon Tech Drive
Macon, GA 31206

NATIONAL CENTER FOR STATE & LOCAL LAW
  ENFORCEMENT TRAINING
Building 67
Glynco, GA 31524

NORTH CENTRAL GEORGIA LAW ENFORCEMENT
  ACADEMY
1672 Old Highway 41
Marietta, GA 30060

NORTHEAST GEORGIA POLICE ACADEMY
150 Ben Burton Road
Bogart, GA 30622

PEACE OFFICER STANDARDS & TRAINING COUNCIL
351 Thornton Road, Suite 119
Lithia Springs, GA 30057

PUBLIC SAFETY TRAINING INSTITUTE
9540 Tara Boulevard
Jonesboro, GA 30236

HAWAII

KE KULA MAKA'L POLICE TRAINING ACADEMY
93-093 Waipahu Depot Road
Waipahu, HI 96797

IDAHO

IDAHO POST ACADEMY
P.O. Box 700
Meridian, ID 83680-0700

PEACE OFFICER STANDARDS & TRAINING ACADEMY
P.O. Box 700
Meridian, ID 83680-0700

ILLINOIS

BELLEVILLE AREA COLLEGE POLICE ACADEMY
2500 Carlyle Road
Belleville, IL 62221

CENTRAL ILLINOIS POLICE TRAINING UNIT
201 SW Adams
Peoria, IL 61635

COOK COUNTY DEPARTMENT OF CORRECTIONS
TRAINING
2000 North Fifth Avenue, Triton College
River Grove, IL 60171

COOK COUNTY SHERIFF/POLICE ACADEMY
1401 South Maybrook Drive
Maywood, IL 60153

EAST CENTRAL ILLINOIS MOBILE LAW
ENFORCEMENT TRAINING TEAM
7th & Jackson Avenue
Charleston, IL 61920

ILLINOIS DEPARTMENT OF CORRECTIONS ACADEMY
1301 Concordia Court
Springfield, IL 62794

ILLINOIS LOCAL GOVERNMENT LAW
ENFORCEMENT OFFICER TRAINING BOARD
600 South 2nd Street, Suite 300
Springfield, IL 62707

MOBILE TEAM FOUR TRAINING CENTER
1201 Seventh Street
East Moline, IL 61244

NORTH EAST MULTI-REGIONAL TRAINING
1 Smoke Tree Plaza, Suite #111
North Aurora, IL 60542

NORTHERN ILLINOIS TRAINING ADVISORY BOARD
420 West State Street
Rockford, IL 61101

NORTHWEST ILLINOIS CRIMINAL JUSTICE
COMMISSION
221 South Peoria Avenue
Dixon, IL 61021

NORTHWEST POLICE ACADEMY
200 East Wood Street
Palatine, IL 60067

POLICE TRAINING INSTITUTE
1004 South Fourth Street
Champaign, IL 61820

SOUTHWESTERN ILLINOIS LAW ENFORCEMENT
COMMUNITY MOBILE TEAM IN-SERVICE UNIT
700 North 5th Street, 2nd Floor
Belleville, IL 62221

TIMOTHY J. O'CONNOR TRAINING CENTER
1300 West Jackson Boulevard
Chicago, IL 60607

TRI-RIVER POLICE TRAINING ASSOCIATION
214 North Ottawa, Room #419
Joliet, IL 60431

INDIANA

INDIANA LAW ENFORCEMENT ACADEMY
5402 Sugar Grove Road
Plainfield, IN 46168

INDIANA STATE POLICE TRAINING ACADEMY
100 North Senate Avenue, Suite N340
Indianapolis, IN 46204

INDIANA UNIVERSITY POLICE ACADEMY
801 North Jordan
Bloomington, IN 47405

IOWA

CEDAR RAPIDS POLICE DEPARTMENT ACADEMY
310 2nd Avenue SW
Cedar Rapids, IA 52404

DEPARTMENT OF PUBLIC SAFETY
East 9th & Grand, Wallace State Office Building
Des Moines, IA 50319

IOWA DEPARTMENT OF PUBLIC SAFETY BASIC
TRAINING ACADEMY
Wallace State Office Building
Des Moines, IA 50319

IOWA LAW ENFORCEMENT ACADEMY
Camp Dodge
Johnston, IA 50131

KANSAS

KANSAS HIGHWAY PATROL TRAINING ACADEMY
2025 East Iron Avenue
Salina, KS 67401

KANSAS LAW ENFORCEMENT TRAINING CENTER
P.O. Box 647
Hutchinson, KS 67504

WICHITA-SEDGWICK COUNTY LAW ENFORCEMENT
TRAINING CENTER
2235 West 37th Street North
Wichita, KS 67204

KENTUCKY

DEPARTMENT OF CRIMINAL JUSTICE TRAINING
Funderbunk Building
Eastern Kentucky University
521 Lancaster Avenue
Richmond, KY 40475

KENTUCKY DEPARTMENT OF FISH & WILDLIFE
1 Game Farm Road
Frankfort, KY 40601

KENTUCKY SHERIFF'S ACADEMY
1536 State Street
Bowling Green, KY 42101

KENTUCKY STATE POLICE TRAINING ACADEMY
919 Versailles Road
Frankfort, KY 40601

KENTUCKY TECHNICAL NORTHEAST SERVICE AREA
09
609 Viking Drive, Rowan State Vo-tech
Morehead, KY 40351

KENTUCKY TECHNICAL NORTHEAST SERVICE AREA
10
4818 Roberts Drive
Ashland, KY 41101

KENTUCKY TECHNICAL NORTHEAST SERVICE AREA
11
508 Third Street, Room 201
Paintsville, KY 41240

KENTUCKY TECHNICAL NORTH CENTRAL SERVICE
AREA 15
104 Vo-tech Road
Lexington, KY 40510-1001

KENTUCKY TECHNICAL NORTHWEST SERVICE AREA
05
505 University Drive
Elizabethtown, KY 42701

KENTUCKY TECHNICAL NORTHWEST SERVICE AREA
06
727 West Chestnut Street
Louisville, KY 40203

KENTUCKY TECHNICAL SOUTHEAST SERVICE AREA
12
101 Vo-Tech Drive
Hazard, KY 41701

KENTUCKY TECHNICAL SOUTHEAST SERVICE AREA
13
235 South Laurel Road
London, KY 40741

KENTUCKY TECHNICAL WEST SERVICE AREA 01
P.O. Box 7408
Paducah, KY 42002-7408

KENTUCKY TECHNICAL WEST SERVICE AREA 02
1033 Sanderson Drive
Hopkinsville, KY 42240

KENTUCKY TECHNICAL WEST SERVICE AREA 03
1901 Southeastern Parkway
Owensboro, KY 42303

LOUISVILLE POLICE DEPARTMENT ACADEMY
2301 Douglas Boulevard
Louisville, KY 40205

LOUISIANA

ACADIANA LAW ENFORCEMENT TRAINING
ACADEMY
P.O. Box 42810
Lafayette, LA 70504

ALEXANDRIA REGIONAL POLICE ACADEMY
315 Bolton Avenue
Alexandria, LA 71301

BATON ROUGE POLICE DEPARTMENT TRAINING
ACADEMY
315 Bolton Avenue
Alexandria, LA 71301

CALCASIEU REGIONAL TRAINING ACADEMY
5400 East Broad Street
Lake Charles, LA 70602

HARBOR POLICE ACADEMY
1 Third Street
New Orleans, LA 70130

JEFFERSON PARISH SHERIFF'S OFFICE TRAINING
ACADEMY
701 South Upland Street
River Ridge, LA 70123

LAFOURCHE PARISH SHERIFF'S REGIONAL ACADEMY
P.O. Box 5608
Thibodaux, LA 70302

LOUISIANA STATE UNIVERSITY BASIC TRAINING
ACADEMY
Pleasant Hall, Room 276
Baton Rouge, LA 70803

MUNICIPAL TRAINING ACADEMY
401 City Park Avenue
New Orleans, LA 70119

NORTH DELTA REGIONAL TRAINING ACADEMY
1900 Garrett Road
Monroe, LA 71202

ORLEANS CRIMINAL SHERIFF'S ACADEMY
2800 Gravier Street
New Orleans, LA 70119

SHREVEPORT POLICE REGIONAL TRAINING
ACADEMY
6440 Greenwood Road
Shreveport, LA 71119

ST. MARY SHERIFF'S ACADEMY
P.O. Box 571
Franklin, LA 70538

MAINE

MAINE CRIMINAL JUSTICE ACADEMY
93 Silver Street
Waterville, ME 04901

MAINE STATE POLICE TRAINING DIVISION
93 Silver Street
Waterville, ME 04901

MARYLAND

ANNE ARUNDEL COUNTY POLICE ACADEMY
3737 Elmer F. Hagner Lane
Davidsonville, MD 21035

BALTIMORE COUNTY TRAINING ACADEMY
7607 Parkwood Road
Baltimore, MD 21222

EASTERN SHORE CRIMINAL JUSTICE ACADEMY
1406 South Salisbury Boulevard
Salisbury, MD 21801

EDUCATION AND TRAINING DIVISION-BALTIMORE
POLICE DEPARTMENT
11001 Owings Mills Boulevard
Owings Mills, MD 21117

HARTFORD COUNTY SHERIFF'S ACADEMY
P.O. Box 150
Bel Air, MD 21014

HARTFORD COUNTY POLICE ACADEMY
P.O. Box 150
Bel Air, MD 21014

MARYLAND POLICE & CORRECTIONAL TRAINING
COMMISSIONS
3085 Hernwood Road
Woodstock, MD 21163

MARYLAND STATE POLICE TRAINING DIVISION
1201 Reisterstown Road
Pikesville, MD 21208-3899

MARYLAND TRANSPORTATION AUTHORITY POLICE
DEPARTMENT
4330 Broening Highway
Baltimore, MD 21222-2258

MONTGOMERY COUNTY POLICE TRAINING
ACADEMY
2350 Research Boulevard
Rockville, MD 20850

MONTGOMERY COUNTY PUBLIC SAFETY TRAINING
ACADEMY
10025 Darnestown Road
Rockville, MD 20850

NATURAL RESOURCES POLICE ACADEMY
306 Marine Academy Drive
Stevensville, MD 21666

SOUTHERN MARYLAND CRIMINAL JUSTICE
ACADEMY
Box 130
Faulkner, MD 20632

WESTERN MARYLAND POLICE ACADEMY
50 North Burhans Boulevard
Hagerstown, MD 21740

MASSACHUSETTS

BARNSTABLE COUNTY POLICE ACADEMY
P.O. Box 746
Barnstable, MA 02630

BOSTON POLICE ACADEMY
85 Williams Avenue
Hyde Park, MA 02136

MASSACHUSETTS CRIMINAL JUSTICE TRAINING
COUNCIL
41 Terrace Hall Avenue
Burlington, MA 01803-3499

MICHIGAN

DETROIT METROPOLITAN POLICE ACADEMY
2110 Park Avenue
Detroit, MI 48201

FLINT POLICE ACADEMY
3420 Saint John Street
Flint, MI 48505

KALAMAZOO RECRUIT ACADEMY
P.O. Box 4070
Kalamazoo, MI 49003-4070

LAW ENFORCEMENT OFFICER TRAINING
ACADEMY
3420 Saint John Street
Flint, MI 48505

MACOMB COMMUNITY COLLEGE POLICE TRAINING
ACADEMY
32101 Caroline
Fraser, MI 48026

MICHIGAN LAW ENFORCEMENT OFFICERS
TRAINING COUNCIL
7426 North Canal Road
Lansing, MI 48913

OAKLAND POLICE ACADEMY
2900 Featherstone Road
Auburn Hills, MI 48326

SOUTHERN MICHIGAN LAW ENFORCEMENT
TRAINING CENTER
2111 Emmons Road
Jackson, MI 49201

WASHTENAW POLICE ACADEMY
4800 East Huron River Drive
Ann Arbor, MI 48106

MINNESOTA

MINNESOTA BOARD OF PEACE OFFICER STANDARDS
& TRAINING
1600 University Avenue West, Suite 200
Saint Paul, MN 55104

MINNESOTA BUREAU OF CRIMINAL APPREHENSION
TRAINING & DEVELOPMENT
1246 University Avenue West
Saint Paul, MN 55104

MINNESOTA STATE PATROL ACADEMY
1900 West County Road I
Shoreview, MN 55126

MISSISSIPPI

BOARD ON LAW ENFORCEMENT OFFICER
STANDARDS & TRAINING
401 North West Street, 8th Floor
Jackson, MS 39201

MISSISSIPPI LAW ENFORCEMENT OFFICERS
TRAINING ACADEMY
3791 Highway 468 West
Pearl, MS 39208

MISSISSIPPI DELTA COMMUNITY COLLEGE
Law Enforcement Training Academy
Highway 3
Moorhead, MS 38761

NORTH MISSISSIPPI LAW ENFORCEMENT TRAINING
ACADEMY
1 Finney Lane
Tupelo, MS 38801

WILLIAM L. SKINNER TRAINING ACADEMY
3000 St. Charles Street
Jackson, MS 39209

MISSOURI

KANSAS CITY REGIONAL POLICE ACADEMY
1328 Agnes Avenue
Kansas City, MO 64127

MISSOURI DEPARTMENT OF CONSERVATION
TRAINING ACADEMY
P.O. Box 180
Jefferson City, MO 65102

MISSOURI HIGHWAY PATROL TRAINING ACADEMY
1510 East Elm Street
Jefferson City, MO 65102

MISSOURI STATE WATER PATROL
2728-B Plaza Drive
Jefferson City, MO 65109

EASTERN MISSOURI LAW ENFORCEMENT TRAINING
ACADEMY
4601 Mid Rivers Mall Drive
St. Peters, MO 63376-0975

ST. LOUIS CO & MUNICIPAL POLICE ACADEMY
1266 Sutter Avenue
Saint Louis, MO 63133

ST. LOUIS POLICE ACADEMY
315 South Tucker
Saint Louis, MO 63102

MONTANA

MONTANA LAW ENFORCEMENT ACADEMY
620 South 16th Avenue
Bozeman, MT 59715

MONTANA PEACE OFFICER STANDARDS &
   TRAINING ADVANCE COUNCIL
303 North Roberts, 4th Floor
Helena, MT 59620

MONTANA STATE HIGHWAY PATROL
303 North Roberts
Helena, MT 59620

NEBRASKA
NEBRASKA LAW ENFORCEMENT TRAINING
   CENTER
3600 Academy Road
Grand Island, NE 68801

NEBRASKA STATE COMMISSION ON LAW
   ENFORCEMENT & CRIMINAL JUSTICE
301 Centennial Mall South
Lincoln, NE 68509

NEBRASKA STATE PATROL TRAINING ACADEMY
3510 NW 36th Street
Lincoln, NE 68524

NEVADA
HIGH SIERRA REGIONAL LAW ENFORCEMENT
   ACADEMY
7000 Dandini Boulevard
Reno, NV 89512-3999

METRO TRAINING ACADEMY LAS VEGAS NEVADA
861 North Mojave Road
Las Vegas, NV 89101

NEVADA DEPARTMENT OF CORRECTIONS
5500 Snyder Avenue
Carson City, NV 89702

NEVADA LAW ENFORCEMENT ACADEMY
2101 Snyder Avenue
Carson City, NV 89701

NORTH LAS VEGAS POLICE DEPARTMENT TRAINING
   CENTER
1301 East Lake Mead Boulevard
North Las Vegas, NV 89030

NYE COUNTY SHERIFF'S OFFICE REGIONAL
   TRAINING ACADEMY
211 West Montgomery Avenue
Beatty, NV 89003

PEACE OFFICER STANDARDS & TRAINING
555 Wright Way
Carson City, NV 89711

SOUTHERN NEVADA LAW ENFORCEMENT ACADEMY
3300 East Stewart Avenue
Las Vegas, NV 89101

NEW HAMPSHIRE
NEW HAMPSHIRE POLICE STANDARDS & TRAINING
17 Fan Road
Concord, NH 03301

NEW HAMPSHIRE STATE POLICE
10 Hazen Drive
Concord, NH 03305

NEW JERSEY
ANTHONY CANALE TRAINING CENTER
5033 English Creek Road
Egg Harbor Township, NJ 08232

BURLINGTON COUNTY POLICE ACADEMY
1 Academy Drive
Westhampton, NJ 08060

CAMDEN COUNTY POLICE ACADEMY
P.O. Box 200
Blackwood, NJ 08012

CAPE MAY COUNTY POLICE ACADEMY
173 Crest Haven Road
Cape May Court House, NJ 08210

ESSEX COUNTY POLICE ACADEMY
250 Grove Avenue
Cedar Grove, NJ 07009

MORRIS COUNTY POLICE ACADEMY
Morris Co. Courthouse, P.O. Box 900
Morristown, NJ 07960-0900

GLOUCHESTER COUNTY POLICE ACADEMY
Glouchester Community College
Tanyard Road
Sewell, NJ 08080

JERSEY CITY POLICE ACADEMY
282 Central Avenue
Jersey City, NJ 07307

JOHN H. STAMLER POLICE ACADEMY
1176 Raritan Road
Scotch Plains, NJ 07076

MIDDLESEX COUNTY POLICE ACADEMY
P.O. Box 1391
Edison, NJ 08818

MONMOUTH COUNTY POLICE ACADEMY
2000 Kozloski Road
Freehold, NJ 07728

MORRIS COUNTY POLICE TRAINING ACADEMY
P.O. Box 900
Morristown, NJ 07960

NEW JERSEY DEPARTMENT OF CORRECTIONS
ACADEMY
Trenton, NJ 08625

NEW JERSEY POLICE TRAINING COMMISSION
25 Market Street
Trenton, NJ 08625

NEW JERSEY STATE POLICE TRAINING ACADEMY
Sea Girt, NJ 08750

NEW JERSEY TRAINING & CERTIFICATION
101 South Broad Street
Trenton, NJ 08625-0809

NEWARK POLICE ACADEMY
1 Lincoln Avenue
Newark, NJ 07104

OCEAN COUNTY POLICE ACADEMY
659 Ocean Avenue
Lakewood, NJ 08701

PASSAIC COUNTY POLICE ACADEMY
209 Totowa Road
Wayne, NJ 07470

PATERSON POLICE ACADEMY
111 Broadway
Paterson, NJ 07505

SOMERSET COUNTY POLICE ACADEMY
209 Cougar Court
Somerville, NJ 08876

TRENTON POLICE ACADEMY
225 North Clinton Avenue
Trenton, NJ 08609

NEW MEXICO
NEW MEXICO DEPARTMENT OF PUBLIC SAFETY-
TRAINING AND RECRUITING
4491 Cerillos Road
Santa Fe, NM 87505

NEW YORK
BINGHAMTON POLICE DEPARTMENT ACADEMY
38 Hawley Street
Binghamton, NY 13901

BLACK RIVER/SAINT LAWRENCE VALLEY POLICE
ACADEMY
1332 Washington Street
Watertown, NY 13601

BROOME COUNTY-ZONE & LAW ENFORCEMENT
ACADEMY
50 Collier Street
Binghamton, NY 13902

BUFFALO POLICE ACADEMY
74 Franklin Street
Buffalo, NY 14202

BUREAU FOR MUNICIPAL POLICE
Executive Park Tower, Stuyvesant Plaza
Albany, NY 12203

CENTRAL NEW YORK POLICE ACADEMY
Onondaga Community College
4969 Onondaga Road
Syracuse, NY 13215-1944

CHAUTAUQUA COUNTY SHERIFF'S ACADEMY
525 Faulkner Street
Jamestown, NY 14701

FINGERLAKES LAW ENFORCEMENT ACADEMY
Sheriff's Office
74 Ontario Street
Canandaigua, NY 14424-1898

KINGSTON POLICE ACADEMY
1 Garraghan Drive
Kingston, NY 12401

MOHAWK VALLEY POLICE ACADEMY
1101 Sherman Drive
Utica, NY 13501

NASSAU COUNTY POLICE ACADEMY
6 Cross Street
Williston Park, NY 11596

NEW YORK CITY POLICE ACADEMY
235 East 20th Street
New York, NY 10003

NEW YORK STATE DIVISION OF CRIMINAL JUSTICE
SERVICE
Executive Power Tower, Stuyvesant Plaza
Albany, NY 12203

NEW YORK STATE POLICE ACADEMY
State Campus Building 24
Albany, NY 12226

NIAGARA COUNTY LAW ENFORCEMENT ACADEMY
3111 Saunders Settlement Road
Sanborn, NY 14132

ONANDAGA COUNTY POLICE ACADEMY
511 South State Street
Syracuse, NY 13202

ORANGE COUNTY POLICE ACADEMY
53 Gibson Road
Goshen, NY 10924

ROCHESTER POLICE DEPARTMENT ACADEMY
Civic Center Plaza, Room 675
Rochester, NY 14614

ROCKLAND COUNTY POLICE ACADEMY
Fireman Memorial Drive
Pomona, NY 10970

SOUTHERN TIER LAW ENFORCEMENT ACADEMY
70 Golf Road
Corning, NY 14830

ST. LAWRENCE COUNTY SHERIFF'S ACADEMY
48 Court Street
Canton, NY 13617

SUFFOLK COUNTY POLICE ACADEMY
550 Mount Avenue
West Babylon, NY 11704

TOMPKINS COUNTY LAW ENFORCEMENT ACADEMY
Cornell University, Barton Hall
Ithaca, NY 14853

WESTCHESTER COUNTY POLICE ACADEMY
2 Dana Road
Valhalla, NY 10595

ZONE 5 LAW ENFORCEMENT ACADEMY
80 Vandenburg Avenue
Troy, NY 12180

NORTH CAROLINA

BURLINGTON POLICE DEPARTMENT ACADEMY
P.O. Box 1358
Burlington, NC 27216

CHAPEL HILL POLICE DEPARTMENT ACADEMY
828 Airport Road
Chapel Hill, NC 27514

CHARLOTTE/MECKLENBURG POLICE ACADEMY
1750 Shopton Road
Charlotte, NC 28217

COASTAL PLAIN LAW ENFORCEMENT TRAINING
  CENTER
902 Herring Avenue
Wilson, NC 27893

CRIMINAL JUSTICE TRAINING & STANDARD
  DIVISION
P.O. Box 149
Raleigh, NC 27602

DEPARTMENT OF CORRECTIONS STAFF
  DEVELOPMENT & TRAINING
P.O. Box 29540
Raleigh, NC 27626

DURHAM COUNTY SHERIFF'S ACADEMY
201 East Main Street
Durham, NC 27701

DURHAM POLICE ACADEMY
505 West Chapel Hill
Durham, NC 27701

GREENSBORO POLICE DEPARTMENT ACADEMY
300 West Washington Street
Greensboro, NC 27401

GUILFORD COUNTY SHERIFF'S DEPARTMENT
  ACADEMY
P.O. Box 3427
Greensboro, NC 27402

LAW ENFORCEMENT TRAINING SERVICE
200 West Jones Street, The Caswell Building
Raleigh, NC 27603-1379

MORGANTON DEPARTMENT OF PUBLIC SAFETY
304 College Street
Morganton, NC 28655

NORTH CAROLINA HIGHWAY PATROL TRAINING
  ACADEMY
3318 Garner Road
Raleigh, NC 27610

NORTH CAROLINA JUSTICE ACADEMY
Eastern Campus
P.O. Box 99
Salemburg, NC 28385

NORTH CAROLINA JUSTICE ACADEMY
Western Campus
P.O. Box 600
Edneyville, NC 28727

NORTH CAROLINA STATE BUREAU OF
  INVESTIGATION
3320 Old Garner Road
Raleigh, NC 27606

RALEIGH POLICE ACADEMY
4205 Spring Forest Road
Raleigh, NC 27604

NORTH DAKOTA

BUREAU OF CRIMINAL INVESTIGATION
P.O. Box 1054
Bismarck, ND 58502

MINOT POLICE DEPARTMENT
515 2nd Avenue SW
Minot, ND 58701

NORTH DAKOTA STATE PATROL TRAINING
ACADEMY
600 East Boulevard, Capitol Building
Bismarck, ND 58505

PEACE OFFICER TRAINING PROGRAM
Lake Region State College
1801 College Drive North
Devils Lake, ND 58301

OHIO

AKRON POLICE DEPARTMENT ACADEMY
217 South High Street
Akron, OH 44308

ASHTABULA COUNTY POLICE ACADEMY
25 West Jefferson Street
Jefferson, OH 44047

BROWN COUNTY PEACE OFFICER ACADEMY
P.O. Box 179
Southern Hill
Georgetown, OH 45121

BUCKEYE HILLS POLICE SCHOOL
P.O. Box 157
Rio Grande, OH 45674

BUTLER COUNTY PEACE OFFICER ACADEMY
3603 Hamilton-Middleton Road
Hamilton, OH 45011

CHOFFIN POLICE ACADEMY
700 West Pete Rose Way
Cincinnati, OH 45203

CLARK STATE BASIC POLICE ACADEMY
40 Severance Circle
Cleveland Heights, OH 44118

CLEVELAND METRO PARKS RANGER TRAINING
ACADEMY
9301 Pearl Road
Strongsville, OH 44136

CLEVELAND POLICE ACADEMY
1300 Ontario Street
Cleveland, OH 44113

COLUMBUS POLICE ACADEMY
2609 McKinley Avenue
Columbus, OH 43204

COSHOCTON COUNTY LAW ENFORCEMENT
TRAINING ACADEMY
P.O. Box 787
Coshocton, OH 43812

CRIMINAL JUSTICE TRAINING & EDUCATION
CENTER
301 Collingwood Boulevard
Toledo, OH 43602

CUYAHOGA COUNTY SHERIFF'S ACADEMY
1215 West 3rd Street
Cleveland, OH 44113

DAYTON POLICE ACADEMY
3237 Guthrie Road
Dayton, OH 45418

EAST CLEVELAND BASIC POLICE ACADEMY
14340 Euclid Avenue
East Cleveland, OH 44112

EASTERN OHIO LAW ENFORCEMENT ACADEMY
67162 Airport Road
Saint Clairsville, OH 43950

GALLIA COUNTY POLICE ACADEMY
18 Locust Street
Gallopolis, OH 45631

GREAT OAKS POLICE ACADEMY
3254 East Kemper Road
Sharonville, OH 45241

GREENFIELD PEACE OFFICERS ACADEMY
300 Jefferson Street
Greenfield, OH 45123

HIRAM BASIC POLICE ACADEMY
11617 Garfield Road
Hiram, OH 44234

LAWRENCE COUNTY BASIC POLICE TRAINING
ACADEMY
115 South 5th Street
Ironton, OH 45638

LOGAN COUNTY SHERIFF ACADEMY
104 South Madriver Street
Bellefontaine, OH 43311

MEDINA COUNTY LAW ENFORCEMENT TRAINING
ACADEMY
1101 West Liberty Street
Medina, OH 44256

MIAMI TOWNSHIP POLICE ACADEMY
2660 Lyons Road
Miamisburg, OH 45342

MIAMI VALLEY REGULATORY LAW ENFORCEMENT
ACADEMY
6800 Hoke Road
Clayton, OH 45315

NEW BOSTON POLICE ACADEMY
3978 Rhodes Avenue
New Boston, OH 45662

NORTHEAST TRAINING ACADEMY INC.
647 East Main Street
Smithville, OH 44677

OHIO CHIEFS OF POLICE ASSOCIATION
6277 Riverside Drive
Dublin, OH 43017

OHIO PEACE OFFICERS TRAINING COUNCIL
1650 State Route 56
London, OH 43140

OHIO STATE HIGHWAY PATROL ACADEMY
740 East 17th Avenue
Columbus, OH 43211-2474

OHIO STATE UNIVERSITY CAMPUS POLICE
DEPARTMENT
2043 Milikin Road
Columbus, OH 43210-1270

PAULDING BASIC POLICE ACADEMY
116 South Main Street
Paulding, OH 45879

PEACE OFFICER TRAINING ACADEMY
P.O. Box 309
London, OH 43140

SALEM POLICE ACADEMY
231 South Broadway
Salem, OH 44460

SANDUSKY POLICE ACADEMY
222 Meigs Street
Sandusky, OH 44870

SHAKER HEIGHTS POLICE DEPARTMENT ACADEMY
3355 Lee Road
Shaker Heights, OH 44120

SHAWNEE-APOLLO BASIC POLICE ACADEMY
3325 Shawnee Road
Lima, OH 45806

SINCLAIR POLICE ACADEMY
444 West 3rd Street, Suite 9321
Dayton, OH 45402

STARK COUNTY SHERIFF'S OFFICE ACADEMY
4500 Atlantic Boulevard NE
Canton, OH 44711

TERRA STATE COMMUNITY COLLEGE
2830 Napoleon Road
Fremont, OH 43420-9670

TRAYNOR'S POLICE ACADEMY
7800 Cranford Street NW
Massillon, OH 44646

TUSCARAWAS COUNTY SHERIFF'S DEPARTMENT
ACADEMY
2295 Reiser Avenue SE
New Philadelphia, OH 44663

VANTAGE POLICE ACADEMY
818 North Franklin Street
Van Wert, OH 45891-1304

WASHINGTON ACADEMY
P.O. Box 305
Reno, OH 45773

WAYNE COUNTY SHERIFF'S ACADEMY
201 West North Street
Wooster, OH 44691

OKLAHOMA

COUNCIL ON LAW ENFORCEMENT EDUCATION AND
TRAINING
P.O. Box 11476
Oklahoma City, OK 73136-0476

LAWTON POLICE DEPARTMENT EDUCATION &
TRAINING DIVISION
10 SW 4th Street
Lawton, OK 73501

NORMAN POLICE DEPARTMENT ACADEMY
201-B West Gray
Lawton, OK 73069

OKLAHOMA HIGHWAY PATROL TRAINING
ACADEMY
P.O. Box 11415
Oklahoma City, OK 73136

OKLAHOMA CITY POLICE DEPARTMENT TRAINING
ACADEMY
800 North Portland Avenue
Oklahoma City, OK 73107

TULSA POLICE DEPARTMENT TRAINING ACADEMY
6066 East 66th Street North
Tulsa, OK 74117-1811

OREGON

BOARD ON PUBLIC SAFETY TRAINING
550 North Monmouth Avenue
Monmouth, OR 97361

OREGON PUBLIC SAFETY ACADEMY
550 North Monmouth Avenue
Monmouth, OR 97361

PENNSYLVANIA

ALLEGHENY COUNTY POLICE TRAINING
ACADEMY
700 West Ridge Drive
Allison Park, PA 15101

ALLENTOWN POLICE DEPARTMENT ACADEMY
2110 Park Drive
Allentown, PA 18103

DELAWARE COUNTY COMMUNITY COLLEGE
TRAINING ACADEMY
Malin & James Road
Broomall, PA 19008

DEPUTY SHERIFFS EDUCATION & TRAINING
BOARD
P.O. Box 1167
Harrisburg, PA 17108

GREATER JOHNSTOWN CAREER & TECHNICAL
CENTER POLICE ACADEMY
445 Schoolhouse Road
Johnstown, PA 15904

HOLY FAMILY COLLEGE TRAINING ACADEMY
Frankford & Grant Avenue
Philadelphia, PA 19136

INDIANA UNIVERSITY OF PENNSYLVANIA TRAINING
ACADEMY
Rear Maple Street, R & P Building
Indiana, PA 15705

MANSFIELD UNIVERSITY MUNICIPAL POLICE
TRAINING ACADEMY
Doane Center, Room 217
Mansfield, PA 16933

MERCYHURST COLLEGE MUNICIPAL POLICE
TRAINING ACADEMY
16 West Division Street
North East, PA 16428

MONTGOMERY COUNTY COMMUNITY COLLEGE
TRAINING ACADEMY
340 Dekalb Pike
Blue Bell, PA 19422

MUNICIPAL POLICE OFFICERS EDUCATION &
TRAINING COMMISSION
75 East Derry Road
Hershey, PA 17033

PENNSYLVANIA LAW ENFORCEMENT TRAINING
SERVICES
32 Maffett Street
Wilkes Barre, PA 18702

PENNSYLVANIA STATE POLICE TRAINING
ACADEMY
175 East Hershey Park Drive
Hershey, PA 17033

PITTSBURGH POLICE TRAINING ACADEMY
Washington Boulevard at Negley Run
Pittsburgh, PA 15206

READING POLICE ACADEMY
815 Washington Street
Reading, PA 19601

STATE POLICE TRAINING CENTER NORTHWEST
195 Valley View Drive
Meadville, PA 16335

STATE POLICE TRAINING CENTER SOUTHEAST
2047 Bridge Road
Schwenksville, PA 19473

STATE POLICE TRAINING CENTER SOUTHWEST
2900 Seminary Drive
Greensburg, PA 15601

RHODE ISLAND

RHODE ISLAND MUNICIPAL POLICE ACADEMY
Community College Of Rhode Island
Lincoln, RI 02865

RHODE ISLAND STATE POLICE TRAINING
ACADEMY
311 Danielson Pike
North Scituate, RI 02857

SOUTH CAROLINA

SOUTH CAROLINA HIGHWAY PATROL
5400 Broad River Road
Columbia, SC 29210

SOUTH DAKOTA

SOUTH DAKOTA TRAINING ACADEMY
500 East Highway 34
Pierre, SD 57501

TENNESSEE

CHATTANOOGA POLICE ACADEMY
3300 Amnicola Highway
Chattanooga, TN 37406

CLEVELAND STATE COMMUNITY COLLEGE BASIC
POLICE ACADEMY
P.O. Box 3570
Cleveland, TN 37320

KNOXVILLE POLICE DEPARTMENT TRAINING
DIVISION
800 East Church Avenue
Knoxville, TN 37915

MEMPHIS POLICE ACADEMY
4731 O.K. Robertson Road
Memphis, TN 38127

METRO NASHVILLE POLICE ACADEMY
2715 Tucker Road
Nashville, TN 37218

TENNESSEE LAW ENFORCEMENT TRAINING
ACADEMY
3025 Lebanon Road
Donelson, TN 37214-2217

TEXAS

ABILENE POLICE DEPARTMENT ACADEMY
P.O. Box 174
Abilene, TX 79604-0174

ALAMO AREA LAW ENFORCEMENT ACADEMY
118 Broadway, Suite 400
San Antonio, TX 78205

AUSTIN POLICE ACADEMY
4800 Shaw Lane
Austin, TX 78744

BRAZOSPORT COLLEGE LAW ENFORCEMENT
ACADEMY
500 College Drive
Lake Jackson, TX 77566

CENTRAL TEXAS REGIONAL POLICE ACADEMY
Highway 190 West
P.O. Box 1800
Killen, TX 76540-9990

CITY OF DALLAS POLICE ACADEMY
5310 Red Bird Center Drive
Dallas, TX 75237

COLLEGE OF MAINLAND TRAINING ACADEMY
1200 Amburn Road
Texas City, TX 77591

COMMISSION ON LAW ENFORCEMENT OFFICER
STANDARDS & EDUCATION
1033 Laposada Street, Suite #240
Austin, TX 78752

CONCHO VALLEY ACADEMY
5002 Knickerbocker Road
San Angelo, TX 76904

DALLAS COUNTY SHERIFF'S ACADEMY
10056 Marsh Lane, Suite 201
Dallas, TX 75229

DALLAS-FT. WORTH AIRPORT ACADEMY
2900 West Airfield Drive
Dallas, TX 75261

EL PASO COUNTY SHERIFF'S DEPARTMENT
TRAINING ACADEMY
800 North Rio Vista
El Paso, TX 79927

GALVESTON COUNTY SHERIFF'S ACADEMY
2026 Sealy Street
Galveston, TX 77550

GARLAND POLICE ACADEMY
4912 East 14th Street
Plano, TX 75074

GARLAND POLICE DEPARTMENT ACADEMY
217 North 5th Street
Garland, TX 75040

GUS GEORGE ACADEMY—FORT BEND COUNTY
SHERIFF'S DEPARTMENT
1410 Ransom Road
Richmond, TX 77469

HARRIS COUNTY SHERIFF'S ACADEMY
2310 Atacocita
Humble, TX 77396

HILDAGO COUNTY SHERIFF'S DEPARTMENT
ACADEMY
413 North 14th Street
Edinburg, TX 78540

HOUSTON COMMUNITY COLLEGE POLICE
ACADEMY
7907 Cowart
Houston, TX 77029

KILGORE COLLEGE EAST TEXAS POLICE ACADEMY
1100 Broadway
Kilgore, TX 75662

LAMAR UNIVERSITY REGIONAL POLICE ACADEMY
4400 Martin Luther King Parkway
Beaumont, TX 77710

LAREDO JUNIOR COLLEGE REGIONAL ACADEMY
West End Washington Street
Laredo, TX 78040

LEWISVILLE POLICE DEPARTMENT ACADEMY
184 North Valley Parkway
Lewisville, TX 75029-9002

LOWER RIO GRANDE POLICE ACADEMY
142 South 7th
Ramondville, TX 78580

LUBBOCK COUNTY SHERIFF'S ACADEMY
1419 Avenue H
Lubbock, TX 79408

LUBBOCK POLICE DEPARTMENT ACADEMY
P.O. Box 2000
Lubbock, TX 79457

MIDDLE RIO GRANDE LAW ENFORCEMENT
ACADEMY
Southwest Texas Junior College
Uvalde, TX 78801

MONTGOMERY COUNTY SHERIFF'S ACADEMY
112 Academy Drive
Conroe, TX 77301

NORTH CENTRAL TEXAS REGIONAL TRAINING
CENTER
624 Six Flags Drive, Suite 125
Arlington, TX 76011

NUECES COUNTY SHERIFF'S DEPARTMENT
TRAINING ACADEMY
P.O. Box 1940
Corpus Christi, TX 78403

ODESSA COLLEGE POLICE ACADEMY
201 W. University Boulevard
Odessa, TX 79764

PANHANDLE REGIONAL LAW ENFORCEMENT
ACADEMY
P.O. Box 447, Amarillo College
Amarillo, TX 79178

PERMIAN BASIN LAW ENFORCEMENT ACADEMY
P.O. Box 60660
Midland, TX 79711

SAN ANGELO POLICE DEPARTMENT ACADEMY
401 East Beauregard, P.O. Box 5020
San Angelo, TX 76902

SAN ANTONIO COLLEGE LAW ENFORCEMENT
ACADEMY
1014 San Pedro
San Antonio, TX 78212

SOUTH PLAINS REGIONAL LAW ENFORCEMENT
ACADEMY
P.O. Box 3730
Lubbock, TX 79452

SUL ROSS STATE UNIVERSITY LAW ENFORCEMENT
ACADEMY
Box C-12, Highway 90 E, Building #202
Alpine, TX 79830

TARLETON STATE UNIVERSITY LAW ENFORCEMENT
ACADEMY
P.O. Box T-1069
Stephenville, TX 76402

TARRANT COUNTY JR. COLLEGE ACADEMY
4801 Marine Creek Parkway
Forth Worth, TX 76161

TARRANT COUNTY SHERIFF'S ACADEMY
100 North Lamar
Fort Worth, TX 76196

TEMPLE POLICE ACADEMY
105 South 5th Street
Temple, TX 76501

TEXAS ABC TRAINING ACADEMY
P.O. Box 13127, Capitol Station
Austin, TX 78711

TEXAS DEPARTMENT OF PUBLIC SAFETY
5805 North Lamar
Austin, TX 78773

TEXAS PARKS & WILDLIFE DEPARTMENT
100 West 50th Street
Austin, TX 78751

TEXOMA POLICE ACADEMY
4501 Dinn Grayson
Denison, TX 75020

TRAVIS COUNTY SHERIFF'S ACADEMY
1010 Lavaca Street
Austin, TX 78767

VICTORIA COLLEGE LAW ENFORCEMENT ACADEMY
2200 East Red River Road
Victoria, TX 77901

VICTORIA POLICE DEPARTMENT ACADEMY
306 South Ridge
Victoria, TX 77902

WEST CENTRAL TEXAS LAW ENFORCEMENT
ACADEMY
1125 East North 10th Street
Abilene, TX 79604

UTAH

PEACE OFFICER STANDARDS AND TRAINING
4525 South 2700 West
Salt Lake City, UT 84119

UTAH STATE HIGHWAY PATROL TRAINING SECTION
5757 South 320th West
Murray, UT 84107

WEBER STATE UNIVERSITY CONTINUING
EDUCATION POLICE ACADEMY
3750 Harrison Boulevard
Ogden, UT 84408

VERMONT

VERMONT CRIMINAL JUSTICE TRAINING COUNCIL
Route 2, P.O. Box 2160
Pittsford, VT 05763

VERMONT STATE POLICE TRAINING DIVISION
103 South Main Street
Waterbury, VT 05676

VIRGINIA

CARDINAL CRIMINAL JUSTICE ACADEMY
917 Central Avenue
Salem, VA 24153

CENTRAL SHENANDOAH CRIMINAL JUSTICE
TRAINING CENTER
211 West 12th Street
Waynesboro, VA 22980

CENTRAL VIRGINIA CRIMINAL JUSTICE ACADEMY
P.O. Box 287
Lynchburg, VA 24505

CHESAPEAKE PUBLIC SAFETY ACADEMY
1080 Sentry Drive
Chesapeake, VA 23323

CHESAPEAKE SHERIFF'S OFFICE TRAINING ACADEMY
401 Albemarle Drive
Chesapeake, VA 23328

CHESTERFIELD COUNTY POLICE DEPARTMENT
ACADEMY
6610 Public Safety Way
Chesterfield, VA 23832

CRATER CRIMINAL JUSTICE ACADEMY
11301 Johnson Road
Petersburg, VA 23805

FAIRFAX COUNTY PUBLIC SAFETY ACADEMY
3911 Woodburn Road
Annandale, VA 22003

HAMPTON ROADS REGIONAL ACADEMY OF
CRIMINAL JUSTICE
1300 Thomas Street
Hampton, VA 23669

HENRICO COUNTY POLICE TRAINING
201 East Nine Mile Road
Highland Springs, VA 23075

HENRICO COUNTY SHERIFF'S OFFICE TRAINING
ACADEMY
4301 East Parham Road
Richmond, VA 23273

INTERNATIONAL ASSOCIATION OF CHIEFS OF
POLICE
515 North Washington
Alexandria, VA 22314

NEW RIVER CRIMINAL JUSTICE TRAINING
ACADEMY
P.O. Box 161
New River, VA 24141

NORFOLK POLICE DEPARTMENT ACADEMY
7665 Sewells Point Road
Norfolk, VA 23513

NORTHERN VIRGINIA CRIMINAL JUSTICE
ACADEMY
45299 Research Place
Ashburn, VA 22011

PORTSMOUTH POLICE DEPARTMENT ACADEMY
1701 High Street
Portsmouth, VA 23704

PORTSMOUTH SHERIFF'S TRAINING ACADEMY
701 Crawford Street
Portsmouth, VA 23704-3888

PRINCE WILLIAM-MANASSAS ACADEMY
9230 Lee Avenue
Manassas, VA 22110

RAPPAHANNOCK REGIONAL CRIMINAL JUSTICE
ACADEMY
3630 Lee Hill Drive
Fredericksburg, VA 22408

RICHMOND CITY SHERIFF'S DEPARTMENT
ACADEMY
1701 Fairfield Way
Richmond, VA 23223

RICHMOND POLICE DEPARTMENT ACADEMY
1202 West Graham Road
Richmond, VA 23220

ROANOKE POLICE DEPARTMENT ACADEMY
309-3rd Street SW
Roanoke, VA 24011

SOUTHWEST LAW ENFORCEMENT ACADEMY
U.S. Route 19
Richlands, VA 34641

VCU POLICE ACADEMY
940 West Grace Street
Richmond, VA 23284

VIRGINIA BEACH POLICE DEPARTMENT ACADEMY
2509 Princess Anne Road
Virginia Beach, VA 23456

VIRGINIA BEACH SHERIFF'S TRAINING ACADEMY
2501 James Madison Boulevard
Virginia Beach, VA 23456

VIRGINIA CAPITAL POLICE TRAINING SCHOOL
9th Street Office Building
Richmond, VA 23219

VIRGINIA DEPARTMENT OF CRIMINAL JUSTICE
  SERVICES
805 East Broad Street, 10th Floor
Richmond, VA 23219

VIRGINIA REGULATORY ACADEMY
805 East Broad Street
Richmond, VA 23219

VIRGINIA STATE POLICE ACADEMY
7700 Midlothian Park
Richmond, VA 23261

WASHINGTON

CRIMINAL JUSTICE TRAINING COMMISSION
P.O. Box 40905
Olympia, WA 98504-0905

SPOKANE POLICE TRAINING CENTER
2302 Waterworks
Spokane, WA 99212

WASHINGTON STATE PATROL TRAINING ACADEMY
631 West Dayton Airport Road
Shelton, WA 98584

WEST VIRGINIA

CRIMINAL JUSTICE HIGHWAY SAFETY DIVISION
1204 Kanawha Boulevard East
Charleston, WV 25301

WEST VIRGINIA STATE POLICE ACADEMY
Academy Drive
P.O. Box 459
Institute, WV 25112

WISCONSIN

BUREAU OF INSTRUCTION & TRAINING
6680 North Teutonia Avenue
Milwaukee, WI 53209

MADISON POLICE ACADEMY
211 South Carroll Street
Madison, WI 53703

MILWAUKEE COUNTY SHERIFF'S ACADEMY
2201 South 7th Street
Milwaukee, WI 53215

MILWAUKEE POLICE ACADEMY
6680 North Teutonia
Milwaukee, WI 53209

TRAINING AND STANDARDS BUREAU
2 East Mifflin Street, Suite 100
Madison, WI 53707

WISCONSIN STATE PATROL ACADEMY
800 South 10th Avenue
Fort McCoy, WI 54656

WYOMING

PEACE OFFICER STANDARDS & TRAINING
1710 Pacific Avenue
Cheyenne, WY 82002

WYOMING HIGHWAY PATROL TRAINING
P.O. Box 1708
Cheyenne, WY 82003

WYOMING LAW ENFORCEMENT ACADEMY
1556 Riverbend Drive
Douglas, WY 82633

Appendix: U.S. Law Enforcement Web Sites

The following Internet Web sites were consulted during preparation of this volume. The URLs provided were active as of press time for the book but may have been revised since then. Inclusion of the Web sites here does not constitute an endorsement of their accuracy or any stated opinions found therein.

Alabama Dept. of Public Safety
http://www.dps.state.al.us/

Alaska State Troopers
http://www.dps.state.ak.us/

American Civil Liberties Union
http://www.aclu.org/

American Police Hall of Fame
http://www.aphf.org/lods.html

Arizona Highway Patrol
http://www.dps.state.az.us/default.asp

Arkansas State Police
http://www.asp.state.ar.us/

Army Criminal Investigation Command
http://www.cid.army.mil/

Army National Guard
http://www.arng.army.mil/

Atlanta (GA) Police Department
http://www.atlantapd.org/

Baltimore (MD) Police Department
http://www.ci.baltimore.md.us/government/police/

Berkeley (CA) Police Department
http://www.ci.berkeley.ca.us/police/default.html

Birmingham (AL) Police Department
http://www.informationbirmingham.com/police/default.htm

Bismarck (ND) Police Department
http://www.bismarck.org/city_departments/department/default.asp?dID=15

Boston (MA) Police Department
http://www.cityofboston.gov/police/

Bureau of Alcohol, Tobacco, Firearms and Explosives
http://www.atf.gov/index.htm

Bureau of Indian Affairs Tribal Police
http://tribaljurisdiction.tripod.com/id9.html

Burlington (VT) Police Department
http://www.police.ci.burlington.vt.us/

California Highway Patrol
http://www.chp.ca.gov/index.html

Chattanooga (TN) Police Department
http://www.chattanooga.gov/74_107.htm

Cheyenne (WY) Police Department
http://www.cheyennecity.org/police.htm

Chicago (IL) Police Department
http://www.cityofchicago.org/police

Cincinnati (OH) Police Department
http://www.cincinnati-oh.gov/police/pages/-3039-/

Cleveland (OH) Police Department
http://www.city.cleveland.oh.us/government/departments/pubsafety/police/policei nd.html

Colorado Bureau of Investigation
http://cbi.state.co.us/

Colorado State Patrol
http://csp.state.co.us/

Connecticut State Police
http://www.state.ct.us/dps/CSP.htm

Copwatch
http://www.copwatch.com/

Dallas (TX) Police Department
http://www.dallaspolice.net/index.cfm

Delaware State Police
http://www.state.de.us/dsp/

Denver (CO) Police Department
http://www.denvergov.org/police

Detroit (MI) Police Department
http://www.ci.detroit.mi.us/police/default.htm

Drug Enforcement Administration
http://www.usdoj.gov/dea/

Environmental Protection Agency
http://www.epa.gov/

Fargo (ND) Police Department
http://www.cityoffargo.com/police/

Federal Bureau of Investigation
http://www.fbi.gov/

Florida Highway Patrol
http://www.fhp.state.fl.us/

Fraternal Order of Police
http://www.grandlodgefop.org/

Georgia Bureau of Investigation
http://www.ganet.org/gbi/

Georgia State Patrol
http://dps.georgia.gov/02/dps/home/0,2228,5635600,00.html;
  jsessionid=9CD46EC003E173E8DC45B1A270986A95

Great Falls (MT) Police Department
http://www.ci.great-falls.mt.us/people_offices/police/

Hawaii Department of Public Safety
http://www.hawaii.gov/psd/

Homeland Security Department
http://www.dhs.gov/dhspublic/index.jsp

Honolulu (HI) Police Department
http://www.honolulupd.org/

Houston (TX) Police Department
http://www.ci.houston.tx.us/hpd/

Idaho State Police
http://www.isp.state.id.us/

Illinois State Police
http://www.isp.state.il.us/

Indiana State Police
http://www.in.gov/isp/

Indianapolis (IN) Police Department
http://www.indygov.org/eGov/City/DPS/IPD/home.htm

Internal Revenue Service Criminal Investigation
http://www.treas.gov/irs/ci/

International Association of Chiefs of Police
http://www.theiacp.org/

Iowa State Patrol
http://www.state.ia.us/government/dps/isp/

Jackson (MS) Police Department
http://www.city.jackson.ms.us/Police/general.html

Kansas Bureau of Investigation
http://www.accesskansas.org/kbi/

Kansas City (KS) Police Department
http://www.kckpd.org/

Kansas City (MO) Police Department
http://www.kcpd.org/

Kansas Highway Patrol
http://www.kansashighwaypatrol.org/

Kentucky State Police
http://www.kentuckystatepolice.org/

Las Vegas (NV) Metropolitan Police Department
http://www.lvmpd.com/

Los Angeles County (CA) Sheriff's Department
http://www.lasd.org/

Los Angeles (CA) Police Department
http://www.lapdonline.org/

Louisiana State Police
http://www.lsp.org/index.html

Louisville (KY) Metro Police Department
http://www.lmpdky.org/

Maine State Police
http://www.state.me.us/dps/msp/home.htm

Maryland State Police
http://www.mdsp.maryland.gov/mdsp/default.asp

Massachusetts State Police
http://www.mass.gov/msp/

Memphis (TN) Police Department
http://www.memphispolice.org/

Miami-Dade County (FL) Police Department
http://www.mdpd.com/

Michigan State Police
http://www.vsp.state.va.us/

Milwaukee (WI) Police Department
http://cms.milwaukee.gov/display/router.asp?DocID=317

Minneapolis (MN) Police Department
http://www.ci.minneapolis.mn.us/police/

Minnesota State Patrol
http://www.dps.state.mn.us/patrol/

Mississippi Bureau of Investigation
http://www.dps.state.ms.us/dps%5Cdps.nsf/Divisions/
   ci?OpenDocument

Mississippi Highway Patrol
http://www.dps.state.ms.us/dps/dps.nsf/main?OpenForm

Missouri Highway Patrol
http://www.mshp.dps.missouri.gov/HP32Web/Index.jsp

Montana Highway Patrol
http://doj.state.mt.us/enforcement/highwaypatrol.asp

Montgomery (AL) Police Department
http://police.ci.montgomery.al.us/

Nashville (TN) Metropolitan Police Department
http://www.police.nashville.org/

National Crime Information Center
http://www.fas.org/irp/agency/doj/fbi/is/ncic.htm

National Law Enforcement Officers Memorial Fund
http://www.nleomf.com/

National P.O.L.I.C.E. Suicide Foundation
http://www.psf.org/

National Sheriffs' Association
http://www.sheriffs.org/

Navy Judge Advocate General's Corps
http://www.jag.navy.mil/

Nebraska State Patrol
http://www.nsp.state.ne.us/

Nevada Highway Patrol
http://nhp.nv.gov/

New Hampshire State Police
http://www.state.nh.us/safety/nhsp/

New Haven (CT) Police Department
http://cityofnewhaven.com/police/home.htm

New Jersey State Police
http://www.njsp.org/

New Mexico State Police
http://www.nmsp.com/

New Orleans (LA) Police Department
http://www.nopdonline.com/

New York City Police Department
http://www.nyc.gov/html/nypd/home.html

New York State Police
http://www.troopers.state.ny.us/

Newark (NJ) Police Department
http://www.newarkpd.org/

North Carolina Highway Patrol
http://www.nccrimecontrol.org/Index2.
   cfm?a=000003,000014

North Carolina State Bureau of Investigation
http://sbi.jus.state.nc.us/sbimain/ncsbi.htm

North Dakota Highway Patrol
http://www.state.nd.us/ndhp/

Oakland (CA) Police Department
http://www.oaklandpolice.com/

Officer.com—The Source for Law Enforcement
http://www.officer.com/

Officer Down Memorial Page
http://www.odmp.org/

Ohio Highway Patrol
http://statepatrol.ohio.gov/

Oklahoma City Police Department
http://www.okc.gov/query.html?police/index.html

Oklahoma Highway Patrol
http://www.dps.state.ok.us/ohp/

Oklahoma State Bureau of Investigation
http://www.osbi.state.ok.us/

Omaha (NE) Police Department
http://www.opd.ci.omaha.ne.us/

Oregon Bureau of Investigation
http://www.state.or.us/agencies.ns/25700/00010/

Oregon State Police
http://www.osp.state.or.us/

Patrolmen's Benevolent Association
http://nycpba.org/

Pennsylvania State Police
http://www.psp.state.pa.us/

Philadelphia (PA) Police Department
http://www.ppdonline.org/

Phoenix (AZ) Police Department
http://phoenix.gov/POLICE/

Pittsburgh (PA) Bureau of Police
http://www.city.pittsburgh.pa.us/police/

Portland (ME) Police Department
http://www.ci.portland.me.us/police/ppd.htm

Portland (OR) Police Bureau
http://www.portlandonline.com/police/

Providence (RI) Police Department
http://www.providencepolice.com/

Puerto Rico Police
http://www.gobierno.pr/PoliciaPR/Inicio/Default

Raleigh (NC) Police Department
http://www.raleigh-nc.org/police/

Rhode Island State Police
http://www.risp.state.ri.us/

Richmond (VA) Police Department
http://www.theblueline.com/feature/VArichmond.html

St. Augustine (FL) Police Department
http://www.ci.st-augustine.fl.us/departments/Police_
Department/

St. Louis (MO) Metropolitan Police Department
http://64.218.68.50/stlouis/newslmpd/viewer.htm

St. Paul (MN) Police Department
http://www.ci.stpaul.mn.us/depts/police/

Salt Lake City (UT) Police Department
http://www.slcgov.com/police/

San Diego (CA) Police Department
http://www.sannet.gov/police/

San Francisco (CA) Police Department
http://www.sfgov.org/site/police_index.asp

Seattle (WA) Police Department
http://www.cityofseattle.net/police/

South Carolina Highway Patrol
http://www.schp.org/

South Carolina Law Enforcement Division
http://www.sled.state.sc.us/default.htm

South Dakota Highway Patrol
http://hp.state.sd.us/

Tampa (FL) Police Department
http://www.ci.tampa.fl.us/dept_Police/

Tennessee Bureau of Investigation
http://www.tbi.state.tn.us/

Tennessee Highway Patrol
http://www.state.tn.us/safety/

Texas Dept. of Public Safety
http://www.txdps.state.tx.us/

Texas Highway Patrol
http://www.txdps.state.tx.us/

Texas Rangers
http://texas.rangers.mlb.com/NASApp/mlb/index.jsp?c_
id=tex

United States Citizenship and Immigration Services
http://uscis.gov/graphics/

United States Coast Guard
http://www.uscg.mil/USCG.shtm

United States Customs & Border Protection
http://www.cbp.gov/

United States Department of Justice
http://www.usdoj.gov/

United States Department of the Treasury
http://www.ustreas.gov/

United States Marshals Service
http://www.usdoj.gov/marshals/

United States Postal Inspection Service
http://www.usps.com/postalinspectors/fraud/welcome.htm

United States Secret Service
http://www.ustreas.gov/usss/index.shtml

United States Securities and Exchange Commission
http://www.sec.gov/

Utah Highway Patrol
http://highwaypatrol.utah.gov/

Utah State Bureau of Investigation
http://sbi.utah.gov/

Vermont State Police
http://www.dps.state.vt.us/vtsp/

Virginia State Police
http://www.vsp.state.va.us/

Washington, D.C., Metropolitan Police Department
http://mpdc.dc.gov/main.shtm

Washington State Patrol
http://www.wsp.wa.gov/

West Virginia State Police
http://www.wvstatepolice.com/

Wilmington (DE) Police Department
http://www.ci.wilmington.de.us/departments/police.htm

Wisconsin State Patrol
http://www.dot.wisconsin.gov/statepatrol/

Wyoming Highway Patrol
http://whp.state.wy.us/

Bibliography

Alexander, Charles. *The Ku Klux Klan in the Southwest.* Norman: University of Oklahoma Press, 1995.

Alix, Ernest. *Ransom Kidnapping in America, 1874–1974: The Creation of a Capital Crime.* Carbondale: Southern Illinois University Press, 1978.

American Civil Liberties Union. *Day of Protest, Night of Violence.* Los Angeles: Sawyer Press, 1967.

Anderson, Jack, and Fred Blumenthal. *The Kefauver Story.* New York: Dial Press, 1956.

Barra, Allen. *Inventing Wyatt Earp: His Life and Many Legends.* New York: Caroll & Graf, 1998.

Bartholomew, Ed. *Wyatt Earp, 1848 to 1880, the Untold Story.* Toyahvale, Tex.: Frontier Book Co., 1963.

———. *Wyatt Earp, 1879 to 1882, the Man and the Myth.* Toyahvale, Tex.: Frontier Book Co., 1964.

Beckett, V. B. *Baca's Battle.* Houston: Stagecoach Press, 1962.

Bell, Susan. *The Facts On File Dictionary of Forensic Science.* New York: Facts On File, 2004.

Berman, Jerry, and Morton Halperin, eds. *The Abuses of the Intelligence Agencies.* Washington, D.C.: Center for National Security Studies, 1975.

Bernstein, Irving. *The Lean Years: A History of the American Worker, 1920–1933.* New York: Houghton Mifflin, 1960.

———. *Turbulent Years: A History of the American Worker, 1933–1941.* New York: Houghton Mifflin, 1969.

Blackstock, Nelson. *COINTELPRO: The FBI's Secret War on Political Freedom.* New York: Vintage, 1975.

Blum, Richard, ed. *Surveillance and Espionage in a Free Society.* New York: Praeger, 1973.

Blum, William. *Killing Hope: U.S. Military and CIA Interventions Since World War II.* Monroe, Maine: Common Courage Press, 1995.

Bopp, William. *"O.W.": O.W. Wilson and the Search for a Police Profession.* Port Washington, Wash.: Kennikat Press, 1977.

Bordua, David, ed. *The Police: Six Sociological Essays.* New York: Wiley, 1967.

Boyer, Glenn. *The Suppressed Murder of Wyatt Earp.* San Antonio, Tex.: Naylor, 1967.

Branch, Taylor. *Parting the Waters: America in the King Years, 1954–63.* New York: Simon & Schuster, 1988.

———. *Pillar of Fire: America in the King Years, 1963–65.* New York: Simon & Schuster, 1998.

Breihan, Carl. *Great Lawmen of the West.* New York: Bonanza Books, 1963.

Burnham, David. *Above the Law: Secret Deals, Political Fixes and Other Misadventures of the U.S. Department of Justice.* New York: Scribner, 1996.

Burrough, Bryan. *Public Enemies: America's Greatest Crime Wave and the Birth of the FBI, 1933–34.* New York: Penguin Press, 2004.

Cannon, Lou. *Official Negligence: How Rodney King and the Riots Changed Los Angeles and the LAPD.* New York: Times Books, 1997.

Cantalupe, Joe, and Lisa Petrillo. *Badge of Betrayal.* New York: Avon, 1991.

Carter, Dan. *The Politics of Rage.* Baton Rouge: Louisiana State University Press, 1995.

Chalmers, David. *Hooded Americanism: The History of the Ku Klux Klan.* 3d ed. Durham: University of North Carolina Press, 1981.

Charns, Alexander. *Cloak and Gavel: FBI Wiretaps, Bugs, Informers, and the Supreme Court.* Urbana: University of Illinois Press, 1992.

Chevigny, Paul. *Police Power: Police Abuses in New York City.* New York: Pantheon, 1969.

Churchill, Ward, and Jim Vander Wall. *Agents of Repression: The FBI's Secret War Against the Black Panther Party and the American Indian Movement.* Boston: South End Press, 1988.

———. *The COINTELPRO Papers: Documents from the FBI's Secret War Against Dissent in the United States.* Boston: South End Press, 1990.

Clayton, Merle. *Union Station Massacre.* New York: Bobbs-Merrill, 1975.

Coates, Joseph. *Nonlethal Weapons for Use by U.S. Law Enforcement Officers.* Washington, D.C.: Institute for Defense Analysis, 1967.

Cohen, Stanley. *A. Mitchell Palmer: Politician*. New York: Columbia University Press, 1963.

Conger, Roger. *Texas Rangers: Sesquicentennial Anniversary, 1823–1973*. Fort Worth, Tex.: Heritage Publications, 1973.

Connelly, William. *Wild Bill and His Era*. New York: Press of the Pioneers, 1933.

Conot, Robert. *Rivers of Blood, Years of Darkness*. New York: Bantam, 1967.

Cook, Fred. *The FBI Nobody Knows*. New York: Macmillan, 1964.

Corson, William. *Armies of Ignorance: The Rise of the American Intelligence Empire*. New York: Dial Press, 1977.

Coulson, Danny, and Elaine Shannon. *No Heroes: Inside the FBI's Secret Counter-Terror Force*. New York: Pocket Books, 1999.

Cox, Archibald. *Crisis at Columbia*. New York: Vintage, 1968.

Cray, Ed. *The Big Blue Line*. New York: Coward-McCann, 1967.

Crichton, Kyle. *Law and Order, Ltd.: The Rousing Life of Elfego Baca of New Mexico*. Glorieta, N. Mex.: Rio Grande Press, 1928.

Criley, Richard. *The FBI and the First Amendment*. Los Angeles: First Amendment Foundation, 1990.

Croy, Homer. *Trigger Marshal: The Story of Chris Madsen*. New York: Duell, Sloan and Pearce, 1958.

Cunningham, Eugene. *Triggernometry: A Gallery of Gunfighters*. New York: Press of the Pioneers, 1934.

David, Henry. *The History of the Haymarket Affair*. New York: Russell & Russell, 1936.

Davis, James. *Spying on America: The FBI's Domestic Counterintelligence Program*. New York: Praeger, 1992.

Davis, John. *The Texas Rangers: Images and Incidents*. San Antonio: University of Texas Institute of Texan Cultures, 1991.

DeArment, Robert. *Bat Masterson: The Man and the Legend*. Norman: University of Oklahoma Press, 1979.

DeLoach, Cartha. *Hoover's FBI: The Inside Story by Hoover's Trusted Lieutenant*. Washington, D.C.: Regnery, 1995.

Demaris, Ovid. *Captive City*. New York: Lyle Stuart, 1969.

DeToledano, Ralph. *J. Edgar Hoover: The Man in His Time*. New Rochelle, N.Y.: Arlington House, 1973.

Dettlinger, Cher, and Jeff Prugh. *The List*. Atlanta: Philmay Enterprises, 1983.

Diamond, Sigmund. *Compromised Campus: The Collaboration of the University and the Intelligence Community*. New York: Oxford University Press, 1992.

Dobson, Christopher, and Ronald Payne. *The Terrorists: Their Weapons, Leaders and Tactics*. New York: Facts On File, 1982.

Domanick, Joe. *To Protect and to Serve: The LAPD's Century of War in the City of Dreams*. New York: Pocket Books, 1994.

Donner, Frank. *The Age of Surveillance*. New York: Knopf, 1980.

———. *Protectors of Privilege: Red Squads and Repression in Urban America*. Berkeley: University of California Press, 1990.

Douglas, C. L. *The Gentlemen in the White Hats: Dramatic Episodes in the History of the Texas Rangers*. Dallas: South-West Press, 1934.

Douglas, John, Ann Burgess, Allen Burgess, and Robert Ressler. *Crime Classification Manual*. San Francisco: Jossey-Bass Publishers, 1992.

Doyle, William. *An American Insurrection: James Meredith and the Battle of Oxford, Mississippi, 1962*. New York: Anchor Books, 2001.

Dray, Philip. *At the Hands of Persons Unknown: The Lynching of Black America*. New York: Random House, 2002.

Eagles, Charles. *Outside Agitator: Jon Daniels and the Civil Rights Movement in Alabama*. Chapel Hill: University of North Carolina Press, 1993.

Edwards, George. *The Police on the Urban Frontier*. New York: Institute of Human Relations Press, 1968.

Elliff, John. *The Reform of FBI Intelligence Operations*. Princeton, N.J.: Princeton University Press, 1979.

———. *The United States Department of Justice and Individual Rights*. New York: Garland, 1987.

Erler, Bob, and John Souter. *The Catch Me Killer*. Wheaton, Ill.: Tyndale House, 1980.

Erwin, Allen. *The Southwest of John H. Slaughter, 1841–1922*. Glendale, Calif.: Arthur H. Clark, 1965.

Erwin, Richard. *The Truth about Wyatt Earp*. Carpenteria, Calif.: The O.K. Press, 1992.

Facts On File Yearbooks, 64 vols. New York: Facts On File, 1941–2004.

Feldman, Glenn. *Politics, Society, and the Klan in Alabama 1915–1949*. Tuscaloosa: University of Alabama Press, 1999.

Fielder, Mildred. *Wild Bill and Deadwood*. New York: Bonanza Books, 1965.

Fisher, David. *Hard Evidence: How Detectives Inside the FBI's Sci-Crime Lab Have Helped Solve America's Toughest Cases*. New York: Simon & Schuster, 1995.

Flinn, John, and John Wilkie. *The History of the Chicago Police*. Chicago: Policemen's Benevolent Assn., 1887.

Foerstel, Herbert. *Surveillance in the Stacks: The FBI's Library Awareness Program*. Westport, Conn.: Greenwood Press, 1991.

Fogelson, Robert. *Big City Police*. Cambridge, Mass.: Harvard University Press, 1977.

Fraley, Oscar, and Eliot Ness. *The Untouchables*. New York: Julian Messner, 1957.

Friedman, Lawrence. *Crime and Punishment in American History*. New York: Basic Books, 1993.

Garrow, David. *Bearing the Cross: Martin Luther King, Jr. and the Southern Christian Leadership Conference*. New York: William Morrow, 1986.

———. *The FBI and Martin Luther King, Jr.: From Memphis to "Solo."* New York: Norton, 1989.

———, ed. *St. Augustine, Florida, 1963–1964: Mass Protest and Racial Violence*. Brooklyn, N.Y.: Carlson Publishing, 1989.

Gelbspan, Ross. *Break-ins, Death Threats and the FBI.* Boston: South End Press, 1991.

Gentry, Curt. *Frame-Up.* New York: W. W. Norton, 1967.

———. *J. Edgar Hoover: The Man and the Secrets.* New York: Norton, 1991.

Giglio, James. *H. M. Daugherty and the Politics of Expediency.* Kent, Ohio: Kent State University Press, 1978.

Gillers, Stephen, and Pat Watters, eds. *Investigating the FBI.* Garden City, N.Y.: Doubleday, 1973.

Gilmore, Christopher. *Hoover vs. Kennedy: The Second Civil War.* New York: St. Martin's Press, 1987.

Golab, Jan. *The Dark Side of the Force: A True Story of Corruption and Murder in the LAPD.* New York: Atlantic Monthly Press, 1993.

Goldman, Albert. *Grass Roots: Marijuana in America Today.* New York: Warner Books, 1979.

Goldstein, Robert. *Political Repression in Modern America.* Cambridge, Mass.: Schencken, 1978.

Gottesman, Ronald, ed. *Violence in America.* 3 vols. New York: Charles Scribner's Sons, 1999.

Graham, Hugh, and Robert Gurr. *The History of Violence in America.* New York: Bantam, 1969.

Green, Ben. *Before His Time: The Untold Story of Harry T. Moore, America's First Civil Rights Martyr.* New York: Free Press, 1999.

Halberstadt, Hans. *SWAT Team: Special Weapons and Tactics.* Osceola, Wisc.: Motorbooks International, 1994.

Halperin, Morton et al. *The Lawless State: The Crimes of the U.S. Intelligence Agencies.* New York: Penguin, 1976.

Heimel, Paul. *Eliot Ness: The Real Story.* Nashville, Tenn.: Cumberland House, 2000.

Helmer, William, and Rick Mattix. *Public Enemies: America's Criminal Past, 1919–1940.* New York: Checkmark, 1998.

Hendrickson, Paul. *Sons of Mississippi: A Story of Race and Its Legacy.* New York: Alfred A. Knopf, 2003.

Hersey, John. *The Algiers Motel Incident.* New York: Alfred A. Knopf, 1968.

Hofstadter, Richard, and Michael Wallace. *American Violence: A Documentary History.* New York: Alfred A. Knopf, 1970.

Hopkins, Ernest. *Our Lawless Police.* New York: Viking Press, 1931.

Horn, Tom. *Life of Tom Horn: A Vindication.* Denver: Louthan, 1904.

Humes, Edward. *Murderer with a Badge.* New York: Onyx, 1992.

Hungerford, Edward. *Wells Fargo: Advancing the American Frontier.* New York: Random House, 1949.

Ingalls, Robert. *Urban Vigilantes in the New South: Tampa, 1882–1936.* Knoxville: University of Tennessee Press, 1988.

Jackson, Kenneth. *The Ku Klux Klan in the City, 1915–1930.* New York: Oxford University Press, 1967.

Jaquith, Cindy, and Diane Wang. *FBI vs. Women.* New York: Pathfinder Press, 1977.

Jeffreys, Diarmuid. *The Bureau: Inside the Modern FBI.* Boston: Houghton Mifflin, 1995.

Jenkins, John, and H. Gordon Frost. *"I'm Frank Hamer": The Life of a Texas Peace Officer.* Austin, Tex.: Jenkins Publishing Co., 1968.

Johnson, David. *Policing the Urban Underworld: The Impact of Crime on the Development of the American Police: 1800–87.* Philadelphia: Temple University Press, 1979.

Jones, Aphrodite. *The FBI Killer.* New York: Pinnacle, 1992.

Jonnes, Jill. *Hep-Cats, Narcs, and Pipe Dreams: A History of America's Romance with Illegal Drugs.* Baltimore: Johns Hopkins University Press, 1996.

Judson, Karen. *Computer Crime: Phreaks, Spies, and Salami Slicers.* Berkeley Heights, N.J.: Enslow Publishers, 2000.

Kaiser, Robert. *RFK Must Die!* New York: E. P. Dutton, 1970.

Kelly, John, and Phillipe Wearne. *Tainting Evidence: Inside the Scandals at the FBI Crime Lab.* New York: Free Press, 1998.

Kennedy, Ludovic. *The Airman and the Carpenter.* London: Collins, 1985.

Kennedy, Stetson. *The Klan Unmasked.* Boca Raton: Florida Atlantic University Press, 1990.

———. *Southern Exposure.* New York: Doubleday, 1946.

Kessler, Robert. *The Bureau: The Secret History of the FBI.* New York: St. Martin's Press, 2002.

———. *The FBI: Inside the World's Most Powerful Law Enforcement Agency.* New York: Pocket Books, 1993.

Kiel, R. Andre. *J. Edgar Hoover: The Father of the Cold War.* Lanham, Md.: University Press of America, 2000.

Kilgore, D. E. *A Ranger Legacy: 150 Years of Service to Texas.* Austin, Tex.: Madrona Press, 1973.

Klaber, William, and Philip Melanson. *Shadow Play: The Untold Story of the Robert F. Kennedy Assassination.* New York: St. Martin's Press, 1997.

Kornweibel, Theodore, Jr. *"Seeing Red": Federal Campaigns Against Black Militancy, 1919–1925.* Bloomington: Indiana University Press, 1998.

Lake, Carolyn. *Undercover for Wells Fargo: The Unvarnished Recollections of Fred Dodge.* Boston: Houghton Mifflin, 1931.

Lake, Stuart. *Wyatt Earp: Frontier Marshal.* Boston: Houghton Mifflin, 1931.

Lane, Roger. *Policing the City: Boston 1822–1920.* Cambridge, Mass.: Harvard University Press, 1967.

Lardner, James, and Thomas Repetto. *NYPD: A City and Its Police.* New York: Henry Holt, 2000.

Lefors, Joe. *Wyoming Peace Officer.* Laramie, Wyo.: Laramie Printing, 1953.

Leinen, Stephen. *Black Police, White Society.* New York: New York University Press, 1984.

Lindberg, Richard. *To Serve and Collect: Chicago Politics and Police Corruption from the Lager Beer Riot to the Summerdale Scandal, 1855–1960.* New York: Praeger, 1991.

Lowenthal, Max. *The Federal Bureau of Investigation.* New York: Sloane, 1950.

Lukas, J. Anthony. *Nightmare: The Underside of the Nixon Years.* New York: Viking, 1976.

Mackay, James. *Allan Pinkerton: The First Private Eye*. New York: John Wiley & Sons, 1996.

Malsch, Brownson. *"Lone Wolf" Gonzaullas, Texas Ranger*. Norman: University of Oklahoma Press, 1998.

Markmann, Charles. *The Noblest Cry: A History of the American Civil Liberties Union*. New York: St. Martin's Press, 1965.

Marks, Paula. *And Die in the West: The Story of the O.K. Corral Gunfight*. Norman: Oklahoma University Press, 1989.

Martin, Jack. *Border Boss: Captain John R. Hughes—Texas Ranger*. San Antonio, Tex.: Naylor, 1942.

Marx, Gary. *Undercover: Police Surveillance in America*. Berkeley: University of California Press, 1988.

Matthiessen, Peter. *In the Spirit of Crazy Horse: The Story of Leonard Peltier and the FBI's War on the American Indian Movement*. New York: Penguin, 1992.

Mayo, Katherine. *The Standard-Bearers: True Stories of Heroes of Law and Order*. Boston: Houghton Mifflin, 1918.

McKennon, C. H. *Iron Men: A Saga of the Deputy United States Marshals Who Rode the Indian Territory*. Garden City, N.Y.: Doubleday, 1967.

McWhorter, Diane. *Carry Me Home*. New York: Simon & Schuster, 2001.

Meager, Sylvia. *Accessories after the Fact: The Warren Commission, the Authorities, and the Report*. New York: Bobbs-Merrill, 1967.

Melanson, Philip. *The Murkin Conspiracy: An Investigation into the Assassination of Dr. Martin Luther King, Jr.* New York: Praeger, 1989.

———. *The Robert F. Kennedy Assassination: New Revelations on the Conspiracy and Cover-Up*. New York: S.P.I. Books, 1994.

Mendelsohn, Jack. *The Martyrs: Sixteen Who Gave Their Lives for Racial Justice*. New York: Harper & Row, 1966.

Messick, Hank. *John Edgar Hoover*. New York: David McKay, 1972.

Metz, Leon. *Dallas Stoudenmire: El Paso Marshal*. Austin, Tex.: Jenkins Publishing, 1969.

———. *Pat Garrett: The Story of a Western Lawman*. Norman: University of Oklahoma Press, 1974.

Miller, Floyd. *Bill Tilghman: Marshal of the Last Frontier*. New York: Doubleday, 1968.

Miller, Nathan. *Stealing from America: A History of Corruption from Jamestown to Reagan*. New York: Paragon House, 1992.

Moldea, Dan. *Dark Victory: Ronald Reagan, MCA, and the Mob*. New York: Viking, 1986.

Mollenhoff, Clark. *Strike Force: Organized Crime in the Government*. Englewood Cliffs, N.J.: Prentice-Hall, 1972.

Monkkonen, Eric. *Police in Urban America: 1860–1920*. London: Cambridge University Press, 1981.

Moore, James. *Very Special Agents*. New York: Pocket Books, 1997.

Morn, Frank. *The Eye That Never Sleeps: A History of the Pinkerton National Detective Agency*. Bloomington: Indiana University Press, 1982.

Morrow, Robert. *The Senator Must Die*. Santa Monica, Calif.: Roundtable Publishing, 1988.

Murray, Robert. *Red Scare: A Study in National Hysteria, 1919–1920*. Minneapolis: University of Minnesota Press, 1955.

Nelson, Jack. *Terror in the Night: The Klan's Campaign Against the Jews*. Jackson: University of Mississippi Press, 1993.

Nelson, Jack, and Jack Bass. *The Orangeburg Massacre*. New York: World Publishing, 1970.

Nelson, Jack, and Ronald Ostrow. *The FBI and the Berrigans: The Making of a Conspiracy*. New York: Coward, McCann and Geoghegan, 1972.

Newton, Michael. *Bitter Grain: The Story of the Black Panther Party*. Los Angeles: Holloway House, 1980.

———. *A Case of Conspiracy: James Earl Ray and the Assassination of Martin Luther King, Jr.* Los Angeles: Holloway House, 1980.

———. *Cop Killers*. Port Townsend, Wash.: Loompanics, 1998.

———. *The Encyclopedia of High-Tech Crime and Crime-Fighting*. New York: Facts On File, 2004.

———. *The Encyclopedia of Kidnappings*. New York: Facts On File, 2002.

———. *The Encyclopedia of Serial Killers*. New York: Facts On File, 2000.

———. *The FBI Encyclopedia*. Jefferson, N.C.: McFarland, 2003.

———. *The FBI Plot*. Los Angeles: Holloway House, 1981.

———. *The Invisible Empire: The Ku Klux Klan in Florida*. Gainesville: University Press of Florida, 2001.

———. *Killer Cops*. Port Townsend, Wash.: Loompanics, 1997.

Niederhoffer, Arthur. *Behind the Badge: The Police in Urban Society*. New York: Doubleday, 1967.

Nunnelley, William. *Bull Connor*. Tuscaloosa: University of Alabama Press, 1991.

O'Connor, Richard. *Bat Masterson*. New York: Doubleday, 1957.

———. *Pat Garrett*. New York: Ace Books, 1960.

———. *Wild Bill Hickok*. New York: Ace Books, 1959.

Ollestad, Norman. *Inside the FBI*. New York: Stuart, 1967.

O'Neal, Bill. *The Pimlico Encyclopedia of Western Gunfighters*. London: Pimlico, 1979.

O'Reilly, Kenneth. *Hoover and the Un-Americans: The FBI, HUAC, and the Red Menace*. Philadelphia: Temple University Press, 1983.

———. *"Racial Matters": The FBI's Secret File on Black America, 1968–1972*. New York: Free Press, 1989.

Owens, Ron. *Oklahoma Justice: The Oklahoma City Police: A Century of Gunfighters, Gangsters and Terrorists*. Paducah, Ky.: Turner Publishing, 1995.

Paine, Albert. *Captain Bill McDonald, Texas Ranger: A Story of Frontier Reform*. New York: J. J. Little & Ives, 1909.

Paine, Lauran. *Texas Ben Thompson*. Los Angeles: Westernlore Press, 1966.

———. *Tom Horn, Man of the West*. Barre, Mass.: Barre Publishing, 1963.

Peavy, Charles. *Charles A. Siringo, a Texas Picaro*. Austin, Tex.: Steck-Vaughn, 1967.

Phillips, Charles, and Alan Axelrod. *Cops, Crooks, and Criminologists: An International Biographical Directory of Law Enforcement*. New York: Checkmark Books, 2000.

Pink, Louis. *Gaynor: The Tammany Mayor Who Swallowed the Tiger*. New York: International Press, 1931.

Pistone, Joseph. *Donnie Brasco: My Undercover Life in the Mafia*. New York: American Library, 1987.

Porambo, Ron. *No Cause for Indictment: An Autopsy of Newark*. New York: Holt, Rinehart and Winston, 1971.

Potter, Claire. *War on Crime: Bandits, G-Men and the Politics of Mass Culture*. New Brunswick, N.J.: Rutgers University Press, 1998.

Powers, Richard. *G-Men: Hoover's FBI in American Popular Culture*. Carbondale: Southern Illinois University Press, 1983.

———. *Secrecy and Power: The Life of J. Edgar Hoover*. New York: Free Press, 1987.

Prassel, Frank. *The Western Peace Officer: A Legacy of Law and Order*. Norman: University of Oklahoma Press, 1972.

Preece, Harold. *Lone Star Man: Ira Aten*. New York: Hastings House, 1960.

Purvis, Melvin. *American Agent*. Garden City, N.Y.: Doubleday, Doran, 1936.

Radlett, Michael, Hugo Bedau, and Constance Putnam. *In Spite of Innocence: Erroneous Convictions in Capital Cases*. Boston: Northeastern University Press, 1992.

Ranalli, Ralph. *Deadly Alliance: The FBI's Partnership with the Mob*. New York: HarperTorch, 2001.

Raymond, Dora. *Captain Lee Hall of Texas*. Norman: University of Oklahoma Press, 1940.

Report of the National Advisory Commission on Civil Disorders. New York: Bantam, 1968.

Reppetto, Thomas. *The Blue Parade*. New York: Free Press, 1978.

Ressler, Robert, Ann Burgess, and John Douglas. *Sexual Homicide: Patterns and Motives*. Lexington, Mass.: Lexington Books, 1988.

Revell, Oliver, and Dwight Williams. *A G-man's Journal*. New York: Pocket Books, 1998.

Richardson, James. *The New York Police: Colonial Times to 1901*. New York: Oxford University Press, 1970.

Riebling, Mark. *Wedge: The Secret War Between the FBI and the CIA*. New York: Knopf, 1994.

Robinson, Charles, III. *The Men Who Wear the Star: The Story of the Texas Rangers*. New York: Random House, 2000.

Rosa, Joseph. *They Called Him Wild Bill*. Norman: University of Oklahoma Press, 1987.

Rothmiller, Mike, and Ivan Goldman. *L.A. Secret Police: Inside the LAPD Elite Spy Network*. New York: Pocket Books, 1992.

Scaduto, Anthony. *Scapegoat: The Lonesome Death of Bruno Richard Hauptmann*. New York: Putnam, 1976.

Schaff, Barbara. *Shattered Hopes: A True Story of Marriage, the Mob, and Murder*. New York: Barricade Books, 1993.

Schlesinger, Arthur. *Robert Kennedy and His Times*. Boston: Houghton Mifflin, 1978.

Schott, Joseph. *No Left Turns: The FBI in Peace and War*. New York: Praeger, 1975.

Sharkey, Joe. *Suspicion*. New York: Simon & Schuster, 1993.

Shecter, Leonard, and William Phillips. *On the Pad: The Underworld and Its Corrupt Police, Confessions of a Cop on the Take*. New York: G. P. Putnam's Sons, 1973.

Shirley, Glenn. *Heck Thomas, Frontier Marshal*. Philadelphia: Chilton, 1962.

Sifakis, Carl. *The Encyclopedia of American Crime*. New York: Facts On File, 1984.

———. *Encyclopedia of Assassinations*. New York: Facts On File, 1991.

———. *The Mafia Encyclopedia*. 2nd ed. New York: Checkmark Books, 1999.

Skolnick, Jerome. *Justice Without Trial: Law Enforcement in Democratic Society*. New York: Wiley, 1966.

Smith, Brent. *Terrorism in America: Pipe Bombs and Pipe Dreams*. Albany: State University of New York Press, 1994.

Smith, Mortimer. *William Jay Gaynor: Mayor of New York*. Chicago: Henry Regnery, 1951.

Sonnischer, C. L. *Roy Bean, Law West of the Pecos*. New York: Macmillan, 1943.

Sowell, Andrew. *Life of "Big Foot" Wallace, the Great Ranger Captain*. Devine, Tex.: Devine News, 1899.

Stanton, Mary. *From Selma to Sorrow*. Athens: University of Georgia Press, 1998.

Stark, Rodney. *Police Riots: Collective Violence and Law Enforcement*. Belmont, Calif.: Wadsworth Publishing, 1972.

Steinberg, Alfred. *The Bosses*. New York: Macmillan, 1972.

Sterling, William. *Trails and Trials of a Texas Ranger*. Norman: University of Oklahoma Press, 1960.

Stone, I. F. *The Killings at Kent State: How Murder Went Unpunished*. New York: Vintage, 1970.

Streeter, Floyd. *Ben Thompson, Man with a Gun*. New York: Frederick Fell, 1957.

Sullivan, William, and Bill Brown. *The Bureau: My Thirty Years in Hoover's FBI*. New York: Norton, 1979.

Summers, Anthony. *Official and Confidential: The Secret Life of J. Edgar Hoover*. New York: G. P. Putnam's, 1993.

Swearingen, M. Wesley. *FBI Secrets: An Agent's Exposé*. Boston: South End Press, 1995.

Swindle, Howard. *Deliberate Indifference: A Story of Racial Injustice and Murder*. New York: Penguin Books, 1993.

Tackwood, Louis. *The Glass House Tapes*. New York: Avon Books, 1973.

Tefertiller, Casey. *Wyatt Earp: The Life Behind the Legend*. New York: John Wiley & Sons, 1997.

Theoharis, Athan, and John Cox. *The Boss: J. Edgar Hoover and the Great American Inquisition*. Philadelphia: Temple University Press, 1988.

Tilghman, Zoe. *Marshal of the Last Frontier*. Glendale, Calif.: Arthur H. Clark, 1949.

Toland, John. *The Dillinger Days*. New York: Random House, 1963.

Truman, Nelson. *The Torture of Mothers*. New York: Beacon Press, 1965.

Turner, William. *Hoover's FBI: The Men and the Myth*. Los Angeles: Sherbourne Press, 1970.

————. *The Police Establishment*. New York: G. P. Putnam's Sons, 1968.

————. *Power on the Right*. Berkeley, Calif.: Ramparts Press, 1969.

Turner, William, and John Christian. *The Assassination of Robert F. Kennedy: A Searching Look at the Conspiracy and Cover-Up, 1968–78*. New York: Random House, 1979.

Ungar, Sanford. *FBI*. Boston: Little, Brown, 1976.

Unger, Robert. *The Union Station Massacre: The Original Sin of Hoover's FBI*. Kansas City, Mo.: Andrews McMeel Publishing, 1997.

Varon, Joseph. *A Matter of Judgment*. Hollywood, Fla.: Lifetime Books, 1994.

Volkman, Ernest, and John Cummings. *Till Murder Do Us Part*. New York: Onyx, 1994.

Wade, Wyn. *The Fiery Cross: The Ku Klux Klan in America*. New York: Simon & Schuster, 1987.

Walker, Samuel. *A Critical History of Police Reform: The Emergence of Professionalism*. Toronto: Lexington Books, 1977.

————. *In Defense of American Liberties: A History of the ACLU*. New York: Oxford University Press, 1990.

Waters, Frank. *The Earp Brothers of Tombstone*. London: Neville Spearman, 1962.

Webb, Walter. *The Texas Rangers: A Century of Frontier Defense*. Austin: University of Texas Press, 1965.

Whitehead, Don. *The FBI Story: A Report to the People*. New York: Random House, 1956.

Wilkins, Frederick. *The Highly Irregular Irregulars: Texas Rangers in the Mexican War*. Austin, Tex.: Eakin Press, 1990.

————. *The Legend Begins: The Texas Rangers, 1823–1845*. Austin, Tex.: State House Press, 1996.

Williams, Robert. *Vice Squad*. New York: Thomas Crowell, 1973.

Wilson, James. *Varieties of Police Behavior*. Cambridge, Mass.: Harvard University Press, 1968.

Wilson, Orlando. *Police Administration*. New York: McGraw-Hill, 1963.

Wise, David. *The American Police State: The Government Against the People*. New York: Random House, 1976.

Woodward, C. Vann. *The Strange Career of Jim Crow*. 3d ed. New York: Oxford University Press, 1974.

Index

Page numbers in **boldface** indicate a main entry; *italic* page numbers indicate an illustration.